Reports
TO THE
GENERAL ASSEMBLY

OF SCOTLAND

THE CHURCH OF

[2001)

KT-214-286

Published in 2001 by
THE CHURCH OF SCOTLAND BOARD OF PRACTICE AND PROCEDURE
121 George Street, Edinburgh EH2 4NY

© The Board of Practice and Procedure of the Church of Scotland 2001

ISBN 0-86153-315-1

British Library Catalogue in Publication Data
A catalogue record for this book is available from the British Library

All Copy Keyed by the Church of Scotland
Type Design, Formatting, Printing and Binding by Lothian Print, Edinburgh
Cover Design by Pointsize Associates, Glasgow
Indexer Peter B. Gunn

Embargoed until 30 April 2001

Authorised for official use
within the Church of Scotland only,
and not for publication until 30 April 2001.

CONTENTS

PRACTICE AND PROCEDURE
MAY 2001

PROPOSED DELIVERANCE

The General Assembly:

1.   Receive the Report.
2.   Record their appreciation of the services of the Very Rev Dr Andrew R C McLellan as Moderator.

ASSEMBLY ARRANGEMENTS

3.   Approve the Order of Business for the first three days (Order of Proceedings).
4.   Agree to apply Standing Order 103 to allow for electronic voting in place of voting by papers.
5.   Instruct Boards and Committees in the preparation of their reports to the General Assembly to have regard to the guidelines set out in Appendix A.
6.   Authorise the Board to make all necessary arrangements for Assembly Services in 2002.
7.   Appoint the Rev R A Baigrie to edit the verbatim record.

LEGAL QUESTIONS

8.   Pass an Act anent Granting and Signing of Deeds as in Appendix B.
9.   Resolve that the meetings of Kirk Sessions shall normally be held in public, with pastoral or disciplinary items taken in private by resolution of the Kirk Session, which shall consider the rights of privacy and freedom of information to which any individual is entitled.
10. Pass an Act amending Act II 1984 as amended (anent Quinquennial Visitation of Congregations) as set out in Appendix C (section 8).
11. Approve the revised Schedule of Guidance for Presbytery visits to congregations contained in Appendix D.
12. Replace Standing Order 117 as set out in the Report (section 8).
13. Amend Regulation I 1999 Anent Nomination of the Moderator of the General Assembly in the manner described in the Report (section 8).

PRESBYTERY BOUNDARIES

14. Receive the report of the Inter-Board Group on Presbytery Boundaries (Appendix E).
15. Instruct the Inter-Board Group and Presbyteries to undertake the consultation process outlined in the report.
16. Instruct the Inter-Board Group to report further, through the Board of Practice and Procedure, to the General Assembly of 2002.

GENDER ATTITUDE PROJECT

17. Receive the Report of the Gender Attitude Project (Appendix F), authorise the continuation of the Project until May 2002 and instruct the Board to bring budgeted proposals for the future of this work to the General Assembly of 2002.

CO-ORDINATING FORUM
18. Approve the changes in the composition of the Co-ordinating Forum detailed in the Report (section 14).

STAFFING
19. Record their appreciation of the long and dedicated service to the Church of Chris Brown and wish her well in her retirement (section 15).

SCOTTISH CHURCHES' PARLIAMENTARY OFFICER
20. Receive the Report of the Scottish Churches' Parliamentary Officer (Appendix G).

THE SCOTTISH BIBLE SOCIETY
21. Receive the Report of The Scottish Bible Society (Appendix H), note the change of name from The National Bible Society of Scotland to The Scottish Bible Society, and its refocused mission.
22. Commend the ministry of The Scottish Bible Society to the prayers and liberality of the Church.
23. Commend The Guild for its significant and generous support of the Bibleworld project and Scripture distribution to ethnic minority peoples in Siberia.
24. Appoint Rev Martin A W Allen, Rev Andrew F Anderson, Rev H Warner Hardie and Rev Norman Maciver to the Scottish Bible Society's Council of Church Representatives.

REPORT

1. Introduction—The Work of the Board

The routine work of the Board is reflected in the titles of its two principal Committees, Legal Questions and Assembly Arrangements. The former deals with issues of church law, practice and procedure and also exercises vigilance in matters of civil law which have a bearing upon the Church. The work of the Assembly Arrangements Committee has been particularly demanding with the move to the Usher Hall. However, this Committee is not simply reactive but is constantly seeking to refine and develop Assembly procedures for the benefit of commissioners. In this connection the Board circulated to all Boards and Committees guidance notes on the subject of reporting to the Assembly. These are printed in Appendix A and it is recommended that the Assembly instruct all reporting bodies to observe these in future.

In addition to the work of its two Standing Committees the Board has established *ad hoc* groups to carry forward four substantial pieces of work, namely the review of presbytery boundaries (see Appendix E), the review of the Presbyteries of Europe and Jerusalem, the marketing of the Assembly Hall *post* Parliament and the Presbytery Clerks' E-mail Project. The Gender Attitude Project continues to find a hospitable and supportive home within the Board. The Project is serviced by the Board, through the Depute Clerk, as were the Special Commissions on Review and Reform and on St. Ninian's, Crieff. Finally, the Board provides support to the Moderator through the Principal Clerk in his role as Secretary to the Moderator.

2. The Very Rev Dr Andrew R C McLellan

Andrew McLellan's nomination as Moderator was warmly welcomed throughout the Church and the expectations awakened by that nomination have more than been fulfilled. A lifetime of commitment to parish ministry, convenership of the Church and Nation Committee and well proven communications skills all came together to match man and moment most effectively. One project which has been particularly acclaimed was a programme of visits to every Scottish prison, but wherever he has travelled, at home and abroad, Andrew has always had the right word for place and people. Throughout the year Irene McLellan has been wholly supportive of her husband but has also made her own gifts and graces generously available. Andrew and Irene have done much good over this past moderatorial year and the Church has cause to be grateful to them.

3. Assembly Arrangements

Following discussions with Sir David Steel and representatives of the Parliament the Board agreed to make arrangements for the 2001 General Assembly to be held in the Usher Hall, thereby enabling the Parliament to remain in the Assembly Hall. This means that the General Assembly is meeting in its third venue in as many years with obvious organisational implications. The Board acknowledges the good spirit of co-operation which has developed between officials of Church and Parliament and also the staff of the Usher Hall and the Sheraton Hotel. Particular appreciation is expressed to the members of the Assembly 2001 Group convened by Ann McCarter. As part of the arrangements agreed with the Parliament a two course buffet lunch will be provided for commissioners each day from Monday to Friday in the Sheraton Hotel. To allow time for this the Board suggests that the Assembly suspends for lunch from 12.45 to 2 p.m. In order to "claw back" this extra fifteen minutes on the lunch break it is suggested that business begin at 9.15 a.m. rather than the traditional 9.30 a.m.

The Assembly Service has been arranged in St. Giles' Cathedral on Sunday 20 May at 10 am with the Gaelic Service on the same day at 12.30 pm in Greyfriars Tolbooth and Highland Church. The Assembly Communion service will be on Monday 21 May at 9.15 am in the Usher Hall.

Commissioners will have been delighted to learn that Her Majesty the Queen intends to be present at the opening of next year's General Assembly in connection with the Royal Jubilee celebrations. The Assembly will meet in the Assembly Hall from Saturday 25 to Friday 31 May 2002.

4. Presbytery Representation

The Presbytery returns show that there are, in all the Presbyteries 1288 Charges, whether vacant or not, and that there are 216 other ministers (excluding retired ministers) who are members of Presbyteries. Representation is calculated for each Presbytery, in accordance with Act III, 2000 and the total number of Commissions is 864 made up as follows: 413 Ministers, 413 elders and 38 deacons.

5. Business Committee

The Board recommends that the Rev David W Lacy be appointed Convener of the Business Committee and that the Rev William C Hewitt be appointed Vice-Convener. The names of others nominated to serve on this Committee will be found in the Order of Proceedings.

6. Commissioners' Subsistence Allowance and Expenses

The Board recommends the following rates for payment of expenses:

Overnight subsistence not exceeding £38.00 for each night

Daily out-of-pocket Expenses:
not exceeding £9.00 in respect of Saturday and Sunday
not exceeding £5.00 per day in respect of an evening meal Monday to Friday

A lunch will be provided each day from Monday to Friday in the Sheraton Hotel

7. Presbyterial Superintendence

Reports from Presbyteries show that Quinquennial Visitations have produced no case requiring action by the General Assembly; and also that Presbytery records are being properly kept.

8. Legal Questions

(a) Freedom of Information

The incorporation of human rights legislation into civil law presents an ongoing challenge to the good practice and standards of the Church, its courts and their agencies. The principle of freedom of information has occupied the attention of the Board, and guidelines for good practice have been issued to all Boards and Committees encouraging the adoption of principles of openness in regard to records, minutes and information, except where obvious requirements of confidentiality dictate otherwise.

In extending these principles throughout the Church, the Board believes it is now right to reverse the existing presumption that the meetings of Kirk Sessions are held in private except for business that particularly merits being taken publicly. Such practice belongs to an era where the business of Session meetings usually related to sensitive disciplinary and pastoral matters, an era that is now past. The Board recommends that the lowest courts of the Church should follow the practice of superior courts, where business is normally taken in open court, with items taken in private where an individual's rights are better served in that way.

(b) Quinquennial Visits

In 2000 the General Assembly approved a booklet produced by the Boards of National Mission and Practice and Procedure concerning the review by Presbyteries of their Quinquennial Visitation procedures. The General Assembly instructed the Board of Practice and Procedure to bring a revised Schedule and Basis of Discussion, with appropriate amending legislation, to a future General Assembly. The Act, Schedule and Basis which appear in Appendices C and D are the fruit of consultations amongst the Boards of Practice and Procedure, National Mission and Ministry and complete the process begun in 2000.

(c) Standing Order 117

The recommendations of the Special Commission anent the Board of World Mission, approved by the General Assembly of 2000, included the following: "That the General Secretary should no longer be a member of the Board of World Mission and that the Board of Practice and Procedure should review Standing Order 117".

In undertaking the review, the Board consulted Boards and Committees of the General Assembly and received no explicit requests for General Secretaries to remain as voting members. One Board helpfully pointed out that the presence of a Secretary, or depute appointed for the meeting, was in fact a responsibility, to assist the deliberations of the Board and provide information and advice. This seemed a proper analysis of the intention of the Standing Order, and reflected the fact that most Secretaries do not exercise their voting rights in practice. Therefore the Board proposes that Standing Order 117 should be replaced as follows:

"**117. Secretaries and Deputes**. It shall be the responsibility of the Secretary of each Board and Committee to attend the meetings thereof, to provide information and advice as requested, and to provide a depute for any meeting that he or she cannot attend. Members of staff shall not have the right to vote at any meeting".

(d) European Directive on Employment

On 17 October 2000, the Employment and Social Policy Council of the European Union produced a draft Directive on equal treatment in employment and occupation. In its earlier draft stages, the Directive appeared to prevent religious discrimination in employment policy without exception, and would have caused difficulties to the Churches in making appointments which required a particular Christian commitment because of the nature of the duties or the ethos of the service-provider.

The Board, along with other member churches of the Conference of European Churches, raised the matter with domestic and European politicians and officials during the autumn of 2000. With the help of pressure from the British and Irish Governments the Directive was amended to provide an exclusion where a legitimate and proportionate occupational requirement justifies a difference of treatment. In particular, Article 4 of the Directive acknowledges the legitimacy of Churches requiring employees to have a loyalty to their ethos.

At the time of writing the Directive awaited incorporation into domestic UK law.

(e) Nomination of Moderator

The General Assembly of 1999 approved new Regulations anent the Nomination of the Moderator of the General Assembly. These have been in operation for two years and the Board agrees with the Committee to Nominate the Moderator that the following alterations are necessary.

It would be preferable were the Committee to be chaired by the most senior of the three former Moderators present rather than the most recent one: the present Regulation could mean that the Committee is chaired by someone who has never previously attended a meeting. The Regulations would require to be amended as follows:

In Section 2 delete 'latest' and substitute 'earliest'.

The Board agrees with the Committee that it would be helpful to move the date of the October meeting from the third Tuesday to the last Tuesday of October, thereby avoiding the school holiday period which affects the availability of Presbytery representatives. The Regulations would require to be amended as follows:

In Section 5 (b) delete 'third' and substitute 'last'.

(f) Civil Registration

In October 2000 the General Register Office for Scotland (GROS) published a consultation paper reviewing the present system of the registration of births, deaths and marriages. The closing date for submissions was February 28, 2001; the submission of the Board of Practice and Procedure was generally favourable towards the review.

The Board welcomed the stated commitment of the registration service to maintaining integrity, dignity and human interaction. The partnership between GROS and local councils was welcomed; the Board called for registration districts to be made contiguous with local authority boundaries to avoid confusion. Formal declarations could also be made before a Registrar (as well as a Notary Public). The Board urged greater consideration for the interests of those for whom English is not a first language.

The Board resisted the introduction of secular "baby naming ceremonies" by registrars as unnecessary. Christian baptism - of infants or adults - has a particular theological and sacramental nature which radically differs from a secular naming ceremony.

The Board recommended that registrars should be allowed to conduct weddings outwith a registration office, within reason. There is often pressure on Church of Scotland ministers to conduct weddings in hotels, mainly because of legal status rather than for any religious reason. Nonetheless, the Board took the view that registrars should not conduct weddings in church buildings or grounds, including ruins (such as Melrose Abbey and St Andrews Cathedral), to avoid inappropriate confusion between secular and sacred ceremonies.

Regarding funerals, the Board noted that the Humanist Society and others already provide non-religious funerals. Although the Church of Scotland does not restrict the conduct of funerals to ministers or deacons, the pastoral care of the bereaved is a concern. The Board does not believe that registrars (with other competing pressures on their time) are best placed to give this. It was the conclusion of the Board that the addition of secular funerals to the range of services offered by local registrars would not add substantially to the ability of bereaved families or individuals to opt for a non-religious funeral service.

(g) Retired and former ministers

The Board is aware of the difficulties faced by parish ministers who find there is an ongoing pastoral relationship between their congregation and one of their predecessors. Even though no malice is intended, the continuing membership of a congregation by a previous minister, or the conduct of funerals or weddings or pastoral involvement by him or her, can make the building of trust and pastoral care by a newer minister particularly difficult. All parties are put in an awkward position by a request for ministerial services from a retired or former minister; though this is usually difficult to refuse, thought should be given to the significance of the call to the present minister, and to the repercussions for future relationships.

When retired or former ministers are asked to take the wedding or funeral of, or be pastorally involved with, a resident of their former parish, they should consider first the pastoral relationship with their successor, as having priority over their own former relationship. It is quite acceptable for a retired minister to refuse such an invitation on these pastoral grounds even if it falls within the definition of 'private invitation' in s.18 of Act II, 2000. Equally, it is acceptable for a Presbytery to instruct individuals to conform to these principles.

The Board of Ministry in its pre-retirement conferences urges carefulness and good practice in this area. The Board of Practice and Procedure recommends to Presbyteries that the following standards should be encouraged when exercising superintendence over its congregations and ministers (including retired ministers).

At the end of a parish ministry, the minister and their spouse should become communicant members (and attenders) of a different congregation, unless remote geography or other exceptional reason makes that impossible. Where a parish minister dies, the widow/widower may wish similarly to transfer membership, unless pastoral need dictates otherwise. Former ministers and the spouses of former ministers should not hold office on the Session, financial court or vacancy committee of a former congregation.

The Board, with the approval of the Board of Ministry, commends these principles to Presbyteries and congregations.

(h) Acts, Regulations and Styles

The General Assembly of 2000 authorised its Clerks to republish the Acts and Regulations of the General Assembly, incorporating amending legislation and bringing language and references up-to-date. This volume replaced the first edition, which was prepared by the clerks of the Assembly in 1994 and expanded each year by the insertion of new pages and the annotation of existing text. The second edition again presents the legislation and regulations as fully amended, fulfils the instruction about language and contains a short section of styles for commonly-used legal documents. The law is

stated as at 1 January 2001, at which date the first edition became obsolete.

The new edition is once more in loose-leaf form, and is available from all Scottish branches of Wesley Owen bookshops and from the Assembly's bookstall. Its purchase price of £25 includes annual posted updates during the lifetime of the edition, and is therefore comparable to the total cost of buying and maintaining the previous edition.

The text is also available on the Church's website.

9. Presbyteries of Europe and Jerusalem

Last year's General Assembly, on the report of the Special Commission anent the Board of World Mission, instructed the Board of Practice and Procedure to look at a number of issues relating to the role and function of the Presbyteries of Europe and Jerusalem and their relationship to the Board of World Mission. The Board has set up a Committee under the convenership of the Rev David Arnott to undertake this remit. A very full consultative process is underway and the Board intends to bring a full report with recommendations to the General Assembly of 2002.

10. Review of Gender Attitude Project

The Report of the Gender Attitude Project is set out in Appendix F.

In 1999 the Project began to be serviced by the Board of Practice and Procedure and accounts for its work through that Board. The Project's five years terminate at this General Assembly, and the Board established a Review Group, comprising a Convener, representative of the Church and Nation Committee, representative of the Committee on Ecumenical Affairs and the Principal of Scottish Churches Open College (none of these having previous involvement with the Project), along with the Co-Convener and one other member of the Project. The Clerk of the Gender Attitude Project serves as Clerk of the Review Group.

The Review Group notes that the Gender Attitude Project Research Project was due to be completed in the

Spring of 2001, and shares the belief of GAP itself that the Project will raise questions that require some further attention. The preliminary conclusion of the review, therefore, is that the Project as a whole should continue for a sixth year until the General Assembly of May 2002, to allow this valuable work to be completed. The Review Group intends to continue its work beyond the General Assembly of 2001, to bring long-term proposals to the Co-ordinating Forum of Autumn 2001 and thereafter to the General Assembly of 2002; this will facilitate a complete review of the whole work of the Gender Attitude Project.

11. Assembly Hall Development

Planning for the commercial development of the Assembly Hall following its hand-back from the Scottish Parliament continued slowly during the year. The Board believes that the Hall will be available in the course of 2003 but the date is not yet precise.

The Board intends to enter a joint venture agreement with the University of Edinburgh through its conference arm, "Edinburgh First" (EF), but has not been able to launch a positive marketing programme. Despite this uncertainty the Board has kept up the momentum of preparations, agreeing a Business Plan and clarifying VAT and contractual issues with the help of the Board of Stewardship and Finance, the Personnel Committee and the Law Department. In the early part of 2001 the Church and EF have begun to develop initial publicity and promotional material and begun work identifying potential customers. This will make it possible to begin an immediate marketing programme when the hand-back date is confirmed. At that point the Board will negotiate contracts for cleaning, security, technical support and building maintenance and will, in due course, recruit a manager for the Assembly Hall.

12. Presbytery Clerks' Project

The Project to provide Presbytery Clerks with E-mail facilities has been completed. A database for the use of Presbyteries has been built and is in the process of being distributed to every Clerk together with initial training in its use. It is intended that the E-mail provision together with the database will enable the electronic transfer of documents and data in the near future. Work is in hand to prepare regular reports and information documents for sending over the internet.

13. Inspection of Records

Last year's General Assembly gave to the Board the task of inspecting the Minutes of Standing Committees of the Assembly. The relevant records have been examined and found, generally, to be in order. Deficiencies have been pointed out and steps taken to remedy these.

14. Co-ordinating Forum

The Forum (a meeting of Conveners and Secretaries of Assembly Boards and Committees) was established by the General Assembly of 1996 under the aegis of the Assembly Council. In 1998 the Assembly passed responsibility for the Forum to the Board of Practice and Procedure with the immediate past Moderator as Convener, the Conveners of the Board of Practice and Procedure and the Assembly Council as Vice-Conveners and the Principal Clerk as Secretary. The Forum has established itself as a useful gathering. It provides a mechanism through which the Board of Stewardship and Finance can consult when drawing up the Mission and Aid Fund budget and it enables Conveners and Secretaries to share information and ideas and to interact at a social level. Recent meetings have also provided an opportunity for theological reflection. It is now the view of the Board of Practice and Procedure, the Assembly Council and the Forum itself that responsibility for the Forum should be passed back to the Assembly Council, the body to which it was originally intended to relate. In light of this it is proposed that the Convener of the Council should be Convener of the Forum, thereby providing an important measure of continuity. The Convener of the

Board of Practice and Procedure would no longer be a Vice-Convener of the Forum (with *ex officio* membership of the Board of Stewardship and Finance and that Board's Budget and Allocation Committee), but would continue to be a member of the Forum alongside other Board Conveners. The General Assembly is asked to approve these recommendations.

15. Chris Brown, MBE, BA

Chris Brown retires following this General Assembly having completed forty-six years of service in the Church offices. Chris entered the service of the Church in 1955 as an office junior in the Home Board. In 1961 she was appointed Secretary to the Rev George Paterson, Secretary Depute to the Home Board and remained with that Board until, in 1978, she became Secretary to the Principal Clerk, the Rev Donald F M Macdonald. The following year she gained the BA degree from the Open University and in 1987 was awarded the MBE in the Queen's Birthday Honours. For the past twenty-three years Chris has served within the Principal Clerk's Office, the responsibilities of which also included for a time the administration of the Church and Nation Committee. Over the years Chris has built up a formidable knowledge of the Church and the General Assembly. Her memoirs would make fascinating reading, though having a natural as well as a professional discretion, those with secrets to hide can probably continue to sleep easily! The Convener of the Board will be inviting the Moderator, at the closing session of the Assembly, to express the thanks of the Church to Chris and to wish her well in her retirement. Meantime the Board places on record its own appreciation and good wishes.

In the name of the Board

DAVID W LACY, *Convener*
WILLIAM C HEWITT, *Vice-Convener*
FINLAY A J MACDONALD, *Principal Clerk*

APPENDIX A

Guidance Notes on Assembly Reports

There is a general complaint that the "Blue Book" is too lengthy. Clearly, the longer the book the higher the publication costs and the greater the challenge to commissioners to assimilate its contents before coming to the General Assembly—but how to reduce its length?

The purpose of the book is twofold:

1. to enable commissioners to prepare for the Assembly;

2. to become part of the permanent record of the Church's work.

To some extent these purposes are in tension. At best commissioners will have one month to absorb the contents of the book before coming to the Assembly. However, once the Assembly is over all the time in the world is available for the purposes of consulting the record. A balance has to be struck so that commissioners do not suffer from information overload, while at the same time ensuring that the record is adequate.

From time to time appeals are made to Boards and Committees to keep their reports as short as possible. However, it was clear from discussion at the Co-ordinating Forum last September, that some guidance from the Board of Practice and Procedure would be useful, in the interests of consistency. The key question is, "What needs to go in the report?".

In an effort to answer this question the Board suggests that each report fall into three sections as follows:

(a) a statement summarising the general work of the Board over the year;

(b) fuller background material relating to **decisions** the Board is seeking from the Assembly;

(c) brief expressions of thanks as appropriate, eg. in respect of retiring Conveners, Vice-Conveners and members of staff, bearing in mind that retiring members of staff are presented to the Moderator at the closing session.

The proposed deliverance would relate to (b) above,

ie. to seeking the Assembly's approval of specific recommendations. "Noting" and "thanking" deliverances would be discouraged.

Conveners would be free, as at present, to use their ten minute speeches as they felt most appropriate in terms of emphasis on (a), (b) or (c). As a general rule the speech might reasonably focus on what was not already in print, on the assumption that what was in print had been read.

Where Boards were presenting substantial reports, eg. from study groups, these could most helpfully be annexed to reports as appendices. This would make them available for the interested reader and ensure that they formed part of the permanent record.

APPENDIX B

Act Anent Granting and Signing of Deeds

The General Assembly, in view of the fact that property belongs to the Church at home and abroad, in respect of which it may be necessary that deeds and other documents should be granted and signed by parties officially representing the General Assembly, hereby authorise and empower the Moderator of the General Assembly, whom failing the Moderator of the previous General Assembly and the Principal Clerk of the General Assembly, whom failing the Depute Clerk, to sign on behalf of the Church all such deeds and documents as may be required up to the date of the meeting of the next General Assembly.

APPENDIX C

Act amending Act II, 1984

Edinburgh, May X, 2001, Sess. X.
The General Assembly enact and ordain that Act II, 1984 as amended by Act VI, 1992 is further amended as follows:

1. Amend the title of the Act to read "Act anent Presbytery Visits to Congregations".

2. In section 1 after "visited" add "in rota".

3. Delete section 3.

4. Amend section 6 to read "The Clerk of the Presbytery or the Convener of the visiting team, after consultation with the minister, shall give notice of the details of the process, which shall be intimated to the congregation at public worship in advance on two Sundays. Copies of the schedule shall be sent to the minister and Session Clerk. One or more of the visiting team shall, during the course of the process of visiting the congregation, conduct public worship, or address the congregation on a week-day, whichever is found more convenient. The congregation shall be given advice as may be considered appropriate and helpful for the promotion of Christian work and fellowship. The minister shall be present on these occasions."

5. The Basis for Discussion appended to the Act shall be amended to read as follows:

BASIS FOR PREPARATION BY CONGREGATION AND DISCUSSION BETWEEN VISITING-TEAM AND OFFICE-BEARERS

A. WORSHIP

1. In what ways do service-times reflect and contribute to the life of the congregation and community? Is worship part of the week-day life of the congregation?

2. (a) Have any new forms of worship been introduced; who leads this worship, and how will this develop in the near future?

   (b) If worship has not changed for some time, what outstanding needs require to be met and how can worship be made more meaningful?

   (c) What provision is made for the place of, and participation by children and young people in, worship?

3. What resources and materials are used in worship, including musical resources? (e.g. choir, instruments)

4. What difficulties if any arise from the administration of the Sacrament of Baptism to infants in accordance with Act V, 2000?

5. What is the frequency of and particular nature of the celebration of the Sacrament of Holy Communion?

6. How can the sacramental life of the congregation be advanced, and what understanding do the congregation have of its significance?

B.   USE AND DEVELOPMENT OF OFFICE BEARERS

1. (a)   Are office-bearers representative of the congregation's life (e.g. age, gender)?

    (b)   How are younger people and non-office-bearers involved in leadership?

    (c)   Are there sufficient office-bearers to allow duties to be spread widely?

    (d)   What are the strengths and weaknesses of the congregation's form of constitution (model deed, etc)?

2. (a)   In what ways do office-bearers become knowledgeable about the wider work of the Church?

    (b)   How can this be resourced?

3. What is the quality of relationship with the Presbytery?

C.   CONGREGATIONAL LIFE

1. (a)   What organisations and groups exist?

    (b)   Are any in need of review or renewal?

    (c)   Are there needs and interests unmet for which new initiatives are needed?

2. What is the membership trend in numbers, age and gender?

3. How many paid staff does the congregation have? Who are they? What are the responsibilities of each and how are these prioritised and shared?

D.   CHRISTIAN EDUCATION

1. (a)   To what extent does the congregation comply with the Church of Scotland Code of Good Practice for the Protection of Children and Young People in the Church?

    (b)   When assessing this, it is important to refer to the Quinquennial Schedule, which is available in Unit 7 section 9 of the Child Protection Handbook. A copy of this handbook was issued to every Session Clerk in September 2000. This schedule describes the practical steps which are required to be evidenced to satisfy the requirements of the General Assembly. Further information and advice is available from the Child Protection Unit, which will be happy to help to identify sensitive ways in which congregations can be assisted to comply with these requirements.

2. Is the responsibility of the Minister and Kirk Session for the Christian education of all age groups within the congregation being exercised? How could this be improved for each age-group, including adults?

3. What resources and educational media are utilised, and what further resources are required?

E.   MISSION

1. What are the missionary needs of the congregation and parish?

2. In what ways is the congregation involved in the life of the community, listening to its needs and responding? What foreseeable changes in the community may make demands upon the congregation?

3. In what ways does the congregation, or groups from it, take part in joint ventures or partnerships with—

   (a) Other Church of Scotland congregations?

   (b) congregations of other denominations?

   (c) community groups?

4. What obstacles prevent good relationships with Christian Churches or groups locally? How can these be overcome?

5. How are members encouraged to share and assume responsibility in the wider work of the Church?

6. What further goals could the congregation pursue in mission?

F. CHRISTIAN LIBERALITY

1. What comments do the office-bearers have about the present financial circumstances of the congregation: do they foresee changes, either within or outside the congregation, which will affect these circumstances?

2. In what ways does the Financial Board keep Christian liberality before the congregation? (For example by planned giving, the use of Gift Aid Forms, etc.) Has a stewardship campaign been undertaken in the last five years?

3. In what ways is the congregation helped to understand its financial commitment to the wider work and witness of the Church nationally and internationally?

G. FABRIC

1. Are the buildings, including Manse, Church, Halls, adequate and used to the full?

2. Manse Fabric. Is this being maintained to the minister's satisfaction?

3. Are the Church and Halls made available to other local organisations and on what basis?

4. Are there any foreseeable changes or developments in the community which would alter the demand or need for the existing buildings?

5. Is there an ongoing, systematic strategy for the maintenance and development of buildings? Have the recommendations in the most recent Property Survey been implemented?

H. MINISTRY SUPPORT

1. <u>Personal Finance</u>: Does the minister feel that he/she is coping financially? Is he/she aware of what help the Church could give?

2. <u>Provision for the future:</u> Is the minister aware of the extent of the Church's provisions for retirement ie pension and housing?

3. <u>Pastoral Issues</u>: Is the minister aware of the range of pastoral support provided by the Church eg Presbytery Pastoral Advisers, CareAssist, Face to Face Counselling?

4. <u>Ministry Development</u>: What plans does the Minister have for his or her own development? How does he or she review his or her work? How is the Minister planning to use Study Leave or pursue other Continuing Education?

5. <u>Administrative Support</u>: Is the Kirk Session satisfied that adequate administrative support is given to the minister?

6. How does the Kirk Session keep Ministry Development and Continuing Education before the Minister and Kirk Session, and encourage him or her in these areas?

7. In what other ways does the Kirk Session support the minister?

APPENDIX D

THE CHURCH OF SCOTLAND

SCHEDULE of GUIDANCE for
PRESBYTERY VISITS to CONGREGATIONS
(Revised by the General Assemblies of 1984 and 2001)

Presbytery .... Congregation ....

Names of Visiting Team ....

Dates of Visit ....

The hallmark of the visit should be the celebration of the Congregation's witness, together with the recognition of its place and role within the Presbytery and the Church in Scotland.

In such celebration the underlying "supervisory" function of the Presbytery should not be overlooked: the skilled and experienced help and encouragement of the Presbytery visitors are charged with bringing to the Congregation can only be properly exercised if the visitors fully and completely understand the composition, strengths, weaknesses, aims and particular projects of the Minister, Kirk Session, Board, Agencies and Members of the Congregation being visited. Thus will the visitors be able to give positive help and encouragement, and constructive criticism where necessary, and to demonstrate to the Congregation the unity of the Church.

The leader of the visiting team should be a person of experience and maturity. The remainder should be chosen bearing in mind both the advantages of experience and the two-way learning process which such visits engender. The numbers and composition of the visiting team will depend on the size, location and strength of the Congregation being visited. Not all members need necessarily be members of the Presbytery, but the majority should be and the whole team should receive such training as the Presbytery deems appropriate.

To conduct the visit satisfactorily and to enable adequate opportunity to be given for full discussion and exchange of views, the visitors will meet with the Minister, other members of a ministry team, the Kirk Session, the appropriate financial board, should meet the office-bearers of other groups within the Church such as the Guild, the Young Woman's Group, Sunday Schools, Youth Fellowship, Bible Class, etc., and should meet so far as possible with other members of the congregation, to give the visitors as broad an experience as possible of the life and work of the congregation and its witness for the future. Presbyteries are free to appoint to visiting teams members of the Church whose skilled or specialist training or knowledge and experience will help and strengthen the discussions to take place, e.g. members of the Presbyterial Council of the Guild, the Education Committee of the Presbytery, Officers of the Boys' Brigade Battalion, School Teachers. A member of the visiting team shall conduct the morning service on a Sunday during the process, at which service the Minister of the congregation shall be present.

The following notes concern details of the process.

Notes for Visiting Team

a.   The leader of the visiting team shall give as much advance notice as possible to the Minister and Congregation of the proposed visit.

b. The visiting team should remain together for the meeting with the Minister, but it may be helpful for individual members of the team to meet with other congregational agencies on occasion(s). During discussion the individual skills and expertise of members of the visiting team shall be encouraged and used – a member experienced in finance might lead the discussion with the Congregational Board.

c. The questionnaire annexed to these notes is to be regarded as an aid to discussion and is not to be regarded exclusively as the basis for discussion and interview.

d. The Minister should be encouraged to express how he or she understands his or her ministry and its properties, how he or she sees the relationship with other churches and with the community at large and how he or she copes with the total workload. The meeting with the Minister should give him or her the opportunity of discussing, in confidence, any problems.

e. The meeting with the Kirk Session should enable them to discuss fully and frankly with the visitors its priorities of work and mission in the community along with their understanding of resources available and required.

f. The purpose of this part of the process is to set goals for the future mission of the congregation.

g. The report of the visiting team to the Superintendence Committee of Presbytery should be full and provide the basis for a detailed discussion concerning the Congregation visited. A copy of the report by the visiting team shall be sent to the Kirk Session before the meeting of the Superintendence Committee. The Congregation shall be entitled to be represented at the meeting of the Superintendence Committee.

h. If any matter of discontent within the Congregation should come to the notice of the visitors, they must act impartially and attempt to bring about a reconciliation. In particular, if any complaint is made against the Minister the visitors should hold a further conference with the Minister before taking any further action. They should, so far as possible, attempt to act as conciliators with a view to resolving the matter before considering the need of any formal report to the Presbytery.

i. The visitors are reminded that one of the Presbytery's chief functions is the superintendence of congregations within its bounds, the Presbyterial visit being one of the methods whereby the General Assembly require Presbyteries to implement this obligation. Therefore all meetings in connection with the visit are called by authority of the Presbytery whose visitors are representatives of a superior court. Accordingly all meetings shall be constituted by a duly authorised member of the Presbytery who shall act as chairman throughout the proceedings.

j. The Presbytery shall be responsible if necessary for paying a pulpit supply fee to enable a member of the visiting team to conduct Sunday worship in the Congregation visited.

Notes for Presbytery Clerks

a. The Superintendence Committee of Presbytery shall meet at least twice per annum, one of such meetings preceding the programme of visits for that year, to enable members of the Committee and visitors to consider and confer about the congregations to be visited and the information to be obtained.

b. The Presbytery Clerk shall provide each member of the visiting team with an extract from the Presbytery records of membership statistics and congregational finances including contributions towards Mission and Aid and Ministry Support and known expenditure on Fabric for a period of four years prior to the date of the visit, together with any policy of Readjustment as far as known.

c. The report of the visiting team to the Superintendence Committee of Presbytery should be full and provide the basis for a detailed discussion concerning the Congregation visited. A copy of the report by the visiting team shall be sent to the Kirk Session before the meeting of the Superintendence Committee. The Congregation shall be entitled to be represented at the meeting of the Superintendence Committee.

d. The Presbytery shall be responsible for paying the pulpit supply fee which enables a member of the visiting team to be free to conduct Sunday worship in the Congregation visited.

e. Presbyteries are referred to Act II, 1984 as amended by Act VI 1992 and Act X, 2001.

Notes for Congregations

a. The preparation by the congregation and its office-bearers is vital to the success of the visitation process and the basis for preparation and discussion should be discussed in detail before the formal process begins.

b. Whilst the Moderator of the Kirk Session retains the right to be present at all meetings of the Kirk Session, it is a right which he or she may waive in order to facilitate frank exchanges between office-bearers and Presbytery visitors. These discussions may, of course, be carried forward in the course of meetings other than a constituted Kirk Session.

APPENDIX E

Report of Inter-Board Group on Presbytery Boundaries

MAY 2001

INTRODUCTION

1.1 The origins of the Group are to be found in the General Assembly of 1999 when it was agreed that the Board of Practice and Procedure, "in consultation with Presbyteries and the Boards of Ministry and National Mission, undertake a fresh examination of Presbytery Boundaries".

1.2 When a Committee established by the Board of Practice and Procedure first met to consider the remit it decided that two options were open to it. The first would be to tinker round the edges of Presbyteries, shifting the occasional charge from one Presbytery to another. Such an exercise would have created minimal stir and would have allowed members of the Committee a quick discharge from their less than onerous duties. However, it was readily apparent to the members of the Committee that the issue was not simply the viability of some smaller Presbyteries but the effective functioning of Presbyteries as a whole within the present Church organisation. This realisation led the Committee to pursue a second and more radical option, namely, to reflect upon the role and function of the Presbytery, its relationship to the congregations within its bounds and its relationship to the General Assembly's Board and Committee structure. The Board of Practice and Procedure acknowledged the legitimacy of this approach and, on its recommendation, the General Assembly of 2000 resolved to take the matter forward through "an Inter-Board Group drawn from the Boards of Ministry, National Mission, Parish Education and Practice and Procedure, with the Board of Practice and Procedure as the lead Board with responsibility for servicing the Group." Subsequently the Group found it helpful to co-opt a representative of the Board of Stewardship and Finance and the Rev Gordon Jamieson, Director of Stewardship, was appointed. In addition, representatives of the Special Commission on Review and Reform, the Assembly Council and the Committee on Ecumenical Relations have attended some meetings. Indeed, we are encouraged by the extent to which our thinking reflects that of the Special Commission. The Group has also been mindful of an instruction given by the Assembly to the Board of Practice and Procedure "to initiate a meeting among SCIFU Churches to explore the feasibility of establishing a Boundaries Commission to harmonise the boundaries of Presbyteries, dioceses, districts and circuits". While the primary focus of the Group's thinking to date has been the operation of our own Presbytery system, the ecumenical dimension has not been overlooked. Having consulted with the Convener and Secretary of the Ecumenical Relations Committee the Group proposes that the consultation process it is recommending should include SCIFU Churches. As a final point in this introductory section it should be noted that the Group has not considered the position of the Presbyteries of Europe and Jerusalem, their roles being the subject of a separate review. No special consideration has been given to the Presbytery of England, the Group considering that its place in a new scheme would be a matter for detailed consultation as would the place of every current Presbytery.

PRELIMINARY STUDY AND ACTION

2.1. With this choice of the second option, the Group began by looking at what it believed to be the essential duties of a Presbytery. We were aware that before we could determine boundaries and therefore, to some extent, the structure of the Church, it was necessary to examine the role of the Presbytery. In the early days of the Reformation Presbyteries did not exist. The Church was governed by the General Assembly, Synods, meeting twice a year, whose territory roughly equated to the medieval dioceses, and Kirk Sessions. There is no mention of Presbyteries in the First Book of Discipline and they only began to be organised about 1580. They were created to offer the synods of the Church help on two fronts. Their first help was to be a spiritual one. Presbyteries were the places where ministers met for

"Spiritual Exercises". Indeed, this was the primary function in these first years of the Reformed Church. But they also were designed to relieve the synods of some of the growing burden of work which went with a rapidly expanding church. History indicates that the nature and function of the Presbytery has changed over the centuries. The Group believes it is time to consider another major change.

2.2. The Group was assisted in looking at the function of the Presbytery by examining the detailed list of duties given in Weatherhead's "The Constitution and Laws of the Church of Scotland". (see page 101) We tried to assess these duties. Many belong to the functions of ministry, many to the supervision of congregations and many to detailed administration of policy which is done hand in hand with Assembly Boards. It was noticed that nowhere in the lists does it allow for Presbyteries to be a place of fellowship and encouragement, even if, in Weatherhead the list is prefaced with the comment that "the Presbytery is responsible for all spiritual matters within its bounds, and should be alert to take suitable initiatives for the advancement of Christ's Kingdom, even if these are neither prescribed by law nor instructed by the Assembly". Nor is there a focus of real power in the Presbytery of today - a place where "the buck really stops here".

2.3.1. Further study and examination led the Group to the point where we started to envisage "the Church being given back to its members" as one member put it - the need for Presbyteries to be allowed to be more active and more responsible than the present set-up of the Church allows. We live in an age of devolution and, even if it is a misplaced analogy to compare the working of the Church to the political processes of Scotland in recent years, nonetheless it is, at least, a parallel for us to see that we live in times when the passing on of certain responsibilities from the centre to more localised bodies (of the Scottish Parliament or the Welsh Assembly) is very much an issue.

2.3.2. The Committee therefore addressed the question of passing power, responsibility and resources from the central Church back to Presbyteries and congregations.

We looked at the balance to be retained in allowing for the maintaining of a proper central structure for the integrity of the National Church while, at the same time, liberating the Presbyteries of the Church to assume far greater responsibility in planning and in the use of resources, financial and other. The obvious consequence of this would be that the boundaries of a Presbytery would need to be sufficiently large to ensure that real resourcing and real power could be responsibly transferred. In short, the Group's vision of the ideal Presbytery is of a body which effectively supports the work of local Churches within a significant regional area, managing its own (substantial) budget, allocating resources and taking the sometimes difficult decisions which that entails, employing appropriate staff (whole-time and part-time, salaried and voluntary) and debating issues arising out of the life of local Churches rather than material "sent down" from Assembly Boards and Committees. Inevitably the question of how many Presbyteries arises and the danger is that the debate then becomes one about numbers. In its discussions the Group has looked at models based on twelve, seven and four new-style Presbyteries. However, the critical thing is that the number be small enough to enable a significant devolving of responsibility and the sustaining of viable regional Church centres. Sensitivity to the requirements of remote areas is also called for.

2.3.3. We were well aware of the size of the task involved in getting from where we are now to the realisation of such a vision of what Presbyteries might become. In particular, we noted that:

(1) We live with the paradox of recognising the need for change yet at the same time being afraid of change. There could be many reasons for this but perhaps the lack of confidence which adheres to a declining body makes our Church and Presbyteries today more anxious to hang on to what we possess rather than to submit our structures and our way of thinking to change which leads us to an unknown future.

(2) We have a tendency to construct our own interpretation of history and therefore to believe that radical proposals for change are an attack on the very basis of presbyterianism which our predecessors so faithfully strove to hand on to the succeeding generations. To suggest new structures which might seem to eliminate from the Church of the twenty-first century any particular Presbytery which is rooted in the seventeenth, eighteenth, nineteenth or twentieth centuries is to strip away our heritage. And so we realise that, though there may be a willingness among some to talk about change, it will only happen, as far as they are concerned, as long as you don't touch me or my Presbytery.

(3) The changes being contemplated by the Group are certainly significant. But, if the basis of this report is accepted, namely that there is a need to effect a significant transfer of decision-making responsibility from the central administration to regional Presbyteries, we must admit from the very beginning that getting from here to there, is not achievable in one single step. Therefore, arguments against radical change will undeniably be able to point to weaknesses in the plan, to potential circumstances of untidiness in the practice of the Church as it goes through any change, and to a higher degree of uncertainty as to where we shall emerge than ever we have experienced in our own lifetime in the Church - though there is no uncertainty that what will emerge will still be national, reformed and consistent with our evolving history.

2.4. As a Group we were aware that we needed as much help as possible. Last June a day consultation was held in Glasgow with representatives of a sample of Presbyteries reflecting different areas of the country, eg. urban, rural, highland, lowland, island and town. The members of the Group held a two-day conference at Troon in November at which we took advantage of the availability of a team of management consultants from the McKinsey Group who were working on a *pro bono* basis with two Assembly Boards. They were supportive of the direction we were taking and helpful in suggesting to us various ways for the Church to address this structural reformation. In addition they advised that, in moving to a different structure, the Church needed also to move to a new way of working. The Group recognises that this must be a major focus of the consultation process. As already noted, we have also been ably helped and encouraged both by the Assembly Council and the Special Commission on Review and Reform. Consultation and shared information have been of the essence of our work. The fact that this interim report is acknowledged and supported by all members of the Group, including the Conveners and permanent staff, is noteworthy.

ACTION AND CONSULTATION POINTS

3.1. The Group proposes the following points for the Church to discuss at Presbytery, Kirk Session and membership levels and also with representatives of the SCIFU Churches. We are more than aware that the discussion points do not comprise a foolproof comprehensive scheme for the reformed Church. But if we have a vision of where we could go in our Church we believe it important that the process of fleshing out the details that are attendant on change needs to be effected by a number of people and agencies. Vital in that process is the contribution of the present Church membership. But what we are prepared to do at this stage is to point the Church in the direction we have been looking and at what we believe to be the possible as well as the desirable.

3.2. The Group has reached a point in its work where it offers the following model as a basis for consultation throughout the Church-

i) that the Church structures itself on a number of Presbyteries small enough to enable a significant shifting of responsibility from the centre and the sustaining of viable regional church centres. These centres would be cities and towns which have good links with airports, rail stations, ferry ports and roads;

ii) that these Presbyteries be serviced and resourced by appropriate teams of full-time and part-time salaried employees and volunteers with specific remits to support and develop the work of the local church in areas such as mission, education, worship, ecumenism, ministry support, property maintenance and financial management.

iii) that Presbyteries would assume responsibility for some of the functions currently dealt with centrally, eg.

the allocation of a ministry budget within the bounds, the deployment of staff resources if demand exceeds supply;

iv) that Presbyteries manage their own budgets, which would be substantial; (the methods of allocation among congregations and collection from congregations to be discussed as part of the consultation process).

v) that, if it is felt that the resultant Presbyteries were too large, consideration be given to ministers, elders and deacons, being commissioned to seats in Presbyteries on a rotational basis as for the General Assembly and that the categories of non-parochial ministers (including retired ministers) entitled to seats in Presbytery be reviewed;

vi) that each Presbytery be divided into a number of Districts - natural areas, eg. a sector of a city, a small town, an island, a group of villages - where a large degree of flexibility and opportunity would be allowed. Districts would bring together representatives of congregations and they would have a basic function of mission, an immense challenge for the Church today and one which calls for imagination and a flexibility of approach. Such Districts would operate under the Presbytery, initiating proposals from their own areas but freed from the bureaucratic and outdated models which are strangling many Presbyteries today. They would not be "courts" of the Church.

vii) that Presbyteries meet two or three times a year, perhaps all day Saturday to encourage the attendance of elders in employment, with districts meeting more frequently and initiating much of the business for the Presbytery, e.g. applications for resources to undertake particular local projects;

viii) that thought be given to the role of Presbytery, not simply as a tier of government but also as a place where local leadership is exercised, and the Church is seen to be powerfully present.

3.3. It is inevitable that the vision we present for revised Presbytery boundaries and, with them, revised responsibilities, will have implications for the structure of the Church at General Assembly level. A number of functions currently carried out by Boards and Committees will pass to Presbyteries. There will be a noticeable shifting of power, authority, responsibility and resources from the centre to the regions. Funding at Presbytery level will be assisted by the greatly reduced costs of Committee and Board travel. While there will be a continuing need for some central committee structure, the membership attending will be much smaller. Indeed, those from whom we have taken advice tell us what many of us already know, that the sorts of numbers attending Committees at present are obstructive to decision-making rather than being helpful. Presbyteries will continue to be represented but with fewer Presbyteries the numbers will be reduced automatically.

NEXT STEPS

4.1   The above is but a skeleton of what might be. The Committee is not afraid to bring such a skeleton idea to the General Assembly because we would value now a process of consultation on the basis of a vision. The people do not perish where the "i"s are not dotted and "t"s are not crossed. The people do not perish if we take a step into the unknown. The people do not perish if we dare to express gratitude for our past and then decide that it is time to move on. Where the people perish is where the Church has no vision. In the last 40 years our Church has lost 30 per cent of its membership. We have Presbyteries now where there are more vacancies than ministers to be Interim Moderators. The business of Presbytery has become largely so routine that many of the best people who could serve do not do so. And it is beyond the point of urgency for us to build on our heritage and offer ourselves the possibility of a new structure. This will not solve the decline in the Church by itself, but it may all the more conclusively assist in that decline being arrested and then turned round. Indeed, this movement from the centre to the regions has the potential to lead to a greater local identification with the work of the Church as a whole with a consequent renewal of energy for mission, outreach and service. We cannot be bound by yesterday's solutions any more. We must not be inhibited by fear of change and drawn back from change by the cautious voice of legalism. These consultation proposals present the Church with a stark challenge. It is either to enter into an adventure for the new century, new wine into a new wine skin, or it is to stay where we are with ever more apparent decline, lack of confidence and the growing inability to function as the Church we think we are and would claim to be for the nation of Scotland.

4.2   The Committee recognises that there is a balance to be struck between drawing up proposals so vague that they offer an inadequate basis for consultation and proposals so detailed as to imply that minds have been made up and consultation will be a mere formality. We hope that in this report we have got that balance about right. If the Assembly authorises a wider consultation process on the basis of the report, the Group intends to consult not only widely, but in depth and detail, beginning with a series of supported consultations throughout the country in late August. These meetings would allow views to be heard on the general thrust of the proposals and a start to be made to the process of fleshing them out. However, the magnitude of this issue is such that the group believes that following these supported consultations with the wider Church, there should be a two stage Presbytery Consultation during 2001–2002. Therefore, it is envisaged, that Presbyteries would consider the matter during the autumn, sending their views to the Principal Clerk by mid-November. In December the Group would draft a further consultation document that would take into account the submissions made by Presbyteries. This second consultation paper would be distributed in time for Presbyteries to provide a second response by mid-February 2002. It will be essential therefore, for Presbyteries to establish a process by which they will be in a position over the next year to make a dual response which will inform the Group as it prepares to bring a more fully developed scheme to the General Assembly of 2002. As any revised scheme would require Barrier Act procedure there would then be further opportunity for discussion and comment between the Assemblies of 2002 and 2003.

Finally, the Group places on record its thanks to the Board of Practice and Procedure for administrative support and for the Board's approval of the proposed consultation process.

In the name of the Inter-Board Group

ALASTAIR H SYMINGTON, *Convener*
DAVID W. LACY, *Convener,*
Board of Practice and Procedure
FINLAY A J MACDONALD, *Secretary*

Membership of the Inter-Board Group

Board of Practice and Procedure
Rev Alastair H Symington, *Convener*
Rev David W Lacy
Mr Michael Gossip
Rev Marjory A MacLean
Rev Finlay A J Macdonald, *Secretary*

Board of National Mission
Rev James M Gibson
Rev Arthur P Barrie
Rev Douglas A O Nicol

Board of Ministry
Rev Professor William F Storrar
Rev John P Chalmers

Board of Parish Education
Rev G Stewart Smith
Mr Iain W Whyte

Board of Stewardship & Finance
Rev Gordon Jamieson, Director of Stewardship
Some meetings of the Group were also attended by:

Mrs Helen McLeod (Assembly Council)

Rev Peter Neilson, Rev Gordon Kennedy (Special Commission on Review and Reform)

Rev Tom Macintyre, Rev Sheilagh M Kesting (Ecumenical Relations Committee)

APPENDIX F

THE GENDER ATTITUDE PROJECT (GAP)

The woman's cause is man's
They rise or fall together. *(Tennyson)*

Who is concerned about gender?

The questions asked about gender, and the discussions within all of the Churches about the roles of women and men, must be viewed against the backdrop of similar discussions within society at large. It is often said that the attitudes apparent in the Churches mirror those of society for the Church is not so distinct from its surrounding culture. This is probably true, although it may also be true that the Church is more conservative in its attitudes and more reluctant to change, so that some women and men find greater openness, acceptance and affirmation outside the Church. It is unfortunate that the Church is not more markedly different in its attitudes for it is called to live with a set of gospel based values and ideals which can be in tension with those of secular culture. Is it possible, therefore, to have a vision of a Church where, one day, women and men worship and work in partnership as equals; where all the opportunities to serve God in the Church are open to women; where the differing gifts of all people, women and men, young and old, are welcomed and nurtured? It is often the world beyond the Church, however, which is more vigilant at tackling questions of discrimination and power, more aware of its attitudes, more willing to put policies in place which counter acts of discrimination and harassment and readier to address the different needs and ambitions of women and men.

The following summations of articles in The Herald (August 22, 2000) provide illustrations of who is concerned about gender.

- **'Female of the species is bookworm' (p4)**
  Surveys show that thirty years ago the level of book reading for men and women was roughly equal but changed as the number of women pursuing successful careers rose. Books are also cheaper than they were and the book buying public is primarily female. Men are spending their time reading newspapers and business reports from work rather than books - a cultural gap is perhaps developing between men and women.

- **'Smoking timebomb as lung disease doubles for women' (p8)**
  Chronic lung disease among women has doubled over the last ten years due to smoking and if the rate of smoking among teenage girls continues the level of disease will continue to rise. Rates for men peaked in the mid-1990s and are now steady but those for women rose every year.

- **'Parent power and boosted morale bridges the gender gap' (p9)**
  A school trying to bridge the achievement gap between girls and boys by boosting the confidence of male pupils was hopeful that its course of action was working. Fourth year boys at St. Modan's High School in Stirling have been receiving additional support and there has been a narrowing of the gap in results between girls and boys. The culture of 'laddism' is perhaps to blame for making a negative attitude acceptable. Parent and son evenings were introduced and a group of male teachers acted as role models and gave encouragement. It was identified that boys are competitive but give up more easily than girls.

It is clear from these accounts that for many professionals and researchers it is important and useful to examine the position of women and men separately, to draw comparisons, and to raise questions about the differences. The year 2000 was the 25th Anniversary of the Sex Discrimination Act and in these years there has been a marked advance of women in many professions - for example, half of all graduating doctors and Church of Scotland ministers are now women. But 'glass ceilings' still exist. Women can advance more easily in professions where there is not such a fixed career structure. The influence of popular culture is certainly a factor in creating what is deemed to be acceptable behaviour for women and men, perhaps more importantly for boys and girls. The pattern of studious girl and unmotivated boy is even present in the Harry Potter books! (Hermione is studious and Ron can't get enthusiastic about libraries at all!)

It is now recognised that, while our sex roles are biologically determined, there are also gender roles that are socially, historically and culturally constructed. The individual is not always free to act as she or he chooses for there are societal forces at play: economic realities and opportunities, expectations we have of ourselves based on gender, our upbringing and our interpretation of our faith. These are human constructions which change and can be changed. There are forms of gender relations, in Church, home and society, which are unjust and in the face of them God's will for humans has to be sought. Neither male nor female is superior or inferior, better or worse and neither has the right to impose its expectations on the other. Sexism is a sin which, like racism, must be challenged and steps taken to eliminate it. GAP is concerned with gender and its work seeks to make the Church aware of gender discrimination and calls upon the whole Church to build gender justice.

What could the Church learn from others who are concerned about gender? For example: most Sunday Schools will be full of girls and bereft of boys—a bit like the adult pews! Why is this case? Is it linked to the situation in schools where girls are more eager to learn, or is it linked to the lack of male role models in our Churches for young boys—or both? It would be interesting to have the statistics for new communicants and GAP suggests that those 'joining the Church' are predominantly female. GAP asks the Church that if this is the situation in your congregation are you able to find out why, and can you take action to encourage men to consider membership? It is already the case that the majority of new elders are women, which is to be welcomed as the balance needs to be redressed. It is similar for those entering the ordained ministry of word and sacrament. This ought not to be feared but there would be valid questions to be asked if, for example, over a number of years there were no men accepted as candidates for the ministry (and equally, if there were no women accepted.) Is there a danger that the Church is becoming largely female? What should be noted is that while women may predominate numerically, men remain dominant in most positions of power and policy making in the Church - and indeed as a minority are even more determined to hold on to that power. There is a real challenge here to become a true community of women and men, working together in partnership and respect.

Gender Attitude Research Project

It is anticipated that some of the concerns raised above will be addressed in the GAP Research Project which will examine the roles played by women and men within the Church and the underlying attitudes and assumptions about what these roles should be. The Research Student began work in the spring of 2000 and the work may have been completed by the 2001 Assembly. The research has been conducted via a combination of interviews, questionnaires and focus groups and GAP is grateful to all - ministers, members and congregations - who gave of their time and were willing to express their opinions.

Complementing the Research Project will be work by an Edinburgh University honours student who has interviewed women ministers from varying age groups to ascertain their different experiences of the Church. It is proposed to publish both pieces of work and make them available to the Church at large. GAP is very grateful to The Novum Trust, The Church of Scotland Guild, The Board of Stewardship & Finance and The Church & Nation Committee for sharing our concerns enough to provide funding.

Paisley Presbytery Retreat

GAP was invited to contribute to a retreat for members of Paisley Presbytery: such invitations are not frequent and are encouraged! Material from the GAP Resource Pack was used; ministers and elders engaged in Bible Study and some personal experiences were shared. It is GAP's impression on all such occasions that people are never very sure what they are going to hear from GAP, appreciate the invitation to reflect on concerns which are new to many and are consequently surprised at the range of topics discussed.

Meetings with Boards and Committees of the Church

GAP has continued to meet with representatives from Church Committees and Boards to open up discussions on how gender issues are addressed within these forums. The meetings (with representatives from The Board of Ministry, The Board of National Mission, The Board of Social Responsibility and the Board of Parish Education) were a useful way to explore a range of questions and in each case members of GAP felt that awareness of the complexity of gender issues had been increased for everyone present. An initial tendency to regard the subject as one of statistics or of interest mainly to women or of simple 'equality' in terms of who does what, changed to a search for the reality of the experience of women and men in the Church. People varied in their response to what is clearly a sensitive subject. For some, it seemed, it was still a matter of: "There is no problem". Others advocated a 'softly, softly' approach, apparently fearing that an open confrontation of continuing sexist attitudes would do more harm than good.

Not surprisingly, in at least one case the discussion moved on to power structures within the Church and how disabling these can be for both women and men. The absence of young men from the Church was often noted as was the numerical predominance of women, encapsulated in a notable phrase: "the role model provided by powerful men in a fundamentally female institution". There was discussion about the roles of lay and ordained members of the Church, about the relationships and attitudes which appear between ministers and deacons and between public, well-known figures and those who choose to serve in quiet ways. These have been important meetings leading to useful and enlightening discussions.

Despite the usefulness of the dialogue GAP has perceived a suspicion of the fundamental purposes of The Gender Attitude Project and has observed that there is a tendency to defend traditional practices and attitudes. This is a matter of concern because unless we can address these important issues together in a spirit of community the problems will remain and people will continue to feel marginalised and even alienated. It is important to ask why some in the Church believe this to be such a delicate subject when it is a matter of informed and robust discussion in civil society. Whether the essence of what was discussed at these small meetings actually has an impact on the Boards themselves, however, remains to be seen.

Contacts with other Churches Concerned About Gender

On a 'lead Church' model, the Gender Attitude Project has provided a focus for gender awareness work which is acknowledged and appreciated in the ecumenical community in Scotland. It has been encouraging and useful, therefore, to discover how such initiatives are pursued in other countries and by Churches there. Contact has been made with the Gospel and Gender Unit of the Uniting Church in Australia (a more highly resourced group than GAP), with a new gender and justice initiative in the Blantyre Synod of the Church of Central Africa Presbyterian in Malawi, and with gender-issues work in ecumenical and para-Church organisations, especially in Europe. These contacts have provided written materials, opportunities for personal contacts, and encouragement for the importance of the group's work. This aspect of the Project's work echoes the original ecumenical thrust behind its establishment.

The World Alliance of Reformed Churches established, in 1997, its Department of Partnership of Women and Men. All member Churches of WARC are "urged to form a continuing committee on partnership of women and men". The work of the WARC Department produces ongoing reminders to us that throughout the Reformed Churches world-wide many women face huge barriers to participation in their denominations. More than this, many women endure sexual harassment and abuse even within the Church. The work of GAP is a reminder to The Church of Scotland that Christians of all Churches have to stand together to combat sexual discrimination and violence in every form.

Men In Crisis?

Today, gender roles are changing: traditional family roles may be reversed; male dominated manual industry is in decline; new jobs are often short-term, part-time and in the service sector or high technology; changes in marriage patterns mean that many boys have few, if any, positive male role models. There is evidence that many men - particularly young men - are unsure of their role in society.

Consider the fact that suicide is now the biggest killer of young males in Scotland: in 1998 suicide killed as many under 35 year-olds as road accidents and drug deaths put together (The Sunday Herald, 28 May 2000.) The number of suicides by men aged 25 to 34 has doubled in the last ten years, as have incidents of self harm among youths aged 15 to 24 (The Herald, 19 May 2000.) This crisis among men has recently been charted by the Centre for Theology and Public Issues at New College, Edinburgh in <u>The Sorrows of Young Men: exploring their increasing risk of suicide</u> (CTPI Occasional Paper No. 45.)

In past times of great change the Church responded to the spiritual needs of men through organisations such as the Boys' Brigade, Toc-H, and the industrial chaplaincy movement. Indeed, it is possible to argue that throughout history the Church served men too well and that it is a patriarchal institution dedicated to keeping women subservient. This patriarchy has turned many women away from the Church. At the same time, many men do not see the Church as a place for them; its style and concerns are perceived as unmanly. Arguably, the Church in Scotland is failing to address the spiritual needs and aspirations of many women and men.

In failing to address the particular needs of men, the Churches are also doing a disservice to women. It is easy to portray issues such as domestic abuse, pornography or prostitution as 'women's issues'. What ought to be recognised is that these are men's issues also - men are the perpetrators of most violence against women and are the customers of pornography and prostitution. Women in Scotland continue to suffer at the hands of men.

In various places around the Church, these issues are beginning to be tackled. The Council of European Churches has asked the European Forum of Christian Men (which represents mainly the men's organisations of the continental European Churches) to attempt to bring a male perspective on these issues. This led to a consultation in Prague in June 2000 which was attended by the Revd. Peter W. Nimmo, with the support of the General Assembly's Committee on Ecumenical Relations. Churches Together in Britain and Ireland (CTBI) held a conference, 'Men's Voices', in Birmingham in September 2000, which again had Scottish representation. The outcome has been the beginnings of an ecumenical network to support those interested in the areas of men's identity, male spirituality, and developing mission to contemporary men.

The Resource Pack

The Gender Attitude Project Resource Pack is still available. It contains Bible Studies and Discussion Material and is ideal for Kirk Sessions, study groups, etc. who wish to raise awareness and explore attitudes. It is available (free of charge for the first copy!) from the office of The Depute Clerk.

Review Group

When GAP was established by the General Assembly of 1995 it was given a five-year life span so it was natural that during the year consideration would have to be given to the ending or the continuation of the project. To this end, GAP requested that The Board of Practice and Procedure establish a small Review Group which would evaluate the work of GAP over the five years and make recommendations. The Board agreed to this procedure and a report from the Review Group will be found in section 10 of the report.

Membership of Group

Two members resigned from GAP during the year and they are thanked for the contributions they made to the work. The Nomination Committee has been asked to recommend two new members, for appointment by the Board of Practice and Procedure, to serve from the General Assembly of 2001.

APPENDIX G

REPORT OF SCOTTISH CHURCHES' PARLIAMENTARY OFFICER

During the year 2000, the Scottish Churches Parliamentary Office established its basic working patterns of resourcing the Churches to engage effectively with the Scottish Parliament and Executive.

In the first half of the year, the high profile public controversy over repeal of "clause 28" was an important part of the workload. The different stances adopted by different Churches certainly complicated the issue for the work of the Office, but may in the end have helped to clarify the role of the Office, as one of enabling and supporting the input of the Churches into the debate. In practice, I was involved in setting up meetings with members of the Executive, making arrangements for evidence to be given to Parliamentary Committees, passing on Parliamentary inquiries to those who could respond on behalf of the Churches, and ensuring that those who were contributing on behalf of the Churches were kept up to date with developments and advised of opportunities. All of that was done for people on both sides of the argument.

Less acrimoniously, and with less publicity, the Office has continued to monitor the wide range of issues in which the Churches have an interest, and to provide information, briefings and advice. Evidence has been given by Church representatives to Parliamentary Committees on housing and homelessness and on asylum-seekers; meetings have been held with the Executive on family law, debt and financial exclusion; Churches have been represented on working parties on police checks for volunteers working with children and on guidelines for sex education; contacts have been made with Parliamentary Committees on matters as diverse as drug misuse and lobbying; responses have been made to consultation papers on topics from the siting of telecommunications masts to education issues; and Churches are involved in several cross-party groups. The Office has also produced a simple Guide to Scotland's Churches as a resource for Parliament and the Executive.

I was also glad to share in organising and supporting a Moderatorial visit to the Scottish Parliament, intended to emphasise the Church's support for people in public life, to deepen awareness of the Church's range of work, and to develop relationships in which conversations about matters of mutual concern can take place. The main features of the programme—which coincided fortuitously with intensive Parliamentary activity on an issue of major concern to the Church (long term care of the elderly)—were (a) personal meetings with each of the Party leaders (b) lunch with the Parliamentary Bureau (c) Time for Reflection (d) meeting with a Parliamentary Committee at the Netherbow (e) reception for MSPs and faith communities and (f) informal lunch with Parliamentary staff. The visit, which was compressed by circumstances into two days (rather than the three originally planned) was warmly received, created several opportunities for follow-up, and provoked encouragement on all sides for something similar to become an annual fixture of Moderatorial and Parliamentary years.

The Scottish Churches Social Inclusion Network (convened and serviced through the Scottish Churches Parliamentary Office) has continued to be one of the best ways in which Churches can share experience and insights, and carry on a conversation with Parliament and the Executive on a range of vital issues. The Office also brought together representatives of the Churches to hear the Executive's proposals for family law reform and share their early reactions to that. In these and other ways, the Office seeks to build trust among the Churches to maximise our effectiveness by working together. That is done by maintaining good working relationships with the various Committees of the participating Churches, and with ACTS; regular working links are also made with the Parliamentary Officers of the Catholic Bishops, Evangelical Alliance, and CARE, as well as links with other faith communities.

The Office, financially supported predominantly by the Church of Scotland but with contributions from the other participating Churches, operated well within budget in 2000 and was reluctant to employ the necessary research assistance until it was clear that other expenses left room in the budget. A part-time Researcher started in January 2001, and will add to the depth of support the Office is able to give.

In common with many bodies, Churches are at times struggling to keep pace with the opportunities to respond to consultation papers from the Scottish Executive and Parliament, especially to do so in ways that draw on the range and depth of the experience in different communities which is a major part of our contribution, and in ways that faithfully reflect the patterns of accountability in different Churches. Being able to participate is clearly something to be valued and encouraged, especially as more imaginative and inclusive forms of "consultation" are tried, but it is also demanding. While dramatic categoric statements catch headlines, patient work reflecting the experience, reflection, faith and vision of the Churches is likely to be a more fruitful contribution. These are issues about which, in Christ's name, we care; the question is whether we care enough to be effective in making the contribution that will make a difference.

The political year of 2000 was, of course, dominated by the tragic death of our first First Minister, whose determination that "there shall be a Scottish Parliament" translated the hopes and commitment of many (in and beyond the Churches) into political reality. Many words - rightly - conveyed the real affection and regard in which Donald Dewar was held by so many Scots, as well as the sense that we will miss his drive and integrity. Among these, the Moderator's pastoral care, and the sensitively crafted words which he and the other participating clergy contributed to the funeral services, spoke well for the Churches, as did the parish minister who expressed his congregation's enjoyment of Donald's participation. As well as passing on supportive messages of sympathy from many Churches, I conveyed on behalf of the Churches our prayerful support to the Presiding Officer and members of the Scottish Executive.

Building on Donald Dewar's frequent description of himself as "culturally presbyterian", the political commentator Iain McWhirter wrote

"Dewar was a 20th century politician. His thinking was fashioned by the politics of the industrial working class and by the morality of the Scottish Presbyterian Church. No great churchgoer, he showed all the symptoms of Presbyterianism, from his disregard for personal appearance to his concern for the disadvantaged. Even his speaking style owed something to the pulpit. His mission was to restore Scottish democracy, but not just for the sake of it. He always regarded the Scottish parliament as a means to an end: social justice and the eradication of poverty. And like all Presbyterians, he worked hard - too hard - at his calling".

The aftermath of Donald Dewar's death brought a strong reaffirmation of the social justice that was his driving force. We should be proud if that commitment is recognised as a symptom of Presbyterianism, or as having wider Christian roots. If the recognition that social justice is what Donald Dewar was about builds a commitment to social justice as what our parliament should be about, that would be a real and fitting legacy which Churches can share in nurturing. If our Parliament has lost its "father", there is all the more reason for its godparents to go on showing we care.

At the end of the year, the new First Minister spoke very warmly of his hopes for regular constructive discourse between Executive and Churches: "it will be a sign of Scotland's growing maturity as a nation if the Government and the churches are able to have a more rational and constructive dialogue on even the most sensitive of issues". It is in developing that dialogue that the SCPO continues to support the Churches.

GRAHAM K BLOUNT,
Scottish Parliamentary Officer

APPENDIX H

REPORT OF THE SCOTTISH BIBLE SOCIETY

After 139 years, the National Bible Society of Scotland decided to change its name. It chose "The Scottish Bible Society" as simpler and more in tune with contemporary Scotland. A leading graphic designer echoed this change with a superb new logo, weaving Scotland's traditional tartan fabric together with the cross.

The fresh name and visual identity were officially launched at a celebratory dinner for 250 guests. The Society's Patron, Her Majesty The Queen, sent a message of greeting: "The Bible has had a significant impact on the history and life of the Scottish nation… I send my very best wishes for the continuation of the valuable work of the Society in promoting even greater awareness of the Bible as we move into the twenty-first century".

Special distributions of Millennium Gospels continued from 1999. Over 200,000 Bibles, Scripture Selections and other publications were sold in 2000, 11 per cent less than the overwhelming demand for Millennium distribution projects in 1999. In one town near Glasgow, local Churches welcomed over 1,000 school children to "Jesus 2000" at a local sports stadium. The Christian message was communicated in song, by clowns and other entertainers, and through the 823 entries to a painting competition. Of course, each youngster received their illustrated copy of Mark to take home!

Faith Comes By Hearing has now benefited over 700 congregations since 1995. There is a growing demand for the recordings in compact disc form (and for the Old Testament, which will soon be available).

Bibleworld, their hi-tech interactive experience for school children, welcomed Bible Society colleagues from Netherlands Antilles, Suriname and Netherlands, where similar projects are being planned (along with Peru, Egypt and Lebanon).

A video competition—*Real to Reel*—has been launched to encourage youth groups to engage with God's Word and its relevance today.

Thanks to a change in UK law, most charitable donations now qualify for tax relief; the Society is seeking to use this to increase its income. A major legacy, together with other special funds, made it possible to support a number of projects in various parts of the world.

Regular fundraising appeals supported Bible work in Cambodia, Mozambique, China (over £100,000) and Haiti. The last was highlighted at the latest series of *Prom Praise* orchestral concerts, which attracted a total audience of 5,500.

The Guild has included a Bible project in Siberia as part of its official outreach for the period 2000–2003.

The Scottish Bible Society greatly appreciates the active presence of the Church of Scotland members on its Council of Church Representatives.

The Rev Dr Graham Houston left his post as Executive Director of the Society by mutual agreement and for personal reasons with effect from 30 June 2000. After a thorough re-assessment process and extensive interviewing of candidates, the Society decided to appoint its own Field Development Officer to the post. Rev M Douglas Campbell, is the youngest leader in the Society's history, having previously served as Associate Minister of New Kilpatrick Parish Church (his wife has a similar role in St Paul's, Milngavie).

PROPOSED DELIVERANCE

The General Assembly

1. Receive the Report and Accounts of the General Trustees.

2. (a) Record their appreciation of the contribution made by Mr Michael E Campbell Penney to the work of the General Trustees, particularly as Convener of their Finance Committee.
   (b) Appoint Rev. E Lorna Hood and Mr C Noel Glen as General Trustees.
   (c) Re-appoint Mr William S Carswell as Chairman and Rev. James H Simpson as Vice-Chairman for the ensuing year and authorise the making of a payment of £1,130 to each of them for their services during the past year (1).

3. Direct that all applications for financial assistance from the Heritage Lottery Fund and buildings related applications to the National Lottery Charities Board made on behalf of congregations shall be sent in the first instance to the Presbytery of the bounds which shall transmit the same to the General Trustees with its comments on the future of the building concerned. The General Trustees will be bound to consult in all cases with the Committee on Parish Re-appraisal and in relevant cases with the Committee on Artistic Matters. If after such consultation, the General Trustees consider that it is appropriate to do so, they are authorised and empowered to transmit the application for consideration (2.5).

4. Remind congregations of the availability of the Better Heating Scheme under which skilled advice can be obtained in the matters of saving money on heating bills and improving the standard of comfort in buildings (4).

5. Approve and adopt the Revised Regulations of the Consolidated Stipend Fund set out in Appendix 2 to the Report (6.1)

6. Approve of the proposal by the General Trustees that they should depart from the general concept of imposing restrictions on the future use of redundant Church property unless such are being conceived to safeguard the use or enjoyment of adjacent or nearby property remaining within Church control (8.1).

7. Rescind the deliverances of the Assemblies of 1965 and 1982 relating to the imposition by local or congregational trustees of restrictions on the future use of redundant Church property, empower such trustees, if so desired, to modify or discharge such restrictions and leave to the discretion of local parties the question of the imposition of restrictions on future sales of locally vested subjects (8.2).

REPORT

1. Introduction and Composition of Trust

The Church of Scotland General Trustees submit to the Assembly their seventy-sixth Report since the passing of the Church of Scotland (Property and Endowments) Act of 1925.

The Trustees regret to report the retirement at this Assembly of Mr Michael E Campbell Penney CA. Mr Penney was appointed a Trustee by the Assembly of 1959 and in 1968 became Convener of the General Trustees' Finance Committee, a post which he held until 1999. The Trustees' present financial position as shown in their Accounts is based on the prudent stewardship of the Committee under his convenership and the Church at large owes him a debt a gratitude.

The Trustees respectfully recommend that Rev. E Lorna Hood, MA, BD of Renfrew: North and Mr C Noel Glen, BL, NP of Cardross should be appointed members of the Board.

The Trustees further recommend that Mr William S Carswell MA, LLB and Rev. James H Simpson BD, LLB should be re-appointed Chairman and Vice-Chairman respectively for the ensuing year and that for their services for the past year they should each receive remuneration of £1,130 as authorised by Section 38 Sub-Section 1 of the 1925 Act.

2. Fabric Matters

2.1 Central Fabric Fund

The following is a synopsis of grants and loans made from the Central Fabric Fund during 2000. In cases where a grant or loan has been made in respect of work at more than one building, the amount involved has been apportioned and the apportioned amounts treated as separate grants and loans for the purpose of the numbers given. As will be seen, the majority of loans were given at interest of 6% per annum but a few, where the circumstances were considered to justify this, were given at the rate of 4% per annum or on an interest free basis. Bridging loans were made at 2% above base rate.

	Total		Churches		Manses		Halls	
	No.	Amount	No.	Amount	No.	Amount	No.	Amount
Grants	155	£683,940	82	£361,028	38	£197,462	35	£125,450
Loans free of Interest	18	£143,474	7	£45,500	7	£83,474	4	£14,500
Loans at Interest of 4%	34	£243,900	11	£62,200	12	£124,000	11	£57,700
Loans at Interest of 6%	59	£1,278,500	33	£876,500	8	£108,500	18	£293,500
Bridging Loans	8	£1,250,955	-	-	8	£1,250,955	-	-

Against the figure of £683,940 voted by way of grants in 2000 has to be offset the sum of £43,510 being grants voted which have lapsed or been cancelled. This means that the net figure which the General Trustees made available by way of grant in 2000 was £640,430—the equivalent figure in 1999 having been £573,528.

2.2 Care of Ecclesiastical Properties

In terms of the relevant legislation, Presbyteries have to report diligence to the General Trustees on fabric matters by 31st December each year. The returns to hand at the time of the preparation of the Report revealed that in 44 Presbyteries, 1380 Property Registers out of 1389 had been examined and all had been found satisfactory. In the same Presbyteries, the properties of 270 congregations had been inspected during the year to 30th June 2000.

2.3 Consolidated Fabric Fund

The Consolidated Fabric Fund was created with effect from 31st March 1996 when the value of each share was £1. The share value at 31st December 2000 was £1.26.

2.4 Millennium Project Fund

The Trustees reported to the Assembly of 2000 that they had set up a Millennium Project Fund which they hoped might be used to provide substantial finance to replace or to modify radically church buildings which, for one reason or another, were no longer suitable for the work of a modern congregation.

Following consultation with representatives of the Board of Stewardship and Finance and the Committees on New Charge Development and Parish Re-appraisal, the Trustees have written to Presbytery Clerks elaborating on their current thinking on the use of the Fund and inviting Presbyteries to put forward schemes for consideration. Particular reference has been made to schemes which:—

(a) are imaginative and creative and which will enable officebearers with vision and enthusiasm to make a real difference to their congregation's work and witness, particularly in the community;

(b) facilitate re-adjustment of congregations by providing a suitable new building or the imaginative regeneration of an existing one;

(c) reduce the number of buildings maintained by a congregation again through the provision of a new building or the regeneration of an existing one or

(d) involve a partnership with the community or another denomination in the provision of accommodation which can be used jointly.

The Trustees have given consideration to the possibility of increasing the size of the fund and at the time of the preparation of this Report were exploring one or two avenues. They think, however, that attracting support for particular projects is likely to be easier than raising money for "a fund".

2.5 The National Lottery

In terms of Act IX 1998, agencies of the Church were authorised to determine for themselves whether or not to make applications for Lottery funding on the basis that such agencies were discouraged from making such applications unless they were satisfied that no suitable alternative funding sources were available. Applications were limited to certain areas, one of which was work in relation to buildings. The General Trustees were authorised, where appropriate, to approve such applications.

In practice there are two bodies to which applications for assistance in respect of buildings related work can be made namely the Trustees of the National Heritage Memorial Fund who administer the Heritage Lottery Fund and the National Lottery Charities Board which administers the portion of the "good causes" fund set aside for charitable purposes. The procedures adopted by these bodies are not identical and since applications were authorised by the Assembly, the Solicitor of the Church has had protracted negotiations with representatives of both bodies with regard to the documentation which has to be contracted on behalf of the Church as a condition of monies being made available. In all cases contracts have to be entered into by the congregation concerned and in the case of grants from the Heritage Lottery Fund the General Trustees also have to assume contractual obligations in relation to buildings vested in them. These obligations are potentially very onerous and include *inter alia* provisions which could result in a requirement, in certain circumstances, to pay back a sum much larger than the grant originally given in the event of the property being sold. In the case of Heritage Lottery Fund grants, the conditions apply for ten years unless the level of grant exceeds £500,000 in which case the period is twenty five years. National Lottery Charities Board conditions can apply for up to eighty years. As a result of the negotiations by the Solicitor it has been possible to achieve concessions on the terms originally proposed, which included an embargo on disposal without consent, but the Trustees administering the Heritage Lottery Fund have not been prepared to depart from their position with regard to clawback and looking to their own trusteeship responsibilities, the General Trustees obtained an Opinion from the former Procurator on the issues which arise.

This Opinion is to the effect that it is not *ultra vires* of the General Trustees or other bodies within the Church to enter into the type of contract which is being required. Given, however, that trustees must exercise that degree of diligence which a person of ordinary prudence would exercise in the management of his or her own affairs, it is considered that each case must be looked at against that criterion. Particular reference is made to the need to consider whether the building is likely to remain in use for the whole of the contract period and to the relative values of the grant aided work and of the building itself.

It is indicated in the Opinion that each contract will require more than a superficial consideration or a *pro forma* approach. It is further recommended that procedures be laid down to regulate such applications and documentation prepared to identify the aspects which must be considered.

At the present time all applications from congregations to the Historic Buildings Council for Scotland require to be channelled through Presbytery to the General Trustees who have been directed to consult with the Committees on Artistic Matters and Parish Re-appraisal as appropriate before approving an application for onward transmission to Historic Scotland. It is proposed that a similar procedure be adopted in relation to applications for assistance from the Heritage Lottery Fund and buildings related applications to the National Lottery Charities Board. Congregations wishing to submit an application would require to pass the same to Presbytery which would be obliged to transmit the application to the General Trustees with its comments on the future of the building concerned. On receiving such application, the General Trustees would consult in all cases with the Committee on Parish Re-appraisal to obtain its views on the future of the building and, in appropriate cases, with the Committee on Artistic Matters, before deciding whether or not the application should be transmitted for consideration. It is envisaged that, as is the case with Historic Buildings Council applications, a form would be issued. This would highlight the relevant considerations and the balancing exercise which must be undertaken between the benefit of obtaining financial assistance and the potential for loss arising from the contractual terms.

3. Determinations under Act VII 1995

The General Trustees report that they have under Act VII 1995 made 95 determinations as set out in Appendix 1 to the Report.

4. Heating, Lighting and Sound Systems

As reported to last year's Assembly, the General Trustees appointed Mr Andrew W MacOwan as their Energy Consultant with effect from January 2000 and he has carried on the good work previously undertaken by Mr Brian Marks and Mr Archie Strang. At 31st December 2000, 1591 surveys (including repeat surveys) of church buildings had been carried out under the Better Heating Scheme and 145 surveys of manses. The Trustees again ask the Assembly to remind congregations that for a modest fee towards which the Trustees offer a subsidy and which is a fair charge on monies held for a congregation in the Consolidated Fabric Fund, Mr MacOwan will provide a survey of buildings incorporating advice on how to save money on heating bills and improve the standard of comfort.

The General Trustees also retain Argyle Energy of Stirling to advise them on energy prices and to negotiate with suppliers with a view to ensuring that congregations obtain advantageous terms for electricity and gas. The arrangement with Scottish Gas relative to electricity referred to in last year's Report was for a period of two years but the arrangement with BP Gas in respect of gas expired at the end of 2000. Negotiations in respect of the year 2001 were initiated in the autumn of last year but proved difficult due to a general increase in gas prices. The Trustees are monitoring the position closely and will report further at the Assembly.

In addition to their Energy Consultant the Trustees have a Lighting Consultant, Mr Hugh J Nicholl and a Sound Systems Consultant, Mr John McDonald who can provide advice to congregations for reasonable fees. Further information regarding heating, lighting and sound systems surveys is available from the Trustees' Secretary's Department.

5. Reallocation of Endowments

The Regulations anent the Application of Stipend and Fabric Endowments (Regulations 5 1995) provide for possible switches of endowments between the fabric and stipend funds. The effect of Determinations made during 2000 was as follows.

(i) Ceres and Springfield: £43,455 from stipend to fabric.

(ii) Gartmore: £10,000 from fabric to stipend.

(iii) Laurencekirk: £41,329 from stipend to fabric.

(iv) Paisley: Sherwood Greenlaw: £100,000 from fabric to stipend.

6. Stipend Matters

6.1 Consolidated Stipend Fund

The Consolidated Stipend Fund (then known as the Consolidated Stipend Endowment Fund) was set up at 1st January 1982 when the value of the capital held was £9,646,816 and the value of each share was £0.9878. The intervening years have seen the capital and share values grow and reference is made to the relevant section in the General Trustees' Accounts. The following statistics reflect the position over the past five years. As will be noted, there has been a fall in total value and share value during 2000.

Capital	Total Value	Value of Share
31st December 1996	£43,459,918	£3.6062
31st December 1997	£50,883,313	£4.0401
31st December 1998	£55,601,217	£4.3764
31st December 1999	£60,573,638	£4.7116
31st December 2000	£59,278,098	£4.5708

Revenue	Net Income	Shares Issued at 31st December	Rate of Dividend
1996	£2,076,408	12,051,552	£0.1625
1997	£2,154,014	12,594,559	£0.1675
1998	£2,388,528	12,704,692	£0.1717
1999	£2,452,284	12,856,323	£0.1803
2000	£2,516,281	12,968,756	£0.1830

In their Reports over the last few years the General Trustees have drawn attention to the likely impact on the Fund of the provisions, announced by the Chancellor in 1997 and effective over the period 1999 to 2004, reducing the total income from UK dividends by 20% as a result of progressive loss of tax credits. They have commented that these might well lead to a reduction in the dividend on the Fund and would certainly make any increase unlikely. An estimate of the income available in 2001 was duly made and the Trustees agreed to hold the dividend at £0.1830 per share. This represents an income yield of 4% on the share value at 31st December 2000 and involves paying a dividend greater than the estimated income on the Fund for the year.

In the light of warnings from the Investors Trust on the level of future income distributions on the Growth Fund, in which the Stipend Fund is very largely invested, the General Trustees commissioned a firm of Actuaries and Consultants to review the investment policy which they have been following. This review was based on the priority being to produce as high an annual income as was consistent with the need to sustain progressive growth in this income in the future, with progressive growth in income being interpreted as at least matching inflation and sustaining that growth as resulting in seeking to maintain the capital value of the Fund in real terms. The Consultants concluded that the current level of support to stipends would not be sustainable in real terms without running a high risk of depleting the capital of the Fund in such terms. On the basis that the Stipend Fund can be viewed on a total return basis, the Consultants came down decisively in favour of continued and, indeed, additional investment in the Growth Fund and against any switch to the Income Fund which, in their opinion, would be likely to result in reductions in the level of the contribution which the Fund would be able to make towards stipend in the future. The firm did not consider that it would be possible, in the medium term of ten years, to increase the contribution towards stipend and suggested that by operating the Fund on a total return basis ie providing for limited access to capital as well as income for the making of distributions it might well be possible to sustain the present rate of dividend. The General Trustees are therefore asking the Assembly to approve Revised Regulations for the Fund which will enable the use of capital as well as income for this purpose. The Revised Regulations for the Fund are printed as Appendix 2 to the Report.

The investment policy which has been recommended by the Consultants and which the Trustees will follow and the revised Regulations have the full support of the Board of Ministry. It is proposed that the policy should be reviewed in 2003 or earlier if need be.

During 2000 the sum of £567,107 was admitted to the Fund in exchange for 121,656 shares.

6.2 Glebes

Farming continues to go through difficult times. In the light of this the General Trustees have been approaching the question of rent reviews selectively and sympathetically. The net income from glebe rents for 2000 was £312,674 which showed an increase on the comparable figure for the previous year which was £301,620.

7. Finance

The General Trustees' Accounts for the year 2000 audited by the Auditor of the Church will be laid on the table at the General Assembly. A synopsis of the position at 31st December 2000 based on the most up-to-date information available at the time of the preparation of this Report is as follows:—

	2000 £	1999 £
Stipend Funds	59,272,991	60,573,638
Glebe Funds	96,650	71,487
Consolidated Fabric Fund	32,872,812	33,691,213
Individual Funds	7,954,470	6,529,249
Central Fabric Fund	6,803,949	6,134,992
General Fund	2,857,841	2,812,531
Millennium Project Fund	1,500,000	1,310,335
	111,358,713	111,123,445

During 2000, £64,484 was received in respect of the redemption of feuduties and standard charges.

The General Trustees intend that the Accountants appointed to audit the Accounts of the Assembly Boards and Committees for 2001 should also be appointed to audit their Accounts for that year.

8. Land Tenure Reform

8.1 Abolition of Feudal Tenure etc (Scotland) Act 2000

In their Report to the Assembly of 2000, the General Trustees referred to the introduction of the Abolition of Feudal Tenure etc (Scotland) Bill in the Scottish Parliament in October of 1999. This Bill became an Act on 9th June 2000. Some of the provisions of the Act came into force immediately but the majority of the substantive provisions are not to come into operation until an appointed day which has not yet been fixed but is likely to be within the next two or three years.

So far as ground burdens, such as feuduties, ground annuals and standard charges are concerned, the position is that they will be extinguished on the appointed day subject to payment of compensation which, in many cases, will be payable in instalments over a period of up to ten years. In an attempt to reduce the administrative burden which will be imposed by the procedures required to constitute a valid claim for compensation the General Trustees offered discounted terms to parties paying ground burdens who were prepared to redeem them at

Martinmas 2000 and reference is made to the figure quoted in the previous section relating to Finance.

More complex issues arise from the provisions of the Act which relate to the possibility of superiors being able to go through procedures which might enable them either to save title conditions which were imposed when a property was sold and which would otherwise be extinguished on the appointed day or to establish a right to compensation for loss arising from such extinction. Given the large number of superiority interests held by the General Trustees an examination of all the titles to identify the cases in which action might be appropriate would be a mammoth task. The General Trustees' Law Committee agreed that two pilot schemes should be undertaken in that regard, one involving the examination of a limited number of titles and the other the making of contact with local parties in selected parishes to ascertain what information was available there. The results of these schemes were being examined by the Committee at the time of the preparation of this Report.

Another matter arising from the legislation is the question of the imposition of title conditions on properties which are being sold. In the past, the General Trustees have made extensive use of the feudal system of land tenure to impose restrictions against what were considered to be undesirable uses of former Church property, conditions to safeguard the amenity of property which was being retained and reservations of the right to participate in a future increase in value in the event of a property being redeveloped. With effect from the appointed day the facilities afforded by the system will no longer be available to the General Trustees. The thinking behind the legislation is that it is appropriate, as a contractual matter, that a party who is disposing of a property should have the right to impose restrictions on the use to which the purchaser of the property may put it. It is not considered appropriate that the original seller should have the right to control what subsequent purchasers of the property may do with it unless the restriction on use has been imposed to safeguard the enjoyment of property which has been retained. Against this background it is the intention of the General Trustees, if the Assembly approve, to depart from the general concept of imposing restrictions against the future use of Church properties for undesirable purposes unless it is appropriate to do so to safeguard the use and enjoyment of adjacent or nearby property. It is envisaged that the Trustees will continue, where appropriate, to incorporate conditions to safeguard adjoining subjects and to secure an additional payment in the event of a property being redeveloped for a more valuable use.

It should be noted that the Scottish Executive is also engaged in a complete overhaul of real burdens incorporated into titles and the General Trustees are continuing to review their position in the light of proposed legislation in that field.

8.2 Restrictive Conditions in Titles on Sale of Locally Vested Church Properties

The General Assembly of 1965 directed that when congregational trustees were disposing of churches which had originated in the former United Free Church they should insert, in the title granted, restrictions against use as licensed premises or for gambling. This was affirmed by the Assembly of 1982 which extended the scope of the earlier direction to the effect that clauses must be inserted on sales by congregational or local trustees of churches vested in them and falling within the ambit of Act XIV 1979 (now Act VII 1995), preventing the subjects from being used as licensed premises, for gambling purposes or for religious or quasi-religious purposes but with power to the General Trustees in any case and after consultation with the Kirk Session and the Financial Court of the congregation concerned and the Presbytery to dispense with, modify or discharge the said conditions in whole or in part.

In the light of the legislation referred to in section 8.1 above the General Trustees propose that the Assembly should withdraw the directions to local or congregational trustees and leave the question of the incorporation of restrictions on future use to local parties operating within the new legislative framework.

9. Insurance

The Church of Scotland Insurance Company Limited, which is owned by the General Trustees, continues to insure

Church of Scotland properties, including those vested in the General Trustees. The Company, either by itself or as agent, provides cover for all classes of insurance.

Congregations are encouraged to have their properties professionally valued for insurance purposes. If such a valuation results in a substantial increase in the sum insured, then the Company will usually agree to restrict the additional premium for up to two years in an effort to assist the congregation concerned. Valuations can also result in the sum insured being reduced. This is because each year the Company, after taking professional advice, indexes sums insured on the basis of the cost of re-instating a stonebuilt church. In the case of a modern building, this may give some scope for shading the sum insured.

Congregations are reminded that it is their responsibility to ensure that their particular sums insured are checked regularly and remain adequate. An automatic increase can never correct a sum which is fundamentally inaccurate.

The Company continues to grant discounts for churches insured for more than £2.5m with a further discount for buildings insured for more than £5m. Discounts are currently being introduced for manses insured for more than £250,000 with an additional discount if insured for more than £500,000.

The number of fire claims is small but malicious fire raising and vandalism have remained constant, being the cause of 60% of claims received. Most of these involve action by children or young persons on an opportunist basis and all buildings should be inspected regularly to ensure that there are no gaps in doors or windows through which matches or lighted paper can be pushed. All doors and windows should be lockfast when buildings are not in use. Claims in respect of fires caused by faulty electrical equipment including a boiler were also received and such items should be checked regularly.

Fabric Conveners are reminded to insist that contractors working with heat on buildings comply with the recommendations of the Loss Prevention Council so that claims arising from this source can be reduced, or even eliminated. The loss of a roof will take a minimum of twelve to eighteen months to restore, often longer, with consequent disruption to the work and witness of the congregation. If plans of buildings are not available it is worthwhile for a comprehensive photographic record to be made, especially of those parts which are not normally seen, such as the roof construction and the interior of spires and steeples. Such records assist in any restoration and should be lodged in a place other than the church building.

The claims experience on classes of insurance other than fire has continued to deteriorate. Statistically almost two out of three congregations claimed on their insurance last year and the insurers of these classes paid out one third more in claims than was collected in premiums. This position would improve if the issues of basic security, referred to earlier, were addressed.

The General Trustees commend the introduction of a scheme for Household Buildings and/or Contents Insurance underwritten by the Ecclesiastical Insurance Office. The scheme is available to members and adherents of the Church of Scotland in respect of cover over their own properties. Not only is it competitively priced but when a policy is taken out, the Insurance Company will issue a voucher for £20 which can be passed to the Congregational Treasurer and used to offset the congregation's insurance costs.

The Insurance Company made an underwriting profit in the year to 31st October 2000 of £1,293,459 compared with £1,277,805 the previous year. The dividends received by the General Trustees from the Company in the calendar year 2000, including tax recovered, amounted to £90,750 and Gift Aid donations and Deed of Covenant income totalled £513,730. The comparable figures for 1999 were £950,000 and £210,000 but the 1999 dividend figure included the exceptional distribution which enabled the Trustees to set up the Millennium Project Fund. Such payments are, of course, at the discretion of the Directors and depend on profitability.

The General Trustees record their appreciation of the significant financial contribution made by the Company to assist the operations of the Trustees and of the work done by the Directors of the Company. They receive no remuneration for the responsibilities which they undertake although the firm of Insurance Brokers of which the Chairman of the Company is a Director receives an annual payment of £6,000 in recognition of the time spent by him on the work of the Company.

10. Whithorn Trust

The Whithorn Trust continues to investigate the development of the early Christian Church and in particular the site at Whithorn. The visitor centre is the main means of passing on information on the subject in addition to a range of publications. In May 2000 the Trust was fortunate to have a visit from His Royal Highness Prince Charles, Duke of Rothesay and this once again focused attention on Whithorn and its association with St Ninian. A small investigation on an area in the Fey Field did not reveal early church building but medieval buildings associated with the Priory. In September 2001 the Whithorn lecture entitled NINIAN and NENDRUM: WHITHORN AND THE EARLY CHURCH IN EAST ULSTER by Dr Ann Hamlin will feature in the St Ninian Festival with concerts, exhibitions of art and the Royal Commission touring exhibition "World of Worship", sculpture and theatre. The Trust welcomes donations, enquiries for information and help in planning visits either by post at 45-47 George Street, Whithorn, Newton Stewart, Dumfries and Galloway, DG8 8NS or telephone 01988 500508 or email butterworth@whithorn1.freeserve.co.uk.

On behalf of the General Trustees

WILLIAM S CARSWELL, *Chairman*
JAMES H SIMPSON, *Vice-Chairman*
ALAN W COWE, *Secretary and Clerk*

APPENDIX 1

Determinations Made Under Act VII
1995

1. General Sales: In the following cases, the General Trustees made determinations authorising the sale or letting of the property concerned and directed that the proceeds should be credited to the benefit of the congregation in the Consolidated Fabric Fund:- Aberdeen: St Ninian's – manse, Abernethy and Dron – former coach house, Airdrie: New Monkland – manse, Ayr: Newton on Ayr – manse, Ballingry and Lochcraig – Ballingry Manse and Lochcraig Church, Banchory-Devenick and Maryculter/Cookney – Cookney Church, Barry – ground at church, Black Mount – manse, Breich Valley – Addiewell Church and Hall, Breich Mission Church, Longridge Church, Hall and ancillary buildings and Stoneyburn Church and Halls, Coalburn – hall, Corsock and Kirkpatrick Durham – Corsock Churchyard, Cullen and Deskford – manse, Dallas – former manse, Dundee: Camperdown – manse, Dundee: West – St Peter's McCheyne Church and Halls, Edinburgh: Portobello St Philip's Joppa – church, Edinburgh: St Cuthbert's – manse, Falkirk: Bainsford – North End Hall, Fraserburgh: Old – manse, Girvan: North – retirement house, Glasgow: Drumchapel St Mark's – manse, Glasgow: Househillwood St Christopher's – manse, Glasgow: Queen's Park – Crosshill Queen's Park Church and Hall, Hamilton: Gilmour and Whitehill – Whitehill Church and Hall, Howe Trinity – Alford: West, Keig and Tullynessle and Forbes Churches, Hoy and Walls – St John's Church, Hutton and Corrie – manse, Inverness: West (2nd Charge) – church, Killearnan – manse, Kilmarnock: St Kentigern's – manse, Kilmarnock: Laigh West High – West High Halls, Kirkintilloch: Hillhead – manse, Lochwinnoch – manse, Moffat St Andrew's – manse, North Knapdale – ground at former manse, North Ronaldsay – New Church, Papa Westray – St Ann's Kirk, Perth: North – ground at halls, Peterculter – St Peter's Church and Hall, Peterhead: Old – manse, Reay – manse, Redding and Westquarter – Westquarter Hall/Church and retirement house, Rothiemay – site of former North Church, Shotts: Calderhead Erskine – former Erskine School building, Skelmorlie and Wemyss Bay – manse and site in church car park, Stonehaven: Fetteresso – manse, Strachur and Strathlachlan – ground at manse, Strathfillan – manse and Strathfillan Church, Tarbat – manse, Urray and Kilchrist – Marybank Church and Whitehills – hall and ground at church.

2. Glebe Sales: In the following parishes, the General Trustees made determinations authorising the sale of glebe subjects and directed that the proceeds should be credited to the benefit of the congregation in the Consolidated Stipend Fund:- Barra, Bowden, Caputh and

Clunie, Cockpen and Carrington, Contin (2), Cromdale and Advie, Dailly, Dunkeld, Elgin: St Giles and St Columba's South, Forgandenny, Gairloch and Dundonnell, Hutton and Corrie, Kilconquhar and Colinsburgh, Kilmore and Oban, Kilmory, Kirkmichael, Straloch and Glenshee, Langholm, Ewes and Westerkirk, Lossiemouth: St Gerardine's High, Mearns, Melness and Tongue, Moffat St Andrew's, Newton Stewart Penninghame St John's, Port of Menteith, Portpatrick, St Andrew's Lhanbryd and Urquhart, Stoneykirk, Terregles and Wishaw: Cambusnethan Old and Morningside.

3. Miscellaneous: The General Trustees made the following miscellaneous determinations:-

a. Aberdeen: Nigg – Sale of church, halls and manse, proceeds to be credited to Central Fabric Fund.

b. Contin – Sale of Strathconon Church, crediting proceeds to the benefit of congregation in Consolidated Fabric Fund and amendment to Scheme 770 of Scottish Ecclesiastical Commissioners.

c. Elderslie Kirk – Crediting to benefit of congregation in Consolidated Fabric Fund of proportion of proceeds of sale of 2 South Park Drive, Paisley.

d. Gillingham St Margaret's – Sale of former manse and crediting of sale proceeds to Central Fabric Fund and successor of National Church Extension Committee.

e. Glasgow: Scotstoun – Sale of congregation's interest in 65 Victoria Park Drive South, Glasgow to Committee on New Charge Development, allocation of £15,000 from the proceeds for fabric purposes in connection with the property and crediting of balance to congregation in Consolidated Fabric Fund.

f. Kilmaurs St Maurs Glencairn – Exchange of land at Glebe.

g. Rousay – Transmission of proceeds of sale of Egilsay Mission Church to General Trustees to be credited to congregation in Consolidated Fabric Fund.

APPENDIX 2

Revised Regulations of the Consolidated Stipend Fund

(A) General

1. A Consolidated Stipend Fund (hereinafter referred to as "the Fund") having been created on 1st January 1982, the following regulations will apply to it.

2. The Fund will be administered by the General Trustees and may be invested through the medium of the Church of Scotland Investors Trust. Any investment policy changes will be put into effect by the General Trustees only after consultation with the Board of Ministry.

3. The General Trustees will be entitled to an administration charge in respect of their intromissions with the Fund of such amount as may be agreed from time to time by the Board of Ministry and the General Trustees or, failing agreement, determined by the Board of Stewardship and Finance.

4. The shares currently held in the Fund for behoof of a congregation will, subject to these regulations, continue to be held for behoof of that congregation.

(B) Distributions from Fund

1. Not later than 31st October in each year, the General Trustees will, after consultation with the Board of Ministry, determine the dividend which it is proposed to pay on each share in the Fund in the following year. It is stipulated for the avoidance of doubt that the General Trustees are empowered to pay a proportion of such dividend out of the capital of the Fund.

2. The General Trustees will account to the Board of Ministry quarterly on 31st March, 30th June, 30th September and 31st December in each year for the amount to be paid by way of dividend on shares.

3. Dividends attributable to vacant charges will be transferred by the Board of Ministry as hitherto to the Board's Vacant Stipend Fund.

(C) Introduction of New Capital

New capital may be introduced to the Fund at the beginning of each calendar month or at such other times as may be determined by the General Trustees and the number of shares to be attributed to such new capital will be ascertained by dividing the total value of the capital of the Fund before the introduction of the new capital by the number of shares in issue at that date, the share value thus produced being divided into the new capital to determine the number of new shares.

(D) Withdrawal of Capital

Capital may be withdrawn from the Fund at the beginning of each calendar month or at such other times as may be determined by the General Trustees by the encashment of shares; the value of the shares to be withdrawn will be ascertained by dividing the total value of the capital of the Fund before the withdrawal of the capital by the number of shares in issue at that date, the share value thus produced being multiplied by the number of shares being withdrawn, in order to determine their aggregate value.

(E) Treatment of Glebe Sales

The net proceeds of glebe land will constitute new capital for the Fund and these will be introduced as provided under (C) above.

(F) Glebe Rents

1. Rents from glebes vested in or administered by the General Trustees (hereinafter referred to as "the Rents") will continue to be collected by the General Trustees but will not form part of the income of the Fund.

2. The General Trustees will be entitled to a collection charge on the Rents of such amount as may be agreed from time to time by the Board of Ministry and the General Trustees or, failing agreement, as may be determined by the Board of Stewardship and Finance.

3. The General Trustees will account to the Board of Ministry quarterly on 31st March, 30th June, 30th September and 31st December in each year for the Rents.

4. The Board of Ministry and the General Trustees are empowered to make such arrangements as may seem appropriate to them from time to time for the funding of expenses falling upon the General Trustees relative to glebes.

(G) Further Endowment of Stipend

1. These regulations are without prejudice to the regulations for creating further stipend endowments by supplementing local capital.

2. Such further endowments of stipend will be introduced into the Fund as New Capital as set out in C above.

(H) Powers of the Church of Scotland General Trustees

For removal of any doubt it is declared that the provisions of these regulations are without prejudice to the powers delegated to the Board of Ministry (coming in place of the Committee on the Maintenance of the Ministry) and to the General Trustees by Act VII 1995 anent Powers delegated to The Church of Scotland General Trustees and Regulations V of 1995 anent the Application of Stipend and Fabric Endowments held by The Church of Scotland General Trustees.

(I) Repeal

Regulations anent a Consolidated Stipend Fund (Rules and Regulations 6 1981 as amended) are hereby repealed.

NOMINATION COMMITTEE
MAY 2001

PROPOSED DELIVERANCE

The General Assembly:

1   Receive the Report

2   Make appointments to Standing Committees and Boards as set forth in the Report, with additions and alterations as follows:—

REPORT

The Committee recommends the following appointments:—

Board of Practice and Procedure

Ministers Retiring Ann Inglis, Andrew Ritchie
Ministers Appointed Ann Inglis*, Ian Watson
Members Retiring Catherine Coull, Alexander MacNiven, David Thomson
Members Appointed Helen Longmuir, Alexander MacNiven*, Andrew Stewart

David Lacy, *Convener*
William Hewitt, *Vice-Convener*

Committee to Nominate the Moderator

Members Retiring Kathleen Forsyth, Mary Sherrard
Members Appointed Eileen Davidson, Flora Little

Principal Clerk, *Secretary*

Judicial Commission

Ministers Retiring Barry Dunsmore, Robert Ramsay
Ministers Appointed Neil Combe, Louden Blair
Elder Retiring Robert Jack
Elder Appointed Kenneth Murray

Douglas Allan, *Chairman*
Alastair McGregor, *Vice-Chairman*

* Denotes second term

Nomination Committee

Ministers Retiring Gillean McLean, Fiona Mathieson, Ria Plate, John Rushton
Ministers Appointed Ian Aitken, Gordon Farquharson, Fiona Lillie, David Searle
Members Retiring Albert Davidson, Sheila Moyes, Charles Munn, Norma Ronald, Elma Stuart
Members Appointed Moira Alexander, Elva Carlisle, Greta Doig, David Fotheringham, Joyce Nicol

Fraser Aitken, *Convener*
Keith Hall, *Vice-Convener*

Assembly Council

Members Retiring   Christine Carson, Neil Gardner, Pauline Steenbergen
Members Appointed   Alison Jack, Christine Carson, Ruth Forbes, Ian Gilmour, Eleanor Hamilton, Fiona Mathieson, Peter Neilson

Helen McLeod, *Convener*
David Dennistoun, *Vice-Convener*

Board of Stewardship and Finance

Ministers Retiring John Lloyd, Alexander Millar
Minister Appointed Ramsay Shields
Members Retiring George Honeyman, Norman Lang, Christine Mitchell

* Denotes second term

Members Appointed Fiona Adamson, Marion Bone (2 years), George Honeyman*, Norman Lang*, James Skinner

Colin Caskie, *Convener*
Vivienne Dickson, *Vice-Convener*

Church and Nation Committee
Ministers Retiring Alison Davidge, Sigrid Marten
Ministers Appointed Jane Barron, Alexander Horsburgh, Sigrid Marten*, Elizabeth Spence
Members Retiring Mukami McCrum, Ian McDonald, Brian Morrison, Duncan Ross, Georgena Wylie
Members Appointed Andrew Currie, Sarah Davidson, Margaret Lunan, Neil McIntosh

Alan McDonald, *Convener*
Morag Ross, *Vice-Convener*

Panel on Doctrine
Minister Retiring Mary Cranfield
Ministers Appointed Joe Kavanagh, Ian Maxwell, Howard Taylor, Ian Walker, Kenneth Walker
Member Retiring   John Innes
Member Appointed   Muriel Wilson

John McPake, *Convener*
Ian Boyd, *Vice-Convener*

Panel on Worship
Ministers Retiring Marion Dodd, Jennifer MacRae, Margaret Millar, Thomas Pollock, Jenny Williams
Ministers Appointed Fiona Douglas, Robert Mackenzie, Jennifer MacRae, Paul Middleton, David Ogston, Laurence Whitley
Members Retiring Suzanne Adam, Lloyd Davies
Members Appointed Suzanne Adam*, Ian Rogers

Gilleasbuig Macmillan, *Convener*
Ian McCrorie, *Vice-Convener*

Department of National Mission
Board of National Mission

James Gibson, *Convener*
Fiona Campbell, John Matthews, *Vice-Conveners*

Parish Reappraisal Committee
Minister Retiring David Clark
Ministers Appointed Alistair Bull, David Clark*, Iain Laing (one year)
Members Retiring Joyce Hannah, Thomas Stephen, Alistair Walker

Arthur Barrie, *Convener*
Noel Glen, *Vice-Convener*

New Charge Development Committee
Minister Appointed Graham Duffin
Member Retiring David Sinclair

Andrew Ritchie, *Convener*
John Collard, *Vice-Convener*

Mission and Evangelism Resources Committee
Ministers Appointed John Jarvie, Christopher Wallace, David Watson
Members Retiring Margaret McBain, Elsie Miller

Colin Sinclair, *Convener*
John Berkeley, Howard Taylor, *Vice-Conveners*

Chaplaincies Committee
Minister Retiring John Fairful
Ministers Appointed Andrew Downie, Ria Plate
Members Retiring Elinor Arbuthnott, Ronald Crawford
Member Appointed Henry Steenbergen

Elinor Arbuthnott *Convener*
James Greig, Stewart McGregor, William Taylor, *Vice-Conveners*

Parish Assistance Committee

Member Retiring Mary Donaldson
Member Appointed

Stanley Brook, *Convener*
Alison Henderson, *Vice-Convener*

Iona Community Board

Member Retiring Richard Frazer
Member Appointed Fiona Gordon

Tom Gordon, *Convener*

Committee on Artistic Matters

Ministers Retiring Richard Frazer, Callum O'Donnell, Brian Ramsay
Ministers Appointed   Brian Ramsay*, Janette Reid
Members Retiring   Sheryl Baxter, Campbell Duff, George Dunnet, Thomas Pollock
Members Appointed   Campbell Duff*, Gordon Hodge, Ronald Jamieson, Iain McCarter

Douglas Laird, *Convener*
Richard Frazer, *Vice-Convener*

Board of Ministry

Ministers Retiring   John Carrie, Douglas Cranston, Norman Maciver, Hugh Ormiston
Ministers Appointed   Russell Barr, Ian Dick, Alexander Douglas, Linda Dunbar, Lezley Kennedy
Members Retiring   Fiona Cameron, Ian Penman
Members Appointed Charles Beattie, Fiona Cameron (2 years), Ian Penman (2 years)

William Storrar, *Convener*
Douglas Cranston, Christine Goldie, William Greenock, Ian Taylor, *Vice-Conveners*

* Denotes second term

Committee on Chaplains to HM Forces

Ministers Retiring   Ian Gough, James Harkness, Matthew Robertson
Ministers Appointed Ian Gough*, James Harkness*, John Miller
Members Retiring   Hugh Arbuthnott, Irene Hill, Philip Macleod
Members Appointed   Hugh Arbuthnott*, Sarah Hankey, Michael Taitt

Iain Torrance, *Convener*
Herbert Kerrigan, *Vice-Convener*

Board of Social Responsibility

Ministers Retiring Douglas Alexander, Graham Dickson, Eric Hudson
Ministers Appointed Graham Dickson*, Eric Foggit
Members Retiring Audrey Dawson, Peter Hinde, William Patterson, Christine Smith
Members Appointed Peter Hinde*, Norman Kinnear, Douglas Martin, Stuart Lynch*, Mary Landells, Ian Waldrum

James Cowie, *Convener*
David Court, Gilbert Nisbet, *Vice-Conveners*

Board of World Mission

Ministers Retiring   Matthew Bicket, Malcolm Cuthbertson, Alistair Keil, John Renton, Douglas Robertson
Ministers Appointed Gillean MacLean, John Renton (2 years), Colin Renwick, Ian Stirling,
Member Appointed   Ian Murray

Alan Main, *Convener*
Elisabeth Cranfield, Alan Greig, *Vice-Conveners*

Committee on Ecumenical Relations

Ministers Retiring   Marjory Macaskill, John Tait
Ministers Appointed Christopher Levison, Margaret Millar

* Denotes second term

Member Retiring   Greta Doig
Members Appointed   Jean Cowan, Peter Lloyd

Thomas MacIntyre, *Convener*
Christine Tait, *Vice-Convener*

Board of Parish Education
Ministers Retiring   George Cowie, Euan Glen, Sally Fulton, Elizabeth Kay, Douglas Paterson, Stephen Smith
Minister Appointed   Sally Fulton*,
Members Retiring   Marilyn Douglas, Julie Green, Ann Lyall, Margaret Shackleton
Members Appointed   Graham Bolster, Roderick Ferguson, Mark Johnstone, Elizabeth McFarlan, Jade MacLean, Iain Young,

John Christie, *Convener*
Lorna Paterson, *Vice-Convener*

Education Committee
Ministers Retiring   James Brown, Alexander Glass, John Paterson
Ministers Appointed   Yvonne Atkins, James Munton
Members Retiring   David Alexander, Marion Martin, Christine Welch
Members Appointed   Janet Allan, David Alexander*, Lesley Donaldson, Marion Martin

John Laidlaw, *Convener*
William Weatherspoon, *Vice-Convener*

Panel of Arbiters
Members Appointed   Grant Barclay, Elizabeth Fox

Graham Philips, *Convener*

Board of Communication
Minister Retiring   Andrew Campbell
Member Retiring   Jane Gray
Members Appointed   Stephen Ogston, Stewart Roy

Jean Montgomerie, *Convener*
Peter Graham, *Vice-Convener*

In the name of the Committee

FRASER AITKEN, *Convener*
KEITH HALL, *Vice-Convener*
FINLAY MACDONALD, *Secretary*

* Denotes second term   * Denotes second term

CHURCH OF SCOTLAND TRUST

MAY 2001

PROPOSED DELIVERANCE

The General Assembly:

1. Receive the Report and thank the members of the Trust for their diligence.
2. Record their appreciation of the services rendered to the Church by the late Mr D D McKinnon as a past Chairman, Vice-Chairman and member of the Trust.
3. Note that in accordance with the constitution of the Trust, Messrs D F Stewart and J A W Somerville retire as members on 31st May 2001 but are eligible for re-appointment.
4. Thank Mr J A W Somerville for 43 years service to the Trust.
5. Re-appoint Mr D F Stewart as a member of the Trust from 1st June 2001.

REPORT

The Church of Scotland Trust, which was established by Act of Parliament in 1932, submits its Sixty-ninth Report to the General Assembly.

1. The Work of the Trust

(a) General

The function of the Church of Scotland Trust is to hold properties outwith Scotland and to act as trustee in a number of third party trusts. During the year it has dealt with various matters which have arisen regarding these properties and trusts.

(b) The Scots Kirk, Paris

The new building on the site of the former Scots Kirk in Paris is near completion. Title to part of the ground floor and the basement of the building will be held in the name of the Church of Scotland Trust. The Congregation have engaged Professor Charles MacCallum, who recently retired as Professor of Architecture at the Macintosh School of Architecture in Glasgow, to design the interior of the building. It is anticipated that the new Scots Kirk will be available for worship in the autumn.

(c) Sea of Galilee Centre, Tiberias

The Trust has been represented at meetings of the Israel Centres Committee.

2. Accounts for 2000

The Trust's Accounts for the year to 31st December 2000 have been audited and copies thereof are available on request from the General Treasurer.

3. Membership

The members regret to say that since the 2000 Assembly they have lost, through death, one of the Trust's very respected members, namely Mr D Douglas McKinnon BSc, FFA, FIMA. Douglas McKinnon died in January 2001 and had served the Trust with distinction since 1974 as a member, Vice-Chairman and later as Chairman of both the pre- and post-1994 Trusts. He devoted much time and energy to the Trust's affairs, particularly during the transitional period brought about by the passing of the Church of Scotland (Properties and Investments) Order Confirmation Act 1994 which established the Church of Scotland Investors Trust and redefined the role of the Church of Scotland Trust.

In accordance with the constitution of the Trust, the following two members retire by rotation on 31st May 2001 but are eligible for re-appointment: Messrs D F Stewart and J A W Somerville. It is suggested to the General Assembly that Mr D F Stewart be re-appointed. Mr J A W Somerville does not seek re-appointment and the members would like to record their gratitude to him for his long service to the Trust since his appointment in 1958.

In the name and by authority of
The Church of Scotland Trust

JOHN M HODGE, *Chairman*
CHRISTOPHER N MACKAY, *Vice-Chairman*
JENNIFER M HAMILTON, *Secretary & Clerk*

CHURCH OF SCOTLAND INVESTORS TRUST

MAY 2001

PROPOSED DELIVERANCE

The General Assembly:

1. Receive the Report.
2. Approve the re-appointment of Mr. A A Aitchison, Mr C M Burnet and Mr W D B Cameron as members of the Investors Trust from 1st June 2001.
3. Receive the Annual Report and Financial Statements of the Investors Trust for 2000.

REPORT

The Church of Scotland Investors Trust, which was established by the Church of Scotland (Properties and Investments) Order Confirmation Act 1994, submits its Seventh Report to the General Assembly.

1. Introduction

The function of the Investors Trust is to provide investment services to the Church of Scotland and to bodies and trusts within or connected with the Church. The Investors Trust offers simple and economical facilities for investment in its three Funds: (a) Growth Fund; (b) Income Fund; (c) Deposit Fund. Investors receive the benefits of professional management, continuous portfolio supervision, spread of investment risk and economies of scale. In deference to the wishes of the General Assembly investments are not made in companies substantially involved in the tobacco, alcohol, gambling and armament industries.

2. Performance Monitoring

Despite the enthusiasm for new economy sectors and the bullish outlook projected by some analysts, the year 2000 was a poor one for UK equity markets with the FTSE 100 Index falling by over 13%. This had an obvious impact on the equity based Growth Fund which, in the circumstances, did well to restrict the fall in the unit price to 3.7%. By comparison, the bond markets ended the year strongly. The Income Fund, which is predominantly invested in fixed interest stocks, produced a total return of 9.1%.

Although the total return from the Growth Fund was 0.0%, this compared favourably with –3.4% for the internal benchmark.

The Income Fund does not have an overall benchmark but is assessed on the performance of its component parts. Accordingly total returns against benchmarks were as follows: Gilts10.1% (benchmark 8.0%); other UK fixed interest stocks 7.8% (benchmark 9.6%) and equities 20.8% (benchmark –5.9%).

The average rate of interest paid by the Deposit Fund was 6.11%, which compares favourably with an average Base Rate of 5.96%.

3. Income Distributions

Previous Reports have highlighted the widening gap between earnings and distributions from the Growth Fund and the reasons, such as adverse taxation changes, have been well documented.

Earnings failed to match distributions for the third year in succession but the shortfall will be covered by reserves. Income distributions for 2001 will be reduced to 14.5p per unit in order that further projected shortfalls in earnings can be offset, over the next four years, by calls on reserves. It is hoped that, in this way, additional cuts in distributions can be avoided.

It is not anticipated that there will be any reduction in the distributions from the Income Fund, which will be maintained at 73p per unit in 2001.

Whilst reductions in Base Rate have been forecast, the impact on the rates of interest payable on the Deposit Fund will be cushioned, to some extent, by the prudent placing of funds over 6, 9 and 12 months at favourable rates of interest. Accordingly, whilst an overall reduction in the average rate paid to investors is inevitable, a higher return than that available from competitive sources, for demand money, is still expected.

4. Growth Fund Management

As a matter of good practice, the Investors Trust reviews the management contracts of its Funds every five years. To assist the Trust in this process, Messrs Hymans Robertson, Investment Consultants were engaged with tenders sought from a wide range of fund managers. From a short list of four, Henderson Global Investors Ltd. were appointed to manage the Growth Fund, with effect from 1st January 2001.

5. Annual Report and Financial Statements for 2000

Copies of the Annual Report and Financial Statements for the year to 31st December 2000 are available from the Secretary.

6. Membership

In accordance with the constitution of the Investors Trust the following three members retire by rotation at 31st May 2001, but are eligible for re-appointment: Mr A A Aitchison, Mr C M Burnet and Mr W D B Cameron.
It is recommended to the General Assembly that Mr A A Aitchison, Mr C M Burnet and Mr W D B Cameron be re-appointed as members.

It is with great sadness that we record the death of one of the Investors Trust's most respected members, Mr D D McKinnon, on 23rd January 2001. Mr McKinnon served for 27 years as a member of the Church of Scotland Trust/ Investors Trust and was highly regarded in the actuarial profession. He brought to meetings a depth of knowledge, an acute mind and a truly Christian approach to the subject matter and to all with whom he came into contact. *In the name and by the authority of the Church of Scotland Investors Trust*

J B M DICK, *Chairman*
D M SIMPSON, *Vice-Chairman*
J L HENDERSON, *Secretary*

THE CHURCH OF SCOTLAND PENSION TRUSTEES
MAY 2001

PROPOSED DELIVERANCE

The General Assembly:

1. Receive the Report.
2. Note that the Actuarial Valuations for all three Schemes are being carried out as at 31 December 2000.
3. Note that the Trustees will commence discussions with the Board of Ministry regarding contributions to the Insured Pension Fund under The Church of Scotland Pension Scheme for Ministers and Overseas Missionaries.
4. Note the improvements made to the benefits under The Church of Scotland Pension Scheme for the Board of National Mission.
5. Note that the Pension Sharing on Divorce Regulations came into force on 1 December 2000.
6. Note that the Trustees have agreed to credit any variable compensation received from Scottish Widows in respect of AVC policies to the Scheme member's individual AVC policy for the Scheme member's own benefit.
7. Re-appoint Arthur John Briggs, William D B Cameron, David Drysdale Fotheringham and W John McCafferty as Trustees.

REPORT

1. Introduction

The Pension Trustees are responsible for the administration and the investments of the three Church of Scotland Pension Schemes with approximately 6,000 members overall and with assets in excess of £230 million:

- The Church of Scotland Pension Scheme for Ministers and Overseas Missionaries
- The Church of Scotland Pension Scheme for Staff
- The Church of Scotland Pension Scheme for the Board of National Mission

The Schemes currently provide different benefits to their members, although an investigation into the feasibility of harmonising the main benefits, which commenced in 1999, continued during the year. All pension schemes are 'Contracted-In', which means that Scheme members will also receive a State Earnings Related Pension.

2. The Church of Scotland Pension Scheme for Ministers and Overseas Missionaries

2.1 With effect from January 2001 the Main Pension Fund Standard Annuity of which a member receives one fortieth for each year of pensionable service was increased from £10,745 per annum to £11,091 per annum.

2.2 The pensions in payment from the Main Pension Fund, the Contributors' Pension Fund and the Widows' & Orphans' Fund were increased by 3.3% per annum from 1 January 2001.

2.3 Following the improvements to the pension under the Main Pension Fund, the original target pension of a half of the minimum stipend and service supplement after 40 years' pensionable service has now been reached. Consequently, due to the Inland

Revenue restrictions there is less scope to provide benefits from the Insured Pension Fund. The 1993 General Assembly noted the intention eventually to phase out contributions to the Insured Pension Fund once the target pension had been reached. The Pension Trustees therefore will commence discussions with the Board of Ministry regarding contributions to the Insured Pension Fund.

2.4 The Actuarial Valuation of the Scheme is being carried out as at 31 December 2000.

2.5 The Pension Sharing on Divorce Regulations came into force on 1 December 2000.

3. The Church of Scotland Pension Scheme for Staff

3.1 The Actuarial Valuation of the Scheme is being carried out as at 31 December 2000.

3.2 All pensions in payment were increased by 3.3% from 1 January 2001.

3.3 The Pension Sharing on Divorce Regulations came into force on 1 December 2000.

3.4 Following the demutualisation of Scottish Widows the Trustees decided that any variable compensation in respect of individual AVC Policies would be credited to the Scheme members' individual AVC Policies.

4. The Church of Scotland Pension Scheme for the Board of National Mission

4.1 The following improvements were made to the Scheme benefits during the year:
- Pensions will be based on actual service in the Scheme and not just years and complete months.
- Pensions on ill-health retirements will be based on prospective service to age 65.
- Children's pensions will be provided on death of a Scheme member's widow(er).

4.2 All pensions were increased by 3.3% from 1 January 2001.

4.3 The Pension Sharing on Divorce Regulations came into force on 1 December 2000.

4.4 The Actuarial Valuation of the Scheme is being carried out as at 31 December 2000.

4.5 Following the demutualisation of Scottish Widows the Trustees decided that any variable compensation in respect of individual AVC Policies would be credited to the Scheme members' individual AVC Policies. Compensation paid to the Trustees in respect of Pension policies purchased by the Trustees was invested in the Pension Investment Fund.

5. Annual Report and Accounts

Copies of the Annual Report and Accounts of each Scheme for the year to 31 December 2000 are available from the Pensions Manager.

6. Trustees

In accordance with the Constitutions of the Trustees approved by the General Assembly of 1997, William D B Cameron and W John McCafferty retire on 31 May 2001. It is proposed that they be re-appointed.

Also the 1998 General Assembly appointed Arthur John Briggs and David Drysdale Fotheringham for a period of three years up to may 2001. It is also proposed that they be re-appointed.

In the name of the Trustees

WILLIAM D B CAMERON Chairman
W JOHN McCAFFERTY Vice-Chairman
Mrs SIRKKA DENNISON Pensions Manager

BOARD OF STEWARDSHIP AND FINANCE
MAY 2001

PROPOSED DELIVERANCE

The General Assembly:

1. Receive the Report.

2. Encourage congregations to promote Christian Stewardship and to use the resources available from the Stewardship Department.

3. Encourage congregations to promote the new Gift Aid scheme among tax-paying members.

4. Receive the 2000 Accounts of the Unincorporated Boards and Committees of the General Assembly.

5. Confirm the appointment of Deloitte & Touche, Chartered Accountants and Registered Auditors, as Auditors of the 2001 Accounts of the Unincorporated Boards and Committees of the General Assembly.

6. Approve the revised Constitution of the Board of Stewardship and Finance, to take effect as from 1st September 2001.

REPORT

1. Stewardship Report

The promotion of Christian Stewardship in terms of time, abilities and money is the function of the Stewardship Department. This promotion is designed to increase the resources available for the mission of the Church at all levels and to ensure that these resources are used in the best possible way for the advancement of the kingdom of God. Christian Stewardship challenges members of the Church to consider God's priorities in the way they use their time, abilities and money. It also challenges the Church at all levels to consider God's priorities in the way the resources provided by members are used.

The Stewardship Department continues to provide resources to assist the promotion of Christian Stewardship. These resources come in two forms – the provision of Stewardship Programmes and the assistance of Stewardship Staff.

Our Stewardship Programmes are currently being reviewed and renewed. The pilot programme 'Time, Abilities, Priorities' has now been renamed 'Fruits of Faith': this is a celebratory programme which focuses on members' time and abilities. The 'Christian Commitment Programme', which is concerned with time, abilities and money, has been revised and renamed 'Commitment Challenge'. Work is progressing on a new money programme to replace 'Sharing Resources'. The 'Stewardship Family Meal' is still available and being used by a number of congregations.

In preparing material for these programmes the Stewardship Department is conscious of the need for programmes to be sufficiently flexible to meet different local situations. It is likely that some material will be produced on compact disc or delivered through the Internet to give congregations the opportunity to use centrally produced material in local congregational literature. One centrally produced leaflet does not meet the need of every congregation.

The three Stewardship Consultants and the Deputy Director continue to be involved in assisting congregational office-bearers carry through the various Stewardship Programmes. During 2000 the staff were involved in over 300 meetings with 105 congregations in

33 mainland Presbyteries. Staff were also involved in meetings organised by the island Presbyteries of Uist and Lewis.

The Director of Stewardship has responded to a variety of invitations to speak on aspects of Christian Stewardship. In the early months of his appointment he was involved in eleven meetings to promote giving through the new Gift Aid scheme.

In July 2000 the Stewardship Staff, together with two members of the Board, participated in the CTBI Stewardship Network Conference at Harlech. This was an opportunity to focus on Christian Stewardship issues with representatives of other Churches, to make useful contacts, and to learn from one another. The Director of Stewardship represents the Church of Scotland on the CTBI Stewardship Network Committee.

The vision of the Stewardship Department is that Christian Stewardship ceases to be something in which congregations engage occasionally, usually when there are financial problems, and becomes part of the ongoing life of the Church, continually challenging us as individuals and as the Church on the way we use God's gifts.

2. Allocating the Mission and Aid Fund

The Board is reviewing the way in which the Mission and Aid Fund is allocated among congregations. In undertaking this review the Board is working alongside the Board of Ministry, which is reviewing the way in which stipend and other ministry costs are levied on congregations.

In our review of the allocation of the Mission and Aid Fund, the main guiding principle has been that the method should be as fair and as simple as possible. In considering what might be the total normal income of a congregation the Board is conscious of the fact that some congregations have considerable reserves while others do not. The Board is considering the possibility of making at least a token allocation to all congregations so that every congregation, including aid-receiving congregations, has the opportunity to support the wider work of the Church.

The outcome of this review will be brought to a future

General Assembly for their approval before a revised method of allocation is put into operation.

3. Congregational Contributions

3.1   Ministry Funds (Appendix 2)

Because a minority of congregations are unable to remit their contributions in full during any one financial year, it is not possible to show the final allocation achievement until at least the end of the next financial year. By 31st December 2000, the net shortfall for **1999** had been reduced to **0.80 per cent,** continuing the excellent achievement of recent years.

At the end of **2000**, the shortfall for that year was **2.07 per cent**, which was marginally higher than the equivalent figure of **1.93 per cent** a year previously. It is expected that the 2000 shortfall will be considerably reduced by late payments in 2001.

It is noted with appreciation that voluntary Aid repayments of **£38,919** were made in 2000 by Aid Receiving congregations, which was higher than the equivalent figure of **£33,845** in 1999.

3.2   Mission and Aid Fund (Appendix 3)

As with Ministry Funds, Mission and Aid Fund statistics are affected by late contributions. An additional, but welcome, factor is the receipt of voluntary extra contributions, which may be undesignated or may be restricted to a particular Board, Committee or project.

Since 1993, shortfalls have been carried forward and the effect of this has been dramatic. In **1991** and **1992** the net shortfalls were over **4.0 per cent**. For the period from **1993 to 1999,** the net shortfalls in each year have been less than **1.0 per cent**.

The contributions position for **2000,** at the end of 2000, was also encouraging, the shortfall at that date being **2.41 per cent**, the second lowest since the establishment of the Mission and Aid Fund. With late contributions already received and still to be received in **2001**, it is hoped that the shortfall for **2000** will be reduced to the low levels of previous years.

The Board expresses its gratitude to all congregations who met their allocations in full and to those who made additional voluntary contributions in 2000. As well as **general undesignated extra contributions of £85,115 (1999 — £84,459)**, congregations gave **extra contributions to specific areas of work within the Mission and Aid Fund of £274,452** in 2000. This was a large increase over the 1999 figure of **£197,291** for designated extra contributions. Particular reference should be made to the generosity of Murrayfield Church in Edinburgh, which donated **£40,000** to the New Charge Development Committee to assist with the cost of building a new church at Cove. In line with past years, the other main beneficiaries of designated extra contributions in 2000 were the Board of World Mission (**£161,205**) and Christian Aid (**£38,646**), reflecting the continuing appeal to congregations of the Church's overseas mission and relief work.

4. Accounting Matters

4.1 Accounts and Financial Overview
As in previous years, separate sets of Accounts for 2000 have been produced for each of the following:

> The Church of Scotland Investors Trust
> The Church of Scotland General Trustees
> The Church of Scotland Trust
> The Church of Scotland Pension Trustees
> The Unincorporated Boards and Committees.

The first three of the above bodies are statutory corporations and the Pension Trustees are an unincorporated body, constituted by the General Assembly. All four bodies are responsible for producing and approving their own Accounts.

The Board of Stewardship and Finance is responsible for preparing and approving the Accounts of the Unincorporated Boards and Committees, which comprise Ministry Funds, Mission and Aid Funds, Miscellaneous Funds, Board of Communication and Board of Social Responsibility.

A Financial Overview, giving a summary of the main features of the Accounts of the Unincorporated Boards and Committees for 2000, has also been produced for Commissioners to the General Assembly.

4.2 External Audit Arrangements
In accordance with recognised best practice, it is the Board's policy to invite tenders for the external audit of the Accounts of the Church at regular intervals. As it was six years since the last tender process, this exercise was carried out again in the course of 2000. Eight firms were approached initially and thereafter three firms were invited to submit formal tenders for the audit. Following interviews with the three firms, the Board appointed Messrs. Deloitte & Touche, Chartered Accountants and Registered Auditors, to audit the Accounts for 2000 of the Unincorporated Boards and Committees of the General Assembly. The Church's three statutory corporations and the Church of Scotland Pension Trustees have also appointed Messrs. Deloitte & Touche to audit their Accounts for 2000. The General Assembly is being asked to confirm the appointment of Deloitte & Touche as Auditors of the 2001 Accounts of the Church.

The present Constitution of the Board of Stewardship and Finance requires the Board to submit annually to the General Assembly, proposals for the audit of the Accounts of the Church for the next financial year. It is felt that the approval of the appointment of auditors by the General Assembly is no longer appropriate and that powers should be given to the Board to proceed with making audit appointments annually, provided that these are subsequently reported to the General Assembly. The revised Constitution of the Board, which is being submitted for approval to this year's General Assembly, has been drafted on the basis of this new procedure applying for the audits for 2002 and subsequent years.

4.3 Attestation of Presbytery Accounts
In 1997 the General Assembly approved Regulations anent Presbytery Finance, which cover the content, audit and attestation of Presbytery Accounts. After the Accounts have been approved by the Presbytery, they have to be submitted for attestation to the Board of Stewardship and Finance, which then has to report to the Assembly. The Board is pleased to report that the 1999 Accounts of Presbyteries showed a further improvement in the standard of accounting presentation.

4.4 Presbytery Attestation of Congregational Accounts

The Law Reform (Miscellaneous Provisions) (Scotland) Act 1990 imposed on charities a new code of law, including specific requirements as to the keeping of Accounts. As part of the central supervisory process, the General Assembly in 1994 approved Regulations anent Congregational Finance and instructed Presbyteries and Congregational Financial Boards to give effect to the Regulations. The Regulations lay down procedures to be followed by Presbyteries in attesting Accounts of all congregations within their bounds.

The reports from Presbyteries on the inspection of 1999 Congregational Accounts indicated continuing progress in achieving compliance with the Regulations anent Congregational Finance. The Board is conscious of the heavy demands placed on voluntary office-bearers but if the Church is to retain its "designated" status and the important exemptions that go with it, it is essential that Congregational Accounts comply with the Regulations and that this can be demonstrated to the regulatory authorities. In this, the Church is heavily dependent upon and appreciative of the diligence of Presbyteries and their Accounts Inspection Committees.

As was reported to last year's General Assembly, the Board is awaiting the outcome of the report of the independent commission on the review of charity law in Scotland, before bringing to the General Assembly new Congregational Accounting Regulations.

5. Child Care Expenses

Last year's General Assembly instructed the Board "to consider financial provision in the future budget of the Church for child care during attendance at meetings of Boards and Committees". This instruction arose from the report of the Gender Attitude Project, which stated that "these expenses would not be payable to serving ministers, since such service falls within their professional duties".

Prior to the Assembly, the Board had already alerted all Boards and Committees to the possibility of paying child care expenses and is presently monitoring the situation to see the level of claims made. The matter was also discussed at the meeting of the Co-ordinating Forum in September 2000 and the point was made that the issue related not only to child care expenses but to any care expenses, e.g. where a Committee member was caring for an elderly relative. It is expected that relatively few claims will be made but it is important that the facility for reimbursement of care expenditure is available for those who otherwise might not be able to serve on Church Committees.

6. Internal Audit

The internal audit function is provided through the services of an independent firm of professional chartered accountants, Messrs Scott-Moncrieff, who have been reappointed for a further three year term. The Internal Audit Committee has continued the appraisal of the financial management controls and activities of the Boards and Committees of the General Assembly, except for the Board of Social Responsibility, which has its own internal audit function, using the same firm of accountants. Systems and procedures covering a wide range of activities of the Boards and Committees are reviewed in accordance with an annual internal audit plan. The Internal Audit Committee is grateful to officials of the Boards and Committees for their positive responses to the internal audit reports and for their ready agreement to implement the recommendations made.

The Internal Audit Committee reports through the Board of Stewardship and Finance but is independent of the Board. It has the right to report directly to the General Assembly, without any modification of its Report. The Board has been informed that there are no issues at this time that the Committee wishes to report directly to the General Assembly.

7. Constitution of Board of Board of Stewardship and Finance

The Board is submitting to the General Assembly a revised Constitution. The major changes in the Constitution are necessitated by proposals being made to the Assembly by the Joint Working Party in relation to the establishment of a new Central Co-ordinating Committee. If approved by the Assembly, the result will be to transfer from the Board of Stewardship and Finance to the Central Co-ordinating Committee responsibility for the Church Offices, at 117–123 George Street, Edinburgh, the General Treasurer's Department and the internal audit function.

By the authority of the Board

LEON M MARSHALL, *Convener*
J COLIN CASKIE, *Vice-Convener*
DONALD F ROSS, *General Treasurer*
GORDON D JAMIESON, *Director of Stewardship*
FRED MARSH, *Administrative Secretary*

ADDENDUM

Mr Leon M Marshall

Leon Marshall retires at this General Assembly after four years as Convener of the Board of Stewardship and Finance. A former Convener of the Budget and Allocation Sub Committee, Leon has added Convenership of the Board to an already committed life as a Reader, member of the Presbytery of Greenock, Session Clerk at Kilmacolm Old, senior partner in a Glasgow firm of Chartered Accountants, and husband of Barbara and a father of three teenagers.

Leon has given of himself unstintingly to the service of the Board during a period of re-organisation and his professional skills have been well used in his chairing of the Board and his detailed submissions to the Co-ordinating Forum. To the many tasks of Convener, Leon has brought to bear depth of insight, a love of people, a warm spirit, clarity of thought and a vibrant sense of humour. Always generous and patient he has put the Board greatly in his debt by the grace and commitment he has shown as Convener.

The Board thanks Leon for all he has done, and all he has been to us over the past four years, and wish him God's richest blessing in the days to come.

In the name of the Board

J COLIN CASKIE, *Vice-Convener*
DONALD F ROSS, *General Treasurer*
GORDON D JAMIESON, *Director of Stewardship*
FRED MARSH, *Administrative Secretary*

APPENDIX 1
Legacies to Central Funds of the Church

	2000 £	1999 £
The Church of Scotland (Unrestricted)	1,740,591	503,459
Social Responsibility	1,224,931	1,202,920
World Mission	646,183	661,754
Housing and Loan Fund	225,693	327,619
New Charge Development	174,186	120
Education for the Ministry	80,295	19,992
Special Trusts	74,412	1,239,983
Mission and Aid Fund	50,604	29,375
Pension Funds	42,052	487,196
Christian Aid	26,974	7,747
Ministry Support	25,739	310,685
National Mission	22,958	268,593
General Trustees	10,420	314,312
Parish Education	1,666	152,146
Chaplains to HM Forces	1,388	75,351
Miscellaneous	599	425
The Guild	-	5,120
Ecumenical Relations	-	418
Total Legacies to Central Funds	**4,348,691**	**5,607,215**

APPENDIX 2

Congregational Contributions to Ministry Funds

Year	Allocated £	Received by 31 Dec £	Shortfall in Year £	%	Contributions received in Later Years £	Net Shortfall £	%
1991	21,429,806	20,927,987	501,819	2.34	409,580	92,239	0.43
1992	23,092,167	22,459,273	632,894	2.74	474,786	158,108	0.68
1993	24,191,147	23,391,116	800,031	3.31	582,258	217,773	0.90
1994	24,760,852	24,090,435	670,417	2.71	529,028	141,389	0.57
1995	26,288,881	25,600,603	688,278	2.62	541,576	146,702	0.56
1996	27,507,754	26,849,322	658,432	2.39	504,835	153,597	0.56
1997	28,168,983	27,594,122	574,861	2.04	413,797	161,064	0.57
1998	29,079,993	28,486,879	593,114	2.04	413,688	179,426	0.62
1999	30,025,114	29,445,071	580,043	1.93	340,420	239,623	0.80
2000	27,272,959	26,708,186	564,773	2.07			

Note: The figures for 1991 to 1999 are inclusive of ministers' travelling expenses. The figures for 2000 exclude ministers' travelling expenses, following the operational changes implemented from 1st January 2000. Congregations no longer receive an annual requirement for ministerial travel (based on estimated mileage) but now are invoiced periodically (usually quarterly) in arrears, based on actual mileage returns from ministers.

Similarly, the figures for 2000 differ from those of prior years in that they are exclusive of the voluntary contributions which congregations make to the Insured Pension Fund on behalf of their minister. This conforms with the treatment of such expenditure as a local, rather than, a central cost in the Co-ordinated Budget.

APPENDIX 3

Congregational Contributions to the Mission and Aid Fund

Year	Allocated £	Received by 31 Dec £	Shortfall in Year £	%	Contributions received in Later Years £	Net Shortfall £	%	Voluntary General Extra Contributions £	Designated Extra Contributions £
1991	7,947,685	7,440,090	507,595	6.39	182,319	325,276	4.09	102,069	109,218
1992	8,513,391	7,936,862	576,529	6.77	224,115	352,414	4.14	91,263	180,240
1993	9,123,848	8,520,794	603,054	6.61	525,926	77,128	0.85	68,392	151,198
1994	9,512,064	9,040,541	471,523	4.96	412,338	59,185	0.62	81,464	167,660
1995	9,222,444	8,835,357	387,087	4.20	346,917	40,170	0.44	85,000	228,529
1996	9,493,627	9,208,986	284,641	3.00	242,649	41,992	0.44	151,207	446,832
1997	9,822,169	9,573,439	248,730	2.53	212,977	35,753	0.36	87,801	173,551
1998	10,170,417	9,923,349	247,068	2.43	206,756	40,312	0.40	95,319	201,829
1999	10,341,879	10,098,505	243,374	2.35	184,777	58,597	0.57	84,459	197,291
2000	10,550,936	10,296,433	254,503	2.41				85,115	274,452

APPENDIX 4
The Church of Scotland
Board of Stewardship and Finance
Revised Constitution 2001

1. Name

The name of the Board shall be the Board of Stewardship and Finance (hereinafter referred to as "the Board").

2. Membership

The Board shall consist of a Convener, Vice-Convener and twenty-four members all appointed by the General Assembly.

A Presbytery representative from and appointed by each of the Presbyteries in Scotland and from the Presbytery of England shall be called to attend meetings of the Board in accordance with Clause 5 hereof.

The Convener and Secretary of the Co-ordinating Forum shall be ex officiis members of the Board and of its Budget and Allocation Committee. *(see foot-note 1)*

The General Treasurer and the Director of Stewardship shall be ex officiis members of the Board and of all its Committees but shall not have voting rights.

3. Terms of Reference

(1) To promote and encourage Christian Stewardship throughout the Church.

(2) To provide programmes and training to assist congregations and their office bearers in visiting members, making known the work of the Church, promoting Christian giving and in administering congregational finances.

(3) To ascertain whether financial resources are or can be expected to be available to support proposals before the General Assembly.

(4) To be responsible for preparing and submitting to the General Assembly a Co-ordinated Budget for the following financial year and a projected Rolling Budget for the next four years. (The details of the procedures to be followed are shown in Appendix 1 attached.)

(5) To be responsible with the Board of Ministry and with Presbyteries for allocating among congregations the expenditure contained in the Co-ordinated Budget referred to in 3.(4) above, and for seeking to ensure that congregations meet their obligations thereto, by transmitting regularly throughout the year to the General Treasurer of the Church contributions towards their allocations. (The details of the procedures to be followed are shown in Appendix 2 attached.)

(6) To set standards of financial management and accounting procedures and to provide financial and accounting services for all Boards and Committees of the General Assembly (except for the Board of Social Responsibility).

(7) To set standards for the production of budgets and management accounts by all Boards and Committees of the General Assembly (except for the Board of Social Responsibility).

(8) To compare budgeted and actual expenditure for all Boards and Committees of the General Assembly (except for the Board of Social Responsibility), on a regular basis throughout the year and to seek explanations of variances therein.

(9) To maintain and up-date such statistical and financial information as is deemed necessary.

(10) To examine the statistical and financial information of such Boards, Committees and Statutory Corporations, the members of which are appointed by and/or answerable to the General Assembly, as the Board shall consider appropriate and to report annually to the General Assembly on the general financial position of the Church.

(11) To make financial arrangements for special projects outwith the Co-ordinated Budget.

(12) To receive and distribute unrestricted legacies and donations in accordance with the following principles:

(a) To receive unrestricted legacies and donations, to maintain therefrom a Contingency Fund of £100,000, and to transfer the balance of unrestricted legacies and donations annually to the Mission and Aid Fund.

(b)   To apply the Contingency Fund to meet exceptional and non-recurring expenditures and deficits outwith the Mission and Aid Fund. Where time considerations are important, payments may be made on the authority of two persons, one of whom shall be the Convener or the Vice-Convener of the Board of Stewardship and Finance, and the other one of whom shall be the General Treasurer or one of the Deputy Treasurers of the Church. A report on all such payments shall be made to the next meeting of the Board.

(13)   To issue annually to each congregation a Schedule of Congregational Financial Statistics, to be completed and returned by a date determined by the Board.

(14)   To report annually to the General Assembly on the attestation of Presbytery and Congregational Accounts.

(15)   To approve and submit annually to the General Assembly the Financial Statements of the Unincorporated Boards and Committees of the General Assembly.

(16)   To appoint Auditors for the Financial Statements of the Unincorporated Boards and Committees of the General Assembly.

(17)   To consider Reports received from the Auditors of the Financial Statements of the Unincorporated Boards and Committees of the General Assembly.

(18)   To ensure that all funds belonging to Boards and Committees of the General Assembly, which are not contained within the Financial Statements submitted to the General Assembly, are audited or independently examined annually.

(19)   To exercise custody over funds and to provide bank arrangements.

(20)   To operate a central banking system for all Boards (except for the Board of Social Responsibility), Committees and Statutory Corporations.

(21)   To consider taxation matters affecting Boards, Committees and Statutory Corporations and congregations of the Church.

(22)   To provide such financial, secretarial and other services as may be required by the Church of Scotland Investors Trust.

(23)   To provide such financial and other services as may be required by the Church of Scotland General Trustees and the Church of Scotland Trust.

(24)   To provide such financial and other services as may be required by the Trustees of the Church of Scotland's Pension Schemes.

(25)   To determine the types and rates of expenses that may be claimed by members serving Boards, Committees and Statutory Corporations.

(26)   To carry out such other duties as may be referred to the Board from time to time by the General Assembly.

4. Committees of the Board

The Board shall form such Committees whether Standing or *ad hoc* as in its discretion it considers necessary for the proper fulfilment of the foregoing terms of reference. Membership of the Committees may include Presbytery representatives as defined in Clause 2, as well as Assembly-appointed members of the Board, provided Assembly-appointed members of the Board shall form a majority of the membership of any Committee.

5. Meetings

Meetings of the Board and of its Committees shall be held as required. At least two meetings of the Board each year shall be attended by Presbytery representatives. At one of these meetings the proposals for the Co-ordinated Budget and the Rolling Budget and the allocation thereof among the Boards, Committees and Statutory Corporations shall be submitted for approval. At meetings of the Board attended by Presbytery representatives, these representatives shall have the full rights of members of the Board.

6. Appointment of Officials

All members of staff of the Board will have the Central Co-ordinating Committee as their employing agency. The Board shall appoint such members of staff to ensure the proper conduct of its business, as may from time to time be considered necessary and expedient. The salaries, length and conditions of service of such appointments shall be determined by the Central Co-ordinating Committee, in consultation with the Board. *(see foot-note 2)*

7. Board Expenses

The net costs of the Board shall be met by the Mission and Aid Fund, from a budget within the General Purposes Fund.

8. Appointment of Presbytery Stewardship and Finance Committees

Each Presbytery shall appoint a Stewardship and Finance Committee or other appropriate Committee.

9. Administrative Arrangements

The Board shall be entitled to frame procedural regulations from time to time to ensure the orderly conduct of its business.

10. Finance and Property

The Board has assumed and shall continue to assume the whole responsibilities in regard to property and the whole rights and assets formerly exercised and enjoyed by the General Finance Committee and the Stewardship and Budget Committee, except that its rights to and responsibilities in respect of the Church Offices at 121 George Street, Edinburgh shall pass to and be assumed by the Central Co-ordinating Committee on 1st September 2001. *(see foot-note 2)*

11. Implementation

The revised Constitution of the Board shall come into effect on 1st September 2001.

APPENDIX 1

Preparation of the Co-ordinated Budget

In fulfilment of its remit to prepare and submit to the General Assembly a Co-ordinated Budget for the following year and a projected Rolling Budget for the next four years, the Board of Stewardship and Finance ("the Board") shall do so by the following procedures and with the following powers:

1. The Board shall prepare Congregational Income Estimates for each of the five years concerned. The Congregational Income Estimates contained in the Rolling Budget will be reviewed and, where necessary, adjusted annually in the light of actual Congregational Income received in past years and projected financial and economic trends.

2. The Board shall submit to the General Assembly proposed allocations of its Congregational Income Estimates for each of the five years among:

   (1) Local Mission;

   (2) Ministry Funds;

   (3) Mission and Aid Fund.

3. In preparing its proposals for
   (a) the allocation of Congregational Income Estimates ("Income Disposition")
        and

   (b) individual budgets within Ministry Funds and the Mission and Aid Fund

the Board shall take account of income from non-congregational sources (including income from and accumulated balances of unrestricted, restricted and endowment funds) available to Boards, Committees and Funds receiving support from the Co-ordinated Budget.

4. The Board shall consult the Co-ordinating Forum on the following matters:

(a) any proposal to vary the proportions in which the Co-ordinated Budget is allocated among Local Mission, Ministry Funds and the Mission and Aid Fund;

(b) matters which involve the transferring of resources from one area of the Church's work to another;

(c) the annual Co-ordinated Budget of the Church for the following financial year;

(d) the Rolling Budget of the Church for the next four years.

5. The Board of Ministry shall advise the Board of the total budget to be incorporated in the Co-ordinated Budget for Ministry Funds. The total of this budget shall not exceed the proposed total share of Congregational Income Estimates allocated to Ministry Funds.

6. The Board shall have powers to issue budget forms to all Boards, Committees, Statutory Corporations and Funds receiving support from the Co-ordinated Budget, in a style and format laid down by the Board, and to require the return of the completed budget forms by dates determined by the Board.

7. The Board shall give Boards, Committees and Statutory Corporations requiring financial support from the Co-ordinated Budget opportunities for consultation about the financial needs of their work. At the meeting of the Board at which the Co-ordinated Budget and Rolling Budget proposals will be presented for the Board's approval before submission to the General Assembly, any Board, Committee or Statutory Corporation having an interest in the proposals for the Co-ordinated Budget and Rolling Budget and wishing to make a submission at this meeting of the Board shall have the right to do so. If any Board, Committee or Statutory Corporation records its dissent from any part of the Co-ordinated Budget or Rolling Budget, the dissent shall be reported by the Board of Stewardship and Finance to the General Assembly, to enable the Assembly to make its judgement thereon when considering the Co-ordinated Budget and Rolling Budget.

APPENDIX 2
Allocation of the Co-ordinated Budget

1. The Board of Stewardship and Finance ("the Board") shall be responsible jointly with the Board of Ministry for the allocation to congregations of the Co-ordinated Budget approved by the General Assembly.

2. It will be the responsibility of the Board of Ministry to allocate, through Presbyteries, all Ministry requirements as detailed in Appendix 1.5, in accordance with the procedures approved by the General Assembly.

3. It will be the responsibility of the Board to allocate, through Presbyteries, the budget for the Mission and Aid Fund among congregations. The Board shall ensure that the Mission and Aid Fund budget, as finally approved by the General Assembly, is fully allocated among congregations.

4. The Board shall determine Allocation Base figures for congregations, calculated from a schedule devised by the Board.

5. Each Presbytery shall return one completed copy of the schedule referred to in Section 4 above for each congregation within its bounds to the Board of Stewardship and Finance prior to 30th April each year. Failure to provide the Board with the required information will give the Board power to provide estimated Allocation Base figures for the congregation or congregations concerned.

6. The Board shall send to each Presbytery by 31st August each year, a list of the proposed figures for the Mission and Aid Fund allocation for the following financial year of all congregations within its bounds.

7. On receipt from the Board of the proposed amount to be allocated for the Mission and Aid Fund to each congregation within a Presbytery, the Presbytery, through its Stewardship and Finance Committee, shall confirm or amend the proposed allocations. In the event of any amendment being made to the proposed allocations, the total sum of the amended Mission and Aid Fund allocations for all congregations in the Presbytery shall be not less than the total sum proposed initially by the Board, unless there is prior consultation with and concurrence from representatives of the Board.

8. The Presbytery Committee shall report its proposed Mission and Aid Fund allocations to the Presbytery Clerk, who shall communicate the particulars to members of Presbytery before the next meeting of Presbytery. At that or a subsequent meeting, the Presbytery shall confirm or adjust the proposed allocations to congregations, provided that the total amount required from congregations within the Presbytery is maintained or that any alteration of this amount has been made with the concurrence of representatives of the Board.

9. The Presbytery shall notify each congregation of its Mission and Aid Fund allocation for the following financial year not later than 15th November each year. The Presbytery shall also transmit copies of its congregational allocations to the Board by that same date each year.

10. The Presbytery shall notify each congregation of its required contributions to Ministry Funds for the following financial year not later than 15th November each year. The Presbytery shall also transmit copies of its congregational requirements to Ministry Funds to the Board of Ministry by that same date each year.

11. The Board of Ministry shall provide figures for congregational contributions to Ministry Funds for the following financial year to the Board by 15th November each year.

12. The General Treasurer shall then issue to congregations in December each year, confirmation of the allocation figures for Ministry Funds and the Mission and Aid Fund for the following year.

Responsibilities of Presbyteries

13. Presbytery Stewardship and Finance Committees and Ministry Committees shall jointly take such steps as they consider necessary to secure that every congregation provides its approved allocations in full. Presbytery Stewardship and Finance Committees shall be required to urge congregations to improve their levels of giving and to be responsible for the education of the membership in a fuller understanding of Christian Stewardship.

14. When Vacancy or Revision Schedules are being completed, the Presbytery will arrange for representatives of its Stewardship and Finance Committee to be present, so that the level of the congregation's giving and the ability of the congregation to meet all its financial obligations may be considered. When considering Vacancy or Revision Schedules, the Presbytery shall obtain from each congregation concerned, and thereafter submit to both the Board of Ministry and the Board of Stewardship and Finance, an appropriate extract Minute from the Financial Board of the congregation, confirming the commitment of the congregation to meet in full its allocations to the central funds of the Church.

15. The Board of Ministry and the Board of Stewardship and Finance shall report annually to each Presbytery Clerk, in relation to his or her Presbytery, all shortfalls in congregational contributions to Ministry Funds and to the Mission and Aid Fund, both those for the latest financial year and any accumulated totals. Each Presbytery shall record annually in the Minutes of the Presbytery all such shortfalls.

16. In all cases where congregations fail to meet their requirements for Ministry Funds or the Mission and Aid Fund, the appropriate Presbytery Committee(s) shall consult with the office bearers, giving opportunity for representatives of both the Presbytery's Ministry Committee and the Stewardship and Finance Committee to be involved.

Responsibilities of Financial Boards and Congregations

17. It will be the responsibility of each Financial Board to inform the congregation of the required figures for Ministry Funds and for the Mission and Aid Fund and to give members information about the work supported by the Mission and Aid Fund.

18. Each congregation shall transmit contributions towards its allocation for Ministry Funds and the Mission and Aid Fund preferably monthly and at least quarterly, by Bank Standing Order or direct debit, wherever possible. Where this cannot be done, then payment should be made by a Bank Transfer or directly to the General Treasurer of the Church. Where a congregation is able to provide more in any year than its approved allocation to the Mission and Aid Fund, that congregation shall be at liberty to allocate its additional contribution to the work of a particular Board or Committee which is funded through the Mission and Aid Fund.

Foot notes:
1) The wording of this sentence is dependent upon the General Assembly approving proposals being submitted on the Report of the Board of Practice and Procedure in relation to the Convenership and Vice Convenership of the Co-ordinating Forum.

2) The wording of this clause is dependent upon the General Assembly approving proposals being submitted on the Report of the Joint Working Party in relation to the establishment of a Central Co-ordinating Committee.

PERSONNEL COMMITTEE
MAY 2001

PROPOSED DELIVERANCE

The General Assembly:
1. Receive the Report.

REPORT

1. SALARIES

The voting members of the Committee, following the normal consultation with the Board of Stewardship & Finance regarding "ability to pay" and taking account of inflation, reviewed the salaries payable to all members of staff for which it is the Employing Agency.

As a result the salary scales were increased by some 3.0 per cent which the Committee believes was a fair and reasonable review for its employees.

The new salaries were implemented with effect from 1st January 2001.

2. PENSIONS

The Committee has undertaken extensive consultations with several interested parties, including staff and management, on the question of the benefits payable under the present terms of the Staff Pension Scheme. It is the Committee's intention to recommend to the Church a revised scheme with benefits which would be more advantageous for its staff.

3. CARS FOR BUSINESS USE

The Committee undertook a review of the factors associated with the provision of cars for business use, taking account of present systems applying in the various Boards and Committees. As a result, three categories of business use were clearly defined according to the number of business miles incurred; namely, essential, regular and casual users. The scheme has been successfully introduced and led to savings in certain Boards where employees have opted to provide a vehicle instead of the Board concerned having to do so.

4. EMPLOYEE STATISTICS

The attached Appendix shows the number of employees under the remit of the Personnel Committee as at 31st December 2000 and the previous two years, for each Board, Committee and Department.

5. CONSULTATION

As an ongoing process, both formal and informal, consultation has continued throughout the year with various Boards, Committees and Departments of the Church as well as with representatives of both the Management Committee and the Staff Association. The Personnel Committee was also represented at all meetings of the Co-ordinating Forum held during the year.

6. JOINT WORKING PARTY

The Convener, Secretary and former Convener, Mr David D Fotheringham represented the Committee as members of the Working Party established by the 1999 General Assembly following the Report of the Special Commission on the Board of Communication. The final recommendations of the Working Party are the subject of a separate report.

7. McKINSEY CONSULTANTS

The Personnel Manager and his staff participated in the organisational review undertaken by the consultancy firm McKinsey for the Boards of Ministry and World Mission respectively. Involvement continues with representatives of these Boards as they seek to implement their decisions following these reviews.

In the name of and by the authority of the Committee,

GRAHAM CHARTERS, *Convener*
GORDON MURISON, *Vice-Convener*
GEORGE B B EADIE, *Secretary*

APPENDIX
CHURCH OF SCOTLAND PERSONNEL COMMITTEE
Employees as at 31 December

Board/Committee/Department	2000 Full Time	Part Time	Total	1999 Full Time	Part Time	Total	1998 Full Time	Part Time	Total
Assembly Council		1	1		1	1	1		1
Church and Nation	1	2	3	1	2	3		2	2
Communication	31		31	27	1	28	28	2	30
Ecumenical Relations	2		2	2		2	2		2
Education	2		2	2		2	2		2
General Trustees	9	9	18	9	9	18	10	7	17
Information Technology	10		10	9		9	8		8
Law	12	3	15	11	3	14	11	3	14
Ministry	17	2	19	18	1	19	16	1	17
National Mission	34	17	51	36	15	51	37	11	48
New College		1	1		1	1		1	1
Office Management	5	5	10	5	2	7	5	2	7
Parish Education	31	8	39	22	12	34	22	12	34
Pensions	3	2	5	3	1	4	3	2	5
Personnel	4		4	4		4	4		4
Practice and Procedure	5	1	6	6	1	7	5	2	7
Scottish Parliamentary Office	2		2	2		2	2		2
Stewardship & Finance									
—Administration	2		2						
—General Treasurers	19	5	24	16	5	21	18	5	23
—Stewardship	7		7	7	1	8	7	1	8
The Guild	3	2	5	3	3	6	3	2	5
World Mission	18	2	20	19	2	21	17	2	19
Worship, Doctrine & Artistic Matters	1	3	4	2		2	2		2
Total Employees	**218**	**63**	**281**	**204**	**60**	**264**	**203**	**55**	**258**
National Missions Groups									
National Mission	13	2	15	12	2	14	12	2	14
Badenoch	1	1	2	1	2	3	1	1	2
St. Ninian's	11	4	15	13	2	15	14		14
Mission and Evangelism	2	5	7	2	5	7	2	5	7
Priority Areas Fund		2	2	1	1	2	1	1	2
Netherbow	6	3	9	6	3	9	6	2	8
Well	1		1	1		1	1		1
	34	17	51	36	15	51	37	11	48

THE GUILD
MAY 2001

PROPOSED DELIVERANCE

The General Assembly

1. Receive the report and thank the office bearers and staff.

2. Commend to the wider church, for use as devotional resources, the forthcoming book and video produced in connection with the Banners 2000 Exhibition, "Hold out the Word of Life".

3. Recognising the benefits of collaborative projects as undertaken by the Guild and its partners, encourage the Boards and Committees of the church to continue their efforts to work co-operatively in mission and service.

4. Recognise the trafficking of persons as an evil practice and encourage the Guild in its support of efforts to combat its growth and care for its victims.

5. Welcome the initiatives undertaken by the Scottish Parliament on tackling domestic violence and urge all ministers and Kirk Sessions, as one contribution to the World Council of Churches' Decade to Overcome Violence, to include this issue in their preaching, prayers and Christian education programmes.

REPORT

1. Introduction

1.1 "How's the Guild doing these days?" asked a minister recently. Usually the General Secretary's response to such kindly enquiries is a polite "Fine thank you", but she was having one of *those* days. The polished veneer had been peeled back and only the unvarnished truth would do. "The Guild", she said, "is breaking out". "Interesting answer" said the startled minister, "tell me more". The answer had not been meant to imply a recent escape from jail or a problem with delayed acne, nor was it given purely for effect. It was simply an apt way of describing the Guild's current activities and initiatives at local and national level.

1.2 Perhaps it is the inevitable pendulum swing following the introspection occasioned by the results of the Questionnaire to non-members which featured in the report to last year's Assembly. Perhaps it is a response to the negative perception of the Guild so bruisingly revealed in that exercise. Perhaps it is simply that several ideas

are coming to fruition around the same time. Whatever the cause, the effect is evident. In various collaborative partnerships and in a variety of areas of witness and mission, a new "can do" spirit is at work and the Guild is increasingly the branch of the Church that likes to say "Yes".

1.3 The Guild began this session by saying "Yes" to a new three year strategy involving a series of annual themes with related topics for discussion and six new projects. The triennium 2000-2003 will see the Guild focusing on the broad theme, *"Strength for Living"*.

2. Annual Theme

2.1 The first annual theme under this heading was launched on 26 August at the annual meeting, "Vision 2000". Lady Christine Eames, World President of the Mothers' Union, was the keynote speaker on the chosen theme for the 2000-2001 session, *"Strength through God's Promises"*. Drawing on the experiences of her term of office, during which she travelled widely in Africa and South America, and on her life in Northern Ireland, where her husband is archbishop of Armagh, Christine Eames gave a moving testimony to her own dependence on God's promises and her recognition of that same source of strength, in difficult circumstances, among those she met.

2.2 Members attending that meeting wrote in great numbers following the event to say how much they had gained from their participation. There was a significant "feel good factor" abroad that day - the sense of a job well done in the magnificent support for the projects in the *"Riches and Poverty"* programme; the inspiration of Lady Eames; the challenges of living as Christians in today's world and today's Scotland outlined by the Moderator and Rev Graham Blount in their talks. There was a feeling of anticipation as new projects were announced and a spirit of appreciation for all that was represented in the banner exhibition, *"Hold out the Word of Life"*, specially diverted from its nationwide tour for a one-day-only appearance at the Royal Concert Hall.

3. Banner Exhibition

3.1 The saga of the banners is a good example of the Guild's "can do" attitude. It started small, an opportunity to involve anyone who so wished, at local level, in an act of creativity and witness during the millennium celebrations. Lots of questions followed the original floating of the idea, lots about how? and when? and where? Significantly few asked "why?", and when they did, they met a resounding "why not?" If Elma Stuart, former vice-Convener of the Guild was the midwife of this idea, Fiona Lange, Information Officer, has been its nanny since birth. To them and to the Banners 2000 Committee, and to several assorted longsuffering and muscular spouses, the Guild and many beyond its membership owe a debt of thanks.

3.2 Over 25,000 visited the exhibition on its tour from Orkney to London. The response has been wonderful and the story will be retold in a commemorative book to be published this year, and a meditative video. Just a few quotations from the visitors' books at the exhibition venues will suffice to illustrate the worth and the impact of this remarkable undertaking :

"What wonderful teaching aids these would be". A mission partner on deputation in Edinburgh.

"So much to think about... back to the Bible for me!" a visitor to Dumfries.

"I didn't want to go at first but I felt I could stay there all day" ... *"I told my mum about them and went with her the next day to get a closer look"*. A primary 7 class at Elgin

"I feel God's grace" a Japanese visitor to Dornoch.

4. Discussion Topic

4.1 The Discussion Topic for the current session has been *"Commitment, What Price?"* As local guilds have addressed the theme of *"Strength through God's Promises"*, they have also been encouraged to look at issues of commitment, or the lack of it, in current society. Why is it so difficult in our culture to commit to another person, to an organisation, to the Church? Why, given God's unchanging promises to us, are we so reluctant to make a commitment to Him? The Projects and Topics Committee prepared guidelines and discussion starters for groups on this whole issue and responses indicate that it touched a chord with many who are concerned about the apparently disposable nature of relationships today.

4.2 Some of these discussion starters were previewed in the *"I'm just looking, I'm not buying"* seminar hosted by the Guild at the 2000 Youth Assembly. Guild members and Youth Assembly delegates shared in this group exercise together. Because experience, attitudes and outlook differed, discussion was not slow to start and became lively, but there was honesty and respect in the exchanges and a fairly steep learning curve for all.

5. Projects

5.1 The second crop of six projects since the Guild departed from the idea of one major project changing annually have now been up and running for almost a year. Under the overall title *"Strength for Living"*, they are:

- The Well : expansion of the facilities for this National Mission initiative among Asian families in Glasgow, providing information and advice in a safe, friendly atmosphere.

- With Wings as Eagles : support for Mission Aviation Fellowship's programme in Papua New Guinea, funding medical evacuations, personnel transport and the training of local people in management.

- A Way of Life : helping the Board of Communication to promote the gospel to the wider world through a dedicated Website and an interactive exhibition

- The Forgotten Frontier : an opportunity to assist the Scottish Bible Society to take the gospel of hope to the isolated and often exploited Nenet people of Siberia.

- The Rainy Hospital : suggested by the Board of World Mission, this project will improve the living and learning conditions of nurses training at the Rainy for health care work there and in the region surrounding Chennai, South India.

- Rebuilding Lives : The Lodging House Mission opens its doors to people from all around Scotland and further afield, who end up sleeping rough in Glasgow. Support for the education and activity programme will help some of them towards purposeful occupation and the chance to re-establish their lives.

5.2 Already there has been a high demand for information and local groups have explored, by means of a variety of resources, the work being undertaken and the underlying issues involved. The donations are beginning to flow in and the total given to date is : £66,981.

6. Training Opportunities

6.1 As a preparation for the use in guilds of both the Theme and the Discussion Topic, training days were held in nine venues on two Saturdays during March and April 2000. This exercise is to be repeated in 2001 as a means of encouraging local leadership teams to use the resources on offer. The 2001 venues will be Oban, Inverness, Aberdeen, Perth, Kirkcaldy, Edinburgh, Glasgow, Ayr and Annan. Each one is led by a member of the national leadership team, supported by experienced local leaders.

6.2 Specific conferences are held annually for Presbyterial Council Conveners and Project Co-ordinators. This year the Conveners' programme included sessions on Trafficking in Women and SCIFU as well as domestic Guild matters. The shocking revelation of the modern slave trade which is trafficking in women, remains a major issue for the **Ecumenical Forum of European Christian Women**, of which the Guild is a member organisation. Support for base level projects in Romania concerned with alerting women to this danger has been offered by the Guild through the Forum. The issue continues to be monitored, particularly in the light of disturbing reports of women entrapped in this way opting for immediate deportation, rather than face possible reprisals from their exploiters.

6.3 The Project Co-ordinators' conference 2000 was particularly important in that it launched the new series of projects with presentations from all the sponsoring bodies. Co-operation in the preparation of resource material and the task of keeping supporting groups informed of progress is vital to the success of the scheme. The effectiveness of the co-ordinating role of the Guild's Information Officer depends greatly on the input of staff members from the sponsoring bodies.

6.4 In addition to these conferences, we are indebted to both the Board of Parish Education, which mounts an overnight conference for Education Representatives from each Council and to the Committee on Ecumenical Relations, which includes the Council Ecumenical Representatives in its day conferences for Presbytery contacts.

6.5 The national leaders are available as individuals, or in small teams, to deliver specific requested training to a

Council or group of Councils and to address Council meetings or rallies. Worthwhile visits have been made this session to the Councils at Kirkcaldy, Gordon, Dunkeld and Meigle West, St Andrews, Annandale and Eskdale, Ayr, Duns, Dunfermline, Stirling and Falkirk, and to the Presbytery of Paisley. Several invitations to centenary celebrations and to Summer Rallies have been extended to the Convener and her team and these opportunities to meet members and share in these special events are very welcome. It seems that no Convener's term can be complete without a visit to the islands and Elva Carlisle's is no exception, a visit to lead a training weekend in Stornoway being planned at the time of writing this report.

6.6 Also of great benefit to members are the all too rare opportunities to spend a longer period of time together, growing in fellowship and allowing for recreational and physical needs to be met as well as the spiritual and intellectual. The overnight meetings for national committee members at Carberry or St Ninian's and the holiday organised as the Badenoch Break for guild members are special times, which achieve far more than is ever recorded in the minute of business completed.

7.   The Team

7.1 The Guild team is currently some 42,939 strong. These are the members, working and sharing in 66 Councils and 1,432 local groups. Each one is valued and to all those who share the tasks of leadership, a particular debt is owed. Each Council nominates a member to serve at national level on one of the Guild's constituted committees and this year these committees have been convened by the following key players :

Moira Alexander, Falkirk Council : Finance and General Purposes

Janette Henderson, Bute Council : Projects and Topics

Margaret Alston, Glasgow NW Council : Programmes and Resources

Isobel Reynolds, Angus East Council : Marketing and Publicity

Valerie Light, Falkirk Council : Matters Relating to Younger Women

7.2 As Convener and Vice-Convener respectively, Elva Carlisle (Glasgow South West) and Elspeth Kerr (Aberdeen) have led the team this session, undertaking speaking engagements and representing the Guild in many areas of Church and Community life. They have done so tirelessly and enthusiastically, supported by the prayers and the friendship of members everywhere.

7.3 The national office has seen several staff changes, notably the retirement of Marion Thomas as secretary to the General Secretary. We are fortunate in that one of the existing staff, Ann Anderson, was appointed as her successor, thus minimising the effect of the loss of Marion's experience. The General Secretary is equally fortunate in having the financial expertise of Maureen Morrish, now the senior staff member (in years of service, if not age!) and the communications skills of Fiona Lange as Information Officer. Newcomer Maureen Scoular completes the team which keeps Alison Twaddle on the right track as General Secretary.

8.   Contributing to the Wider Community

8.1 The Guild values very much its involvement across the mission of the Church through its representation on various Boards and Committees. Project work with sponsoring agencies such as the Scottish Bible Society and ecumenical initiatives through its participation in the **Network of Ecumenical Women in Scotland** serve to widen that involvement. Guild members will be taking part in a special "Fruits of the Spirit" service at Dunblane Cathedral to celebrate the achievements of the ecumenical projects, imaginatively mounted by the "Good News 2000" group of NEWS to mark the millennium

8.2 Other examples of a positive stance being adopted towards collaborative initiatives have been in the sponsoring of delegates from Eastern Europe to this summer's Conference for Teachers of Religious Education in Edinburgh and our offer of support to the Board of Parish Education's "Year of the Child" initiative.

8.3 In the longer term, discussions have been held with Christian Aid Scotland, with a view to putting the Guild's network at their disposal when the "Trade for Life" campaign is launched later this year. There is an exciting possibility of some jointly produced resource material in a co-branding of ideas rather than merchandise. In this kind of partnership the Guild will be mirroring the involvement of the Mothers' Union south of the border, another link in the chain of shared service and co-operation.

8.4 One measure of the Guild's commitment to the mission of the church is its financial support both to congregational schemes and to the wider work of the church through the Mission and Aid fund and the projects. Details for the current year are given in Appendix A below.

8.5 Beyond the Church communities, the Guild shares in national life through its membership of the **Women in Scotland Forum** and the **Women's National Commission**. Recently we have accepted invitations to comment on issues of concern to members, including submissions on the *"Parents and Children"* white paper on family and divorce law reform and on the consultative document *"Redressing the Balance"*, dealing with procedures in rape trials. In December 2000, the Guild was represented by former Convener, Catherine Nelson, at a major conference hosted by the WNC in London, on the government's Strategy for Women. This has been an ongoing involvement, developing from the Guild's participation in the wide-ranging *"Listening to Women"* consultation of 1999. It was gratifying to see the Guild's contribution on gender stereotyping in education quoted in the final published report, *"Future Female, A 21st Century gender perspective"*.

9. Seizing the Opportunities

9.1 Most of what is recorded above, in sections 2-8, reflects the basics of the Guild; they are the annual events and programmes which form the framework of the Guild's life and work. What isn't included in this kind of check list of major headings is reference to the opportunities for new ventures and initiatives which come out of left field to challenge and disturb. They land on the desk or arrive by phone or e-mail asking questions which begin : "Would the Guild be interested in….?", "What's the Guild doing about….?", "Can the Guild help with….?"

9.2 The great trick is not to feel threatened by those who seem to be doing more, or inhibited by those who seem to have so much more expertise, but to be alive to the opportunities which are presented and to embrace the mission initiative behind many of them. Valuable new links are forming all the time. An example of this is the building of connections as a result of the World Council of Churches' call for a Decade to Overcome Violence, beginning in 2001.

"Overcoming Violence"

9.3 This came to the attention of the Guild initially through our representation on the Committee for Ecumenical Relations. How could we contribute? What were we already doing in this field? Where could we offer support to those more specifically involved?

9.4 The Projects and Topics Committee was already exploring the possibility of making Reconciliation the subject of the annual Discussion Topic for 2001–2. This was largely due to the participation of the Committee's Convener and the General Secretary in a Conference mounted by Women Together Moving On, a remarkable movement of women in Northern Ireland, first introduced to the Guild through its involvement in the Women's National Commission. This Conference, on the theme *"Building Relationships across the Isles"*, addressed a range of issues, raised in the context of Northern Ireland, but applicable to situations of violence and prejudice anywhere.

9.5 The Guild already had links with Vashti, (Scottish Christian Women against Abuse), and had been concerned with the issue of Trafficking in Women through its membership of the Ecumenical Forum of European Christian Women (see para 6.2 above). Following the Northern Ireland conference, an approach was made to the Centre for Non-violence at Dunblane, which led to further valuable exchanges of resource material. Some limited financial support has been offered to some of these groups and in return a body of useful background material has been built up.

9.6 Links with sister organisations in other denominations also came into play when we were able to send a representative to the Conference on "Women and Violence" mounted in Leeds by the Methodist Network. Through Jubilee 2000 we learned of a group of women and men working towards reconciliation between the genders in Nicaragua and there may be the possibility of further exchanges of information and resources.

9.7 All of these links and co-operative ventures have meant that, when the decade is launched, Guild members will be aware of it and will have resource material to hand to help them address issues, not just concerning the abuse of women, but issues of violence in its widest sense. The Projects and Topics committee has now produced guidelines for the 2001-2 Discussion Topic under the title, *"Overcoming Violence"*. This will be a foundation from which guild members may explore, in subsequent years of the decade, other aspects of violence and fear and of the implications of the Biblical injunction to *"Seek peace and pursue it"*. Racial justice, for example, has already been suggested as a possible future topic.

9.8 It is worth noting, in connection with violence perpetrated in the home, that the Scottish Executive's Social Justice Department has adopted a strategy "to eradicate domestic abuse entirely". In her concluding remarks during the parliamentary debate, Margaret Curran MSP made a passionate commitment, both personally and on behalf of the Executive, to see domestic abuse gone from Scotland forever. *"We want a Scotland"*, she said, *" where no woman waits in fear for the sound of a key in the lock and where no child cowers under the bedclothes, terrified about what is being done to his or her mother. Let parliament show that it has the political will to make that happen."* Amen to that. And let the voice of the church be no less prophetic than that of the parliament.

10. Conclusion : Freedom to act

10.1 When the Guild was invited to comment, along with others, on the various reviews of the Church which have been underway in recent months, our response was one born of actual experience of the management of change.

That experience has been that it is a mistake to assume that structural change can effect real change in the life of an organisation. All that structures can do is help or hinder the progress towards accepted goals.

10.2 Three or four years on from debilitating argument over structures, we are now experiencing the liberating effect of uniting individuals behind personal and shared goals. Where structures are helpful, we use them—for communication, for training. But it is empowering to realise that there is no "one size fits all" blueprint model for a guild group. The role of central services vis à vis local groups differs according to each group's perceptions of its own needs. Some groups function best for the individuals concerned when they are solidly plugged in to the support system of central resources—it's good stuff, they use it well, they get things done, they grow. For other groups, devolution of responsibility from the centre is an attractive and exciting prospect. They have their own needs and ideas and they go for it, sometimes weakening the umbilical link to the point of complete separation. This need not be a cause for tears and recriminations. The Guild's aim is couched in terms of enabling and encouraging *individuals* to explore their commitment to their faith, not in terms of supporting an organisational structure.

10.3 The freeing up of central structures means that policy decisions, once taken by those who represent the members across the country, can then be applied imaginatively by those entrusted to carry out these policies. Therefore, because the Guild's Executive Committee endorses the concept of Christian nurture and support of children, an immediate "yes" can be given to sponsorship of the first issue of Parish Education's "CHOK". In addition, the committee looking at the needs and interests of younger women can explore further this whole area, following its identification as a priority in their recent survey of members' concerns. Similarly, the idea of a single member to launch a prayer initiative for young people across Scotland can be acted upon in the very next issue of the Newsletter.

10.4 The next step—and one possibly not far off—may be to offer groups at presbytery and congregational level, the opportunity to seek support for local projects and initiatives consistent with the movement's aim. This may mean using financial reserves to break new ground, but how can we *not* do that if we really mean to enable people, in the words of our aim, "to express their faith in worship, prayer and action"?

In the name of the Guild

ELVA A. M. CARLISLE, *National Convener*
ALISON M. TWADDLE, *General Secretary*

APPENDIX A
Financial Contributions

Sums given by guilds were as follows :

Mission and Aid Fund	£197,989
Congregational Funds	£557,539
Work of the Church (including projects)	£253,401
Work outwith the Church	£ 96,090
TOTAL	£1,105,019

(Amounts based on most up-to-date information available at the time of preparation of this report.)

ADDENDUM 1

At the General Assembly of 2001, Elva Carlisle completes her year as National Convener of the Guild. Her leadership has been strong and energetic. As an experienced presbytery elder and member of Assembly Boards, Elva was no stranger to the structures of the Church and has represented the concerns of the Guild, in every forum, with confidence and clarity. It is her great gift that she has been able to combine this effective leadership with a warmth for the members and the staff which has reflected her personal faith and caring character. Who can forget her all embracing "Welcome to Glasgow" at the Annual Meeting? It was clear she meant to enjoy herself that day and joy has indeed been the watchword of her term as Convener. In recording our gratitude for her contribution to the life of the Guild, we have to say, "Thank you Elva, it's been a lot of fun."

ELSPETH H. KERR, National Vice-Convener
ALISON M. TWADDLE, General Secretary

ASSEMBLY COUNCIL

MAY 2001

PROPOSED DELIVERANCE

The General Assembly

1. Receive the Report.

2. Note with approval the level of co-operation there has been between the Assembly Council and the Special Commission anent Review and Reform in the Church.

3. Thank all those who responded to the Council's paper "Change or Decay?" and all those who participated in consultations in the course of the year.

4. Encourage congregations to take risks and be more daring in realising their vision for change.

5. Encourage Presbyteries to consider ways in which "good news" stories and new ideas can be shared between congregations.

6. Welcome the continuing work of the Panel on Doctrine on the topic of Church Membership and instruct them to take account of the strong opinions on this issue coming through the Council's consultation process.

7. Commend central Boards and Committees for their willingness to engage in radical thinking for the future.

8. Amend Standing Order 110.12 to read: instead of "Convener, Vice-convener and ten members", substitute "Convener, Vice-convener and fourteen members".

9. Give thanks for the life and service of the Rev Duncan McClements.

REPORT

1. Building the House

"The desperate need of the church today is the Holy Spirit. We need individual Christians filled with the Spirit. More than that, we need revival, a mighty supernatural visitation of the Holy Spirit in the community. Nothing else will save our church from its spiritual torpor or our country from lapsing into complete paganism."

John Stott, quoted in David Watson *One in the spirit*

"What is ending in Christian Britain… is something more elemental than merely the churches failing to attract the people to worship… the culture of Christianity has gone in the Britain of the new millennium. Britain is showing the world how religion as we have known it can die."

Callum Brown: *The Death of Christian Britain*

"There is no ebb-tide
without a full-tide after it.
The tall white bride
accepts the fresh waters."

Iain Crichton Smith: *Collected Poems*

1.1 The Council has been listening intently over the last year to members from all over Scotland. We have been told that the images we shared in last year's report were helpful. We wish to share two other strong images this year, the ebb and flow of the sea, and the church as the House of God, filled with the living Spirit of God.

1.2 The Council has been told on many occasions that what the church needs is to be more open to the Holy Spirit; that the key to the future is spiritual renewal – of individuals, of congregations, of the whole church. But at the same time we are told that the crisis we face is one of belief itself and the possibility of its existence in our present society. It is not a case, according to this thesis, of engaging more effectively in mission, having a more committed membership, or of getting the structures right, but recognising the fact that culture and society have changed so fundamentally in the last 50 years that there is nothing we can do about it.

1.3 If these analyses are correct then it may seem that we are helpless. On the one hand, if the need is for spiritual renewal then we cannot demand that the Spirit effect a new revival. On the other hand, if the problem is the perceived crisis of belief in our contemporary culture then there may be little point in the Council or others planning for the future or proposing changes which at best may effect only small differences while using up time, energy and resources in the process.

1.4 What we can all do, however, and what the Council would argue that we have a duty to do, is to strive to build a house for the Spirit's dwelling; a house where men and women and children may encounter God in imaginative and disturbing worship; a house with open doors which shelters people in all the events of their lives, in celebration and in sorrow; a house which offers unconditional friendship and care and the chance to speak of the deep longing of the human spirit; a house in whose windows the candles burn brightly during what has been called this ebb-tide of faith, while we await the day when the tide will turn.

1.5 Such a house will not be built through deliverances or Acts of the General Assembly. It must be built locally by people in their own place and in their own way and in partnership with the ever-renewing and ever-disturbing Spirit of God. What committees can do is to try to order our organisational life so that there is space for this to happen and resources to help it happen. It seems to be agreed that the present organisation does not do this, may even be a barrier to it, and there is a positive mood around that things could be different. The Council is convinced that this is a time of critical opportunity for the church and that much can be achieved in the present atmosphere of apparent willingness to contemplate change. But it is also conscious that it could also be a time of pain and cost for many and that we should be aware of the need for pastoral care and concern for those most affected by the process.

2 "Preparing the Way…"

2.1 Last year as a result of the Assembly Council report the General Assembly encouraged Presbyteries, Kirk Sessions and congregations to discuss the issues raised in that report – issues of a renewed vision for the Church, issues of change and how we relate to it.

2.2 The reasons for this initiative were twofold:

2.2.1 The Council report had argued that the key to the future was for a renewal of vision in the local situation: "The Council is convinced that local vision is important if the Church of Scotland has to change – because that is where things are happening and have to happen." While recognising that a great deal is already happening in the way of creative worship, imaginative renewal of buildings, and committed community service, it was felt that everyone would benefit from discussing these big questions in the context of their own situation and in the context of the national church. It was hoped that the insights of those who had made some progress in articulating a local vision would benefit those who were still seeking the way ahead.

2.2.2 The second purpose was to raise awareness of the need for change and prepare the way for major proposals likely to come in the report of the Special Commission on Review and Reform in the Church due to come to the Assembly of 2001. Last year's Council report underlined the importance of involving as many people as possible in the thinking through and planning of change: if people have contributed to the working out of ideas and participated in the debate and discussion at an early stage then proposals for change are far more likely to be accepted and owned. Or to be more Scriptural and to borrow from the Committee of Forty report of 1974: "Growth and therefore change of the body means not direction from above, but every single part working according to its function so that the whole builds itself up in love."

2.3 It is recognised that previous Commissions and other bodies (eg the Anderson Commission in 1971 and the Committee of Forty throughout the 70s) brought forward imaginative and forward-thinking ideas, including proposals on team ministries, area churches with smaller groups for fellowship, moderation of call and tenure, less dependence on expensive buildings and on full-time salaried workers. Many of these ideas were not argued down nor tried and found to be wanting, but merely left unimplemented.

2.4 The Council was concerned that a similar fate should not befall the proposals of the present Special Commission if these were accepted by the Assembly. The Council and the Commission have continued to co-operate with each other over the past year. While the credit for the Commission report belongs entirely with the members of that body, the Council hopes that it may have made a useful contribution to the process, first of all by identifying those issues which people consider to be the important ones, and second by preparing the way through raising the expectation for change and encouraging local vision-building.

3 "Permission to talk…"

The Council's listening role

"…we would like to thank you for giving us the opportunity to discuss these things and for listening to our voice."

"This has been a worthwhile exercise and we thank the Council for its engineering of this opportunity for Kirk Session and parish self-evaluation and, hopefully development."

"The Assembly Council's consultation process…is in itself a positive sign."

"It was felt to be a sign of hope that we were sitting discussing such questions and that the Church of Scotland was facing up to the situation."

3.1 To facilitate discussion of last year's report "Change or Decay?" the Council produced a leaflet outlining the main issues and posing questions under different headings to initiate debate.

Single copies were sent in the first instance to presbytery clerks, ministers, session clerks, guilds, youth workers, youth assembly representatives and boards and committees. The initial print run of 10,000 copies proved to be insufficient to meet demand and a second print run of 2,000 was done. Council members have travelled to different parts of the country to facilitate meetings held to discuss the report and this has formed a large part of the work of the present year.

3.2.1 Responses to the report ranging from short paragraphs to detailed accounts of discussions have been received by the Council.

3.2.2 In total, the Council received 202 responses (some 450 pages), some of which reflected a discussion involving more than one group. The vast majority came from Kirk Sessions or congregations. There were also returns from Presbyteries, Guilds and other sources (youth groups, house groups, individuals etc).

3.2.3 Although a small percentage of the returns were negative in attitude either towards the process, the questions asked, or the content of the Council report, the overwhelming majority of responses were accompanied by the kind of comments quoted above. Many groups had special meetings or a series of meetings to address the matter. A fair number indicated that the first discussion had prompted a wish to continue and develop the themes with particular reference to their own local situation. Many have asked that the Council keep in touch with them. At least two Presbyteries are using the "Change or Decay?" paper as part of local discussions on a Presbytery Plan.

3.2.4 A detailed analysis of the responses is given in the appendix to this report. The main findings are as follows:

Strong tendencies:

- *Almost uniform agreement on the need for change in the Church of Scotland.*
- *Overwhelming desire for the release of centrally held funds.*
- *Great enthusiasm and support for team ministries.*
- *A widespread wish to get people, both elders and non-ordained people, involved in worship, visiting, necessary administration and the planning and leading of church and community activities and projects.*
- *Many are in favour of a complete or partial overhaul of the membership system.*

Other areas of concern:

- *The selection and training of ministers.*
- *Flexible and community oriented use of buildings.*
- *A widespread feeling that ministers should be in parishes, not in 121, busy doing administration or tied up in committee work.*
- *Need for radical review of the call and tenure of ministers.*
- *Support for flexibility and openness to new and differing styles and formats of worship.*

- *Widespread concern about the perceived absence of young people in the Church.*
- *A feeling that the media image of the Church needs updating and strenghtening, suggestions including changing the role or tenure of the Moderator.*
- *Broad support for the Church remaining the "national" church.*
- *Agreement that the Church should be outward-looking and oriented to the wider community.*
- *A wish for the Church to listen more to its grass-root members and adherents and to take them seriously.*
- *A feeling that there is a general lack of effective communication within the Church.*
- *While there seems to be a lot of support for ecumenical relations in the abstract, in practical terms most respondents prefer any ecumenical initiatives to be locally originated and managed.*
- *Agreement that the Church is altogether too bureaucratic, too full of red tape and that its operations are hindered and slowed by a surfeit of boards and committees.*

3.3 Website questionnaire

3.3.1 At the same time a questionnaire has been running on the Council pages on the church website, inviting people to send in their thoughts and ideas about the future of the church. In spite of some technical problems with the site this has produced a small but steady flow of returns averaging six per month. The results of this were shared with the Special Commission on Review and Reform. The Council feels that this venture has been a promising one. The material has been collated and analysed and the results are presented below. Among the opinions offered were these:

- *The Church should listen more to ordinary members and allow them to get involved in all aspects of Church life, using their individual talents and experiences.*

- *The Church tends to be too concerned with secondary issues (buildings, committees, church history) at the expense of essentials (Gospel, people, outreach).*
- *The Church is ageing and needs to change and update itself. However, there is a feeling that many in the Church are resistant to change.*
- *The Church needs to be more approachable, welcoming and inclusive.*
- *The Church needs to stand up for Christian values in society, and stay true to the message of the Gospel at all times.*
- *Falling numbers are of great concern, and the lack of young people is a problem with regard to the future.*
- *Ministers should concentrate on their local parish, not central committees and administration.*
- *The Church should go to people where they are rather than wait for people to come to them.*

3.3.2 It is hoped that this promising start will encourage people to continue sharing their opinions and ideas with the Council via the website. In the future, the Council hopes to make more opportunities for communication available in this way, possibly in the form of further questionnaires, a newsgroup or a chatroom.
The questionnaire is at:
www.churchofscotland.org.uk/boards/assemblycouncil/ assemblyquestion.htm

3.4 Time for action

3.4.1 The Council is aware that many of the ideas and suggestions coming through all our consultations are not new, indeed some have been debated in the Church for some 30 years or more. The fact that issues debated by the Anderson Commission and the Committee of Forty in the 1970s are now being discussed on a congregation level is evidence of a trickle-through effect that operates slowly but thoroughly, allowing ideas time to take root and congregations time to make them their own. The Council is convinced that the process of listening and consulting must be coupled with action, real tangible consequences, in order not to lose its credibility and appear just another paper-shuffling exercise. In view of the trickle-through effect and the attitude changes it has apparently effected, the Council feels that the time of talking is in some respects over and that the time is ripe for action.

3.4.2 It is also to be noted that while some wished-for change might require General Assembly decisions, many other issues lie within the power of local groups to achieve. To take but a few examples – varied patterns and times of worship, participation of more people in worship, giving members and adherents a voice and making more use of individual gifts and talents, increased local ecumenical co-operation, ministry teams of different kinds, imaginative use of buildings can be accomplished, and in fact, are taking place through local initiatives in different parts of the country. Congregations should therefore be encouraged to take matters into their own hands and do what they can to carry through the changes to which they aspire.

3.5 Good News stories

3.5.1 The Council also invited people to send in "good news" stories via the website – for whatever reason this has been less successful. However a fair number of the groups responding to the last year's report did tell us of positive local developments. For example, many told us of exciting new experiments in worship, of thriving Sunday Schools and Youth Groups. Many also had successful efforts at outreach going on in their parish. In one area, a new charge's experiments provide inspiration and an example of bottom-up change to its neighbours. Several told of successful, inter-denominationally organised Alpha groups, and one spoke of how taking part in the Jesus video project had helped to break down sectarian barriers.

3.5.2 There is clearly good news to be told, but we find as we go round the country that people are diffident about seeing their positive accomplishments as anything out of the ordinary, or find it difficult to identify what is happening in their area. We all need to work harder at emphasising the positive, communicating what is happening and sharing ideas with each other.

3.6 Other consultations during 2000

3.6.1.1 At last year's **General Assembly** the Council held focus-groups of first-time commissioners which reflected on their own experience of the church and also on their reactions to the Assembly. The Council has passed on the comments made about the Assembly to the Assembly Arrangements Committee of the Board of Practice and Procedure. For most people the experience had been a very positive one in terms of worship and learning about the work of the Church, but for many it had also been a lonely one. For this reason the Council has taken the initiative this year together with the Assembly Arrangements Committee of arranging an introductory social evening on the Friday before the Assembly starts to welcome new commissioners and to enable them to meet a range of different people.

3.6.1.2 As regards the wider discussion on the contemporary challenge facing the church, the groups' views reflected much that the Council has heard elsewhere. Most agreed that change was necessary. The strongest desire was to see elders and members more involved in the mission and worship of the congregation – this was said by every group. A longing for more varied forms of worship was expressed, more opportunities for exploring faith, and for concentrating more on the gospel and less on the "Church". Team ministries of varying kinds were seen as the way forward and there was a call for a reform of presbyteries and vacancy procedures. Opinion was almost equally divided between the need to rationalise church buildings and the importance of keeping them for as long as possible. There was concern about the poor image of the church portrayed in the media and a wish that the church could speak with one voice. There was a call for more effective communication so that more people know what is happening in the church, especially the good things which are happening. There was a feeling that the central organisation of the church was a long way from the local situation.

3.6.2 Meetings with **ecumenical and overseas visitors** to the Assembly also produced useful experience to pass on and valuable insights into the way others see us. One memorable comment was that the Church of Scotland seemed less complacent than in the past: it was now humble enough to admit that it was seeking for answers and that might be the sign of a real new beginning.

3.6.3 The consultation at last year's **Youth Assembly** produced slightly different emphases. Alongside the frustration with what is seen as old-fashioned formality, outdated traditions, rigid structures and regulations, too many committees, too much talking and not enough action, there was again a call for inspiring and relevant worship with alternative timings and patterns, more involvement of the people and more modern presentations of teaching and preaching. There was plea to listen to young people, to use them more and to involve them more in decision-making. There was also a very strong support, expressed over and over again, for ecumenical unity.

3.6.4 In January of the present year the Council held another consultation with **Presbytery Clerks**, which at the time of writing is still to be analysed.

3.7 Vision

In last year's paper, the Council suggested that the Church needed to define a vision for itself, a vision that could be shared by everyone. This wish, we now find, is echoed in our consultations. It seems to the Council that a vision is indeed taking shape, and that some of the following characteristics could be included in a definition of it:

- *A dynamic, proactive church taking the shape best suited to the local situation, firmly rooted in prayer, faith and worship.*

- *A church with a degree of autonomy and flexibility in methods, activities and worship, allowing it to cater to diverse needs.*

- *A community of faith which is outward looking to the global community and to the community in which it is placed, and that is willing to go out to where people are.*

- *A church that is open to all and where all feel welcome whether they come regularly or occasionally.*

- *A forum for exploration and growth rather than an institution with set rules and beliefs.*

- *A witness to the truth of the Gospel by what it does as well as by what it says.*

- *And with other layers of church government – regional and national – there to support and resource the local church.*

4 Thinking...

4.1 Although suffering a severe blow from the untimely death of its convener, Duncan McClements, the study group has continued the thinking which produced last year's report.

4.2 The Gospel message in the present context

4.2.1 Duncan's invaluable contribution was especially evident as the group reflected upon the way in which the Gospel can be meaningfully presented in today's society. The group affirmed that the Good News of God's love cannot be communicated solely in propositional or formulaic terms. Rather we would see the need for the Church to listen better to people's stories and relate these to the Gospel, as well as enabling people to discover how the Gospel relates to their stories.

4.2.2 There are key questions which the Church must ask itself with regard to how we meet and relate to those with whom we have contact. Can the Church contemplate being in the business of meeting needs when asked, without looking for any further response? Can the Church take the risk of "blurring its boundaries" and becoming vulnerable? Do we sometimes seem to be so preoccupied with doctrine, law and structure that we effectively exclude those to whom God is reaching out in love?

4.2.3 The central message of the Gospel is of the God who is love. This is the love of unconditional acceptance, the love that never rejects, such as we see depicted, for example, in Hosea chapter 11.

4.2.4 And yet it is also recognised that the message of Good News calls for a response. Following Jesus involves a commitment to prayer, to caring for the earth and its people, to working for justice and peace, and to sharing this Good News with others. In the communication of the Good News of God's unconditional love and in the context of our present society, how and when is it appropriate to introduce the challenge of commitment?

4.2.5 In raising these questions we do not seek to come to easy answers, but we do wish to challenge the church to continue to reflect on these issues.

4.2.6 In the present ebb-tide of Christian faith in our society, it may well be that the church of the immediate future will be a smaller church, but – we would venture and hope – a church turned outwards to society. However the ebb-tide is followed in time by the full-tide. The question, indeed the challenge for the church might be whether it has the will and the courage to be patient and wait for the tide to turn, meantime acting in such a way as to maintain the credibility of both church and belief as we await and prepare for the turning of the tide.

4.3 Spirituality

The Study Group and the Council have become aware of a growing number of voices within the church urging us to consider how a renewal of "spirituality" might be encouraged. Increasingly there is concern that the reformation of the church be understood as more than simply a matter of structural adjustment. There is a cry for a true spiritual renewal, a fresh understanding of God's grace, a focus on the spiritual life, and a recovery of prayer.

We acknowledge this growing concern and the study group will be giving further consideration to this in the coming year.

4.4 Other group work

4.4.1 Two other issue-based groups were formed in the autumn following an examination of the points raised in last year's consultations. Much had been said in these consultations about the emphasis on the "journey" of faith and the need for discipleship rather than membership. A second major concern had been ministry in its widest sense: the ordained ministry, the ministry of the people, how to sustain parish ministry throughout the country. These relate to two key stages for people who are seeking a spiritual dimension in their lives: first the point at which they come into contact with the Jesus story. In an increasingly secular society we must provide wide and varied opportunities for this, and we have to recognise that some will explore it and then reject it. But some will have their interest and perhaps their soul engaged and will want to learn more; opportunities for deeper faith exploration must also be available; and perhaps we might question whether this is the point to make demands of involvement in institutional activities. However worship opportunities, fellowship and relationships are all key to this situation.

4.4.2 The second key point is when interest and commitment is sufficiently engaged for a person to want to devote time and energy to a greater or lesser degree to serving Christ in the world, and perhaps also in the church. (It is important to remember however that a clear division between those who are in the church and who meet other people's needs and those who are outside and have needs to be met is unreal. People inside the church also need space and the chance to reflect on their own faith – perhaps to admit to doubts and differences of view-point which arise as the years pass and the experiences of life make their mark.) But the fact remains that if worship is to take place and if the gospel message is to be heard, then that requires a committed core of people to give service and resources to enable that to happen. In a situation where fewer are entering the ordained ministry and where those who are in are increasingly pressured and over-worked, there needs to be a realistic assessment of how this service is to be provided.

4.4.3 The groups are therefore looking at issues of belonging/membership and service/ministry.

4.5 Belonging/Membership Group

4.5.1 Any discussion on membership must be done against a background of a changing society. In a culture of non-commitment, gone are the days when there was an almost automatic flow of people graduating from Sunday School to Bible Class to the communicant classes to become members of the Church. The demographic make-up of the group of people who become members of the Church has changed, and now demonstrate a greater diversity than before. Where there were teenagers, we now see young couples, perhaps parents, or even middle-aged people who have found their way back to the Church after a period of absence.

4.5.2 The process of becoming a member of the Church is described within Act XV, 1992 in the following way:

> "In accordance with the law and practice of this Church, a Kirk Session is obliged to test the response of faith of a baptised person before authorising admission to the Lord's Table. The Kirk Session normally requires to be satisfied that the baptised person has received instruction in the faith and order of the Church, is of Christian character, and is ready to make public profession of faith, whereupon such person is admitted to the Lord's Table and his name is added to the Communion Role".

4.5.3 However, during its discussions the group has become convinced that this narrow and legalistic definition does not necessarily cover reality on the ground. In our initial discussions and consultations we have identified a number of instances where we feel that formal membership may be unhelpful.

- The tendency to view the attaining of traditional membership as a "goal" can be counter-productive to lifelong discipleship.

- Some people, particularly young people, see themselves first and foremost as Christians rather than having an allegiance to one particular denomination and may see no need to become members of one Church.

- Traditional membership does not take account of new mission ventures eg Alpha courses, mid-week worship, and community projects, which are often offered – and taken – on a no-expectations basis.

- The increased mobility of people today is at odds with the static nature of traditional formal documentation.

- In some congregations adherents can form a significant presence and constitute a great potential resource. Traditional membership excludes adherents from several different kinds of participation and service.

4.5.4 The group has studied various models of membership in different denominations, and found that several of these are similarly engaged in a rethinking of their systems. During this and other discussions the group has become convinced that the way forward lies in an emphasis on belonging rather than membership. The signs of belonging to the Church could consist of worship, fellowship, service, profession of faith and a willingness to witness through daily living.

Membership, the group feels, should enable those who feel they belong to the Church to journey in faith, to see themselves as part of a faith community and not some exclusive club where some are "in" and others are not.

4.5.5 Views on membership formed a very strong thread in the responses which the Council received from congregations (see Appendix 1, para 3.12). While some felt that the present membership system still has a role to play, many more were in favour of a complete or partial overhaul. Organisational change is secondary to attitude change and this seems to be a case where the attitude required is already in place and the time is thus ripe for action. However the Council is aware that the Panel on

Doctrine is considering the issue of membership at the moment with the intention of reporting in 2002 and would not wish to pre-empt that study. The Council will pass on to the Panel the numerous views and comments received on this subject.

4.6 Serving/Ministry group

4.6.1 Last year's report by the Board of Ministry reaffirmed the belief in the "ministry of the whole people of God": "only the membership of the whole church can demonstrate all aspects of the one ministry of Jesus Christ in and to the world". The ministry of the people is a phrase which is in common currency but about which there are many different views and interpretations. Some assume that it means church members doing "ministerial" tasks; others react against what they see as the "clerification of the laity". This is an area which requires much more exploration and debate.

4.6.2 The development of collaborative patterns (within which the ordained minister has a part) was also encouraged in that report. This relates to opinion widely-held in the church as reflected in the Council's consultation. Church structures already allow for team ministries to develop and the group was impressed by a number of initiatives which are already in place in some congregations. One charge has a paid staff of a minister, a part-time counsellor and an administrator, supported by voluntary worship and visiting teams; another employs a counsellor, youth worker and administrator alongside the minister; two linked charges in a rural situation united at their own request with a team of minister, Reader and administrator; one congregation operates a system of "worship by the people for the people" where different members of the congregation are responsible for different parts of the service each week (and the minister may not feature at all). In all these situations each member of the team brings something different and special and the whole adds up to more than the sum of the parts. All spoke of the sense of openness, vulnerability and trust in their relationships with each other and with the congregation. The point was also made that different training is required for this type of situation, and stress laid on having aims and objectives and submitting these to an ongoing process of appraisal. It should also be underlined that all these initiatives have arisen from local people working out together how to be the church in their place.

4.6.3 The Council is aware that some of these teams are staying in contact with each other to exchange ideas and give support. It would be good if some kind of network could be established so that people who want to try things out could be put in touch with those who have already done so.

4.6.4 The group was also very conscious of the fact that any discussion of the need for change in the church may seem to hold an implicit criticism of the present ordained ministry. Ministers are already under increased pressure due to increasing workload and changing expectations and it is important to be sensitive to feelings of being undervalued and misunderstood. However it is important to note that other professions such as social work, education and the medical profession have similar pressures to contend with. It might be useful to explore experiences with them. In all these professions sharing of work and responsibility provides support in withstanding difficulties – and so we return to the collaborative situation again. This seems to offer a solution to so many of the problems highlighted in research done, by, eg the Rev Donald Macaskill, on the practice of ordained ministry in the Church of Scotland. A willingness on the part of ministers to embrace this concept would offer positive ways forward for the future.

4.6.5 We emphasised above that much can be done by local people taking initiatives in their own place, and it is important to work out ways of encouraging a culture of permission, and of changing perceptions about the role of the minister in relation to the congregation. However there also remains a question of whether current church practices may restrict or hinder such developments. It

seems clear that a congregation's present right of call and the current tenure situation may prove a block to imaginative team situations and new models of working. The present vacancy procedure was also a subject which both the group and many people who responded to the consultation felt required reform. These are all areas which certainly require investigation.

5 "...and joined-up thinking"

The Council's co-ordinating role

5.1 We hear on all sides a plea for "joined-up thinking", for a rationalisation of work and resources, a concern that there are so many overlaps in the work of boards and committees, sometimes unconsciously promoted, a worry that so many separate bodies (of which the Council is one) are thinking about the future of the church.

5.2 The Co-ordinating Forum (consisting of the Conveners and Secretaries of the Boards and Committees) was established in 1996 to try to answer some of these concerns. It originally came under the aegis of the Council but was passed to the responsibility of the Board of Practice and Procedure at a time when it was thought that the Council might cease to exist. It has had a role in the last few years for advising the Board of Stewardship and Finance about the budget of the church. At the September meeting last year there was a shared feeling that decisions about priorities should come before budget decisions and the Forum agreed to have an extra meeting in December to address the subject of priorities. That meeting made some progress towards deciding strategic initiatives and at the time of writing it is hoped that the scheduled meeting in March will produce some decisions which can be brought in a supplementary report to the Assembly.

5.3 It is understood that the Board of Practice and Procedure is proposing that the Forum should be returned to the responsibility of the Council and the Council welcomes this, as it has a responsibility for assessing priorities. The Boards and Committees are making real efforts to rationalise their structures, to work together and to put the good of the church before sectional interests. They are to be commended for this.

5.4 As well as the interaction provided by the Forum, members of the Council have also had a series of meetings with representatives of Boards and Committees over the last year. The Council is grateful for their willingness to give this time and has benefited greatly from their experience and their particular perspectives on the work of the Church nationally.

5.5 The Council has in the past year sponsored meetings of some of the groups doing forward planning to try to foster the desired "joined-up thinking". This enabled an exchange of information about current work, and a pinpointing of possible areas of overlap. These meetings have now been overtaken by the new initiative in the Co-ordinating Forum and this is to be welcomed.

6 The Council's role

The Council has become increasingly comfortable over the past year with the role it has established. The **listening** facet of that role remains a key one: it is important for the church to listen to itself, to have a neutral listener without a particular line to canvass. As well as listening to what people are saying, it involves processing what is heard, passing on and adapting ideas and reflecting them into the ongoing debate. It also involves passing on concerns expressed to us to the proper quarter.

It has an **enabling** role – facilitating other work and encouraging people to find their own vision as in the process over the past year of the discussion of last year's report.

It has a **thinking** role, focusing on key issues and exploring them or encouraging others to do so. There is too a place for constantly **challenging** accepted thinking.

It has an **affirming** role, encouraging and supporting what is good, rather than operating through confrontation and criticism.

It has a **co-ordinating** role, taking an overview of church life without the promotion of any specific aspect, making suggestions where planning could be more co-ordinated or where work is duplicated. It is hoped that this will be developed productively in the Co-ordinating Forum.

One other important part of the Council's remit is the **identification of priority areas and tasks**. Once a vision is identified and accepted (and the Council looks forward to this year's Assembly to achieve this) the establishing of strategic initiatives and practical tasks can move forward. Again the Co-ordinating Forum has a significant role to play here and as is indicated above has already made a start on the process.

7 Membership

The Council has 12 members including the Convener and Vice-convener with the Principal Clerk in attendance. This would probably have been adequate in less-pressured days when most people could make most meetings most of the time. The reality is that due to work commitments almost always there are a few people missing. In a large Board this makes little difference, but in a group of 12 and even more so in some of the smaller working groups it has considerable impact. The Council is therefore asking the Assembly to increase its membership to 16 to take account of this.

8 The Rev Duncan McClements 1940–2000

Duncan McClements was a son of the manse and an alumnus of Edinburgh University where he graduated in Classics and Divinity. His first charge was Hurlford in Ayrshire followed by Grahamston Church Falkirk which called him in 1976. He went on to build up the United Congregation of Grahamston, a union of two Church of Scotland charges and the nearby Congregational and Methodist congregations. Duncan played a key role in many church initiatives over the years: Industrial Mission, Kirk Care Housing, ACTS, SCIFU. He served on many Assembly Boards and Committees including the Board of Social Responsibility and the Committee on Ecumenical Relations of which he was the first Convener. He also took a large part in Falkirk church and community life and was Clerk to Falkirk Presbytery for many years.

It is appropriate that tribute should be paid to Duncan McClements in a gathering in which he was such a well-known figure and influential presence. Indeed he was probably one of the best-known figures in the Kirk: many felt that they knew him without knowing him personally, because of the impact he made on any situation in which he was present. Everyone will have strong impressions and memories because no one could be indifferent to him. And that was because he himself was not indifferent or detached in any way – he immediately engaged with people, with issues, with the business in hand.

Last year the Moderator asked that the theme for the year might be " a passionate church in a gentle Scotland" – surely there was never a better representative of the passionate church than Duncan: – passionate about the faith and about the institutional church which he loved; passionate about justice – social justice, political justice, ecumenical justice; passionate about getting things right whether in the working out of the big issues or in the observing of procedures; passionate about caring for people.

Although he spoke often and forcefully, he spoke from knowledge and experience and good sense and with the spiritual wisdom which comes from having the right things in perspective. He was a very kind and generous man both to his friends and those who were not of that number. And in spite of the workload he carried locally, in Presbytery and nationally he was never heard to complain of stress and overwork.

With his sudden passing in September 2000, the Council has lost a wise and supportive Vice-convener and together with many in the Church and beyond a warm, humorous and true friend.

We give thanks to God for the privilege of working with him.

References

Brown, Callum G: *The Death of Christian Britain*, London: Routledge, 2001

Smith, Ian Crichton: *Collected Poems*, Manchester: Carcanet Publishers Limited, 1995

Macaskill, Donald: *The Practice of Ordained Ministry within the Church of Scotland: a summary report with recommendations*, unpublished, 1999

McClements, Duncan: *The Gospel Message in the Present Context*, Unpublished, 2000 (available from the Council Office)

In the name of the Council

HELEN McLEOD, *Convener*
DAVID DENNISTON, *Vice-convener*
KARIN LUNDGREN, *Research and Development Officer*

Appendix 1

1 Introduction

1.1 Consultation is the Assembly Council's way of fulfilling its role as a listening body. Attempting to discover what people want and what they feel is important is crucial not just for sound decision-making but also in itself: it allows people to talk, to be heard and above all to be involved. This was, in part, the specific aim of the project.

1.2 This appendix presents the preliminary results from the consultation. In its 2000 report the Council asked Presbyteries, Kirk Sessions and congregations to discuss Appendix 1 to the Report, a paper titled "Change or Decay?". To aid discussion, the Council also produced a leaflet summarising the paper. The data gathered from the responses will form the basis for further discussion and analysis in the future.

2 Methodology

2.1 Sampling

2.1.1 The sample is self-selected – the Council has had no control over or influence on who chose to respond. This inevitably leads to a degree of skewing, which has to be borne in mind when interpreting the results. While we can know who chose not to respond, we cannot know why or what they would have said if they had responded.

2.1.2 While the form and content of the responses are often influenced by questions or statements from the report or the leaflet, there was no effort to make the style of the responses comply with any predetermined guidelines. The result is a wide variety of styles, from extremely detailed and extensive narrative reports of discussions to concise and economical bullet points. The reason behind this method of working was both a wish to *let people talk* with as few restrictions as possible, and a wish to obtain the richest data possible. At the time of analysis, this was proven to be a good methodology, as the material has yielded data of great quality and depth.

2.2 Conducting

The data was analysed using content analysis, a time-consuming but highly sensitive method of evaluation. It involved close and careful reading of all the material and breaking it down into some 300 categories. The categories were then analysed by frequency and relation until a pattern emerged. It is in part a creative process and it yields data that cannot easily be quantified. The majority of the findings are therefore presented in text form as opposed to statistical charts and tables.

3 Preliminary results

3.1 Introduction

3.1.1 Given the small and self-selected nature of the sample, it is impossible to make sweeping generalisations from this data. Neither do we imagine that it is the authentic "voice of the people of the Church" or anything such. It cannot, in short, be said to be representative. It is merely an indication, a hint of the greater truths that may or may not exist "out there". This data cannot be used to authenticate findings in the name of the general public. It is made up of opinions, impressions and ideas, not facts. This must be borne in mind lest the findings be misunderstood.

3.1.2 This, however, should in no way detract from the weight and importance of the data, rather it should reinforce its authority. Data of this kind, carefully analysed, can give real insights into people's minds and thoughts. Every part of this data represents something someone said to us, a real voice of a real person, offering us her or his opinion. We hope that this project can offer something in return: attention to that voice, and in some cases, the strength of many voices speaking together. We hope thus to have established a valuable and ongoing relationship with the people who have offered us their contributions.

3.1.3 The majority of the respondents welcomed the opportunity to discuss issues relating to the future of the church, and many told us how engaged and lively a debate they had enjoyed. Many also intended to keep the discussion going in their Kirk Session or congregation, even after the deadline for the responses had passed. Some, however, had found the task difficult, although the majority of the respondents relished the challenges this presented.

3.1.4 The results give a valuable and interesting insight into the issues that are closest to people's hearts. This appendix will try to give an idea of the topics raised and the opinions offered, which will influence the future thought and work of the Council.

3.2 The Need for Change

One of the most striking aspects of the material collected is the almost uniform agreement on the need for change in the Church of Scotland. Perhaps this is not surprising considering the nature of the sample, but the data is interesting nonetheless, since despite the agreement in the general, there is some variety in the particular. While the majority prefer change to be slow and gradual, some say that the time for evolution is past and it is now time for revolution, suggesting that radical change is the kind most likely to endure. The most common caution is against the principle of change for change's sake, and against discarding things merely because they are old. Some also emphasise that for change to succeed, it is vital that the change is owned by the people concerned and not imposed from above.

3.3 Society

Many respondents recognise the need to move with the times and to understand and adopt to changing social conditions. Many fear, however, that this will mean a dilution of the central message of Christianity – some feel that they can already see this happening. Among the changes readily apparent to people are the perceived lack of interest in the Church, the different attitude to Sundays, the many alternative attractions with which the Church finds it hard to compete (especially where children and teenagers are concerned) and the perceived general reluctance among people today to join and to commit. Many feel that the Church and its activities are perceived as irrelevant by the general public.

3.4 Finance

There is strong support for the release of centrally held funds. The majority of those who specify how they think the funds should be used are in favour of it being given to local congregations for local projects in the community. Generally, there is concern that money should be equally distributed and used carefully, while a few feel that individual congregations should have more control over what funds they generate or at least be told more exactly what happens to the money.

3.5 Ministry

3.5.1 In general, there is strong support for team ministries as a way of getting more people involved, taking the weight off over-worked ministers and allowing rural parishes a chance to survive. A fair number agree that the call and tenure of ministers is in need of radical review. The shortage of ministers already ordained as well as candidates for the ministry is a concern for many. Another widespread feeling is that ministers should be in parishes, not in 121, tied up in administration or committee work.

3.5.2 The strongest trend with regard to ministry is the wish to involve other people, both Elders and non-ordained people, in worship, visiting, necessary administration and the planning and leading of church and community activities. This comes through especially clearly in the strong support and enthusiasm for team ministries of various kinds. It links in with themes in the paragraphs on membership (3.12) and worship (3.7).

3.5.3 With regard to elders, some feel that there ought to be more flexibility, for example in the form of finite terms of service. Some wish for more elders in their thirties and up – one suggested that a new designation for the office be found that fits better with the image of a younger, more flexible and "modern" eldership.

3.5.4 On the issue of the selection and training of ministers, there is some support for an overhaul of the selection process. Some also feel that ministers' training ought to include skills such as communication, leadership and management alongside traditional theology and other academic subjects. A few suggested that there should be alternative paths into the ministry besides academia, and that the age at which training is available should be more flexible. Many also feel, some from personal experience, that vacancy procedures need to be reviewed and in particular, that it takes much too long to fill a vacancy.

3.6 Buildings

The vast majority is in favour of flexible and especially community-oriented use of churches and church halls. Some mention ecumenical sharing. A fair number feel that despite the difficult and sometimes painful decisions involved, the Church must dispose of some buildings that may be beyond economical repair, too expensive to heat and maintain, or impossible to adapt to different uses. Others feel that the Church sometimes tends to focus on the buildings rather than the people worshipping in them. Some feel that churches ought to be open more often. Many support adaptation and changes to interiors, in particular the removal of inflexible and uncomfortable pews, which would make old buildings more welcoming and comfortable.

3.7 Worship

3.7.1 The majority of the respondents are in favour of a degree of flexibility and openness to new and differing styles and formats of worship. Most seem to find the model of traditional and new co-existing side by side the most successful and satisfying. This answers the common concern of alienating loyal long-standing members with new and unfamiliar ways. Most are also in favour of increased informality, both in dress and manners. In particular, people want plain everyday language, especially in the sermon, perhaps clarified with hand-outs, or bullet points on a screen or overhead projector. There are indications of a growing support for house groups and other small, informal, friendly worship arrangements, and a wish for young people to be more involved in the planning and participation in services.

3.7.2 Most of the changes experienced in this area in the past are looked upon, at least in retrospect, as positive developments. In particular people mention the increased informality in minister-congregation relations, women ministers and elders, new music and the fact that people now attend church because they choose to and not because they are expected to.

3.8 Young People

Most of the respondents are concerned about the perceived absence of young people in the Church. "Young" is defined by respondents as anything from children to people in their 30s, 40s or even 50s, but the age group most are concerned about is 15-40. There is an overwhelming felt need to attract more young people, but much confusion and vagueness about how to go about this. The data indicates a lack of understanding, in parishes and congregations, of how teenagers and young adults think and feel, although some run very successful and thriving youth initiatives.

3.9 Image and Media

3.9.1 There is little definite agreement in this area, but some patterns still emerge. The issue of a spokesperson is debated from several angles: many feel the need for a stronger, more authoritative voice to speak for the Church. Some recognise the tension between Presbyterianism and the perceived need for a spokesperson. Some suggest that changing the Moderator's remit or electing him/her for a longer period of time would solve the problem. For others, there is an alternative in a stronger, unified voice, speaking out on current issues and debates, thereby ensuring the Church its share of the media attention.

3.9.2 Quite a few people feel that the general image of the Church needs updating, that it is seen as old-fashioned and out-of-touch. Some feel that other denominations speak more clearly or command more of the media's attention. A few feel resentful of the portrayal by the media of the Church and religious institutions, which is often perceived to be hostile and misleading.

3.10 National Church

The majority of respondents are in favour of the Church remaining the "national" church, much as it is today. The most common reason given in favour of national status was the church's presence throughout the country and the opportunity to serve and be available for everyone, whether a member or not. Others claimed that national status gives the Church authority, visibility, publicity, recognition and respect as well as influence over political and public opinion. One or two respondent groups admitted to confusion as to exactly what national status entails, and a handful wanted the Church to be more vocal on ethical, social, medical and moral issues.

3.11 Community

3.11.1 There is great enthusiasm for churches becoming more involved with the wider community. A great many respondents were in favour of more outreach, more co-operation with other churches as well as with non-religious organisations, and felt that the Church should go where people are and not wait for people to come to them. Some were unclear as to exactly what this meant, but the majority responded with enthusiasm. Several highlighted opportunities of ministry and outreach in contexts such as sport, shopping centres, places of work, factories, pubs and clubs. Quite a few talked about the need for new methods of teaching and outreach, and new ways of presenting the timeless message of Christianity.

3.11.2 A very few were uncomfortable with non-members of the Church or the congregation requesting funerals, baptisms or weddings, fearing that the minister's time would be taken up with such events rather than with ministering to his own flock. Others, however, felt that such occasions were great opportunities for reaching people who would otherwise never have come into contact with the Church at all.

3.12 Membership

3.12.1 While a lot of people still find falling numbers a great concern and express a wish to find a way of halting the decline, there is a growing number who regard numbers as only one of the measurements of the health of a church. Many point out that the remaining people are more committed, and that quality is more important than quantity.

3.12.2 While some feel that membership still has a role to play, and would not like any changes to be made, many more are in favour of a complete or partial overhaul of the membership system. Among the sources of dissatisfaction are that the rolls seem to bear no relation to reality, that nominal membership is a weakening influence on the Church, that Communion ought to be more open and that the rules and regulations put potentially interested people off. Many agree that rules and regulations emphasise the wrong aspects of the life of the Church, and that the emphasis should be on journeying, not arriving; discipleship not membership. There is still a feeling, though, that commitment in some form will always be important, and indeed many feel that current members ought to be more committed and involved.

3.12.3 A very few feel that it is the lack of discipline rather than an excess of it that puts people off and leads to the falling away of current members. They fear that a lack of clear standards and criteria sends the wrong message to the community about the value the Church puts on membership.

3.12.4 Here, as elsewhere in the data, there is a strong insistence that anyone worshipping in a congregation should be allowed to become involved and to use their talents, experiences and skills in the work of the Church. It is coupled with a wish for the Church to listen more to its grass-root members and adherents and to take them seriously.

3.12.5 Another small number feel that the communion roll is helpful in administrative matters and some wondered where funds would come from if the roll did not exist.

3.13 The Church Experience

People are very concerned that church should be welcoming, friendly and inclusive. A great many also feel that whatever changes the future may have in store for the Church, it is vitally important to stay true to the central message of Christianity, to keep mission going and to keep on being salt and light for the community. There is also a feeling that local congregations should have more scope for experimentation and risk-taking in their own strategies. The notion that church should be based on community and relationships received a lot of support.

3.14 Communication

Quite a few people feel that there is a general lack of effective communication within the Church. In particular, some feel that the "ordinary people in the pews" know very little about Church organisation and the work of the Boards and Committees, or even of the General Assembly. With regard to congregations, some called for more adult Christian education, and some recognised that far fewer members of the general public have a working knowledge of Christianity or the Bible than could be assumed in the past.

3.15 Ecumenical Relations

While there seems to be a lot of support for ecumenical relations in the abstract, in practical terms most respondents prefer any ecumenical initiatives to be locally originated and managed. Also, many seem to prefer a model of co-operation in which, while sharing in community work, projects or even worship, different denominations nevertheless remain separate and never actually merge. A very few objected on doctrinal grounds to any sort of ecumenism, and an equally small number said clearly that they would not lend their support to any nationwide ecumenical initiatives.

3.16 "121"

Many people feel that "121" is remote from their daily lives and activities within the Church. Some admit openly not knowing what goes on in the building. The data indicates that there is disagreement over whether "121" is really needed, and what, if any, changes could be made to how it works. There is as much support for it being needed as there is for it being superfluous. Generally speaking, a common suggestion is that "121" should be downsized, the perception being that it appears to be growing as the Church is shrinking. It is suggested by some that its role might be more limited to administration, finance, redistribution of resources and the kinds of expert advice that cannot be provided by parishes themselves. There is also a perception that "121" should be serving and supporting parishes and congregations, not vice versa, and that this is not always the case.

3.17 Structure and Organisation

3.17.1 The most common opinion in this area is that the Church is altogether too bureaucratic, too full of red tape and that its operations are hindered and slowed by a surfeit of boards and committees. However, there are also indications that some people are largely unaware of the work done by these boards and committees and so would be unable to decide exactly which are unnecessary. Another common concern, which for some appears to be rooted in personal experience, is of overlap in committee work and of poor communication and co-operation between boards and committees.

3.17.2 On the question of possible decentralisation, opinions are divided. The general feeling is that more decisions should be left to Presbyteries, Kirk Sessions or congregations, supported by another tendency to see the present organisation as top-heavy and over-centralised. Comparatively few, however, provide any detail as to how exactly they think this should be achieved or what it should involve. Since a fairly small number engaged with this topic, and even fewer in any depth or at any length, it is difficult to draw any clear conclusions. In short, the data is inconclusive beyond the broadest generalisations.

4 Conclusion

4.1 Future Research Plans

4.1.1 The above consultation is viewed by the Council as part of an ongoing process. A number of respondents asked for feedback on the results of the consultations, and some offered to keep us informed of any further developments in their parish or Presbytery resulting from their discussions. The Council will continue to consider ways in which further contact with congregations would be of benefit to both.

4.1.2 The Council considers the consultation initiated by last year's Report a success, and it hopes that this progress is an indicator of a more open and co-operative climate within the Church, where ideas and opinions can be shared and exchanged more freely and easily. It also hopes that the relationship established between the people of the Church and the Council, between the talkers and the listeners, so to speak, will be a lasting and mutually rewarding one.

4.1.3 The Council would once again like to thank everyone who took part in the above consultations, the Presbyteries, Kirk Sessions and their Clerks, the congregations, the Guilds and their Presidents, the youth groups and youth leaders, the house groups and the individuals. We hope that they feel that their trust has been repaid, that they agree with some of our conclusions and that they feel that their taking part was a worthwhile exercise.

CHURCH AND NATION
MAY 2001

PROPOSED DELIVERANCE

The General Assembly

1. Receive the Report and thank the Committee and those who by their support and shared concerns have helped in this work.

ACTION TAKEN

2. Encourage support for the forthcoming conference on weapons of war.

3. Encourage the Boards involved to pursue their discussions on debt relief for the poorest congregations in the Church, and to report to the General Assembly of 2002.

4. Instruct that, as a matter of course and as a matter of principle, fairly traded tea and coffee and other fairly traded produce should be available in the Church Offices.

INTERNATIONAL ARMS TRADE

5. Urge Her Majesty's Government (HMG) to act on the findings of the Scott Report and implement the recommendations made by that report.

6. Welcome the openness of HMG as shown in the publication of the Annual Reports on Strategic Export Controls and encourage HMG to provide more detailed information.

7. Encourage HMG to establish and publish a register of arms brokers, as well as creating legislation which would stipulate that all arms brokers would be required to obtain written permission for each transaction.

8. Encourage HMG to recognise the important role that the UK should play in international co-operation, as a member of the EU and of NATO, and as a nation with a permanent seat on the UN Security Council, on questions of arms control and in the curtailment of the international arms trade

JERUSALEM

9. Affirm the right of Israelis and Palestinians to live within secure and fixed boundaries in states of their own; and of those refugees who wish to do so to return to the land from which they fled.

10. Recognise the fundamental difficulty represented by the fact of occupation or illegal annexation of territory by Israel, and reaffirm that the withdrawal from such occupation is the first step towards a just and peaceful resolution of the conflict.

11. Encourage HMG to use its influence with the Israeli government and the Palestinian Authority to bring about an end to the violence that has enforced the occupation and the violence that accompanies the resistance to it.

12. Encourage HMG to put just treatment for all occupants of Jerusalem high on its agenda.

13. Record particular concern over the abuse of individual human rights perpetrated both by the Israeli and Palestinian security forces, and encourage HMG, in conjunction with its partners in the EU, to make economic and trade concessions to Israel and Palestine contingent upon concrete moves to a just peace.

14. Encourage individuals and church groups to pray for and to visit our Christian, Muslim and Jewish sisters and brothers in Israel and Palestine.

15. Instruct the Board of World Mission, the Panel on Doctrine and the Committee on Church and Nation to initiate a joint study into the theology of land.

SRI LANKA

16. Call on HMG to give support and encouragement to the work of the Peace Envoy Eric Solheim, that a just and peaceful settlement may be negotiated in Sri Lanka.

17. Call on HMG to recognise the dangerous situation of Tamil refugees returned to Sri Lanka.

RACIAL JUSTICE

18. Commend the Boards and Committees of the Church for their work to promote cultural awareness and racial justice, and encourage Church members to involve themselves in this work whenever the opportunity arises.

19. Commend the continuing financial support of ecumenical work for racial justice, and commit the Church to the way forward outlined in Section 6 of the report.

20. Call on HMG to abandon the Voucher Scheme for asylum seekers and replace it by a cash scheme based on income support levels.

21. In the light of Sodexho's close involvement with the Voucher Scheme, encourage the Office Management Committee of the Church Offices to re-examine its contract with that company.

22. Recognise migration as both an historical and a current fact of human life which represents hope and promise much more than threat or danger.

23. Commend the many congregations who have worked so hard to make refugees welcome in Scotland.

HUMAN RIGHTS COMMISSION FOR SCOTLAND

24. Commend the creation of a Human Rights Commission for Scotland and call on the Scottish Executive to move swiftly to its implementation.

THE POLITICAL PROCESS

25. Re-affirm the place and value of public service in a democratic society.

26. Recognise the worth of those who stand for and are elected to public office, and of those members of political parties whose efforts sustain the democratic process.

27. Affirm that civil servants have valuable skills and a key role in securing effective communication between government and people in promoting openness, transparency and accountability.

28. Urge those engaged in the political process to demonstrate standards of conduct which justify public respect for the process.

29. Welcome the Scottish Executive's commitment to public consultation in all areas of proposed legislation; and urge that it be carried out in a way which takes account of adequate timescale, public involvement at the earliest stage, meaningful communication, effective feedback and maximum inclusiveness.

30. Welcome the Scottish Executive's review of public bodies and urge that the following areas be addressed:
    - the purpose and accountability of Non-Departmental Public Bodies;
    - the oversight of NDPBs by the Scottish Parliament, with particular reference to appointments to and monitoring of NDPBs;
    - the review of the method of remuneration to establish a fair and consistent regime;
    - the recruitment and selection of members with a view towards improved inclusiveness and accountability.

31. Recognising the democratic accountability of local government, urge the Scottish Executive in its review of NDPB responsibilities to give primary consideration to local government as a provider of public services.

32. Urge the Scottish Executive to take account of the lessons to be taken from the case of the Scottish Qualifications Authority, not from the perspective of blame, but to avoid a repetition of such problems.

33. Welcome the action taken to date by Her Majesty's Government and the Scottish Executive to ensure that local authorities have the capacity to play an effective and accountable role in relation to the Scottish Parliament and the Scottish Executive, and look forward to the enactment of the necessary legislation.

34. Call for the introduction of the Single Transferable Vote system for elections to local councils at the earliest practicable date, coupled with a related programme of voter information and education.

35. Emphasise the importance of reforming local government finance in order to enhance accountability of councils to citizens, welcome the inquiry initiated by the Local Government Committee of the Scottish Parliament and call upon the Parliament to support comprehensive and innovative proposals to this end.

36. Welcome the development of community planning so as to give councils a leading role in local governance.

37. Recognise the important role of local council employees in the provision of public services and the need to ensure fair levels of remuneration.

SOCIAL INCLUSION

38. Welcome the Scottish Executive's commitment to put Social Justice at the heart of its policy making and urge it to keep the issue of poverty in mind at all times.

39. Commend all those working in Social Inclusion Partnerships for their commitment to their work and encourage them in their efforts.

40. Urge the Scottish Executive to be more flexible in its approach to fixing the geographical boundaries of SIPs.

41. Urge the Scottish Executive and other funders to have regard to the severe difficulties caused by short-term funding when allocating their grants, and to plan for sustainability.

42. Commend the involvement of churches and church members at all levels in SIPs and encourage Presbyteries, Kirk Sessions and members to develop their involvement in them.

ROAD FUEL PRICING

43. Re-affirm the present position of the Church in favour of direct taxation, recognise the part that taxation can play in influencing fuel use, and call on HMG to recognise that current fuel tax levels could be causing hardship to many.

44. Urge Her Majesty's Government to agree to the ring-fencing of a sizeable proportion of road fuel taxation revenue for environmental renewal, rural infrastructure and development of public transport.

45. Welcome the Transport (Scotland) Act 2000 and urge local authorities to take advantage of the opportunities it provides for establishing integrated transport and concessionary travel schemes.

46. Recognising the considerable environmental advantages of alternative fuels: welcome recent developments and encourage vehicle designers and manufacturers to continue their efforts, urge Church members to consider not only how much they use their car but the fuel used for it, and urge HMG to use taxation policy and grants to achieve significant conversion to alternative fuels.

THE TEXTILE INDUSTRY

47. Recognise the difficulties presently being experienced by the textile industry; and welcome the positive action being taken by government and those at all levels of the industry to promote Scottish textiles in a much changed marketplace.

48. Given the importance of the textile industry in Scotland, urge members of the Church whenever possible to support the industry at this difficult time

PUBLIC SERVICE BROADCASTING AND REGIONAL BROADCASTING

49. Welcome the opportunities for communication in the new digital technology, recognise the potential for using the same technology to do good or ill, and encourage members of the Church to offer their commendation and their concern to broadcasters whenever either is merited.

50. Call on HMG to require the BBC to consult regularly with the Scottish Parliament.

51. Welcome the White Paper, *A New Future for Communications*, and urge HMG to secure the future of public service broadcasting and regional broadcasting by maintaining universal access, ensuring quality and promoting diversity in Britain's broadcasting.

DISTRIBUTION

52. Instruct the Committee to send copies of the Report with the Deliverance to appropriate Government Ministers, Members of the Scottish Parliament, Scottish Members of the UK Parliament, Scottish Members of the European Parliament, and others involved in the issues addressed by the Report.

REPORT

ACTION TAKEN BY THE COMMITTEE

The Committee's work this year has been characterised by a significant amount of movement around the country and beyond. Meetings have been held with various people in Larkhall, Galashiels, Hawick, Cumnock, Prestwick, Glenrothes, Kirkintilloch, Lochgilphead, Glasgow, Dundee, St Andrews, Edinburgh, London, Belfast, Brussels, Amman, Damascus, Jerusalem and Bethlehem. We have met representatives of political parties in both London and Edinburgh, consulted with civil servants, discussed issues with local councillors and union representatives, heard from business people and enterprise companies, talked with community activists, listened to academics, and contributed to debates in the media and in public fora.

Many of these meetings were part of the gathering of evidence towards the reports below. The Committee also visited the Presbytery of Ayr, following our custom of meeting with at least one presbytery every year. The arrangements for this visit were made by the Church and Community Committee of the Presbytery and we would like to record our thanks to them.

1. Matters from the General Assembly

1.1 *Poverty*

Following the decision of last year's General Assembly, we distributed and gathered in petitions on the need for Minimum Income Standards; over 2000 signatures came from the Church of Scotland to be added to those collected from other individuals and organisations around the United Kingdom. This campaign has the support of the Scottish Select Committee and the Social Security Select Committee. We have also been involved in the launch of the Scottish part of the Debt on our Doorstep campaign which aims, after the success of Jubilee 2000 in Britain, to bring to the attention of everyone the vast amount of personal debt under which poor people in our own country struggle. The Debt on our Doorstep campaign was one of the subjects raised during our visit to Westminster (see below).

1.2 *Debt*

The theme of debt was raised with us in a very direct way by one congregation. The suggestion was that the Church of Scotland, having been concerned with Jubilee 2000 and Debt on our Doorstep, should now look seriously at those poorer congregations who are heavily indebted to the central funds of the Church. The Committee, while aware that an increasing number of congregations are heavily supported from central funds, and that debt can be written off when a congregation becomes vacant, nevertheless is continuing conversations with the Boards of Ministry and Stewardship and Finance concerning how this matter can be further pursued.

1.3 *Fair Trade Produce*

At last year's General Assembly the matter of the provision in the Church Offices of Fair Trade produce was raised. The situation is that Fair Trade instant coffee is available if specifically requested. It is, however, neither available as a matter of course nor advertised as being available. The Committee, along with Christian Aid and the Board of World Mission, believes that the coffee and tea provided should all be fairly traded and discussions with the Office Management Committee are continuing.

1.4 *Civil Peace Service*

Following last year's deliverance which *encouraged the Committee... to take further the development of the concept of a Civil Peace Service*, the Committee is now in touch with Peaceworkers UK. The hope is that the Global Nonviolent Peace Force, based in the USA, and the Global Peace Services project in Sweden can be merged with the European Civil Peace Corps. There is much interest from churches in many countries and considerable interest also from the United Nations. Although much work will be required to bring these various organisations and interests together, it is work which promises a great deal. The Committee intends to be involved in this work in Scotland alongside the Scottish Centre for Nonviolence.

1.5 *Access to Affordable Food*

Last year's General Assembly asked the Committee *to pursue the question of adequate access to the food necessary to maintain a healthy diet as part of local authorities' planning and anti-poverty strategies*. Further to the publication of the Scottish Diet Action Plan by the Scottish Office Department of Health (July 1996) and "Social Inclusion: Key Activities and Good Practices by Scottish Councils" by CoSLA (2000), promotion of healthy eating strategies can be seen in a range of activities. Individual local authorities are involved in a range of healthy eating initiatives including breakfast clubs, cookery classes, fruit and vegetable co-operatives, Scotland's Healthy Eating Choices Award Scheme, and a range of projects within schools. CoSLA, HEBS and the Scottish Executive have collaborated to fund two public health posts to provide advice on health improvement and to work with local authorities in drawing up good practice guidance.

Improvement of diet is both important and long-term work involving many different strands and strategies. Local authorities are indeed responding positively in many ways to food poverty. It will be important to remember that the encouragement and promotion of healthy eating must take account of what food is available locally and of the restrictions on many household finances. The Committee will therefore continue to look for the use of planning powers to address the issue of food supply.

1.6 *Humanitarian Intervention*

The General Assembly of 2000, *recognising the dilemma*

surrounding the practice of military intervention for humanitarian purposes, encouraged the Church to continue to explore the issues involved, in collaboration with key decision-makers. In response to this the Committee was delighted to be offered a place at a conference on this very subject. The conference involved participants from, among others, the Ministry of Defence, the Department of International Development, the Foreign and Commonwealth Office and the United Nations.

1.7 *Trident*
In furtherance of numerous statements by the General Assembly over many years concerning the moral and theological illegitimacy of nuclear weapons, their use or threatened use, the Convener was present at a demonstration at Faslane in February. The Committee was glad to see that many others from the Church of Scotland, including the Moderator of the General Assembly, were also in attendance on this occasion.

As part of the study promised to the 2000 General Assembly on weapons of war, the Committee has begun to plan for a major conference in the next year on this subject.

2.   Civil and Political Contacts

2.1 *Scottish Parliament*
We continue our membership of two cross-party groups within the Scottish Parliament—the group on Asylum Seekers and Refugees, and the group on Human Rights. The opportunity to build close working ties with MSPs and others is, we feel, a great advantage—and one which will develop with the passing of time. The Committee continues to be supportive of the work of the Parliament, believing that its arrival was long overdue, that it has already delivered significant progress in a number of areas, and that its value to Scotland will develop and mature in the years ahead.

2.2 *Westminster*
We paid our annual visit to Westminster in November and included, for the first time on such visits, a meeting with the Secretary of State for Scotland. We had been pleased to hear of the election to the Speaker's chair of Michael Martin MP, a long-time friend of the Committee. We were delighted when the Speaker gave us the use of his chambers for our meetings with MPs and assured us that this could now be an annual arrangement.

The meetings with back-bench MPs were, as usual, helpful and stimulating. A total of 31 MPs attended, an indication of the value of these meetings to the politicians concerned. We expect that this number will rise once the temporary phenomenon of dual-mandated MPs and MSPs ceases.

At the request of the Board of Social Responsibility we raised the matter of the Royal Commission on the Long-Term Care of the Elderly—and the possibility of a differentiated response to it from Holyrood and Westminster. Only one politician (a Conservative former member of the Cabinet) seemed to take on board the thought that Scotland's decision on this might cause consternation in London—but he seems, with hindsight, to have been the perspicacious one.

2.3 *Scottish National Party*
Our meeting with representatives of a political party in Scotland was this year with the Scottish National Party; this being particularly worthwhile as it had not been possible to meet with SNP MPs during our visit to London.

2.4 *Civic Alliances*
The Committee continues to be represented on the Civic Forum, an organisation which is beginning to find its feet and to establish itself in Scottish life. The Committee also arranged a meeting with the Chief Executive of CoSLA, a meeting which linked in well with the reports on Local Government and on Social Inclusion being prepared this year.

2.5 *Consultations*
Since the last General Assembly we have responded to consultations on:
• Ferry Services
• Judicial Appointments
• Agricultural Strategy
• Public Appointments
• Powers of Local Government

- Communications White Paper
- Advertising Prohibitions (ITC).

The Ferry Services issue has since moved on. On 23 January 2001 Sarah Boyack, Minister of Transport in the Scottish Executive, announced her proposals formed in response to the consultation document. She believes that these proposals conform to EU regulations and she has submitted them to the European Commission for their approval. We hope that this approval is granted. The main points are: (1) that Caledonian MacBrayne should remain in public ownership; (2) that all its routes, including mainland to mainland routes, should be regarded as being consistent with public service obligations; and (3) that the network should be put out to tender as a whole. These points represent the overwhelming view of those who responded in the consultation process. The Committee welcomes the progress made so far and intends to keep this matter under review.

2.6 *Holocaust Remembrance Day*
The Committee supported the principle of a day of remembrance for the genocides of the last century. It is to be hoped that the seriousness with which the first such occasion was conducted can remain as a hallmark for the future. We were gratified to note that the television coverage of the day did not omit our own nation's past problems with anti-Semitism and our continued ambivalence concerning refugees.

3. Co-operation

3.1 *UPA Hearings*
During the past year the Board of National Mission held a series of hearings in Urban Priority Areas. The Committee was grateful to be invited to participate in these, and glad to be able to do so.

3.2 *The Moderator's Visits to the Prisons of Scotland*
The Committee was pleased to be involved in Dr Andrew McLellan's welcome initiative in visiting all the prisons of Scotland and was keen that the results of this should be taken forward in the best way possible. At the time of

writing a joint meeting with the Moderator and with Prison Chaplains has been organised at which plans can be made about what needs to be done next and by whom.

3.3 *Ecumenical Co-operation*
The Committee is part of the ACTS Commission on Justice, Peace, Social and Moral Issues, of the CTBI Church and Society Forum and of the CTBI Peace Forum. In addition, the Committee is involved with other co-operative efforts, such as the Scottish Churches Social Inclusion Network.

3.4 *Financial Support*
The Committee gave financial support this year to the following organisations:

- Centre for Theology and Public Issues
- Refugee Survival Trust
- Council on Christian Approaches to Defence and Disarmament
- Church Action on Poverty
- Debt on our Doorstep (Scotland)
- Scottish Environment Link
- Scottish Churches Housing Agency.

4. Reports

4.1 *Racial Justice*
The preparation of reports remains the principal task of the Committee. This year we include a report on Racial Justice prepared with the co-operation of representatives of other Boards and Committees. As was reported last year, the Church and Nation Committee was asked by the Co-ordinating Forum to act as the lead committee on this subject, and this report and its preparation represent the first fruits of this new way of working. We hope that this will be the beginning of a pattern of co-operation able to develop and to take us forward.

4.2 *Report Requests*
The subject reports now follow. As well as the report on Racial Justice, the Committee was glad to be able to respond to requests from other parts of the Church for reports to be compiled. Thus the report on Sri Lanka is

at the instigation of the Board of World Mission, that on Road Fuel Pricing at the suggestion of the Rural Committee of the Board of National Mission, and that on Textiles at the request of the Presbytery of Hamilton.

THE INTERNATIONAL ARMS TRADE

1.   The scope of the problem

1.1   The launching of the World Council of Churches' Decade to Overcome Violence in January 2001 means that this, the first of our reports about the scale of armaments, from hand-guns to weapons of mass destruction, comes at a most opportune time. It also comes in response to last year's General Assembly deliverance encouraging the Committee, *to initiate a new study of the issues surrounding nuclear and other weapons in the wider context of modern warfare.*

1.2   The international arms trade, and in particular the proliferation of small arms, is one of the most tragic features of our modern world. Children, sometimes as young as six, are among those who, with virtually no training, use the guns, rifles and mortars which have been responsible for the vast majority of the 23 million deaths which have occurred in the 149 wars estimated to have taken place since 1945. The majority of these wars are in the impoverished South, with most of the deaths being of civilians rather than military personnel. The effect on development in the world's poorest countries has been catastrophic, as can be seen from the Department for International Development's 1999 report which states that:

A major obstacle to the eradication of poverty is the persistence of violent conflict, or its legacy, in many of the poorest countries. Reducing the incidence, duration, and effect of armed conflict is essential.

1.3   Recent figures for the last decade have been just as depressing as those that have gone before:

- 39 major conflicts during the 1990s alone with more than 4 million killed and 9 out of 10 casualties being civilians.
- 200,000 child soldiers in the world

- the 70 million AK-47s outnumber the world's teachers—and AK-47s are simply one brand of automatic rifle, which is but one type of infantry weapon.

There can be few clearer signs of that flaw in human nature that we call sin.

2.   The role of HM Government

2.1   Few people therefore would doubt the pressing moral need for stricter arms control, not only of the weapons of mass destruction, but of the multitude of small arms in circulation internationally. HM Government is on record as wanting to have an ethical dimension to foreign policy.

2.2   The 1997 Labour Party Manifesto declares, among other things:

- that it "will not permit the sale of arms to regimes that might use them for internal repression or international aggression";
- that it "will increase the transparency and accountability of decisions on export licences for arms";
- that it will "support an EU code of conduct governing arms sales".

These pledges began to be acted upon in September 1997 with the Chancellor announcing that export credit guarantees would no longer be given for non-productive exports to the 41 poorest countries. The moratorium was extended to a further 22 highly indebted poor countries in early 2000, but the Department of Trade and Industry has yet to make a convincing moral or economic argument in any circumstances for underwriting and effectively subsidising (contrary to public policy statements) arms sales to such countries.

2.3   It was particularly disappointing that in the Queen's speech at the State Opening of Parliament in December 2000, the long-expected proposals for arms export legislation were completely missing. Ever since the Scott Report into the "Arms to Iraq Affair" expectations about increased controls over arms exports have been steadily rising. Now the lack of progress continues to be reflected in the damning words of the February 2000 joint parliamentary committee (made up of MPs from the Trade and Industry, Foreign Affairs, International Development and Defence Select Committees):

We are dismayed that the Government should not have afforded greater priority to bringing forward a Bill to implement the recommendations made four years ago ... We are frankly appalled at the dilatory approach to legislating on the Scott Report.

2.4 For the problem to be taken more seriously more publicity needs to be given reports like the UN Report by Russet and Sylvan *The Effects of Arms Transfers on Developing Countries*, which suggested that for an average developing country each £200m spent on arms imports adds 20 infant deaths per 1,000 live births, decreases life expectancy by 3-4 years, and results in 14 fewer literate adults for every 100 people. This also puts a responsibility on the West, with organisations like the UK's Defence Export Services Organisation and its 600 employees committed to persuading foreign governments to buy British, to try to change the situation where some countries, and indeed whole sections of continents, are described as "awash with arms".

3. The significance of the arms trade for the British economy

3.1 One of the arguments that has traditionally been used to justify the UK's position as the second biggest European arms producer and fifth largest in the world (along with the other four permanent members of the UN Security Council—China, France, Russia, and the USA) is that it helps the national economy in a significant way. But in recent years there have been an increasing number of challenges to that argument.

3.2 One example is Professor Paul Dunne's inaugural lecture in November 1999 at the London School of Economics. Talking about the national defence industrial base, he argues persuasively that the MOD's estimate of 400,000 jobs directly or indirectly connected with the arms industry (150,000 of them linked to exports), while representing about 10% of manufacturing employment, represent less than 2% of total employment. He

concludes that therefore the industry is not as important to the economy as might be thought. In addition he points out that there are all kinds of hidden costs that are not included in press releases, including export credit guarantees, marketing and other support, offset arrangements, aid budgets, commissions and questionable inducements, and technology transfer and licensing. He agrees with the findings of various researchers that there is in actual fact a large subsidy for the arms trade. Estimates of this subsidy range from £228m (in 1995 by Stephen Martin, a defence economist at York University) to £1,000m (in 1996 by the Campaign Against the Arms Trade).

3.3 The arms industry represents a pool of highly skilled labour which could be deployed elsewhere. For example engineering skills for developing the Challenger II tank could, with imagination and effort, be redeployed in improving rail infrastructure, while skills in arms electronics could be transferable to aspects of communications systems. But nothing can happen without the political will to re-direct these skills into other kinds of production.

4. The need for increasingly tight Governmental control

4.1 Another major area of concern, in spite of the controls that HM Government have set up over the years, is the existence of loopholes that are regularly exploited, particularly in the fields of arms brokering, licensed production, and ineffective end-user control. The existing law governing UK arms exports was introduced as an emergency measure at the beginning of the Second World War in 1939 and today new loopholes, undreamt of at the time, give considerable scope to those determined to export arms to questionable destinations.

4.2 Bodies like Amnesty International, with its concern to stop the export of torture equipment and arms which might be used for internal repression, draw attention to the Gallup International poll conducted last year which found that 87% of the public believe the government should introduce tighter controls on arms sales as soon as possible. With regard to arms brokering consider, for example, the quite feasible situation quoted by the UK United Nations Association:

> *In some cases the arms will be delivered by a shipping firm based in one country, with its aircraft registered in a second, which flies out from a third, will pick up arms in a fourth, re-fuel in a fifth, be scheduled to land in a sixth, but actually will deliver its lethal consignment in a seventh.*

4.3   The situation can be just as conveniently confusing when it comes to licensed production, and can lead to the former German manufacturer, Heckler and Koch, now owned by Royal Ordinance, which in turn is owned by British Aerospace, having sub-machine guns produced under license in countries as diverse as Turkey, Iran, Myanmar, Pakistan, Saudi Arabia, and Mexico. Reports show arms from these places turning up in such sensitive destinations as Algeria, Sudan, and Angola, as well as in the producer countries.

4.4   When it comes to end-use control the situation is far from satisfactory. The certificates, which are meant to be a guarantee that the arms are for the sole use of the importer, are known to be abused far too frequently. In HM Government's second Annual Report on Strategic Export Controls, covering 1998, Jordan and Singapore both received a large number of export licences despite having in the past been notorious transit routes to Iraq and Iran respectively. In this context what are we to make of stun grenades to the Channel Islands (which received more licences for small arms than France), submachine guns for San Marino and heavy machine guns for the Bahamas?

4.5   Some other countries are well ahead of us in their arms control legislation. US law, for example, stipulates that all arms brokers must obtain written permission from the Government for each transaction and applies to US citizens wherever they live and any foreign nations living in the US. Germany, Sweden, the Netherlands and Luxembourg also have significant controls on arms brokering. An important first step for the UK would be to establish a register of brokers.

4.6   The greater openness on the part of Government, promised in 1997 and seen in the publication of the Annual Reports on Strategic Export Controls, is to be welcomed as a significant step in the right direction. Nevertheless there needs to be a tightening up of some of the details. Actual quantities and end-users of weapons should be listed, rather than just saying, for example, that "assault rifles" were licensed to Zimbabwe, leaving it unclear whether there were 10 or 500 and whether they were to be used by the police, armed forces, or game-wardens.

4.7   Large quantities of light weapons in circulation are known to contribute to exacerbating civil conflicts, banditry, and crime in dozens of countries, and the export situation cannot be scrutinised thoroughly enough. The organisation Saferworld has made a country by country audit of arms exports about which it is concerned and lists 36 different situations where it has significant concerns about the export of arms to what it calls "sensitive countries". What are needed are arms contracts with legally binding assurances preventing the misuse of the arms for human rights violations or their diversion to third parties, where any breaking of the contract would lead to it becoming null and void and further deliveries and repair services cancelled. This already happens in Sweden. If our exports of beef can be labelled and tracked all the way from the producer to the consumer, there is no reason why there cannot be legislation requiring arms shippers to have cargo and documentation authenticated by officials at each stage.

5.   The example of South Africa

5.1   Terrible though the cumulative effect of the international trade in small arms is, there are also major concerns at the level of the supply of aircraft and ships, which can be illustrated by the case of South Africa. South Africa faces chronic social problems of unemployment, poverty, and crime, yet in January 1999 it announced the Cabinet's provisional approval of the decision to re-equip the South African National Defence Force. Items to be procured included 28 Gripen fighters, 24 Hawk trainer fighters, 4 corvettes, 3 diesel submarines, 4 super-Lynx helicopters, and 40 light helicopters (now reduced to 30), with a total value of £3bn to be spread over 15 years, representing a 20% increase in the military budget.

5.2 This re-arming of South Africa is viewed by the West as enabling it to be the policeman of sub-Saharan Africa, but little cognisance is taken of the fact that it simultaneously increases the sense of insecurity of neighbouring states and the possibility of violence within the country itself. If the question is asked why South Africa is viewed by the West in such a favourable light, it is difficult to avoid the conclusion that western strategic interests are being pursued at the expense of South Africa's immediate neighbours.

5.3 Over and above the build-up of arms for its own use South Africa is continuing the export of arms to all kinds of questionable destinations world-wide. The international organisation Economists Allied for Arms Reduction (Ecaar) points out that the state-owned Armaments Corporation of South Africa (Armscor), which was greatly expanded after the UN Security Council imposed an arms embargo on South Africa in 1977, boasted in 1994, literally the day after the UN arms embargo was lifted, that it intended to triple exports of weapons. Within two months Armscor was caught selling surplus Chinese AK-47s to Yemen, which turned out to be merely the transhipment point for weapons supplies to Croatia, in violation of another UN arms embargo. Since that time exports have gone to such sensitive destinations as Algeria, Colombia, India, Israel, Pakistan and Turkey, as well as illicitly to Unita in Angola, the African Great Lakes region, the Democratic Republic of Congo and other countries in conflict.

5.4 Another sinister aspect of the situation is that BAe Systems, now the world's second largest arms contractor, has been transferring its production to newly industrialising countries such as South Africa to bypass mounting British criticisms of its involvement in such places as Saudi Arabia and Indonesia. South Africa is certainly ignoring Desmond Tutu's words:

> *Abolishing the world's budgets of death and destruction would give all God's children everywhere a clean water supply, enough to eat, decent education, adequate health care and a roof over their heads. Let the children have peace.*

6. Inter-governmental control

6.1 However much the UK does on its own to act responsibly in this whole complex field of arms control, it also has a major role to play in terms of international co-operation. As one of the major countries of the EU, as a key member of NATO, and with a permanent seat on the UN Security Council, the UK still wields significant influence in international affairs. Our national policy for arms control is therefore of crucial importance in terms of its overall effect on world peace. Also, if our commitment to human rights expressed in our subscription to the UN Declaration on Human Rights and our recent commitment to European human rights legislation is to have any meaning at all, we must as a nation play our full part in working for the curtailment of the international arms trade.

7. Conclusion

7.1 While acknowledging the moral challenge posed to the Christian Church by those of its members who are convinced pacifists, the majority of Christians would accept the need for countries to make a certain amount of provision for their legitimate self-defence. The problem with the arms trade is that, although it is set in the context of a desire for ethical dimensions to foreign policy, it is in fact driven by the most powerful of profit motives and by the desires of politicians and military chiefs around the world for personal power and aggrandisement, both of which are heavily disguised under persuasive talk about "national interest".

7.2 The Church, recognising the capacity of sinful humanity for self-deception, has therefore a prophetic role to play in challenging the demonic extent of the arms trade. It should do so both in terms of stating the obvious grotesqueness and immorality of that trade seen as a whole, and also by pressing for the individual, point by point, changes in legislation that need to be made systematically and drastically to reduce it, inspired at all times by Jesus' words in the Sermon on the Mount:

> *Blessed are the peacemakers, for they shall be called God's children.*

JERUSALEM

1. Introduction

1.1 The Church and Nation Committee has presented reports on the Israeli-Palestinian conflict to the General Assembly on a number of occasions, most recently in the form of a longer report in 1998.[1] This report noted the previous occasions on which the Church and Nation Committee of the Church of Scotland had addressed the issue at length in an Assembly context. All of these reports have expressed the fundamental conviction of the General Assembly that the modern state of Israel, like all states, has the undeniable right to exist as an independent state. However, the 1998 report to the Assembly ended on a gloomy note, stating that [t]*ime is not on the side of peace*.[2] Israel has continued in its efforts to impose a settlement to the conflict whilst ignoring and procrastinating over negotiations: the refusal to allow refugees to return, the refusal to withdraw from territory acquired by war, the refusal to refrain from constructing further settlements are all indicative of this. Although many in the West hailed the May 1999 election victory of Ehud Barak as Prime Minister over Binyamin Netanyahu as greatly improving the chances for peace, Barak consistently failed to live up to expectations and in reality the situation deteriorated on all fronts.

1.2 The territories occupied by Israel in 1967 (the Gaza Strip, the West Bank, East Jerusalem and the Golan Heights) all remain under effective Israeli control. Even where parts of the Gaza Strip and West Bank have supposedly been handed over to Palestinian control under the interim Oslo agreements, they have in fact been shown clearly to be under Israeli control in the course of recent unrest, and Israel has entered them at will in pursuit of its military objectives.[3] The Oslo "peace process" has resulted in a "bantustanisation" of the Occupied Territories: the creation of small enclaves of Palestinian-controlled territory surrounded by Israeli settlements, roads, and military outposts. Comparisons with South African apartheid abound.[4] Although many commentators had foreseen this,[5] it would appear that a number of Palestinian negotiators and many in the West had not, or were unwilling to see it. When Ariel Sharon,

the leader of the Israeli Likud party made a provocative visit to the Noble Sanctuary/Temple Mount[6] at the end of September 2000 and the next day a number of Palestinian demonstrators were shot at the same location by Israeli forces, many ordinary people in the Occupied Territories took up active protest against the occupation; this became what is known as the al-Aqsa intifada. This uprising can only be interpreted as a clear rejection of the Oslo process, which culminated in the failed summit at Camp David, Maryland, USA, in the summer of 2000. Though significant progress was lacking on many of the outstanding issues of the conflict, many of them focussed on the issue of Jerusalem, particularly the city's holy sites in the Old City, as the principal stumbling bloc that led to the failure of the summit. In many ways, Jerusalem serves as a microcosm of the Israeli-Palestinian conflict.

2. The concentration of issues in Jerusalem

2.1 The most significant issues that contribute to the conflict can all be represented by looking at Jerusalem, where they are all concentrated. Broadly, these can be summarised as:

- sovereignty/occupation
- settlements/land resources
- refugees.

(We return later to the status of Jerusalem as a holy place for three faiths.)

2.2 *Sovereignty/occupation*

2.2.1 Under international law,[7] Jerusalem is a *corpus separatum*, an international zone administered by the UN, and neither Israeli, nor Palestinian.[8] At the end of the 1948 war, Israel was in possession of the western part of the city, and Jordan was in possession of the eastern part, including the Old City. Thereafter, in defiance of UN Resolution 303,[9] Israel moved its government from Tel Aviv to Jerusalem and the latter was declared the capital city with retroactive effect from 15.5.1948. After the 1967 war, Israel was in possession of the eastern part of the city as well.[10] Shortly after the war, Israel formally annexed the eastern part of the city, expanded it considerably, and declared this entity to be the "eternal and undivided capital of Israel" (this expansion included approximately 70km2 of the West Bank including villages and property belonging to Bethlehem and 28 other villages around the city which had previously not been regarded as part of Jerusalem – this tripled what was now known as Jerusalem[11]). Under all applicable international laws, this was and remains illegal, and so far virtually no state has recognised Jerusalem as Israel's capital: embassies remain in Tel Aviv.

2.2.2 Israeli offers of a "form of sovereignty" or "shared sovereignty" over East Jerusalem are non-starters. Most Palestinians think, understandably, that restricting their demands to the lands occupied by Israel in 1967 is in itself a concession, since even in 1948/9 Israel acquired far greater territories than were allocated to it under the UN partition plan. Under these circumstances, it is to be expected that most attempts by Israel to return less than what was taken in 1967 will simply be a recipe for perpetual conflict, though the Barak government would possibly have allowed Palestinian control of the Noble Sanctuary as long as Israeli control of the Western Wall could be assured.[12] The Oslo process appeared to offer a negotiated way out of this conflict situation, but the way in which Israel continued to create settlements, violate human rights and refuse refugees the right to return means that, although appearing to negotiate, in fact a position was being entrenched which would make any negotiation meaningless. Jerusalem as the "cause" of the breakdown can be seen as being simply symbolic of the refusal of Israel to give ground on the substantive issues.

2.3 *Settlements/land resources*

2.3.1 As Israel has taken over swathes of land around Jerusalem and subsumed it into its annexation of East Jerusalem to form what it sometimes calls "Greater Jerusalem," the resources of these lands have also been directed to Israel's usage, regardless of the consequences for Palestinian needs. For example, over the last 34 years, thousands of Palestinian olive trees have been uprooted and destroyed to make way for new settlements or roads to the settlements. Olive oil has been one of the traditional agricultural products that Palestinian families have been engaged in producing for centuries and for many represents their livelihood. Settlements around Jerusalem have increased at a startling rate, and the current plans available from the Jerusalem municipality show ever greater expansion for the future. With the beginning of construction a short while ago at Jebel Abu Ghneim, called Har Homa by Israel, there is a more or less complete ring of Israeli settlements around Jerusalem, including East Jerusalem. This ring will make it extremely difficult for Palestinians to reassert their authority over Jerusalem in any final status negotiations. The ring of settlements not only encloses Jerusalem, but also extends far beyond it. One of the largest settlements, Ma'ale Adumim, stretching eastwards behind the Mount of Olives, is planned eventually to reach across the West Bank and to the Jordan river, dividing the West Bank into two segments, the connection between them being in Israel's control. Already it is extremely difficult, and often impossible, for Palestinians to travel between the southern part of the West Bank (*eg* Bethlehem) and the northern part (*eg* Ramallah) since Palestinians from the West Bank may no longer enter Jerusalem without a permit— Jerusalem being the natural link between them. Every settlement in East Jerusalem has been built on expropriated Palestinian land. Often, such land has initially been declared "Green Land" by the municipality, which prevents anyone from building on it. However, at a later date the municipality has re-zoned the land and allocated it to Jewish developers.

2.3.2 Settlement activity has also taken place in and around the Old City. There are a number of settlers who have taken control of properties in the Muslim Quarter, as well as, for example, in Silwan near the Noble Sanctuary/Temple Mount. Ariel Sharon has himself taken a house in the Muslim Quarter.[13] In almost all of these cases the families have been forcibly evicted or the properties sold without clarity about who was behind the purchase, it later turning out to be settlers. The Israeli government has actively supported such activity, using public funds to do so.[14] Former US President Carter summed up the position with regard to the success of negotiations in a recent article: "An underlying reason that years of U.S. diplomacy have failed and violence in the Middle East persists is that some Israeli leaders continue to "create facts" by building settlements in occupied territory."[15] A writer in a Middle East Council of Churches publication stated that: "The establishment of Israeli settlements in Jerusalem constitutes a flagrant violation of UN General Assembly Resolutions 181 (II), 194 (III) and 303 (IV)... which have never been abrogated. The establishment of settlements further violates several other U.N. resolutions, the Hague Regulations of 1907, the Fourth Geneva Convention of 1949 and international law generally."[16]

2.3.3 Water, an increasingly scarce natural resource in the Middle East, is controlled by Israel in all the Occupied Territories, with Jewish areas receiving far more than Palestinian areas. Israel uses large quantities, has seriously depleted its own resources, and currently draws heavily on the groundwater under geographical Palestine, including the West Bank. Groundwater consumption currently exceeds replenishment at a rate of 15% *per annum*– a catastrophe in the making, as senior Israeli hydrologists have repeatedly stated. It is also taking much more water than Jordan and Syria from the Jordan river. Palestinian towns and villages are regularly left without proper running water, whilst settlements receive more than adequate supplies. In any final settlement, equitable use, control, conservation and recycling would need to be clarified; sole Israeli control would be a serious potential cause of conflict.[17]

2.4 *Refugees*

2.4.1 Although the summit at Camp David in the summer of 2000 supposedly broke up because of disagreement over Jerusalem, the possibly still more contentious issue of refugees has only recently begun to be addressed openly by the parties. UN Resolution 194 specifies that the Palestinian refugees must be allowed to "return to their homes" or be compensated – the choice being an individual and not a collective one. This Resolution has long been seen as the basis for a just resolution of the refugee situation. It should be noted that the current American proposals reflect a wholesale adoption of the Israeli position that the implementation of the right of return be subject entirely to Israel's

discretion. However, 194's call for the return of Palestinian refugees to "their homes," wherever located— not to their "homeland" or to "historic Palestine" —cannot be ignored if a resolution to the conflict is to be successful. In fact, the right of return's essential element is that of choice: Palestinians should be given the option to choose where they wish to settle, including return to the homes from which they were driven. The refugees' "dream of return," does not mean becoming Israeli citizens in an Israeli state in which most of their original villages have either been destroyed (*eg* numerous Galilee villages) or have been taken over and changed beyond all recognition (*eg* the lands around Jerusalem that Israel has annexed) —that would be a painful and alienating experience, something of which most Palestinians are aware.[18] This makes the issue of choice between compensation and the right of return all the more important. There is no historical precedent for a people abandoning their fundamental right to return to their homes whether they were forced to leave or fled in fear and it is unlikely that Palestinians will set this precedent—nor should they be expected to do so. However, there have been a number of detailed discussions between Israelis and Palestinians regarding the resolution of the refugee problem in such a way that would implement this right whilst accommodating Israeli concerns. It is perhaps problematic that the current US suggestions appear to revert to an earlier Israeli position and ignore progress made on the issue so far.

2.4.2 Recognition of the right of return and the provision of choice to refugees is a pre-requisite for the just and final ending of the conflict.

3.   Palestinians Living in Jerusalem[19]

3.1 Although Israel has declared Jerusalem to be its "united and eternal capital" it treats its Jewish and Palestinian residents very differently. Only those Palestinians actually in Jerusalem at the time of annexation were granted permanent residency status. Although they are entitled under certain circumstances (including swearing allegiance to Israel) to become Israeli citizens, most, for political reasons, choose not to do so. It is impossible in the context of a brief report such as this to note the full details of such discrimination, but it covers all areas of life, including housing, infrastructure, welfare, health provision and amenities.

3.2 For example: in terms of housing, only 7% of East Jerusalem is available for Palestinian building, and most of this is in already-existing Palestinian areas. Planning permission for new construction can take years to be granted, and often it is not. This leads to construction without permission, with Israel regularly destroying houses built in this way. The municipality deals unequally in this regard too. Although Palestinians are responsible for less than 20% of illegal construction in Jerusalem, 60% of demolitions are of Palestinian homes. Partly because of this overcrowding is a major problem, with over ten times as many Palestinian households (almost 25%) with three or more people per room than Jewish households (1997 figures). In total, there are 634,000 people in Jerusalem, of which 200,000 are Palestinian; nearly half of all Jews in the city live in areas occupied and annexed after 1967.

3.3 Regarding infrastructure, some simple examples illustrate Jewish predominance: in 1999, "Jewish" areas had 743 residents per km of sewer piping, "Palestinian" areas had 2,809 (there are whole Palestinian suburbs without adequate sewage facilities); Jewish residents per km of road numbered 710, Palestinians numbered 2,448; Jewish residents per km of pavement numbered 690, Palestinians numbered 2,917. This situation is not improving: of the 423 million New Israeli Shekels (£71m) of the 1999 Jerusalem Development Budget, a mere 40 million NIS was to be allocated to Palestinian areas.

3.4 Although Palestinians in East Jerusalem are theoretically entitled to similar provision of welfare and health services as Jews, this is not the case in practice. Palestinians have to prove their residential status in Jerusalem before the state will pay medical bills. During the course of the investigation bills must be paid by the patient. Investigations into residency status regularly result in Palestinians losing their residency rights for spurious reasons, and this then jeopardises their right to remain in the city. Israeli Jews, on the other hand, are not subject to any investigation and may live for any length of time anywhere in Israel, in a settlement, or abroad,

without it affecting their rights to welfare provision. "Israel", to use the words of a human rights group in a report describing the lack of care for pregnant women and newborn children, "is a state that violates the rights of some of the most vulnerable people in its charge, pregnant women and their newborn. The state… needlessly … [causes] financial hardship to many relatively disadvantaged families and potentially puts at risk the health of countless Arab children in the city."[20]

3.5 In terms of amenities, one can note simply that "Jewish" areas of Jerusalem in 1999 had a total of 36 swimming pools, 531 sports facilities, 26 libraries and 1,079 parks; "Palestinian" areas had no pools, 33 sports facilities, 2 libraries and 29 parks.

3.6 For Palestinians, the difficulties involved in living in Jerusalem have led many to leave. Under Israeli regulations, once a Palestinian has moved out of Jerusalem it is extremely difficult, if not virtually impossible, to return. Well over half of those who have left the city since 1967 have been Christians, and at the current rate of emigration the complete disappearance of the Palestinian Christian community, which has been steadfastly keeping the faith since the days of the Apostles, is foreseeable.

3.7 In summation, Israel has over many years consistently and methodically discriminated against Palestinians living in Jerusalem and continues to do so. This is not simply a random and arbitrary form of discrimination, but a matter of deliberate policy designed to make life as difficult as possible for the Palestinian population in East Jerusalem and, if possible, to reduce that population in number.[21]

4.   The Next Steps in Trying to Resolve the Conflict

4.1 In spite of heroic and sincere efforts on the part of many negotiators on both sides, there needs to be a recognition that the Oslo peace process has failed. Whilst the two sides negotiated, Israel's withdrawal (at times this was actually redeployment rather than withdrawal) from territory has been minimal, with massively increased settlement activity and increasing violations of human rights. The longer this continues, the more intractable the situation becomes. As the UN has reaffirmed on numerous occasions, a just resolution to the conflict should be based on the Resolutions that it has passed at various times in the past, including 194 and 242.

4.2 A renewed European role

4.2.1 The United States of America positioned itself, despite its closeness to Israel, as an "honest broker" in the negotiations between Israelis and Palestinians. In this it has failed. It has found it impossible to provide uncritical support and massive economic and military aid to Israel whilst simultaneously purporting neutrally to assist negotiations between it and parties with whom it is in conflict.[22] The United Nations, the European Union and Russia have all been sidelined by the US in the Oslo process, the Europeans being restricted mainly to subsidising the ailing Palestinian economy.

4.2.2 The European Union has not acted as outlined in our 1998 report.[23] We continue to believe, as there, that economic pressure should be brought to bear, and we continue to encourage HM Government to work with its partners along the lines described in 1998.

4.2.3 At the time of writing (February 2001) the direction foreign policy under the new American president will follow is not clear, though many assume that attention in the Middle East will move away from Israel-Palestine to Iraq. Whilst this probably does not herald good news for Iraq, it may mean that in terms of Israel-Palestine a renewed role could be found for the Europeans and perhaps even the United Nations.

4.3 The churches' role

4.3.1 Churches in the West, our own included, have continued to struggle to reach an understanding of the contemporary conflict in Israel-Palestine. Some of this struggle has been due to the idea that the contemporary state of Israel can be assumed to be coterminous with the Ancient Israel found in the Bible. The consequence of this is then presumed to be that as Christians we must support the modern secular state of Israel. This interpretation then colours the understanding of Israel's treatment of Palestinians and Palestinian land, asserting a special right of modern Israel to the land and its resources over and above the rights of all others. The General Assembly of 1991 stated that whilst the "rights and claims to justice and self-determination" of the Palestinians "should be kept in the forefront of attention... sensitivity must be shown to the rights and security of the state of Israel". This means that, whilst recognising the right for the modern state of Israel to exist, issues regarding its theological justification remain to be resolved, including Israel's treatment of Palestinians.

4.3.2 We consider that a study of a theology of land and of covenant might prove very useful in this question, not only for the Church of Scotland, but perhaps also for others. More generally, it is imperative that we work towards a greater understanding of the origins and nature of the present conflict and do not allow simplistic analyses to stereotype people one way or another. Ongoing promotion and support of balanced news and opinion is to be strongly encouraged, whether from Christian sources or not; equally, distorted coverage should be criticised. We encourage reflection on the possibility of establishing a UK or European network of churches supporting moves for peace in the Middle East.[24]

4.3.3 The churches have a pastoral concern for both parties to the conflict: for Palestinians still suffering under the effects of over fifty years of dispossession and oppression, and for Israelis unable to experience life in a normal and secure context as their leaders continue to rely on increasing militarisation in order to retain their country's position of supremacy – this latter is inevitably a cause for concern, not least in terms of its effects on the young people serving in Israel's military forces. The churches can have a role here, in supporting those bodies working to address people's pastoral and material needs.

4.3.4 The Church and Nation Committee strongly welcomed the December 2000 pastoral visit to Church of Scotland staff and institutions by the Moderator accompanied by the Convener of the Church and Nation Committee. We also welcomed the March 2001 visit by representatives of Churches Together in Britain and Ireland to the Middle East, a trip including Israel-

Palestine. The Convener of our International Affairs Sub-Committee was a part of that delegation. It is hoped that our sisters and brothers in the churches in the region feel supported and cared for by Christians in this country and that our concern for the wellbeing of all parties can be adequately communicated. Whilst the Committee is well aware that this is seen as a dangerous time to visit the region, we nevertheless would encourage members and congregations of the Church of Scotland to make a conscious decision to visit now as an expression of faith and solidarity, and therefore consider not only their own safety, but also the importance of such a visit to the local Christian communities.

---

[1] Church of Scotland, *Reports to the General Assembly 1998*, Edinburgh 1998, 19/51-19/58

[2] Church of Scotland, *Reports to the General Assembly 1998*, Edinburgh 1998, 19/57

[3] *eg* the "closure" policies (sealing off a town/village) which further Israel's control of Palestinian territory; references to records of entry into Area A territory can easily be located if required

[4] *eg* David McDowall, *The Palestinians*, Minority Rights Group International Report, London, 1998, p28; Jeff Halper, "The Road to Apartheid" *News from Within*, Vol XVI No 3, May 2000, published by the Alternative Information Centre, Jerusalem

[5] *eg The Independent's* Robert Fisk, the academic and commentator Edward Said, and many others

[6] The Noble Sanctuary (Haram al-Sharif) is the third holiest site in Islam, containing the Dome of the Rock, from which Muhammad is said to have ascended into heaven, and the al-Aqsa Mosque. It is regarded by Jews as the site of the last temple. The Western Wall (sometimes known as the Wailing Wall), is regarded as the only remnant of the Temple.

[7] The following instruments of international law are primarily applicable to the conflict: Hague Convention 1907, UN Charter 1945, Universal Declaration of Human Rights 1948, Fourth Geneva Convention Relative to the Protection of Civilian Persons in Times of War 1949. Israel has accepted her obligations under these international instruments, signed the Universal Declaration of Human Rights soon after being admitted to membership of the UN, and ratified the Fourth Geneva Convention on 6.7.1961.

[8] General Assembly Resolution 181, 29.11.1947 (the UN partition plan)

[9] It was UN Resolution 303 of 9.12.1949 that declared Jerusalem a *corpus separatum*.

[10] The wider Arab-Israeli conflict has been discussed in several previous reports. The 1991 report includes a description of the Arab view of the 1967 war as a *pre-emptive strike by Israel against the build up of Arab forces* and of the Israeli view of the war as *resistance to Arab aggression*. The 1968 report states clearly that *armed force must not become the criterion by which any nation may keep or annex territory for itself.* And the 1984 report aligns the Church with United Nations Resolution 242, saying *the Resolution is based on two principles: the necessity for Israeli withdrawal from occupied territories; and the right of every State in the area (including the State of Israel) to live in peace within secure and recognised boundaries.*

[11] B'Tselem, *A Policy of Discrimination: Land Expropriation, Planning and Building in East Jerusalem*, B'Tselem Report No. 15, January 1997, Jerusalem, p18. Pages 17-28 contain excellent background material on Jerusalem, including its status in law. The remainder of the report contains detailed analysis of Israeli government statistics and other materials, providing a damning account of expropriation *etc* in East Jerusalem.

[12] Yezid Sayigh, http://www.iiss.org/pub/sp/sp00030.asp. It should be noted that whilst Muslims and Christians have historic holy places in Jerusalem, "the Jews do not possess actually any Holy Places in Jerusalem" – as acknowledged by Chaim Weizmann (c.f. Henry Cattan, "The Status of Jerusalem Under International Law and United Nations Resolutions" in *MECC Perspectives*, July 1990, Middle East Council of Churches, Limassol, Cyprus, pp43-51, p48)

[13] Nazmi al-Ju'beh, "A Tour in the Old City" in *Sharing Jerusalem*, eds: Amneh Badran, Daphna Golan, Jack Persekian, published by The Jerusalem Link: A Women's Joint Venture for Peace, Jerusalem, ca. 1997, pp56-58, p58

[14] Amir S Cheshin, Bill Hutman, Avi Melamed, *Separate and Unequal: The Inside Story of Israeli Rule in East Jerusalem*, Harvard, 1999, pp215-6

[15] Washington Post, 26.11.2000

[16] Henry Cattan, "The Status of Jerusalem Under International Law and United Nations Resolutions" in *MECC Perspectives*, July 1990, Middle East Council of Churches, Limassol, Cyprus, pp43-51, p46

[17] David McDowall, *The Palestinians*, Minority Rights Group International Report, London, 1998, p28

[18] Khalil Shakiki, *Jerusalem Report*, 15.1.2001.

[19] Unless otherwise indicated, most of the statistics in this section are taken from the B'Tselem document *Jerusalem: Injustice in the Holy City*, December 1999

[20] LAW, *The National Insurance Institute and the violation of the rights of pregnant women and their newborn in East Jerusalem*, Jerusalem, 1999, p30

[21] Amir S Cheshin and Avi Melamed, two Jewish Jerusalemites involved for many years at a high level in the city's planning environments and Bill Hutman, a Jewish Jerusalemite who covered Jerusalem as a reporter for the *Jerusalem Post* newspaper, have described this is in considerable detail in their book *Separate and Unequal: The Inside Story of Israeli Rule in East Jerusalem*, Harvard, 1999

[22] Patrick Seale, "Farewell to Dennis Ross", *Middle East International*, No 638, 24.11.2000, pp23-25

[23] Church of Scotland, *Reports to the General Assembly 1998*, Edinburgh 1998, 19/56

ETHNIC CONFLICT IN SRI LANKA

1. Last year the General Assembly was greatly moved by the appeal of the Rev. Ebenezer Joseph of Sri Lanka to be concerned at the effects on his country of 18 years' civil war in which more than 85,000 deaths have been recorded. This is an ethnic conflict, which began as a movement for self-determination on the part of the Tamils who make up 15% of the population, but escalated into civil war with the 85% Sinhalese. On the one hand the Liberation Tigers of the Tamil Eelam (LTTE) represent the militant arm of the Tamil minority based mainly in the North and East of the country, but particularly active in the Jaffna peninsula. On the other hand the army of the Sinhalese majority has responded with force. The Rev. Ebenezer Joseph spoke movingly of 800,000 people spending ten years in refugee camps, of widows and orphans, of the ratio of women to men in Jaffna as 10 to 1.

2. The Committee on Church and Nation has taken up this issue because the civil war, and the role of the Christian churches within that, are not matters which are widely known or politically acute in Britain. Yet there are many refugees seeking asylum in this country. Further, the conflict is an instance of a distant war for which other countries provide the weapons. It is reported that some weapons come into Sri Lanka from Pakistan with Indian acquiescence, but most originate in former Soviet states which have many weapons but little money. Others come from earlier war zones where fighting has ceased.

3. In the situation left by Britain at independence there were some seeds of the future conflict. The British had already distinguished very clearly between the ethnic groups, preferring Tamils for civil service posts, while the bequest of a Westminster-type parliamentary system was found not to work well with such unequally-divided ethnic groups. But in the present there are three major and immediate barriers to peace in the country:

- *Party politics*
  Although an agreement facilitated by the British Foreign Office was reached in 1997 that issues concerning the ethnic conflict would be approached jointly by the two main political parties, this has not been honoured. Victory at the next election appears more important than co-operative peace making.

- *Development of "extremism"*
  On the one hand the LTTE have practised terrorism; on the other there are developments among the Sinhalese of groups such as the National Movement Against Terrorism, whose aim is to eliminate every terrorist by terrorist means.

- *Hardening of attitudes*
  Even without the extremists the terrorism of the LTTE has hardened general opposition among the Sinhalese, while the actions of the Sinhalese army, which include harassment and reported torture, harden general Tamil attitudes.

4. Devolution of power to the Tamils in the north and east has been proposed, but no satisfactory version has been found. Scottish-type devolution has been cited as an example, but the counter-argument runs that all parts of the country need some form of devolution. The people of Sri Lanka undoubtedly want peace, traumatised as they are by suffering injury, death and economic hardship, but up to now there has been little agreement, and less political will, concerning its achievement. The peaceful co-existence of different languages, histories and religions is not in sight thus far.

5. The most hopeful present possibility has come from Norway, which unilaterally, without any international organisation behind it, is attempting unbiased third party mediation at the request of both the President of Sri Lanka and the leader of the LTTE. Erik Solheim resigned his seat in the Norwegian Parliament to become a "peace envoy" charged with mediating between the warring sides and encouraging public debate on ways towards a negotiated settlement. His efforts, however, are at an early stage.

6. And what of the Sri Lankan churches in this situation? They form only 7.5% of the population while Buddhism is the major religion of the Sinhalese. Yet that majority feels itself threatened by the millions of Tamil Hindus in India beyond those in north Sri Lanka. Another 7.5% of the country is Moslem, and they are caught up in the maelstrom too. In 1990 the LTTE ordered 75,000 Moslems to leave their homes in the north. They are still in refugee camps. Given that Buddhists and Hindus are the main combatants, they must be the main actors in negotiating peace. But the local churches, of which the Roman Catholic is much the largest, do take initiatives in bringing their own ethnically mixed congregations together and encouraging further co-existence. Ebenezer Joseph emphasised that only in the Christian community do Tamils and Sinhalese come together for worship, while the churches also take on the humanitarian tasks of relief and rehabilitation. But because they welcome and are hospitable towards both sides they are also attacked by those hostile on both sides. Thus far Protestant and Catholic churches tend to work separately rather than ecumenically, and that may decrease their total impact.

7. Churches in Britain have their own role to play too. As a response to the Rev. Ebenezer Joseph's plea, and with sympathetic understanding of the situation, we may affirm in prayer and deed our solidarity with the churches of Sri Lanka, and with the multiple ethnic and religious groups, all of which have suffered. Further, though many Tamils may find it difficult to leave their country openly, and may face imprisonment if they return, many still seek asylum here. Last year about 5,500 Tamils applied for asylum in the UK, the second largest category of applicants after those from the former Republic of Yugoslavia. Since 1993 most applications for asylum from Sri Lanka people have been refused on grounds such as that there is no state of war in the country, though recently about half of these decisions have been overturned on appeal.

8. The Church could, moreover, be more concerned about the global trade in small arms. In the report on the International Arms Trade, attention is drawn to the frightening quantities of armaments readily accessible all over the world. The LTTE has been very astute in obtaining large numbers of arms by purchase from the global network of arms traders and by capture from the Sri Lankan army. Our tolerance of the export of UK manufactured weapons and the lack of effective UK and international control of the global arms trade help to make possible the atrocities committed by both sides in Sri Lanka. Finally, the Church of Scotland may encourage the UK Government to use its still significant influence in the region to encourage both sides to adhere to international laws concerning the conduct of war, the inadmissibility of torture and the implementation of human rights.

9. Sources

Sri Lanka: Making Peace Possible, Churches' Commission on Mission, Churches Together in Britain and Ireland, 2000.

Address to the General Assembly 2000, Rev. E. Joseph *Illicit Transfer of Conventional Weapons: The Role of State and Non-state Actors in South Asia, Small Arms Control*, UN Institute for Disarmament Research, Ashgate Press, Aldershot.

Caught in the Middle, a Study of Tamil torture survivors coming to the UK from Sri Lanka, Medical Foundation for the Care of Victims of Torture, 2000.

RACIAL JUSTICE

1. Introduction

1.1 In 1992 the Education Committee reported to the General Assembly on *Racism and the Church*. This report set out to provide guidelines for the Church as an employer, a guide to good practice for the committees and congregations of the Church, and a "racism-awareness" checklist for those involved in producing Church publications. There is no information recorded of how that report was taken up or of how it influenced the work of the Church. This year's report does not seek to diminish the importance of anything said at that time; rather its aim is to set the Church's concern for issues of racial justice in a wider context and to encourage an increased understanding of and involvement in that context.

1.2   Also in 1992, the Scottish Churches Agency for Racial Justice (SCARJ) was established to assist ACTS and its member churches to pursue racial justice work on an ecumenical basis. Funding for this work has never been set on a firm, reliable and long-term basis and last year the funding base provided by the churches all but disappeared, with only the Church of Scotland and the Methodist Church providing donations of appreciable size. This was to provide the impetus for a review not only of SCARJ and its work but also the work and commitment of the churches in Scotland to racial justice work in general. This review was carried out by the Rev Norman Shanks, Leader of the Iona Community, at the request of ACTS and his review and conclusions are considered later in this report (section 6).

1.3   Since 1992 there have been many changes in the churches and in the society they seek together to serve. Perhaps the most influential document to have been produced in that time has been the Stephen Lawrence Report, written by the McPherson Commission in the wake of the murder of Stephen Lawrence, the subsequent shambles of the police enquiry and the scandal of the failure to bring his assailants to justice. That report did more than any other to bring into popular parlance the concept of "institutional racism". Britain as a whole has since been viewed through the prism of this concept— and has in many instances and in many ways been found wanting. The churches, with the help of the Churches Commission for Racial Justice (CCRJ) of Churches Together in Britain and Ireland (CTBI), have tried also to look at themselves in the same way. CCRJ has held

two conferences on the subject; the Catholic Bishops' Conference of England and Wales produced a pamphlet in 1999 entitled *Serving a Multi-Ethnic Society* to help the Roman Catholic Church there to review its working in the light of the Lawrence Report; and the Church of England has instituted cultural awareness training for all levels up to and including its Archbishops.

1.4   In 2000 the Runnymede Trust[25] published the Parekh Report: *The Future of Multi-Ethnic Britain*, including a chapter on "Religion and Belief". "Multi-ethnicity" is in itself a concept just as defining as "institutional racism". It is a fact of and a function of globalisation, itself a descendant of imperialism, that economies and markets and therefore people become ever more intricately involved with one another. There are still, however, those in many parts of the world who try to hang on to monoethnic dreams; and we only have to look at the example of the former Yugoslavia, or of Fiji or Austria or Rwanda or Indonesia or Sri Lanka, to understand the dangers such dreams encapsulate for humanity. In these and other places there are destabilising forces at work, which attempt to divide people on the basis of race or religion or ethnicity. In our own country too such forces are never far from the surface.

1.5   A useful summary of the progress being made by the United Kingdom on matters of racial justice is provided by the observations of the United Nations Committee on the Elimination of Racial Discrimination. A brief account of these is included (section 3) which acknowledges progress as well as pointing up deficiencies.

1.6   It is perhaps in relation to immigration, refugees and asylum seekers that the most obvious opportunities arise for those who would wish to divide humanity. The iniquities of the voucher system for asylum seekers, the problems of racial abuse, the behaviour of some in the press and among politicians, all point to continuing problems in this area which require to be addressed. A speech last year by Home Office Minister Barbara Roche began to explore the benefits of immigration for a nation and we will want to develop that a little further (paras. 4.9–4.10). The 1981 Nationality Act, however, stands in direct opposition to any such development; it exercises a wide and malign influence on much that is done in our name and this report (para. 4.8) adds its weight to that of others who wish to see a complete overhaul of this piece of legislation.

1.7   Finally, what is the Church of Scotland to do in this area of concern and work? There are examples of good practice to follow, some of them our own. We hope that we can as a Church find new ways to make clear in all that we say and do that in Christ there is neither Jew nor Greek, and that all humanity is made in the image of God.

2.   The Lawrence and Parekh Reports

2.1   The Lawrence Report speaks of the setting of aims and targets and of establishing measures against which attainment can be set. For churches this means an analysis of the training of ministers and of the practices of management; it means an audit of the church in terms of its membership; and it means education for all in cultural awareness. Churches are challenged to make progress in all of these areas. There are certain prerequisites for doing this. Not only must we be open about what we do, we must also be open to doing things differently. As an organisation and as individuals we need enough humility to be able to be told when what we do or how we do it needs to be understood in a new way. One of the best avenues for this is to be found in the building of relationships. The work of The Well is described later in the report, but perhaps there is a need to repeat this kind of work on a wider area and on a greater scale.

2.2   Scotland has been described as the second whitest country in Europe (next to Iceland) and it has often been tempting to hide behind this to say that racism and racial justice are not issues here "because there are not enough of them". Such a way of thinking suggests that racism is caused by the presence of people from ethnic minorities. The truth, of course, is that victims should never be seen as the authors of their victimhood.

The murder in Edinburgh in 1989 of Axmed Abuukar Sheekh, and the subsequent court case, caused a crisis in community relations. The death in 1998 of Surjit Singh Chhokar, and the subsequent court cases, have had the same kind of effect. In the case of the latter it is to be hoped that the formal inquiries which have been ordered by the Lord Advocate can have an overdue influence in making Scotland take seriously its own problems.

We do our country no favours by trying to paint a false picture which encourages its people to ignore the truth and thus to do nothing to change it. To do this is to connive in injustice.

2.3   Racism is at its heart not an ethnographic issue but rather a spiritual one. If I experience fear, hesitancy, disdain, suspicion or even hatred merely because of the colour of a person's skin, that is an issue within me, which needs to be addressed. It is also a spiritual matter for the nation as a whole and the Church has a responsibility to help the nation tend its spiritual health. To pretend that we do not need to address such issues only makes the spiritual necessity all the more urgent.

2.4   The CTBI response to the Lawrence Enquiry suggests small, structured, relaxed group meetings taking place over a period of weeks during which people from different cultural backgrounds share the leadership of the group as well as sharing stories, faith, culture and time. The aim of such meetings is to break down the presumptions we make about one another, to see each other as people who have a great deal in common before we see one another as members of groups with different backgrounds and customs.

2.5   The *Parekh Report,* however, stresses the importance of giving due weight and importance to group belonging. The model for society commended there is that of "a community of communities":

> *The fundamental need ... is to treat people equally and to treat them with regard and respect for difference; to treasure the rights and freedoms of individuals and to cherish belonging, cohesion and solidarity. Neither equality nor respect for difference is a sufficient value on its own. The two must be held together, mutually challenging and supportive. Similarly, neither liberty nor solidarity is sufficient on its own. They too must be held together, qualifying and challenging each other, yet also mutually informing and enriching.* (Para. 8.5)

The simultaneous nurturing of equality and diversity is the challenge set down for the nation—to offer without threatening, to accept without feeling threatened.

2.6 When turning to the place of religion and belief within this community of communities, the Parekh Report recognises the important role played in Britain by churches and other faith communities. It acknowledges the resources which churches put at the disposal of the communities they serve. And it notes the traditional stance against racism adopted by the churches—as evidenced by such bodies as CCRJ and by its work to promote Racial Justice Sunday. It notes the specific religious anti-discrimination measures which are in place to protect Jews and Sikhs, asking why such legislation is not in place for other groups, notably Muslims. It questions the dominant role of the Church of England and perhaps, by extension, the Church of Scotland. And it examines "closed" and "open" views of "the other", a distinction and an examination which could be useful in discussing many kinds of division within society. The report also makes some specific recommendations concerning religious discrimination urging, in particular, that faith communities should ensure close connections between anti-racism and inter-faith work.

2.7 With much in this report, it will be easier for the Church to address issues concerned with the nation than to do so with those directly concerning the Church itself. Yet if we are to make a firm commitment to a society which is proud of its multi-cultural nature, we will have to be able as part of that to examine our own, many would say privileged, position. No particular recommendations are made about this here, save to plead that a conversation and a serious consideration be begun.

3. The Government's Record

3.1 The United Nations High Commissioner for Human Rights, Mary Robinson, has within her department the Committee on the Elimination of Racial Discrimination. In August 2000, this committee considered the record of the United Kingdom Government. They welcomed many developments since their last report. These included:

- the introduction of higher maximum penalties for racially motivated crimes;
- the introduction of a Human Rights Commission for Northern Ireland;
- the incorporation of the European Convention for the Protection of Human Rights and Fundamental Freedoms;
- the action plan occasioned by the Stephen Lawrence enquiry;
- the pro-active approach within the New Deal to introduce young members of ethnic and national minorities to the labour market;
- the recognition given to Irish and Roma travellers;
- the setting of targets for the employment of members of ethnic minorities in the Home Office, the police and prison services, the fire service and the armed forces.

3.2 There were matters, however, which they did not regard quite so positively:

- they expressed concern at continued racial harassment and increased feelings of vulnerability among members of ethnic minority communities;
- there was a feeling that the police service was not responding well to the recommendations of the Lawrence enquiry, indeed reference was made to a "backlash" among officers;
- a continuing worry about deaths in police custody was recorded and fully independent investigation into complaints against the police was called for.

3.3 Progress was also needed with regard to the high levels of unemployment among ethnic minority groups, racial harassment and bullying in schools and the disproportionately high levels of exclusion from school of ethnic minority members.

3.4 Turning to the matter addressed in section 4 below, the United Nations Committee recommended that the Government should *take leadership in sending out positive messages about asylum seekers and in protecting them from racial harassment*. They were also concerned that the effect of the dispersal of asylum seekers would be to separate them from expert legal advice and other appropriate services. This echoes the concerns outlined above and clearly represents an immediate problem which ought to be addressed with urgency.

3.5 The *Parekh Report* also has a long list of recommendations for action by government and others.

These are built around the central concepts of cohesion, equality and difference. They echo the United Nations worries concerning policing; they call for a review of the differences in sentencing policy in the courts; they ask schools and further and higher education establishments, in particular the inspectorate, to address issues of exclusion, language teaching, recruitment, teacher training, education for citizenship; they suggest a huge increase in translation services in the health service. They recommend, as we do below, that UK law on nationality be brought into line with international human rights standards. We recommend anyone interested in these and related issues to read the entire report, published by the Runnymede Trust.

4. Asylum and Immigration

4.1 The Church and Nation Committee has looked at the issue of asylum before. The Committee produced in 1997 a pamphlet entitled *Welcoming the Refugee* which addressed, among other matters, the issue of offering sanctuary to those facing deportation. Much work went in to that report at the time and the General Assembly supported it in spite of the controversy it aroused. The issue of asylum seekers has since then moved even further up the political agenda. Last year the General Assembly asked editors of newspapers to be careful about the language they used and to be accurate in the information they supplied. The language used by newspapers and by politicians has been generally more measured in the time since then. As a recent opinion poll showed, however, the perception of the public on issues concerning asylum seekers is a long way from the truth. The respondents overestimated by many times both the number of asylum seekers in Britain and the degree of support to which UK law entitles them.

4.2 Last year the Scottish churches, through the work of the Scottish Churches Parliamentary Office, supported a petition to the Scottish Parliament which called on the Parliament to restore the level of support to which asylum seekers had been entitled in Scotland before various pieces of Scottish legislation had been amended by the Asylum and Immigration Act 1999. Although these matters are reserved to Westminster, the Scottish Executive has undertaken to review the working of the Act in Scotland eighteen months after its introduction. Meanwhile the Social Inclusion Committee decided unanimously to follow up the petition which had been presented and to launch its own investigation, calling among its witnesses those who had raised the matter with them.

4.3 The Church of Scotland is represented by the Church and Nation Secretary and by The Well's Community Worker on the Scottish Parliament Cross-Party Group on Refugees and Asylum Seekers. The Scottish Churches Parliamentary Officer is also a member, as is a representative of SCARJ. This group seeks to monitor the work being done in Scotland to support those asylum seekers who have been dispersed to Scotland with a view to ensuring that the Scottish Parliament is kept abreast of developments; it also seeks to monitor the work of the Scottish Parliament committees where it comes into the area of the group's concern.

4.4 The Cross-Party Group made a submission to the review by the Home Office of the voucher system. This is a major concern for all those involved in this area as it means that asylum seekers have to use vouchers rather than cash to buy food and other essentials. This immediately marks them out as different, makes transition to a new society—already complicated—even worse. Additionally, the supermarkets and shops where the vouchers are used are not allowed to give change. This is both degrading and unfair. The submission argued that:

> *The voucher system must be abolished in its entirety. It is inefficient, costly and degrading and we cannot see any rationale for continuing with its use.*

This position was supported by all the members of the group and also by the Church's Board of Social Responsibility.

The company entrusted by the Government to administer this scheme is Sodexho who, coincidentally, run canteen facilities for both the Scottish Parliament and the Church of Scotland Offices. Sodexho insist that the target of protest ought to be the Government rather than themselves. The Church and the Parliament, however, will have to take note of the position.

4.5 Another continuing feature of the lives of asylum seekers is harassment and intimidation. The tradition of Scottish hospitality, a warm myth with which we like to console ourselves, often does not seem to be particularly well or even particularly alive. Even communal drying greens can become battlegrounds—literally a turf war—where other residents intimidate asylum seekers (usually women with young children). Public telephone boxes known to be used by asylum seekers become points of ambush by young men seeking to boost their own flagging self-esteem by attacking others. A report from the Scottish Refugee Council and the Save the Children Fund (*I Didn't Come Here for Fun, 2000*) indicates not only that official policy discriminates against the children of asylum seekers (contrary to the United Nations Convention on the Rights of the Child) but also a near universal experience among these children of verbal and physical harassment. There is a real and continuing need for the Church both to condemn such behaviour and also to support the work of many people of good will who seek to provide a real welcome and tangible help.

4.6 The work of Glasgow the Caring City is worthy of special mention here. It has, with the warm endorsement of the Presbytery of Glasgow, brought together a huge amount of practical aid from several congregations in Glasgow, many of them far from well-off. The effect of this is not simply to be measured in food or clothes but in the witness it provides to fellowship and common humanity. These congregations have opened their doors to asylum seekers coming in to their midst, and have found themselves enriched in the process. Working ecumenically they have been showing Christ's love through the offering of hospitality and the provision of English classes. This aid needs to be given sensitively and with care, taking account of the legal position of the recipients.

Less well known is the work of the Refugee Survival Trust, of which the Convener of the Church and Nation Committee is *ex officio* a trustee. The Trust provides grants to those whose situation leaves them without the means to survive, usually either because they are awaiting support from DSS or because DSS provision does not meet their needs (there is a glaring example of this in the case of pregnant women and mothers with new-born babies).

4.7 The Home Office made public in December 2000 a plan to use the former Dungavel Prison in South Lanarkshire as a detention centre for those awaiting deportation. Talks between the Home Office and South Lanarkshire Council are taking place at the time of writing. Reactions locally have focused on the hope for employment and concern for the local population. Just as important, however, will be the wellbeing of those who will be detained there. It is hoped that a Prison Visiting Committee can be reinstated to watch over their welfare. The Church will have an important rôle in undertaking chaplaincy work.

4.8 Christian Action for Justice in Immigration Law (CAJIL) believes that UK immigration law is in urgent need of review - and we agree. The first port of call for such a review ought to be the British Nationality Act 1981. The Act was introduced at a time of prejudice and xenophobia and was, in effect, an immigration measure based on excluding UK citizens from Britain on the basis of colour and ethnicity. The result of it is now that there are six categories of British national, only one of which carries any rights, particularly the right of entry to the UK. CAJIL has been correct to campaign for immigration legislation to be subject itself to the Race Relations Act and to comply fully and without restriction to the European Convention on Human Rights.

4.9 Immigration law and the regime which puts it into force has traditionally been based on the premise that immigration is a bad thing which therefore needs to be kept to a minimum, its harm kept under firm control. This presumption is one which has for a long time been in need of challenge. Britain is indeed a nation of immigrants—even the Celts came across Europe from the Russian Steppes. There is no reason to suppose that the movement of people around the world—whether for reason of war, famine, or simply looking for a better life—is a new phenomenon or intrinsically a bad thing. Those who went, and continue to go, from Scotland to other parts of the world looking for better standards of living or simply for jobs were not and are not described as "economic migrants" or as "scroungers"; they are seen simply as enterprising people trying to look after their families in the best way they know. We should not see those who come to these shores any differently.

4.10 We are becoming gruesomely accustomed to images of the trafficking in humanity which, feeding off desperation and profiting from suffering, disfigures our age. Immigration can, however, be seen both as a necessity and as a positive good. Barbara Roche, Home Office Minister, made a speech in September 2000 in which she began to acknowledge the positive aspects of immigration. She called for a debate about the rôle of immigration in our society and cited the view that immigration into the United States of America (11 million people in the 1990s) *has been the key to sustaining America's longest ever economic boom.* She pointed to the fact of labour shortages in Britain and to Britain's ageing demography. She included, in our view, still too much of an attempt to see immigration as good if the immigrants are rich and bad if they are poor: the Minister spoke of entry being dependent on a job offer *at a sufficiently high level* and of the number of millionaires among those who have come to Britain in the last forty years. We welcome, however, the attempt to move the debate on to a level which acknowledges the positive impact of immigration on our country.

5. The Church Response

5.1 The Board of Ministry recognises the importance of ministers having an informed awareness of issues of racial justice. There are four ways in which the Board can encourage such awareness, both directly and indirectly:

- by encouraging ministers to devote study leave to the pursuit of activities, either locally or overseas, which would enhance their knowledge of this aspect of ministry and subsequently by disseminating the experience of these ministers more widely through various available media;
- by including appropriate sessions on racial justice in their standard conference programme;
- by incorporating a racial awareness element in the initial training of ministers (along the lines of child

protection training);
- by making available additional resources to address the particular issues raised for ministers whose parishes have high concentrations of refugees, asylum seekers or people from ethnic minorities.

The Board of World Mission, through its Faithshare Programme, is also involved in setting up Study Leave opportunities to enable ministers to experience the work of our Partner Churches overseas. Both Boards will continue to encourage these developments.

5.2 The Board of National Mission supports the work of The Well in Glasgow. Local Christians who volunteer at The Well are made aware of racial justice issues through contact with their Asian neighbours; and the staff seek to raise awareness of racial justice issues when they share their work with church groups. The Well is also involved directly in supporting people who have suffered racial harassment and it is part of a pilot scheme initiated by Strathclyde Police which allows for third-party reporting of racial incidents through community agencies. The Well has been involved in asylum issues through the Scottish Churches' Parliamentary Office and gave evidence to the Scottish Parliament's Social Inclusion Committee about concerns in this area.

5.3 The Mission and Evangelism Resources Committee of the Board of National Mission last year noted the need for the Church to be trained in cultural awareness, recognising that we live in a multi-cultural society. It was therefore remitted to Catriona Milligan, Community Worker at The Well, to develop materials appropriate for use throughout Scotland. This work is in progress with support from other denominations and agencies who already have training programmes in place.

5.4 The Guild Discussion Topic for 2001–2002 is "Overcoming Violence". Within this issues of racial justice are raised. It is possible that a future Discussion Topic will take up the theme directly as a further contribution to the World Council of Churches Decade to Overcome Violence.

5.5 The churches in Scotland have co-operated in matters of racial justice through the ACTS agency, SCARJ. In 2000 this agency faced a financial crisis caused by the withdrawal of financial support from the Scottish Episcopal Church and the Roman Catholic Church in Scotland. It seemed that this was a good time, therefore, to undertake a widespread consideration of how the Scottish churches have engaged with issues of racial justice. Norman Shanks was asked to conduct such a review.

5.6 The Shanks Review was commissioned by the Central Council of ACTS. We were therefore very grateful for the opportunity to read what was in effect a piece of work still in process and to incorporate its findings in our report.

6.   The Shanks Review

6.1 The Review pays tribute to the work achieved since 1992 by SCARJ and draws attention to its wide range. Importantly it points out that it has never been the aim of SCARJ to be involved in issues of racial justice *on behalf* of the churches, but rather to be the means by which the churches involve *themselves* in that work. This point is then used to narrow what SCARJ itself might hope to achieve. Thus, in the three areas set out by the SCARJ Committee in 2000 (mainstreaming racial justice work, creating alliances between member churches and black communities to tackle racial disadvantage, challenging institutional racism), it is recognised that the bulk of work in all of these areas is the work of the churches themselves. The rôle of SCARJ in the achievement of these aims is:

to be a catalyst and resource, to stimulate, encourage, support and help co-ordinate the efforts and activities of the churches working within and on behalf of their own constituencies and campaigning where necessary together.

6.2 There is wide agreement that this cannot and will not be achieved without an employed person - and we come therefore to the issue of finance. It is suggested that a new arrangement be entered into whereby a worker be employed and supported by CCRJ using money contributed by the churches both to SCARJ and to CCRJ. (The combined total of money to these two organisations from the Church of Scotland in 2000 was £13,480.) It will be vitally important for all the churches in Scotland to maintain a financial commitment to this work—

approaches in recent time to trusts have elicited the fair and obvious response that, if the churches want this work done, the churches should be paying for it. It is always good to put our money where our mouths are.

The creation is also suggested of a Scottish Reference Group to work alongside CCRJ and its Scottish worker; this group would continue much of the current work of SCARJ.

It is perhaps helpful here to quote in full the recommendation concerning the worker:

The primary task of the worker should be focussed on raising awareness and activity concerning racial justice within the Scottish churches, so that familiarity with church structures as well as experience and commitment on racial justice issues should be prerequisites for the person appointed. Such other aspects as involvement in political campaigning and combatting institutional racism, and direct engagement with black and minority ethnic communities, whether locally or nationally, should be regarded as for the churches themselves, with the worker providing support and resource material.

6.3 This suggested arrangement holds much promise and is a positive way forward for the vital and necessary work in this field. We believe this not only because it puts the work of an ecumenical agency on a clear and firm footing, but also because it makes clear the responsibility of the churches, individually and collectively, to carry on their own work for racial justice - not simply relying on others to do this on their behalf. It is proposed to hold a meeting involving CCRJ, church representatives and SCARJ Committee members to map the next steps in some detail. The Church of Scotland should commit itself to this meeting, to the structures suggested by the Review, and to continued funding at or above the current level.

---

[25] The Runnymede Trust was founded in 1968 and is the foremost UK-based independent think tank on ethnic and cultural diversity. It sees its rôle as being to challenge racial discrimination, to influence anti-racist legislation and to promote a successful multi-ethnic Britain. It is funded by voluntary donations.

A HUMAN RIGHTS COMMISSION FOR SCOTLAND

1.1 At the 1999 General Assembly the Church & Nation Committee presented, as part of its Report, a paper on Human Rights illustrating and explaining them and giving a theological perspective on them. This part of the Report ended as follows:

We accept that understanding what such a commitment [to universal human rights] means in practical terms will involve us in a continual intellectual struggle; trying to live out our commitment in what we say and do as a church, as congregations and as individuals, will involve us in continuing effort and in finding a willingness in ourselves to give up what we prize as our own rights. The vision which beckons us, however, is of a world where human rights are not defined by their absence but one where the wholeness of creation is celebrated in community with each other and in our relationship with God who loves us all.

1.2 Related to this part of the Report the Assembly approved a number of deliverances, of which two were as follows:

46. Recognising that upholding human rights involves a continuing theological and practical struggle to maintain a balance between the rights of individuals and of communities, encourage Church members to take responsibility through prayer and action for the rights of others.

47. Encourage the Scottish Parliament to make respect for human rights integral to its work.

1.3 It might be thought that this issue, having been examined so recently by the Committee, warranted no further examination for a while. However, matters have since moved on considerably, requiring the subject to be re-visited.

2.   Legal background

2.1 The 1998 Human Rights Act enshrines into United Kingdom law all the rights set out in the European Convention on Human Rights. This Act came into force on 2nd October 2000. The rights protected by the Convention are very extensive, including among others the right to life, the right to privacy and the rights to freedom of expression, to a fair trial, to education and to freedom from discrimination.

2.2 Since 1st July 1999, as a result of the 1998 Scotland Act, the Scottish Executive has been open to challenge in the courts in Scotland if, in its decisions or its failure to act, it has infringed any of these rights and freedoms. The result has been a number of well reported challenges to the Executive.

2.3 Now, however, every public authority in Scotland—and indeed, throughout the United Kingdom—and any body fulfilling a public function (which might include many private companies, voluntary organisations and churches) is also liable to challenge by any member of the public if he or she believes that this body has infringed their rights under the Convention. This has significant implications for all such bodies, not only for the Executive, not only for public authorities but also, for example, for hospitals, prisons and, as stated, many others when fulfilling a public function.

2.4 As yet there is widespread ignorance, not only among the public in general but also within many public authorities, concerning the effect and importance of these provisions.

2.5 Against this background the Scottish Human Rights Forum (an informal group of organisations which include ACTS) has been pressing for approximately two years for the creation of a Human Rights Commission for Scotland. The Justice Minister of the Scottish Executive has accepted the need to issue for circulation a Consultation Paper on this subject so that, it is hoped, such a Commission might be established if questions of funding, independence and function can be resolved.

3.   Benefits of a Commission

3.1 In an area of such importance the Church should, we believe, lend its support to those pressing for the creation of such a Commission, for the following reasons:

• Such a Commission would raise awareness within the

general public of what rights they have and could provide advice and information on them, although we would not envisage it having a "campaigning" role. To enable it to achieve such awareness, of course, there would need to be accessibility and openness for the public to the Commission, but this should be possible to attain.

- Such a Commission could provide benefits to the voluntary sector by giving guidance in this area of the law, which is a grey area for many at present.
- Such a Commission could benefit the Scottish Parliament by providing an independent expert view on legislation.
- Such a Commission could also benefit the Scottish Executive along similar lines, though it would require to be fully independent of the Executive.
- Such a Commission could benefit public authorities in Scotland who must not act in ways that are incompatible with the Convention. Advice on this could prove invaluable to authorities.
- Finally, such a Commission could help advance the aims of both deliverances set out above and approved previously by the Assembly.

3.2   Although it might be argued that as no such Commission is yet proposed for England and Wales and that Scotland should await that event first, we see no advantage in delay. It should be noted that a Human Rights Commission already exists in Northern Ireland. Contrary to expectation, it deals with a very broad range of issues, not only matters relating to the Troubles or the Peace Process. Human Rights legislation is now in force here and in order to advise on it, to oversee its effectiveness and to bring about public awareness in Scotland of these rights, there could be no more effective means than a Human Rights Commission. Further, given that there will often be a particularly Scottish dimension to the issues raised, a Commission for Scotland seems essential.

3.3   Nor do we see any insuperable difficulties in dealing with such issues as funding or the Commission's relationship to other bodies. The Scottish Human Rights Forum has already prepared a helpful discussion paper exploring these issues—*A Human Rights Commission for Scotland: March 2000*—and with good will on all sides it should be possible to resolve any problems presented. We would wish to stress at this stage that it is our wish that the Commission be made answerable to the Scottish Parliament (not to the Executive) and that it should be given adequate resources to enable it to function effectively, receive adequate powers for its task and be capable of responding urgently when a situation requires this.

3.4   We would commend the creation of a Human Rights Commission for Scotland to the General Assembly. In our view, there would be no better way of implementing the deliverances of 1999 and no better way of showing how seriously the Church of Scotland takes such rights than for us to give our backing to it.

THE POLITICAL PROCESS: COMMUNICATION, CONSULTATION, INVOLVEMENT AND ACCOUNTABILITY

Constitutional change in Scotland has taken place against the backdrop of other, wider changes in government and in the political culture. Whereas devolution took place at a specific time, which allows for relatively straightforward analysis, other developments in the political system have emerged gradually, and continue to evolve. Inevitably, one has an effect upon the other and it is not always possible to separate devolution-related changes from those which have their source in other shifts.

The themes which arise—communication, consultation, involvement and accountability in the political process—are not exclusive to Scotland. There is much to discuss and to cause concern in the relationships between the UK government and the media, and in what has been called the dumbing down of democracy. As part of the UK, Scotland is affected by these trends (if they exist) and cannot escape national and international influences of these kinds. Yet as a country with a devolved parliament and distinct systems, Scotland has its own set of circumstances and this merits separate consideration.

We attempt, therefore, in this Report to survey the progress being made and the problems being faced in the Scottish political process today. Section 1 deals with the Parliament and its attempts to live up to the expectations invested in it. Sections 2 and 3 look at the vexed question of Quangos and at the issues of accountability they raise, particularly as evidenced by the events of last summer concerning the Higher results. Section 4 picks up the subject of local government reform. These can all be examined separately, but they are presented here together because they ought to form a coherent whole. Where the different pieces of government machinery do not fit neatly together or grind one another down, there is clearly something amiss. Parliament, Executive and Council need to work together for the good of the people.

This Report needs also to be read in conjunction with last year's report on Public Life in Scotland Today. There we affirmed our support for those engaged in or employed in public life. It is because we believe that public life is important and indeed vital for the well being of the nation that we believe it important for the Church to understand and comment on how it is organised. We need to assure ourselves that the people of Scotland are being served well.

1.   The Scottish Parliament

1.1   As we approach the second anniversary of the establishment of the Scottish Parliament, we have the opportunity to consider what parts the Parliament and the Scottish Executive have come to play in post-devolution Scotland, and the ways in which they are shaping and adapting to the evolving political environment.

1.1.1   At the time of the referendum, and leading up to the Scottish Parliament elections in 1999, there was much discussion of "the new politics" or "consensus politics". Coalition, or partnership, government—not seen in the United Kingdom since the war—added to the idea that the practice of consensus politics was possible. But, properly understood, consensus politics goes deeper than one party, denied an overall majority by a new system of proportional representation, coming to an agreement with the smallest party in the Parliament. The new politics, we were told, would involve listening to the people and an abandonment of party political squabbling. Now,

nearly two years on, commentators ask, "Is this really the new politics?" or "Can there be such a thing as the new politics?"

1.1.2   Questions about the nature of our politics go to the heart of what it means to live in a democratic society and to be governed by elected representatives. Is there a central paradox? The servant of the people must lead the people. Should the government follow public opinion, or form public opinion? Should it attempt to do both, or neither?

1.1.3   In one sense, the Church is peculiarly well placed to offer comment on the service of leadership. Christ, the servant King, listened and led, listens and leads. Christ, who washed the feet of the disciples and who sought no glory in leadership, taught and guided and inspired. The Church, in attempting to follow this pattern, ought to know something about the difficulty of serving and leading. As a Church, we are also familiar with the competing demands of working simultaneously with the poor and the rich. Our calling is to share Christ's bias to the poor and to speak for those who have no voice, but we recognise that the temptations of power are very great. As a Church we struggle, and sometimes fail, to get the balance right. We may find ourselves too keen to be popular and to be in with the leaders, and neglect the difficult and lonely task of saying what is right. This enables us to recognise the challenge which faces those in power in the choice between comfortable focus group approval and uncomfortable adherence to principle

1.1.4   There is an argument that government is not about leadership at all. Rather, it is argued, government exists to facilitate the functioning of society and should do no more than the minimum necessary to defend the nation, maintain law and order and, perhaps, to make some provision for the destitute. "Big government", it is argued, is expensive, intrusive, and threatens our rights and freedoms. We believe, however, that leadership is a critical function of government and that it is essential to the health of the nation for there to be a democratic structure at the pinnacle of which are responsible and accountable leaders. Furthermore, we believe that public service of this kind is honourable and is to be upheld. As Christians, we owe a duty to our leaders, as a minimum, to support them in prayer.

1.1.5 Of course, it is equally an essential part of a healthy democratic process that the nation's leaders heed the concerns of their electors. And as Christians, and as a Church, we also have a duty to speak clearly on what we believe to be just and right.

1.1.6 Are our politics truly new? It might be argued that in one sense our politics are new. There is much discussion of ideological divisions being eroded and of there no longer being a left and a right. Political analysis seems to focus on the battle for the middle ground and on "the third way". In a different sense, it may be thought that the new constitutional settlement has been accompanied by a new culture. There is, however, a danger in characterising devolved Scottish politics as new and good and Westminster politics as old and bad. The difference is not that easy. Certain simplified procedures, the higher profile of Committees, public involvement in the legislative process and greater accessibility are to be very warmly welcomed. The ways in which the founding principles of the Consultative Steering Group have thus been given effect are to be applauded. At the same time we recognise that MPs continue to play a valuable role. As a Committee, we have maintained our annual Westminster visit and we have been encouraged by the responses of MPs from all parties. When visiting Westminster we meet backbenchers and have the opportunity to discuss issues of importance which are reserved to Westminster. This is very valuable to the Committee and we are very grateful to the MPs we meet for giving us their time and for sharing their views. We place a high value on this continuing contact and we appreciate the benefits which are gained through speaking to politicians from all parties at Westminster.

1.1.7 Taking decisions closer to home is an advantage for the Scottish Parliament and the Scottish Executive. But is this advantage used to the full? In the present circumstances in Scotland, any government, and a parliament of any composition, would have difficulty in meeting expectations. Devolution was and is about much more than a new style of politics. The Executive and the Parliament are having to cope with unprecedented demands, and from different directions. They are having

to deal with a huge range of "firsts", with pressure to be different from London, and to conform to London practices, and with pressure to be as good as or better than London. They also have to deal with cynicism and with impatience. Perhaps the defensiveness of those involved in pointing to the record of the first year is understandable. And, objectively, in terms of legislative progress, the record is creditable. The Parliament has approached major areas of law reform responsibly and has dealt with important, heavyweight legislation without fuss. There may not always have been a lot to read in the newspapers about the Standards in Scotland's Schools Act or the Adults with Incapacity (Scotland) Act, but these measures were necessary, and demanding in terms of scrutinising consideration. Condemnations of the "it's achieved nothing" type are simply inaccurate.

1.2 *Consultation*

1.2.1 Consultation is one of the political catchwords of the past three years. As a notion and as a process, it has been taken up enthusiastically in Scotland. The obligation on the Scottish Executive to consult on its legislative proposals is reflected in the Standing Orders of the Scottish Parliament. (Rule 9.3 provides that the Policy Memorandum accompanying an Executive Bill must set out the consultation, if any, which was undertaken on the objectives of the Bill and the ways of meeting them or on the detail of the Bill and a summary of the outcome of that consultation.) The same Standing Orders provide for the Committees of the Scottish Parliament to take evidence on Bills at the Stage 1 consideration of general principles. That evidence, on form so far, has come from a wide range of sources. Given that the opposite is the imposition of law with no regard to public feeling and that, in that way, we end up with measures as unpopular as the poll tax, consultation is to be welcomed. However, for it to be meaningful, consultation must be of good quality. Certain questions need to be asked.

1.2.2 Who is being consulted? All of the Scottish Executive consultation papers are published on its website and "those interested" are invited to respond. Sometimes the consultation paper makes it clear that responses from certain types of groups, or people, will be particularly welcome. Some consultation papers are specifically sent to certain companies and organisations. How are these mailing lists drawn up? Can you apply to be put on a mailing list? Who decides whose views are to be given special regard? We warmly welcome the moves made by the Scottish Executive to bring coherence to the consultation system, and, in particular, we are encouraged by the direction of the Scottish Executive's Policy Unit project on civic participation.[26] We welcome the fact that civil servants and ministers are giving thought to methods of improving the consultation process. The commitment made by the then Finance Minister in June 2000 to clear rules for consultations—and perhaps especially to the minimum 12 week period—is a very positive step.

1.2.3 Should all consultation responses be regarded equally? If not, who determines the ranking? Some consultation papers are wide open; others much more narrowly focused. Is it the rôle of the Executive to say, "Please select A or B" or should we be given blank sheets? At what stage of policy formulation should consultation take place? This goes to the heart of the question about the role of government leadership. Crucially, does the Executive come with its own agenda, for which it seeks public approval, or is it looking for new ideas? If it doesn't have its own proposals, why not? And if it does, will it stick to them in the event of an adverse reaction? Which principle takes precedence? The principle on which the policy is based, or the principle of acting in accordance with public wishes?

1.2.4 Concerns have been expressed from many directions about the volume of work involved in responding to consultations. Consultation papers are, or appear to be, issued in increasing number and with increasing frequency. In addition, the time allowed for responding is often very short. Whilst it is important to move ahead with legislation, rapid fire consultation will not produce quality responses and will lead to disenchantment with the process. It may be that in some cases where the matters are very complex, the 12 week minimum will be insufficient. Where voluntary organisations and other institutions are being consulted, particular issues arise. First, most organisations have their own structures of accountability and responses must be agreed within them and with the involvement of a number of people. This can take time. Secondly, for many organisations, this has serious implications for resources.

1.2.5 Feedback is extremely important. For consultation to be meaningful, it is essential that the consulted are truly involved. The purpose of the consultation should be made clear at the outset. There ought to be no expectation on the part of the consultee that his or her contribution will be accepted in its entirety, acted upon and incorporated in legislation. However, there is a legitimate expectation that each serious contribution will be considered and that a response will be issued. For the health of the process, it is important to ensure that each response is acknowledged. Summaries of responses received are useful. More importantly, reasons for the choice of a particular course of action should be issued. The format of the consultation needs to be considered. The written word is very efficient, and is the most widely used communication tool, but it may not be appropriate in all circumstances. The articulate enjoy a special advantage and the needs of those who experience difficulties in communication for whatever reason must be considered.

1.3   *Public involvement*

1.3.1 Consultation is perhaps the most obvious way in which the government involves the public in its programme. Consultation papers are not the last word and there must be ever evolving ways of communicating. Perhaps it is the relatively small size of Scotland which leads to a culture of "the usual suspects". Élites exist. Paradoxically they struggle not to be élitist, but it is easier to talk to the same, known people. The Church is involved in that struggle too. The efforts of those who do try to be inclusive are of great value and all support should be given to them.

1.3.2 Time, money and hope have been invested in the Civic Forum, an organisation which aims to meet the needs of numerous bodies in the voluntary sector and in wider society in their communications with the Scottish Parliament and with the Executive. It is to be hoped that the role of the Civic Forum will continue to evolve and that it will come to play a helpful, linking part in the processes. It is not yet possible to say whether this promise will be fulfilled.

1.3.3 One aspect of public involvement not often addressed, other than in the weeks leading up to an election, is voter turnout. Voter apathy does receive some attention, but merits more. We are concerned that disinterest quickly deteriorates into cynicism. It is not good enough to retreat from responsibility by saying that one lot of politicians is as bad as the next and that none deserves a vote. This attitude undermines public service as a whole and demeans the state and society. Civic education is to be encouraged and we would welcome steps to improve this type of development. Disillusionment in the democratic system is a serious concern to the Committee; and this is an area in which we plan to develop our work.

1.3.4 An associated question concerns the decline in membership of political parties. In our eagerness to get away from party political bickering, there is a danger that we lose sight of the value of party membership. Political parties can be campaigning organisations, not just power vehicles. Credit should be given to those behind the scenes whose commitment to an ideal, perhaps in the face of disillusionment, keeps democratic party structures functioning. Is there a place for such commitment in acceptance of consensus politics? We believe that there is.

1.3.5 We recognise that changing ways in government place pressures not just on politicians but on those whose job it is to maintain the links between government and people. We are privileged as a country to have a civil service with a commitment to duty. And, as the Committee said in last year's report to the General Assembly, we believe that public service is a good to be cherished. Although many civil servants feel that they are doing their work best when they are invisible, this can lead to the perception that they are not subject to scrutiny and that their activities are secretive and protective of their positions. Where this meets with reality, it is to be deplored, but to see this as the chief characteristic of the civil service is to diminish and degrade the important work carried out by dedicated officials.

1.4   *Public action*

If low voter turnout is a problem and it appears that too few people are interested in the welfare of the country, can we complain when individuals organise in less conventional ways to put across their points of view? Political expression takes different forms. We have been concerned in our approach to consider ways in which the government relates to and communicates with the people. It is equally important to consider how the people respond to and communicate with the government. It is our intention in the future year to give consideration to the changing ways in which members of the public express their views. Also, as a Church, communication is a continuing challenge. We need to maintain our awareness so that the part we play is full, informed and responsible.

2.   Quasi-Autonomous Non-Governmental Organisations

2.1   Introduction

2.1.1 In our Report to the General Assembly 2000 on Public Life in Scotland Today, the Committee indicated that the involvement and accountability of quangos in the provision of public services needed to be examined.

2.1.2 In undertaking such an enquiry, the Committee recognises that a more general study is required than the system of making public appointments. This is especially so since the Scottish Executive has announced a review of the system of selection and begun to look more rigorously at the organisational concept.

2.1.3 The recent adverse publicity affecting the Scottish Qualifications Authority (SQA) and the Scottish Tourist Board has raised concern amongst the public as to the efficiency, responsibility and accountability of quangos to Ministers, the Civil Service and the Parliaments of the United Kingdom. In turn Ministers have been sucked into crisis management and political embarrassments from the actions of bodies which were originally set up as buffers to implement policy established by Ministers. So important are the issues arising from the SQA debacle that section 3 is devoted to that specific discussion.

2.1.4 The role of quangos also interacts with that of local government and the delivery of local services. Elected councils have lost many functions to new non-elected bodies which have been established by central government to by-pass local government and the views of local electors. It is therefore important to study the emergence of what has been called the "quango state" and its impact on the organs of government following the creation of the Scottish Parliament.

2.2 The Quango State

2.2.1 In recent years there has been an explosion in the number of quasi-autonomous non-governmental organisations. That term, however, is applied to a range of bodies with different powers and different relationships to government so that the term has largely been replaced in official publications as NDPB or a non-departmental public body, which the Cabinet Office describes as *a body which has a role in the process of national government.* This means a national or regional public body operating independently of Ministers, but for which Ministers are ultimately responsible. Such bodies are not part of a government department and function independently at arm's length from them. They therefore operate, to a greater or lesser extent, at arm's length from Ministers. They are neither administered by the civil service nor are they civil servants, although civil servants may be seconded to them. Employees are the employees of the quango and responsible to the quango or its board.

2.2.2 There are executive quangos like Scottish Enterprise and the SQA, advisory quangos like the Local Government Boundary Commission, tribunal bodies like the children's panels, and a myriad of others like some housing associations and all health trusts. But they all have something in common. They are appointed by government patronage; they obtain their funds from central government; and they are accountable, directly or indirectly, to central and not local government.

2.2.3 Quangos are very useful bodies for Ministers. They recruit expertise to put flesh on government policies and give valuable cover to Ministers over the allocation of public funds and the delivery of public services. If they did not exist, they would have to be invented! There

are around 120 quangos operating in Scotland today with an annual budget of £6.5 billion, close to one third of the Scottish Executive spending.

2.2.4 A reason why quangos have expanded so readily within the body politic is encapsulated in this quotation from *Political Power and Democratic Control in Britain* (Stewart Weir and David Beetham) pp.203-4:

> *as they are by definition adaptable and easily established, quangos allow central government fairly easily to set up mechanisms outside existing structures and relatively free from political opposition and formal checks in order to meet its political needs and carry out its policies. They are in this sense the flexible friends of central government. The creation of new hierarchies of control in school and further education show how quickly this political scaffolding can be rigged up.*

2.3 Scrutiny and Openness

2.3.1 A cloak has been thrown over the extent to which ministers and civil servants are involved in the supervision of the bodies which they have established. Ostensibly, these organisations are supplied with their own boards and staff. They are given funds and they publish reports which are circulated to MPs, MSPs and the press, previously occasionally laid before Westminster and even more occasionally discussed in an Estimates Day in the Scottish Grand Committee.

2.3.2 Prior to the establishment of the Scottish Parliament, the Scottish Office was perceived to be a secretive, somewhat arrogant, organisation which was allowed to be so because of the absence of both Ministers and MPs in London. It was only rarely that its impenetrable workings broke into the public gaze. Even within the relatively short time the Scottish Parliament has been in place, a fuller picture is emerging. There are now many active politicians quarrying information from the Scottish Executive and the Committee system promises to put Ministers and civil servants through the hoops. In common with other institutions in Scotland, the civil service is having to accommodate itself to a challenging transitional phase.

2.3.3 A break-through in relation to quangos came with the demands by the Parliament and its Committees for civil service papers relating to the advice given to the Education Minister prior to the investigation of the Scottish Qualifications Authority scandal. Although the outcome in October 2000 was a compromise under which the Committee Convener and Deputy Convener were able to scrutinise papers on behalf of their Committee, nevertheless the rules of the Parliament give it power in future to obtain primary documents blocked to Westminster under the Civil Service Code. It is likely therefore that the great benefit to government of the inscrutability of quangos will be lost.

2.3.4 The First Minister Henry McLeish announced on 13 November 2000 that the whole operations and existence of quangos were now to be re-examined.

2.4   The Patronage State

2.4.1 Quangos have become embarrassing. Bad publicity (the Scottish Arts Council budgeting, the nature of the appointment of the Caledonian-MacBrayne chairman, the Scottish Tourist Board and the SQA to give a few examples) has been accompanied by an impression of sleaze and political patronage which could do damage to a government working in the light of the Nolan Report and under the watchful eye of the Neil Committee.

2.4.2 While many people serve on the various organisations without reward, it is equally well known that a sinecure on a quango can be a good way of topping up a pension. When governments change one set of office-holders departs to be replaced by more politically reliable friends, if not party colleagues in need of an opportunity. And in all of this the processes of selection bring in the professional élites with very little recruitment from the people at large, despite the notional advertising. They are also not accountable to the public they serve.

2.4.3 While the boards may have around 3,900 members, it is reckoned that the real power is wielded by around 100 people who form the narrow professional and political elite available to a small country. Some quango

members hold more than one office and, with processes of selection in the hands of a range of unaccountable people, there is a danger of self-perpetuating oligarchies. It is estimated that quango boards are predominately male, middle aged, and middle class, with only 0.05% of membership coming from the ethnic minorities.

2.4.4 We recognise the value of the work done by many people in the provision of public service, the majority of whom give their time without remuneration. In cases where members do receive remuneration, it is variable and inconsistent. We do not disagree with remuneration in itself in appropriate circumstances. We do believe, however, that the system should be transparent and subject to scrutiny by the Parliament.

2.5   The Future

2.5.1 There is a view that many quangos have gone past their sell-by date and that something must be done. The problem is what will replace them. Many quangos provide essential services. The fabric of society could be harmed by their unthinking demise.

2.5.2 In any review, we must go back to first principles and answer three tests: Does the quango serve any useful purpose and does it deserve to remain? If it does, to whom should it be accountable? Could the work be done better by local government or under direct control of ministers?

2.5.3 The whole skein of government in Scotland has changed with the creation of the Scottish Parliament. Opportunities exist now to change the way we are governed in a new democratic, open and accountable fashion. There should be no rigid thought processes from the past. The administration of government should be seen as an integrated process with local government, central government and the Parliament all working together. It may be more efficient for certain national functions to become the responsibility of Ministers through the Civil Service or through executive agencies, and answerable to Parliament and the Committees of the Parliament.

3.   Accountability: The Scottish Qualifications Authority as a Test Case

3.1 In *Responsibility and Christian Ethics*, William Schweiker says that accountability is *important for the discourse of praise and blame*; it is, he says, *basic to assigning culpability to persons, to establishing the grounds and the limits of praise and blame*. Nothing could illustrate that more vividly than the first Scottish Parliamentary debate on the SQA/exams crisis, as one politician after another argued that "somebody must be called to account for what has happened." The urgency over the fairly complex issue of accountability, following the debacle of late and inaccurate results, seemed very much to be about who the blame could be pinned on, or who should resign.

3.2   *Governance of the SQA*

3.2.1 The SQA was established by statute in 1996, merging the previous Scottish Examination Board (SEB) and Scottish Vocational Education Council (SCOTVEC). Its general functions are (a) to devise qualifications; (b) to determine the entitlement of individuals to SQA qualifications and, where a person is so entitled, award and record such a qualification; (c) to keep under review and develop SQA qualifications; (d) to approve education and training establishments as being suitable for presenting persons for SQA qualifications; and (e) to make arrangements for, assist in or carry out the assessment of persons undertaking education and training.

3.2.2 The arrangements for the governance of the SQA and its relationship with Ministers have been seen by Parliamentary Committees as "reasonably standard for an NDPB", that is there were formal Ministerial powers to control and to give directions (as defined by statute), more specific arrangements contained in a Management Statement and Financial Memorandum, and regular meetings. The Ministerial power to *give directions of a general or specific character with regard to the discharge of its functions* was a key point of conflict in the debate, at least in the early stages, especially after the Minister declared to Parliament that he had "absolutely no powers to instruct the SQA to do anything." Clearly, there was a

lack of clarity about responsibilities (as the Committee reports note). It appears that Ministers and their civil servants were unclear as to the precise scope of their powers with regard to the SQA—how much could they probe behind the assurances they were given that everything would be "all right on the night", and how much could they legitimately direct the SQA as to how to go about its business? There is no express power to enforce any directions given; and the Executive and the SQA apparently saw the power to direct as a "measure of last resort" (though it is hard to see what circumstances would justify its use if those of last summer did not). There can be no doubt that lack of clarity and the tensions which came from that contributed to the problems.

3.2.3 The Committees also recognised the distinctive, almost unique nature of the SQA as an NDPB. Distinctive areas include (a) funding, only 21% of which comes from the Executive (b) the large number of "stakeholders" closely involved in management through Board membership (c) shared responsibility between two Executive Ministers and (d) the role of assessing Executive performance. The Committee felt that this encouraged the SQA to take a *rather more robust attitude with the Executive than might be expected of a wholly dependent organisation*. That "robust attitude" meant that the Executive did not have the "hard core" information about SQA performance which might have provoked a more pro-active policy. At times, it seems, the Executive was phoning the SQA to check on information it had gleaned from the media. However, both Committees found that the Executive had become more and more interventionist as the problems emerged; this was described by a senior civil servant as bearing *no relation to the normal relationship between an NDPB and the (Executive) department*.

3.2.4 The Education Committee had to conclude that the Executive had been *ineffective in preventing the problems*; and the SQA had clearly failed to deliver on its core business. In the aftermath of these problems, the faith that moving such bodies to arm's length would secure effective delivery of services seems evidently misplaced. The reports argue for new management strategies and structural changes towards making SQA work more effectively, but there remain ongoing issues of accountability or responsibility.

3.3   *Accountability*

3.3.1 Is accountability just a part of the culture of blame, a pointer on the road to litigation or recrimination? Does it fuel the partisan break up of the Committee's consensus by making the Executive parties defensive and the opposition seek to score cheap points? Or is it an ingredient of good governance?

3.3.2 Some of those angered by the Minister remaining in post, as the Chief Executive resigned and further mistakes were revealed, thought wistfully of Presidents who believed that "the buck stops here", and of old-fashioned Westminster ideas of ministerial responsibility. But this was an "arm's length" agency, not, it was said, subject to the direction of the Minister(s). Since the Committees did not find the Minister culpable, his task was to ride out the storm and to get the agency back on track. One academic lawyer gave evidence to the Committee that *Whereas the Minister is obliged to give an account of anything that has gone wrong within the area of responsibility, it does not follow that the Minister is personally culpable for all errors of administration, far less obliged to resign when such errors occur.* Yet the Scottish Executive's own evidence on the nature of NDPBs states that *the Minister is ultimately answerable for the performance of an NDPB.*

3.3.3 As the Executive largely succeeded in moving the debate on to securing the future rather than raking over the past, and in moving the Minister on to new responsibilities, accountability dropped down the agenda. It figured hardly at all in the independent Deloitte Touche report, which focused much more on effective management strategies, and the Parliamentary Committee reports were very much oriented to effective operation in future, although there does seem to be momentum in reviewing the position of quangos or NDPBs.

3.3.4 Clear definition of responsibilities seems an important part of the solution, but in which direction should matters be clarified? Sam Galbraith, then Minister

of Education, put it this way: *Whatever happens, the Minister gets it. The question that is often asked is "if Ministers are going to get it, why don't they just take responsibility for the organisation".* Many people would agree that accountability has to depend on power, that is that ministerial responsibility only makes sense on the understanding that Ministers ultimately have the power to get the job done in the way they want it done. If we believe that they should not have that power (because political interference gets in the way of getting the job done), we should accept that they cannot be held responsible when things go wrong. The democratic deficit is, then, the price to be paid; and accountability belongs to the person with the operational power, the Director or Chief Executive.

3.3.5 What is apparent here is that there are questions of whose accountability, and to whom. Ministers are accountable democratically, to Parliament and thereby to the people as a whole, but what does this amount to? A lack of effective scrutiny, or its side-tracking by party political pressures in both directions, has not convinced people that the doctrine of Ministerial accountability is effective beyond the occasional demise of a Minister following a scandal, presumably *"pour encourager les autres".* The accountability of directors or chief executives of large companies does not seem to offer a much more convincing model. And in a public body, the situation is complicated by the various "stakeholders" to whom accountability might be felt to be owed. In the case of the SQA, for example, should accountability be to the students, the parents, the schools, the universities and colleges, prospective employers, taxpayers, or a wider community.

3.4 *Theological Context*

3.4.1 Might there be any theological light in this confusion? There is a vital understanding of accountability to God running through the Biblical narrative from the moment Adam seeks to offload responsibility ("she gave me to eat"), via discussion of accountability for the welfare of others ("am I my brother's keeper?"), to the New Testament stewardship parables, several of which hinge on a day of reckoning. There is a strong link between this accountability and God's judgement: accountability does not allow excuses to be offered nor bucks to be passed; just as judgement seeks not to punish but to put things right. Both accountability and judgement are within the context of the originality of sin: they are part of our understanding of human existence, where wrongdoing must be acknowledged and, importantly, overcome.

3.4.2 There is also a rich Biblical understanding of leadership and of shared, communal responsibility that goes beyond the individualism that has undermined contemporary understanding of ministerial responsibility. When Moses returns from the mountain to find the people building idols in their impatience for results, he is clearly not individually culpable, but accepts responsibility and accountability to God for what has happened.

3.4.3 Accountability is not, then, about divine or human blaming—because blaming does nothing to put things right. It is essentially, in the Old Testament, an aspect of good government (see, for example, Daniel 2) and in the New Testament the accountability of leaders to God is a major part of our obligation to obey them (Romans 13 and Hebrews 13). If we belong to God, we are accountable to God in ways that have at least as much to do with our responsiveness to God on a daily basis as with any final judgement. If we belong together, we are mutually accountable in ways that enable us to respond to each others needs, and indeed faults, in the knowledge that fear has been cast out by love. Our responsibility to God and to one another is therefore not to be part of continuing the problem, whatever it may be, but to be part of the solution.

3.5 *Conclusion*

3.5.1 So what could this mean for the SQA and good governance in Scotland? Accountability is part of what has been called the "pious vocabulary" of the new politics, to which the churches have given support, and it has good Biblical basis. But the SQA debate has shown that it needs closer examination. Clearly, the existence of the Scottish Parliament has enabled far deeper scrutiny of the SQA than would have happened under Westminster, and the Committee reports (which achieved consensus on everything except ministerial responsibility) were examples of Parliament at its best. However, neither Parliament nor Executive was able to prevent the mess from occurring and it remains to be seen whether the First Minister's brave undertaking that "it will not happen again" will prove more accurate than the SQA's more cautious pointing to continuing problems. Indeed, it seems strange that when the reports were debated, Parliament was simply asked to note them and to urge the Executive to give urgent consideration to their findings.

3.5.2 We need forms of accountability that are enabling, not disabling, of good governance. Perhaps we should focus more on mutual responsibility, and democratic responsiveness, rather than the accountability that is more concerned with pinning individual blame for the past. We certainly need clarity on issues of responsibility, and structures that inhibit the corralling of accountability by powerful pressure groups. We need to look hard at issues of transparency too, and of freedom of information, so that scrutiny can be effective.

3.5.3 The painful impact on thousands of lives of the SQA's failure to deliver one of its core services is a reminder that these issues are not simply interesting niceties of political philosophy. They are about how effectively we show we care.

4. Local Government Reform

4.1 *Introduction*

4.1.1 Since the 16th century the Church of Scotland has prided itself on continuing to rely on a system which brought governance close to the people. The Bible emphasises the value placed by Jesus on the views of ordinary people. In the 20th century the Church has espoused devolved government and, in the last decade, the concept promoted by the European Union of subsidiarity (the exercise of power as close as possible to the people). In discussion of the new political settlement in Scotland it is too easy to concentrate on the Parliament and the Executive and thereby ignore what could be regarded as the democratic foundation of any such settlement—local government. It is our belief that this foundation needs to be valued and strengthened.

4.1.2 In response to consultation exercises carried out by The McIntosh Commission on Local Government[27] and by the Scottish Executive[28], the Committee expressed the following views:

- The need for a covenant governing relations between the Parliament and local authorities;
- The need to remove the party whip from non-ideological decisions to be taken by local authorities;
- The desirability of using the Single Transferable Vote proportional system for local elections;
- The need to monitor continually the boundaries of local authorities;
- A code of conduct for councillors.

4.1.3 The Committee's Response to the Executive on the Report of the Commission on Local Government focused on:

- The need to foster education in citizenship
- Its regret that the Executive rejected the Commission's recommendation for an independent inquiry into local government finance. The Committee stated that it was "concerned about local government finances and will return to the subject in its report on local government";
- The need for a power of general competence for local authorities;
- The advantages of holding local elections every four years, in the mid-term of Scottish Parliament elections;
- Opposition to directly-elected council leaders;
- The status quo on council employees being elected, and on the salary threshold at which the ban on this applies.

4.1.4 Many of these aspects of local government reform are now in course of implementation by the Scottish Executive and by local authorities, or being actively considered by them, or are subject to inquiry by the Local Government Committee of the Scottish Parliament. The Reform of Local Government, as defined by the McIntosh Commission, is thus well underway.

4.2 *The Objectives*

4.2.1 The Committee is convinced that powerful, representative and independent local authorities are essential to providing high quality services which respond both to the demands and needs of the Scottish people. To achieve these objectives, councils must be so empowered as to occupy the lead position among agencies, quangos and the voluntary sector in the provision of services: in other words, they should be the "community portal" for such provision.[29]

4.2.2 Throughout the campaigns and debates which led to the re-establishment of the Scottish Parliament, local authorities expressed concern that the advent of the Parliament might serve to diminish their powers and status in the structure of government in Scotland. It was therefore essential that their relations with the Parliament and the Executive be considered in depth and this was achieved in the report and recommendations of the McIntosh Commission.

4.2.3 Although the Commission was precluded from studying the question of local government finance, it recorded its view that the present system was subject to strong criticism by reason of the control exercised by central government over areas formerly within local discretion, such as the business rate and the capping of council tax increases by central government. Further criticism was directed at the imbalance in Council revenues, where council tax accounts for only 10% of revenue, and also the complexity of the system of local authority finance. The Commission recommended that an independent inquiry should be launched immediately into local government finance.[30]

4.2.4 To be representative of the views of citizens, councils should be elected by a system where votes cast are reflected in seats won. This calls for a proportional system. The operation of the existing system, for example in 1999 in Glasgow (when 50% of the vote for one party resulted in the election of 74 out of the 79 councillors) can hardly enable the views and aspirations of citizens who support other parties to be represented. As a result councils in this situation forfeit the support or acceptance of substantial numbers of their citizens, and turn-out in local elections is dismally low.[31]

4.3 *Themes*

4.3.1 Given the multifarious aspects of local government reform, the Committee has confined itself to the concept of accountability, expressed in the following five themes:

- the relationship of councils with Parliament and the Executive;
- the use of proportional representation for local elections;
- local government finance;
- Community Planning;
- the position of council employees.

4.3.2 Members of the Committee visited Argyll & Bute, City of Glasgow, Fife, and East Dunbartonshire Councils. These areas were chosen to include, respectively, councils for a large area with a difficult topography; a major city; a mixed urban and rural area; and a smaller area divided into two parts by the boundary revision of 1994. We are grateful for the welcome we received and the valuable information garnered during these visits.

4.4 *Authorities, the Parliament and the Executive*

4.4.1 Because the devolution settlement in Scotland has resulted in a new fluidity in the exercise of power between local authorities, the Scottish Parliament, the Executive and quangos, the true bounds of the powers exercisable by the Parliament have not yet been set. But it is clear that, with Ministers backed by the experience of the erstwhile Scottish Office in winning and wielding power, and the Parliament backed by the provisions of the Scotland Act and by its own ambitions, councils are vulnerable.

4.4.2 Only by insisting therefore on full implementation of the major proposals made by the McIntosh Commission and of the supplementary proposals made by the Kerley Working Group, and by themselves embracing change wholeheartedly, are councils likely to survive with at least their existing powers in an age of devolution, rapid technological development and heightened consumer expectations. The Commission itself stated in regard to its recommendations:

...we have deliberately designed them as a single package, whose elements are intended to work together and to reinforce each other.[32]

4.4.3 The Committee is convinced that local authorities' powers and functions should in fact be extended, so as to re-launch local democracy by passing powers and competences from the Scottish Executive to local level. This calls for a series of self-denying ordinances by the Executive in order to reverse the leaching of powers from local level to Edinburgh. The Executive is now accountable to Parliament as never before, and the Scottish Parliament has the obligation and responsibility to ensure that powers are returned to local authorities, together with finance adequate to exercise them, so that democracy in Scotland is rebuilt from the bottom up, rather than from the top down.

4.5 *Representation and Legitimacy*

4.5.1 If councils are to assume the leading role in Community Planning, and to sustain it, they must be recognised as legitimate bodies, fully representative of and acceptable to, voters in their area. By embracing proportional representation (PR) for elections to devolved assemblies in Scotland, Wales and Northern Ireland, the present and previous UK governments have acknowledged its advantage in securing closer representation of various interests, groupings and individuals, and thus in achieving wider support for such assemblies. The same arguments apply to elections to councils. The McIntosh Commission stated:

It is critical that the democratic credentials of councils should be no less strong than those of the Parliament.[33]

4.5.2 It was argued during the Committee's visit to Glasgow that the use of PR would sever the link between citizen and councillor, in that if the Single Transferable Vote (STV) system were to be used (as recommended by the Kerley Working Group), the number of councillors in any ward could be between three and five, thus confusing the person seeking a councillor's help.

4.5.3 While, as with any innovation, citizens may have to adjust to a new electoral system, as Scots did with conspicuous success to the PR system used for the election to the Scottish Parliament in May 1999, five points can be borne in mind. First, citizens could under STV choose to seek help from one or more of up to five councillors, a choice of councillor at present denied to them. Second, political parties worth their salt should select candidates who relate to different areas in a multi-member ward, thus rendering them if elected acceptable to a large number of citizens in these various areas. Third, some Scots will recall the system of election to local councils before 1975, where the first-past-the-post system was used to elect councillors in multi-member wards. The use of STV will, however, ensure fairer representation of parties and individual candidates than did the pre-1975 system. The McIntosh Commission expressed the view that:

> the multi-member ward can be considered to be an improvement in representation for individual constituents.

Fourth, the use of STV in the Irish Republic and Northern Ireland, two territories with particularly close links with Scotland, where PR has been in use for some decades, has not prevented either those elected or the electors from communicating with each other[34]. Finally, all member states of the European Union conduct local elections by some type of proportional system, and none appear to have plans to introduce a first-past-the-post system.[35]

4.5.4 On the basis of its own and other commissioned research, the Kerley Working Group assessed the Single Transferable Vote as against the Additional Member System (AMS) used to elect the Scottish Parliament. Applying the criterion of the councillor:ward link to the systems, it found that under STV the citizen might be confused by having two or more councillors elected in a large ward. Under the AMS, on the other hand, while the citizen might benefit from a councillor elected specifically to represent the ward (as at present) he or she might be confused by the presence of councillors elected from lists, who claimed also to represent the ward. The existence under the AMS of "Ward Councillors" and "List Councillors" might also be more disadvantageous for the administration of the Council than the existence of "constituency" and "list" members appear to be to date for the Scottish Parliament.[36]

4.6 *Local Government Finance*

4.6.1 *The present system of local government finance confuses accountability, creates dependency and has too many central controls—and any review of the system must take a holistic approach.*

This was the view of the Convention of Scottish Local Authorities (CoSLA), as expressed to the Local Government Committee of the Scottish Parliament. It is clear that if local government is to be reformed, the system of financing it must be included. The Committee regrets the refusal of the Scottish Executive to set up an independent inquiry into this matter and welcomes that launched by the Parliament's Local Government Committee.

4.6.2 Scots are at present ill-served by the incoherent and out-dated methods used to finance local authorities. These, added to the over-exercise of control by the Executive, the over-reliance on Government grants, and the formulas for distribution create a serious lack of accountability in local government finance. The Committee is seriously concerned at the financial pressures imposed by central government upon local authorities, which have resulted in severe cuts in services, notably deterioration in care for the elderly and infirm, in remuneration of teachers and local authority officers, in the condition of school premises and in provision of vital aids to education such as books, and in the state of the homeless.

4.6.3 The Committee obtained first-hand evidence in its visits to four local authorities of the severe pressures imposed on their finances. In East Dunbartonshire, a small excess of expenditure over the guidelines had resulted in reductions in the Council's budget which had had to be made very rapidly and had caused disproportionate cuts in services. Glasgow had suffered a reduction in its budget since 1996 of 20%, which conflicted with its responsibility for providing city centre services for the two million people who travel to it for work and leisure purposes each day. Fife Council opposed hypothecation, or the "ring-fencing" of grants for particular services, which would reduce Councils to becoming solely the deliverers of services on behalf of the Executive.

4.6.4 The Committee on Church and Nation therefore welcomes the Inquiry by the Local Government Committee of the Parliament into local government finance, whose report is due in January 2002. It emphasises the fundamental importance of re-building local democracy by instituting a system of local government finance based on accountability. This system should liberate Councils from oppressive central control, permit them to raise revenue by a more progressive taxation system, acknowledged by taxpayers to be fair and which lifts burdens from the disadvantaged, and offers citizens the assurance of good quality local services.

4.7 *Community Planning*

4.7.1 *Community planning provides a process through which a local authority and other local partners, including community, voluntary and private sector groups, come together to develop and implement a shared vision for promoting the wellbeing of their area.*[37]

With a view to legislation, the Scottish Executive has sought views on the shape of legislation necessary to underpin Community Planning. The Committee learned, in particular from its visits to Fife and Glasgow, that Community Planning implies partnerships between the Council and, for example, the Health Boards, Local Enterprise Companies, Scottish Homes and the voluntary sector.

4.7.2 The Committee welcomes the evolution of Community Planning, as it gives a leadership role to the sole elected body in a council area, thus ensuring a stronger voice for council tax-payers, and greater accountability for appointed quangos; it should result in optimal service delivery and measurable financial savings; it enables a coherent, cross-cutting approach so that the Council and diverse agencies can jointly formulate and implement policy on, for example, children, the elderly, drugs and social inclusion.

4.7.3 Effective Community Planning depends to a great extent on local authority boundaries being co-terminous with those, for example, of Health Boards, local enterprise companies and Water Boards. The re-drawing of local authority boundaries in 1994 has not proved helpful in this regard. The Committee heard of the difficulties resulting from the separation in East Dunbartonshire of the Bearsden and Milngavie area from the eastern area round Kirkintilloch. The mismatch of boundaries is particularly serious in West Central Scotland, Ayrshire and Dundee, but other areas are also affected. We believe that this is an issue which will have to be addressed as Community Planning develops. From another perspective the facts, for example, that Thurso is 120 miles by road from Inverness and that the problems facing the people of Caithness and Sutherland differ considerably from those facing the people of Lochaber, call for imaginative responses to be sought by the Highlands Council. Much development work remains to be done on Community Planning, but it commands widespread support amongst councils, and should help to bring quangos within a new framework of accountability. But it will call for more extensive training for councillors and the assurance of remuneration for them adequate to match their new leadership responsibilities.

4.8 *Employees of Councils*

4.8.1 The Committee met representatives of trades unions, and is grateful for the opportunity to hear their views.

4.8.2 The picture presented to the Committee was bleak. Morale is low among council workers, due to staff cuts and multiple reorganisations. Existing staff are obliged to work longer hours against a background (until recently) of remuneration lagging for years behind inflation. The public regard for councils and council workers was said to have diminished with the obvious loss of councils' powers to the private sector through Private Finance Initiatives, housing associations, and diverse quangos, from Water Boards to Health Boards. Council work does not therefore attract as many high quality entrants as it should, throwing further pressure on existing staff and potentially stunting the ability of councils to adapt to new systems of governance such as Community Planning.

4.8.3 On the positive side, trades union representatives argued that Councillors should be better paid and trained if they were to assume the lead in local partnerships, and also should be able to return to their former employment if defeated at an election. Union members also urged better education in schools in citizenship, and a higher profile for local issues to be given by political parties and the Scottish Parliament.

4.8.4 The Committee is convinced that, however visionary and attractive are plans on paper for local government reform, a failure to retain and to recruit to council service candidates of high calibre, and to create for them terms and conditions of work which offer fulfilment, and a just reward in terms of salaries and prestige in society, must threaten the prospect of success for such reform.

4.9 *Conclusion*

4.9.1 Within the necessarily confined compass of this section the Committee has offered its views on areas of local government reform in which scope remains for discussion, for decision and for action. It accords major importance to the issue of reform of local government finance and will continue to engage in the ongoing discussions on this subject.

4.9.2 As an end-piece, the Committee emphasises the importance it attaches to training for citizenship as part of the schools curriculum and of action by councils. It has recently been formalised in the schools curriculum in England. The McIntosh Commission recommended that *Parliament and local authorities alike give further study to the development of civic education*[38] and the Committee responded positively to this proposal in 1999. In developing their procedures for consultation of the people, such as citizens' panels and forums, councils should also take the opportunity of explaining not just new approaches to local governance, but its basis, objectives and place in the structure of Scottish democracy.

---

[26] "Civic Participation—A Policy Unit Project"—Scottish Executive document 17 March 2000

[27] Church & Nation Committee. Response to Consultation Paper 2 issued by the Commission on Local Government and the Scottish Parliament; adopted 23 February 1999.

[28] Church & Nation Committee, Constitutional Sub-Committee. Response to the Scottish Executive; adopted 23 November 1999

[29] The Community Portal: Democracy, Technology and the Future for Local Governance. The Scottish Council Foundation and the New Local Government Network, 2000.

[30] Report of the Commission on Local Government and the Scottish Parliament (The McIntosh Commission) June 1999, Chapter 3, paras. 53-57

[31] McIntosh Commission Report, *op cit.*, para. 183.

[32] McIntosh Commission Report, *op cit.*, para. 76.

[33] McIntosh Commission Report, *op. cit.*, para. 83.

[34] *Does Ireland need a new electoral system?* by Michael Gallagher, Trinity College, Dublin. Irish Political Studies, vol.2, 1987, pp31, 35, 46.

[35] The Constitutional Status of Local Government in other countries, prepared by the Institute of Local Government Studies, University of Birmingham. The Scottish Office, 1998.

[36] Report of the Renewing Local Democracy working group, chaired by Richard Kerley, June 2000, paras. 86, 95-96.

[37] A Power of Community Initiative, Community Planning etc. A Consultation Paper. The Scottish Executive, November 2000, para. 24.

[38] McIntosh Commission Report, *op. cit.*, paras. 116

SOCIAL INCLUSION PARTNERSHIPS

1. The Context

1.1 In the last two reports to the General Assembly, the Committee has written about welfare reform and about minimum income standards. Last year the Board of Social Responsibility considered social inclusion from the point of view of its own work. These are all reflections of the centrality that social exclusion and inclusion have assumed in the thinking not only of the nation but also of the Church. This is not surprising; as the Board report said last year: *Social inclusion is the very essence of the Christian faith.*

1.2 The context for all this is, as the Committee has pointed out before, the dramatically widening gap between the rich and the poor which has been witnessed over the last two decades. A remarkable increase in the general standard of living has not been shared equally over the population as a whole, meaning that there was an increase in the proportion of the population below half mean contemporary income (before housing costs) from 7% in 1979 to 18% in 1998/9.

1.3 The Scottish Executive published statistical indicators to show the underlying causes of exclusion: 1 in 6 Scottish children live in families where no one has a job; half of lone parents and half of people from ethnic minorities and who are of working age have no job; 1 in 7 among young people between 16 and 19 are neither in education nor training nor employment; 25% of pensioners live in households which have an income of less than 60% of UK average income. Also, there are concentrations of all these figures in areas where few are in work, where work is low-paid and where stress and poor health are high.

1.4 The political response to the existence of such concentrations has been to attempt to target resources. The Urban Programme grew out of this strategy in the early 1970s. In the late 1980s four of Scotland's poorest peripheral estates (Wester Hailes, Castlemilk, Whitfield and Ferguslie Park) were selected for the establishment of "regeneration partnerships". Under the leadership of the Scottish Office, these partnerships brought together the public and private sectors with representatives of the local community to prepare and implement a regeneration strategy for each area. Based on the experience of the Urban Programme and these pilot projects, Priority Partnerships were created in the 1990s. These and others have recently been formed into the current Social Inclusion Partnerships (SIPs).

1.5 SIPs continue to attempt to target resources in specified multiply deprived areas and to co-ordinate attempts to improve the quality of life in the area. The Scottish Executive has committed itself to *the elimination of child poverty, full employment by providing opportunities for all those who can work, securing dignity in old age* and *building strong, inclusive communities.*[39] It sees work on education, housing, healthcare, employment, drugs, justice, fuel poverty and economic development as parts of its social inclusion agenda and is aiming to co-ordinate efforts on all these policy areas and others.[40] Social Inclusion Partnerships are seen as a key part of delivering on these policy commitments. It is expected that, in response to funding from the Scottish

Executive, local spending will be "bent" to assist in achieving the agreed aims of the strategy and effect long-term change.

1.6 There are currently thirty-four area-based and fourteen thematic Social Inclusion Partnerships. Having decided to study their working, the Committee decided to visit three: East Ayrshire Coalfields, Dundee, and Glasgow East End. These were chosen to try to achieve a balanced sample. We would like to thank all those, including members of the local churches, who helped us and offered us their time and hospitality during these visits.

2. The Experience

2.1 *East Ayrshire Coalfields Area*

2.1.1 People involved in the delivery of social inclusion projects here are "at the coal face", a phrase which acts as a reminder of the pride in their heritage still felt in these communities. The Committee met with the Provost and the deputy Chief Executive of East Ayrshire Council, with the SIP manager and with staff of several projects which are, at least in part, funded through SIP money.

2.1.2 East Ayrshire is a new authority following local government reorganisation in the mid 1990s but it is not a naturally distinct area, having no history as a recognisable unit. Agriculture was formerly a major employer. It is also an area where the dominant industries, mining and textiles, have gone, a factor which has contributed to it recording some of the highest levels of unemployment and poverty in Scotland and the UK as a whole. Just being in the area provided a vivid reminder of the scale of problems faced. Large areas of derelict ground intersperse the housing. We learned of a local GP's surgery operated in a community hall, in which the only running water is unheated and is in the toilet.

2.1.3 One of the points which was made repeatedly was that social exclusion does not recognise geographical boundaries. SIP money is targeted, mainly in the south of the area, but there are also areas of great need in the north which do not qualify for funding. This is a source of considerable frustration to council and SIP personnel alike, who spoke of the need to "roll out funding" over the entire East Ayrshire area. This feature of SIP funding is actually contributing to inequality, rather than overcoming it. Mention was made of "bending the spending"—in other words trying to find ways of spreading the benefits of SIP funding—and this has met with some success. Experience has also shown that SIP funding can attract other investment and so the money actually spent in a number of projects greatly exceeds that which is available purely through SIP funding.

2.1.4 Another regular theme was the problem of rural transport. Buses run infrequently. As well as the difficulty that this poses to people who rely on public transport for getting to work, it also increases the sense of isolation felt by many in the scattered villages of the area.

2.1.5 One of the benefits of the partnership approach was that it was said to promote joined up thinking, a practical example of which was the use made by various projects, particularly those targeted at young people and the elderly, of vehicles owned by the health board and the council at times at which they would otherwise be idle, such as evenings and weekends. Through SIP funding, new "disabled friendly" vehicles were being brought into use.

2.1.6 Innovative work is being undertaken with young people and we were privileged to visit Yipworld.com, a centre where children and teenagers could access state of the art computer equipment for study and learning IT skills. They could also develop a range of other skills—including parenting skills and basic household management. Health education and training for employment are also on offer. The centre is a focus for projects aiming to educate young people about drugs and other matters concerning responsible citizenship. It has 1,100 children and teenagers registered with it, of whom about 400 are seen each week.

2.1.7 All those with whom we met displayed a passionate enthusiasm for their work and a real belief in it and a great deal of credit for success must go to the individuals involved. Several spoke about the benefits of being a part of a SIP in terms of it enabling several agencies, which previously had worked separately, to co-ordinate their efforts more effectively. The fact that high level staff in the health board and the council were involved in the Partnership Board spoke of the commitment these bodies are showing and this commitment was felt by many to be quite genuine.

2.1.8 However, the same problems kept being referred to:

- The ring fencing of money to particular areas creates problems as some may access services but others not. Freedom to spread funding out over the whole community would be warmly welcomed.
- Obtaining funding for capital projects was considered to be exceptionally hard but perhaps of most concern was the fact that SIP funding is only given for comparatively short periods. Much work has been put in to working out strategies to continue projects after SIP funding ends. There was even the suggestion that provision of certain projects in the short term and then withdrawing them is potentially more harmful in the long term than had they never been provided at all.

2.1.9 Empowerment of local communities is at the heart of Scottish Executive rhetoric on social inclusion and the Committee was interested to hear views on how this was working in practice.

- Representatives of the Coalfields Community Federation told us of the involvement of various community organisations and about their own work which centred on establishing and keeping open lines of communication within the communities of the former Coalfield area, and between these communities and the local authority and SIP Board.
- Those who were involved spoke of a real sense of partnership. Fears that their presence on the SIP Board might be merely token appear unfounded.
- Frustration was expressed that so few people came forward to participate in the decision making process but those who are involved seem determined to keep up the work, shouldering a great burden on behalf of the whole community.

2.2 *Dundee*

2.2.1 Meetings were held with representatives of

Dundee Anti-Poverty Forum, Dundee Money Advice Support Team, Linlathen and Mid-Craigie Social Inclusion Partnership Group, Maxwelltown Information Centre and Hilltown SIP Group. We were also joined by the Rev Colin Strong, minister of Mid-Craigie Parish Church.

2.2.2 It became very quickly apparent that, in the view of the people involved in SIP projects, the fundamental problem, faced by the people they were working with, is lack of money. Debt is a huge problem and so income maximisation is the priority.

2.2.3 The Committee's questions concentrated not so much on the particular projects but on the overall working of the partnership system. The Committee heard more about the perceived outcomes of the system than about particular projects.

- With increased police involvement in SIP areas, crime is down and people are less afraid.
- Levels of unemployment and of benefits claiming are lower in SIP areas since their inception.
- A lot of good work is being done, many people are being helped and there is a very strong belief that the work undertaken by the SIP supported projects is worthwhile.

However, problems with the system dominated discussion.

- The "nonsense of postcodes"—being the way SIP funding is targeted, meaning that people on one side of the road may be eligible while those on the other are not—was a recurring theme.
- Mention was made of the shifting of population which causes "morphing"—the spreading of problems outwith the SIP areas. While some are moving because of increasing financial resources, many, particularly the young and members of ethnic minorities, are moving without problems being resolved.
- Housing has been demolished, rightly, but new building is not keeping pace. The result is that deprivation is not as concentrated as it was when SIP areas were first established and therefore the ability

of SIPs to address problems has suffered.

- In some cases, the work of SIPs can appear successful, and at times it is. But in too many cases, people are just being moved from one category of problem to another. Different ways of defining problems only serve further to obscure matters.
- We heard of a "lack of joined up thinking."
- There had been disputes between partners which had led to funds being withdrawn and the Committee was given the impression that these disputes need not necessarily have led to this outcome.

2.2.4 On the issue of community involvement, differing views were expressed.

- Some project employees said that community representation was only "token" and "shockingly low", citing as reasons for this the lack of a democratic process for appointing community representatives and their consequent lack of accountability. The process of becoming a community representative was described as "daunting" and so it is difficult to get people involved in this "very complicated" work.
- Regret was expressed that local people who had learned new skills through their involvement with SIPs but were still unable to find employment within the local community.
- More opportunities for "on the job" training are needed, particularly for those for whom college attendance is not an option.
- The costs of voluntary work to those involved were highlighted. In spite of this, many are making quite considerable efforts.
- Community representatives spoke of excellent relationships with MPs, MSPs and councillors and of generally feeling that they were being taken more seriously by other partners in SIP Boards. There are able people demonstrating commitment to the community through serving on SIP Boards. They spoke warmly of the funding mechanism of SIPs in that it gave local people, with real experience of life in SIP areas, a seat at the table at which funding decisions are taken.
- Despite this, pleas were made for the agenda to be set locally for community development projects and

for them not to be based so much on local authority or government priorities.

On the subject of funding, the ability of SIPs to attract funding for projects greater than their own budgets was mentioned but funding overall was not felt to be adequate. There was a considerable sense of frustration that so much work is needed which cannot in fact be undertaken and that pressure on staff meant that existing clients were not necessarily receiving the attention their cases merited. Uncertainty over continuity of funding cripples projects, particularly when much time has to be taken up with attempting to secure funding for subsequent years. Community representatives spoke of good projects folding through lack of finance and of momentum lost. Success can count against projects when funding is reviewed.

2.2.5 Community representatives, while recognising that individual church members were active in SIP Boards, asked for more visible church involvement. This may be more a problem of communication than of actual lack of involvement, parishes being very active in the whole field of social inclusion. Individually, many local activists are church members. Perhaps a greater degree of integration with the SIP Boards, rather than just at project level is needed, particularly so that duplication of provision of certain services can be avoided.

2.2.6 The Committee also heard of feelings of isolation in Dundee from the centres of decision making. It is important that those who work on social inclusion on a macro level encounter the micro level, as the Committee can testify. We were particularly pleased to hear that the Scottish Parliament's Social Inclusion Committee has held a full meeting in Dundee at the Happyhillock Neighbourhood Base but were disappointed to learn that this had been the only time this committee had met outside Edinburgh.

2.3   *Glasgow East End*

2.3.1 Representatives of the Committee visited the east end of Glasgow and met with SIP project workers, representatives of Scottish Enterprise Glasgow, local church leaders and the MSP, Frank MacAveety, at various locations around Dalmarnock, Calton, Bridgeton, the Gallowgate and central Glasgow. This particular visit followed up discussions which had begun at the Committee's conference in Dunblane in September, at which Frank MacAveety had been a speaker.

2.3.2 Of the three visits, this was perhaps the one of greatest contrasts in attitudes towards the concept and practice of Social Inclusion Partnerships. On the one hand, there is a clear emphasis put on using SIP funds for long term strategic planning rather than to seek to fund short term projects. Long term change is the aim of the SIP Board and they see their rôle as creating the right conditions for funding targeted at specific projects to be brought in. Some believed that this approach was working well but from others we heard the opinion that the whole SIP philosophy was flawed and a waste of effort. With such diametrically opposed views, the truth probably lies somewhere in between.

- The real problems of sustainability of projects is being recognised and addressed but the fact that it was only about eighteen months since the Social Inclusion Partnership had been formally inaugurated meant that strategy was still at an early stage in development.
- The larger partners such as the Health Board, Local Authority, and Local Enterprise Company are increasingly conscious of the need to work in partnership and are beginning to see the benefits of this.
- The area covered by the Glasgow East End SIP was formerly designated a Priority Partnership Area. The difference becoming a SIP has made is that there is a much greater feeling of commitment from government and the focus is not primarily on the physical environment, the economic situation, training or jobs but on people. This was thought to promote a culture of joined up thinking.
- Consultation was given a high priority as it is important that people see that they are being listened to. There was a huge job to be done as there is a deep-seated suspicion of professionals arising from occasions when consultation has only been token. Attempts to overcome this have sometimes resulted in a tendency to "consult people to death." Local people were

"cautious and confused" according to one local minister, having been let down so often in the past. There was talk of the "authorities walking over us."

- Among people working in SIP supported projects, there was concern that the levels of bureaucracy are stifling and that too much time and energy were going into that rather than into delivery of services. Some were very dismissive of the SIP while others spoke positively about it. It is probable that the views expressed reflect the relative strengths of the different projects represented. Those which were perhaps least financially secure and operating with the fewest staff were most warm about their involvement in the SIP while the larger, more financially viable projects had a more "go it alone" mentality.

2.3.3 As before problems with the system were a recurring theme:

- Nobody can be sure that any new initiative will last for long enough for it to be worth doing.
- The implications of joined up thinking have yet fully to sink in.
- It is not easy to engage with the community. For the community truly to be at the heart of the SIP process, the problems of huge demands being placed on a limited number of activists will need to be overcome. However, members of the SIP board were sometimes perceived to be parochial and just there to defend their own interests. Whether true or not, it is a perception that needs to be tackled.
- It is very difficult to measure long term results or quantify success and this presents problems when seeking further funding.
- SIPs were said to need to be more transparent.
- It is important to remember that the implementation of Social Inclusion policy has brought in very little new money. Most of it is funding that has been renamed but that does not conceal the fact that it is not enough. The fact that many projects rely on a "cocktail of funding" contributes to their instability. The agendas of the various funders inevitably clash at times and this can lead to harmful competition among projects for funds.

- Provision of jobs is not enough. The jobs need to be appropriate.
- Many people need continuing support after making the transition into employment. It should never be thought that getting a job is the end of problems. Employers need to be more aware of issues surrounding coming off benefit and into wage earning and the particular hardship this can cause initially as benefits stop before the first pay packet comes in.
- Many local people know little about the SIP in their area and are not seeing their expectations being matched by what is being done.
- People have been used to things being done for them rather than having agencies and projects working with them. There is a need for a change in culture so that the philosophy of partnership affects all levels of the community and is not just seen as a partnership between funding agencies.

2.3.4 It was salutary to learn that when local people were consulted at the beginning of the SIP process, few said they had problems relating to poverty. This simply indicates how low expectations are. A little deeper probing found that some 33% of residents experienced real money problems in any two week period. Money advice is one of the most heavily used SIP supported services. Overall, the visit highlighted the scale and diversity of the problems faced in the east end of Glasgow. While there was no doubt about their nature and severity, there was little unanimity on how to tackle them. One man spoke with considerable exasperation when he said, "The system doesn't matter—it's about the people." It is about people, but the system, whatever it is, needs to be the best it can be.

3. Key Points

There are certain key points which can be drawn out of these visits:

- The staff working in the partnerships and in the associated projects were able and enthusiastic. They were making serious efforts to make a change in their communities and to involve the people living in the SIP area in the process of preparing a strategy, implementing it and monitoring the results.

- Senior officers represented the main partners at board meetings of the Partnership, reflecting an important commitment to the work on behalf of their organisations. Representatives of the local communities were involved in all the Partnerships and we were very aware that they gave an enormous amount of time and energy to that work.

- The work of the partnerships is new and developing and, given the diverse nature of the areas we visited, there will be advantages in continuing the exchange of ideas and experience.

- However, there were criticisms about the bureaucratic nature of the organisation and of the competitive nature of the selection process of projects for financial support.

- The real involvement of the community in the Partnerships was questioned on several occasions, though it was recognised that that it was not easy to involve the often diverse facets of a community.

- The amount of time, effort and skill required from a community member on a SIP board was also drawn to our attention.

- Fixed boundaries were mentioned as a problem more than once. It is not unknown for services to be available to people on one side of a street but not to those on the other. Low income is not a problem reserved to those living within a SIP boundary.

- The short-term nature of funding was often mentioned as it leads to difficulty in recruiting and retaining staff, and to an inordinate amount of time lobbying for continued support rather than getting on with the job.

- SIPs, with their limited budgets, are not likely to have any major impact unless they have the full support of the public sector partners and really succeed in "bending the spending".

4.   Social Exclusion

4.1   The Committee welcomes the commitment of the Scottish Executive to reducing social exclusion and tackling poverty and injustice in our society; and we recognise that the figures quoted in paragraph 1.2 do not measure the effect of more recent measures. We recognise too that there are many policies and programmes being pursued by both the UK Government and the Scottish Executive of which SIPs are but one strand.

4.2   Wendy Alexander MSP, the then Scottish Executive Minister for Communities, in a speech given at Strathclyde University on 16th June, 2000, indicated that in the Executive's view, social exclusion was not a matter just of income but of expectation. She wished to redefine the terminology in terms of "social justice", meaning by that that inequality in economic and other matters was a primary concern. The language used changes regularly. Talk of social exclusion has given way to social inclusion which is being replaced by the term social justice. But as one project worker we met in Dundee said, "No matter what you call it, it has always been about poverty and always will be." The language often seems to move away from talk of poverty and, while commending the Scottish Executive for trying to see the broadest possible picture, we are nevertheless concerned that references to adequacy of income are few and far between. Attempts to avoid this issue will not ultimately serve Scotland's poor.

4.3   Social Inclusion Partnership projects may have many aspects to them; but in their broader work the Government and the Executive seem to concentrate heavily on paid work as the way to promote social integration. The definition of social exclusion or inclusion can then easily be narrowed to the issue of participation in paid work and not question why people who are not in employment are consigned to poverty. Benefit increases, for example, are not seen as a method of reducing poverty. Because only a distinction between employed and unemployed is then made, questions of exclusion arising from poor pay are not considered, obscuring inequalities between men and women and between different classes in the labour market. The value of unpaid work is not considered, undermining the legitimacy of non-participation in paid work such as full time caring for children or a dependant relative. The chief problem with this is, of course, lack of work, but neither is there much regard given to the suitability of the work on offer.

4.4   Although avoiding the crass attempt to blame the

victim by suggesting that poverty and exclusion are simply the result of individual inadequacy or moral degeneracy, nevertheless there is here an understanding which can end up using paid work as a method of social control and can, indeed, continue to promote inequality as an incentive to greater competitiveness.

4.5 There is, however, an alternative. This is to concentrate on poverty and to seek to address it through redistribution. This way of thinking promotes a reduction in poverty by using benefit levels and tax regimes to redistribute wealth. The value of unpaid work as a means of tackling exclusion is recognised through not adhering rigidly to a view that the only way to tackle poverty is through employment. It takes the position that citizenship is about social engagement and is therefore the obverse of exclusion. By recognising social, political and cultural citizenship as vital for the wellbeing of all within society, it understands social exclusion as being more than economic. It thus critiques inequality, understood as more than material inequality, and focuses on the processes which lead to inequality. Redistribution is therefore a strategy to reduce inequality of both resources and power.

4.6 This alternative takes seriously the innate worth of each person within society by emphasising that the well being of all is vital for the health of the whole of society. It does not see people as purely economic units in terms of the work each is able to perform and values the contribution of people to society, even if they are not creating wealth. Redistribution is the means by which wealth is shared to support all the people.

4.7 The social teaching of Jesus insists that people be measured by far more than their economic contribution. Rather they are to be enabled and empowered to belong. The Committee remains of the view that this enabling and empowering is bound up with an adequate level of income, meaning that a measure of what is "adequate" continues to be urgently needed. This would also enable a realistic and truly "minimum" wage to be set that would allow a reasonable standard of living for those for whom it was the sole source of income.

4.8 When we discuss social inclusion, we are speaking about a society in which the processes of dehumanisation are defeated. We are speaking of an understanding of humanity which sees personal wholeness and social wholeness as inextricably linked. We uphold a vision of social being where each of us is caught up in and by the life of those around us. Such a vision is encapsulated in the New Testament word *koinonia*. Koinonia represents the antithesis of the individualism by which we have learnt to set such store. It insists that the way to understand human life is as one body where no part can say to another that they are not needed.

4.9 This is vitally important when the Church looks at how the nation promotes social inclusion. What we must insist on is that the whole of society is damaged by poverty, not only those who are materially and financially disadvantaged. Equally, our view is that it is simply not acceptable that some can use their material prosperity to opt out of the society in which they are set, to turn their backs on those who have lost out. Once social inclusion is understood not simply as a circumlocution allowing poverty not to be mentioned, but as koinonia, as an existence in and for others, a living out of the phrase "I am for you", we can bring a much more searching light to bear on the policies and strategies designed to bring this existence into being.

4.10 In this light we can ask not only what effect social inclusion policies have on the poor, but also what effect they have on the rich. We can enquire about ideas of responsibility, both personal and social. We can ask about work and wealth, about whether or not it is true that, as Paul says, we work principally in order to have something to share. Is it true, as it was for Nehemiah, that celebration is only possible when provision is made for those who have nothing? Can we speak of a truly inclusive society when the gap between rich and poor continues to grow wider? Is the bridging of that gap to be a matter of charity or one of justice?

4.11 We live in a world and a society where many live in ignorance of the plight of their fellow citizens, where many are excluded from the basics of life, where others go to great lengths to avoid those whose poverty judges the riches they enjoy. In such a world, we as a church require not only to examine carefully what those elected to govern our land do in this area of policy but we also need to ensure that inclusiveness is the mark of our theology and our church life. Because these issues lie not only at the heart of government policy but also at the heart of our faith, this is a task not simply for one report to the General Assembly, but one to be revisited time and again.

---

[39] The Scottish Executive: *Social Justice . . . a Scotland where everyone matters, Annual Report 2000*
[40] Ibid.

ROAD FUEL PRICING

1. When the Committee decided to examine the issue of the rising price of petrol in June 2000 we were not to know that within a few months the crisis would threaten to bring the country to a halt. While we take account of the issues that gave rise to last September's blockade in this report we concentrate on three issues that were and are central:

- The allegedly high cost of fuel *per se*
- The cost of fuel in the UK compared to the rest of Europe
- The considerably higher pump prices in rural areas compared to prices in towns

We also considered possible future developments. In addition to studying reports by Government and other agencies, members of the Committee sought to obtain at first hand the views of both those who retail and distribute as well as those who use fuel and those who use and work in public transport.

2.   Present Church position

2.1 It is widely agreed that worldwide consumption of carbon based fuels must be drastically reduced. Global warming is now accepted worldwide as a reality. Its effects are clearly being seen in many parts of the world, and even now in Scotland. New evidence is coming almost weekly of what we are doing to our health, safety and environment by burning fossil fuels without limit. The fastest growing sources of global warming are the emissions from air traffic and from our cars and lorries.

2.2 The emissions of acid and organic pollutants from vehicle exhausts have also brought urban pollution levels back towards levels we thought had gone forever when we stopped burning smoky coal. Sheer increased car use is outstripping the gains made from catalytic converters and fuel efficiency. The damage to our health is a high price to pay for the convenience of cheap fuel. The pump price has never reflected the real environmental and health costs we are paying for global warming and urban pollution by our daily car journeys. For years we have presumed on having cheap petrol and diesel, at the expense of the environment and human health. We fill up because it is convenient, and ignore the consequences. We cannot do so any more.

2.3 Fuel tax rises were intended to reduce car use by deliberately making it expensive. It has not worked well. A major reason is that the Government has not "ring fenced" the fuel tax revenues, visibly to set aside a substantial proportion for environmental renewal, rural infrastructure and public transport. Indeed, last summer the Government was defending its fuel taxation policy by claiming that the cash raised was funding our hospitals and other public services. The General Assembly in 1995 accepted a report from the Committee which argued the case against such indirect taxation. We would continue to argue for that position. People may not accept higher fuel prices if they cannot see anything in return that they value. There is a need also to recognise that there are vast rural areas where public transport either does not exist or is not a realistic alternative to the car.

2.4 The Church has traditional concerns in this area: care for the poor, both at home and abroad, and care for the earth. Although we recognise the difficulties for industry and individuals of increasing fuel costs, we do not believe that reducing fuel prices significantly across the board (thus boosting demand and consumption) would help the balance of these concerns. Such a course of action would be highly irresponsible in the light of the damage it would cause. We as individuals need to move away from thinking selfishly and in the short term. The Government needs to encourage us to do so.

2.5 We welcome the fact that broad based discussions continue to be conducted with many and varied solutions being advanced not only by politicians of all parties but also by many other groups and individuals. We know that there is no simple and quick fix available but a long-term view must be sought and agreed. We wish to encourage those involved in the democratic process in this endeavour, as it is only in that process that progress can and should be achieved.

2.6 We have already put forward some practical suggestions:

- Much of the freight of the road hauliers could be on the railways, not on the roads. An active promotion of rail freight, subsidised by fuel tax if necessary, and a better integration with local distribution networks would reduce the road hauliers' share of pollution.
- The "ring fencing" of duty is essential so that a significant proportion is seen to be used on alleviation of the damage from road transport, on direct investment in public transport, and on infrastructure in rural areas. This has been proposed by numerous authorities for many years, including most recently the Joseph Rowntree Foundation.
- A national scheme for subsidising public transport costs for the elderly and those on low incomes and benefits (as advocated by the Scottish Affairs Committee in their report *Poverty in Scotland*) would be an advance in social care.
- Crucially, accelerated public transport development and integration is central to any serious strategy aiming to care for the earth and the poor.

3.   Fuel retailing

The Committee set out to establish how fuel retailing operates.

3.1   *How the customer pays*

Cash and credit card sales are the usual means of payment for private motorists. Bulk sales to business customers are of two main types:

- *Agency card* for small business users. The petrol companies each have their own schemes that seek to tie the holder into buying a particular brand in return for discount. Retailers do not receive their usual margin (2.2p a litre) but receive instead their wholesale

price plus a handling charge of around 0.75p a litre. The holder of an agency card has an option of either paying notional "national rates" or the local pump price. National rate may well be higher than pump price in the Central Belt but will be considerably lower than pump rate elsewhere.

- *Bunker* deals are used mainly by freight companies and bus operators; payment is direct to the supplier— BP, Shell etc.—and as with all bulk purchases attracts a considerable discount.

Small stations in rural areas may refuse to take agency cards because of low margin allowed on such sales.

3.2   *Types of petrol station*

- *Directly Company owned*—usually large Central Belt site, operated by a manager. Pump price is dictated centrally.
- *Franchise site* - "Owners" instead of 2.2p per litre will get about 0.5p but will make their money from their volume sales and other site activities. All advertising costs etc. are paid for.
- *Privately owned sites,* local shop, garage or other privately owned petrol station—Here the seller is allowed a 2.2p litre mark-up from which all overheads including costs of promotional schemes must be paid. Such owners negotiate individual deals with their supplier. Some will settle for a lower basic margin but will gain bonuses if pre-agreed targets are reached; some will have their credit card costs covered (around 1.9%).

Each of these is locked into dealing with a single oil company, in the case of franchise sites, usually for 5 years. So even if an alternative supply source at a cheaper rate became available it could not be used.

There is general agreement that margins for those selling petrol are very low. The manager of one private petrol station to whom we spoke estimated that non-fuel products are 10% of sales but mean 34% of profit. In launching its new logo on 24th July 2000 BP announced the aim of generating 50% of its market profits from non-fossil fuel sales.

3.3   *Price support*

This is used by the oil companies to preserve market share.

It can operate in several ways e.g. Esso "Pricewatch" or other direct subsidy; the supplier may agree to absorb the seller's Agency and Credit card costs (presently 1.9%); or may also offer a cash bonus if pre-agreed targets are met and also help with costs of special promotions. Privately owned filling stations negotiate their own deal. The Esso "Pricewatch" and other campaigns operate by the supplier altering what he charges the retailer to take account of any reduction the latter has to make to meet local prices. This is done on a daily basis. Support may be withdrawn and if others in the area follow suit a price increase sticks. Offers to replace pumps or shop refurbishment are also used as incentives to stay with a particular company.

3.4 *Reasons for price variation*

Not surprisingly, people ask how, in an allegedly competitive market, petrol prices always seem to rise in unison—normally as soon as possible after a rise in the price of crude oil—yet fail to fall as speedily when the reverse is the case. To some extent this is due to the very small profit margins that apply to the supply of petrol, but also to the low cost of crude oil relative to the retail price (see Section 6). The total sales in Caithness (population *circa* 25,000) are estimated at 7million litres a year. This compares to figures from one City petrol station that sells 21million litres a year. The latter can survive on a small margin; rural stations cannot. The more you sell the easier it is to live on 2.2p a litre or less. Fuel deliveries are paid for "up front" so how much can be taken will depend on cash flow as well as storage capacity.

3.5 *Economies of scale and rural areas*

Sales at one Highland village station are 100,000 litres a year. Even adding a higher margin of 5p a litre the revenue is only £5,000 a year from sales, from which sum all overheads have to be met. Another Sutherland village station sells around 125,000 litres a year; thus the same 5p margin produces around £6,250 in revenue. Such margins, whether in rural or urban filling stations, are set by the retailer. There is a need for local supply to retain tourism as well as to serve local populations, yet it is impossible on these figures to make a decent living only selling petrol. Large filling stations have daily supplies from tankers but a small rural station will take a part

load (1,200 litres) and will incur a surcharge of 0.8p a litre as a result. This surcharge, as well as any extra mark-up, plus VAT, will of course be added to the pump price. Caithness and Sutherland (population *circa* 40,000) has 33 petrol outlets—26 BP, 1 ESSO, 6 Shell—needed because of its vast area, but has not the potential customer base of the Central Belt. In this area BP distributes about 5million litres of petrol and 2.5million litres of diesel a year.

4. Fuel prices at home and abroad

4.1 The pump price comprises net cost from which oil producers, distributors and retailers make a living, duty and VAT, *e.g.*:

Net	25.99p
VAT	13.90p
Duty	48.82p
Gross pump price	87.90p

The Oil Companies claim their margin on distribution is around 1.7/2p a litre. All claim to be working to small margins. The Government gains in VAT on a rise in fuel price or increase in retailer's margin. There has thus been a considerable gain in VAT take as the price of crude oil has risen. This, however, will disappear if the price of crude oil falls.

4.2 *Comparative fuel prices over time—UK average (per litre) at constant 1995 prices*

1989	52.09p
1991	51.73p
1993	52.63p
1995	54.58p
1997	56.35p
1999	63.19p

Source—DTI

4.3 Unleaded Prices within the UK (per litre)

Scotland	84.60p
Rural Scotland	88.04p
Midlands	85.00p
UK average	85.00p

Source—AA Research June 2000

In calculating this figure, the AA states:

> *The AA fuel price survey is predominantly a survey of prices in the main centres of population ie where most fuel is bought. The listed UK average excludes prices in Scotland Remote Areas since they are generally higher and distort the results.*

The high price of fuel in "Scotland Remote Areas" is not simply a statistical inconvenience, but bears most heavily on those who have no alternative to the car.

4.4   Petrol prices Autumn 2000 (per litre)

Stornoway	94.50p
Wick	92.50p
Badenoch	89.90p
Thurso	88.90p
Inverness	86.90p
Perth	82.70p
Peebles	81.90p
Edinburgh	78.90p

While prices have fluctuated in the meantime the differentials have remained similar.

(From the Committee's own research)

4.5   The Office of Fair Trading report published in July 2000, *Petrol and Diesel Pricing in the Highlands and Islands*, declares that with the exception of the Western Isles they found no evidence of excessive or unfair profit-taking and claim that the higher pump price in rural areas is due only in part to the higher cost of delivery, but mainly due to the higher margin taken by a retailer because of his smaller volume of sales. With regard to the Western Isles the report says:

> *... it cannot be concluded that the market in the Western Isles is working competitively. Prices are higher than elsewhere and this cannot be explained in terms of lower volumes or by what we currently know about costs ...*

As a result, the Office of Fair Trading is to undertake further research in this area.

4.6   *Unleaded prices across Europe as at June 2000 (converted into sterling as at June 2000)*

Austria	53.59p
Belgium	63.34p
Czech Republic	59.33p
France	72.81p
Germany	62.88p
Irish Republic	61.60p
Norway	86.03p
Spain	53.19p

Figures from AA

Exchange rates subject to fluctuation, as are prices. It should be noted that oil is priced in dollars and the pound has remained reasonably constant against the dollar, whilst the euro lost approximately 30% of its value against the dollar between its launch and Autumn 2000.

4.7   It is not just in rural areas that the high price of fuel hits hard. While those who can afford it will continue to run their cars no matter the price, there exist both rural and urban poor for whom the car is no luxury. In urban peripheral housing schemes, for example, the cost of public transport—especially for a family—is such that a car may make sound economic sense. Taxis are likewise not a luxury but a legitimate means of public transport. In rural areas a taxi is both more economic and more environmentally friendly than an almost empty bus; in cities they may well be both a safer and more convenient means of travel home after a shopping trip. Taxi owners have faced significant cost increases because of rising fuel costs, but since fares are regulated by local authorities, have not always been able to recoup such costs.

5.   Red diesel

Schedule 1 of the Hydrocarbon Oil Duties Act 1979 allows "excepted vehicles" to be fuelled with rebated gas oil (red diesel). The most common type of such vehicle is an agricultural tractor, a tractor either totally used in fields or if on the road solely for agriculture horticulture or forestry. If any other work is undertaken, such as haulage, then the vehicle's excepted status is void. Such diesel is stained and Customs & Excise can and do check that the farmer's other cars are not stained. VAT can be reclaimed and duty is only 3.13p a litre. The price of red diesel has gone up from around 11p a litre to 20p a litre in the last year, mainly due to rise in the price of crude oil.

6. Alternative fuels

6.1 Alternatives to fossil fuels have been researched for several decades and some important advances have now been made. One area is hybrid electric-petrol vehicles, which use both batteries and a conventional engine. The other is fuel cell vehicles which burn hydrogen and produce only water as emissions. To be effective in greenhouse gas terms, the source of electricity or hydrogen needs to be renewable energy or nuclear power. This would imply a need to expand renewable electricity and not reduce the nuclear component.

6.2 All current fuels generate large quantities of carbon dioxide and contribute to global warming. Road and air transport is the fastest growing source of greenhouse gasses. Petrol and diesel are also significant pollutants with sulphur impurities, partially burnt volatile organic and particulate emissions. There is no doubt that the modern car with "lean burn" engine and catalytic converter is much more fuel-efficient and less polluting than its predecessor. Since 1993 the increasingly strict emission targets have greatly reduced emissions. Carbon dioxide, however, is not filtered out. If no further measures are taken it is forecast that by 2010 gains will be cancelled out if growth and fossil fuel use is unchecked. Ultra Low Sulphur Diesel is now widely available and the Chancellor of the Exchequer announced in his Autumn Statement that the Government was launching a drive to make Ultra Low Sulphur Petrol similarly available. To encourage its use, the duty on ULSP and ULSD will be reduced by 2p in the Spring of 2001. Welcome though it is to reduce sulphur oxide emissions and therefore acid precipitation, ULSP is still oil, contains only less sulphur, and carbon dioxide emissions are unchanged.

7. Liquid Petroleum Gas (LPG)

7.1 LPG has considerable relative environmental advantages over petrol and diesel. It is primarily a liquefied hydrocarbon gas so it has fewer impurities. Hence it generates less of many of the main pollutants, for example 5% less carbon monoxide, 85% fewer hydrocarbons, 40% less oxides of nitrogen, 10% less carbon dioxide and 87% less ozone forming potential. Although much cleaner, it is not, however, clean in global warming terms because it still produces almost as much carbon dioxide as petrol.

7.2 LPG is less dense than petrol, thus requiring a larger volume to produce the same amount of energy. There is only a slight loss of power in a LPG car; manufacturers claim that the average motorist will notice no difference. There is a loss of about 25% of useable boot space to accommodate the extra tank in a Vauxhall Omega or Ford Focus for example. Cars cannot run solely on LPG but are started on petrol with LPG being used soon thereafter, thus are designed for dual fuel use.

7.3 In July 2000 it was estimated that there were about 10,000 vehicles in the UK equipped to burn either LPG or petrol as against over 1 million in Italy and 500,000 in France. There is clearly room for improvement in this country. In July 2000 Scottish Office Minister Brian Wilson launched a campaign in conjunction with Gleaner Oils to introduce LPG to 20 fuel stations in the Highlands. Similar schemes are underway elsewhere but at the time of writing this Report we are nowhere near the promised "half hour drive" between LPG stations.

7.4 In addition to availability there is also the economic obstacle to be overcome. Mr Wilson promised that the Government would ensure that the pump price of LPG remained 30p a litre below that of unleaded petrol. It is not clear that this will be a sufficient incentive to motorists to drive dual fuel cars.

7.5 The fuel consumption figures for a Ford Focus 1.8l engine over the "combined cycle " of urban and open road motoring are:

	Diesel	LPG	Petrol
Litres per 100km	5.4	11.2	7.6
Miles per gallon	53.2	25.2	37.2

Those for a Vauxhall Omega 2 litre are:

	Diesel	LPG	Petrol
Litres per 100km	7.8	7.1	9.3
Miles per gallon	36.1	39.8	30.3

7.6 Unlike Ford, Vauxhall do not market "conversion" of engines to LPG but design and build LPG engines. Our inquiries suggest further that LPG is at its most competitive in large cars which are not designed for good fuel consumption. Vauxhall's promotional literature is aimed at the large mileage fleet company which will see the greatest financial gain.

7.7 There is also the capital cost of either a new LPG car or conversion of an older car. In 1993 the Government set up the Energy Saving Trust as an independent company in association with major energy companies, to promote the more efficient use of energy in the UK. The Powershift Scheme makes grants of between 25%-75% of the additional cost of a "clean fuel vehicle" subject to conditions which include "the availability of funds." This scheme has been operated in Scotland since last year by the Scottish Executive. In December 2000, some firms involved in converting cars claimed that funds had dried up in Scotland. We would hope that this will soon be remedied. Grants are calculated on the cost excluding VAT which makes them less beneficial to private users. Grants are available for new cars and lorries or cars not more than one year old. It is those who are poorest who are less likely to own cars which qualify.

7.8 The extra cost of a factory-converted Ford Focus or Mondeo (Dec 2000) is £1,995 including VAT; of a Vauxhall Omega £2,000 including VAT. If this scheme is to be more widely used there has to be a clearer financial advantage to the motorist. The EKOS report mentioned below argues for a 50p a litre price difference as being the point at which it becomes economic to consider conversion. Only if demand for LPG vehicles is increased will it be worthwhile for more manufacturers not only to offer conversions but to design and build vehicles that are at their most efficient on LPG.

7.9 The cost of installing LPG pumps at a garage is around £15,000. We mention below a grant scheme for fuel outlets in rural areas but clearly this cost could inhibit the spread of LPG outlets.

8. Fuel Cell Technology

This has been researched for over 30 years. Vehicles powered by electricity are a far cry from the milk float of yesteryear. General Motors, Ford, Daimler/Chrysler and BMW are all running hydrogen powered fuel cell vehicles in prototype form and expect to have them in the show rooms within five years. The main problem has been to reduce the size of the generating unit. The technology is as simple as it is clean. Hydrogen from an on board tank reacts with oxygen from the outside air to produce a small amount of electricity and water. The current is multiplied through a stack of fuel cells which powers the vehicle. The sole exhaust product is water. Only customer demand and a sympathetic tax regime will turn these prototypes into a daily reality.

9. Rural issues

In rural areas the fuel price hits hard on those with low incomes. There is a high level of car dependency because of the inadequacy of public transport. Yet it is in rural areas that the price of fuel is highest. *Car Dependence in Rural Scotland 1998* (Central Research Unit, Scottish Office, Report) found that 88.8% of journeys were made by car in Rural Scotland. They further noted that of the households with an income of less than £10,000 a year, 32.5% had no car. The EKOS report declares in respect of the Highlands:

Per head of population 75% more road miles are travelled in the Highlands than in Scotland as a whole - 65% of the population are at least one hours drive from a main centre, compared to 10% in Scotland as a whole...

9.1 *Assistance available to rural filling stations*

For three years from 1998/99, as part of the Rural Transport funding package, £400,000 was made available to rural filling stations. A grant scheme started in 1998 and last year £300,000 is allocated. To qualify, a petrol station must be:

- at least 30 minutes' drive from the edge of an Urban Area (population over 30,000)
- have a throughput of less than 1m litres per year
- be at least 8 miles from nearest competitor, and
- sell both lead free and diesel.

Grants cover up to 50% of costs of replacing tanks, meeting modern regulations etc.

9.2 In April 2000 the Scottish Executive expanded the scheme to include installation of LPG equipment, but the rules are still as above except that the second of them will not be enforced. This scheme will enable petrol stations in rural areas to continue to trade but will have little effect on the pump price. Rate relief for rural shops would help those shops which sell petrol stay open but the effect on pump price would be negligible. Highland Council is looking at expanding its present scheme of bulk buying fuel for small fishing boats to bulk buying road fuel for sale to rural communities.

9.3 In October 2000, EKOS economic consultants produced a report *Assessing the Fuel Price Difference in the Highland and Islands Option Appraisal* on behalf of the Highlands and Islands Action Group on Hydrocarbons. This document is well worth study. Among its recommendations is *an immediate implementation of a reduction in Vehicle Excise Duty … for permanent householders in special transport tax zones.* This proposal has the advantage over variable VAT rates in that it ensures that saving is passed on to the customer and is not absorbed by distributors or retailers whose margins are under pressure. While benefiting the essential small mileage user, it also gives proportionally less benefit to those who undertake long journeys that could in part be undertaken by public transport. The link between fuel consumed and tax paid, which we support on environmental grounds, is thus maintained.

10. Future taxation policy

10.1 The Government is already committed to a policy of revising Vehicle Excise Duty (VED). From 2000 cars with small engines (up to 1100cc) presently enjoy a £55 reduction; the qualifying engine size is to be increased in the 2001 Budget. At the same time a new VED regime is to be introduced for all new vehicles in which the amount of Duty paid will be related to the amount of CO_2 emissions produced. This is a welcome reform on the basis that the polluter pays and hopefully will encourage further reductions in pollution. We have some reservation with the idea that smaller cars should always pay less. It is not obvious that an aged small engine car is necessarily less polluting than a modern lean burn engine car.

10.2 If there is a shift to more environmentally friendly cars can we be assured that the Government will not then seek to make up the lost revenue by reducing or abolishing the tax advantage? It is vital that the Government continue to encourage less polluting cars and fuels and that the tax regime is used to this end. Traditionally the Treasury has been opposed to hypothecation (ring fencing) of any tax raised. Yet in the 2000 Budget the Chancellor agreed to the ring fencing of the extra tobacco duty decreeing that this should be allocated to the NHS. We believe that a similar policy in regard to fuel taxation would enable consumers to make a clearer connection between their car use and the cost to the wider community.

11. Integrated fuel policy

11.1 Decisions about road fuel price and taxation policy should not be made in isolation but will ideally be made as part of an integrated energy policy. Such a policy could also assist the UK to meet its target of a 20% reduction of greenhouse gas emissions. The capacity of a government to intervene in energy policy is not helped by the present structure of the industry.

11.2 Given the nation's growing dependency on electricity supplies and petroleum-based fuels, it is perhaps surprising that the Government is so reluctant to develop anything which could be represented to the public as an energy policy.

11.3 The essential vulnerability of the global market place to price movement and supply variability has been amply demonstrated by the events over the past year. Without a guaranteed energy supply and a reliable distribution system any nation can quickly be brought to its knees. It is clear that no government can any longer provide the absolute assurances that most people would be seeking under the terms of a national energy policy. However, this does not absolve the Government of its responsibility to think and plan for the longer term contingencies and uncertainties in the world energy market.

11.4 Although an integrated energy policy for the UK is a very distant prospect given the conflicting requirements of housing, transport, health services, industrial and commercial applications, together with the proposed responses to climate change, a new focus is needed within the currently responsible department—the Department of Trade and Industry—to avoid further episodes of acute crisis management. A National Energy Forum should be quickly established to address this deficiency in the machinery of government.

11.5 This need was highlighted in the recent report of the Royal Commission on Environmental Pollution published in June 2000 under the title *Energy—The Changing Climate* (Royal Commission on Environmental Pollution 22nd Report). The Royal Commission specifically recommended that:

> ...*a Sustainable Energy Agency should be set up to promote energy efficiency more effectively in all sectors and co ordinate that with the rapid development of new energy sources.*

Looking toward the Scottish Parliament, the Royal Commission also recommended that:

> *The devolved administrations should review and improve their arrangements for promoting energy efficiency and renewable energy, taking into account our recommendation that a Sustainable Energy Agency should be established, and if necessary should seek additional powers in this field.*

We would argue that any policies in relation to fuel pricing should be framed in the context of wider energy decisions.

12. Transport (Scotland) Act 2000

12.1 Events in Autumn 2000 revealed the need for considerable investment in our railway system but this must be done on an integrated and planned basis. If people are to be persuaded to exchange their cars for public transport, many changes are needed to the present system.

12.2 This Act became law on 21st December 2000. It is in the main an enabling Act empowering local authorities to introduce measures rather than seeking to impose a single national structure. The original proposals for workplace parking charges and motorway tolls have not reached the statute book because it is claimed there was neither public nor business support for such measures. At the time of writing it is not clear if any additional funding or borrowing consent is being made available to local Authorities to introduce the measures intended. What is clear is that the funding that could have come from workplace parking charges and road tolls will not be available in Scotland. The introduction of congestion charging is possible (Edinburgh has considered such a scheme) and if funds thus realised are used for further development of public transport this will be welcome.

12.3 It remains to be seen how successful local authorities are in implementing integrated transport schemes, and the various transport agencies are in introducing flexible ticketing systems and providing clear reliable timetable information. The setting of national standards for concessionary travel is long overdue and welcome. The Committee will keep this matter under review.

13. The cost of fuel

13.1 Scotland is a net exporter of energy and yet is hard hit by the present taxation regime. As well as the health of our citizens we need to have regard to the health of the economy, many sections of which have to bear the high cost of fuel. We do not deny that there is a high cost to be paid for environmental health. But this cost will only be seen as a price worth paying if a significant part of the taxation raised is specifically designated and re-invested in environmental renewal, rural infrastructure and public transport, as well as helping to assist the poorest and hardest hit by rising fuel prices.

13.2   The cost of road fuel varies widely across Europe as the table in 7.6 shows. Fuel cost is, however, only one component of road transport costs.

13.3   In much of Europe VED or its equivalent varies from region to region as well as nationally. When this and road tolls are taken into account, accurate direct comparison is difficult.

13.4   In regard to the higher cost of fuel in isolated areas, while it is easy to see the difficulties thus caused, especially since public transport may not be a valid alternative to the car in such areas, it is not easy to see a simple solution. The higher cost is in the main due to the higher margins required by retailers and subsidy of rural filling stations would bring with it a further series of anomalies.

13.5   Nonetheless, we would urge the Government not to overlook this issue as it seeks to frame taxation and fuel policies.

THE TEXTILE INDUSTRY

1.   The Presbytery of Hamilton asked the Committee to consider the problems of the Textile Industry in June last year. DAKS Simpson had been the major employer in the Larkhall area for over 50 years but in May 2000 had declared 598 of the 1,500 workforce, redundant. In January 2001 a further 262 workers were declared redundant. DAKS Simpson had been a family firm for over 50 years but in 1992 had been bought out by a Japanese concern. Apart from their own product, DAKS had made for Marks & Spencer, Simpson's and Burberry. Following the decision by M&S to buy from non-UK manufacturers, the DAKS Simpson contract was ended. This specific issue coincided with the Committee's continuing interest in the textile industry. Last year we were in contact with parts of the knitwear sector in the Borders. Members of the Committee visited the Borders in January and a visit to Ayrshire is due in March 2001.

2.   The problem at DAKS Simpson is part of a larger problem. The clothing retail industry is undergoing massive change. In June 2000 C&A announced the closure of all its UK stores; in July 2000 the Arcadia group (including Wallis and Principles) closed 400 of its stores. Several firms in Ayrshire are also experiencing difficulties; Falmer's Jeans no longer trades as a brand name and following a management buy-out now trades as AGM Casual Wear, supplying Arcadia among others. It has to be said that as well as decline there is growth; change in all around there may be but not total decay. The revolution in the retail sector, and the change in buying habits, is the major cause of the difficulties in the manufacturing sector. Members of the Committee have met and continue to meet with those involved.

3.   Difficulties are not confined to the Clothing sector. The Scottish Executive commissioned a study published in June 2000 by DTZ Pieda Consulting and their report covers not only the garment sector but knitwear, weaving, Harris Tweed, dyeing and finishing, spinning, carpets, leather, lace and soft furnishing. This report, published in June of last year, includes the following details (figures are from 1997, the latest year for which full figures were available):

- The Textile Industry is the fourth largest manufacturing sector in Scotland but has declined from employing 57,000 in 1984 to 33,800 in 1997. This rate of decline is almost twice that of manufacturing as a whole.
- Since 1997 a further 5,000 jobs have disappeared. Cambridge Econometrics forecast that by 2010 the number employed will fall to 2,000.
- In some areas, such as the Borders, the textile industry accounts for 50% of manufacturing jobs.
- The industry is a low wage sector (10% below average), this only partly explained by the high number of female employees.
- The industry is a major exporter (£498 million in 1998). It accounts for 3% of Scottish manufactured exports. 28% of its output is exported.

4. The DTZ Pieda report details the problems faced by each sector of the industry, but the following are common to all:

- The difference in labour costs between the UK, the Far East, Eastern Europe and North Africa
- The change in demand in the UK market
- Fluctuations in the economies of the major export markets
- Fluctuations in exchange rates, especially the continuing weakness of the Euro, which has lost 30% of its value between its launch and Autumn 2000.

5. Cashmere can be taken as an example not only of the problems of the industry but also of the way solutions can be found. It is of particular importance in the Borders and is also a major component of our export trade. The cashmere sector faces problems from the following:

- The end of the Multi-Fibre Agreement (MFA). The MFA was introduced in 1974 to regulate import quotas and "protect" markets from a flood of cheap imports from the developing world. Many saw this as not only an unfair restriction of trade but also a major handicap for the developing nations. The Trade and Development Centre claims that about a third of developing nations have substantial export interests in textiles and for one in seven such countries textiles make up the majority of their export earnings. As a result of the World Trade Organisation's (WTO) latest agreement on textiles and clothing such quotas will be phased out over a ten year period and by 1st January 2006 should no longer exist. While we welcome the advantage this will bring to poorer nations we need to be aware of the consequences for the British textile industry. Scottish Cashmere may face a major inflow of cheaper cashmere (from, for example, China) when the MFA ends.
- The threat arising from a continuation of the so-called "Banana War". The WTO found in favour of the USA and against the EU over the matter of European banana quotas. Europe has so far not conformed to the WTO ruling and as a result the USA has introduced tariffs that discriminate against European exports to the USA. There have been threats to include cashmere products in this tariff war. Whatever

be the rights and wrongs of the banana issue, it is clear that the Scottish cashmere Industry could finish up as a totally innocent victim.

- With cheaper labour costs as well as raw materials in developing nations, increasing industrialisation adds to the problem. China, for example, not unreasonably now aims to manufacture finished products rather than just export wool.

6. On 6th June 2000 the Scottish Executive launched a package of measures aimed at offering help to the Industry, this to run in tandem with a raft of measures from the DTI. In launching the measures Henry McLeish, then Minister for Enterprise and Lifelong Learning, said, "We fully acknowledge the setbacks which the industry has experienced in recent years. … I believe this package provides the foundations for the textile industry to fight back and safeguard the futures of the thousands which it still employs."

7. The Borders visit enabled the Committee to find out how both the DTZ Pieda report and the Government's response had been received. There was general acceptance that DTZ Pieda research provided a sound basis on which to proceed and that the Government's response was welcome. While there was little new funding—rather a re-packaging of what was already on offer—this was welcome as it made companies aware of what aid was available.

8. Most Borders firms are small to medium-sized businesses with about 3,800 people employed in 80 or so firms. Exports are important. The European Union is the main market, followed by the United States and the Asian Pacific countries. The supply of high quality products, often cashmere, to these niche exports and to home markets is seen as the future direction for the industry. There is an optimism that the decline in the industry has now bottomed out and that there are continuing opportunities for development.

- The establishment at Galashiels of one of the Centres of Manufacturing Excellence by Heriot-Watt University was good news. Design is one of the areas in which the Scottish Industry can succeed. Apart from training, this centre organises competitions for students of Design and in co-operation with Scottish Enterprise Borders, graduates of the Centre may be provided with small business units in which they can set up.

- Scottish Enterprise Borders has been given the lead role in developing a "Textile Strategy for Scotland".
- The establishment of the Scottish Textiles Forum brings together most sections of the industry.
- The development of the *Made in Scotland* logo and making this mean quality is also welcome.
- The problem of shortage of labour with the necessary skills is being addressed by varied training and re-training schemes. Of special note is the *Behind the Label* scheme, a programme aimed at school-leavers encouraging them to think of the Textile Industry as a positive career choice, which most no longer do.

It remains to be seen how effective these and other measures are.

9.　　The Labour Research Department confirmed that between May 1997 and May 2000 around 18,000 jobs had been lost in Scotland in the whole range of manufacturing. Clearly, the textile industry is undergoing a process of change. In the Borders, for example, 45% (8,500) of jobs in textiles have gone over the last 20 years. The estimated loss to the Borders economy in wages is £6-£7 million a year; indirect loss of income is put at £26.8 million. We need to understand what is happening and sympathise with those whose traditional way of life is threatened. There is obvious frustration that there appears as yet no obvious alternative employment in many affected areas. Change there is and such change needs to be managed, and managed with sympathy and understanding. There may well be no simple single answer. The textile industry, as well as farming, mining and other traditional industries, is changing before our eyes. We in the UK cannot hope to compete with low wage economies in the developing world, nor should we want to. The hope for textiles would appear to be in the design and manufacture of a quality product and in making *Made in Scotland* synonymous with quality. When we speak, as we often do, of the stewardship of resources, we speak not only of money or land or possessions but also of people. The story of the textile industry, in

common with many others, is a story which speaks to us of the need to recognise and to cherish the riches we have been given - riches of skill and tradition and natural resources - and to invest in them adequately. They then have the chance to produce their harvest and to weave it into the tapestry of human life.

PUBLIC SERVICE BROADCASTING AND REGIONAL BROADCASTING VISION FOR THE FUTURE

1.　Public Service Broadcasting in the New Communications Context

1.1　We have grown up in a country and in an age where public service broadcasting (PSB) has been the presumed norm. John Reith, General Manager of the BBC, said in 1924:

> *As we conceive it, our responsibility is to carry into the greatest possible number of homes everything that is best in every department of human knowledge, endeavour and achievement.*

1.2　Public service broadcasting has been about the accessibility of good quality broadcasting and ensuring universal access, maintaining diversity and plurality and securing quality. Public service broadcasters must be willing to deliver these qualities regardless of their commercial viability. The Peacock Committee reported a consensus among public service broadcasters on the duty to "inform, entertain and educate" and on the principle of geographical universality.

1.3　However, there is grave doubt about the willingness of television companies to continue to provide the present level of service in the areas of public service broadcasting and regional broadcasting. Many producers have concerns that the increasing market pressures will threaten quality public service broadcasting. Existing regulatory bodies such as the Independent Television Commission (ITC) have had difficulty in attempting to sustain even light-touch regulation in the face of commercial pressure. This is in part because some of the reasons which justify regulation in the past no longer exist, or are not seen as desirable in the new era.

1.4 Broadcasting is undergoing a profound revolution. Digital technology now permits many more channels to be carried, both by traditional terrestrial transmitters and by satellite. As technology surrounding the Internet improves, moving pictures can be accessed via simple phone lines. The distinction between radio, television and internet has become less clear. The potential for change and greatly increased choice is now with us, but there remains uncertainty as to what kind of change will result from the combination of finance, technology, and consumer demand.

1.5 As the new channels compete for audience attention, some would argue that when technical restrictions are gone there will be opportunity for the market to deliver what people want, unfettered by regulation. But these restrictions have not yet gone. Most of the population, for reasons of availability, choice or cost, or a combination of these, still receives only four or five channels via the analogue terrestrial network of transmitters. When digital reception is a reality for everyone, there are issues of competition to be addressed, such as the commercial advantage of existing channels in having established themselves, and the power of carriers, cable and satellite, who are also owners of individual channels.

1.6 Plans are currently being considered for BBC3 and BBC4. These have to balance on the one hand the need to create channels which are established and secure by the time all viewers have access to digital transmission, and on the other the need to deliver a universally accessible service to viewers who are meanwhile not capable of receiving digital channels. Planning appropriate evolution to BBC3 and 4 requires a clear signal from the Government as to when analogue switch off is planned. It will not be acceptable for many viewers to have the less commercial elements of the BBC's output delivered on channels with limited audience potential and much smaller budgets. The BBC, funded as it is by the public via their licence fees, is clearly a cornerstone of public service broadcasting. In the face of multi-channel environment where channel "branding" will become increasingly important, the BBC's diversification into new channels is clearly necessary if it is not to become an "optional add-on", as PSB appears to be in the United States.

1.7 As Andrew Graham and Gavin Davies assert in *Broadcasting, Society and Policy in the Multi Channel Age, Public service broadcasting is not an optional add-on, but central to the health of all broadcasting.*

2. The White Paper

2.1 Amid this climate of change and uncertainty, the Government published a White Paper in December 2000: *A New Future for Communications*. For the first time, it is not a broadcasting white paper but a communications white paper. It argues that: *It is vital that government has a clear policy framework for this rapidly developing sector, which will be so central to our economy, democratic life, culture, entertainment and education.* (1.1.23)
　The Committee responded to it at the appropriate time, and now seeks to stimulate wider thinking about vision for the future.

2.2 The Government in its White Paper makes the following general points:

- *Our world is changing and communications are central to this change;*
- *We want to ensure the widest possible access to a choice of diverse communications and services of the highest quality;*
- *We will make sure that people can continue to receive much-loved broadcasting channels;*
- *We will strengthen the regional dimension to UK broadcasting and continue to support the independent production sector, as well as consider new plans for community media.*

2.3 Because the boundaries of the broadcasting industry are not so clearly defined as they once were there is a huge difference from the way most of us have perceived broadcasting up until now. The framework for which the White Paper argues would have very strict guidelines and be able to be implemented. Thus rather than try to combine existing regulators the Government proposes the radical measure of creating, as the White Paper puts it:

a single regulatory body for the communications and media industries—an Office of Communication (OFCOM)—which will cover telecommunications, television and radio. Its remit will cover both content and communications network. It will promote competition and manage spectrum.(1.3.6)

This new body, however, will not cover the BBC who will still be regulated by a Board of Governors.

2.4 With the huge changes taking place and with the end of spectrum scarcity, some people are suggesting that the end of public service broadcasting is imminent, simply because of the competition in a vibrant market. However the existing terrestrial channels have public service obligations laid upon them in return for the privileges granted to them. In the case of the BBC the privilege of the licence fee and in the case of ITV, Channel 4 and 5 the limited spectrum available for transmission has limited the number of channels. Although digital and cable and eventually the Internet will provide opportunities for transmission of many more channels, these terrestrial channels remain uniquely privileged in competitive terms in having access to analogue spectrum. Therefore their public service obligations remain.

2.5 The White Paper insists that:

Public service broadcasting will continue to have a key role to play in the digital future, potentially an even more important rule than it has now. However the way public service broadcasting is regulated and delivered by the broadcasters will have to change to reflect the new conditions in which they operate. (5.1)

2.6 The new structure of regulation, it is proposed, *would allow broadcasting to adapt quickly and efficiently to change,* and clearly backs the maintenance of the PSB statutory commitment for quality, variety and levels of PSB. OFCOM is expected to ensure that it will be possible for all channels to carry the entire range of public service broadcasting.

2.7 The White Paper assures us that: *We will give OFCOM powers to ensure that public service broadcasting channels are given due prominence on devices such as electronic programme guides and that*

access to them is easy. Accessibility to public service channels, however, is also vital. If the viewer cannot access them easily they will not watch. The broadcasters may use this as lack of public interest and in turn use this as an argument for dispensing with them altogether. This accessibility includes the issue of the listings of public service channels and whether this should be by genre as well as by channel. These arrangements would refer to the channels already mentioned but [*the Government*] *will retain the right to add new public digital services to this list, where we consider that these are essential for full social inclusion.(3.5.1)*

2.8 The key elements, therefore, of the proposed regulatory framework are:

- to create a system which allows flexibility for public service broadcasters
- to maintain mixed, varied and high quality schedules, and
- to ensure a level playing field for different broadcasters who have different aims and objectives and funding sources.

The White Paper sees this mixture as a national treasure:

By having a mixture of publicly owned, publicly regulated and purely commercial broadcasters, the UK has in many ways had the best of both worlds. The competition from commercial broadcasters has been a spur to innovation and serving consumers. The public service broadcasters have provided a guarantee and benchmark of quality for the rest of the market, halting any slide towards lowest common denominator content. That mixed ecology of broadcasting is worth fostering, indeed is essential for the digital world.(5.3.12)

2.9 The White Paper retains a commitment: *to ensuring that public service TV channels are available to everyone, as now, free at the point of consumption, both before and after the switchover to digital television.*

Because more than 99% of the population has access to most television channels, the Government wants to maintain that kind of service and will work actively to ensure that everyone has easy access, *either free at the point of delivery or at an affordable price.(3.2.1)*

3. The Perspective of the Church

3.1 The Church comments on these matters from the basic belief that people matter as people. All else, including commercial considerations, is therefore secondary. As this is so, then inclusion must be a guiding principle. For us this will mean that neither geography nor income should separate people from the society in which they are set (ensuring universal access); it will mean that they are worthy of good broadcasting (securing quality); and it will mean that their own local culture is worthy of attention in its own right—saved from the fate of metropolitan homogenisation (maintaining diversity and plurality).

3.2 The Church, with its network of contacts in the presbyteries and parishes across the land, has set universality of access as a watchword for its own organisation and is therefore aware that, likewise in broadcasting, universality of access to high quality programmes, regardless of their commercial viability, is important to people.

3.3 We therefore welcome the assurance of the Foreword of the White Paper that the Government is keen: *to ensure the widest possible access to a choice of diverse communication services of the highest quality …We want to include every section of our society in the benefits of these services, and use to the full the opportunities now available for enhancing their diversity and quality.*

3.4 Having less commercial appeal should not be assumed to be the same as being less popular. All broadcasters measure *ratings*, the number of people watching a given programme at any one time, and *share*, the percentage of the watching public tuned in to a channel at any given time. These are the most common means of measuring audience, and the means used by advertisers. But they are not the only measurement of value or popularity. Broadcasters also measure *AI* (Appreciation Index) the level of satisfaction a programme gives, and *reach*, the number of people who may watch some part of a series or channel at some time over a given period. However viewers may be at least as concerned that, say, a factual series can be relied upon to be of a high standard when they watch it, even if they do not watch every programme in the series. A mark of public service must be valuing the *AI* and the *reach* as much as the *share* or *rating*.

3.5 The White Paper seeks views on ownership of channels and specifically on whether the restriction on ownership of channels by religious bodies should be preserved. The Committee does not feel it should be. In a multi-channel environment where anyone with conviction and capital can set up a channel it would be anomalous to prohibit religious bodies from doing so. However, the Committee does not believe that religion as a subject should be confined to religious channels. High quality factual programming, part of public service, should include specifically religious programmes. Other factual and drama programmes should make an effort to ensure appropriate reflection of the religious dimension of life, and not assume that religious departments or channels are looking after the subject to the exclusion of all other programme makers and genres.

4. Ensuring Universal Access

4.1 Public service broadcasting should be for everyone's benefit but not everyone is willing to pay for more than the programmes they already know, such as sports and films. For the majority of viewers at present, traditional terrestrial distribution remains the principal means of receiving television programmes and in the future there will be many viewers who will choose not to pay for additional channels. There may also be a question of power within a household where one member may be in a position to dictate which channels are bought whereas at present terrestrial television channels are available on all television sets. The development of digital television is to be encouraged provided that everyone benefits from the improved service.

4.2 The White Paper promises that: *We will maintain and extend obligations to secure the carriage of public service channels over cable and satellite.* But perhaps it is more important to define what is meant by PSB. Do cable and satellite providers mean the same as the Government does? This issue will be especially important after the switchover to digital as many people with digital will want all services through the set top box they have without needing additional equipment for terrestrial signals. For this reason cable and satellite operators will also deliver PSB.

4.3 Not only is the range of programmes available important, viewers and listeners should have a choice of providers for these services. Digital technology makes this plurality much easier and gives rise to competition between providers. This, it is hoped, will encourage innovative investment leading to the excellent delivery of services that society requires. However, without a regulatory oversight, investment may only be made in the more popular programmes and therefore the full diverse service which we now enjoy would not be available.

4.4 The Committee urges that a measure of public service should be a channel's willingness to use as a criterion for scheduling not just ratings or share but reach, for reach is about valuing the viewer. Factual, including religious, programmes may not always achieve the ratings of a soap, but there is clear evidence that their reach is significant. The audience will not be well served if such programmes are squeezed to the margins of both budget and schedule. In many ways the BBC World Service, to which there are to be no changes in existing arrangements, is an excellent example of quality where reach, rather than ratings, must be a measure of its success.

4.5 While not being complacent about the future of public service broadcasting, the fact remains that it has been a major and valued part of UK broadcasting for all of broadcasting's life. Developments that have already taken place with the multi-channel revolution have made improvements, especially in the areas of films, sport and news. And PSB has proved thus far to be the best way of making original UK programmes that people want to see. The White Paper notes that, *The public service broadcasters still command 61.6% of the total audience in multi-channel homes and 70% in peak time.*

4.6 These programmes are the basis of much of the programming for digital channels, as these television and radio programmes are what economists call "public goods". Once a programme has been completed extra copies are virtually free and with access virtually free at the point of use, the programme can be repeated many times without increasing cost. The public interest is best served and access not restricted by continuing the practice of everyone paying for television through advertising or the licence fee.

4.7 But if the economic argument hold good so does the democratic one. Public Service Broadcasting ensures that the interests of all viewers are taken into account and we should not tolerate a market that results in exclusion. This means ensuring that the best programmes remain available to the maximum number of people.

5. Securing Quality

5.1 The White Paper's concern about quality is that *...increased diversity may harm the quality of programming available and reduce standards of decency.*(1.1.22) In ensuring universal access the Committee is concerned that the access is to a product worth having. An increasing emphasis on entertainment to win audiences may reduce the number and quality, for example, of high-quality factual programmes on network, including religious programmes. Factual programmes have been seen as a measure of commitment to public service. For example, current affairs and religious programmes have been increasingly squeezed out of peak time transmission.

5.2 OFCOM will combine the functions of the current regulators (Broadcasting Standard Commission, Independent Television Commission, Oftel, Radio Authority, Radio Communications Agency) thus simplifying oversight. OFCOM has a further specific role—to develop good links with the relevant policy committees and executives of devolved assemblies, to ensure that regional as well as national voices are heard. The BBC will retain a Board of Governors with modified responsibilities. A big advance would be for the BBC also to be given a legal requirement to consult with the Scottish Parliament.

5.3 The media are important in representing the views of a nation and the fact that broadcasting is not a devolved power makes this issue an essential component of the work of OFCOM. This is especially so if it is to be an effective regulator for the Government: to oversee UK broadcasting and to ensure the retention of the important place of public service broadcasting and regional broadcasting.

6. Maintaining diversity and plurality

6.1 Regional programmes need to be included in the commitment to maintain a quality of service, for it not only plays a part in stating a region's identity, it is the place where people learn about local issues and should be encouraged to participate. As it states in the White Paper: *It [regional broadcasting] is an intrinsic element of public service broadcasting in the UK.*(3.3.2)

6.2 "Nations" and "regions" are terms now used by all broadcasters in their policymaking for production from outside London. The nations referred to are Scotland, Wales, and Northern Ireland, and the regions are the regions of England. While England is significantly larger than the other nations, it should be remembered that the regions of Scotland are also diverse and distinct. The Borders are distinct from the Central Belt, the East Coast from the West, the Northern Isles from the Western Isles and the Highlands from the Lowlands. The ITV network has traditionally borne significant responsibility for reflecting this.

6.3 If public service is about delivering quality regardless of commercial considerations, and if there are to continue to be public service requirements laid upon ITV, then the new regulator must have both the resources and robustness to ensure public service requirements, and regionality in particular, are not compromised by inevitable commercial pressure. This may mean more constructive means of assessment than the current system of merely counting minutes.

6.4 It has to be said, of course, that the regional broadcasting provision is not perfect. Often geographical problems mean that some people cannot at present receive the regional programmes best suited to their area. With the use of digital broadcasting it is hoped that this issue can be resolved and the Government is to initiate discussion to this end, with relevant broadcasting companies. It is to be hoped these discussions are soon and worthwhile.

6.5 ITV does have particular obligations in delivering regional programmes and the White Paper makes it clear that these will continue. Regional production is inevitably less economic than network production and factual programmes less expensive than drama and entertainment, so regional outputs on ITV are mostly factual. The question of finance is also raised because the 1990 Broadcasting Act removed the financial incentives previously offered to ITV companies to make their regional programmes with higher budgets and to higher standards. Post 1990 there is intense commercial pressure on ITV companies to cut programme costs wherever possible. The Act has not been rigorously implemented and so regulation and intervention by the ITC to maintain quality has been much harder. There are therefore issues about the quality being assessed by subjective standards, the variety of regional programmes on ITV and light touch regulation which should also be discussed in the Government talks.

6.6 Delivering programmes on network which reflect the cultures of all the nations of the United Kingdom is clearly another mark of public service, and the White Paper's acknowledgement of regionality is welcome. The EU has legislation to ensure restriction on what otherwise would be the domination of our screens by imported American programmes. So legislation is required to ensure there remain healthy production bases in, and input from, all the nations and regions of the UK. The regional dimension for each ITV Company will be stated in the licence conditions and OFCOM at a time of subsequent take-over will be required to review the regional obligations.

7. Scotland

7.1 This is especially relevant to Scotland when the

merger of Scottish Television and Grampian Television is recalled. In the report to the General Assembly in 1998 the Committee stated: *This media domination within Scotland has aroused fears of the erosion of regional identity. Many viewers in the Grampian transmission area are concerned that the distinctive character of the region may be submerged with a loss of editorial independence and more centralisation of resources and a reduced presence in Aberdeen.* These fears have been realised. The ITC upheld complaints from MPs, MSPs and the trade unions and, following their own monitoring of the situation, criticised Grampian Television in May 2000 for cutting the number of regional programmes. The report found that over the last two years there had been a substantial reduction in programmes of special interest to North of Scotland viewers in prime time slots. The Government also wants to see regional aspect developed further by other public service broadcasters, with BBC and Channel 4 increasing their commitment to the nations and regions. This is to be welcomed and targets are to be set and monitored by OFCOM.

7.2 Scotland's geography compared with the rest of the UK deserves particular attention which the White Paper has not acknowledged. The Highlands and Islands and the Borders have many small communities separated from each other by hills and mountains. This makes the communities distinct in character as they are geographically defined and these small pockets of population can be served easily with radio stations whose signals are contained by the hills.

7.3 The White Paper talks of the potential for community level services in television and radio. Scotland already has a number of highly successful community radio stations, largely run by volunteers and in which local churches often have involvement. Regulation should acknowledge their distinctiveness and facilitate further growth in these areas. Community television could also be available with the new technology and the Government does want to encourage broadcasters in this area. Some cable companies do offer local services but there are questions of quality, supply, demand and supervision which would need to be examined.

8. Gaelic

8.1 The desire to meet the needs of different communities led to the establishment of the Gaelic Broadcasting Task Force in 1999. It reviews the current provision of programming in the Gaelic language and considers future options. With this great revolution in broadcasting it is now simpler to advocate a separate Gaelic language channel and many Gaelic speakers themselves would support this because they are aware that there is resistance from non-Gaelic speakers about the air time Gaelic programmes have and the compromise of putting English subtitles on Gaelic programmes has not been acceptable to the native speakers. The Committee has noted concerns expressed about the demise of Telefios, the Gaelic news service on Grampian/ Scottish. The compromises which the 1990 Act introduced, whereby ITV was required to carry Gaelic programming in peak time, have clearly not been resolved, and the White Paper's intention to give further consideration to structures for Gaelic broadcasting are welcome.

In the name and by the authority of the Committee

ALAN McDONALD, *Convener*
ERIK CRAMB, *Vice-Convener*
DAVID SINCLAIR, *Secretary*

ADDENDUM

Erik Cramb has served for the past two years as Vice-Convener of the Church and Nation Committee. In that time his wise advice and ready wit have helped to keep the Committee both focused on its task and happy in its work. Erik has brought wide experience of church and nation to bear and the Committee has been the better for it. As a support for Convener and Secretary he has been invaluable in his ability to combine the insights of his "day job" in Industrial Mission with the analytical task of the Committee. He has decided to stand down to lessen the "middle-aged, clerical and male" image of the Church and Nation officebearers. We thank him for his commitment to the Committee and the time he has given; and we wish him well as he returns to his day job and to the support of his football team, Partick Thistle Nil.

ALAN McDONALD, *Convener*
DAVID SINCLAIR, *Secretary*

PANEL ON DOCTRINE
MAY 2001

PROPOSED DELIVERANCE

The General Assembly

1. Receive the Report.

2. Instruct the Assembly Council: (a) to study the Report, and in particular those sections which relate to the eldership; (b) to undertake a review of the office of elder in the Church of Scotland, with a view to enabling the whole church to rediscover the full significance of the eldership as a spiritual office; and (c) to bring proposals for the implementation thereof to a future General Assembly.

3. Welcome the commitment of the Board of Ministry to producing a report on non-stipendiary ministry in consultation with other Boards and Committees, and instruct the Board to draw upon the Panel's Report in its further thinking.

4. Instruct the Boards of Ministry, Parish Education and National Mission, together with the Panel on Doctrine to collaborate in a comprehensive review of local recognised ministry (Report 5.4), in consultation with Presbyteries, and to bring a joint Report to a future General Assembly.

5. Accept the view of the Panel that ordination should be extended to the diaconate and remit to the Board of Practice and Procedure, in consultation with the Board of Ministry, to prepare legislation for the introduction of the ordination of deacons.

6. Remit to the Panel on Worship to review the services for the ordination of ministers of Word and sacrament and for the ordination of elders, and to prepare an order of service for the ordination of deacons.

7. Affirm that no change is necessary to Act III 1999 anent Moderators of Presbytery (Appendix).

8. Accept the Report as fulfilling the Panel's remits on ordination.

REPORT

Ordination in the Church of Scotland

1. Introduction

1.1 The Panel's remits and the 2000 Report

The subject of ordination was remitted to the Panel in two stages: first in 1997, when the matter of ordination to the Diaconate was raised; and secondly in 1998, when the Panel was asked "to examine the concept of Ordination as it applies to or may apply to the Ministry, the Auxiliary Ministry, the Eldership, the Diaconate and the Readership". The Panel brought an interim Report on the Diaconate to the General Assembly of 1999. In 2000, it presented the first part of a final Report, under the title, "The Doctrine of Ordination". In this, the concept of ordination was examined in the context of reflection on church and ministry. The General Assembly endorsed this Report as "a sufficient statement of the church's understanding of the doctrine of Ordination at this present time". There are important matters remaining to be addressed, however: in particular the principles of the 2000 Report must now be applied to the ministries mentioned in the remit.

1.2 Process

The Panel's Working Party on Ordination has continued to meet over the last year, with ongoing representation from the Boards of Ministry, Parish Education, and National Mission. The Working Party has benefited from contacts with other churches, and is grateful in particular for contributions from the Rev. Dr. John Clark of the United Reformed Church, the Rev. Douglas Kornahrens of the Scottish Episcopal Church and Fr. Michael McMahon of the Roman Catholic Church. We are also grateful for the significant contribution from the Rev. Steven Mackie, formerly of the University of St. Andrews and of the staff of the World Council of Churches, who was co-opted on to the Working Party at an early stage.

2. Revisiting the 2000 Report: "The Doctrine of Ordination"

2.1 Background: a variety of ministries

The 2000 Report noted that throughout its forty year history the Panel on Doctrine has repeatedly been asked to study the subject of ministry. The Panel thought it wise to begin by reviewing this history, as it might shed light on the underlying concerns which had given rise to the remits on ordination. One issue which emerged was the inter-relationship between the various offices which have grown up in the Church of Scotland. While offices like the Ministry and the Eldership have a long history, and are well established in the Church's structures, the present offices of Reader, Deacon and Auxiliary Minister have emerged more recently. The Panel detected a concern in the Church that we perhaps no longer have a coherent understanding of ministry. It is widely felt that the character and inter-relationship of the various offices is less than clear; and that this situation hinders the Church as it seeks to enable and support Christian service in and through these offices. The question of ordination highlights this problem, for only ministers, auxiliary ministers and elders are ordained, and the method of ordination is not uniform. Deacons, meanwhile, are commissioned, while readers are set apart. There is much confusion in the Church about what these different terms signify, and perhaps even a suspicion that the avoidance of the term ordination for certain ministries signifies a reluctance to grant them "full status" alongside the others.

A second issue which emerged as a long-standing concern was the role and position of the Diaconate. The Panel on Doctrine's work on ministry in the 1980s derived from a remit agreed following the Report of the Diaconate Board in 1982, the latter having expressed unease about the future role and position of the Diaconate. The Panel's 1980s Reports did not propose significant change for the Diaconate. The main change which has taken place since then arose from the Report of the Diaconate Committee in 1989, which successfully proposed the admission of deacons into the Courts of the Church. While this has broadly been welcomed, it has arguably created a more anomalous situation than before, since deacons are the only members of the Courts of the Church who are not ordained.

2.2 Background: the ministry of the whole people

The 2000 Report also considered how far the remits had arisen from contemporary concerns about ministry within the church. It came to the conclusion that the remits do indeed reflect current concerns, which raise very serious issues of theology and practice. During the twentieth century the world-wide church experienced a rediscovery of the insight that ministry is the task and calling of the whole church. In earlier ages ministry was seen as the task of the few; the Reformers did not disagree with this, affirming explicitly that the priesthood of all does not mean the ministry of all. This remained the largely unchallenged view of the churches right into modern times: in 1927, the first World Conference on Faith and Order in Lausanne affirmed five propositions on ministry, but there is no hint in them that ministry might be the calling of the whole people of God. Indeed the fifth of these states: "Entrance into the work of ministry is by an act of ordination by prayer and the laying on of hands to those gifted for the work, called by the Spirit and accepted by the Church". The ensuing decades, though, have brought an enormous shift: the ministry of the few who occupy particular offices is no longer seen as the whole ministry of the church; nor, arguably, as the primary ministry of the church. Rather the primary call to ministry is understood to be the calling of the whole church, and the ministry of those who occupy particular offices is understood as summoning and serving that prior call to ministry.

The Panel believed that this shifting perspective, even more than concerns about specific offices, lay behind the remits and required to be addressed. Indeed the two are related, for the emergence of the Diaconate, the Readership and the Auxiliary Ministry can be interpreted as a response to the growing conviction that ministry is something wider, not restricted to a few. However, it was important to realise that a broader range of offices was only a partial solution. It was not, on its own, a sufficient response to this new insight. For the claim that ministry belongs to the whole people put serious questions to the very notion of ordination. Why, if ministry is for all, do we appoint some to particular offices? Why do we recognise publicly the call of some to ministry, when we don't do this for everyone? Why do we ordain some but not others? Ordination was formerly understood to be the gateway to ministry; but, if all are called to ministry, what then is ordination?

This new understanding required not only fresh attention to the doctrine of ordination, it required a fundamental rethinking of the nature and practice of ordained ministry. This kind of re-visioning process is indeed ongoing throughout the church. No-one engaged in ordained ministry today can be entirely exempt from it. The danger was very real, though, that our official positions as a church, and consequently our structures, would not keep tempo with the changing perceptions and needs of the church at large; and the resulting lag would hinder and disperse the winds of the Spirit which had brought us this far.

2.3 Ministry in the church

The 2000 Report, therefore, took the view that the doctrine of ordination needs to be examined in the context of serious reflection on the nature of the church, and the nature of ministry. It borrowed a structure for this reflection from the Panel's 1980s Reports: that such

reflection must recognise the mission of God, in creation, reconciliation and redemption, as its starting point; it must identify Christ as the true agent of ministry, the one who fulfils God's purpose; and it must recognise the church's task of ministry (which is, fundamentally, the calling of the whole church) as derived from Christ's ministry, neither identical with nor independent of it, but serving and bearing witness to Christ's reconciling presence in the world.

2.4 Witness and service

Since its earliest Reports on ministry in the 1960s, the Panel has consistently supported the insight that ministry is the calling of the whole church. The 2000 Report discussed some of the issues raised by this affirmation. It argued that the terms "ministry" and "service" must be understood broadly, and indeed it argued that these terms are largely interchangeable. If divisions have grown up on the basis of a distinction between these terms - between the ministry of the Word, perhaps, and the ministry of service in the world - such divisions are in fact groundless. The whole church is called to bear witness to Christ, and to serve him in the world. To bear witness to Christ is to serve him; to serve Christ is to bear witness to him. Of course there is a variety of gifts within the church, and there must be some distribution of functions; but the practical distinctions which must be drawn are not the distinction between witness and service. To speak of the ministry of the whole people of God is to say that the whole church has the character of service. The work of Christian ministry or of Christian service is not for a few, not even with the assistance of the many. This work is the responsibility of the whole church, and the task of the few who are set apart to particular ministries is to lead and support the whole church in its witness to and service of Christ's ministry of reconciliation.

2.5 The doctrine of ordination

The New Testament, particularly in passages like 1 Corinthians 12-14 and Ephesians 4, offers a picture of a variety of ministries in the church, grounded in a variety of spiritual gifts, each serving to strengthen and unify the church. The picture is of an attractive freedom in which gifts could be expressed and exercised without formal authorisation. The development of a more rigid ordering of ministry may seem like a retrograde step. It is worth noting, however, that the burden of Paul's argument in 1 Corinthians 12–14 was that the church's gifts and ministries must be used in an orderly way, for the good of the whole.

It was important to affirm, then, that the appointment of some to particular spheres of ministry, or to particular responsibility for ministry, was not precluded by the affirmation that the whole church is called to ministry. Indeed such appointments may be required by it. For the fact that the church has a definite character and calling meant that it may or may not remain true to its character and calling. It may forget or deny that it is called into being to serve Christ's ministry, and through it the divine purpose in creation, reconciliation and redemption. The 2000 Report argued that the practice of ordination is grounded in the need for the church to hold firm to its character and calling. It quoted *Baptism, Eucharist and Ministry* in this regard: "In order to fulfil its mission, the Church needs persons who are publicly and continually responsible for pointing to its fundamental dependence on Jesus Christ, and thereby provide, within a multiplicity of gifts, a focus for its unity".[1]

The 2000 Report surveyed the doctrine of ordination in Reformed thinking and in the history of the Church of Scotland. It then affirmed the inauguration of ministries by ordination, an act which expresses the grounding of ministry in the gifts of the Holy Spirit and in divine calling. It explicated the notion of ordination for life not on the basis that the ordained have a new status either before God or society (the Report explicitly disavowed any distinction between clergy and laity), but on the basis that gifts and call come to persons: "Implicit in these notions of gift and call, however, is the fact that the *person* is called. The gifts of the Holy Spirit are not extraneous additions to one's personality and abilities. To speak of the gifts of the Spirit here is to recognise that our personal abilities are God-given. They may need to be nurtured and developed; they are never so secure or self-sufficient that we do not need to depend on God; and we cannot on the strength of "natural" abilities, without grace, presume to be able to do God's work. But it is through the instrument of *persons*, with their particular abilities and limitations, that God works. We are not called to make available to God abstract abilities or skills, without personal commitment. Gifts and call come to *persons*".[2]

2.6 Criteria for ordination

The 2000 Report, then, defends an understanding of church and ministry in which it is appropriate not only that there are some particular ministries in the church which are set apart and publicly recognised, but also that it is right and good to inaugurate some such ministries by ordination. The question then arises: which ministries ought to be ordained? The 2000 Report suggested four criteria - ordained ministries are those which: i. are concerned not just with one part of the church's life, but with keeping the church true to its nature and calling; ii. are understood to be ministries of the universal church; iii. have their vocation to ministry tested and affirmed by the church; iv. endure through time. These four criteria are intended to express the conviction that ordination is not the gateway to ministry as such, but rather the gateway to certain ministries which are concerned with the character of the church *as the church*. Ordination gives order to the church's ministry. Ordained ministries are concerned with the identity of the church, its unity through time as well as its unity throughout the world, its calling to be Christ's witness and servant in the world. These ministries exist to hold the church to its true nature and calling; therefore they operate not in isolation or distinction from the church and its calling, but as a part of it charged with particular responsibility.

2.7 Work in progress

The 2000 Report aimed, then, to present an account of ordination appropriate to an age which believes firmly in the ministry of the whole people of God. It had to set the doctrine of ordination in the wider context of reflection on church and ministry, since the insight that ministry is the calling of the whole church puts serious questions to existing teachings and practices. The Panel believes that such questions not only lie behind the remits it has received in this area, but also that they are prompting much reflection on the nature and practice of ministry throughout the church, and will continue to do so.

Indeed the 2000 Report held back from making concrete proposals about ordination and particular offices, partly because of a fear that to rush to such conclusions would divert attention away from the seriousness of the issues at stake. The priority for the church is not to tinker with its offices, but rather to en-vision ministry in the Church of Scotland, including ordained ministry, in new ways. In its 2000 Report the Panel attempted to contribute to this process. If this further Report will shortly go on to make concrete proposals in relation to particular offices and their inauguration, we would emphasise that these are not to be regarded as the fundamental subject matter before the Panel and the Church. Even if the Panel urges the Church to take certain concrete actions, it would urge the Church even more strongly to reflect on the issues which have given rise to these two Reports, to reflect on the nature of the church and its calling to ministry today. This further Report, as much as the 2000 Report, is intended to stimulate and encourage this kind of reflection.

3 Oversight

3.1 Ordination and oversight

Ministry (or service) is the calling of the whole church; and baptism can be seen as the act by which this call to ministry is recognised and publicly affirmed.[3] Ordination would therefore be superfluous were its task only to recognise and authorise ministry. It requires a deeper grounding; and that deeper grounding is found in the need for the ordering of the church's ministry. In other words, all are called to ministry; and some are called to remind the church of that, and to give guidance and focus to the whole church's ministry.

This much the Panel argued in its 2000 Report. Ordination is not the gateway to ministry as such, but the gateway to leading the church in its ministry. We must be careful about how we understand leadership in this context, however. Leadership is never the exercise of unregulated authority. It is answerable, and in two directions: towards God and towards the church. Authority in the church, as the 2000 Report stressed, takes the form of service. It is always derived from, and accountable to, God, exercised through the gifting and enabling of the Spirit. Moreover the fact that service is the calling of the whole church means that those who lead do so as a part of the church, with an accountability towards the whole church.

The term leadership, although legitimate, perhaps struggles to express all this. It might be better, then, to say that ordained ministries are ministries of oversight or superintendence. These latter terms have their own history and resonances within the churches, but they are useful in this context, so long as they are interpreted with a broad meaning. Another word for the ministry of oversight which is in common use today, particularly in ecumenical discussions, is *"episkopé"*, a transliteration from Greek.[4] A further alternate term with strong roots in our own tradition might be "church-government". While this sometimes has a narrower meaning, indicating specifically the structures for decision making, it can also have wider reference, such as the Westminster Assembly's *The Form of Presbyterial Church-Government* (1645), which outlines a structure of church courts and describes the nature and duties of different offices of ministry, and the means of their inauguration.

The point is that whatever term one uses, the dimension of oversight is what justifies and calls for ordination. Ordained ministries do not differ from one another, or from non-ordained ministries, in rank or prestige, but they may indeed vary in character and scope. Ordination indicates and ensures that such ministries are exercised by those whose calling and preparation has been tested and accepted by the church. It also indicates that the oversight of the church is a responsibility which calls for deep personal commitment. Ministries of oversight may have different dimensions: there is the government (in the narrower sense of decision making) of the church, whether local or wider; there is pastoral oversight of the people; there is witness to Christ, in preaching, and the signal reception and celebration of grace in the sacraments. While the oversight of the church must always have these dimensions, that is not to say that each dimension will be present in the same way in every ordained office: the distribution of responsibilities among particular offices may for example reflect the dynamic of the Gospel, in which the proclamation of Christ in preaching and sacraments is met by the obedient response of faith.

3.2 Varieties of oversight

Our tradition has given us two distinct, long-established ordained ministries: the ministry of Word and sacrament and the eldership. Despite the great differences between these, even extending to the manner of ordination, it is clear that both of these are ministries of leadership or oversight. Indeed it has to be said that the degree of difference between these two offices can be troubling if one wishes to understand both as part of a unified structure of ordained ministry. The duties of the two offices are different of course, and one is part-time and non-stipendiary while the other is traditionally full-time and stipendiary. But it is more than that: what it means to hold ordained office is quite different in each case. For example, the selection, training and serving of an elder normally all take place in the congregation in which he or she is already a member, without any involvement of the wider church. Ministers, though, have their call tested by the wider church; during their education they are placed in other congregations; and their ordination involves the agreement and action of the wider church. Ministers very rarely exercise their ministry in the same congregation in which they were initially a member.

The degree of difference between the offices has in the past led to the suggestion that it is not sensible to inaugurate both by ordination, which cannot be the same thing in each case. The Panel felt the force of this argument, even if it did not in the end take the same view. We are conscious, though, that the account of ordination given in the 2000 Report does not fit the two offices equally well. The Panel has considered the thought that we ought perhaps to take steps to harmonise the way the Church regards these two offices. For example, is there not a way in which the wider church, perhaps in the form of the Presbytery, could have a role in the ordination of elders? As we reflected on this, however, another point emerged: if ordination has to do with the leadership or oversight of the church, perhaps there is something important in the difference between the two offices, something to be appreciated and maintained, rather than minimised. Our polity embodies the conviction that the responsibility for leading the church does not fall solely on those who are called to preach and to administer the sacraments. This responsibility of oversight is shared with others in the church, whose gifts to share in oversight are recognised by the local church. This practice did not develop by accident, and it is of some importance.

In other words, leadership emerges in different ways. There is a primary place in the oversight of the church for those appointed to ministries of the Word, because their calling, to bear witness to Christ in preaching and sacraments, reminds the church of its identity as Christ's servant, and calls the church to be true to its nature. But there is also a crucial role in the oversight of the church for those who, within a particular church, can lead and guide the community's response of faith, building communion, encouraging and exemplifying a spirit of service. Our offices of minister and elder, though different, lead the church's life and service in complementary ways. The ministry of Word and sacrament maintains the church by exercising a personal ministry of proclamation and presidency, ensuring the faithfulness and continuity of the church grounded in the unchanging gospel. The eldership, on the other hand, is a means by which leadership may emerge within the life of the local church; the ministry of the eldership is exercised not personally, primarily, but rather collegially, elders acting with one another and with ministers of Word and sacrament. Drawn from within the local church, elders are a reminder to the church that the call to service is addressed primarily to it, to the whole people of God.

4 The Eldership

4.1 Eldership past and future

The Reformers sought a grounding for the eldership in New Testament references to what they took to be an office of government or leadership: Calvin refers to Romans 12:8 and 1 Corinthians 12:28, and speaks of "elders chosen from the people, who were charged with the censure of morals, and the exercise of discipline along with the Bishops".[5] Eldership was conceived, and developed, along different lines in different Reformed Churches. In Scotland, the *First Book of Discipline* called for the election of elders annually. The *Second Book of Discipline*, though, took the significant step of providing for the admission of elders for life. Elders in this view are not simply representatives of the congregation (or even of the wider community), but are holders of a permanent, spiritual office in the church.

There is a good deal else that can be said about the history of the eldership, and about different understandings of the office which have been advanced at one time or another. However, much of this ground has been covered by the Panel in previous Reports, and there is no particular value in repeating their contents here.[6] For, whatever theories of eldership have proved popular at different times, it was the *Second Book of Discipline* which provided the basis for the enduring office of eldership. And it happens also to have given what is perhaps the most enduring rationale for the eldership as a spiritual office: "As the Pastors and Doctors should be diligent in Teiching and sawing the Seid of the Word, so the Elders should be cairful in seiking the Fruit of the same in the people".[7] The important point about this is that it suggests a distinct ministry of the eldership which is complementary to, but also closely related to, the ministry of the Word. The church is the church not only in speaking the Word but in first hearing it; there is a dynamic here which is real, even though the hearing and speaking are never separate, but always present in each other. The great value of the office of the eldership is that it gives real expression to this movement in which the church lives.

Theories of eldership which assimilate it to the ministry of Word and sacrament (such as the view that elders and ministers are part of a single office of "presbyter", the former called ruling elders, the latter adding the function of teaching elder) may obscure this character. Indeed if there is another office in the church which the eldership is closely related to, it must be the office of deacon. T.F. Torrance has commented that "the nature of the office elders hold and the kind of functions they perform bear a close resemblance to the office and functions of the *deacon* described in the Pastoral Epistles and Early Church documents".[8] When the Reformers distinguished between elders and deacons, and when the latters' responsibility for distributions to the poor meant that they were restricted to financial matters, the integrity of the earlier notion of the deacon's ministry was lost.

T.F. Torrance argues for a renewal of the eldership based on the recognition that its theological character is diaconal. A renewal on these lines, he writes, "would have the much needed effect of deepening mutuality and complementarity between the Presbyteral ministry of the Word and Sacrament and the diaconal ministry of shared obedience to Christ".[9] Torrance paints an attractive picture in which elders have "a more central ministry in the responses of God's worshipping people, in leading their praise and thanksgiving, in guiding their intercession and witness, and in the translation of their love to God into a living liturgy of service in the depths of human need".[10]

4.2 Eldership today

The Panel believes that a proper understanding of the eldership as a distinctive office requires appreciation of this diaconal character, and also of the local character indicated in section 3.2 above. We affirm that a local, diaconal ministry should have an enduring role in the oversight of the church, and as such can legitimately be an ordained office. While we are happy to make this affirmation, we feel it is necessary at the same time to ask some questions. For the description of the eldership given above is not fully reflected in the practical exercise of the office throughout the church. On the contrary, there are areas where the eldership seems to be some distance from the conception we have outlined. Professor Torrance's appeal, a quarter of a century ago, for a renewal of the eldership bears repeating. The Panel wonders, therefore, whether it might be desirable that a more wide-ranging review of the office of elder be undertaken in the church.

It might be helpful if we indicate a number of issues which we believe merit attention. First of all, we believe that questions are raised by the very significant numerical expansion of the eldership which has taken place over the last hundred years. Comparative statistics show that in 1901 the Church of Scotland had 25,808 elders and 1,163,594 communicants, which means one elder for every 45.1 members. By 1998, however, there were 44,388 elders and 641,340 communicants, or one elder for every 14.4 members. This figure is particularly striking when we bear in mind that the active worshipping congregation in most places is much smaller than the communion roll.

In the absence of research into these remarkable figures, the Panel suspects that an important factor has been changing notions of pastoral care and district visiting, along with increasing demands on people's time. These have made it harder to maintain the traditional structure of district visiting, and in order to maintain coverage Kirk Sessions have grown steadily. The Panel believes this is an issue which needs to be studied carefully. Is it good for the church that the number of persons ordained to the lifelong spiritual office of the eldership is influenced less by a thoughtful consideration of the work of leading the life of the church, or by a careful discernment of gifts for oversight, than by the need to cover the districts? It concerns the Panel that Kirk Sessions, consciously or otherwise, may be acting on the principle that one has to be an elder in order to participate in the work of pastoral care. Perhaps there is a need here for greater attention to the point that ordination is not the gateway to service, but to leadership of the church's service.

The Panel is aware that there are congregations which have faced this issue: some, for example, have appointed members to undertake pastoral visitation other than elders; the Kirk Session, which may then remain a smaller body, is then free to oversee the whole life and service of the church. This is only one of a number of directions in which the Church might move. We mention it as an example of change arising from a reconsideration of the nature of eldership and the role of the Kirk Session. The Panel is not asking the Church to proceed immediately down this road. It has drawbacks too: many would regret any weakening of the link between eldership and pastoral care. (Certainly, it cannot be said too often that leadership in the church is not about power but about service.) We would, though, urge the Church to consider seriously whether some such development would not be helpful in the continuing rediscovery of the spiritual nature of the office, and its renewal in the life of the church. After all, ordained ministries cannot model and enable the service of the whole people if they undertake all the work themselves.

A further, and perhaps related, issue which has concerned the Panel is the expectation of lifelong commitment to essentially the same duties. We have mentioned above that the *First Book of Discipline* provided for the annual election of elders. In its 1989 Report, the Panel noted that the *Second Book of Discipline*, while providing for lifelong appointment, still allowed for elders to be relieved of duties for a while.[11] Such a suggestion has reappeared on a number of occasions in recent times. For example the Committee of Forty in 1976 and the Panel itself in 1989 both suggested a system of fixed terms of office. The Panel is aware that these proposals for change were firmly rejected. However, we believe that it is time to look again at this area, giving weight both to the arguments for change and the arguments for the *status quo*.

One point we want to make clear is that we are not proposing the cessation of ordination to eldership - which was the principal cause of concern in 1989. Moreover, we believe that the passing of time has seen a significant shift of attitudes. For example in 1989 the Panel made the point that there is no good reason why elders can't be granted sabbatical leave from their duties; but it also noted that "in practice, very few elders seem to avail themselves of this opportunity of refreshment".[12] There is a good deal of anecdotal evidence that it is increasingly common for elders either to seek release from duties for a time, or even to resign from a Kirk Session with the hope that they will be able to serve again at some future date. The Panel believes that such options, which were regarded negatively in the past, are increasingly viewed with a healthy realism. It is more widely understood today that to serve for a term on a Kirk Session, rather than permanently, is not to dispense with the notion of service for life. It is simply to acknowledge that lifelong service may be given in different ways at different times. All Christians, after all, are called to lifelong service.

The Panel is aware that even calling for a review will be controversial; others in the Church may have different ideas of where the eldership might go. Many may wish it to stay just where it is. The Panel believes that the last of these is the one option which is not realistic. The appearance of unchanging continuity is an illusion. Change is constant, although it is mostly gradual and evolutionary. The office of the eldership has changed enormously over the years. In many places it has altered a good deal in the last 25 years, since the Committee of Forty bemoaned the poor representation within it of women and young people. That Committee, though, identified problems which arguably are still with us. It spoke, on the basis of returns to its survey of the eldership, of "a dilemma, almost a crisis, of leadership".[13] It detected in the eldership at that time a distrust of centralised power and decision making. This, the Committee believed, was "not matched by obvious willingness to take responsibility for shaping and leading the life of the Church by Kirk Sessions: on the contrary it appears to reflect a fearfulness and lack of confidence which erodes all kinds of openness". Such comments, though strongly worded, do not constitute a criticism of elders. Rather they indicate a problem in the way our structures of service—the eldership and other offices—are operating. They indicate an environment in which flexibility and imagination are often stifled rather than encouraged. The Panel's impression is that this problem has not gone away. We would repeat that we do not blame elders for this situation; however, we would suggest that the best way to address it would be for the Church to carry out a thorough review of the nature of the eldership to enable the whole Church

to rediscover the full significance of its character as a spiritual office.

4.3 The manner of ordination

Finally there is the narrower question of the manner of the ordination of elders. At present the selection, appointment, and ordination of elders all take place without any involvement of the church beyond the bounds of the local congregation. This is not to say that the wider church is not involved. It is the Church of Scotland, understanding itself as a part of the universal church, which has defined and which regulates the office of elder. When elders are ordained, they are not appointed simply to a role within that particular congregation; they are ordained to an office of the church, recognised across the whole of the Church of Scotland. However, the Panel wonders whether there might be merit in the ordination of elders expressing more clearly this character of the eldership, as an office of the church. We say this not out of a desire to assimilate the eldership to any other office. We believe the distinctive character of the eldership, as a ministry which emerges within the local church, to be important.

Nonetheless the fact of ordination implies the catholicity of the church, and there might be much to be gained from elders being ordained in a manner which gives expression to this dimension. One suggestion, noted earlier, would be that elders be ordained by the Presbytery. However, there would be drawbacks here, particularly if it took ordination out of the local congregation. A simpler solution might be to develop a practice in which, while ordination remains within the local congregation, an appropriate representative of the Presbytery could attend; or perhaps representatives of neighbouring churches could be invited, and even included in giving the right hand of fellowship.

5. The Ministry of Word and Sacrament
5.1 The full-time ministry
It was stated above that ordained ministries cannot model and enable the service of the whole people if they

undertake all the work themselves. This applies also to the ordained ministry of Word and sacrament. (Indeed it could be argued that there is a need for the church to rediscover the specific spiritual character of the ministry of Word and sacrament, as indicated in this designation.) The Panel has no hesitation in stating that the commitment and abilities of its ordained ministers has been and remains one of the Church of Scotland's greatest gifts. Nonetheless there are many who would argue that a culture has developed in which ministers are expected, by themselves and others, to do far more than is good either for themselves or for the church. The Committee of Forty described it this way: "because the ministers of Word and Sacrament are the only whole-time ministers in most situations, they come to be regarded as the repositories and guardians of all the gifts, and have to attempt to be all-rounders in a way that neither God nor St. Paul ever intended".[14] That Committee took the view in 1978 that there was an urgent need for action, and suggested several routes, including revitalising the eldership and developing the diaconate.

It also argued for the development of part-time ministries of Word and sacrament. It stated confidently that "the old pattern of one minister to one congregation is being much modified".[15] In retrospect, this last remark seems premature; it indicates, however, that even 23 years ago this pattern, which has served the Church so well for so long, had begun to be perceived as a barrier to desirable changes. The Committee of Forty spoke of the need for ministers to "learn a new flexibility and readiness to work together in teams".[16] It is notable that this assessment of the direction in which the Church needs to move is in substantial accord with the principles affirmed in the Board of Ministry's Report to the General Assembly of 2000.

If little progress has been made in the intervening 22 years, the Panel would simply ask whether there can be any significant change while the strength of the bonds between "one minister" and "one congregation" (or charge) remains undiminished. Is change possible without a serious re-examination of long cherished principles, such as a congregation's right of call, and the security of

ministerial tenure? It takes courage to contemplate the possibility that principles which were valuable and important in one age may no longer be so. It is possible for one era's founding principles to become a later era's pointless taboos. The Panel is not asserting categorically that this is the situation we face. We are, however, making the point that our patterns of ministry are extremely deeply embedded. Change will not happen merely because a Report says it is desirable.

5.2 Non-stipendiary ministries of the Word: the Auxiliary Ministry[17]

One of the Committee of Forty's principal ideas was the setting up of a part-time ministry of Word and sacrament. This proposal led directly to the establishment of the Auxiliary Ministry in the early 1980s as an ordained ministry of Word and sacrament, exercised on a part-time, non-stipendiary basis, and under supervision. The Panel believes that the Auxiliary Ministry has been beneficial for the Church, and has been a vehicle through which much valuable service has been given. However, it is undoubtedly true that it has not developed to the extent originally hoped for. The number of auxiliary ministers has remained small, something which the Church has noted often in recent years.[18] Recruitment is in the hands of Presbyteries. A number of these were strongly opposed to the office at its inception, and some appear to have maintained their opposition.[19]

During its short life, the Auxiliary Ministry has had to cope with a succession of different conceptions of its nature, rules for its training and deployment, and reviews of its future. The idea was proposed by the Committee of Forty in 1977 and 1978; it was implemented by an Act of 1980, supplemented by regulations of 1981; and this was consolidated by a schedule and statement of conditions in 1985. However, in 1986 a review was agreed, which resulted in a new Act governing the Auxiliary Ministry in 1987. In 1989 the Panel on Doctrine called for a review of the relationship between the Readership and the Auxiliary Ministry, and in 1992 the Committee on Education for the Ministry delivered this. In 1994 the Assembly Council initiated a review of the Auxiliary

Ministry; it produced an interim Report in 1995 - a valuable document asking important questions. It promised a full review in 1996, but this seems to have been lost at sea, as the Assembly Council found itself blown off course.[20] The remit was passed to the Committee on the Maintenance of the Ministry in partnership with the Board of National Mission. Nonetheless in 1996 a new training scheme for auxiliary ministers was agreed, on the Report of the Committee on Education for the Ministry.

In 1997 the Committee on the Maintenance of the Ministry and the Board of National Mission reported separately that they had taken on the work begun by the Assembly Council, and that this was ongoing. The remit had by this time broadened under the title "New Forms of Ministry". However, the most striking feature of these brief reports in 1997 is that while they refer to ministers and other church workers (the Board of National Mission report mentions "whole and part-time paid ministry"), and while they even mention elders, office bearers, and members, the Auxiliary Ministry is not mentioned at all. Somehow, it seems to have dropped out of this review entirely. In any case, no results of this process have since been reported to the General Assembly. In 1999 responsibility for selection and training transferred to the new Board of Ministry, which was also, on an overture from the Presbytery of Dumfries and Kirkcudbright, given a remit to consider the "status, role and functions of auxiliary ministers" and to consider "the extension of non-stipendiary ministries within the Church". In 2000 the Board of Ministry indicated that its Committee on Education and Training intends to review again the training of auxiliary ministers. Moreover, the Board of Ministry's major policy statement in 2000, *Ministers of the Gospel*, indicated the Board's intention to continue theological reflection, with particular regard to its responsibilities for stipendiary and non-stipendiary ministry. The Panel understands that the Board established a Committee in June 2000 which has commenced this work.

The Panel welcomes the Board of Ministry's ongoing work, and in particular its desire to examine ministry across the division between stipendiary and non-stipendiary forms. However, the main point we would make, as the Auxiliary Ministry reaches its twenty-first birthday, is that it has had to endure a most unhappy childhood. With regard to the history related above, we can only say that this has been a dreadful way to seek to develop a new form of ministry. The Auxiliary Ministry has lacked support and promotion, without any body responsible for its oversight and development. Instead, all responsibility for recruitment was entrusted to Presbyteries, despite the strong opposition many of them had shown to the idea. Year after year the Reports of the Committee on Education for the Ministry noted disappointingly low recruitment figures. Nine years ago, a Working Group of that Committee identified "a lack of enthusiasm on the part of Presbyteries" as one of the chief reasons for this. It added: "Few Presbyteries have any positive conception of Auxiliary Ministry, and few have any strategy of ministry and mission in which auxiliary ministers feature".[21] It also suggested that it would be helpful if the Board of Ministry took on a role in the superintendence of auxiliary ministers. None of this was acted upon at the time. Instead there has been a series of reviews, placing question marks over the Auxiliary Ministry, but leading so far to very little action.

Surveying the history of the Auxiliary Ministry, it is difficult to get a sense of the vision which prompted its creation. The Panel has therefore turned to the Reports of the Committee of Forty. Doing so has revealed significant differences between the original vision and the Auxiliary Ministry which was actually established. For one thing, the Committee of Forty was wary of multiplying offices within the church. Although it did not propose any change to the Readership, it did state clearly that it believed it "anomalous that a man or a woman may be licensed to preach the Word to God's people, without any expectation that he or she may subsequently be given authority to administer the sacraments in signal fulfilment of that Word".[22] The Committee clearly hoped that there would be a natural and easy route for readers to enter this further ministry, and that to do so would be a natural progression for at least some readers.

Another crucial element of the Committee's vision was that such ministries would not be "imposed from outside a situation of need, but would grow organically out of the Church's life in a particular place".[23] In other words where there was a need or opportunity for such ministry, the person to supply that need would be identified within the local situation. Kirk Sessions could nominate someone from their own congregation or perhaps a neighbouring one. Such a local grounding was central to the Committee's desire that this ministry would be a paradigm of the giftedness of each member and thereby encourage the development of the church's gifts.

The Committee's vision was of a flexible ministry, adaptable to different local circumstances. In rural locations a part-time minister might take the primary role in maintaining a preaching and sacramental ministry in a community; supervision would be exercised from a greater distance than in an urban situation, in which the part-time minister would very much be part of a team. The Committee of Forty's view, then, was not just that part-timers could plug the gaps; rather it saw existing structures as failing to liberate the gifts present within the church, and forcing the full-time ministry into an unhelpful pattern, in which it is expected to be in personal possession of all the church's gifts. The Committee called for the establishment of a part-time ministry as a means towards a new understanding of congregational life, bridging the gap between ministers and people.

Much of this vision has not been reflected in the subsequent history. Critically, when legislation was first drafted there was a great weakening of the expectation that the needs of the church in a local situation would be met within that local situation. An office was created which, from the beginning, had the potential for rivalry with other ministries in the church. This was particularly so since no simple route was provided for readers to become auxiliary ministers. The continuation of this situation has contributed to frustration. In 1998 the Board of Parish Education commented that "at present, someone who is trained as a Reader and qualified for attachment to a charge nevertheless has to undertake the full three years of training for the Auxiliary Ministry if

called to a ministry of sacrament as well as of Word". It added that the Board's Readers Committee took the view that "for as long as the Church feels it right to maintain both forms of ministry, greater flexibility is needed, with a 'conversion course' available for those already working as readers, and qualified for attachment to a charge, whose Presbyteries also wish them to exercise a wider ministry of sacrament and pastoral care".[24] Such a provision would be very much in line with the vision of the Committee of Forty.

Why was the original vision not realised? To some extent, one could point to an ambiguity within the Committee of Forty's ideas. On the one hand, it was proposing a ministry which would be ordained, which would have sacramental authority and which would carry membership of Presbytery. In these respects, such ministers would have greater authority and recognition than readers. On the other hand, however, the Committee's proposals were for a ministry growing up and being exercised within the local situation. With hindsight, the two sides of this vision tended to pull in opposite directions. A split developed: the elements of wider authority were preserved at the expense of the local character.

Perhaps with more attention to this issue, the vision could have been realised fully. It could be argued, though, that the shape taken by Auxiliary Ministry amounted to the domestication of a radical vision of ministry, pressing it into a form in which it reflected the church's existing patterns and structures. A threat was assimilated and thereby disarmed. As we noted above, the church's existing patterns of and assumptions about ministry are very deeply embedded. The Panel does not doubt that the Auxiliary Ministry has been valuable. We repeat what we stated above: that much good and committed service has been given by auxiliary ministers over the last two decades. However, we wonder whether the office might not have been more valuable still, and flourished much further, if it had been designed in a way that preserved more of the original vision of a flexible, local form of ministry. The legislation of 1980 (and 1987), rather than enabling a new, more flexible kind of ministry, seems only to have added a further variation on the established pattern, and one which is even more tightly regulated than existing offices.

5.3 Non-stipendiary ministries of the Word: the Readership

At the Scottish Reformation an office of Reader was established to sustain the church's worship at a time when there were not enough Reformed ministers available. These readers were authorised to read a service, rather than to preach. The office was seen as a solution for unusual times, and it duly died out in the course of the seventeenth century. The modern Readership, which dates from 1918, also originated as a solution for unusual times, which were experiencing a shortage of ministers. However, in other respects it was quite different. Lay Readers, as they were called until 1958, were authorised to preach; they differed also in that their ministry was generally itinerant, providing pulpit supply where and when it was needed. The office has not only survived but developed. For most of its life the Readership has been a solution of last resort: retired and student ministers had priority in the pulpit supply pecking order. This has changed more recently, as have training requirements, which have increased and been standardised. The Readership today is governed by an Act of 1992, which has opened up new possibilities for deployment: readers can now be attached to a charge, working regularly in one place.[25] What has not changed is that readers are "set apart" to their ministry rather than ordained; nor has there been any change in the identification of the Readership as a ministry of the Word, but without a sacramental ministry. Recruitment for the Readership is currently buoyant.

There is some uncertainty in the Church about why readers do not have sacramental authority. Many would argue that it is undesirable to divide Word and sacrament in this way. We have already noted the Committee of Forty's opinion in 1977 that this situation is "anomalous".[26] This view was, of course, part of that Committee's justification for its proposal of a new non-stipendiary ministry, but it inevitably raises a question about the Readership. Some (although clearly not all) readers continue to ask the question: the Readership Committee reported in 1997 that it had heard from many readers who "feel that their ministry is hampered by their inability to conduct the sacrament of Holy Communion".[27] If the question is asked why they do not seek to transfer to the Auxiliary Ministry, the answer would probably be that readers are reluctant to begin another demanding process of selection and training from scratch. In both 1997 and 1998 the Readership Committee appealed for a simpler way of taking the step into sacramental ministry.[28]

There is also uncertainty in the Church about whether it is right to continue with the Readership and the Auxiliary Ministry as distinct offices. Certainly there has been a considerable convergence between the two. This derives particularly from the new legislation on the Readership introduced in 1992. That legislation had its origins in the Panel on Doctrine's 1989 Report, which called for greater co-ordination between the two ministries. The remit resulted in a Working Group being established by the Committee on Education for the Ministry. Its Report in 1992 noted a number of unjustifiable anomalies in the way the Church treats the two offices, and also recognised that the Readership could be used more fully and effectively. It successfully proposed a new Act governing the Readership, addressing these concerns. Under this Act, selection of readers remains the responsibility of Presbyteries, but the Board of Parish Education has a role in the process, increasing the consistency of the system. Training of readers was standardised, the normal route being the TLS course (Training for Learning and Serving) provided by the Scottish Churches Open College (as it now is). The most significant change of all, though, was the new Act's provision for readers to be placed in particular appointments, serving for a time in one place.

The Act therefore brought about a good deal of convergence between the two ministries. In that sense it co-ordinated them, although it did not provide for easier movement between the two. The Working Group did not propose any substantive change to the Auxiliary Ministry.

How did it see the relationship between the two offices, then? It affirmed the distinctness of the Readership and the Auxiliary Ministry, and did so on the basis that "the level of commitment and training required of the Reader would remain considerably less than that required of the Auxiliary Minister".[29]

It has to be asked whether this remains the case today. For readers trained under the new arrangements and attached to a parish, the difference may seem particularly small. There have in recent years been some changes in the organisation of the TLS course through which readers are trained. The course is now run by the Scottish Churches Open College, which has a collaborative relationship with Napier University. In September 1996 SCOC introduced the CertHE (Certificate of Higher Education) in Church Studies, which is a certificated route through the TLS programme for those who, like all Readership candidates, take the two-year Foundation Course plus a one-year Specialist Course. In 1997 the Readership Committee agreed that all Readership candidates should register for the Certificate. Auxiliary Ministry training has also developed. Since 1996 the regular course has been the Certificate in Christian Studies, offered through the Divinity Departments of the Universities of Glasgow and Aberdeen, formerly with the involvement of the Scottish Churches Open College. This is also a three year part-time course at CertHE level.

As far as the degree of commitment is concerned, the norm for auxiliary ministers is that they are expected to devote an average of ten hours per week to their duties. When the attachment of a reader to a charge was made possible, it was presumably intended that they would have a smaller time commitment than Auxiliary ministers. No specific statement was made on hours of service, though, and there is nothing to prevent an attached reader giving the same time to their duties as an auxiliary minister would.

5.4 The future of non-stipendiary ministries of the Word

In the light of these developments, the Panel believes that the Church urgently needs to look again at the two offices of Reader and Auxiliary Minister. There are several issues which require to be addressed. There is the question of whether readers might have a sacramental ministry. There are anomalies such as the fact that readers are paid, while auxiliary ministers are not. There is the problem of the failure of the Church to envision a mission strategy in which these ministries (particularly the Auxiliary Ministry) have a role. There is the unresolved question of the relation between the two, made all the more pressing by the convergence of the two offices. There is the fact that, despite the 1992 Report's desire for greater co-ordination, there is no easy path to move from one to the other. And there is the loss of the original vision of the Committee of Forty, and the fact that neither office provides for a ministry which grows organically out of the local situation.

The Panel believes that for the sake of those serving the Church as auxiliary ministers and readers, and for the sake of the Church, which has much to gain from the development of non-stipendiary ministries, it is essential that we resolve these issues. A clear way forward needs to be identified. The Panel believes that the Church urgently needs to undertake a major review which addresses the Readership and the Auxiliary Ministry in a co-ordinated way. This must include both ministries, and have a sufficiently wide scope to address the development of more local ministries of the Word, as well as relating these offices to the stipendiary ministry of Word and sacrament. In particular it must address the six issues identified below:

5.4.1 *Local ministry*

The Panel believes that there is a scope for, and a need for, the growth of local ministries of the kind envisaged by the Committee of Forty. Such ministries could be important not only in themselves but also in modelling the gifted service of the whole people. The Panel in fact endorsed this vision in 1989, when it said:

> What of members who have no special commission from the Church? In the past there were sound practical as well as theological grounds for limiting preaching and celebration strictly to the ordained.

It was a safeguard against heresy and against ignorant exposition in days when very few enjoyed the privilege of much education. Now there are likely to be many members in a congregation who are at least as articulate and educated as the minister; also with many insights into the complex issues of modern life, born of experience the minister has not shared. There are likely also to be many of a greater spiritual maturity than the minister has yet acquired … By condemning to silence its experts, its saints, even its probing questioners, the Church has lost many God-given insights. … The current law of the Church … leaves the minister in charge of worship, but with freedom on occasion to delegate and to involve others. … If this kind of co-operation is invited by the minister and planned with a degree of ministerial help and oversight, it can use and develop talents which previously had no place in Scottish worship. The minister's task is to nourish the faithful; which does not necessarily mean serving every meal.[30]

5.4.2 *Two ministries or one?*

When the church establishes a new, additional office, it may appear that this serves to recognise and encourage a greater variety of types of ministry. The Panel believes that this appearance can be misleading. Where there are multiple offices, tightly defined and regulated, with relatively small differences between them but large barriers in the way of those who would move between them, you arguably have less flexibility rather than more. You have the fragmentation of the church's ministry, rather than its liberation.

There are many forms in which ministries of the Word can be exercised, from the local form described above through to the full-time ministry of Word and sacrament. Such ministries can be equipped by varying degrees of education and training, have varying amounts of responsibility, operate in a variety of situations, in various ways, in varying relationships of supervision, support and collaboration with others. At one extreme, the church could choose to have a large number of offices, each designed for a particular situation. At the other extreme

you could have a single office, but which incorporated great variety within it. The Panel's point here is that the latter may in fact be more flexible than the former. This is not to say that distinct offices are never justified. There are times when a variety of offices will indeed serve and support a variety of forms of ministry. What we would say, though, is that such distinctions as are drawn must serve some clear purpose. There is a serious question about whether the distinction between Readership and Auxiliary Ministry currently enables more service than it frustrates. Any review of these ministries must consider seriously whether there should be two offices in the future, or whether there should be a single office of non-stipendiary ministry, in succession to the existing Readership and Auxiliary Ministry.

5.4.3 *Sacramental ministry*

The clearest reason for having two offices at the moment is that one is principally a preaching ministry, while the other adds a sacramental ministry. But is it right to have the former without the latter? The Panel is clear that in principle the division of a ministry of the Word from a sacramental ministry is undesirable. It tends to obscure the relationship between Word and sacrament, rather than serve it. However, there is more to the issue than this single principle. There are varieties of preaching ministry, as noted above, and there is a case for saying that not all should have authority to administer the sacraments. The Panel's treatment of ordination stresses the connection between ordination and oversight. There is a case for granting sacramental authority not to all who may take some share in the church's public speech, but to those whose preaching ministry is associated with a share in the oversight of the church. This seems to have been the principle on which the Committee of Forty operated, in proposing a sacramental ministry which would be ordained, and be admitted to the Courts of the Church. There is also the fact that the Church has sought to avoid authorising ministries which will not in fact be exercised. The Readership developed out of a need for preaching ministries, but there was not the same need for extra sacramental ministries.

The Church's present solution to these issues is undermined not by the mere principle of the unity of Word and sacrament, but also by the difficulties placed in the way of readers wishing to be admitted to a wider, sacramental ministry. The recent developments in the selection, training and deployment of the Readership have increased the pressure here. The current solution is also put under pressure by the renewed sense in the church at large of the unity of Word and sacraments, and the resulting increase in the frequency of celebration of Holy Communion. The possibility of wider authorisation of sacramental ministry is therefore something which a review will have to examine closely.

5.4.4 Non-stipendiary ministry

The Panel regards the present financial arrangements for these two ministries as unsatisfactory. The Church's interpretation of the term "non-stipendiary" as meaning that no payment other than expenses may be made to auxiliary ministers is bizarre. There are many forms of payment which are not stipends. The Panel sees no reason why auxiliary ministers should not receive some payment in recognition of the service they give, just as readers receive pulpit supply fees, and those attached to a charge can receive a fee. These fees, after all, have never been described as stipends. The Committee of Forty's proposals did not specify that a new ministry would have to be unpaid; the original Act of 1980 referred to the possibility of pulpit supply being paid. It was in rules introduced the following year that the current interpretation was introduced. This was reaffirmed in the revision of the legislation in 1987, despite the fact that the committee which carried out this review was quite critical of the principle of non-remuneration. The 1992 review by the Education for the Ministry Committee was also critical of the lack of remuneration; it proposed a modest book allowance, which was a welcome step, albeit a small one. The Assembly Council's Report of 1995 also criticised the *status quo*, and proposed that auxiliary ministers be paid for the hours served. Indeed it is hard to find any serious comment in favour of the present arrangements. A review must ensure that this weight of opinion translates into action.

5.4.5 Mission strategy

A Review will also need to address the Church's attitude to these ministries. Adjustments to the legislation on non-stipendiary ministry will be worthless unless there is a willingness in the church at large to accept these ministries. The 1992 Review made some important points: it criticised the lack of attention to recruitment and called for Presbyteries to "adopt a more pro-active approach towards the recruitment of both Auxiliary Ministers and Readers".[31] There would be no point in increasing recruitment, though, if there was no way to use those recruited. The 1992 Review also, therefore, argued that in planning and overseeing the mission of the church, with regard to every congregation and parish, the question should be raised of where and how readers and auxiliary ministers might be deployed. Unfortunately no procedures to develop such a practice were introduced.

5.4.6 Barriers

Whatever solution is chosen to these problems, it must be one which aims at genuinely flexible ministries, which can be exercised in different ways according to need, and with scope for imaginative development. It must be a solution that dismantles unnecessary barriers between those who serve. There is surely something seriously wrong with a system which authorises readers to a ministry of the Word, but gives no weight to their selection, training and experience for that ministry when the question of progression to a sacramental ministry is raised. Yet, when someone seeks to serve in a way that involves a greater responsibility, there is a question of further selection and training. The structure should be one of successive steps on a road, which can, where possible, be taken naturally as the needs and circumstances of the church and the individual dictate.[32] The current structure of selection and training for readers is a useful model. Instead of an "all or nothing" selection at the commencement of training, there are two stages, the second a year after the first. This involves a similar principle to the new Enquiry Process being introduced by the Board of Ministry, which also moves away from a single selection event to the affirmation of call in successive stages.

What is needed is for the church's ministries of the Word to be co-ordinated with one another in line with this principle. The selection and training of a person for one office, and their service in that office, must be given serious weight if they offer themselves for another office. It will not count for everything; but it must not count for nothing.

A further area where barriers should be lowered is between non-stipendiary ministries and the stipendiary ministry. Again, it does not make sense that someone whose call and qualifications have been acknowledged to the point of Auxiliary Ministry should be starting from scratch again if they wish to serve full-time. Further selection and education are appropriate, but these ought not to amount to starting over again from the beginning. Moreover there is a need to consider the possibility of a full-time minister taking other employment, and being eligible for appointment to a non-stipendiary position. Again it is a case of lowering unnecessary barriers. Only in this way can the church move to more flexible patterns of ministry, away from the fracturing of ministry which occurs when multiple offices are defined in ways which make no provision for growth from one into another.

Questions are also raised in this area by the recent introduction of part-time stipendiary ministries. These will need to be addressed. Another issue which may well arise is whether there is scope for non-stipendiary ministries to work more independently in some circumstances, as was originally suggested by the Committee of Forty.

It will be apparent from the above comments that the Panel believes that a much wider review is necessary than that already remitted to the Board of Ministry by the General Assembly in 1999. We are convinced that only a review which treats the whole area of non-stipendiary ministry in a co-ordinated way—including both the Readership and the Auxiliary Ministry – can produce the results which the church needs. There have been too many reviews over the last twenty years which have addressed only part of this area; despite much valuable work, the problems persist. We believe they will persist further, until the church undertakes and implements a review which addresses all the issues identified above.

6. The Diaconate

6.1 The Diaconate in the Church of Scotland

The question of whether or not deacons should be ordained was the subject of the original remit to the Panel in 1997, later widened to include other offices. In acknowledgement of this, the Panel included a section on the Diaconate in its Report in 1999, indicating some of the work of its Diaconate Working Party which had met over the two preceding years. That Report included brief comment on the origins of the Diaconate in the Church of Scotland in the late nineteenth century, and it also described more recent discussions of the nature of diaconal ministry, particularly three phases of this: first, in the early 1970s, in the aftermath of the admission of women to the ministry of Word and sacrament; secondly in the Panel on Doctrine's Reports in the 1980s; thirdly in ecumenical discussions, such as the *Windsor Statement* of 1997. It is perhaps advisable to recapitulate briefly some of this.

Professor A.H. Charteris played a key role in the establishment of an office of Deaconess, which he understood as a revival of a New Testament and early church office. The first deaconess, Lady Grisell Baillie, was set apart by the Kirk Session of Bowden in 1888. Other forms of service developed for women, notably the Parish Sisters, and, in the United Free Church, the Church Sisters. These streams combined in 1950 to form a single Order of Deaconesses, and it was also around that time that all deaconesses were commissioned to their work by Presbyteries. Discussion about the nature of the Order, as it was then described, continued: in 1954 a Commission on the Order of Deaconesses was established, which reported to the General Assembly in each of the following three years. This served to consolidate the position of the Diaconate, and established its pattern for the following decades. It is worth noting that the question of whether deaconesses should be ordained was addressed, but not answered clearly, in 1957.[33] That question re-emerged on other occasions prior to the Panel's current remit, for example in 1964, when the Panel suggested that the Diaconate be enhanced by the use of the term ordination, the laying on of hands, and admission to the Courts of the Church; it was raised also in 1976, on the initiative of the Deaconess Board.[34]

In the 1970s, discussion about the character of the Diaconate had gained new energy following the admission of women to the ministry of Word and sacrament. There were, no doubt, some in the Church who had regarded the Diaconate as a vehicle for the service of women, given that they were barred from entering the ordained ministry, and who therefore expected the Diaconate to shrink away after this situation changed in 1968. It is particularly significant, then, that in 1972 the Deaconess Board presented a substantial Report to the General Assembly, affirming the Diaconate as a distinctive ministry, complementary to the ministry of Word and sacrament, and calling for its renewal on this basis. In 1979 the General Assembly declared the office of the Diaconate open to men as well as women. Deacons were admitted to membership of the Courts of the Church in 1990, as noted previously.

6.2 The diaconate in an ecumenical setting

It is important to realise that much of this history in the Church of Scotland has been mirrored in other churches. The establishment of the Order of Deaconesses in the 1880s followed in the wake of similar developments across much of Europe, beginning in Germany fifty years earlier. Likewise the consolidation and development of the diaconate in recent decades is part of a wider recognition of the distinctive contribution which deacons can make. In the Roman Catholic Church, for example, in which the diaconate had for long been no more than a stage on the way to the priesthood, the Second Vatican Council provided for the restoration of a permanent office of Deacon. Similar developments have taken place within the Anglican communion. This trend was sufficiently strong even twenty years ago for *Baptism, Eucharist and Ministry* to say: "Today there is a strong tendency in many churches to restore the diaconate as an ordained ministry with its own dignity and meant to be exercised for life".[35]

Given this trend, it is not surprising that much recent exploration of the nature of the diaconate has been carried out ecumenically. The *Windsor Statement* is an example of this, having been produced by a process in which the Church of Scotland participated along with Roman Catholic, Anglican and Methodist partners. It makes important affirmations: "We increasingly perceive our role to be pioneering and prophetic, responding to needs, proactive in opportunity through commitment to mission and pastoral care within and beyond the Church."

6.3 The ministry of deacons

The Panel, both in its 2000 Report and earlier in this Report, has argued for an understanding of ministry grounded in the dynamic unity of witness and service, in the speaking which is also a listening for the Word, and in the serving which is also a receiving of Christ's service. The church's speaking, its proclamation of the gospel in preaching and in the sacraments, always exists in relationship with its serving, its obedient response of faith. The distinction between them is always relative, never a separation, since the church's proclamation is also part of its response of faith; and its service is also a form of witness. Yet a distribution of tasks is necessary, and in practice this distribution must reflect the variety of the gifts of the Spirit. The distribution of tasks also, though, reflects the dynamic in which the church lives. Some are given particular responsibility for the church's proclamation; others, by no means necessarily the same persons, will have particular gifts for leading and enabling the church's service, for guiding and supporting its life as a faithful response to the reconciling ministry of Christ.

The Panel sees in this distinction a very strong grounding for the ministry of deacons. There is an underlying unity between kerygmatic and diaconal forms of ministry, yet each has its own particular focus, the former in witness, the latter in service. This description of ministry establishes a clear identity for what we might, rather tautologously, call diaconal ministry. This is not something exclusive to deacons, but belongs to the whole church. The office of Deacon is grounded here, though, in leading and guiding the church's character as *diakonos* or servant. The office of Deacon is therefore quite distinct from the ministry of Word and sacrament—a point we cannot stress too strongly. Equally it is complementary to the ministry of Word and sacrament, and always related to it—this also we cannot stress too strongly. The distinction and relation are indicated by the comments of T.F. Torrance on the eldership: "While ministers are ordained to dispense the Word and sacraments *to* the people, elders are set apart to help the people in their reception of the Word and in their participation in the sacraments, and to seek the fruit of the Gospel in the faith and life of the community".[36]

Two comments must be made on this. First of all, while this implies that diaconal ministry is concerned with the church's response to God, it should not be concluded that it is therefore merely reactive or passive, or that it is led and directed by the primary ministry of proclamation. That would be a serious misunderstanding of the nature of ministry. All ministry is reactive in the sense that the initiative in salvation is God's. But this means that proclamation is a reaction or response, just as much as any act of service. Equally, the church's service can be extremely pro-active—it may take great imagination, initiative, courage and commitment to stand for Christ and his reconciliation. Diaconal ministry may indeed have to be, as the *Windsor Statement* says, "pioneering and prophetic, responding to needs, proactive in opportunity through commitment to mission and pastoral care within and beyond the Church". Moreover, in appointing particular persons to a diaconal office, not to engage in ministry but to lead and guide the church in *its* ministry, there is all the more need for them to be able to give active leadership to the church's life. Ministries of witness and service are mutually complementary. Diaconal ministry, in any form, is not about taking second place to a preaching ministry.

The second comment which needs to be made here is about the relationship between the eldership and the diaconate. We have identified both as diaconal ministries, and indeed stressed the importance of this character which they share. We believe this to be consistent with much that the Panel has said in the past, and with much

that is emerging in ecumenical discussion of diaconate. The question arises, then, of the difference between them. Our answer would be that the differences lie not in the theological character, but in other areas - primarily in the fact that the eldership is local in character, while the diaconate is not. Instead, it offers the church a flexible, mobile ministry, through individuals whose call has been tested by the wider church, and who have undertaken far more extensive education and preparation.

6.4 An ordained diaconate

In the light of all these considerations, the Panel believes that it is appropriate for the church to have an office of full-time diaconal service, and that this should be an ordained office, sharing in the oversight of the church's service.[37] Ordination of deacons should be carried out by the appropriate Presbytery. The Panel would hope that the continued development of this office would strengthen a collaborative approach in and among all the church's ordained ministries, and greatly encourage an understanding of ministry which will liberate ministries among the whole people of God.

In conclusion, while this Report has stressed the connections between the diaconate and the eldership, it is equally important also to stress the distinction between the diaconate and the ministry of Word and sacrament. Certainly, deacons are authorised to conduct worship – and it would surely be unduly restrictive if it were not so, given their gifts and training, and given the underlying unity of ministry; but it would be regrettable if the church lost sight of the distinctive character of the diaconate. It would be particularly regrettable if the pressure to maintain existing structures led to deacons being used to plug gaps when they appear. A developing Diaconate can help the church to recover a fuller vision of ministry, but it will not do this if it is used to shore up a partial one. The church needs to learn better what the diaconate is, in order that it might learn what it is itself—the servant of Christ, who came to serve.

7 Ordination issues

The Panel has approached its remits on ordination on

the assumption that they could only be discharged responsibly by a thorough consideration of the character of particular ministries, and that this must be done in the light of careful reflection on the theology of ministry and ordination. However, we also need to address some practical questions about the act of ordination. The 2000 Report spoke of ordination as having a dual character, divine and human: divine in that it presupposes and recognises the call of God and the gifts of the Holy Spirit, fitting that person to service; human in that it is the church's authorisation of that person to engage in particular service. Ordination is a liturgical act following on the church's testing of vocation and appropriate preparation for ministry. Its centre is prayer for the graces of the Spirit, and, in some cases, the laying on of hands, which is the apostolically given sign witnessing to the Holy Spirit and the church's obedience.

There are four questions in particular which require some comment:

7.1 *Ought elders to receive the laying on of hands?*

The 2000 Report described the hesitation felt by the church in the aftermath of the Scottish Reformation regarding the laying on of hands, and even in regard to the term ordination. However, with time the Scottish church developed the confidence to follow Calvin's solution in the *Institutes* of 1559, in which he set aside his own earlier hesitation and affirmed the imposition of hands, regarding it as "useful for the dignity of the ministry to be commended to the people by this sort of sign". It was instituted by the apostles, he noted, to indicate "that they were offering to God him whom they were receiving into the ministry". The apostles also used this sign, he adds, "with those upon whom they conferred the visible graces of the Spirit."[38] The laying on of hands is seen then not as the core of ordination – that is the prayer of ordination itself – but as the church's act, a sign of the appointment of a person to a particular ministry, and of the call and grace of the Holy Spirit enabling that appointment.

The Panel can see no clear reason why the arguments in favour of this sign should not apply to the ordination of

elders. All that can be said in its favour applies to elders as much as to other ministries. It is used in the commissioning of deacons, and indeed (with different intention) in the service of confirmation and admission to communion. Its omission from the service of ordination for elders is perhaps an unhelpful anomaly. Why then has it been omitted? Perhaps out of a desire to distinguish the two ordinations, or possibly out of a fear that it would be interpreted as having transmitted a power possessed by the agent into the recipient – a kind of spiritual "contagion". On this theory, the imposition of a minister's hands would "make" a minister – and it ought therefore to be omitted from the ordination of an elder! Surely, though, this is not a good reason. This "contagion" theory is most definitely not the view of the church; but to omit the imposition on these grounds will tend to give credence to it. Including the imposition, by contrast, would encourage a healthier view, and, more importantly, encourage an understanding of different offices as complementary and collaborative.

7.2 *Who ought to preside and lead the prayer of ordination?*

There is a difficult balancing act to be achieved in discussing the character of different ministries. On the one hand, it is unhelpful to overemphasise differences. It is wrong, for example, to use the distinction between witness and service, which is always a relative distinction, to erect and sanctify barriers between different functions in the church. Those who occupy a diaconal office still bear witness to Christ. Those who occupy a preaching office still serve Christ. Nonetheless, different offices do have distinct characters. They require different gifts. We need to get away from the notion that a few people in the church have all the gifts, and restore the church's confidence in the diverse gifting of the whole people. Therefore while it is unhelpful to erect barriers between offices, it is equally unhelpful to deny that different offices have different characters and roles.

However awkward and awesome this may sound, those who are called to proclaim the Word in preaching and sacraments represent Christ to the community. They are called to speak, "from God to the people", even though they can only speak in and through their humanity. The Panel therefore takes the view that the person who presides at an ordination, and who leads the prayer of ordination, ought to be an ordained minister of Word and sacrament. If the church is going to trust someone to articulate the words "…we ordain…" it ought first to have entrusted that person with a ministry of Word and sacrament. Such a person's presidency in ordination is a demonstration of the fact that the words "…we ordain…" are not simply enacting a decision of the Presbytery, but are witnessing to the call of God and the gifts of the Spirit. It might be regretted that when an elder or deacon is Moderator of a Presbytery this will divide the Moderator's traditional role in two. The Panel sees this as unavoidable. While the Moderator is generally understood to speak for the Presbytery and act for it, there is nothing to prevent a Presbytery asking someone other than its Moderator to represent it and act for it in a particular matter such as an ordination.

7.3 *Who lays on hands?*
The established practice in the ordination of ministers is that it is not the whole Presbytery but only the ministerial members who participate in the laying on of hands. This goes back to the *Form of Presbyterial Church-Government*, and its famous phrase "those preaching presbyters to whom it doth belong". Justification for this has been sought in an argument similar to the one used above: imposition of hands belongs to ministers in their representative capacity, signifying the gifts of the Holy Spirit.

The Panel doubts that this argument is sustainable, and would suggest that other considerations count in favour of a change in our practice. The above argument does not give due weight to the difference between the ordination prayer when the words "…we ordain…" are uttered, and the imposition of hands, which is best understood not as enacting ordination, but as a sign of it. The imposition of hands is best seen as an act of (or on behalf of) the church, a sign of the church's appointment of a person, in obedient recognition of the call and gifts

of the Holy Spirit. The Panel would therefore be happy to see other ordained members of a Presbytery participate in the imposition of hands. This would also have the benefit of avoiding the impression that imposition is about the transmission of something, or constitutes admission of the ordinand to a closed society. A change in our practice here might also help to suggest a collaborative relationship amongst the church's ordained ministries. In addition, as noted in the 2000 Report, there are precedents for this broader imposition in our tradition; indeed the most likely interpretation of the *Second Book of Discipline* on this matter is that it included elders in the imposition. The only word of caution we would give here is about the practical arrangements. The attempts of large numbers of ministers to participate in the laying on of hands can sometimes threaten the dignity of the moment of ordination; a much larger number, swelled by elders and perhaps deacons, might require the Church to consider how best to balance the different requirements. One point which emerged in the Panel's discussions of this was that a congregation's representative elder on the Presbytery should be clearly involved, perhaps taking a prominent role in the act of imposition.

A related matter which might arise is the question of who would lay on hands were imposition to be introduced in the ordination of elders. Here the Panel would suggest that the best solution is that the presiding minister alone act in the laying on of hands. There is no likelihood here that such an act will be interpreted as transmission of a power possessed by the minister, nor that the act will appear like admission to a status or a society. However, were the whole of a Kirk Session to join in the imposition, both of these dangers might become very real.

7.4 *Ordaining deacons*
The Panel, in the light of the arguments contained in the section above, suggests that if the Church indeed proceeds to the ordination of deacons, then the laying on of hands should be treated in the same manner as in the ordination of a minister: i.e. with the participation of ministers, elders and deacons. Nonetheless it would be appropriate if those deacons present were to take a prominent place in joining

the Moderator in the imposition of hands.

This would constitute a significant change from the current practice: at present, when a deacon is commissioned, only deacons participate in the laying on of hands. The Panel believes that this practice is unhelpful, and runs the very real risk of suggesting that some "transmission" is taking place, or that the deacon is being admitted to a society.

A further issue requires some comment: should existing deacons, who have been commissioned to the office, now receive ordination? The Panel believes that this would be an appropriate step for serving deacons. In calling for the ordination of deacons, we are not saying that commissioning and ordination are equivalent terms. It is clear that the Church's previous avoidance of the term "ordination" in the inauguration of a deacon's ministry reflected a hesitation about acknowledging the Diaconate as a permanent office in Christ's church. Therefore deacons who have been commissioned, even with the laying on of hands, cannot simply be counted as having been ordained. Were ordination not offered to serving deacons, this might have the effect of creating two "classes" of deacon, and this situation could persist for many years. An objection might be raised that ordaining a serving deacon implies some lack in their present ministry. The Panel would say that this is not so – the only thing lacking has been the Church's unqualified affirmation of the office.

We would suggest that each serving deacon should be consulted by the Presbytery of the bounds, and, with the deacon's agreement, a service of ordination should be arranged. Where more than one deacon serves in any Presbytery, that Presbytery could, with the agreement of the deacons involved, ordain them at a single service. The Panel believes that these services would be important, not only in affirming the ministry of individual deacons, but as a visible demonstration of the place of the Diaconate as an office in the Church. It would, of course, be difficult for the Church to insist on ordination against a deacon's wishes. However, the Panel suggests that if ordination is declined during the life of an existing appointment, it would nonetheless be the appropriate method of inauguration if that deacon takes up a new appointment in the Church.

Other Matters

Work on Baptism and on the meaning of membership is now advanced, as is the study of the nature and purpose of the church, based on a recent Faith and Order paper from the World Council of Churches and on initiatives made possible by the former Priority Areas Fund, and it is hoped to bring reports on these matters in the near future. The Joint Commission on Doctrine, involving representatives from the Roman Catholic Church and from the Committee on Ecumenical Relations as well as the Panel, is now re-established. Further, a first meeting has taken place to explore the setting up of a bilateral series of discussions on faith and order issues with the Church of England, again in partnership with the Committee on Ecumenical Relations. The Panel also contributed in March of this year to a consultation of British and Irish Reformed Churches on the theme of "Identity and Partnership".

During the year, the Panel said a regretful farewell to the Very Rev. Professor Robert Davidson, who had been the representative from the University of Glasgow on the Panel. Professor Davidson served the Panel for many years and had contributed willingly and substantially to a number of enquiries, including most recently that on the interpretation of Scripture.

The Panel was sorry also that during the year its Vice Convener, Mrs. Katharina Nimmo, had to resign for personal reasons. Mrs. Nimmo had been a most thoughtful contributor to the work of the Panel and had convened one of its working parties.

Finally, the Panel records the signal contribution of the Rev. Dr. Ian Boyd who for most of its life was convener of the working party on Ordination, the second of whose reports is presented to the Assembly this year.

In the name of the Panel,

JOHN McPAKE, *Convener*
DOUGLAS GALBRAITH, *Secretary*

[1] *Baptism, Eucharist and Ministry*, p. 8, quoted in *Reports to the General Assembly 2000*, p. 13/6.

[2] *Reports 2000,* p. 13/19-20.

[3] This idea was noted in the Panel's 2000 Report. See *Reports 2000*, p.13/5. On the history of this idea in ecumenical discussion, see *Patterns of Ministry* by Steven G. Mackie (London: Collins, 1969), p. 58.

[4] See for example *Episkopé and Episcopacy and the Quest for Visible Unity: Two Consultations*, ed. Peter C. Bouteneff and Alan D. Falconer (Geneva: 1999, WCC Publications, Faith and Order Paper no. 183). The association of the term *episkopé* with an episcopal form of church-government should not mislead us here. Oversight or *episkopé* can and must be exercised in the local church as well as at the regional level; and at the regional level it can be exercised collegially, for example by church courts, as well as personally, by an *episkopos* or bishop.

[5] *Institutes* IV, iii, 8.

[6] See for example the Panel's 1989 Report, in *Reports to the General Assembly 1989*, pp. 198-203. A valuable discussion is also contained in T.F. Torrance's *The Eldership in the Reformed Church* (Edinburgh: Håndsel Press, 1984).

[7] The *Second Book of Discipline* I,6,5.

[8] Torrance *The Eldership in the Reformed Church*, p. 9.

[9] Ibid., p. 14.

[10] Ibid., p. 14.

[11] This is one respect in which the provisions of the *Second Book of Discipline* have not been reflected in later practice.

[12] *Reports 1989*, p. 201.

[13] *Reports 1977*, p. 494.

[14] *Reports 1978*, p. 502.

[15] *Reports 1978*, p. 502.

[16] *Reports 1978*, p. 502.

[17] The Panel uses the term 'non-stipendiary' to refer to both the Auxiliary Ministry and the Readership. In doing so we interpret it broadly—we do not take it to exclude payment of any form. A stipend is a living, and the fees paid to readers do not constitute a living. We would ideally prefer to use the term part-time ministries; however, this would be more confusing, since there are now part-time stipendiary ministries in the Church of Scotland.

[18] In the 2000/01 Church of Scotland Year Book, 31 auxiliary ministers are listed; in the Board of Ministry's Report to the 2000 General Assembly, it was stated that there were 14 candidates in training (p. 17/34). For comparison, the 2000/2001 Year Book lists 278 readers. In January 2001 there were 82 candidates training for the Readership.

[19] See *Reports to the General Assembly 1980*, where the comments from Presbyteries on the Overture which had been sent down are a valuable commentary on the wide range of views within the Church at the time.

[20] In 1996 the General Assembly repealed the Act which had established the Assembly Council, and established in its place a new Assembly Council with a smaller membership and a more restricted remit. The ongoing work on the Auxiliary Ministry was remitted to the Committee on the Maintenance of the Ministry in partnership with the Board of National Mission. See the Report of the Special Commission to review the Assembly Council and the Board of Practice and Procedure, *Reports 1996*, pp. 30/1–8.

[21] The Report of the Working Group on auxiliary ministers and readers to the 1992 General Assembly: *Reports 1992*, pp. 501–507.

[22] *Reports 1977*, p. 498.

[23] *Reports 1977*, p. 498.

[24] *Reports 1998*, p. 25/36.

[25] The 1992 Act arose from a Working Group of the Committee on Education for the Ministry; its remit arose from the Panel on Doctrine's 1989 Ministry Report, which called for study of the relationship between the Auxiliary Ministry and the Readership.

[26] *Reports 1977*, p. 498.

[27] *Reports 1997*, p. 25/23.

[28] See *Reports 1997*, p. 25/23 and *Reports 1998*, p.25/36.

[29] *Reports 1992*, p. 504.

[30] *Reports 1989*, p. 197.

[31] *Reports 1992*, p. 504. Incidentally, the effectiveness of more active recruitment activities has recently been

made clear: the Board of Parish Education has begun increased nation-wide promotion of the Readership, and has seen a sharp increase in applications. In January 2001 there were 82 candidates at some stage of Readership training.

[32] For the sake of clarity, the Panel would affirm explicitly that while there are barriers which need to be lowered in the area of selection and training, we would not wish to see a lowering of educational standards.

[33] See *Reports 1957*, p. 512.

[34] See *Reports 1976*, p. 143.

[35] *Baptism, Eucharist and Ministry*, p. 27.

[36] *The Eldership in the Reformed Church*, p. 14.

[37] For the sake of clarity, the Panel affirms that inaugurating the ministry of deacons by ordination does not imply that they will thereafter have sacramental authority. The description of the ministry of deacons in section 6.3 is intended to make clear the distinctive character of their office. Ordination does not change this.

[38] *Institutes* IV,iii,16.

APPENDIX

ACT III 1999 Anent Moderators of Presbytery

The General Assembly declare, for the avoidance of doubt, that in accordance with practice the Ordination of a minister shall be led by a minister who shall, if the Moderator of the Presbytery be not a minister, be appointed by the Presbytery from among its ministerial members.

PANEL ON WORSHIP
MAY 2001

PROPOSED DELIVERANCE

The General Assembly

1. Receive the Report.
2. Receive the Report of the Church Hymnary Trustees.

REPORT

1. Publications

By publishing the *Ordinal* in a temporary and loose-leaf format, and distributing this to Presbyteries, the Panel has left the door open for the further revision which is likely to become necessary as work is concluded on the diaconate, on non-stipendiary ministries, on procedures leading towards ordination and on related matters.

A compact disc and audiotape of 27 items from *Common Ground*, recorded by a variety of choirs and singing groups, are now in circulation, and should assist congregations wishing to introduce material from the collection. A book of instrumental parts, designed with maximum flexibility to suit local combinations of instruments, is also now available, and can be ordered from the Panel's office.

The Panel has returned to a monthly format for the publication *Pray Now*, providing a cycle of prayers, practical assistance in private prayer, and information about resources, including those available from other boards and committees of the Church. A pattern of production and marketing has been agreed with Saint Andrew Press by which each new issue will be published in time for Advent. Currently, discussions are taking place with the editor of the Church's website concerning the possible inclusion of devotional material based on *Pray Now*, together with comment and views on matters related to spirituality, drawing both on recent editions of *Pray Now* and on previous Reports of the Panel. Also under consideration is the possible provision of appropriate prayer and devotional material for young people aged between 16 and 25, which may include exploring not only traditional book-based resources but Internet and CD formats.

Also now available is a pamphlet on Baptism, sister to that on Marriage, outlining the service and offering practical information and assistance about the event. This is designed for handing to those preparing for their own Baptism or for parents bringing their children for Baptism, and to facilitate this the cost has been kept as low as possible. A further publication is nearing completion, intended for those wishing to read more about Baptism, and consisting in the main of a detailed commentary on the Orders for Baptism, the Public Profession of Faith and Admission to the Lord's Supper, together with discussion on related issues—similar in style to the commentary on Holy Communion in *Why can't we share?* produced by the Committee on Ecumenical Relations.

2. Ongoing work

The Panel has recently returned to an earlier remit from the Assembly regarding "all-age" worship. It undertakes this work aware that renewal in worship today requires more than making room for all generations but that worship must be "inclusive" in other ways also. Depending on the outcome of these deliberations, which will be conducted with maximum consultation, the Panel would hope to draw attention to or produce suitable materials. Parallel to this enquiry are the consultations with the Board of Communication, acting upon a remit from the Assembly of 2000, on the subject of multimedia worship.

3. Presbytery conferences

The Panel has been interested to observe, and in different ways to participate in, conferences arranged by presbyteries on the subject of worship. It will perhaps be useful to other presbyteries who might be planning such conferences to record here the variety of format, each in its own way effective. In one case members gathered in the morning for a presentation of a theological basis for worship, with discussion, while after lunch they participated in creative workshops using movement, sound, silence and objects in innovative ways in preparation for a seasonal act of worship, with which the afternoon closed (Falkirk). In another, representatives from congregations within the bounds of the presbytery gathered for an evening which opened with presentations relating to the encounter between tradition and innovation, continued with groups focusing on music, on drama and on the sharing of ideas which had worked locally, and ended with a panel discussion (Buchan). Another heard from three of their own number describing contrasting approaches to worship in their congregations and giving some account of the principles by which worship was approached. This continued with a visiting presentation centering on the relationships between history, theology and practice in worship (Perth).

The Panel has no doubt that other presbyteries have also planned gatherings or conference sessions on worship and would be interested to hear of these. Members of the Panel stand ready to assist as requested, whether the focus is mainly musical or on wider aspects of worship, understanding the task as being the recognition and utilisation of gifts and insights in each local situation

In the name of the Panel

GILLEASBUIG MACMILLAN, *Convener*
COLIN RENWICK, *Vice-Convener*
DOUGLAS GALBRAITH, *Secretary*

Retiral of Vice-Convener

The Panel wishes to place on record the substantial contribution made by its Vice-Convener, the Rev. Colin Renwick, over these past three years. As well as his enthusiastic convenership of the Music Committee, for which his own skills have so amply qualified him, the Panel as a whole has greatly benefitted from his kindly and steadfast support, and is much in his debt.

GILLEASBUIG MACMILLAN, *Convener*
DOUGLAS GALBRAITH, *Secretary*

COMMITTEE TO REVISE THE HYMNARY
MAY 2001

PROPOSED DELIVERANCE

The General Assembly

1. Receive the Report and the Supplementary Report.
2. Thank the Committee, especially the Convener, and Secretary.
3. Remit the Draft List to Presbyteries for comment, their comments to be sent to: The Secretary of the Committee to Revise the Hymnary, Manse of Canongate, Edinburgh, EH8 8BR by 31 December 2001.

REPORT

1. Introduction

The Committee's long task of selecting and editing material is now within sight of completion. All the hymn books known to the members of the Committee, together with pamphlets and other publications and a large number of manuscripts submitted to the Committee, have been carefully examined. The material selected from these sources has been ordered according to the Table of Contents which was submitted to the General Assemblies of the participating Churches and sent down to Presbyteries for comment in 1998. The resultant draft List of Hymns, in the form of a Supplementary Report, is now offered to the Assemblies in the hope that it will be remitted to Presbyteries for comment, the comments to be received by the 31st December 2001.

2. The Draft List

Responding to the List

Most people, when presented with a list of the contents of a new book of church praise, will scan it in search of familiar and treasured hymns. The absence of any of these loved and valued hymns will generate feelings of regret, and perhaps leave little room for celebrating the new items in the list. Indeed, regret for the passing of the old may even prompt feelings of reservation about the new, reservations which may have little or nothing to do with the quality of the text or the music, but which arise solely from the fact that the new material conjures up nothing for us: it conveys no fond associations of good or determining experiences which can filter into our consciousness.

For the fact is that hymns carry not only the faith of the Church but also our own personal history. One line of text, or of music, may open for us the wounds of grief or the joy of childbirth, the yearning for a better life or the once fervent devotion which is now lukewarm. In hearing or singing a hymn we can be transported back to our first child's baptism or to the moment when we first felt the hand of God upon us.

But because each personal history is *de facto* an individualistic experience, it cannot be expected that the hymns and songs will resonate in the same way in every individual who sings them. While one person may lament the non-appearance of a particular hymn 'of great importance' (to the objector), another may not understand what the fuss is about.

With this in mind, the Committee was keen that the Church should know at the earliest possible moment which items from CH3 were likely to be excluded from the new hymn book. That information was published in the Exclusion List presented to the General Assemblies and to Presbyteries in 1996, and the List was amended in the light of the comments received. Yet, despite the advance warning of likely exclusions, some people will still be surprised and disappointed by the absence of one or more hymns which they deem to be essential to the life of the Church.

To such disappointment, two palliatives can be offered. The first is that almost nothing excluded from *CH3* or *RCH* cannot be reproduced: copyright on a text or tune lapses seventy years after the death of its author or composer.

The second is simply that the proposed list is not yet final. The Committee would welcome comments and suggestions, particularly in respect of (i) hymns relating to aspects of Christian life and witness which are not sufficiently well represented, (ii) children's hymns suitable for congregational singing, and (iii) hymns in contemporary musical idioms.

Material still needed

The first of the three categories for which material is still sought is 'Christian life and witness'. This includes hymns reflecting the life and ministry of Jesus, contemporary hymns of personal faith, and hymns about such things as the care of creation. The Committee has scoured almost every hymnal produced in English-speaking nations in the past two decades, and all bear witness to a lack in these areas.

The second category is children's hymns, which continue to present a challenge. The difficulty does not lie in any shortage of material: there are children's hymns in abundance, but many have a limited shelf-life, while the text of others makes them embarrassing to adults. The Committee is not finding it easy to identify items of quality and possible longevity. This is not to say that churches should be discouraged or prevented from using simple songs and choruses which are suitable for, and enjoyed by, children at school or Sunday School. For as long as there have been hymn books, there have been book of hymns and songs specifically for infants and young people, as the revered Carey Bonnar volumes witness. But adult hymns, psalms, and biblical paraphrases are important in helping children grow into the Church's faith. The challenge is to find texts and tunes which are accessible and fulfilling for use by people of all ages in the context of congregational worship as distinct from Sunday School services or school assemblies.

Much of the material in the third category of hymns and songs, contemporary styles of music, is intentionally short-lived. Commercial Christian music publishers are influenced, for example, as many other businesses are, by the power of market forces and popular trends; and are perhaps driven more by the search for something new and immediately accessible than by words and music which will speak across cultures and centuries.

Again, the Committee would not want to discourage people from using such material, but, because the new hymnary is expected to have a life of at least 20 - 25 years, it is important that discernment is used when it comes to choosing songs in contemporary or commercial musical styles.

This is particularly important in two further respects. The first is that much contemporary Christian song is performance-orientated, and may also be performer-dependent.. In other words, the song may be a great favourite, but it may be one which people prefer to listen to rather than to sing; or, it may depend on the skill of the musician or group of musicians to effect its purpose, whereas a hymn or folk song should be able to stand on its own with or without accompaniment.

The second is practical and commercial. Many new worship songs take up, in terms of lay-out, a greater number of pages than traditional hymn equivalents. A song such as 'Here am I, Lord', which is included in the proposed list, takes three pages of music while, say, 'Abide with me' takes only one. The Committee, aware both of the availability of popular worship songs in other publications and the financial constraints on any substantial publication, must take this factor into account when deliberating on the contents.

In spite of these difficulties, the Committee hopes that the new book will represent the best in contemporary styles of worship songs. It was said of CH3 when it appeared in 1973 that it did not reflect the explosion in English-language hymn-writing which had begun at Dunblane and was promoted by such people as Ian Fraser,

Fred Kaan, Fred Pratt-Green, and Brian Wren. Precisely to avoid that kind of imbalance, the Committee is keeping its eyes and options open until the last.

3. Frequently Asked Questions

The reasons as to why the Church should have a new hymnary were rehearsed when the project was proposed at the 1995 General Assembly. Here, however, it might be appropriate to answer some of the most common questions still being asked with regard to the new book.

a. 'Why can't we just use "Mission Praise" or "Common Ground"?'

There is nothing to prevent congregations using these and similar books. But "Common Ground" (and "Songs of God's People") were provided by the Church as *supplements* to the Church's song, allowing some material to be tested on Scottish congregations and introducing material (for example, such songs as 'Here I am, Lord,' and 'Gather Us In') from established writers not previously commonly known throughout Scotland.

Books such as "Mission Praise" and "Songs of Fellowship", are avowedly commercial publications where the criteria for selection of materials are very different from those directing the compilation of a denominational hymn book. For example, most denominational traditions aspire to ensure that their congregations know and sing or recite the full gamut of the psalms, sing portions of scripture paraphrase, and draw on material from throughout Christendom where it is agreeable to the theology of the particular tradition. And most traditions would expect that a proportion of the material would emanate from writers within that nation and denomination to which the Church belongs. It is not always easy to see these criteria reflected in the above-mentioned books. They contain few psalms of lament, few substantial paraphrases, few hymns and songs which come from Africa, Asia, Latin America or even North America, and few hymns which could claim a presbyterian, let alone a Scottish, provenance.

The Committee feels that it is vital that the new hymn book should provide a canon of hymnody which reflects the history, the theology, the spiritual aspirations, the culture and creativity native to these shores, and the global awareness which are all part of our developing heritage.

b. 'Why not just use overhead projectors or service sheets?'

Again, there is nothing to prohibit people from using either, so long as copyright is not infringed. The *exclusive* use of these, however, raises at least three concerns.

(i) A hymnary is not simply a song book. It is a collection of texts, some of which come straight from the Bible, which are aids to spiritual growth and personal devotion. To be able to thumb through a hymn book is to have access to a treasury of spiritual wisdom which might not otherwise be available to the majority of worshippers who do not have anthologies of religious thought on their bookshelves.

(ii) The exclusive use of overhead projectors tends to diminish the usefulness of the text. No sooner has the verse been sung than the words disappear, and the worshipper cannot look back and muse on what has been sung, as is possible with a hymn book. Ministers and leaders of worship should be particularly aware of this, given that their choice of material for the overhead projector comes through their ability to reflect on written texts - a privilege which is denied to the worshippers.

(iii) When overhead projectors and service sheets are used as a substitute for hymn books, there occurs something very like a centralisation of power in the hands of a few, namely those who choose the hymns and songs. This could be seen as being contrary to the reformed understanding of the shared priesthood of the congregation. The drive in the 16th and 17th centuries to furnish not just the choir but the whole congregation with psalters was indicative of the belief that all worshippers should have access to materials which would nourish their spirits. The making of overheads and print-outs from the galaxy of hymn books and supplements on the manse shelf might well result in the congregation being fed on the diet preferred by the minister; but it might also deprive the worshippers of the opportunity of supplementary vitamins being available, an opportunity that would exist if all the people had access to all the resources.

(c). 'Is there going to be four-part harmony in the new book?'

Yes, there will be four-part harmony, where appropriate. But the Church has never made four-part harmony mandatory, nor has it ever provided a hymnary where every song was in four-part harmony. For example, the favourite tunes, 'Veni Immanuel' ('O come, O come Immanuel') and 'Sussex Carol' ('On Christmas night all Christians sing') have never been fully harmonised for Soprano, Alto, Tenor, and Bass (SATB). The intention of the Committee is that the book should be published with musical settings appropriate to the tune and text.

The Committee further hopes that it may be possible to publish three versions of the hymnary, though it recognises that the final decision on this matter will have to be made in conjunction with the publisher and with the Church Hymnary Trust, since questions of marketing and cost are involved. The popular or pew version would have a unison melody line, guitar chords if and when appropriate, and some shorter songs (for example, 'O Lord, hear my prayer') in harmony. A standard choral and accompaniment version would be provided for choirs, organs, or keyboards. And subject to funds being available, a musician's compendium, with background information to the text, tune, and performance, would provide alternative harmonisations for organ, and settings for instrumental descants which could be photocopied for use in public worship.

(d). 'When is the new book coming out, and how much will it cost?'

At the moment, the Committee's work is on target: the aim was to submit to the General Assemblies in the year 2001 a draft list of the contents of the new book. The time it takes thereafter to print and publish the book will depend largely on the publisher's schedules, but it is the Committee's earnest hope that the new book should be available for the General Assembly of 2003.

It would be foolish to state a price before the book has been costed. However, it should cost no more than:

- two best seller novels which most people will read only once;
- a stand ticket at Ibrox or Easter Road;
- the average price of a three course meal in an Indian restaurant;
- a CD of John Rutter's Choral music, or;
- a year's subscription to "The People's Friend".

The Committee, in conjunction with the Church Hymnary Trust which is funding the publication, hopes to make an announcement as to price at the earliest possible moment. In the meantime, congregations are encouraged to start a New Hymn Book Fund, and to lay aside realistic sums against the day when the new hymn book appears.

The Committee is grateful to the Church Hymnary Trust for its continuing encouragement and for its funding of the Committee's work.

In the name of the Committee,

JOHN L BELL, *Convener*
CHARLES ROBERTSON, *Secretary*

COMMITTEE ON ARTISTIC MATTERS
MAY 2001

PROPOSED DELIVERANCE

The General Assembly:

1. Receive the Report.

2. Instruct the Committee to appoint a review group, co-opting members with a wide representation of interests, to make proposals for the management of sacramental vessels held locally by congregations.

REPORT

SACRAMENTAL VESSELS: A NEW SITUATION

1. Earlier legislation

The matter of the sale of Communion vessels first came before the General Assembly in recent times in 1960, when, in response to reports that Communion vessels had been 'displayed for sale as antiques', it was resolved that all surplus items should be retained by the congregation concerned or passed to another Kirk Session for its use. In 1971, however, it was acknowledged that difficulties had been experienced locally in conforming to this ruling, and it was agreed that congregations could apply to the General Assembly, through the General Administration Committee, for permission to dispose of surplus vessels. Two years later the issue was again raised and the Committee asked to consider the matter further.

In 1974 it was reported that, in the pursuance of this instruction, a survey had been undertaken to ascertain the number and nature of items of plate held by congregations, in conjunction with the National Museum of Antiquities. The result was that in the following year, the Committee brought for the first time to an Assembly guidelines by which applications to sell surplus Communion plate would be judged. These were that: the historical significance of such items must be recognised; only truly surplus items might be sold; and the proceeds of the sale must be applied to something of more than passing value. As examples of this last, the preservation of an historic church building, the

endowment of a fabric fund, or the further endowment of stipend were given. The Committee intimated that in addition it would be enquiring into the possibility, firstly, of valuable items being lent to museums and, secondly, of establishing in a few suitable centres treasuries in which such plate could be displayed.

Over the next 17 years, applications were received at an average of 4 per annum. Many were agreed outright and some were agreed under certain conditions; a few were instructed to invest the proceeds of the sale with the General Trustees. In 1985, an additional guideline was agreed, to the effect that "the opinion of the applicant's Presbytery should be sought with regard to the application". In 1991, it was further agreed that application should be made to the General Assembly not only when a congregation wished to sell Communion vessels but also when it was proposed to give these away. After 1992, the Board of Practice and Procedure was given freedom to make decisions without reference to the Assembly, bringing before it only difficult or controversial cases.

2. Calling the guidelines in question

In 1997, at the point of asking the Assembly to transfer the responsibility for dealing with applications to the Committee on Artistic Matters, the Board predicted that such applications were likely to increase in number. Its Report also expressed the view that, having considered the effectiveness of past and current procedures, there was need for a revision of guidelines in the light of changing circumstances. The present Committee has continued to apply the guidelines inherited from the Board of Practice and Procedure, and the experience gained in the past four years has led it to confirm that it would indeed be advantageous to review procedures. A number of factors may be cited.

2.1 In approaching each case, the Committee's first enquiry is whether the cups might not be used, both as a vivid reminder of the continuity of our Christian worship and witness and as an eloquent symbol of the sharing that is at the heart of Holy Communion (the right of any member of the Church to take Communion from a common cup remains on the statute book). With the continuing rationalisation of church buildings, however, some congregations are accumulating more items of communion ware than they feel able either to use or to care for. Even if there is a wish to make these accessible, many items are too valuable to display safely.

2.2 The second avenue is to discuss the possibility of significant items being lent or sold to a museum, so that they remain in the public domain and can be examined and appreciated. Here too the situation is changing, as both local and national museums are experiencing a severe restriction in funds for purchase. As more examples are offered, storage space becomes limited. It is therefore becoming less and less likely that difficulties experienced by congregations can invariably be solved by museums.

2.3 Some congregations feel that the situation is changing, also, with what they see as escalating costs of storage and insurance. While difficulties are certainly being experienced, it is important to state the facts. It is true that in the case of one bank, storage is now contracted out, and while the bank itself makes no charge in the case of churches and charities the security company concerned quotes fees for reclaiming items each time they are needed for use. Two of the other main banks retain items on the premises: while one makes charges beginning at a rate of £25 per annum with a small fee for removing and returning items, the other does not charge in the case of

churches and charities. With regard to insurance, some have suggested that this is often difficult to arrange or too expensive to contemplate. Not all would agree. The Church of Scotland Insurance Company, for example, advises that insurance is readily and easily obtainable, a typical annual cost being £22.50 per annum for an item valued at £10,000. Nevertheless, with a considerable variety of practice, many congregations are experiencing difficulties in storage and insurance.

2.4 A final consideration is the increasing demand locally on financial resources. This ranges from difficulty in maintaining the level of contribution to stipend to the need for the provision of disabled access. (The Committee has just produced an advisory leaflet on this matter entitled *Open Church: access for the disabled*.)

3. Questions of value

The Committee considers that the value of sacramental vessels can be measured in several different ways, a view we believe is widely shared in the Church. While it is not surprising that some congregations might see in their, often, unused sacramental vessels a source of finance in crisis or missionary opportunity – as "realisable assets" – there are other aspects to be considered.

3.1 For one thing, these items may supplement the written historical record. Inscriptions may give information about donors, incumbents or practices. These need not be in words only. One such example is the collection of Communion and Baptismal plate belonging to the Trinity College Church, which had originally stood on the site of Waverley Station and of which until very recently the custodians had been Holy Trinity Church, Wester Hailes. For some years, these have formed the centre-piece of the Museum of Scotland's *Reformed Church* display. On the silver bread plates are not only words but also pictures, unique engravings depicting a celebration of Holy Communion in the early seventeenth century. The most striking feature of these is that at the table, set for the sacrament, is a kneeling figure. It takes us to the heart of a time of turmoil in the Church of Scotland, with James VI and then Charles I attempting to introduce worship practices that conformed to those in the Church of England. The most deeply unpopular section of the Five Articles of Perth was the one which called for kneeling at Communion, focusing the fury felt by Scottish people which culminated in the signing of the National Covenant of 1638. The minister who commissioned the plate, Thomas Sydserff, was clearly a supporter of the King, and was made Dean of Edinburgh on the way to becoming Bishop of Brechin. A further feature of interest is that in the engravings are representations of actual vessels acquired by the church. Thus it is not just the individual items that are of importance but the whole group.

3.2 Another "value factor" is artistic importance. Just as interesting as what is engraved on our cups and plates is what is behind them. An Act of Parliament of 1617 stipulated that each parish was to provide itself with cups, cloths and tables for Communion, as well as basins and ewers for Baptism. Many of the finest items date from this period as congregations hastened to comply. The result was a unique eye into history which puts paid to any notion that after the Reformation there was a distrust of things of beauty in the church. What's more, with no comparable domestic corpus of silver now surviving, our church silver is a major proof of what was an unexpectedly rich period of Scottish craftwork. Equally significant is the fact that before 1850 such items were probably made locally rather than centrally and in some cases may be the only surviving examples of the craftwork of a particular town. They speak of a high creativity and deep Christian conviction lying at the heart of the local community.

3.3 Also to be borne in mind is the fact that the original instigators and users of the vessels might not be a congregation in today's narrow sense but the whole local community. A congregation seeking to sell or give its vessels needs to have in mind that it is responsible not only to those currently on their roll but, in many cases, the wider community of today. The town council minutes

of Dunbar record how a collection was taken (which appears to be of silverware as well as coins) to melt down into, or go towards the purchase of, enough silver to make the four cups - still in use - inscribed "For the bwrugh of Dwmbar 1657". Cups of the Barony of Glasgow bear the city's coat of arms and the prayer, "Lord let Glasgow Flourish through the preaching of thy Word". Church made common cause with city. There is some obligation upon us to consider this dimension in any discussion about disposal.

3.4 There is value too for a family who might have given these items in the past. For them, the vessels may recall someone whose generous Christian spirit enriched the life of church and community. It may be in such cases, if descendants are known, consultation should be sought.

4. A shared responsibility

Congregations generally take a very responsible position towards the sacramental vessels of which they are custodian. They are aware that they hold such things in trust - for the people of the past who caused them to be made, and for the people of the future who might value them in more than monetary terms. How can we be responsible to them as well as to our own immediate and pressing tasks and calling?

It is because of the importance of this part of our heritage that the General Assembly (through the Committee on Artistic Matters) shares responsibility with the congregation when consideration is being given to selling such items. This does not just reflect the seriousness of the decision in any one case, but suggests also that what we are dealing with is a single possession of the whole Church. It is important to approach the matter in terms of the totality of the situation. A collective approach is needed rather than one that proceeds case by case.

In approaching this joint task, the contribution of both Assembly and local congregation help ensure that certain balances are kept. The needs of the present day church seem urgent, but how will they rate in the long term?

We are told that the town council of Stirling sold its pre-Reformation silver to mend the holes in the road. These items have vanished, but one still encounters contraflows on the M9! We may despair of keeping up with our fabric or become anxious about being able to contribute to a minister's stipend, and see the solution lying unseen and unused in the bank vault. That is understandable, but we need to be aware of what are our successors might say about our stewardship when the roof yet again needs repair or the congregation flourishes under the guidance of a non-stipendiary minister.

Another balance to be kept is in the relative importance of *all* we have inherited. We tend to give precedence to our buildings, perhaps because of their solidity, but the truth is that a congregation may "wear out" several churches in the time covered by its set of Communion or Baptismal ware. We already agree that important historic buildings should be "listed" and protected. Perhaps we need to accord at least the same importance to silver and pewter as we do to stone and lime.

An important aspect of any discussion about disposal is how the proceeds will be applied. From the start, guidelines have insisted that these should be applied in a way commensurate with the significance of the items, a significance found both in the central acts of the church that they serve as well as the often costly witness of our forebears in the faith. To cite as example the recent case of the vessels from the old Trinity College Church, there the proceeds went towards seed capital for the Trinity Centre Project in Wester Hailes, which aims to provide community help and support to one of the most socially disadvantaged and deprived areas of the city of Edinburgh.

Reference to these vessels raises the question of means of disposal. Here the sale was not to "the highest bidder" but was negotiated with the National Museums of Scotland who were able to attract grant aid to purchase them, both because of their historic and aesthetic value as well as because of the destination of the money which would be realised. In an ideal situation, such 'negotiated sales' might be preferred over auction, avoiding the danger of items of national importance "vanishing" into private collections in this country or overseas—although that is not to say that items in private hands are never offered for display. Of course, as in the case of museums, the increasing availability of such items could depress the market.

5. Conserving our heritage

It is because the Committee fears that the earlier average, quoted above, of four approaches per year may increase and that the guidelines currently followed may again become difficult to operate that it asks the Assembly to authorise a fresh look at the matter, in which ways may be sought of preserving this part of our heritage while protecting the freedom of congregations to deploy these resources in the way they consider most responsible.

In the first place, there are good arguments for returning to the task, begun by the Rev. Thomas Burns in 1892 and continued by the General Administration Committee in 1974, namely the gathering of information on the totality of what the Church holds in this regard. In this way, one can begin to identify those items which are of particular significance and whose disposal, if desired, must be carefully managed. This of course would also identify items which might be more readily disposed of. What is required is a congregation-friendly system of recording what is currently kept by the Church as a whole. There are indications that the National Museums of Scotland and the Scottish Museums Council, the body which supports and regulates local museums, would be willing to advise and assist such a process. Other bodies with expertise and a shared interest would be the Scottish Churches Scheme, Scottish Church Heritage Research Ltd., and the churches section of the National Association of Decorative and Fine Arts Societies (NADFAS).

Among suggestions that have been made, in the context of the increasing difficulty that museums have in funding, has been the creation of a central Church fund to purchase and retain the most important of the items where there is a good case for disposal. Although seed money would need to be found, such a fund could be increased through congregations being required or requested to give a percentage from the sale of sacramental vessels, say the same percentage as an auctioneer might expect to take.

The acquisition of the most significant items by the Church as a whole would raise questions of storage and display. The suggestion made in 1975 has been noted above, that central treasuries be created for such a purpose in the event of museums being unable to assist. Even if this prove unworkable, it should be noted that some cathedrals in England and on mainland Europe, have their own treasuries, assisted by external funding. A few churches in Scotland, of course, display items in secure cabinets.

There are other matters which have been raised, for example relating to insurance, storage and display on which it would be beneficial to gather advice for the guidance of congregations.

To deal adequately with the setting up of such a survey, with the feasibility of establishing a central fund, with matters of public display, the gathering of the best advice in insurance and related matters, not to mention assisting congregations discover and appreciate what treasures they may have, it would be desirable to invite together a review group representative of many interests and areas of expertise, from church and from nation. The Committee has already encountered much good will from bodies who share parallel interests in the secular field and do not think it will be difficult to access what is required in this particular instance.

6. Thanks

Many consultations, within and without the Church, have taken place in exploring this matter and in producing this Report. As well as colleagues in the Board of Practice and Procedure, the General Treasurer's Department, the Law Department, the General Trustees and the Board of Stewardship and Finance, the Committee expresses particular appreciation to: George Dalgleish, Curator of Scottish Decorative Arts, National Museums of Scotland; Jane Ryder, Director of the Scottish Museums Council; Professor John Hume OBE, former Chief Inspector of Buildings, Historic Scotland; James Napier of the Church

of Scotland Insurance Co. Ltd.; and Kirkpatrick Dobie, an elder with particular expertise in Scottish sacramental silver.

DOUGLAS LAIRD, *Convener*
ROY WILSON, *Vice Convener*
DOUGLAS GALBRAITH, *Secretary*

Rev. Roy Wilson, D.A., A.R.I.B.A., A.R.I.A.S., Vice Convener

Rev. Roy Wilson, one of the Church's auxiliary ministers, retires at this Assembly. Throughout his many years of service, as member, Vice Convener, and for a spell Acting Convener, his enthusiasm and vigour infected not only the Committee but also the many congregations he has visited. He was always concerned to leave a workable, and very often an ingenious, solution to a local problem, and made many friends for the Committee in the bygoing. He will also be remembered by the Committee for his series of searching and moving meditations relating to the Committee's work which became a feature of its monthly meetings.

DOUGLAS LAIRD, *Convener*
DOUGLAS GALBRAITH, *Secretary*

PROPOSED DELIVERANCE

The General Assembly

1. Receive the Report.
2. Affirm the theological perspective and profile of the Diaconate as set out in the *'Deacons of the Gospel'* Report. (Section 2)
3. Instruct the Board of Ministry to use this Report, in conjunction with the *'Ministers of the Gospel'* Report (General Assembly Report 2000, page 17/3, section 2) for the development of its policies in all areas of its work relating to the recruitment, education and development of the Diaconate. (Section 2)
4. Instruct other Boards and Committees of the General Assembly to use this Report in the development of their work in relation to the Diaconate. (Section 2)
5. Pass an Act anent Selection, Training and Admission of Deacons as set out in Appendix I. (Section 2.9)
6. Approve the proposals contained in the outline of the Enquiry, Appraisal and Assessment Scheme. (Sections 6.3 & 6.4)
7. Approve the amendments to Act V 1998 as set out in Appendix II. (Section 6.4.6)
8. Instruct the Board of Ministry to keep a watching brief on changing legislation in Data Protection and Human Rights, and ensure that its processes and the processes of Presbyteries conform to the highest standards of the law. (Section 6.5)
9. Approve the changes proposed to the processes of dealing with the admission and readmission of ministers to the Church of Scotland and transmit the Overture set out in Appendix III for the consideration of Presbyteries with returns by 31st December 2001. (Section 6.8.4)
10. Encourage the Committee on Education and Training in its support for candidates in training and its continued consultation with them regarding the most appropriate provision of educational and developmental opportunities. (Sections 7.1 & 7.2)
11. Express gratitude to those who act as supervisors of candidates in placements. (Section 7.3.1)
12. Commend the Committee for its commitment to the continuing development of supervisory training. (Section 7.3.2)
13. Affirm the importance of the close consultation with Presbyteries regarding candidates, and look forward to receiving the Board's proposals regarding the continuation of candidature. (Section 7.4)
14. Encourage Presbyteries to follow the Guidelines set out in Appendix VI anent Long-Term Illness of Ministers in Charge (Act X 2000). (Section 8.2.4)
15. Instruct the Board, in consultation with the Board of Practice and Procedure, to revise the Act anent Long-Term Illness of Ministers in Charge, with a view to bringing to the General Assembly in 2002 a more effective revised Act for the future. (Section 8.2.4.3)
16. Approve the new Scheme for Pastoral Advisors and Colleagues and affirm the Guidelines in Appendix VII. (Section 8.3)
17. Welcome the opportunities for ecumenical co-operation afforded by the Scheme. (Section 8.3.7.3)

18.   Instruct Presbyteries to work co-operatively in the effective implementation of the Scheme. (Section 8.3.7.4)

19.   Instruct the Board to provide training, support and resources where necessary to maintain the integrity of the Scheme. (Section 8.3)

20.   Note the Minimum Stipend and other related allowances declared for 2001. (Section 8.4)

21.   Approve the principles set out in the Future Stipend Research Group's Report. (Section 8.5.3.3)

22.   Note the levels of Travelling Expenses in 2001 for cars, motorcycles and pedal cycles. (Section 8.6.1 & Appendix IX)

23.   Welcome the new structure of conferences to support ministers during the first five years of their ministry. (Section 9.2.1.3)

24.   Urge Kirk Sessions to encourage participation by ministers in Study Leave. (Section 9.2.2.1)

25.   Alert Presbyteries to the possibility of increasing numbers of ministers becoming eligible, and applying, for extended periods of Study Leave requiring longer-term planning for cover and resources. (Section 9.2.2.2)

26.   Note the special financial arrangements to assist ministers from remote Presbyteries with travel when applying for study leave. (Section 9.2.2.4)

27.   Affirm the ongoing pilot of a ministerial review process and, pending satisfactory evaluation and amendment, encourage the Committee responsible to give consideration to wider extension. (Section 9.4)

REPORT

1.   INTRODUCTION

1.1   The acceptance by the General Assembly in 2000 of the Board's Report on *'Ministers of the Gospel'* has been the basis for every area of new work undertaken in 2000/2001. Conscious of the many changes of recent years, the Board undertook a comprehensive review of its structures and staffing needs in October and November.

1.2   The management consultants, McKinsey and Co., generously agreed to assist the Board in this task, and on a no charge basis provided three members of their staff to conduct this review. In December 2000, the Board unanimously accepted the recommendations of McKinsey and Co. and is pleased to announce that major developments have already taken place. The Board of Ministry wishes to put on record its thanks to McKinsey and Co. for this *pro bono* work and for their sensitive and collaborative approach and their willingness to base their work on the *'Ministers of the Gospel'* principles.

1.3   Change always brings concern, but Board members and staff are working together for the good of the Church and the full support of ordained ministers and commissioned deacons and their families. It is firmly believed that the revised structures and the more appropriate use of staff will all contribute to a better service and a visionary approach to the ministry of all God's people.

2.   WORKING GROUP ON MINISTRY— IMPLEMENTING *'MINISTERS OF THE GOSPEL'* REPORT

2.1 Preamble

2.1.1   In its Report to the General Assembly of 2000, the Board of Ministry presented a Report entitled *'Ministers of the Gospel'* in which it articulated a theological understanding of the ordained ministry of Word and Sacrament. Critical to that Report was the conviction that *"ministry is the service of the whole people of God, sharing in the one ministry of Jesus Christ, sent by the Father in the power of the Spirit to fulfil God's mission in the world"* (General Assembly Report 2000, page 17/4, section 2.2.1). This Report was approved by the General Assembly and the Board was instructed to *"use this Report for the development of its policies in all areas of its work"*. The Board of Ministry appointed a Working Group to consider the issues surrounding the Diaconate and Auxiliary Ministry. The Board submits a Report this year on the distinctive ministry of the Diaconate under the title *'Deacons of the Gospel – A Vision for Today: A Ministry for Tomorrow'*. The Working Group hopes to present an interim report on Auxiliary Ministry for the consideration of the General Assembly in 2002, and a final report on Non-Stipendiary Ministry in 2003. It is hoped that the report on Non-Stipendiary Ministry will be produced after further consultation and co-operation with the Board of Parish Education, the Panel on Doctrine, the Board of National Mission, the Readership and Auxiliary Ministers. The Board has undertaken the work on the Auxiliary Ministry as a result of the decision of the General Assembly of 1999 regarding this, in which the Board was instructed to address the matter of Auxiliary Ministry in dialogue with the various parties involved.

2.1.2 In developing its theological understanding of ministry, the Board now turns to the distinctive ministry of the Diaconate.

DEACONS OF THE GOSPEL

A Vision for Today : A Ministry for Tomorrow

2.2 Introduction

2.2.1 The Working Group on Ministry wishes to express at the outset its recognition of the distinctive ministry of the Diaconate and its vital role in the changing patterns of ministry in the life of the Church of Scotland today.

2.2.2 In its remit for this Report, the Working Group was charged with developing the following:

- a theological reflection on the distinctive ministry of the Diaconate;
- a vocational profile of the deacon;
- a set of theological and vocational criteria for the selection, education and training of the Diaconate; and
- a scheme for selection, education and training.

2.2.3 It was not part of the Working Group's remit to address the question of the ordination of deacons. This question is being addressed by the Panel on Doctrine who will report to the General Assembly in May 2001.

2.2.4 In undertaking this work, the Working Group recognises that it is not covering this ground for the first time. It acknowledges the work of previous committees and the insight gained from them in preparing this Report. Furthermore, those in the Working Group, who comprised representatives of the Board of Ministry and the Board of National Mission, express their appreciation of the consultations with the Board of National Mission, the Panel on Doctrine, the Board of Practice and Procedure and the Diaconate Council, and their collaboration in the drafting of this Report.

2.2.5 It is hoped that the adoption of this Report will address contemporary concerns about this particular, distinctive ministry within the Church of Scotland while, at the same time, establishing a process of fair practice which, from initial enquiry to final deployment, will be free of anomalies and incongruities.

2.3 Theological Reflection on the Distinctive Ministry of the Diaconate—The Nature of Diaconal Ministry

"I am in the midst of you as one who serves."
(Luke 22:27)

2.3.1 The model for diaconal ministry is Jesus Christ, *"one who serves"*. Servanthood is the key to understanding the "call" to diaconal ministry.

Servanthood ministry is a call and empowerment by God to enable people to experience God's gracious power and love. This is based on an understanding of God whose love and care extends to all people. It is a call to be in relationship with God, God's Word and God's world, to accept, support, comfort, equip and encourage others to use their own gifts to fulfil their potential in service and in life.

2.3.2 In the Church the people of God gather as a community to worship and are sent out to serve. God calls us to worship and be nurtured. God sends us out to nurture others. It is a constant movement of gathering and dispersing. The sending out or diaconal nature of the Church expresses its life and purpose. The ministry of the Diaconate involves the two aspects of the Church— the people of God gathered as a community and the Church acting in the world as Christ's servants.

2.3.3 Within the life and worship of our Church, the distinctive role of diaconal ministry is to see needs in the world and to call the Church to respond. In practice this has meant that deacons have been involved in pastoral care, social service, evangelism and mission, wherever their particular gifts and service can be used to encourage and enable the whole people of God.

2.3.4 Servanthood, as expressed by diaconal ministry, is positive and a privilege. It is not to be confused with servitude or slavery! *"Now that I, your Lord and Teacher, have washed your feet, you also should wash one another's feet."* (John 13:14) It is a ministry that enables others also to do ministry. Ministry is fruit-bearing when it draws others into ministry.

2.3.5 As Christ identified with the suffering of the world, with injustice, with poverty, with the disenfranchised, with the abused, so the Diaconate calls the people of God to see the suffering of the world and to be involved. We are to bear one another's burdens, not to make others dependent, but to express solidarity and support and to be agents of healing and hope. There is a call to persevere in ministry and to be faithful. The Diaconate, like the ministry of Word and Sacrament, is committed to collaboration, so that it works with all the people of God and others in ordained and commissioned service to proclaim the Gospel, not just by what we do but by who we are. Ministers of Word and Sacrament are expected and called to work in a collegial manner with members of the Diaconate to ensure that a variety of gifts and forms of service are harnessed for the proclamation of the Gospel and the care of God's people.

2.3.6 Through reflection, the Diaconate is engaged in asking some of the deep and important questions about Church and society to enable the Church to be a living witness to the Gospel in the years ahead; and, through training and ongoing commitment to growth and development, it is dedicated to the formation of the people of God in the community. *"To prepare God's people for works of service, so that the body of Christ may be built up until we all reach unity in the faith and in the knowledge of the Son of God and become mature, attaining to the whole measure of the fulness of Christ."* (Ephesians 4 vv 12-13)

2.4 Vocational Profile of Deacons

2.4.1 Introduction

2.4.1.1 Deacons are called to serve Christ through the worship and witness of the Church. In the Church of Scotland deacons typically practise ministry in a team situation and most are currently employed in a parish setting. There are exceptions to this, however, and some deacons are to be found working in industrial or hospital chaplaincy, the armed forces or in other forms of ministry approved by the Church.

2.4.1.2 In our efforts to understand as fully as possible the range of skills and qualities expressed in the ministry of the Diaconate, we consulted with the deacons presently employed by the Church of Scotland and with the Board of National Mission's Parish Assistance Committee. This consultation exercise was carried out in a number of ways including formal meetings and discussions with representatives of the Diaconate Council, a questionnaire to all serving deacons, a study of the role of the Diaconate internationally, as well as informal conversations with deacons. These consultations helped to clarify the distinctive contribution that the Diaconate makes to the ministry of the Church of Scotland and have informed the following vocational profile.

2.4.2   Collaborative Approach

2.4.2.1 Deacons work in team situations alongside other ministers and with members of a local congregation, church groups and community. Team working is not an optional exercise for the Diaconate, it is a core skill, critical to the distinctive ministry of the Diaconate. These collaborative skills embrace such diverse qualities as planning, organising, supporting, encouraging, enabling, resourcing and motivating and they are typically practised across the whole age range.

2.4.3   Pastoral Skills

2.4.3.1 The Diaconate is an office of the Church which involves a wide range of pastoral skills and responsibilities, not just for the community of the faithful, but for others outside the Church from all walks of life. In their care of the elderly and pastoral support of the bereaved, deacons often work alongside those ordained to the ministry of Word and Sacrament. Deacons are also employed in encouraging others to fulfil these pastoral tasks and here the role of the deacon becomes one of instructor and enabler, sharing skills and equipping other people for the task of pastoral ministry.

2.4.4   Ecumenical Dimension

2.4.4.1 Although an integral part of the Church of Scotland's tradition and practice of ministry, there is an ecumenical and international dimension to the ministry of the Diaconate. In common with their colleagues in the ministry of Word and Sacrament, deacons require a breadth of outlook that will seek to engage with those in other churches and traditions. Ecumenical awareness and engagement is one of the important features of the Diaconate.

2.4.5   Worship Skills

2.4.5.1 It is generally expected that deacons will be able to lead worship and offer prayer in a variety of contexts such as a nursing home, hospital ward, private home, school assemblies and services. Preaching is also an activity in which a number of deacons are actively engaged, although few deacons would see preaching as one of their core activities.

2.4.6   Christian Education

2.4.6.1 It is often the case that deacons are involved in the provision of Christian education to various groups within the Church and in school settings. An understanding of education principles in relation to the Christian faith is necessary.

2.4.7   Social and Cultural Awareness

2.4.7.1 Many deacons are engaged in working with the local community and this demands an awareness of the social context in which the particular congregation is operating and the prevailing culture in which the Church exists. The meeting place of Church and world is often the daily task of deacons and their work can involve them in collaboration with social and community workers, district nurses and health visitors, community education officers, credit unions and youth and pensioner groups outwith the life of the local congregation.

2.4.8   General Education

2.4.8.1 Like their colleagues in the ministry of Word and Sacrament, deacons are committed to life-long learning. Given the significant changes in the opportunities for further education, and acknowledging the range of skills and abilities needed for the ministry of the Diaconate, the Board is of the opinion that, from now on, graduate training will be the accepted requirement for the Diaconate, although consideration will always be given to applicants with other formal qualifications and relevant life experience. All candidates are expected to maintain a commitment to ongoing training and development.

2.4.9   Conclusion

2.4.9.1 As part of the ministry of the Church, the deacon has an historic role to fulfil. Deacons bring to the practice of ministry a variety of skills and interests that complement the ministry of Word and Sacrament. The focal point of diaconal ministry is service and through this service to encourage the Church to fulfil its calling to serve. As such, diaconal ministry contributes to the continuing ministry of Jesus Christ in the world.

2.5 Characteristics of a Potential Deacon

2.5.1 Intrinsic

- evidence of a maturing faith;
- a sense of vocation;
- a sense of commitment to the Gospel;
- a commitment to being part of a collaborative ministry;
- an ability to reflect and integrate personal faith journey with that of the wider Church.

2.5.2 Knowledge and Understanding

- of the Christian faith;
- of the organisation and structures of the Church of Scotland;
- of the principles and practice of team ministry in the Church of Scotland;
- of the role and special contribution of ministers of Word and Sacrament, deacons and other paid or authorised staff;
- of the organisation of our society; and salient contemporary social problems and needs.

2.5.3 Formative

- an openness to personal growth and professional development;
- ability to envision possibilities to see "what might be" and to innovate in order to achieve what needs to be done;
- capacity for study and subsequent application of knowledge and ideas.

2.5.4 Collaborative

- ability to work with others, including persons in authority;
- capacity to work as an effective team member, observing mutual accountability and ability to respond constructively with colleagues;
- capacity to communicate with groups/audiences, large or small;
- capacity to enlist and motivate others.

2.5.5 Reflective

- a capacity to be self-reflective in practice;
- possession of some awareness of personal strengths and weaknesses;
- ability to demonstrate an insight into the dynamic relationship between who we are and what we are.

2.6 Diaconal Selection Process

2.6.1 In the recent past, since the Board of Ministry took over the selection, recruitment and training of the Diaconate, a process of involvement in the selection conference programme of the Church of Scotland has been instituted. It is the view of the Committee that this process, which has been developed by the Committee on Vocational Guidance, should continue. It is also recommended that those who have expressed an interest in diaconal ministry should be invited to be part of the Enquiry Process, to allow them to explore the parameters of diaconal and other ministries and forms of service within the Church of Scotland. As a result of engaging in the Enquiry Process, along with others who are interested in the ministry of Word and Sacrament and other forms of service, those who express interest are invited to take part in a journey of vocational exploration that may lead them to apply for consideration as a candidate. In order to underpin the team work and collaboration that lies at the heart of the Board's understanding of ministry, it is proposed that the age requirements for selection and training to the ministry of Word and Sacrament will also apply to the Diaconate.

2.6.2 After completion of the Enquiry Process, which will include field assessment and a parallel process of experience, review and assessment, as required for potential ministers of Word and Sacrament, an enquirer may submit an application; the applicant, normally a member of the Church of Scotland, would be invited to a selection conference, in which there would be a group or groups of applicants with assessors who had particular training and background materials, including deployment, on the Diaconate. The application at this point would be accompanied by a report from the applicant's minister and Presbytery. The vocational profile and details of this report would form the criteria for assessment. The exercises of the selection conference process would helpfully explore the issues of a collaborative, reflective and formative ministry and highlight the characteristics and issues of diaconal service that the Church has agreed are critical.

2.6.3 The actual details of the process of the selection conference would be designed by the Vocational Guidance Committee, drawing on its past experience of running selection conferences over the last thirty or more years, in particular the recent experience of diaconal selection processes. Full cognisance would be taken of the reports from the applicants, Presbyteries, congregations and relevant referees. Involvement in the Enquiry Process would ensure that those who had expressed a wish to be selected for diaconal service had an adequate and appropriate knowledge of the boundaries and practice of diaconal ministry within the Church of Scotland. The recommendation from the selection conference would be made to the appropriate committee of the Board of Ministry for consideration and would be reported through the Board to the individual and Presbytery concerned.

2.7 Course Proposals
2.7.1 Introduction
2.7.1.1 If we are agreed that the Diaconate needs to be a group of widely skilled, competent and confident people who have gifts to offer to the whole people of God in their ministry, we must be certain that the training they have equips them to serve in a particular and helpful manner for the good of the Church. Such a training will include divinity topics to allow deacons to work from a strong theological base. Training will also include social science topics to enable insight into social and cultural issues.

2.7.2 Core Course
2.7.2.1 Any core course should include the following:

- Old and New Testament Study;
- Introductory Course in Practical Theology including Mission, Evangelism, Pastoral Care Counselling, Worship of the Church, in particular the Church of Scotland, and Sociological and Ecclesiological Issues;
- Church History with special reference to the Church of Scotland;
- Systematic Theology in the areas of the Principal Doctrines of the Christian Faith, including, for example, Trinity, Salvation, Redemption, Doctrine of God and Christology;
- Practical Placements;
- History and Contemporary Understanding of the Diaconate (Church of Scotland and Ecumenical);
- Law and Practice of the Church of Scotland;
- Christian Education;
- Voice and Communication Skills;
- Attendance and Participation at Diaconate Council.

2.7.2.2 While a faculty of divinity or an institute of higher learning with a religious studies department would normally offer such courses, flexibility would be allowed to acknowledge a candidate's previous study in these areas prior to commencing any course or preparation for the Diaconate.

2.7.3 Additional Courses
2.7.3.1 A list of options would be possible to encourage the development of particular skills in the candidates for the Diaconate. Included in this list would be:

- Youth Work;
- Christian Spirituality;
- Hospice and Hospital Care;
- Industrial Chaplaincy;

- Management Analysis and Systems;
- Work with Elderly;
- Developmental and Co-operative Enterprises with Secular Agencies for Community Projects.

2.8 Acknowledgement of Work Experience

2.8.1   While many of our candidates may well have completed a degree at one of the four faculties of divinity, the Scottish Churches' Open College or another institution of higher learning, it would be important to agree that some time in training (in a practical sense and through conference work) was undertaken with other candidates for ministry, so that they are acquainted with the issues, and have challenged others by their presence, participation and witness regarding the ethos and understanding of diaconal service.

2.8.2   This would be fulfilled through the candidates for diaconal ministry attending the conferences for candidates for the ministry of Word and Sacrament which are held each year in September, as well as undertaking practical placements where they work alongside others in ministry. If a candidate has completed his or her academic training in all areas prior to acceptance as a candidate, we would expect at least one year of full-time training in an institution recognised for training by the General Assembly, involving other candidates for the ministry. This would allow candidates to undertake either a Diploma, a Certificate in Ministry or perhaps even a Master's Degree, and would provide opportunities for interaction with candidates training for other ministries.

2.9 Act Anent Selection, Training and Admission of Deacons (Appendix I)

2.9.1   The Board of Ministry places before the General Assembly at this time an Act to change various previous pieces of legislation affecting the Diaconate. The Board presents this proposed legislation for the approval of the Assembly in the hope that it will enable the Board of Ministry to undertake the effective recruitment, training and support of potential deacons for the future benefit of the Church as a whole.

2.10 Other Issues

2.10.1   It would be important that the training devised acknowledged the changes in Scotland and the challenges that will develop in the future in any form of ministry in this country. Perhaps being rigidly prescriptive would be a mistake; instead, candidates should be encouraged on an individual basis to develop particular skills in sociological and psychological development, to prepare them for understanding the multitude of needs in society and in individuals whom they seek to serve as deacons.

2.10.2   Any regulation of the core course might be left flexible and open to determination by the Working Group on Academic Questions which will advise the Education and Training Committee and the Board in 2001 regarding the educational requirements of all candidates for ordination or commissioning.

3. INTERIM MINISTRY

3.1   The Board is pleased to report that there is continuing positive work being done by its Interim Ministry Team. There is no need to continue the practice of detailing each appointment with a pen sketch of the issues being faced in each situation. However, it is important continually to remind congregations and Presbyteries of the opportunity that exists to conduct a serious inventory of congregational life and vision under the guidance of an Interim Minister.

3.2   It is particularly important to see the process and aims of such ministry as being relevant at the point of almost every vacancy. This is not a troubleshooting ministry. To describe it as such is a great misunderstanding of the scope of this work.

3.3   The Church in almost every place is facing the challenge of setting relevant priorities in order to extend its mission. Along with this comes the challenge of planning and bringing about major changes in our congregational life. We need to plan our church life in partnership with our Church of Scotland and our ecumenical neighbours. None of this is easy, yet under an Interim Minister it is possible to focus on some of these issues and hence lay the foundation for the future.

3.4 The Board is working in a variety of ways to develop this ministry and it would encourage congregations and Presbyteries to give serious consideration to a wider use of this resource.

4. PROTECTION OF CHILDREN AND YOUNG PEOPLE

4.1 The Board is pleased to report that, in accordance with the instructions of the General Assembly of 1998, 1096 ministers have successfully completed the approved one-day training course in the Protection of Children and Young People. This has been a formidable task which could not have been accomplished without the sterling endeavours of trainers and facilitators, as well as the co-operation of Presbyteries, which provided locations for the meetings. Inevitably, some ministers have fallen through the net for reasons such as illness or overseas service and annual opportunities will be offered for them to participate when their situations permit. The very few who have failed to undertake the course without apparent cause are being pursued through their respective Presbyteries. The course is now integrated with the education and training of prospective ministers.

5. STAFF

5.1 The Board wishes to express its sincere thanks to all members of Staff who continue to meet the wide-ranging needs of ministry. Their continued detailed, courteous and helpful responses to the many important and diverse situations which have arisen have been greatly appreciated by many of those who contact the Board.

6. THE COMMITTEE ON VOCATIONAL GUIDANCE

6.1 The Need for Change

6.1.1 Over the past two years the Board has reported in some detail on the need for a new approach to recruitment and selection. The Board's Report on *'Ministers of the Gospel'* only serves to make the task of review more urgent. In this Report the Church of Scotland has for the first time set down some fundamental criteria for its future ministry. In short it has called for a ministry which is:

- able to communicate the Gospel in ways appropriate to varied contexts;
- prepared for a deeply collaborative style of leadership;
- open to continuing vocational development and appraisal.

(General Assembly Report 2000 page 17/14, section 2.3.4.1)

6.1.2 It is now a matter of some urgency that the Church addresses its mind to providing a framework in which future ministers can be assessed against these standards.

6.2 Enquiry Process

6.2.1 In a spirit of positive collaboration the Board of Ministry, together with the Board of National Mission, the Board of Parish Education, the Board of Social Responsibility and the Board of World Mission, has engaged with more than 130 members of the Church pursuing an interest in discerning their vocation.

6.2.2 Enquirers' Conference

6.2.2.1 An Enquirers' Conference was run as an overnight event during the first weekend of September 2000. 103 enquirers attended this event where they engaged with a programme which covered the topics that were set before the General Assembly in 1999 (Board of Ministry Report Page 17/9). Of these 103 enquirers, forty-three are, under the auspices of the Board of Ministry, further exploring their sense of vocation to ordained or commissioned service through a period of accompaniment alongside a trained Co-ordinator. Some, without this period of accompaniment, are proceeding directly to Selection Conference, while others are now exploring some of the different avenues of service that were highlighted by the other Boards.

6.2.2.2 Early signs show that this has been one of the most valuable exercises carried out by the Church in recent years. Feedback from the Enquiry Conference showed that this was a helpful experience for almost every participant. At the time of writing this Report a second Enquiry Conference is at the planning stage. The five Boards, which constitute the main employing agencies of the Church, anticipate that such Enquiry Conferences will continue to be held twice a year. In the case of the Board of Ministry, it proposes that in future all applicants for ordained or commissioned ministry will have attended an Enquirers' Conference before embarking on a process of assessment and selection.

6.2.2.3 It is clear that being engaged in an Enquiry Conference and a period of accompaniment helps to widen perspectives and present realities. It is also clear that such a process helps would-be applicants to test out their gifts, skills and sense of Call. This alone constitutes a major step forward in our vocational guidance procedure. However, the knowledge gained from this pilot scheme and the evidence collected in the Board's consultation with Presbyteries leads us to believe that the Church is ready for more far reaching change to our processes of assessment and selection.

6.3   The Proposed Enquiry, Appraisal and Assessment Scheme

6.3.1   Presbytery Consultation

6.3.1.1 As a major part of its developmental thinking, the Board carried out a Presbytery consultation. In the consultation document Presbyteries were given a detailed account of the proposals which were beginning to emerge. In addition, a response was invited to a number of key questions. This exercise proved to be extremely fruitful and, following a detailed analysis, it was gratifying to find a large measure of concurrence emerging.

6.3.1.2 With only one exception, the Presbyteries that responded (forty-two) were broadly supportive of the introduction of regular Enquiry Conferences and of the proposals for a period of co-ordinated enquiry and assessment. There was also broad agreement around the proposed areas of life and practice that should be examined during the assessment of an applicant for ministry.

6.3.1.3 Divergence of opinion emerged around:

(a)   The issue of confidentiality
(b)   The decision making authority of the Local Review
(c)   The make-up of and apparent lack of Presbytery involvement in the Local Review.

However, in spite of a width of opinion on these matters, clear and substantial majority conclusions emerged.

(a)   The issue of confidentiality

On the matter of the length and compulsory nature of the enquiry period the Board has acknowledged the need to build in some flexibility. There may be circumstances (including an individual's need for confidentiality at this stage) which make it advisable to shorten, or in some cases omit, the first Extended Enquiry part of the process, thus allowing the process of co-ordinated assessment to begin soon after attendance at an Enquirer's Conference. More generally, the Board accepts that some enquirers will continue to have worries about confidentiality but believes that these will have to be handled as sensitively as possible in the circumstances of each individual case. However, any permission to omit this step would be given only after consultation with a member of the Vocational Guidance staff and with a Presbytery representative.

(b)   The decision making authority of the Local Review

While five or six Presbyteries had some anxiety about the prospect of a Local Review being able to veto an applicant's right to attend an Assessment Conference, the vast majority clearly expressed the view that the Local

Review should have full decision making powers. The Presbytery returns make it clear that Presbyteries are willing for a critical decision to be taken at a Local Review. Therefore, as well as recommending a scheme in which material gathered during the period of co-ordinated assessment should be forwarded to the national Assessment Conference, the Board is also recommending a scheme in which a Local Review, with significant input from Presbytery representatives, should make a decision on whether an applicant is ready to proceed to such an Assessment Conference.

(c)   The make-up and apparent lack of Presbytery involvement in the Local Review

On the final point a substantial number of Presbyteries questioned the significance of the role of Presbytery in the Local Review. Many Presbyteries felt that their input in this Review was minimal. Here, for the sake of clarity, it is worth spelling out the role and authority of the Local Review. In the first instance it should be seen as the first part of the Church's national Assessment Scheme. The presence of an Assembly appointed Assessor and the input of the psychologist assessor are to help ensure consistency and objectivity of practice. In addition the presence of a non-assessing member of the Board's staff at such reviews is aimed at maintaining continuity and consistency across the country.

The Assessment Scheme Committee would continue to be the body responsible to the General Assembly for this, as for the rest of the process. Any appeal against a decision of the Local Review would therefore be to that Committee, not to the Presbytery. However, the Board's scheme, in contrast to existing arrangements, is designed to give scope for local parties (appointed by Presbytery), who have built up a relationship with an applicant and learned a lot about how s/he performs in sensitive and challenging situations, to make a substantial contribution to the assessment process. In addressing this issue the Board would highlight the following points:

(i)   The scheme as now presented allows Presbyteries to assign up to two representatives to take part in the Local Review.

(ii)   Presbyteries who feel that this is not enough involvement are still at liberty to interview an applicant and send a report (separate from the Review Report) to the Assessment Conference.

(iii)   Even after Assessment and Selection at national level, Presbyteries are still required finally to decide whether or not to promote an applicant to the status of Candidate in Training.

6.4   Proposed Changes

6.4.1   The final proposal of the Board, which now requires the approval of the Assembly, is for a three stage Enquiry, Appraisal and Assessment Scheme. There are three major changes at the heart of these proposals:

- Through an **Enquirers' Conference** and the availability of a period of **Extended Enquiry** it will be possible for members of the Church to embark on a period of self-appraisal aimed at helping them to discern their vocation.

- A major part of the assessment of every applicant for ordained or commissioned ministry will take place during a period of **field assessment.**

- This period of **field assessment** will culminate in a **Local Review** that will make a determination on whether an applicant is ready to proceed to a national **Assessment Conference**.

6.4.2   Stage One

6.4.2.1 Enquirers' Conference and Extended Enquiry

6.4.2.1.1   Prior to considering application for recognition as a candidate in training for the Ministry of Word and Sacrament or Diaconal Ministry, all 'would-be' applicants would have to become **Enquirers**. As such they would make two visits within their Presbytery and reflect on their experience of each with a Presbytery representative. One visit would be to observe worship in a church, if possible with a different style of worship to their own, and the other would be to a local church project or centre *etc*. The Enquirer would also complete a questionnaire for their own personal use that would help them begin to identify their own strengths and weaknesses.

6.4.2.1.2 On completion of the above, an Enquirer would attend an Enquirers' Conference that would focus attention on:

- The major challenges facing the Church today;
- The need for gifted and able people to work in a variety of key roles throughout the life of the Church;
- The rigours of facing full-time education, training or re-training;
- The importance of personal integrity in all areas of life and ministry.

6.4.2.1.3 Enquirers' Conferences would be likely to be held twice a year. They would be overnight events, with the Church funding the cost of the conference. Participants would normally be expected to meet their own travel costs. As reported to the Assembly in 1999, these conferences would act both as a focus for issuing the call to service and as a forum for presenting the challenges of ministry with candour and realism.

6.4.2.1.4 Following attendance at this conference the process of Enquiry would normally be extended into a further period of reflection and self-appraisal that will be provided through a period of **Extended Enquiry**. This period would be **'enquirer driven',** and its length (up to a maximum of six months) would be determined by the **Enquirer**. Such a period of extended enquiry could be as little as one month in length or as long as six months. The Board, in consultation with Presbytery, would make arrangements for a suitable placement alongside a trained co-ordinator who would act in a mentoring role during this time of reflection and self-appraisal. Normally such enquiry placements will be in a church other than the Enquirer's home congregation.

6.4.2.1.5 There would be no element of Church assessment in this part of the process. It would be designed for the specific purpose of enabling the Enquirer to make decisions about the nature of her/his vocation and whether or not s/he should proceed to become an **Applicant** for recognition as a candidate for ordained or commissioned ministry.

6.4.3   Stage Two

6.4.3.1   Co-ordinated Field Assessment

6.4.3.1.1 Should an Enquirer become an **Applicant** for recognition as a candidate for ordained or commissioned ministry, the Board of Ministry in consultation with Presbytery would thereafter place her/him in a local setting where the process of Assessment of suitability for training for ministry will begin.

6.4.3.1.2 The applicant would be assigned to a local Co-ordinator (not in their home congregation nor with the co-ordinator who might have been involved in Stage 1), and here would begin a process of up to five to six months in which the local parties in partnership with an Assembly appointed assessor and a psychologist assessor would begin the process of open and continuous assessment of suitability.

6.4.3.1.3 The Co-ordinator would be a minister, deacon or other appropriately trained person who would lead the **Applicant** through a series of activities and exercises designed both to allow the applicant to continue in a process of self-assessment and to allow the Church to assess the person and their potential as a candidate for ministerial training.

6.4.3.1.4 The Presbytery consultation process showed a great deal of consensus about the areas of assessment around which the Church should be concentrating. In summary these come under five main headings:

- integrity of faith and life
- openness to learning
- interpersonal skills
- reflective skills
- coping with change.

6.4.3.1.5 Near the beginning of the placement the applicant would be interviewed by a psychologist assessor who would be particularly interested in assessing development potential. If practical, the psychologist would then be present at the Local Review, however, if this was not possible, the psychologist would at least see the applicant again towards the end of the placement and feed a written report into the Local Review. At appropriate stages during this period of assessment another member (or two members, as a Presbytery may see fit) of Presbytery would join the Co-ordinator in order to facilitate both a process of reflection on the journey of the applicant and to extend their experience of the applicant. Finally, at the end of the placement, the Co-ordinator, Presbytery Representative(s) and an Assembly appointed Church assessor would meet with the applicant, review their application and make a decision on whether the applicant is ready to proceed to a national Assessment Conference.

6.4.3.2 Training of Personnel

6.4.3.2.1 Every Presbytery emphasised the need for thorough training of all the personnel involved in the scheme. The Board, acknowledging this fact, can think of few enterprises that merit any greater investment of time and resources. The Board has already begun the process of training and, should the Assembly endorse these proposals, is ready to tackle the next phase of preparing the necessary personnel. In dedicating resources to the training of personnel, the Board envisages eventually having access to an extensive network of people who would be able to work in any one of the vital roles required by the scheme. In other words every Presbytery would have a body of people capable of acting as co-ordinators at any stage of the process, Presbytery Representatives or locally based Church assessors. The Board will continue to consult with Presbyteries to identify suitable people for training. Further, Church assessors (past and present) could be placed on standby to help conduct Local Reviews.

6.4.3.3 Sharing of Expertise across Presbytery Boundaries

6.4.3.3.1 It is also interesting to note that nearly every Presbytery that responded indicated a willingness to share expertise across Presbytery boundaries. This is good to know, since it will be essential, in the case of small Presbyteries or to accommodate an Enquirer or Applicant who is working or studying outside of their home Presbytery, to share resources and expertise as widely as possible.

6.4.3.4 The Local Review

6.4.3.4.1 It is easy to see how effective a well trained local Review Team could be in helping to discern the suitability of applicants for ordained and commissioned ministry. The presence of a Church Assessor from the national team together with the input of a psychologist assessor would help to ensure objectivity as well as providing another layer of expertise. It is also hoped that because of the local nature of this Review, it will take place in a setting more conducive to seeing the applicant in a relaxed and natural way. The Review will aim to:

- enable an Enquirer and representatives of the wider Church together to reflect on the particular vocation of the individual;
- review the experience of an Applicant during the period of Enquiry through conversation and receiving reports;
- communicate clearly with an Applicant regarding the way in which others experience that individual in relation to giftedness for ministry.

6.4.3.4.2 Together, this team would work to ensure that an applicant, before proceeding to the next stage, was an individual in whom:

- person and practice are well integrated;
- is demonstrated maturity of faith, soundness of judgement, healthy self-awareness and sensitivity toward the needs of others;
- the Church could rely to be collaborative in their approach, reflective in their practice and committed to lifelong formation (General Assembly Report 2000, page 17/17, section 2.4ff).

6.4.3.5 Presbytery Involvement

6.4.3.5.1 It is hoped that Presbyteries will feel that input through their members on the Local Review will be sufficient in providing the national Assessment Conference with information on an applicant. In most cases this process will be more thorough than current practice. However, if a particular Presbytery feels it should continue to interview candidates separate from the Local Review, then it should be aware that it will be necessary to share the content and recommendation of that report with the applicant. In any event, it is not envisaged that a Presbytery in open court will hear a report on an applicant until after they have attended an Assessment Conference (see Section 6.5 on Data Protection and Human Rights Legislation).

6.4.3.6 The Decision Making Authority of the Local Review

6.4.3.6.1 A key part of these proposals is the decision making power of the Local Review. It is clear from the consultation process that the majority of Presbyteries wish to participate in the decision of whether or not an applicant is ready to proceed to a national Assessment Conference. It is also essential that this review process be as open and honest as possible. Human Rights Legislation already means that a body such as Presbytery can no longer supply a negative report on an applicant without the applicant being aware of the content of that report (see Section 6.5). The same standard must apply to the work of this Local Review, which will be responsible for sharing their report with the applicant following their deliberations.

6.4.3.6.2 Therefore, as the final element in the process of 'field assessment', the Review group will provide the applicant with a written report making one of the following decisions which would be reported to the Assessment Scheme Committee:

(i) The Applicant is ready to proceed to be considered at Assessment Conference.

(ii) The Applicant is given an extended period of Field Assessment prior to a final decision.

(iii) The Applicant is informed that s/he is not ready to proceed to an Assessment Conference at this time (leaving open the possibility of up to two more periods of field assessment after a specified time).

(iv) The Applicant is informed that final consideration has been made in the Local Review and that it will not be possible to proceed to Assessment Conference. (Such a decision would only be reached where the Local Review Group was

convinced beyond all reasonable doubt that proceeding to Assessment Conference could not be permitted.)

6.4.3.7 Right of Appeal

6.4.3.7.1 An applicant would of course have a right of appeal against the decision taken by the Local Review. The process of appeal would be through the Assessment Scheme Committee and would follow the course set out in Act V 1998 Section 6e.

6.4.4 Stage Three

6.4.4.1 The Assessment Conference

6.4.4.1.1 Following the Local Review, all Applicants given permission to proceed will be required to attend an Assessment Conference. Such a Conference would continue to provide the Church with a consistent procedure which would be applied to all those who apply for recognition as candidates in training for Ministry.

6.4.4.1.2 Up to this stage we hope that every applicant will have been dealt with in a more open and constructive way than ever before. We particularly hope that those who have not been accepted will nonetheless feel affirmed in their Christian service and may find another direction in which to develop their service. Now it becomes more important than ever to deal appropriately with those who attend an Assessment Conference.

6.4.4.1.3 While this is an event which comes at the culmination of an assessment process, it is crucial that it is not seen as a rubber stamping of a decision that has already been made. There will be people who will be disappointed with the outcome at this final stage. It is crucial, therefore, that this Conference is well informed of the strengths and weaknesses of each applicant and that the outcome of this assessment is properly documented and, as soon as possible after the event, placed in the hands of the individual applicant.

6.4.4.1.4 In the first instance the applicant would be aware of all that had been said in relation to their assessment up to this point. In the second instance all such information would be passed on to the Assessment

Conference for use in that context. In such a way the Assessors will, before the Conference begins, be much better informed about the background of an applicant. Many of the attributes, gifts and skills of an applicant will already have been put to the test and been the subject of the report generated by the Local Review. The national Assessment Conference will therefore have a different and more specific purpose than before. It may also be expected that it will be shorter and less expensive than the present arrangement.

6.4.4.1.5 The Assessment Conference will, however, continue to be a vital part of the Church's Assessment of its applicant. As with the present Selection Conference, this event will present a unique opportunity to:

- See the applicant in a group context, assessing their ability to relate, integrate and collaborate with others;
- Examine with complete objectivity, away from the local setting, the character and beliefs, vocation and general suitability of each applicant;
- Examine further, areas of life, doctrine, faith journey etc, which may have been highlighted by the Local Review;
- Allow an opportunity to address what might be the appropriate education and training needs of each individual applicant;
- Ensure consistency of assessment and help to eliminate any variations in the approach of Local Review Groups.

6.4.4.1.6 An applicant could be permitted to attend Assessment Conference up to a maximum of three times. If the Assessment Scheme Committee felt that further information was required on an individual before reconsideration could be given to their application, it would be at liberty to insist that, prior to a further attendance at Assessment Conference, the applicant should undergo a further period of field assessment.

6.4.4.1.7 Finally, in line with the Board's proposals contained in the *'Ministers of the Gospel'* Report, the Assessment Conference would form the gateway to a process of continual assessment that would apply throughout a candidate's period of Education and Training.

6.4.5 Evolution of the Process

6.4.5.1 As at present through Act V 1998 Section 6(a) the Board, through its appropriate sub-committee, shall be responsible for working out the fine detail of each part of the assessment process. Much of this work has already been done during the period of the pilot enquiry scheme and much of what has been done over the last three decades will continue to serve the new scheme. However, as always, the Board presents this Scheme to the Church as a developing process. It will continue the work of evaluation and further review. Year on year the Board will keep the Assembly informed of any major changes in the Scheme, and it pledges itself to continual dialogue and collaboration with Presbyteries and congregations as this process is introduced.

6.4.6 Amendment of Act V 1998 (Appendix II)

6.4.6.1 As a consequence of the introduction of the Enquiry, Appraisal and Assessment Scheme, the Board also brings forward an appropriate amendment to the Act anent Selection and Training for the Full-time Ministry and Eligibility for Ordination.

6.4.6.2 Essentially, this is an amendment of Section 2 of the Act that effectively removes the 'three year membership rule'. However, it replaces this requirement with the need for all would-be applicants for the Ministry of Word and Sacrament to become Enquirers (in accordance with Stage One of the new Scheme) before submitting an application for recognition as a candidate in training. Furthermore, in Section 5 and 6(a) the Act makes way for the addition of a period of field assessment that shall culminate in a Local Review with powers to decide whether or not an applicant is ready to proceed to an Assessment Conference. The Board submits this Act for the approval of the General Assembly.

6.4.7 Implementation

6.4.7.1 This Act will apply to all applications received after 1st June 2001. However, in accordance with the usual practice of the Church of Scotland, this change in practice will not be made retrospective. Therefore, although all pending applicants shall be encouraged to enter this new Enquiry and Assessment Scheme, they shall, nonetheless, be entitled to complete their current application under the terms of the legislation as it stood at the time of their application.

6.5 Data Protection, Human Rights Legislation and Freedom of Information

6.5.1   Over the last year, the Committee on Vocational Guidance has been particularly exercised over forthcoming changes in the Data Protection Act and in the introduction of Human Rights and Freedom of Information Legislation. These changes make a significant impact on the work of the Vocational Guidance Committee, the way in which records are handled and the approach required by the personnel who operate our processes.

6.5.2   The Assembly should be aware of some of the most immediate issues that have to be addressed:

- Reports on an applicant—made by Presbyteries, Local Review Groups and at the Assessment Conference itself—should be shared with the applicant. One consequence of this will be providing non-accepted applicants with a written feedback report, and in future it may well be that reports from each stage of the process should be made available in full to an applicant.
- Reports from previous Selection Conferences should no longer be cited as evidence at subsequent Selection Conferences. Only evidence which is available to both the applicant and the assessors, namely, the feedback report from a previous Selection Conference, should be cited in the case of a returning applicant.
- Archive material on all applicants should be kept to a minimum. An organisation like the Church is only entitled to retain such information as is absolutely necessary on its applicants, candidates, students and ministers.
- Application, reference and report forms should be

reviewed to ensure that the information being sought on an applicant is essential and not extraneous to the task of assessment and selection.

6.5.3   These are just some of the matters being tackled by the Committee. In this work the Board has been indebted to the valuable work and advice of the Solicitor of the Church and her colleagues. Together they have provided training input for our assessors and valuable guidance to the Committee on Vocational Guidance. The Board would simply assure the Assembly that in continued co-operation with the Law Department, it will work to ensure that its procedures meet the appropriate standards.

6.6 Selection Conference Assessors

6.6.1   At this time the Board reports that it has begun the process of recruiting and training new Selection Conference Assessors. The appropriate Presbyteries from the rota and members of the Board have been approached to submit names of those suitable for consideration. The process of selection and training has now begun, and the Board will bring the names of new Assessors to next year's Assembly for approval and appointment.

6.7 Feedback

6.7.1   Following last year's Assembly the Board has begun its work on evaluating the process of giving feedback to non-accepted applicants. This has revealed a number of interesting facts that are now being examined by the Committee on Vocational Guidance. It is unquestionably true that non-accepted applicants do appreciate hearing something of the reasoning behind the decision that is made at Selection Conference. However, most would appreciate an even more open reporting system. That thought has been at the forefront of the mind of the Board in the development of the new Enquiry and Assessment Scheme process. More work has to be done on the analysis of the data received from a variety of sources. However, as already mentioned, other events have overtaken this evaluation process and it is envisaged that in any event the future practice of the Committee will be to provide written feedback reports to all applicants.

6.8 The Committee on Admission and Readmission

6.8.1 Certificates of Eligibility

6.8.1.1 The Committee on Admission and Readmission reports the issue of the following Certificates of Eligibility:

Richard Campbell, United Free Church of Scotland
Anne Job, United Reformed Church
Brian McDowell, United Reformed Church
Leslie Milton, Igreja Evangelica de Cristo em Mocambique
Kim Mislin, United Church of Christ, USA
Derek Morrison, Associated Presbyterian Church
Angus Morrison, Associated Presbyterian Church
Ben Pieterse, Nederduitse Gereformeerde Kerk of South Africa

6.8.2 Petitions

6.8.2.1 The Committee has interviewed three persons who had intimated their intention to petition the General Assembly for admission or readmission as a minister in the Church of Scotland.

6.8.3 Completion of Course

6.8.3.1 The petitioner the Rev Professor Louis Bezuidenhuit has now completed the course stipulated by the General Assembly in 1999 and has been called to a charge.

6.8.4 Revision of Act III 1995 anent Admission and Readmission of Ministers and Eligibility for Nomination, Election, Call and Appointment (Appendix III)

6.8.4.1 Through its Committee on Vocational Guidance the Board has been working steadily on the principles that should govern the admission and readmission of ministers and deacons. Act III 1995 has quickly outgrown its usefulness. For example, the Church of Scotland will soon have no office of Licentiate, yet under this Act it is still possible to petition the Assembly as a Licentiate of another church.

6.8.4.2 There is also general agreement that those who would enter the Church of Scotland from another denomination or re-enter the ministry having resigned or been deprived of their status, should be held up to the same exacting standards that have been set for ordinary applicants. The General Assembly, in its adoption of the Report on *'Ministers of the Gospel'*, has set out the high standards of integrity it expects of its ministers and deacons. It has also laid down some of the qualities and characteristics that it requires in those who would interpret the Gospel in the context of a fast changing post-modern Scotland. So, just as it has been necessary to review and revise the process by which ordinary applicants are assessed, it has also been necessary to review and revise the way in which others enter or re-enter the ministry of the Church of Scotland.

6.8.4.3 As stated in last year's Report, *"it is not the intention of the Board to deprive the Church of Scotland of the richness of being able to draw from other branches and traditions of the Church. On the contrary, the Board believes that the Church of Scotland has been enriched by many of those who have come from overseas or from other denominations in the United Kingdom"*. However, it is the intention of the Board to give the Church a process that will thoroughly assess the potential of all those entering the ministry of the Church of Scotland. It is in that spirit that the Board brings forward the new Act Anent Admission and Re-admission of Ministers contained in Appendix III of this Report. This new Act attempts to deal appropriately and consistently with a number of different categories of people who currently seek admission through the Committee on Admission and Readmission and the General Assembly.

6.8.4.4 The most significant aspect of these proposals is to ask the General Assembly to give powers to the Board of Ministry, acting through its Assessment Scheme Committee, to deal with and dispose of all applications for Admission and Readmission without bringing petitions to the General Assembly. The Board is already entrusted with this responsibility in respect of ordinary applicants. It conducts in-depth assessments and determines whether or not applicants should proceed to training for ordained or commissioned ministry. Given that all applicants have a right of appeal to the Church's highest court, it is only a short step to extend the remit of the Board to include applicants for admission or readmission. In this regard, the Assembly should note that in recent history its Committee on Admission and Readmission has never brought a recommendation to the Assembly that was not upheld. This seems to point to an effective way of working which, if affirmed by a majority of Presbyteries, would have the effect of removing unnecessary business from the floor of the Assembly.

6.8.4.5 In framing these proposals, the Board has sought the advice and guidance of the Committee on Ecumenical Relations. In this matter, the Board is pleased to report that it will be happy to liaise with the Committee on Ecumenical Relations in the ongoing review of those Churches which should be included in Schedule A of this Act.

6.8.4.6 Proposed Changes

6.8.4.6.1 The fundamental changes being proposed are as follows:

(i) **An Assessment Scheme Committee**
Presently, the Board of Ministry has two Committees that deal with applicants for ministry in the Church of Scotland. The Assessment and Selection Committee deals with ordinary applicants and the Committee on Admission and Readmission deals with applications from ministers of other Churches and with former Church of Scotland ministers who are seeking to have their status restored. Since these proposals seek to bring some consistency of criteria to bear on all applicants for ordained and commissioned ministry, it is proposed that in future, one committee, namely an Assessment Scheme Committee be responsible for overseeing the progress of all applications.

(ii) **Certificates of Eligibility**
Presently, a Certificate of Eligibility is only issued to a qualifying applicant after s/he has received a Call or been appointed to an appropriate appointment in the Church of Scotland. In the future it is proposed that a Certificate of Eligibility should be applied for and issued prior to making application or being considered for ministerial posts in the Church of Scotland. It is also proposed that such Certificates should only be issued after thorough examination of each applicant, and that the validity of such Certificates should be time limited to three years. After three years a Certificate will have been deemed to have lapsed, requiring a fresh application to be made to the Assessment Scheme Committee.

In every case the Committee would only have the right to issue a Certificate of Eligibility. Ultimately, a Presbytery would have to decide whether or not to sustain a Call or admit to membership a minister working in a post as referred to in Act III 2000 anent Membership of Presbytery.

(iii) **Introduction of a Review Panel**
That the present criteria in respect of the issue of a Certificate of Eligibility namely (i) completion of a university course acceptable to the Committee on Education and Training (ii) completion of not less than five years' service in a qualifying church (iii) be in good standing within that church (iv) never previously refused entry to the Church of Scotland ministry, be extended to include the need to be interviewed by a Review Panel that would make a recommendation to the Assessment Scheme Committee on whether or not a Certificate should be issued.

(iv) **Conditional Certificates**
That in the future, Certificates of Eligibility could be issued conditionally. Presently, this is not the case. Therefore it is possible that some ministers enter or re-enter the Church without any period of familiarisation or training appropriate to ministry in the Scottish context. It is therefore proposed that in future a Certificate of Eligibility could be issued

subject to certain conditions, such as completion of a course in church law or a period of supervised familiarisation within the Church of Scotland being met. This is of particular importance, since some applicants approach the Church of Scotland with little or no knowledge, far less experience, of what it means to minister in a parish setting.

(v) **Schedule 'A' Churches**
Presently, the issue of Certificates of Eligibility is restricted to ministers of certain churches in the UK and to ministers whose churches are members of the World Alliance of Reformed Churches. It is proposed that this category be extended to include churches with whom the Church of Scotland may have some other accord. A list of such churches would be kept as Schedule 'A' to the new Act and this list would be added to and subtracted from as the Board, in collaboration with the Committee on Ecumenical Relations and the Board of World Mission, reported to the General Assembly year on year.

(vi) **Ministers of the Presbyterian Church in Ireland**
In the interest of consistency it is proposed that ministers of the Presbyterian Church in Ireland should also be subject to application for a Certificate of Eligibility. Therefore, in addition to meeting the current requirement of Act V 1984 Sec 13(9) they also submit to interview and assessment by a Review Panel as in section (iii) above.

(vii) **Ministers from Churches outwith Schedule 'A' and Ministers having resigned or been deprived of their Status**
Those ministers from churches outwith Schedule 'A' of the new Act and ministers having resigned or been deprived of their Status should also become subject to the process outlined in Section (iii) above. The Committee would still be charged with the responsibility for the fullest investigation of such an applicant's suitability. They would be interviewed by a Presbytery, as in the present process, whose report would be sent to the Review Panel. The Review Panel would then interview the applicant, following which their names (if they are being recommended for the issue of a Certificate) would be circulated, as at present, to all Presbyteries for comment, prior to a final decision being made by the Assessment Scheme Committee. This process would effectively mean that at least one category of applicant would not have to appear as petitioner before the General Assembly.

It is felt that a small group, such as the Assessment Scheme Committee or its Review Panel, would be in a much stronger position than the General Assembly to cross-examine in detail a particular applicant. The General Assembly has already entrusted the matter of selection and assessment of ordinary applicants to the Board of Ministry; it is consistent therefore, to extend this trust to the application of ministers in this category. In recent memory, the General Assembly has always accepted the recommendation of the Committee, so it is in the spirit of appropriate devolution of unnecessary business from the floor of the Assembly that the Board, with the support of the Board of Practice and Procedure, brings forward this recommendation.

(viii) **Licentiates and Graduate Candidates**
Since the Church of Scotland no longer has the Office of Licentiate, and since Licentiates and equivalent Graduate Candidates of other Churches have no track record of ministry, it is recommended that such applicants should no longer approach the Church through the procedure of this Act, but should be assessed through attendance at a Church of Scotland Selection Conference. Very often such applicants have not been exposed to the same rigorous assessment and many have quite a bit of 'catching up' to do in respect of their academic and church training. The Board believes that those with a genuine call to service in the Church of Scotland

have nothing to fear from exposure to our regular selection procedures.

(ix) **Licentiates or Graduate Candidates of the Church of Scotland who have not completed their training; Licentiates who have not maintained their name on the roll of Licentiates; and Graduate Candidates whose Graduate Candidate's Certificate has been withheld**

Currently, this category of applicant has to apply for a Certificate of Eligibility in order to restart training under the supervision of the Board of Ministry. This process too, is unsatisfactory. Often a considerable period of time has elapsed before application is made, and a Licentiate or Graduate Candidate may have travelled a considerable life journey since attending a Selection Conference. It is therefore proposed that for such applicants, whose suspension, whether imposed by a Presbytery or adopted by personal choice, has extended beyond three years, should have to return to an Assessment Conference to be reassessed. Thereafter, an accepted applicant shall undertake whatever course of training or familiarisation may be set down by the Board.

(x) **Deacons**

At present there is no properly regulated process of dealing with deacons who fall into categories similar to those set out above. Accordingly, it seems right to take the step of regularising this process through this new Act, so that it would be equally applicable to deacons who wish to enter or re-enter ministry in the Church of Scotland.

(xi) **The Review Panel**

It is envisaged that the Review Panel would be made up in much the same way as the Assessing teams at a Selection Conference. This would bring together a psychologist assessor with two trained Church assessors from the Board's team of assessors, who would meet with the applicant and bring forward a recommendation for consideration by the Assessment Scheme Committee. Such interviews could take place at various times throughout the year and would not be subject to the timetable constraints of the present process.

(xii) **Appeals Process**

In all cases where an applicant is not satisfied that s/he has been dealt with fairly, there will be a right of appeal using the process as it is set out in Act V 1998 Section 6e and 12.

(xiii) **Form of Certificates**

It would be for the Board of Ministry to produce a Certificate of Eligibility in a form and style appropriate to the category of successful applicant.

6.8.4.7 The Legislative Act

6.8.4.7.1 The Board is happy to submit to the General Assembly, for its approval and transmission under the Barrier Act, the Overture as set out in Appendix III of this Report. Also attached to this Report is a helpful diagram of the process as envisaged (Appendix IV).

7. THE COMMITTEE ON EDUCATION AND TRAINING

7.1 The Committee has diligently carried out its responsibilities in the education and training of candidates for the Ministry of Word and Sacrament, auxiliary and diaconal ministries and has endeavoured to extend appropriate care and support to such candidates. The Committee strives to maintain the best practice in formation for ministry, both for the good of candidates and the Church as a whole, and is grateful to all those who support this process.

7.2 New Scheme of Theological Education

7.2.1 This new scheme, approved by the General Assembly in 1999, is now well established and generally working well. The remaining small number of candidates under the old scheme will complete their studies this summer and will attend the same conference programme during their probationary period as those now completing courses under the new scheme.

7.2.2 The first full-time summer placements under the new scheme were undertaken by a number of candidates during the summer of 2000 and these have initially proved to be very fruitful in giving experience to candidates whilst not having to cope with the pressures of academic life at the same time.

7.2.3 Another feature of the new scheme is that candidates have to submit reflective papers on previously issued assignments, designed to help integration of theology and practice. To date these papers have been of a high standard overall and are proving helpful in candidates' formation for ministry.

7.2.4 The first annual eight-day conference for candidates for the Ministry of Word and Sacrament was held in St Andrews in September 2000, preceded by a two-day introductory conference for new candidates. Candidates in training for Diaconate and auxiliary ministry also attended this conference during the first weekend. The conference covered a number of topics which are vital in formation for ministry and many other topics will be raised as appropriate in future training conferences. The conference served well in encouraging a sense of belonging to the Church and developing peer group formation. Through evaluations and consultation with candidates valuable insights have been gained to be incorporated in future conferences, the main one being that the conference be split into two, with one part in September (Friday to Wednesday) and the other in March/April (Monday to Friday). The eight-day conference was deemed to be too long and intensive which did not create the most productive learning atmosphere and produced difficulties for those with family commitments, hence the suggested alternative.

7.2.5 The Board's Education and Development Officers continue to work in close conjunction with the university faculties of divinity and supervising ministers, as well as keeping contact with presbyteries, to ensure appropriate support, assistance and encouragement is given to candidates during their training and whilst serving in placements. The Education and Development Officers regularly visit the candidates at the divinity faculties and arrange meetings with candidates and supervisors as appropriate, involving Committee members who read reports on the candidates.

7.2.6 The Committee has consulted with candidates about the training process and will continue to do so to ensure that their views are heard and considered. In addition to Committee members being involved in meetings with individual candidates, the whole Committee also meets with all candidates at least once per year in a day conference, and a representative from each faculty has attended the March Committee meeting.

7.2.7 The Committee is in the process of evaluating its ways of working with candidates, including the reporting system, in order to better reflect in the training process the principles stated in the Board's *'Ministers of the Gospel'* Report to the General Assembly 2000.

7.3 Supervision

7.3.1 The Committee once again would like to extend its gratitude to those ministers who act as supervisors to candidates for their expertise and diligence in ensuring good supervision. The Committee continues its policy of only using ministers who have been trained in basic supervision and are committed to ongoing training.

7.3.2 The Committee's working group on supervision has looked carefully at this area of work and the Committee is now taking steps to act on its findings, including the need to offer ongoing support and resources for supervisors, to arrange review days for supervisors and develop further training in supervision, all within different geographical settings.

7.4 Candidature

7.4.1 The Board undertook to explore the issues relating to candidature at the 2000 General Assembly. Issues have been explored through the Committee, however, this whole area has proved to be complex and therefore no specific proposals are brought to the Assembly at this time.

7.4.2 The Committee has consulted with the Law Department regarding terms and conditions for placements and these have been agreed. These will be issued for all placements commencing this summer.

7.4.3 The Committee affirms the need to continue its vital policy of consulting with presbyteries where difficult issues arise concerning candidates.

7.4.4 The Committee believes termination of candidature may be justified in certain circumstances; however, it raises legal questions and constitutional issues that must be thoroughly addressed, including recent European Human Rights Legislation. The Committee is presently consulting the Principal Clerk, the Deputy Principal Clerk, the Procurator and the Church's Solicitor to discuss the issues of candidature relating to the law of the Church of Scotland at present and will report in due course to a future Assembly.

7.5 Bible Examinations

7.5.1 The Committee undertook a limited review of these examinations in regard to extending the examination period and the number of examination diets. It decided to increase the time allowed from two to three hours in accordance with most university examinations. It was noted that some candidates were delaying sitting these examinations to a later date, with some failing to pass, resulting in special arrangements having to be made for students to resit these examinations in order to receive an Exit Certificate. The Committee agreed, therefore, that all candidates should sit a Bible examination at the annual September conference in each year of study, with a suitable time in February/March for any necessary resits.

7.6 Probationers

7.6.1 The Committee has continued to provide conferences for probationers of the Church and has received reports on their progress. It has been encouraging to note that probationers generally have found their placements fulfilling, offering excellent

grounding and time for reflection prior to ordination. The following table indicates the progress as at 31st January 2001 of those candidates who began in 1999 and have had their placements sustained:

Parish Ministry	15
Associate/Assistant Ministry	0
Community Ministry/Chaplaincy/Alternative Form of Ministry	1
Seeking a Call	8

7.7 Auxiliary Ministers

7.7.1 The Committee has maintained its work with auxiliary ministers in training, providing support of their academic and placement work and involving them in the Candidates Annual Conference. A review of training for auxiliary ministers, in the light of the scheme for full-time candidates now operating, has still to be undertaken. A report will follow in due course to a future Assembly. There are at present twenty auxiliary ministers in training, eight of whom are probationers.

7.8 Deacons

7.8.1 The recruitment of deacons has been suspended since May 2000 pending approval by the Assembly this year of the Report of the Working Group on Ministry. At present there are three candidates for diaconal ministry undertaking academic studies.

8. THE COMMITTEE ON MINISTRY SUPPORT

8.1 The Committee has as its prime objective the overall support of the ordained and commissioned ministry and this is reflected in the following Report. A very important aspect of the work since the last General Assembly has been to develop a future stipend policy, and an interim Report is contained in Section 8.5. In the meantime, the Committee will endeavour to maintain the value of ministerial income at least at its present level. Pastoral care has also been high on the agenda and at this Assembly we present a modified scheme for the provision of Pastoral Advisors for ministers and deacons (see Section 8.3).

Following an instruction from the General Assembly of 2000, we have also compiled Guidelines for the Act Anent Long-term Illness of Ministers in Charge (Section 8.2.4).

8.2 Pastoral Support
8.2.1 Board and Staff Support

8.2.1.1 The Board, through the staff in the Church offices, provides continual and wide-ranging support and help in co-operation with presbyteries. It is important that wherever possible information regarding need should be notified to the Department as soon as possible. The pastoral care of ordained and commissioned ministers and their families has a high priority in the overall work of the Board, and as responsibilities change and develop, this policy will continue.

8.2.2 Medical Panel and Occupational Health Physician

8.2.2.1 The Board, on the advice of the Medical Panel, continues to use the services of Salus Occupational Health, but will continue to keep this under review.

8.2.3 FirstAssist and Face-to-Face Counselling

8.2.3.1 The 24-hour telephone counselling service provided by FirstAssist is still proving to be of great help to a small number of ministers and manse families and the Board feels fully justified in continuing to provide this service.

8.2.3.2 There has only been a small take-up in the Face-to-Face Counselling Service but a survey of those who have used it indicates that it is essential in the overall pattern of pastoral care being provided.

8.2.4 Guidelines for Act Anent Long-Term Illness of Ministers in Charge (Appendix VI)

8.2.4.1 The General Assembly of May 2000 instructed the Board of Ministry to issue guidelines to Presbyteries on the implementation of the Act Anent Long-Term Illness of Ministers in Charge (General Assembly Report 2000, page 31/1). Through its Ministry Support Committee, the Board sought to produce such guidelines, incorporating the comments forwarded by Presbyteries.

8.2.4.2 From the comments received, the Board of Ministry recognised that what Presbyteries sought was guidance and a step by step process for implementing the Act. It is the Board's opinion that what is required is a re-drafting of the Act. However, in the short term, and to fulfil its remit, we present guidelines in Appendix VI.

8.2.4.3 The Board now seeks the approval of the General Assembly to consult with the Board of Practice and Procedure with a view to bringing a revision of the Act to the next General Assembly. It is convinced that unless this is done, there will not be uniformity in practice, and that even with the proposed guidelines, there is the potential for serious differences in application around the Presbyteries.

8.3 New Pastoral Support Scheme

8.3.1 In May 1990 the General Assembly approved the following proposal about the appointment of 'Pastoral Advisors' in Presbyteries:

"The Council therefore proposes that the Assembly should require each Presbytery to appoint, by the 1st of September 1991, at least one Pastoral Advisor. These Pastoral Advisors will be required to meet individually and on a regular basis with each minister who is in the first five years of his or her ministry. These Advisors will encourage and enable those ministers to share their thoughts and concerns on pastoral problems, but not just with a focus narrowly on, or restricted to, the congregation. The ministers will be guided to a development of their own spirituality and to a deepening of their own devotional life. The role of the Advisors will not be judgmental but reflective and enabling." (General Assembly Report 1990, page 84, Assembly Council)

8.3.2 Through its Ministry Support Committee, the Board of Ministry has endeavoured to support Presbyteries in the implementation of this scheme for ministers in the first five years of ministry. The Board's recently adopted policy statement, '*Ministers of the Gospel*' (General Assembly Report 2000, pages 17/3-17/25), has prompted all Committees to look again at their work and to ensure that the principles enshrined in the statement form the basis for their ongoing work. The theological perspective outlined in the Report emphasises the crucial role of "*integrity of person and practice*" in ministry, as well as affirming an approach to ministry which is "*collaborative*", "*reflective*" and committed to ongoing "*personal formation and development*".

8.3.3 While the Board of Ministry affirms the work which has been done in implementing the Pastoral Advisor scheme over the past decade, the results of a recent survey of ministers who have participated in the scheme (both as Advisors and as Advisees), reveal that the need exists for a reappraisal of the scheme, even in Presbyteries where it might appear that the scheme is functioning well. Given the findings of this survey and noting the principles in the Board's policy statement, the Ministry Support Committee has taken time to reconsider some aspects of the existing structure and to bring recommendations aimed at strengthening the effectiveness of the scheme into the future. The proposals contained in this paper also seek to take account of the desire expressed by many Presbyteries and individual ministers that the scheme should be extended in its scope to take in all those serving in ordained and commissioned ministries. This desire is congruent with the theological perspectives noted above.

8.3.4 In making this proposal, it is necessary to distinguish to some degree between those in the early years and those who have more experience. This is reflected in the change of nomenclature from Pastoral Advisor to Pastoral Colleague at the point of transition. It is important to stress at the outset that the changes to existing structures proposed in this document and the proposals for a scheme beyond the early years are made out of a desire to offer the best practice possible to Church of Scotland ministers. The proposals should not be seen as a criticism of those who have offered willing and able support of the existing scheme, but rather as an opportunity for building on good practice and extending it to all those serving in ordained and commissioned ministries.

8.3.5 This Report seeks to outline the following:
- A set of guidelines for the role of Pastoral Advisors to ministers and deacons in their first three years of ministry;
- Guidelines for pastoral support beyond the first three years through a system of Pastoral Colleagues;
- The relationship between the roles of Pastoral Advisor and Pastoral Colleague, and the main points of difference;
- The relationship between the support which Presbyteries are asked to provide and the services which the Board is able to offer on a wider scale.

8.3.6 Pastoral Advisors : The First Three Years

8.3.6.1 The existing scheme provides for the pastoral care of ministers in their first five years of ministry. The decision to opt for five years arose at a time when there were no plans for provision of a comprehensive network of pastoral support. In the light of the revision of the scheme, it is proposed that the initial period in which a Pastoral Advisor would be appointed to relate to newly ordained and commissioned ministers, should be seen as one of up to three years.

8.3.6.2 The appointment of the Pastoral Advisor is the responsibility of the Presbytery. Some guidelines are appended (Appendix VII(a)) as to the kinds of qualities sought in a Pastoral Advisor and the responsibilities which are involved in engaging in the role. Above all, the Pastoral Advisor should seek to establish a relationship of trust with the Advisee, such that a warmth of friendship and genuine respect as colleagues is fostered.

8.3.6.3 The revised scheme aims to ensure that the Advisee moves smoothly from the relationship with a Pastoral Advisor into the longer-term support system of the Pastoral Colleague scheme. It is envisaged that for many this point of transition will be reached before the three-year mark, but Presbyteries are asked to ensure that all Advisees move into the second phase of the scheme no later than three years from the date of ordination. Part of the intention of the Pastoral Advisor relationship is to prepare the Advisee for entry into the Pastoral Colleague scheme.

8.3.6.4 The Pastoral Advisor scheme is intended to be pro-active, in the sense that the onus of responsibility for initiating and maintaining the relationship lies with the Advisor throughout a period of up to three years. The role is one primarily of befriending and support rather than 'mentoring', but should it be sought, the Pastoral Advisor may offer advice on matters of concern to the Advisee. The scheme should not be seen in any sense as part of an appraisal system, or as having any contact with the Presbytery's cycle of (quinquennial) review.

8.3.6.5 There are parts of the role of Pastoral Advisor which are, of necessity, functional. These may include checking that the newly ordained minister is fully aware of her/his entitlements and duties in relation to such areas as sickness, holiday, maintenance of the manse, what may rightly be expected of the Kirk Session or Congregational Board, and such other matters as may be of practical relevance to the smooth functioning of parish and/or family life. It is again important here that Pastoral Advisors be people who can offer support and advice with sensitivity and in an atmosphere of trust built on strong lines of confidentiality.

8.3.7 Pastoral Colleagues: An Ongoing Support Network

8.3.7.1 When a minister moves to a new Presbytery, or at the latest at the end of the first three years of ordained ministry, that Presbytery should be responsible for ensuring that a Pastoral Colleague relationship is established for all ministers and deacons. Guidelines concerning the qualities and functions of such a Pastoral Colleague are appended (Appendix VII(b)), but above all, this is a relationship of equality between colleagues. It is based upon mutual recognition of skills and aptitudes, a willingness to listen attentively to the needs of the minister and an availability to respond in appropriate and sensitive ways when such response is commonly acknowledged as potentially helpful. The

relationship seeks to enable free conversation and support in areas of the personal, emotional, relational and spiritual development of the minister. It is not intended that the Pastoral Colleague attempt to act as a professional 'Counsellor' to the minister. A full range of counselling services is available to ministers and their families under the auspices of the Board of Ministry.

8.3.7.2 The Pastoral Colleague scheme works on the basis of response to the initiative of the minister or deacon, though the Pastoral Colleague may on occasion feel it important to make the first move, especially at the beginning of the relationship. Although it may be helpful in some instances for the Pastoral Colleague to have contact with the manse family (where one exists), this should only be at the invitation of the minister, and within reasonable time-parameters for the Pastoral Colleague. The scheme is designed in the first instance as a support scheme for ministers, other forms of support being more widely available through the resources of the Board of Ministry.

8.3.7.3 The appointment of the Pastoral Colleague should be overseen by the Presbytery, but ministers may be asked to nominate persons with whom they would be happy to form such a relationship, including ecumenical colleagues where appropriate. (Different Presbyteries will wish to adopt procedures relevant to their size and organisational structures.) The scheme depends on the goodwill of both parties, so its implementation needs to be seen to be collaborative rather than a matter of imposition.

8.3.7.4 The Board recognises that the introduction of this Scheme will have resource implications for all Presbyteries, but particularly so for some rural Presbyteries, where the wider geographical spread may raise significant issues. The Board also encourages Presbyteries to work co-operatively across boundaries where this is to the overall benefit of the efficient functioning of the Scheme.

8.3.8 The Relationship Between Pastoral Advisors and Pastoral Colleagues

8.3.8.1 The qualities and responsibilities required

of Pastoral Advisors and of Pastoral Colleagues are fundamentally the same. The major differences in role may be summarised as follows:

- A Pastoral Advisor has the duty to be pro-active in the relationship, while a Pastoral Colleague will largely be responsive to the initiative of the minister to whom s/he relates, though regular contact needs to be maintained;
- A Pastoral Advisor will, at least initially, bring a much greater functional dimension to the role, whereas the Pastoral Colleague may only wish to enter into this kind of area at the express request of the minister to whom s/he relates;
- A Pastoral Advisor will normally be a member of the Church of Scotland, whereas a Pastoral Colleague may be drawn from an appropriate wider ecumenical circle.

8.3.8.2 Normally it will be beneficial for a different person to take on the role of Pastoral Colleague when the period of relationship with a Pastoral Advisor comes to an end. Only in exceptional circumstances, with the approval of the Presbytery pastoral committee (or equivalent), should this be handled otherwise. Another point of difference is in the method of appointment. Pastoral Advisors are appointed by the Presbytery, while Pastoral Colleagues may be nominated by the minister. In both instances, however, close collaboration and mechanisms for checking out the ongoing effectiveness of the relationship need to be in place.

8.3.8.3 It is vital to the functioning of both these relationships that Pastoral Advisors and Pastoral Colleagues observe the strict boundaries of confidentiality. Matters should only be taken beyond the relationship with the express permission of the minister or deacon.

8.3.9   Models of Good Practice
8.3.9.1 There is a clear recognition by the Board of Ministry that no blueprint exists for the provision of good pastoral support for ministers. Whatever shape the scheme takes at a local Presbytery level will need to be flexible and sensitive to the demands of local culture,

availability of people and resources, and the particular needs of the individuals to whom the scheme relates. The scheme outlined in this document is thus offered in a spirit of humility and good faith. The Board has received a number of models of good practice already adopted by different Presbyteries across the country and these are available from the Department of Ministry on request.

8.3.9.2 The primary expectation arising from the adoption of this scheme is that all Presbyteries will of necessity adopt a scheme which is available to all ordained and commissioned ministers within their bounds, and which builds upon the models of good practice which have been tried and tested in other places. The Board continues to be grateful for the co-operation of Presbyteries in this matter, and is glad to receive from time to time such other models of good practice as may be tried and proven within Presbyteries, with a view to disseminating these to the wider Church.

8.3.9.3 Annually, Presbytery Clerks are responsible for reporting diligence in respect of the scheme. From time to time they should also keep the Board of Ministry informed of the scope of the scheme which they have adopted.

8.3.10   Wider Support Networks
8.3.10.1 In addition to the local Pastoral Colleague scheme, the Board of Ministry offers a number of wider support networks which make use of resources at a national level. These resources are explained in detail in the annually updated leaflet '*Manse Family Counselling Agencies*', which has been made available to all ordained ministers and manse families and will continue in future to be available to both ordained ministers and deacons, and their immediate family.

8.4   Stipend and Service Supplement
8.4.1   The level of minimum stipend for 2001 has been declared at £18,016 and a manse, with the real value of ministerial remuneration being maintained through the increase in the minimum stipend as detailed in Appendix VIII.

8.5 Future Stipend Research

8.5.1 In the Board of Ministry Report to the General Assembly in 1999, a clear commitment was given to researching and bringing forward a new stipend structure (General Assembly Report 1999, page 17/16, section 9.4.2). Through its Ministry Support Committee, the Board wishes to present the broad principles of a new structure. Following the General Assembly, discussion will continue with the Board of Stewardship and Finance, the Pension Trustees and the Housing and Loan Trustees with a view to bringing to next year's Assembly fully worked out costings for a new scheme, which could become effective from 1st January 2003.

8.5.2 Where We Are

8.5.2.1 The General Assembly of 1994 introduced a new stipend structure whereby ministers received:

Stipend (based on the income of a charge)
plus
Service Supplement (based on the number of years of qualifying service).

8.5.2.2 This was a bold and imaginative initiative which allowed the Church to take a big leap forward in its remuneration of ministers. It should be noted that with the introduction of the service supplement, the Church introduced a 'salaried' element to stipend—funded from self-supporting congregations and not linked to the individual charges. During the phasing in of service supplement, the range of stipend was reduced so that the maximum stipend became limited from forty per cent to fifteen per cent above minimum.

8.5.2.3 The system introduced to implement service supplement succeeded in increasing a minister's remuneration by £4,166 (for ten years of qualifying service). However, this system cannot be adapted easily to be used five, six or seven years later, the main difficulty being the conflict between ensuring at least inflationary rises to stipend while stipend is tied to congregational income bands. Also, during the introductory period, stipends were limited to inflationary increases, and throughout, service supplement has remained unchanged.

This has resulted in a falling behind, in terms of the original targets for stipend levels.

8.5.3 New Stipend Structure

8.5.3.1 Right from the outset it was agreed that comparisons should not be made with other professions. Every profession is different and therefore it is impossible to determine which should be used for comparison. What the Church should try to achieve is the very best possible for its ministers.

8.5.3.2 In researching a new structure, various questions were looked at:

- Should stipend be related to the income of a charge?
- Do we keep the present 10 Bands for stipends?
- Do we keep Bands from minimum to minimum plus 15 per cent?
- Should we move away from a range within each Band and replace it with a fixed amount?
- Should service supplement be retained as a separate component, or should it be incorporated into stipend?
- Should Ministry costs be gathered as a fixed percentage of actual stipend?

8.5.3.3 Each of the above questions was looked at in detail and, where appropriate, costings and examples sought. From these, the Research Group began work to determine possible principles for a new structure:

- No minister will remain on minimum stipend throughout his/her ministry;
- No minister should have his or her income reduced as a result of any new scheme;
- Each charge should be appraised in terms of burdens and responsibilities;
- The minister's performance should be appraised;
- Stipend and service supplement should be merged into one;
- Stipend should not be linked to the income of a charge;
- Congregational contributions to Ministry costs should be linked to income.

8.5.3.4 The first two principles have been long held and need no explanation. The most difficult of these principles to deal with are the ones connected to appraisal.

It quickly became apparent that there was neither the mechanisms nor the will to link pay to specific workplace or performance. However, sight should not be lost of this issue. As noted in the '*Ministers of the Gospel*' Report (General Assembly Report 2000 page 17/25, section 2.5.5.1). "*...tomorrow's ministers will need to be open to continuing appraisal of their development in the knowledge, skills and personal growth required in ministry.*"

8.5.3.5 Merging of stipend and service supplement would make payments to ministers more straightforward and, as a result, less confusing. Various possibilities were explored to try and combine stipend with what is a salaried element. This proved to be very difficult, trying to keep within present minimum and maximum stipends and stay within the Co-ordinated Budget. Our proposal is that ministers would begin their ministry on a Year 1 stipend and would receive nine annual increments to Year 10 (this Year 10 stipend would be the figure used for calculation of Pensions etc). Receiving increments after Year 1 rather than Year 5 will be of great help to recently ordained ministers, who often begin their ministry with a substantial burden of debt from their student days. In addition to stipend, congregations would still be able (after consultation and agreement of Presbytery, and having met all their costs) to supplement stipend by up to fifteen per cent.

8.5.3.6 While this new stipend structure is straightforward and easy to understand, such a scheme can only be introduced if it can be adequately funded.

8.5.4 Funding a New Structure

8.5.4.1 In 2001, to be a self-supporting charge costs £26,938. However, with service supplement, it costs £30,500 (based on full service supplement) for each minister in a charge. This results in only thirty-eight per cent of charges meeting the full costs of a minister, with the necessity of supporting the other sixty-two per cent at the same time. In other words, while there are (at the time of writing) 285 Aid Receiving charges, 775 charges could be classified as not meeting the real costs of ministry.

8.5.4.2 The Board is proposing that the concept of Aid Receiving disappears and that all charges see themselves as contributing. This would, it is hoped, change the negative associations connected with ' Aid Receiving.'

8.5.4.3 In order to make this a reality, Ministry Costs will have to be linked to income. Various schemes have been investigated in detail, all of which would result in Aid being collected as part of Ministry costs. This will be much simpler than at present where some Aid is collected through the Mission and Aid Fund and the rest through the service supplement Levy. Discussions are ongoing with the Board of Stewardship and Finance to ensure that we work in tandem while they investigate a new scheme for collection of what we know as Mission and Aid.

8.5.4.4 Consultations have also been held with the Pension Trustees. It had been hoped that the twenty per cent contribution to the Main Pension Fund would soon be at the point of being reduced. In order to ascertain whether any reduction would be advisable in 2003, the Trustees have instructed a valuation to take place as at the end of December 2000. The result of this valuation will not be known until after this General Assembly, and therefore it is impossible to give a detailed costing for funding at this time.

8.5.4.5 It should be noted, however, that unless new money is found, there is little likelihood of any significant increases in stipend. What is hoped is that those on lower stipends will be able to benefit from an increase under the new scheme and that charges who wish to give additional benefit can (within limits).

8.5.5 Difficulties

8.5.5.1 A minister's remuneration is not only stipend and service supplement payment, but also Insured Pension Fund contributions and a manse. We look to our Pension Trustees to advise on the future of the Insured Pension Fund now that pensions are significantly better than ever before. Manses, though, continue to be a difficult issue. There are undoubted benefits but, unfortunately, there are negative aspects as well. Huge heating costs, poor state of repairs, living attached to church and/or halls can take its toll on ministers and their families. It is with regret that no report on the future of manses is being presented at this time, but it is still on our agenda.

8.5.5.2 Repeated calls have been made for an equalisation of stipend. Calls have also been made for congregations to have freedom to set stipend without restriction. Neither of these, we believe, is an option.

8.5.5.3 Equal stipend for all is an admirable notion but not a realisable reality. Differences in costs associated with the manse (which is at present part of stipend), different levels of contribution (if any) to the Insured Pension Fund, and paid Chaplaincies mean that there will always be differences. Indeed there is concern that while the differential in stipends has reduced, some ministers enjoy a significant financial benefit from other approved appointments.

8.5.5.4 Likewise, allowing local congregations to decide would result in large differentials which is something the Church over the years has moved away from. Giving permission for charges, with agreement of Presbyteries, to supplement stipend by fifteen per cent allows for local input into a minister's stipend.

8.5.6   Where Now?

8.5.6.1 Once the principles of a new stipend structure are agreed, it is proposed that full costings for every congregation will be worked out. Once these costings are available, a series of Roadshows will be conducted across the country to explain how the new scheme will affect congregations. This will give an opportunity to hear feedback and identify teething problems before returning to the General Assembly next year for approval to introduce the new scheme in 2003.

8.6 Ministers' Travel

8.6.1   Travelling Expenses

8.6.1.1 This scheme remains unchanged for 2001 (see Appendix IX).

8.6.2   Car Provision Scheme

8.6.2.1 The Board, after careful consideration and in the light of changing circumstances, has decided that it will no longer provide a car fleet. It is clear that in the light of the other options now available this is in the best interest of the resources of the Board and the needs of ministers. All fleet users have been advised that no further replacement cars will be provided after June 2001, except in very exceptional circumstances.

8.6.3   Car Loans

8.6.3.1 Car loans are still in considerable demand and the Committee will continue to offer these to all serving ministers. Once again, it has not been possible to increase the level of loans as previously planned, due to changes in fiscal policy. The Committee will, however, increase loans when it is appropriate to do so.

8.6.4   Car Leasing Scheme

8.6.4.1 The Board continues to make available to ministers, deacons and Church staff information regarding various leasing offers. It is important that all those considering this method of car provision should do their homework carefully since the contracts are between the company chosen and the minister, deacon or member of staff. The experience to date is that this alternative is of considerable benefit to those using one of the schemes. The Board will continue to seek out other offers as they become available with a view to giving the widest possible choice.

8.7 Pulpit Supply

8.7.1   There has been no alteration to Pulpit Supply arrangements and the detailed regulations are contained in Appendix X.

8.8 Maintenance Allowances

8.8.1   Four Maintenance Allowances were provided in 2000.

8.9 Further Endowment

8.9.1 During 2000, the following grants were set aside:

Congregations	Consolidated Stipend Fund Shares
20	4,402

8.9.2 The Committee submits the following amendments to the Regulations for Further Endowment so that a grant may be given:

The limits for investment in Further Endowment for stipend to be as follows:

a) Following the approval of the grant, the average of the charge's contribution to stipend over the previous three years, together with the current year's endowments, must be not more than £17,300 and the endowments must be raised to not more than £4,200.

b) Further Endowment capital will be bought directly into the Consolidated Stipend Endowment Fund and the relevant Grant allocated every quarter. The predetermined price will be the previous quarter's price, any movement in price being met by the Committee.

8.9.3 Dividends are payable from the date of entry into the Fund at the rate of return quoted from the Consolidated Stipend Fund.

8.10 Endowments for Stipend Purposes

8.10.1 In terms of Act XXVII 1953 and of the Regulations governing the Consolidated Stipend Endowment Fund, the Committee considered every vacancy involving the use of endowments and reported that agreement was reached with the Presbytery in every case.

9. THE COMMITTEE ON MINISTRY DEVELOPMENT

9.1 Aims

- To provide and evaluate appropriate post-ordination training for ministers at key stages in their ministry;
- To offer opportunities for further study to update existing knowledge or to develop new areas of expertise relevant to the minister's work;
- To facilitate exchange of experience among ministers;
- To assist ministers in evaluation of their ministry;
- To direct all its activities to enable ministers to fulfil the aspirations of the Board's seminal statement, 'Ministers of the Gospel'.

9.2 Methods

9.2.1 Programme of Courses and Conferences (see Appendix XI)

9.2.1.1 The Committee continues to experiment with times of year and venues because conferences are run in order to satisfy as many as possible of the appropriate cohort of ministers. One conference, held further north than usual, was much appreciated by those who normally have to travel longer distances and appeared to pose no problems for others. Dates are, however, subject to many external constraints.

9.2.1.2 A Rural Ministry Conference proved successful, although sparsely attended. In addition to the normal programme, the Committee is planning two further specific conferences: one on Congregational Management (2001) and the other on Worship (2002). The Committee is reflecting on ways of responding to requests from other Boards for inclusion of themes in Board of Ministry conferences.

9.2.1.3 The new programme of conferences for ministers in their first five years will alternate one-day events with residential events.

9.2.2 Study Leave Programme (see Appendix XI)

9.2.2.1 The Study Leave Programme is achieving increasing levels of popularity among ministers, some of whom have now participated in the scheme. The variety of uses to which Study Leave is put is particularly gratifying. The Committee has attempted to encourage applications from ministers by holding a series of Open

Days involving previous participants, along with Board staff. Also fifty ministers who had not applied for Study Leave were visited and interviewed to ascertain the reason. Among outcomes of this exercise were decisions to improve communication about the scheme and to involve Kirk Sessions in encouraging their ministers to participate.

9.2.2.2 Although numbers applying to date have been satisfactory and manageable, the Committee is concerned that substantial numbers of ministers may (quite legitimately) be saving up their allocation until the maximum allocation of fourteen weeks is available. It is desirable that the financial implications and the ability of Presbyteries to provide cover should be addressed well in advance of this occurrence. The Committee therefore recommends that application for Study Leave periods in excess of eight weeks should be made at least one year in advance, with full Presbytery consultation, and the Committee will amend its regulations accordingly. Even with such precautions, it will not be possible to guarantee approval of every request. Although there are no strict requirements of Study Leave reports, some are proving so interesting that a short anthology has been printed for wider circulation.

9.2.2.3 The Committee has increased the number of closing dates for applications throughout the year from three to four with a view to enhancing flexibility and minimising the need for late applications. The period of notice required continues to be proportionate to the length of leave proposed. Presbyteries should note that the published timetable is the minimum required by the Board for administrative purposes but individual Presbyteries may insist on longer periods if they feel it is necessary.

9.2.2.4 The Committee on Ministry Development has recognised that ministers in particular areas of Scotland are disadvantaged by virtue of the cost of travel to significant libraries and to certain study leave destinations. Applications for Study Leave from ministers in the Presbyteries of Orkney, Shetland, The Western Isles, Sutherland, Caithness, South Argyll and other remote Presbyteries will be given special consideration and additional funding will be available to enable Study Leave plans to come to fruition. Special application for this should be made to the Board of Ministry.

9.3 Links with Princeton Theological Seminary
9.3.1 The 2000 Joint Institute of Theology in Princeton, organised jointly by the Board of Ministry and Princeton Theological Seminary, was much appreciated by the sixteen Scottish ministers who were present. Many utilised Study Leave allocations to facilitate attendance and some combined the Institute with experience of congregations in the United States. The 2001 Institute will be held in St Andrews from 20th–31st August and it is hoped that Church of Scotland ministers will be represented more numerously than on the previous occasion two years earlier.

9.4 Personal Ministerial Review
9.4.1 The Committee is pleased to confirm that the Review Process has made considerable progress since the previous Assembly. Nearly fifty ministers agreed to participate in a pilot scheme and a further group of about twenty accepted invitations to become reviewers. A residential training course was provided for the latter, who determined first to review one another before contacting the original group of volunteers. The first round of the process, which should be completed during the year 2001, will be closely monitored and evaluated prior to extension to a wider client group.

9.5 Directory of Ministry Development Opportunities
9.5.1 Continuing efforts are being made to enhance the user-friendliness of the annual Directory which aims to provide ministers with a comprehensive summary of all provision made on their behalf by the Committee. Dates of courses and conferences, closing dates for Study Leave applications, other relevant information about activities and brief pen portraits of the

Education staff members are all included. Staff are always receptive to enquiries about development-related topics.

In the name of the Board,

WILLIAM F STORRAR, *Convener*
CHRISTINE M GOLDIE, *Vice-Convener*
WILLIAM GREENOCK, *Vice-Convener*
SHAW J PATERSON, *Vice-Convener*
IAN TAYLOR, *Vice-Convener*
ALEXANDER McDONALD, *General Secretary*
JOHN P CHALMERS, *Depute General Secretary*
NIGEL J ROBB, *Director of Educational Services*

ADDENDUM

Staff Developments—The Very Rev Dr Alexander McDonald

As set out in the Introduction to the Report, the Board of Ministry carried out a review of its structures in the autumn of 2000 and unanimously agreed to implement the integrated set of recommendations from its consultants. In the interests of implementation, Dr McDonald graciously offered to step down from his post as General Secretary and take up an interim appointment with the Board as Senior Adviser (Ministry Development and Pastoral Care) until his retirement in November 2002. The Board accepted this offer and appointed Dr McDonald to this interim post, from the starting date of his successor as General Secretary. Dr McDonald will continue to offer his widely respected pastoral gifts, experience and skills in this pioneering interim appointment, allowing the new General Secretary to focus on the management role agreed by the Board. There will be opportunity in due course for the Church to express its thanks to Dr McDonald for his long and valued service of the Board of Ministry. At this time, the Board of Ministry acknowledges a profound debt of gratitude to Dr McDonald for his leadership through a period of transition and his willingness to undertake fresh duties for the sake of the ministry he loves and serves with distinction.

Rev Shaw J Paterson

Rev Shaw Paterson has served the Board of Ministry for eight years and for the last three years as Vice-Convener. His special knowledge of stipend structure made him the ideal choice as Convener of Ministry Support. Shaw has taken a very active interest in the pastoral care of ministers and manse families and from his own experience knows just how demanding ministry can be on the manse family as well as on the minister. The Board and the Church owe him a special debt of gratitude for all his work, including in particular future stipend research, interim ministry development and his passion for pastoral care.

In the name of the Board,

WILLIAM F STORRAR, *Convener*
CHRISTINE M GOLDIE, *Vice-Convener*
WILLIAM GREENOCK, *Vice-Convener*
IAN TAYLOR, *Vice-Convener*
JOHN P CHALMERS, *Depute General Secretary*
NIGEL J ROBB, *Director of Educational Services*

APPENDIX I

Working Group on Ministry

ACT ANENT SELECTION, TRAINING AND ADMISSION OF DEACONS

The General Assembly enact and ordain as follows:

Definitions

1. Act V 1998 (as amended) section 1 shall apply to the Diaconate subject to the deletion of subsections (d), (h), (i), (j) and (k) and the second sentence of subsection (g), all for the purposes of that application only.

Selection and Training of Deacons

2. Act V 1998 as amended, sections 2–11, 12(a), 12(b), 16, 18–25 and the Rules of Procedure for Panel of Arbiters appended thereto, shall apply to the Diaconate.

   For the purposes of this Act:

   (i) references to 'the Ministry of the Church of Scotland' or 'the full-time ministry' shall be understood as referring to the diaconal ministry of the Church of Scotland

   (ii) references to Universities shall be deemed to include any institution of higher education approved by the Board of Ministry for the training of deacons.

Academic and Practical Training of Deacons

3. (a) Each Candidate shall have a Course prescribed by the Committee on Education and Training immediately following acceptance as a Prospective Candidate.

   (b) The Candidate shall satisfy the Committee on Education and Training of competence:

   (i) in all areas of study prescribed from time to time by the Committee, which shall always include the interpretation and use of Holy Scripture (both Old and New Testaments), the development and growth of the Church including special reference to the Church of Scotland, the principal doctrines of the Christian faith (their interpretation, their defence and their application), the constitution and laws of the Church of Scotland, the history and contemporary understanding of the Diaconate in the Church of Scotland and ecumenically, practical theology (including mission, evangelism, pastoral care and counselling, the worship of the Church (especially the Church of Scotland), and the contemporary understanding of Church and society), and voice and communication skills;

   (ii) in further optional courses approved from time to time by the Committee on Education and Training and selected by the Candidate;

   (iii) in all areas of practical knowledge required by the Committee on Education and Training, by satisfactory participation throughout their candidature in such residential courses and conferences as are prescribed by the Committee;

   (iv) in attendance and participation at the Diaconate Council defined in s.10 of Act VIII 1998;

   (v) in the practice of the diaconal ministry, by completing to the satisfaction of the Committee on Education and Training the three placements prescribed below.

Placements during Training

4. (a) As part of the Church requirements, three periods of placement work shall be undertaken by the Candidate, and must be completed to the satisfaction of the Committee on Education and Training which shall determine the length and

content of each placement. The placements shall normally include two during the academic course (of which one shall be part-time and shall last not less than twenty-five weeks and one shall be a full-time summer placement lasting not less than ten weeks) and one full-time placement of twelve months commencing on the first day of July, August, September or October in the year of completion of the prescribed academic course; the Committee shall have power in exceptional circumstances to vary this arrangement. The candidate will not normally be permitted to engage in academic study through a university or college or in remunerative employment or office during the course of the twelve months full-time placement at the conclusion of the academic course.

(b)   The supervisor of each placement will be chosen by the Committee on Education and Training and shall undertake training as specified by the Committee. The supervisor shall be responsible for supervising the placement according to the guidelines and standards established by the Committee and University, and shall produce assessment materials as required.

(c)   The assessment materials shall be assessed by the Committee. It shall be competent for the Committee to refuse to sustain a placement.

Sustaining the Course

5. (a)   The Committee on Education and Training shall obtain from the universities or colleges lists of those Candidates who have satisfactorily completed their prescribed Course, whereupon the Secretary may inform candidates that they have permission to commence their final placement.

(b)   The Committee shall, in consultation with the Presbytery decide whether to sustain the final placement after nine months.

(c)   Commissioning shall be according to the procedure set out in Act VIII 1998, section 5a.

6. The Board shall maintain a list of those who have satisfactorily completed their training in terms of this Act and Act V 1998 (as amended). An individual who has completed training, who has not been commissioned as a deacon in terms of Act VIII 1998 and who has not applied to be removed from the above list, shall for the purposes of superintendence and discipline be treated in the same manner as a Graduate Candidate as defined in Act V 1998 (as amended) sections 26 and 27, and all Acts and Regulations of the General Assembly relating to the superintendence or discipline of a Graduate Candidate shall apply to such individuals.

Admission and Readmission of Deacons

7. Act III 1995 as amended, sections 1, 3, 4, 5, 6(1)–(2), 6(4) and 8, and the Regulations appended thereto, shall apply to the Diaconate. For the purposes of this Act:
    (i)   references to 'the Ministry of the Church of Scotland' shall be understood as referring to the diaconal ministry of the Church of Scotland
    (ii) in section 6(4), the words 'either (a) inducted to a charge or (b)' shall not apply to the Diaconate.

Retirement Age

8. Deacons shall retire from appointments under the jurisdiction of the Church no later than their sixty-fifth birthday.

Repeals

9. Act VIII 1998 sections 3 and 4 are hereby repealed.

APPENDIX II

Committee on Vocational Guidance

ACT AMENDING ACT V 1998 AS AMENDED

The General Assembly enact and ordain that Act V 1998 as amended is hereby further amended as follows:

1. In section 1 (b) "The Assessment Scheme Committee" is the Committee to which the Board delegates authority to determine matters relating to assessment and selection.

   Add new 1(l): " "Enquirers" are those who have registered for enquiry in terms of section 2(a) hereunder."

2. Delete Section 2 and substitute:

   Pre-Application Enquiry Process

   2 (a) A person wishing to apply for recognition as a Candidate in Training for the Ministry of the Church of Scotland shall first register as an Enquirer with the Assessment Scheme Committee of the Board of Ministry and with the Clerk of the Presbytery in which he or she currently resides. Where such a person resides outside Scotland, the enquiry shall be registered with the Presbytery of Edinburgh.

   (b) The Enquirer shall undertake the prescription for the period of Enquiry as set down by and from time to time reviewed by the Board of Ministry.

   (c) The Committee shall determine all questions relating to the implementation of this section, subject to the right of appeal set out in section 6 (e)(I) hereunder.

3. Amend Section 4 as follows:

   After the first occurrence of the word "applicant" add the words "who has fulfilled the requirements as set out in section 2 (b) above".

4. Delete Section 5 and substitute:

   5 (a) The Committee, in consultation with the Presbytery, shall make suitable arrangements for a period of field assessment of up to six months duration, which shall be by a placement different from that undergone for any purposes of Section 2 above. The co-ordinator of each placement will be chosen by the Committee and shall undertake such training as may from time to time be specified by the Committee. The co-ordinator shall be responsible for supervising the placement according to the guidelines and standards established by the Committee, and shall produce assessment materials as required.

   (b) The assessment of the candidate during and at the end of the field assessment shall be by a psychologist assessor and a church assessor appointed by the General Assembly and allocated by the Committee, the local co-ordinator and up to two representatives appointed by the Presbytery.

   (c) The assessment at the end of the field placement shall be referred to as the Local Review, and out of this Review one of the following written decisions shall be reported by the Review to the Committee:

   (i) That the Applicant is ready to proceed to Assessment in terms of section 6 hereunder;

   (ii) That the Applicant should undergo further field assessment before a decision to proceed can be made;

   (iii) That the Applicant is not yet ready to proceed to Assessment in terms of Section 6;

   (iv) That the Applicant is not suitable to be assessed in terms of Section 6.

   (d) Applicants in respect of whom a decision is made in terms of Section 5 (c) (iii) may apply to be taken on field assessment on a further two occasions, after which it shall no longer be open to the assessors to make such a decision.

(e) Applicants shall have the right to appeal against the decision reached in section 5(c) above. The appeal process is as set out in Section 6 (d) and (e) of this Act.

(f) (i) All materials received by the Committee from the field assessors in terms of sub-section (c) above shall be available to those making consideration in terms of section 6 (a) below.

(ii) No individual shall serve as an assessor for the same Applicant more than once.

(iii) Notwithstanding its responsibilities in terms of Section 5 (b) above, the Presbytery shall be entitled to submit to the Committee written comments on the Applicant's character and beliefs, vocation, motivation and general suitability.

APPENDIX III

Committee on Vocational Guidance

OVERTURE ANENT ADMISSION AND RE-ADMISSION OF MINISTERS AND OTHERS

The General Assembly adopt the Overture, the tenor whereof follows, and transmit the same to Presbyteries for their consideration under the Barrier Act, directing that returns be sent in to the Principal Clerk not later than 31 December 2001.

1. In this Act the following definitions apply:

(a) "Applicants" are persons who have submitted an application in terms of this Act

(b) "The Board" is the General Assembly's Board of Ministry

(c) "The Committee" is the Board's Assessment Scheme Committee

(d) The "Review Panel" is a body appointed by the Committee but does not contain any of the Committee's voting membership. Its function is to assess the character and beliefs, education and experience, vocation, motivation and general suitability for ministry of those applicants referred to it by the Committee in terms of this Act, and to make recommendation to the Committee about each application.

2. Applications in terms of this Act shall be submitted in the first instance to the Committee which is empowered, subject to the provisions of this Act, to make such Regulations for its procedure and to require such fees from applicants as it sees fit. The Committee shall issue a statement of such Regulations and Fees, the dates of the meetings of the Committee and the latest submission date for applications to be considered within a particular cycle of the Committee's meetings, for the guidance of applicants and for its own use.

3. Applications shall be presented in keeping with the style required by the Committee. They shall give full particulars as to the applicant's age, present Church connection, educational curriculum, medical history, ministerial career and other employment, together with a statement indicating the reasons for the applicant's wish to be admitted to the ministry of the Church of Scotland and the form of service which the applicant wishes to exercise. The application shall be accompanied by all the documents (originals, extracts or copies) necessary in the opinion of the Committee to substantiate the facts set forth, by the names of three referees, and by a statement indicating willingness to submit to a medical examination if this is considered necessary by the Committee.

Ministers—Standard Procedure

4. (1) Ministers referred to in section 4(2) shall have their application considered in terms of sections 6 and 7 below. It shall be the responsibility of the Committee to determine whether the applicant's ordination is recognised by the Church of Scotland before referring his or her application to the Review Panel. Such determinations shall be subject to the right of appeal set out in section 12 below.

(2) This section shall apply to the following categories of person:

(a) Ordained ministers of other churches, except those specified in section 5 below

(b) Former ministers of the Church of Scotland referred to in section 8 below

Ministers—Abbreviated Procedure

5. Ministers of churches listed in Schedule A or who in the view of the Committee fulfil the criteria set out in subsection (4), (6), (7), (9) or (10) of section 13 of Act V 1984 (as amended), shall have their applications considered in terms of section 6 below. Determinations by the Committee in respect of a minister's fulfilment of the above criteria shall be subject to the right of appeal set out in section 12 below.

Consideration by the Committee

6. (a) It shall be the duty of the Committee to examine each application and such other documentation as it may require, to refer applications to the Review Panel as defined in section 1(d) above and receive its recommendation in respect of each applicant and to grant, with or without conditions, or refuse a Certificate of Eligibility. All decisions made by the Committee in fulfilment of this section shall be subject to the right of appeal set out in section 12 below.

(b) A "Certificate of Eligibility" entitles the holder to apply for charges, appointments open to ministers of the Church of Scotland and appointments to office outwith the jurisdiction of the Church of Scotland (provided such office is one which, if held by a minister of this Church, entitles the holder to membership of Presbytery in terms of Act III, 2000). Admission to the status of minister of the Church of Scotland shall take effect at the point of admission to membership of Presbytery. Certificates of Eligibility shall be valid for three years from the date of issue.

Consideration by Presbytery

7. (a) In respect of applications made in terms of section 4 above, following the interim decision of the Committee, it shall be the duty of the Secretary of the Committee to inform the applicant of that decision and invite the applicant to determine whether or not s/he wishes to continue the application or appeal the decision.

(b) When the Secretary of the Committee receives from the applicant an indication of her/his desire to proceed with the application, s/he shall forward to the Presbytery of residence, or in the case of an applicant who has not resided in Scotland for three months prior to the date of the application to the Presbytery of Edinburgh, and to any Presbytery within whose bounds the applicant may have been permitted to be employed as a minister pending the outcome of the application (a) a copy of the application in full (b) copies of any documents used by the Committee and (c) the interim decision of the Committee. The Secretary shall also intimate to all Presbyteries the applications that have been received, for their information and comment before the date of the meeting of the Committee at which the application is to be considered.

(c) For the purposes of this Act, "the appropriate Presbytery" shall be the Presbytery in Scotland in which the applicant resides. In the case of an applicant not residing in Scotland at the time of submission of the application, the appropriate Presbytery shall be the Presbytery of Edinburgh.

(d) In the event that the interim decision of the Committee is not to allow the applicant to proceed, it shall be open to the applicant to appeal, as set out in section 12 below.

Ministers—Readmission Procedure

8. An applicant who has been a minister of the Church of Scotland but who has resigned that status or been judicially deprived thereof, notwithstanding that he or she may also belong to one of the categories specified in section 5, shall make application in terms of this Act, which application shall be considered in terms of sections 6 and 7 above, subject to the right of any Presbytery to require that the decision of the Committee be confirmed by the Commission of the General Assembly, at which the said Presbytery shall be required to appear and be heard.

Licentiates and Graduate Candidates of the Church of Scotland

9. (1) This section shall apply to the following categories of person:

(a) Holders of an expired Certificate of Entitlement granted in terms of Act V 1985 (as amended) section 58,

(b) Licentiates whose names no longer appear in the Roll of Probationers/ Licentiates maintained by the Board of Ministry,

(c) Candidates in respect of whom more than three years have passed since any formal training was undertaken in terms of Act V 1985 (as amended) or Act V 1998 (as amended), or

(d) Graduate Candidates in respect of whom a Graduate Candidate's certificate has been withheld by the Presbytery in terms of Act V 1998 (as amended) section 27(a).

(2) Act V 1998 (as amended) sections 3–12 shall apply to those referred to in section 9(1), and upon acceptance and nomination they shall be obliged to fulfil any training or familiarisation process determined by the Committee.

(3) Upon completion of the requirements of section 9(2), those referred to in section 9(1) shall have the status, privileges and responsibilities of a Graduate Candidate as defined in Act V 1998 (as amended) sections 26 and 27.

Licentiates, ordinands, etc of other churches

10. Licentiates, ordinands, graduate candidates and those of comparable status, from Churches whose ordination is recognised by the Committee, shall be subject to the provisions of Act V 1998 (as amended) sections 3–12. For the purposes of this Act the Committee shall determine how to apply those provisions to applications in terms of this section, subject to the right of appeal set out in section 12 below.

11. A successful applicant shall be admitted to the status of Graduate Candidate as defined in Act V 1998 (as amended) sections 26 and 27, subject to the completion (at the applicant's own cost) of such academic requirements, placements or other practical training, course work or conference work determined by the Committee, subject to the right of appeal set out in section 12 below.

Appeals

12. For the purposes of this Act, the Appeals Procedure shall be that set out in sections 6(e) and 12 of Act V 1998 (as amended), which shall for the purposes of this Act be construed in conformity with it. Recourse to the Panel of Arbiters shall for the purposes of

this Act be available only in respect of appeals taken against the final decision of the Committee or any conditions attached to such decision, and shall not be available in respect of intermediate appeals.

Confidentiality

13. Each application and all procedure under this Act shall be taken in private by the Committee and by Presbyteries.

The Diaconate

14. The provisions of this Act shall apply to members of the diaconal ministry of the Church of Scotland and other Churches. The Committee shall be responsible for determining the interpretation of this Act consistently with the provisions of Act VIII 1998 and Act (the new one about the diaconate) 2001; such determinations shall be subject to the right of appeal set out in section 12 above.

Repeals and Amendments

15. (1) Act III, 1995 and the Regulations appended thereto, are hereby repealed.

    (2) Act V 1998 (as amended) section 28 is hereby repealed.

    (3) The Act Anent Discipline of Ministers, Licentiates, Graduate Candidates and Deacons, 2001 shall be amended as follows:

    Section 1(1)(h)(iii) shall be amended to read 'removal of status, subject to restoration only by application in terms of the Act Anent Admission and Readmission of Ministers and Others, 2002 section 8.'

Interpretation of Acts

16. Act XI 1994 shall be interpreted in conformity with this Act.

APPENDIX IV

Committee on Vocational Guidance

ADMISSION AND READMISSION—PROCESS OF ADMISSION

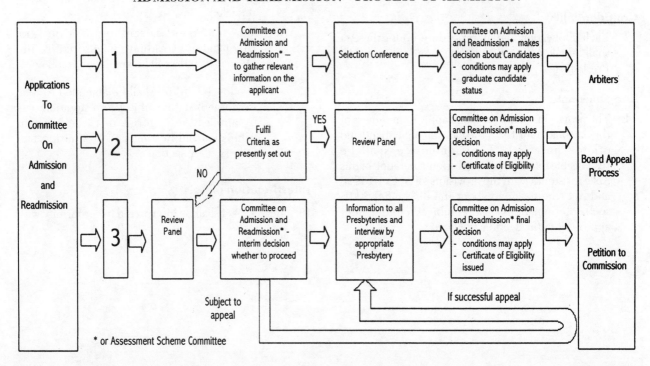

NOTES

Box 1:

- Licentiates, Ordinands and Graduate Candidates and those of comparable status from Churches whose ordination is recognised by the Committee.
- Holders of an expired Certificate of Entitlement (Act V 1985 as amended, section (58)).
- Candidates in respect of whom more than three years have passed since any formal training was undertaken in terms of Act V 1985 (as amended) or Act V 1998 (as amended).
- Graduate Candidates whose Graduate Candidate Certificate has been withheld (Act V 1998 as amended, section (27)).
- Licentiates whose names no longer appear in the Roll of Probationers/Licentiates maintained by the Board of Ministry.

Box 2:
- Ministers of Churches listed in Schedule A or who in the view of the Committee fulfil the criteria set out in sub-sections (4), (6), (7), (9) or (10) of Act V 1984, section (13) as amended.

Box 3:
- Ministers of Churches listed in Box 2 who do not fulfil the criteria as laid down in Act V 1984, section (10) as amended.
- Former ministers of the Church of Scotland seeking restoration.
- Ordained ministers of other Churches except those specified in Box 2.

APPENDIX V

Committee on Vocational Guidance

SELECTION CONFERENCE STATISTICS

Acceptance Statistics for the Full-Time Ministry for 1996–2000 are as follows:

	1996	1997	1998	1999	2000		
					Male	**Female**	**Total**
Applicants	56	57	45	47	39	25	64
Accepted	15 (27%)	20 (35%)	18 (40%)	17 (36%)	14 (36%)	12 (48%)	26 (41%)
First time Applicants	31	37	31	29	28	14	42
Accepted	10 (32%)	16 (37%)	7 (23%)	15 (52%)	11 (39%)	7 (50%)	18 (43%)
Returning Applicants	25	20	14	18	11	11	22
Accepted	5 (20%)	4 (20%)	11 (79%)	2 (11%)	3 (27%)	5 (45%)	8 (36%)

APPENDIX VI

Committee on Ministry Support

GUIDELINES FOR ACT ANENT LONG-TERM ILLNESS OF MINISTERS IN CHARGE

In the terms of the Overture, the Act anent Long-Term Illness of Ministers in Charge sought to deal with the problems of both persistent absence and continuous absence due to illness, with concern being expressed for both minister and congregation. The following guidelines seek to clarify the terms of the above Act while ensuring privacy for all ministers and at the same time relieving Presbytery Clerks of unnecessary administration. The guidelines likewise seek to underline the pastoral support for the minister and also the manse family who may find this Act threatening, while at the same time seeking to come to terms with illness. It must be emphasised that the Department of Ministry is available at all times to offer advice and practical help. Good communication between the Department, Presbytery Clerk, the Church's Occupational Health Physician and the minister is essential at all times. **Ministers will receive full co-operation from the Pension Trustees and the Housing and Loan Trustees so that they can be fully appraised of the pension and housing benefits which are available.**

1. All absences due to illness *must* be intimated to both the Department of Ministry and to the Presbytery Clerk.

2. The section entitled *'Procedures in Cases of Illness'* in the Minister's Handbook should be strictly followed, especially in regard to medical certificates. The Ministry Department shall inform the Presbytery Clerk when a certificate has been received, though not necessarily the reasons for absence.

3. On receiving such a medical certificate, leave of absence is being taken as having been automatically granted by Presbytery to that minister. It is possible for ministers also to be granted leave of absence on compassionate grounds (for example, death in the family, illness of spouse etc) and this should not be included in any cumulative record of absence due to illness.

4. The Presbytery Clerk shall keep a record of such absences but should not deem it necessary to inform Presbytery until:

    a) The length of time is such that an Interim Moderator is appointed. This would normally be after an absence of six weeks but could be earlier.

    b) A pattern emerges of frequent absences which taken together may give rise for concern. The complete record of such absences should then be noted in the Presbytery Minutes retrospectively.

5. The start date for leave of absence shall normally correspond to the first notification of absence.

6. The expiry date for leave of absence shall normally correspond to the length of time indicated on the medical certificate.

7. At the point when the minister is due to consult with the Church's Occupational Health Physician, Presbytery shall refer the matter to an appropriate committee (which should not be the Superintendence Committee), or form an *ad hoc* committee. This committee shall not only consult with the minister but also ensure appropriate pastoral support. This committee shall also ensure that full support and suitable advice have been offered by the Department of Ministry.

8. Clauses 2 and 3 of the Act state *'the minister shall consult'*. Such consultations would be initiated by the Department of Ministry or appropriate Presbytery Committee with the minister concerned. In the case of a minister refusing to consult, the matter would be referred to the Presbytery's Superintendence Committee for further investigation.

9. With regard to section 4b, the time limits referred to in the Act should be adhered to and the ministry should be terminated by Presbytery unless there are exceptional circumstances prevailing, in which case Presbytery shall have discretion in regard to termination.

10. If Presbytery decides to extend the time limits, then there should be a likely date of return to work and there must be a reasonable projection that normal duties would be resumed on a permanent basis. The Church's Occupational Health Physician would need to give a view in this regard.

11. In terms of clause 4 and 5 of the Act, no minister shall have his/her ministry terminated without Presbytery being satisfied that the minister and his/her family have received appropriate help and advice from the Department of Ministry.

12. **At all times the minister concerned shall be entitled to privacy and confidentiality. All information divulged to the Department of Ministry, the Presbytery Clerk and the appropriate Committee of Presbytery shall be kept in strictest confidence.**

APPENDIX VII (a)

Committee on Ministry Support

GUIDELINES FOR APPOINTMENT OF PASTORAL ADVISORS— QUALITIES, SKILLS AND RESPONSIBILITIES

Some Qualities and Skills to be Sought in Pastoral Advisors

- Listening skills
- Able to maintain confidentiality
- Common sense/wisdom
- Ability to empathise
- Availability
- Knowledge of own limitations
- Honesty
- Respect
- Patience/generosity
- Sensitivity
- Integrity
- Genuine interest
- Non-judgemental attitude
- Willingness to be a friend
- Imagination
- Local knowledge

Responsibilities of Pastoral Advisors

- Make initial contact with the Advisee within two weeks of appointment.
- Continue to take initiative in maintaining contact over the period of relationship (up to three years).
- Ensure that meetings take place in a comfortable, private and appropriate environment.
- Set time parameters to regular meetings (a minimum of three meetings per year).
- Indicate availability at other times.
- Ensure that Advisee is able to set the agenda and that it is a manageable one.
- Help identify areas for mutual exploration.
- Ensure space is given for evaluation of the relationship.
- Ensure the Advisee is fully aware of her/his entitlements and duties in relation to such areas as sickness, holiday, maintenance of the manse, what may rightly be expected of the Kirk Session or Congregational Board, and such other matters as may be of practical relevance to the smooth functioning of parish and/or family life.
- Help prepare the Advisee for transfer into the ongoing Pastoral Colleague scheme.
- Maintain confidentiality.
- Engage with the appropriate Committee in regular appraisal, including feedback from the Advisee.
- Make an annual report of diligence to the Presbytery.

Guidelines for Relationship of Pastoral Advisors and Advisees

- The relationship is essentially with the Advisee but should acknowledge, with interest, the life of the family as a whole (where applicable).
- There should be a basic assumption of confidentiality, only taking any matter beyond the relationship with permission of the Advisee, the aim being to develop a culture of secure openness.
- The task should be seen as part of a creative process, not as problem centred.
- The mutuality and quality of the relationship will determine its effectiveness. There needs to be warmth, trust, genuineness and respect between the parties involved—and a willingness to listen with attention and respond with sensitivity.
- The Pastoral Advisor should have support in this work from an appropriate external resource. This could be a minister, but there are many others who are appropriately experienced.
- Either the Advisee or the Pastoral Advisor may request an end to the relationship. The Presbytery is responsible for ensuring that a new appointment is made as soon as possible.
- The relationship should seek to foster both personal and professional growth.

APPENDIX VII (b)

GUIDELINES FOR APPOINTMENT OF PASTORAL COLLEAGUES— QUALITIES, SKILLS AND RESPONSIBILITIES

Some Qualities and Skills to be Sought in Pastoral Colleagues

- Listening skills
- Able to maintain confidentiality
- Common sense/wisdom
- Ability to empathise
- Availability
- Knowledge of own limitations
- Honesty
- Respect
- Patience/generosity
- Sensitivity
- Integrity
- Genuine interest
- Non-judgemental attitude
- Willingness to be a friend
- Imagination
- Local knowledge

Responsibilities of Pastoral Colleagues

- Make initial contact with the minister/deacon as soon as possible following appointment.
- Be responsive to the minister/deacon's requests for meeting time.
- Ensure that meetings take place in a comfortable, private and appropriate environment.
- Agree time parameters for regular meetings and indicate availability at other times.
- Ensure that the minister/deacon is able to set the agenda.
- Help identify areas for mutual exploration.
- Ensure space is given for evaluation of the relationship.
- Maintain confidentiality.
- Engage in mutual reflection on and appraisal of the process.
- Make an annual report of diligence to Presbytery.

Guidelines for Relationship of Pastoral Colleagues and Ministers/Deacons

- The relationship is essentially with the minister/deacon but should acknowledge, with interest, the life of the manse family as a whole.
- There should be a basic assumption of confidentiality, only taking any matter beyond the relationship with permission of the minister/deacon, the aim being to develop a culture of secure openness.

- The relationship should be seen as part of a creative process, not as problem centred.
- The mutuality and quality of the relationship will determine its effectiveness. There needs to be warmth, trust, genuineness and respect between the parties involved—and a willingness to listen with attention and respond with sensitivity.
- The relationship should function within a framework of collaboration and should model reflective patterns.
- The Pastoral Colleague should have support in this work from an appropriate external resource. This could be a minister, but there are many others who are appropriately experienced.
- Either the minister/deacon or the Pastoral Colleague may request an end to the relationship. This should be reported to the Presbytery, which is responsible for working with the minister to appoint a new Colleague as soon as possible.
- The relationship should seek to foster both personal and professional growth.

APPENDIX VIII

Committee on Ministry Support

STIPEND AND SERVICE SUPPLEMENT

1. Level of Minimum Stipend in 2001

The Committee has declared the minimum stipend for 2001 at £18,016, an increase of 4%, and a manse. In making this declaration, the Committee recognised the need to maintain the real value of the stipend plus service supplement and taking this into account the average increase for ministers is 3.7%.

2. The Service Supplement

The Service Supplement now fully implemented is not being increased.

3. Island Allowances

The Committee has declared the Inner and Outer Island Allowances to be increased by the RPI (April 3%) to the following levels:

Inner Island Allowance	£520
Outer Island Allowance	£1,302

4. Manse Disturbance Allowance

The Committee has declared the Manse Disturbance Allowance to be £1,500.

APPENDIX IX

Committee on Ministry Support

MINISTERS' TRAVEL

1. Cars

The Committee has declared travelling expenses for 2001 as follows:

A capital Allowance of £960 will be paid in twelve equal payments with the necessary Tax and National Insurance being deducted at source. Travelling expenses will then be paid at the Inland Revenue levels which do not incur further Tax and National Insurance irrespective of the miles travelled:

40p per mile for the first 4,000 miles
22.5p for all additional mileage
22p per mile for Pulpit Supply.

2. Motorcycles

In the case of those who use motorcycles, their Travelling Expenses are based on fifty percent of those provided for car users.

3. Pedal Cycles

In the case of those who use pedal cycles, the level of Travelling Expenses in 2001 will be 7p per mile which relates directly to the rates supplied by the Inland Revenue. Ministers claiming Travelling Expenses for pedal cycles should do so from local Treasurers and not from the Committee. It is not proposed to set up a centralised scheme for the payment of Travelling Expenses for pedal cycle users.

6. Where weekend board and lodging are agreed as necessary, these may be claimed for the weekend at a maximum rate of that allowed when attending the General Assembly. The fee and expenses should be paid to the person providing the Supply before s/he leaves on the Sunday.

APPENDIX X

Committee on Ministry Support

PULPIT SUPPLY 2001

1. In charges where there is only one diet of worship the Pulpit Supply Fee shall be a Standard Fee of £45 (or as from time to time agreed by the Board of Ministry).

2. In charges where there are additional diets of worship on a Sunday, the person fulfilling the Supply will be paid £10 for each additional Service (or as from time to time agreed by the Board of Ministry).

3. Where the person is unwilling to conduct more than one diet of worship on a given Sunday, s/he will receive pro rata payment based on the total available fee shared on the basis of the number of Services conducted.

4. The fee thus calculated shall be payable in the case of all persons permitted to conduct Services under Act II 1986.

5. In all cases, necessary Travelling Expenses shall be paid. Where there is no convenient public conveyance, the use of a private car shall be paid at 22p per mile and updated from time to time by the Board of Ministry. In exceptional circumstances, to be approved in advance, the cost of hiring may be met.

APPENDIX XI

Committee on Ministry Development

1. **Conference Attendances (2000/2001)**

Conference	Number Attending	As % of Number Invited
Recently Ordained	34	76%
Five Year	33	72%
Eight Year	22	56%
Fifteen Year	28	62%

2. **Study Leave**

   2.1

| Applications Received | | | Applications Approved |
Male	Female	Total	
116	27	143	142

2.2

By age group	No of Applications		By Year of Ordination	No of Applications
30-34	5		1950's	0
35-39	14		1960's	6
40-44	31		1970's	35
45-49	34		1980's	61
50-54	28		1990's	41
55-59	28		Total	143
60+	3			
Total	143			

CHAPLAINS TO HER MAJESTY'S FORCES

MAY 2001

PROPOSED DELIVERANCE

The General Assembly:

1. Receive the Report of the Committee.
2. Reaffirm the commitment and support of the church to the concept of chaplaincy in the Armed Forces and to those who serve the church in this way.
3. Encourage the church to uphold in prayer those who face tension, separation and danger as they serve their nation, that they may protect the ends of justice, truth and peace.
4. Note that the Reverend John M A Thomson, minister of Lanark, St Nicholas', was deployed to Bosnia on Operation Palatine, and that the arrangements agreed at the Assembly of 2000 have worked satisfactorily.
5. Instruct the Committee to consult with the Inter-denominational Advisory Committee and the RAF Heads of Denominations, to form a view on the satisfactory working of the RAF Chaplains' Branch, and to report to the Assembly of 2002.
6. Note the spiritual needs of those who serve in the armed forces but are not of the Christian faith, and acknowledge that service chaplaincy need not exclusively be Christian.
7. Endorse the foundational principle of the Creedy Report that service chaplains be the authorised agents of a recognised body, to whose authority they remain answerable in spiritual matters.
8. Endorse the principle that it is incumbent upon service chaplains unstintingly to give themselves pastorally to those who are not of their faith, and to hold each other in respect.
9. Encourage the Ministry of Defence to consult and to draw up guidelines and templates to cover ceremony and speech at public military occasions where the official representatives of faiths other than Christian may expect to have a part.
10. Encourage the Ministry of Defence to consult and to elaborate guidelines for the accommodation of religious observance within the confines of service life.
11. Welcome the re-appointment of the Venerable Simon Golding QHC RN as Chaplain of the Fleet.
12. Thank the Rev Dr Charles Stewart for outstanding service as Chaplain of the Fleet and Director General Naval Chaplaincy Service.

REPORT

1. The Air Training Corps and the Sea Cadets.

At the Assembly of 2000, several commissioners asked why reference was not made to chaplains of the Air Training Corps in the Committee's report. It was explained that this was because ATC chaplains do not hold The Queen's Commission, and are not appointed under the auspices of the Committee, which thus has no more authority to report on them than it has to report on the activities of any of the other outstanding uniformed organisations which foster the development of young adults. Army Cadet Force chaplains hold a Territorial Army (Class B) Commission in the RAChD, and so are under the authority of the Assistant Chaplain General (2 Div). Unlike their colleagues in the ATC, they are Chaplains to the Forces and come directly under the remit of the Committee.

Despite this difference, because ATC officers (other than chaplains) all hold RAF commissions and because the RAF sponsors the Air Training Corps, it makes sense for this Committee's report to be the place where ATC chaplaincy is noted and encouraged. There is a section in the report of the senior Church of Scotland and Free Church Chaplain in the RAF relating to the invaluable work of these chaplains who are distinctive in that they are entirely voluntary. The Naval Chaplaincy Service has no connection with or influence over any chaplain serving with the Sea Cadets, so any kind of report here is beyond the Committee's remit.

2. Report on Bosnia

Under the arrangements agreed at the Assembly of 2000, The Reverend John M A Thomson, minister of Lanark, St Nicholas', was deployed on Operation Palatine to Sipovo in Bosnia from 29 September to 14 December 2000. In a very full report, he informed the Committee how much he had enjoyed and learned from the deployment. His presence was immensely appreciated by the units to which he ministered and demonstrates yet again the invaluable contribution offered by TA chaplains and the importance of their ability to be deployed. He reported that the various financial and other arrangements agreed at the Assembly of 2000 had worked smoothly.

3. Implementation of the McGill Report

As was reported to the Assembly of 2000, in May 1999 Brigadier Ian McGill CBE, at the request of the Adjutant-General, submitted the *Spiritual Needs Study: An Investigation into the Need for Spiritual Values in the Army*. The McGill report has now been accepted in full, and is in the process of being implemented.

Ian McGill, as a former Royal Engineer (not a Chaplain), was invited to take a robust look at the role of and need for spiritual values in today's Army. He pointed to the fact that the British Army is currently deployed on operations where the roles are complex and sometimes difficult to understand. The Balkan conflicts are a paradigm instance. Even very junior soldiers are frequently exposed to situations where they need *more* than a clear understanding of the commander's intent. They need to acquire judgement and a human dimension if events are to be handled sensitively and resolved professionally.

The acquisition of maturity and character is a mysterious process which, in a fragmented postmodern culture, cannot be taken for granted. The military communities may—and do—amass an array of procedures, but it could be literally fatal to mistake these for a substantive ethic. Character is more fundamental than rules, and the motivation and character which are founded on spiritual values are wider than specific religious commitments.

The McGill Report thus distinguished between (broad) spiritual values, of which there are a number of secular varieties and which must, in some measure, be possessed by all members of the armed forces of the responsible democracies, and the narrower band of specifically religious values which sustain Christians or subscribers to the other faiths. The fostering of spiritual values—that is, enabling people to make the almost indefinable leap between following a procedure obediently and doing something intelligently and humanely because it is believed in—is a key part of the duty of every commander, no matter how junior. Christian chaplains do not have a monopoly in eliciting and inspiring spiritual values: nonetheless, they are a principal resource in today's armed forces, and provide an example of lives where there is an integration of belief and practice.

Within this broad distinction between the perceived need for spiritual values, and the vocation of Christian chaplains to nurture the responsibilities and changed behaviour which is a response to the preaching of the Christian gospel, McGill endorsed the work of the Royal Army Chaplains' Department.

Specifically, he recommended that all deployable formations and major units, as well as training schools, require their own chaplain. Acceptance of the report means that the Army is now seeking to recruit 24 additional chaplains. There will be continued use of an additional 6 retired chaplains and 3 additional officiating chaplains. This, together with additional staff support at Ministry of Defence Chaplains leads to a total projected spend of £1.995 million.

At a time of financial stringency, this is a resounding endorsement for the work of RAChD, and a recognition of the efforts and vision of the current and previous Chaplain General.

Chaplaincy in the armed forces is a part of Christian mission, and the Church of Scotland, along with the other denominations, is being invited to respond to the challenge to send additional chaplains (women and men) to discharge this calling.

4. Distinction between Christian chaplaincy and spiritual needs: the implications of the McGill Report for support of spiritual values which are other than Christian.

As is sketched above, McGill distinguished between chaplaincy (currently only Christian) and spiritual needs. This raises the issue of the needs of religiously committed persons who are not Christian. Currently, none of the three armed forces provide regular or TA chaplains who are not Christian, though there is one part-time officiating chaplain representing the Jewish community, who operates on a tri-service basis. It follows that there are scant opportunities for that particularly close nurturing of values and behaviour which may arise in a worshipping community for those soldiers who are religiously committed but not Christian. Two questions follow: (1) What genuinely adequate provision may be made for them? (2) How, in the close-contact world of the armed forces, may the Christian chaplain most helpfully represent those who are committed practitioners of other faiths on occasions when there may be public ceremony?

Currently, the Ministry of Defence provides (external) religious *advisers* or counsellors for servicepeople who are Moslem, Jewish, Hindu, Sikh and Buddhist. It may be necessary, at some future date, for religious representatives of the different faiths to be fully integrated into the armed forces on equal terms with Christian chaplains. Because currently only Christians are chaplains,

and the distinctive role of *service chaplain* (which is itself an historical construct) is defined by their dual citizenship in their sending *church* and role in the Army, for any such discussion to be taken seriously, the current major stakeholders (among whom we are) must step back and ask if we are unwittingly involved in a sectarian construction of the role of 'chaplain'. To further that discussion, and to inform the Church, a short account is given below of how representatives of the different faith communities are fully integrated in the US armed forces.

5. The arrangements in the United States Armed Forces.

Returning from a theological conference in Nashville in November 2000, the Convener spent two days as a guest of the US Navy Chaplains' Corps in Norfolk, Virginia, at the largest naval base in the world. His object was to understand something of the pluralism in the US Armed Forces. At Norfolk he was shown very great kindness and hospitality by the chaplains and given access to an invaluable range of documents. He is much indebted especially to Chaplain David Gunderlach (Command Chaplain, Naval Station, Norfolk) who made the visit possible, and to Rabbi Chaplain Seth Phillips (Naval Station, Norfolk, Chapel, and his wife, Rabbi Chaplain Karen Soria) who acted as guide during his visit. It was a pleasure also to meet again The Reverend John Beadle, the RN chaplain at Little Creek. He is also most grateful for the kindness of Chaplain James Magness (Chaplain to the US Atlantic Fleet), Chaplain Victor Smith (Mid-Atlantic Regional Chaplain) and Chaplain Terry Gordon from the Resource Branch who produced umpteen electronic documents.

There are over 900 different religious groups in the US armed forces, with 110 different organisations being represented (for example) by the Chaplains Corps of the US Navy.

This means that the distinction between Christian chaplaincy and wider spirituality is not only permitted, but allowed to flourish. In the US forces, servicepeople are positively encouraged to worship and celebrate in their own ways. This is seen as a source of strength, not as a weakness.

How is such pluralism managed within the constraints and disciplines of a service environment?

The appointment of chaplains is taken very seriously and responsibly, as would be expected. Chaplains are professionally qualified clergy, who are appointed to provide for the free exercise of religion for all members of the military services. Specifically, they minister to personnel of their own faith group, 'and facilitate ministries appropriate to the rights and needs of the persons of other faith groups in the pluralistic military environment' (Department of Defence Directive 1304.19, dated 18 Sept 1993).

Chaplains must be certified by a faith group which the Department of Defence (DoD) recognises *as an ecclesiastical endorsing organisation*. Such an endorsing organisation 'possess(es) ecclesiastical authority to grant or withdraw initial and subsequent ecclesiastical certification' (DoD Directive 1304.19). It follows from this that, like our own chaplains, all US chaplains are ecclesially situated. They are not independent free operators, but act as the agents of a recognised organisation which has the authority to withdraw endorsement and thereby cancel a chaplain's armed forces role. This is similar to the Creedy principle in the British army that chaplains have dual citizenship and are ultimately answerable to their sending church. It is this which permits them an element of spiritual independence from a military chain of command and thus allows them to be recipients of confidentialities.

The endorsing agency attests that the chaplain is 'willing to support directly or indirectly the free exercise of religion by *all* members of the military services, their dependants and other authorised persons'; is educationally qualified by possession of a bacclaureate degree (an undergraduate degree) and has completed three resident years of graduate professional study in theology.

In a move from which we could well learn, the vitality and range of different worshipping groups is sustained *at sea* (i.e. where there is no available shore-based religious

agent) by the appointment by the Commanding Officer of a number of Lay Leaders. The task of the Lay Leader is to facilitate prayer and/or worship by an identified group of people when and where an appropriate chaplain is not available. This may be seen as an attempt to enable the worship of the whole people of God.

In a crucial regulation (DoD Directive 1300.17 dated 3 February 1988 and updated by Secretary of the Navy Instruction (SECNAVINST) 1730.8 dated 31 December 1997 [http://web7.whs.osd.mil/pdf/d130017p.pdf] it is undertaken that it is the policy of the Navy 'to accommodate the doctrinal or traditional observances of the religious faith practised by individual members *when these doctrines or observances will not have an adverse impact on military readiness, individual or unit readiness, unit cohesion, health, safety or discipline'*.

Thus, where at all possible, observance of Sabbath and holy days is accommodated. A calendar of significant holy days is published. Following consideration of religious doctrines and traditions, separate rations may be authorised. Immunisation requirements may be waived, though religious objection is balanced against the medical risk to the individual and military unit. Religious items which are not visible may be worn with uniform provided they do not interfere with the performance of military duties. Visible items of religious apparel may be authorised except when the item is not 'neat and conservative' (these terms are defined). Thus, a yarmulke may be worn by Jews with uniform whenever military headgear is not prescribed. It may also be worn beneath military headgear.

At a personal level, chaplains of the US Armed Forces agree to a covenant approved by the collective Endorsing Agents (what we would call 'the sending Churches') in December 1994. Together, they then represented 245 religious bodies recognised by the Armed Forces. The covenant includes the clauses:

- I will hold in trust the traditions and practices of my religious body.
- I will carefully adhere to whatever direction may be conveyed to me by my endorsing body for maintenance of my endorsement.

- I understand as a chaplain in the Armed Forces that I must function in a pluralistic environment with chaplains of other religious bodies to provide for ministry to all military personnel and their families as entrusted to my care.

- I will seek to provide for pastoral care and ministry to persons of religious bodies other than my own within my area of responsibility *with the same investment of myself as I give to members of my own religious body*. I will work collegially with chaplains of religious bodies other than my own as together we seek to provide as full a ministry as possible to our people. I will respect the beliefs and traditions of my colleagues and those to whom I minister. When conducting services of worship that include persons of other than my religious body I will draw upon those beliefs, principles and practices that we have in common. [*Emphases* added.]

- I will not proselytise from other religious bodies, but I retain the right to evangelise those who are nonaffiliated.

Use of this covenant is illustrated in an agreement of the US National Conference of Christians and Jews over considerations to be taken into account before offering *public prayer*. Christians and Jews agreed to remember that in public prayer one is calling upon God's presence on behalf of *all* of those present. Together Christians and Jews plead for use of common language and shared symbols which were acceptable and understandable and not offensive and unintelligible. Together, they agreed to seek the 'highest common denominator' and the best level of inspiration without compromise of conscience. For beginning *common prayer*, they suggested use of such forms as 'Dear Creator, Source of all life' …, 'O Lord, our God and Sustainer' … , and for concluding, the phrases 'In your name, we pray' … 'in our Lord's name' … .

6. The next step.

Though we share a common language, our culture is not the same as that in the United States. They are both more Christian and more pluralist than we are; we are more post-Christian and less pluralist. Nonetheless, an important conversation is taking place, and we may do well to learn from American experience in enabling different groups to worship by means of Lay Leaders, and in expecting denominational and other-than-Christian chaplains both to work together collegially and to give themselves positively to those who are not of their faith. As part of that discussion, we offer the following as preliminary guidelines within the Ministry of Defence, for action by our ministers on public military occasions, where members of other faith groups may wish their representatives to take part:

(a) No chaplain may be obliged to act against his/her conscience on any such occasion, nor should any member of HM Forces, whether Christian or a member of another faith group, ever be ordered to take part in such activity if he or she believes it to be against his or her conscience.

(b) Any act of multi-faith activity should be notified well in advance. Those being invited to attend should be given ample notice to enable them to decide whether or not to participate in such activity. Those who decide they cannot in conscience attend must be given— where possible—an opportunity to worship according to their particular traditions.

(c) Where Christian chaplains are involved in multi-faith activity they should be satisfied that such activity does not contain material which is contrary or hostile to the claims of the Christian faith. Likewise, material put forward by Christian chaplains should follow the same principles with regard to the sensitivities of members of other faith groups. The order of service for such an occasion should be agreed by those leading the service well in advance, and be strictly followed.

(d) The order should be 'themed', in the sense that there would be a Christian section followed by other sections given wholly over to the ceremonies of other faiths. This would have the advantage of marking the ownership and leadership of different sections.

6. The Reverend Dr Charles Stewart

The Church records its debt to The Reverend Dr Charles Stewart who retired from the post of Chaplain of the Fleet and Director General Naval Chaplaincy Service on the 24th of August 2000. A double graduate of Strathclyde (BSc and PhD), Charles Stewart studied Divinity at Glasgow (BD) and Edinburgh (MTh). After an assistantship at Bearsden South, he was ordained by the Presbytery of Dumbarton and appointed as a chaplain to the Royal Navy in February 1976. Thereafter he served with immense distinction, being involved in chaplaincy during the Falklands conflict and later during the Bosnian conflict. He achieved a notable number of 'firsts', being in 1996 the first non-Anglican to be officially appointed as chaplain to a warship in the Royal Navy, the first non-Anglican Director General of Naval Chaplaincy Service in 1996 and Chaplain of the Fleet in 1998, thereby achieving the full potential envisaged in the creation of the Naval Chaplaincy Service in 1992, where Roman Catholics, Anglicans, the Church of Scotland and the Free Churches came together in a model now followed by the Royal Air Force. On retirement from active service, Charles Stewart achieved another 'first', becoming the first non-Anglican to become chaplain to the Royal Hospital School at Holbrook, Ipswich. Royal Navy Chaplaincy and the General Assembly are much in his debt.

In the name of the Committee

IAIN R TORRANCE, *Convener*
DOUGLAS M HUNTER, *Secretary*

CHAPLAINCY IN THE ROYAL NAVY

A highlight of the year has been the Moderator's visit to the Royal Navy. While in Portsmouth, Dr and Mrs McLellan were hosted by the Second Sea Lord. They began their visit onboard HMS VICTORY then moved to HMS RICHMOND (from the oldest to the newest frigate in commission in the RN). After the ship visit, the Moderator visited HMS SULTAN, the Marine Engineering training establishment, the Armed Forces Chaplaincy Centre, the Royal Marines Commando Training Centre at Lympstone and, in Plymouth, HQ 3 Commando Brigade and HMS RALEIGH, the Navy's new entry establishment for sailors.

Throughout the visit, the Moderator highlighted the friendly and helpful attitude of those they met. He likened the atmosphere to that of a hard working but close family. He was also impressed by the relaxed but professional attitude shown by staff and trainees alike.

Work continues to develop the concept of Chaplaincy provision for the major UK non-Christian faith groups. The first stage is the provision of Chaplaincy care, on a part time basis, by Specialist Religious Advisers from the Buddhist, Hindu, Jewish, Muslim and Sikh faiths. Full time Chaplains will be able to draw on the expertise of the SRAs in making provision for facilities for service members of these faith groups and arranging pastoral contact when required. It is intended that this provision be put in place during the coming year.

NCS is pleased to announce that as of 8 January 2001, NCS is at full strength. However, the projection for 2002 is that at least 12 Naval Chaplains will retire. It is therefore vital that we continue to recruit during the coming year.

A major reorganisation is underway in the operational structure of the Navy. The Commander-in-Chief Fleet, who has overall operational command throughout the Royal Naval and the Royal Marines, is currently implementing his Fleet First restructuring, which will rationalise the Command and Control of the operational Navy. For Chaplaincy this is a major advantage to our role.

The primary duty of the Naval Chaplaincy Service is to serve service men and women in the front line. While it is important to offer spiritual and pastoral support to those serving ashore and to their dependants, the priority is to minister to those at sea in ships and submarines, with the air stations and the air groups embarked on the aircraft carriers and ships, and with the Royal Marines in their many different theatres of operation. Utilising Fleet

First, gone will be the requirement for a Chaplain to care for a squadron of 6 or more ships; in its place every ship on a directed task will carry a Chaplain throughout the deployment. To achieve this, NCS has increased the number of Chaplains appointed to front line units, and now the Chaplain will join for the initial work-up, remain through the full deployment and only leave when the ship returns home. This increase will mean that over 50% of our Chaplains will be working in frontline appointments.

This is not, of course, to denigrate the very important work being done by the home based Chaplains who continue to give major support in Naval Bases, in training establishments, hospitals and headquarters units. They are, in fact, complementary.

The NCS is very grateful for the help and support given by the Chaplains' Committee during the year. During his visit, the Moderator assured the Chaplains and the service men and women of the prayers and good wishes of the Kirk. That support is very important to us and we are very grateful for it.

Locations of Royal Navy Chaplains

Retirement:
The Reverend Charles E Stewart QHC BSc BD MTh PhD
Now serving as Chaplain to the Royal Hospital School, Holbrook.
(Presbytery of England)

Newly joined:
The Reverend Stan Kennon RN
From Stow: St Mary of Wedale and Heriot
(Presbytery of Melrose and Peebles)

The Reverend Donald Keith RN
Continues to serve with the Fleet Royal Marines Protection Group (formally COMMACHIO Company RM) at RM CONDOR, Arbroath, and at HMS CALEDONIA at Rosyth.

When the FRMPG moves from Arbroath to Faslane in early summer 2001 he will move with them and become part of the ecumenical Chaplaincy team at Faslane, while continuing to minister to HMS CALEDONIA.

The Reverend Scott Rae MBE RN
Continues to serve as Naval Director at the Armed Forces Chaplaincy Centre at Amport House, Andover, where he is Programme Director.

He provides pastoral care courses for all ranks of the three services as well as offering a variety of conferences and in-service courses for Chaplains and associated welfare agencies. During 2001 he will exchange with a Presbyterian Chaplain from the Royal Australian Navy and will serve for four months in Australia.

The Reverend Alison Britchfield RN
Now serving as Chaplain to HMS FEARLESS.

She provides spiritual and pastoral care to the ship's company of 520, with an additional 300–400 embarked when the ship is operational. Other duties include providing resettlement advice to those leaving the Service and acting as Education Officer. Alison (nee Norman) was married in April 2000.

The Reverend Scott Shackleton RN
Continues to serve as Staff Chaplain to Commandant General Royal Marines, based with the 3rd Commando Brigade in Plymouth.

During the Autumn and Winter he served in Kosovo as co-ordinating Chaplain, responsible on a tri-service and an international basis for the provision of Chaplaincy to all service personnel serving in that theatre.

The Reverend Scott Brown RN
Continues to serve at HMS SULTAN.

A new project for the Chaplaincy team is the development of an Internet Suite and Coffee Bar, providing trainees with entertainment facilities, an electronic means of communicating with families and friends and an informal contact point where they can meet with the Chaplains for care and support. An ecumenical Service has been started for the trainees on a Monday evening, in addition to the growing Sunday CSFC congregation. He has become a member of the Spiritual and Personal Development Working Group, which is redesigning the RN Religious Education syllabus.

The Reverend Rory MacLeod RN

Continues to serve at the Commando Training Centre at Lympstone, Devon. His routine involves the pastoral care of recruits, training teams and families, both at home and in the field, with Christian education and worship at the core. The Chaplaincy team is developing a cyber café for recruits to use. His work is ecumenical and he has been developing interfaith initiatives as well. He is developing a Cultural and Religious awareness programme as part of the Chaplaincy syllabus, preparing recruits for overseas service and trainers for recruits from other faith communities within the UK.

The Reverend lain McFadzean RN

Continues to serve at the Clyde Naval Base at Faslane, Helensburgh. He has been involved in the development of projects aimed at making Chaplaincy more accessible to sailors and their families and helping them to integrate into the local community. One Christian community outreach project, "Back Chat", is a drop-in centre for teenagers from the naval housing estates. He has moved his focus for Sunday worship into the local community close to the base.

The Reverend Stan Kennon RN

Having joined the Navy in September, he completed his new entry training at Britannia RN College in December 2000. This included 6 weeks Initial Sea Training on HMS CAMPBELTOWN. After specialist pastoral training, his first appointment is to serve at HMS SEAHAWK, the RN Air Station at Culdrose in Cornwall. RNAS Culdrose is the home to the RN's new helicopter, the Merlin.

Presbyterian Church In Ireland

The Reverend Terry Maze QHC RN

Promoted to Principal Church of Scotland and Free Churches Chaplain in May 2000, he is also Director (Training and Programmes) for the Naval Chaplaincy Service. In addition to his pastoral care for the CSFC Chaplains, he has overall responsibility for the training given to all Naval Chaplains and the training delivered by them to naval personnel, including the Spiritual and Personal Development syllabus.

CHAPLAINCY IN THE ARMY

Church of Scotland Chaplains serving in the Royal Army Chaplains Department, as Regular Army Chaplains, are currently serving in Germany, Cyprus, England and Scotland. Some have been deployed on operational tours in Kosovo, Bosnia, Sierra Leone and Northern Ireland.

Territorial Army Chaplains have been training in Germany and America, involved in Annual Camps and various other activities in Scotland. Some have also volunteered for Full Time Reserve Service in Bosnia.

Army Cadet Force Chaplains continue their sterling work with Scottish teenagers on weekend training and Annual Camp

Recruiting has been buoyant. Regular Army Chaplains are fully up to strength. There is at present only one vacancy in the TA at the Lowland Volunteers. Four new ACF Chaplains have been commissioned, the Reverend Elizabeth A Fisk, the Reverend Iain A Sutherland, the Reverend Irene A Charlton and the Reverend Arthur Sherratt. There are three vacancies to be filled.

During his year as Moderator, Dr Andrew McLellan, visited Catterick and Fort George, Inverness. On Tuesday, 29 August the Moderator and Mrs McLellan visited HQ 2nd Division at Craigiehall. They were met by the General Officer Commanding, Major General R D S Gordon CBE They were briefed on the 2nd Division which stretches from Chester to Shetland by Colonel H C G Willing and travelled by helicopter to Catterick, escorted by Colonel A K Miller. At Catterick Garrison they met the Reverend J W Aitchison, Senior Chaplain, 2nd Bn ITC who works with the Army's recruits. They then moved on to visit I Highlanders and met their Chaplain, the Reverend B J A Abeledo.

On Friday, 24 November, the Moderator and Mrs McLellan visited Fort George, Inverness where they met the 1 RHF Chaplain, the Reverend D K Prentice. After lunch in the Officers Mess the Moderator had the opportunity to meet soldiers and learned of the regiment's new mountain warfare role.

Location of Army Chaplains

Rev B J A Abeledo — 1 Highlanders
Somme Barracks
Catterick Garrison
N Yorks DL9 3AQ

Rev J W Aitchson — 2nd Bn ITC
Helles Barracks
Catterick
N Yorks DL9 4HH

Rev R N Cameron — Church Centre
BFPO 40

Rev A R Cobain — 1KOSB
Salamanca Barracks
BFPO 53

Rev D Connolly — 1AandSH
Redford Barracks
Colinton Road
Edinburgh EH13 OPP

Rev Dr D G Coulter — RCMS
Shrivenham
Swindon
Wilts SN6 8HD

Rev J R Daillv — DACG
HQ 42 (NW) Bde
Fulwood Barracks
Preston PR2 8AA

Rev D V F Kingston — 1 PWO
Dale Barracks
Liverpool Road
Chester CH2 4BD

Rev A J R McCulloch — 3RHA
BFPO 38

Rev S L Mackenzie — 1RS
Ballykelly
BFPO 802

Rev C A MacLeod — 1 SG
Wellington Barracks
Birdcage Walk
London SWIE 6HQ

Rev R N MacLeod — Army Training Regiment
Glencorse Barracks
Penicuik
Midlothian EH26 0NP

Rev P L Majcher — Sen Chap Soldier Training
AG Corps Centre
Worthy Down
Winchester
Hants S021 2RG

Rev Dr A M Martin — HQ ARRC
JHQ
BFPO 40

Rev D K Prentice — 1RHF
Fort George
Arderseir
Inverness 1V2 7TE

Rev J P Whitton — Assistant Chaplain General
Army Headquarters
Scotland
Craigiehall
South Queensferry EH3O 9TN

Also serving from the Presbyterian Church in Ireland

Rev N G McDowell	1BW Fallingbostel BFPO 38
Rev P W Paterson	26 Regt RA BFPO 113

Territorial Army Chaplains

Rev Dr I C Barclay	HQ 2nd Division
Rev S A Blakey	32 Sig Regt (V)
Rev A R Forsyth	71 Engr Regt (V)
Rev J M Gibson	205 (S) Fd Hosp (V)
Rev L Kinsey	205 (S) Fd Hosp (V)
Rev J M A Thomson	105 Regt RA (V)
Rev I C Warwick	51st Highland Regt (V)

Army Cadet Force Chaplains

Rev D M Almond	Glasgow & Lanarkshire Bn
Rev J E Andrews	Lothian & Borders Bn
Rev Dr I C Barclay	BW Bn
Rev R D M Campbell	Argyll and Sutherland Highlanders Bn
Rev I A Charlton	Shetland Indep Bty ACF
Rev E A Fisk	BW Bn
Rev J L Goskirk	1 Hldrs Bn
Rev I M Homewood	Argyll and Sutherland Highlanders Bn
Rev A Sherratt	West Lowland Bn
Rev I A Sutherland	1 Hldrs Bn
Rev S Swindells	2 Hldrs Bn
Rev M A Whyte	West Lowland Bn
Rev G N Wilson	Glasgow & Lanarkshire Bn

CHAPLAINCY SERVICES RAF

Revised Management Structure

The new management structure has been running successfully for the part two years. On reflection the Branch has enjoyed improved working relationships and a more open style of government. Internal communications with those members of the Branch Management Team who are rusticated has not proved to be the problem it was anticipated to be. It should be noted that the Inter-Denominational Advisory Committee will need to meet with the Heads of Denomination to discuss the way forwards as the trial period will be completed before the General Assembly meets in 2001.

Training Review.

The CSFC Principal completed a review on Chaplaincy Training. The recommendations made to Chaplaincy Services will mean considerable changes and enhancements to Chaplaincy Training (CT). In brief, the training will be subdivided into three areas.

(1) Professional Competence which includes management and staff training at particular career points.
(2) Pre employment training for particular task attached to certain posts.
(3) Vocational and Theological Reflection which will encourage chaplains to study and critically reflect on the theological context of their day to day employment.

Revision of Terms and Conditions of Service. The new terms and conditions of service bring Chaplaincy Services in line with the wider Air Force. In brief they mean a chaplain remains longer in the relative rank of Flight Lieutenant and is boarded for promotion to relative rank of Wing Commander rather than time promoted.

Location of Church of Scotland Chaplains

The Revd (Wg Cdr) Duncan Shaw remains at Lossiemouth at the time of writing this report although, on return from his detachment to Ali Al Salem in September, will probably move. Duncan was our project officer for the Tri Service Millennium Appeal for Mozambique. The final figure raised by the RAF was in excess of £38,000 which is more than double the target set.

The Revd (Wg Cdr) Peter Mills is senior Chaplain RAF Bruggen and will remain there until its closure at the end of this year. This has been a good move for Peter and one that he and Sheila have enjoyed.

The Revd (Wg Cdr) Gordon Craig is now the College Staff Chaplain and Senior Chaplain at Royal Air Force College Cranwell. This has been a good post for Gordon and given him the first taste of Chaplaincy from the management perspective.

The Revd (Sqn Ldr) Andrew Jolly is at RAF Halton and is part of the chaplaincy team who are engaged in delivering the Beliefs and Values Programme to the Recruits. Andrew has risen to the challenge of this posting well and is doing a superb job.

The Revd (Flt Lt) Chris Kellock successfully completed his SERE Training at Cranwell indeed he was awarded the Deadalus Trophy on Graduation—an award given to the Leading Officer Cadet (SERE). He is the only chaplain in the history of the Branch to do so. Chris with Monica and Scott are located at Cottesmore and he with other chaplaincy colleagues form the Cottesmore/ Wittering Chaplaincy Team.

Recruitment, overall, has continued to be brisk; but unfortunately Church of Scotland candidates have been few and far between. The notional posts they may have filled have been allocated to other CSFC Denominations to ensure Chaplaincy Services fill its establishment.

Report on the Air Training Corps

Since 1941 the Corps has boldly lived up to its motto of 'Venture Adventure' and has enriched the lives of tens of thousands of young men and women who have passed through its ranks. Over these sixty years the object of the Corps has been to promote and encourage among young people a practical interest in aviation, to provide a training which will be useful in civilian or Service life and, by fostering the spirit of adventure, to develop qualities of leadership and good citizenship.

As part of this great object the Chaplaincy Service to the Air Training Corps continues to serve both the Cadets, the Officers and the Adult Instructors, making the most of the opportunities provided both by special Church Parades and ordinary meetings of the Squadrons. More and more use is being made of informal contacts and talks, rather than set periods of religious instruction. In this way helpful links are being formed with not a few who, in the context of modern living, would otherwise have little contact with the Church, and no chance of speaking thus directly, on free and friendly terms with a minister. It is the responsibility of the Squadron Commanding Officer to encourage Cadets to pursue the religious faith to which they belong and 'to further this purpose the CO is to secure the services and the appointment of a suitable Chaplain'.

ATC Chaplains are honorary appointments—they are not commissioned and therefore they neither wear uniform, nor do they receive pay—but they are eligible to receive certain allowances. For administrative purposes within the Corps, Scotland is linked with Northern Ireland. There are 117 Squadrons within this Region and 83% have Chaplains. In Scotland there are a number of vacancies, some of which are caused by the movement of ministers from one parish to another, and the Chaplains' Committee of the Corps would appeal to parish ministers to consider carefully the claims of this service, with the opportunities it offers as an extension of their parish work, not only among the young people but also with their officers and instructors. The five geographical areas of Scotland are served by experienced Wing Chaplains and the Regional Chaplain for Scotland and Northern Ireland is the Rev. T.W. Tait, who can be contacted through Air Cadets Regional HQ at 25 Learmonth Terrace, Edinburgh, EH4 1 NZ.

I conclude by thanking my fellow Heads of Denomination and the Church of Scotland Committee for their co-operation and support.

TRUSTEES OF THE CHURCH OF SCOTLAND HOUSING AND LOAN FUND FOR RETIRED MINISTERS AND WIDOWS AND WIDOWERS OF MINISTERS

MAY 2001

PROPOSED DELIVERANCE

The General Assembly:

1. Receive and approve the Report and thank the Chairman, the Trustees and Staff.

REPORT

1. Aim of the Fund

1.1 The Fund exists to support retired ministers and widows and widowers of ministers in need of help with their housing. The Trustees endeavour to provide assistance by way of either a house to rent or a house purchase loan.

1.2 The Trustees own and regularly acquire additional houses for leasing at concessionary rents to those retired ministers and widows and widowers of ministers with insufficient resources available for house purchase. Alternatively, loans at very favourable rates of interest are granted up to seventy per cent of the house purchase price, but with overriding normal maximums of £25,000 for Standard Loans and £59,500 for Shared Appreciation Loans.

2. Houses

2.1 The Trustees own 199 houses. Nineteen houses were purchased during 2000 at a cost to the Fund of £1,515,159 and eight houses were sold in the year for £387,972.

2.2 Currently Rents are chargeable to ministers at forty per cent of Market Rent and for pre-1989 leases seventy per cent of Fair Rent; and to widows and widowers of Ministers at twenty per cent of Market Rent or thirty-five per cent where Fair Rent is still the basis.

3. Loans

3.1 Three Standard Loans, three Shared Appreciation Loans and two additional advances were made in 2000. These amounted in all to £226,000. Fourteen loans (including one part-repayment) were repaid totalling £210,005.

3.2 The Fund provided Short Term Bridging support in two instances to the extent of £58,000.

3.3 Interest only Standard Loans continue to be granted up to a normal maximum limit of £25,000. Current rates of interest are five per cent in the case of a minister, and two and a half per cent in the case of a loan granted or passing to a minister's surviving widow or widower.

3.4 Shared Appreciation Loans, which link loan values over their term to the value of the property concerned over the same period, can be granted up to a normal maximum limit of £59,500. Current rates of interest for these loans are three per cent for ministers, and one and a half per cent on loans granted or passing to a minister's surviving widow or widower.

4. Survey Undertaken by the Trustees

4.1 To assist the Trustees with forward planning, a brief Questionnaire was distributed in November 1999, with a short covering letter, to 820 ministers in active service who were aged forty-five and over. The response rate over the early part of last year was a quite remarkable ninety-six per cent and the Trustees are grateful and heartened.

4.2 Analysis of the returned questionnaires has indicated that:

- Projected Ministerial Retirements over the twenty year period to 2019, which information may prove of interest and help to the Church in general, shows a fairly steady level of expected retirals at around the forty mark each year.
- Fifty-five per cent of parish ministers in this age group expect to make application to the Fund for some help with a house for retirement occupancy.
- Forty-four per cent of those responding, or their spouse, own a house which is considered suitable for retirement housing. But of those, approximately one sixth envisage making application for assistance, mainly to enable repayment to be made of an existing mortgage.
- Rental Housing is the expressed choice of thirty-eight per cent overall. This response indicates a move from Rental Housing to Loans over the next twenty years but, however, this belies the trend over the past ten years.

4.3 Comparison with a previous similar survey, held in 1995, suggests a slight but welcome fall in the proportion of ministers who believe application for support will be necessary in due time.

4.4 The need by retiring ministers for help from the Fund seems unlikely to diminish significantly in the foreseeable future and remains challenging.

5. Donations, Bequests etc.

5.1 The Trustees are gratified to acknowledge the receipt of £2,791 during the year from donations, grants and income from trusts, and of £225,693 from bequests.

6. Accumulated Funds

6.1 Net outgoing resources for the year to 31st December 2000 amounted to £7,823. Realised and unrealised investment gains reduced the net adverse movement in Funds to £4,623.

6.2 Long Term Loan advances at the year end numbered 160 which, together with two outstanding Short Term Bridging Loans of £58,000 amounted to £3,128,215.

6.3 Investments at Market Value and deposit balances at 31st December 2000 amounted to £4,532,534.

6.4 Commitments for further house purchases and loans approved by the year end, but still to be met from Funds, amounted to £1,680,500.

7. Further Information

7.1 Application forms and further information and guidance may be had from The Secretary, Mr Ronald C Mather, at the Church Offices.

In the name of the Trustees

WILLIAM McVICAR, *Chairman*
RONALD C MATHER, *Secretary*

BOARD OF NATIONAL MISSION

MAY 2001

BOARD OF NATIONAL MISSION

MAY 2001

PROPOSED DELIVERANCE

The General Assembly:

1 Receive the Report and thank the Conveners and members of the Board and Constituent Committees and Sub-Committees.

2 Thank all staff, especially those who retired in 2000, and commend the work of the staff to the prayerful support of the whole Church.

3 Remit to Presbyteries Section 7.1.5 of the Report for consideration and for response by 13th December 2001. (Sec 7.1)

4 Resolve that the Scheme of Ministry with Deaf People as detailed in Section 7.2 of the Report becomes an ongoing part of the Ministry and Mission of the Church of Scotland. (Sec 7.2)

5 Agree that the main focus of Field Staff appointed as Advisers in Mission and Evangelism should be on enabling congregations for mission rather than on Presbyteries and on "Presbytery Partnerships". (Sec 7.3)

6 Recognise Rev James C. Stewart, Perth: Letham St Mark's, as a part-time evangelist, commend his services to the whole Church, and invite Presbyteries to identify others who might in the future be so recognised. (Sec 7.4)

7 Agree that development of the Netherbow Arts Centre together with John Knox House, 43-45 High Street, Edinburgh, as a National Cultural Centre is a priority for the Church and authorise the Board of National Mission to proceed when appropriate, in consultation with the Board of Stewardship and Finance. (Sec 7.5)

8 Welcome the "Statistics for Mission" initiative and instruct Presbyteries to advise the Board of National Mission on changes made to parish boundaries which occur outwith the scope of Act IV (1984). (Sec 7.6)

9 Express thanks for the dedicated service of prison chaplains in providing pastoral care and religious services to prisoners, and appreciation of their role in promoting links between congregations and prison communities. (Sec 7.7)

10 Welcome the discussions and exploratory work which have taken place between the Board and the Scottish Prison Service in the development of prison chaplaincy and care of prisoners; endorse the general direction agreed by all denominations and the Scottish Prison Service; and instruct the Board to implement the new structures for the provision of chaplaincy to the Scottish Prison Service. (Sec 7.7)

11 Welcome the initiative of the Board to establish a Scottish Mission Studies Centre. (Sec 7.8)

12 Approve the continuation of the work of Project Rejoice! for a further five years. (Sec 7.9)

13 Amend the Constitution of the Board of National Mission as detailed in Appendix 1.

14 Receive the Appendix headed "Analysis of a Survey of Healthcare Chaplaincy in Long Stay Units" in fulfilment of the instruction of the General Assembly of 1999 "to review chaplaincy provision and responsibility in the light of the Community Care Act" and encourage Presbyteries and congregations to respond positively to the report's recommendations. (Appendix VI)

Society, Religion and Technology Project (Sec 3.10 and Appendix V)

15   Affirm that there are limits to how far we may genetically engineer animals for medical benefit, on the grounds of animal welfare, and because animals have inherent value as God's creatures.

16   Affirm that genetic engineering of farm animals to produce pharmaceuticals in milk and eggs is ethically acceptable, subject to welfare considerations in each case.

17   Recognise that the use of genetically modified pigs as a source of human organ transplants is justified only if there is a realistic chance of substantial human benefit.

18   Express concern at the large increase in the use of genetically modified mice in human genetic research, and urge the Home Office to adopt tighter controls in the purposes for which it issues licenses in this area.

19   Urge the Home Office not to allow the genetic modification of primates for medical research.

20   Urge HM Government to bring forward with urgency primary legislation to ban human reproductive cloning, to press for such a ban internationally, and to impose tight restrictions on the use of nuclear transfer cloning methods in stem cell research in the UK.

21   Oppose the use of nuclear transfer to create hybrid human-animal embryos.

22   Urge HM Government to increase its efforts to combat climate change and to ring fence fuel tax revenues for environmental remediation, promoting energy saving and renewable energy use, public transport and rural infrastructure.

23   Welcome the launch of the Eco-Congregation initiative in Scotland and urge all congregations to take part in the scheme.

Scottish Churches Community Trust (Appendix X)

24   Encourage congregations, working together, to seek support from the Scottish Churches Community Trust to help to strengthen disadvantaged communities and enable them to tackle local needs.

25   Appoint Rev Ian Moir as the Church of Scotland's representative to the Board of the Scottish Churches Community Trust for a further year.

REPORT

1.   Travel to the New …

1.1   The celebration of the Year 2000 is now at a close—but reflections on the past and hopes for the future continue! These past reflections and future hopes colour our interpretation of the facts of the present.

1.2   In the work of the Board the facts do not present a uniform picture:

- On the one hand, Presbyteries throughout Scotland are reporting to the Committee on Parish Reappraisal a shortage of ministers with some experiencing a record number of vacancies.   (In December 2000 the Presbytery of Glasgow alone reported 26)

- On the other hand, while the Church might despair of reduced numbers of ministers and members, the Committee on Chaplaincies reports that the secular agencies of the land are offering more financial resource for quality chaplaincy (almost 60 ministers engaged whole-time in chaplaincy - and the number of appointments is growing).

The contradictions are there, but these contradictions coalesce in a challenge to the Board in just two of many areas of concern.

1.3   In this Report to the General Assembly the Board seeks to encourage the Church to rise to the challenge of present concerns and to **travel to the new** in confidence and faith.

1.4 Travelling to the New ... Millennium

Such confidence and faith was present in 1992 when the Board began thinking about journeying into a new millennium. Realising that there would be much attention given to the time when the world changed from the 1900s to the 2000s the Board established an AD 2000 Working Party with the task of encouraging the Church to be imaginative and enterprising in its evangelistic efforts focussed on the Year 2000. Appendix IV gives detailed information about what happened and what was achieved and it is the hope and prayer of the Board that the momentum gathered in seeking to proclaim "Jesus Christ, the same yesterday, today and forever" will be maintained in the Church's mission as we travel on in this third millennium.

2. Travel to the New ... in the staffing of parishes.

2.1 Parish Reappraisal:

2.1.1 The staffing of the parishes of Scotland is the responsibility of the Committee on Parish Reappraisal which works in close co-operation with the Committees on New Charge Development and Parish Assistance.

2.1.2 The Committee on Parish Reappraisal reports that in its ongoing work it is seeking to assist congregations, Presbyteries and the whole Church to **travel to the new.** Much of the Committee's work is giving consideration to decisions of Presbyteries taken under Acts IV (1984) and V (1984) and a full record of decisions taken is given in the Tables in Appendix II. During 2000 the Committee concurred with 57 unrestricted calls, 24 calls with restricted tenure, 12 bases of linking and 13 bases of union.

2.1.3 The Committee always seeks as much information as necessary to make its decisions. In requests for concurrence with unrestricted calls the Committee always requests completed Congregational Survey Forms. When such forms are incomplete the Committee often defers a decision and so the importance of fully completed Survey Forms being submitted with decisions of Presbyteries cannot be over-emphasised.

2.1.4 In order that decisions regarding congregations are not taken in isolation the Committee continues to stress the value of Presbytery Planning. At the end of 2000 40 Presbyteries had Agreed Plans with the Committee and all other Presbyteries were engaged in the process of planning. When the Committee agrees a Plan with a Presbytery it is stated that "the Plan is a statement of intent of the Presbytery which does not infringe the rights of ministers in charges and the rights of congregations". As Scotland and the Church of Scotland continues to change, planning has become an ongoing process and throughout 2000 the Committee has been involved at the request of Presbyteries in many discussions on planning.

2.1.5 The Committee continues to work closely with the General Trustees in the fulfilment of the Regulations for Control of Work at Ecclesiastical Buildings. In 2000 well over 60 requests for work over £50,000 were considered and the Committee records warm appreciation to the General Trustees for their co-operation in the fulfilment of the regulations.

2.1.6 Warm appreciation is also expressed by the Committee to many others who have assisted the Committee in its work. Presbytery Conveners and Clerks have facilitated effective communication; the Deputy Secretary to the Board of Practice and Procedure, the Rev Marjory A. MacLean, has greatly assisted the process of the revision of Acts IV (1984) and V (1984); the Rev Martin Johnstone, Urban Priority Area Adviser of the Board has offered valuable insights to the Committee; and a lesson from the Church overseas has come from a study of the life and work of the Cariboo Presbyterian Church of Canada offering insights into rural ministry.

2.1.7 Summer Student Appointments:

2.1.7.1 Each Summer the Committee appoints students to serve in a number of rural and UPA parishes in a scheme entitled "Summer Student Appointments".

2.1.7.2 Students are paid at 60% of the current Minimum Stipend and accommodation and travel costs are met.

2.1.7.3 Those appointed give invaluable support to ministers and congregations in the most remote and the most hard-pressed parishes in Scotland. A declining number of Divinity Students available to undertake appointments has had an effect on the numbers of appointments which can be made but the Committee is pleased to report that 21 such appointments were made in 2000.

2.1.8   Part-time Charges:
2.1.8.1 The Committee reported to the General Assembly of 2000 that it was continuing to monitor the progress of part-time charges and now reports that during 2000 a survey of the Ministers and Kirk Sessions of part-time charges has been undertaken.

2.1.8.2 A range of both positive and concerning responses was offered and the need for training to be available for ministers in part-time charges was highlighted.

2.1.8.3 As a first step towards meeting the needs of ministers serving in part-time charges the Committee is planning a conference for such ministers in the Spring of 2001. Representatives of the Board of Ministry will be invited in the hope that a collaborative approach will offer solutions to the concerns of some.

2.2   Parish Reappraisal Day Conferences:
2.2.1 In early October 2000 the Committee organised Day Conferences in Dundee, Glasgow and Inverness. All but one Presbytery as well as other Constituent Committees of the Board were represented and the Committee found the reflections at the Conferences on current issues of great value. Topics for discussion included "Issues about Terminable and Reviewable Tenure", "Additional Appointments", "Presbytery Plans", and "Multiple Linkages".

2.2.2 In discussions on issues about Terminable and Reviewable Tenure there was agreement on the need for such tenures in the Church though particular importance was placed on the need for a clear statement of the reasons for a review being stated. In order to facilitate such reviews the Committee will be preparing a national database of reviewable and terminable tenure and will remind Presbyteries a year before a review is due. Guidelines for reviews will also be prepared and both the national database and guidelines will be available in September 2001.

2.2.2.1   The Committee is mindful of the instruction of the 2000 General Assembly to the Board of National Mission in these terms:

"Recognising the need for flexibility of tenure, instruct the Board in consultation with the Board of Ministry to give consideration to ways in which this flexibility can be balanced by greater support for ministers and families affected by such flexibility and bring proposals to a future General Assembly".

Matters relating to this instruction were considered at the Day Conferences and the thinking will be reflected in the work currently being undertaken by the Board of National Mission in consultation with the Board of Ministry and the Depute Secretary of the Board of Practice and Procedure on the revision of Acts IV (1984) and V (1984).

2.2.3 In the discussion on Additional Appointments those attending the Conferences expressed the view that all parish appointments should come under the scope of new legislation. Noting a request for clarity on issues such as contracts and Mission and Aid Fund relief the Committee has included a report on these discussions in the review of Acts IV (1984) and Act V (1984) already reported.

2.2.4 Discussions on Presbytery Plans included recommendations that five year plans would be of greater value than ten year plans since they gave more opportunity of responding to changing circumstances; and the importance that congregations are involved in the process of planning and consequently know about their future in a plan. Considering the importance being given to Presbytery Plans in the early stages of the work on reviewing Acts IV (1984) and V (1984) the Committee has included a report on these discussions in the papers for the group undertaking the revision.

2.2.5 The belief that in the future teams will have a greater part to play in ministry was emphasised in discussions on "multiple linkages". Such teams would include Ministers, Deacons, Readers, Elders, and others and it was suggested that short-term ministries as a basis for encouraging and training lay people to be more involved should be encouraged. The advantages of unions over linkages in rural settings were often highlighted.

2.3   National Mission Appointments:
2.3.1 The General Assembly of 2000 approved proposals for National Mission Appointments to replace appointments of ministers through "New Forms of Parish Ministry" and Parish Assistance placements. The year 2000 has been a year of transition.

2.3.2 The last appointments or re-appointments of ministers through "New Forms of Parish Ministry" were made during the year and were:

- Rev Michael Edwards was appointed as Community Minister in the Govan area of Glasgow and as Chaplain to the Braehead Shopping and Leisure Park
- Rev Tom Houston was appointed as Associate Minister at Glasgow: Priesthill and Nitshill
- Rev Alan McKenzie was appointed as Associate Minister at Glasgow: Drumchapel St Andrew's
- Rev Paul McKeown was appointed as Community Minister in the Queen's Cross area of Glasgow

The Committee places on record warm appreciation to these ministers and to all other ministers who have served through "New Forms of Parish Ministry" over recent years.

2.4   Parish Assistance:
2.4.1 The task of assessing parishes and projects which apply for a National Mission Appointment to support their mission and outreach vision is given to the Committee on Parish Assistance. This Committee is deeply aware of the challenge to recruit the right people, at the right time and in the right place.

2.4.2 53 Deacons are among the 76 who are supported by the Committee on Parish Assistance, and the Committee keeps terms and conditions constantly under review. Flexible working, professional and personal development, and team training are only a few of the issues recently considered.

2.4.3 New National Mission Appointments include ones at:

Cowdenbeath: Trinity: where a Development Project Worker has been recruited to assist this newly united congregation to achieve their aim of being a missionary congregation.

Glasgow: Gorbals: where two part-time appointments are supporting a congregation which is serving a parish soon to rise to a population of 17,000.

Paisley: Wallneuk North: where a worker assists in the development of a project begun by a Deacon.

Patna Waterside: where a Deacon is supporting a congregation during a transition period.

2.4.4 Other applications are presently being considered and fresh ones are encouraged.

2.4.5 The General Assembly of 2000 approved the following instruction to the Board of National Mission:

"Instruct the Board to formulate guidelines and criteria for the five yearly reviews of all National Mission Appointments and establish a procedure for personnel appraisal to run alongside these reviews".

The Board remitted consideration of this instruction to the Committees on Parish Reappraisal and Parish Assistance and at an early stage in discussions the Committees noted that "five yearly reviews" were no longer appropriate in the light of the new regulations for National Mission Appointments. These discussions continue and a Report will be offered to a future General Assembly.

2.5   New Charge Development

2.5.1 The passing of Act XIII 2000 by the 2000 General Assembly recognised a change in the way in which the Church is creating new charges. Not only are they being erected in what might be seen as traditional sites for new charges, the expanding housing developments of Scotland, but new charges are also being created on 'brownfield sites'. These are places where the Church may have had a congregation for some years which has found it difficult to adapt to changing circumstances or where the needs of its parish make it necessary to adopt a new identity for a new situation.

2.5.2 In Aberdeen the parish of Stockethill has been existence for some fifty years but in 1998 it became apparent to the Presbytery that it could no longer sustain congregational life as it is traditionally conceived. With the agreement of the congregation it was decided to dissolve the charge so that a new church could be created. In 1999 the Rev Ian Aitken was inducted and he has been seeking new ways of being church for that community.

2.5.3 An example of the second 'brownfield' development is Perth: Riverside which was created in March 2000. The parent congregation of St Andrew's and St Stephen's worshipped in a Victorian building on the edge of the parish and had made few significant inroads in the parish. The new charge now worships in the local school and a new building to be completed in 2001 is under construction. The Minister, Rev Fred Drummond, and the core team of Riverside are engaged in new ways of worship and are seeking to evangelise the parish from within rather than from outwith the community. The local YMCA have recently appointed a youth worker who will also work in the community in close co-operation with the people of Riverside.

2.5.4 In both these instances, and in all New Charge Developments, the charge is supervised and encouraged in mission by its own Commission as defined in Act XIII (2000). The Committee would wish to pay warm tribute to the men and women who serve on these Commissions in various parts of Scotland. There will be a growing need for New Charge Commissions as new charges are created and the Committee is always willing to hear from people with a vision for new and exciting ways of communicating the Gospel to become involved.

2.5.5 In the past year discussions have taken place with the following Church Extension Charges to change status to New Charge Developments: Aberdeen: Cove, Aberdeen: Bridge of Don Oldmachar, Paisley: St Ninian's Ferguslie and Dundee: Whitfield. The congregation of Greenock: Cartsdyke, a congregation in Full Status, is also in the process of changing status to that of a New Charge Development. In each instance this has been precipitated by a desire to better equip the local church for the task of serving Christ in a new age. The Committee is grateful to those ministers and office-bearers who have caught the vision and shown themselves willing to seek change.

2.5.6 The work that the Committee is supporting throughout Scotland is an exciting one. Jim Ritchie, the minister at Bridge of Don Oldmachar writes:

"When we arrived in Bridge of Don on 4th January 2000, and subsequently started work at Oldmachar in February, Maggie and I believed that God had called us here for a very specific reason; to build a new Church in a new way for a new millennium and to work with New Charge Development to help create a Scottish model of 'New Church' which could both challenge and encourage the National Church.

Almost one year on, there is so much to be thankful for; real answers to prayer, exciting challenges met, and many of the foundations put in place to secure a solid and exciting future for the congregation of Oldmachar.

In the first few months I felt that the primary responsibility was to get the public worship and prayer ministry right, both to encourage the congregation as to where we were going, and also to create an environment which would be welcoming, attractive, relevant and effective in communicating the Gospel to any new people from the community who would come as we began to reach out. So I restructured Sunday morning worship to be as contemporary and all-age friendly as possible, with a large emphasis on music, sharing, healing and the preached Word.

We now have in place a first-class praise team which has 16 members (8 musicians and 8 singers) who lead all of the worship. In most services I leave space for people to stand up and share the story of what God has been doing in their lives. On top of that we regularly give people the opportunity to come forward for prayer for healing and to share needs with the congregation to pray for. The preaching of the Word is obviously very important, but here too the style is contemporary and dialogical. Hopefully with the installing of 'Power-Point' in the next few months this too will develop.

Beyond Sundays I started a Wednesday evening Prayer and Worship time at which 35-40 people regularly attend. We had a month of early morning prayer from 7-8 am every day in June which again was supported by over 40 people, and we have introduced a weekly prayer time for everyone who takes part in the leading and planning of worship Maggie has developed a ladies house group at the manse on Monday mornings for young mums, and around 12 ladies come together to talk pray and study the Bible. We hope to increase the small-group ministry this year.

We also started a youth club on Monday evenings which attracts 75–80 teenagers. Again with additional resources the youth ministry will expand significantly in 2001.

The response to all of these new initiatives has been very encouraging, and there has been real growth around the church in every way. Numbers attending worship have grown considerably, we have admitted 45 new members (15 by profession of faith), givings have increased significantly, and there have

been many new people coming to worship, and it has been our greatest privilege to regularly lead people to faith in Jesus Christ as Lord.

As far as outreach is concerned, we had four concerts with contemporary Christian musicians throughout the year. A community barbecue and a children's club were held in July, an outreach weekend in September, and at both Easter and Christmas we took adverts in the local press and delivered quality printed invitations to the whole community inviting people to special outreach services. The response to all of these ventures was very encouraging.

Our task from here is to further expand all that is in place, and to continue to develop and nurture all areas of ministry, outreach and community involvement within our present vision statement.

To become a Christ-like community in this place, who honour God, worship Jesus, and go out in the power of the Spirit to make disciples and share the Father's love.

2.5.7 At the time of writing new buildings are in the process of being erected in Perth: Riverside and Kilwinning: Mansfield Trinity. Both of these have been designed in co-operation with those who will ultimately use them and will enhance the mission of the Church in those areas. The Committee believes that buildings are not simply bricks and mortar but expressions of our faith for the future. At a time when most people only hear of church buildings closing, the opening of new buildings is a sign that the Church is alive and, indeed, expanding. Through our buildings the Church also serves the community in which it is set. Through this interaction with its community the Church discovers how to be the Church for that place and better ways of communicating the Gospel to the people.

2.5.8. In this coming year the Committee will be holding a national conference for Ministers of New Charge Developments, their Presbytery Clerks and Conveners of Commissions so that we might review how the work is going and how better it might be both organised and expanded.

2.5.9 As we **travel from the old** to the new the support and development of new causes in the communities of Scotland must lie at the very heart of what we do as a Church. There can be no substitute for the enhancing and supporting of local mission by local Christian men and women. The structures offered by the new Act allow the Committee to offer this support, to permit innovation, to question why things are done so that the Church in the new areas of our land and the Church in the areas of growth and change might better be the Church of today.

3.   Travel to the New ... in resources for Mission and Evangelism.

3.1   'Encouraging mission and evangelism in Presbyteries and parishes through congregations of the Church of Scotland by means of research, development and training' is, within the policy of the Board, the responsibility of the Committee on Mission and Evangelism Resources which also seeks to develop a vision for this work in Scotland and to identify, originate and support projects in mission and evangelism in key areas of Scottish life.

3.1.1 The Committee on Mission and Evangelism Resources and its components offer support to the Church for missionary engagement in the areas of urban priority and rural congregational life; in the fields of science, technology, story-telling, drama and the visual arts; and of mission to the Scottish Asian communities. Through the Team of Advisers in Mission and Evangelism, the Missions Co-ordinator and a working group tackling the apologetic task of 'Why Believe?', people, ideas, programmes and resources are made directly available to congregations and Presbyteries across Scotland. It remains the policy of the Board that the prime agents for mission and evangelism throughout the land are strong congregations, adequately resourced.

3.1.2 During 2000, at the close of the Decade of

Evangelism, the Committee engaged in reviews of its key programmes and of the remits of a number of its senior staff and the support of the General Assembly is requested for conclusions reached with regard to:

- The Presbytery Development Process and a Decade of Evangelism
- Recognition of Rev James C. Stewart as a further part-time Evangelist
- Re-developing the Netherbow as a National Cultural Centre for the Church of Scotland

These are reported in detail in Sections 7.3, 7.4 and 7.5 respectively.

3.2   Why believe?

3.2.1 During the year, the Apologetics Committee was re-constituted and entitled 'Why Believe', with a remit to produce resources to equip congregations in the task of giving a reason for the Christian faith and to engage in the work of apologetics in key areas of Scottish thought and culture. In our very secular and sceptical age its vision is to provide resources and encouragement to those in Christian leadership positions so that they too can be confident in commending the Christian faith as 'true and reasonable'. (Acts 26:25). To accomplish this the Committee has been:

- developing a web page
- gathering together audio tapes (mainly for the use of ministers)
- forming a 'response group' to write letters/articles replying to press articles
- seeking the best response to the New Age phenomena especially as seen at Findhorn

3.3   Advisers in Mission and Evangelism

3.3.1 From their contacts with congregations and Presbyteries across Scotland, the team share their experience of entering a period of real transformation in church life and urge that it is essential to maintain focus on Mission and Evangelism. The picture world-wide is not quite as bleak as it sometimes seems to be in Scotland and in the UK generally. Spectacular church growth in

Asia, Africa and South America means that the overall picture is one of growth. It so happens that Britain is one of the most difficult mission-fields nowadays—what a challenge for our churches!

3.3.2 As we travel into the unknown future for our Church the Team of Advisers in Mission and Evangelism report that the following essentials of Mission and Evangelism will serve us well:

- Christianity, not 'churchianity'

  We want people to "come to Christ" not just come to church. In one congregation a new member was heard to say—"Hardly anyone talks about Jesus!" Could your Church be accused of that? Evangelism is about sharing Jesus, not about promoting the church.

- Evangelism is part of our overall mission

  God's word encourages us to be "doers of the word". Christ's mission was to 'free the prisoner', to 'bring healing and wholeness to the sick', to 'bring justice to the oppressed'. The local Church should be known in its local community for at least one way in which it is trying to be involved in Christ's mission to the world—an act of service to the local community or perhaps supporting the poor abroad, or even showing solidarity with the 'outsider' or 'outcast'. This may also include today looking after God's creation or standing alongside those at the sharp edge of contemporary life.

- "Some are evangelists …"

  It is fine to say that this particular calling is not for me—as long as you are prepared to accept that God does give each one of us some spiritual gift, and you endeavour to find out what that gift is and put it to good use. But we have overlooked and ignored this gift to our shame. Some are now suggesting that as many as 1 in 10 may have the gift of evangelist.

- "…. but all are witnesses!"

  Every ordinary Christian is called to be a witness to Jesus—to "gossip the Gospel". We spend most of our time at work, at home or in our leisure pursuits, and in quite natural ways when the opportunity arises, we have the privilege of sharing the good news. We need a holy dissatisfaction with the way we have been doing things. On too many occasions we are too polite. We ought to be "unashamed of the Gospel".

- Sunday worship is a key "shop window"

  Is it friendly and welcoming? Will I want to come back? Is there a good mix of ages? Many of the growing churches have put a lot of effort into making their basic Sunday service as accessible as possible to visitors and outsiders, and have also found that people are very open to an invitation to attend—perhaps initially special services at Harvest, Christmas or Easter. Some churches are holding services at times other than Sunday morning.

- 'Ministry by all the people of God'

  It is becoming increasingly important that although the minister has an important part to play and calling to fulfil, yet the recognising of the gifts of others means that many churches now have a rota of Bible readers, people who may offer prayers or have a gift in communicating with the children. Some congregations have a Sunday where the elders will be responsible for worship. It is about freeing up the people of God to discover the ministry already given to you and me.

In times of decline of church attendance these are very difficult days for everyone. But these are the days and this is the time that God has given to us. They are therefore also exciting and challenging times as we **travel to the new**.

3.4 Urban Priority Areas
3.4.1 Church life within the context of community change

Over the past three years the Urban Priority Areas Committee has reported on the immense demographic and environmental changes affecting many inner city areas and housing schemes. Within the context of these changes, the Church in the UPAs has an increasingly precarious existence. In line with housing stock, schools and other community facilities, many church buildings in UPAs have come to the end of their useful life and are in need of considerable renovation and in some instances, demolition. Local congregations do not have the financial resources to undertake these major works of refurbishment and redevelopment. Furthermore, in areas where poverty is most prevalent, congregations tend to be much smaller than in the past, some with fewer than 50 members attending worship weekly. Against this background some congregations feel that they lack the necessary resources to meet the challenges presented both by the church and community. Others have begun to let go of more traditional church organisations and programmes which they feel are no longer effective and are seeking new ways to share in the life of the wider community and proclaim the Gospel. Some of the most innovative work going on in the Church today is happening in UPA parishes.

3.4.2 Mission in time of change

In recent years, often with the assistance of the Priority Areas Fund, new projects linking church and community have come into being. The early signs are that these new developments, which can be life changing to the individuals involved, and which contribute so much to the life of the community do not bring people in great numbers to church membership. However it is clear that those who participate in them have a sense of belonging to the church. Within these contexts faith is nurtured; opportunity given for people's gifts to be expressed and the grace of God experienced in many ways. At this time when UPAs are changing so rapidly and radically, the Church may be tempted to focus its mission and place its hopes on newcomers to the private and more settled areas of these parishes. Such a focus may indeed secure the future of the Church but in turning from those who are most in need the Gospel as 'Good News to the Poor' will not be so clearly heard. The UPA Committee affirms the mission character of new projects bridging the gap between the Church and some of the poorest people in Scotland. In some of these projects new forms of church life are beginning to be seen.

3.4.3 The UPA Hearings

In response to an instruction of the General Assembly of 1999 "to investigate the building and wider needs of congregations in UPAs" four Hearings have been between Autumn 2000 and Spring 2001 in Glasgow, Dundee and Edinburgh. At the time of writing two Hearings have taken place. These one-day events in Garthamlock and Mid Craigie have given representatives from the wider Church the opportunity to see some UPA parishes at first hand, to listen and to engage in dialogue with people living and working in them. It is hoped that from this process proposals will emerge that will enable these parishes to continue to be truly recognised and resourced as Urban Mission Priority Areas. The Board intends to report to the General Assembly of 2002.

3.4.4 Presbytery Consultations

During the year ten consultations were organised by the UPA Committee in conjunction with Presbytery Mission Committees. They have taken place in Dundee, Irvine and Kilmarnock, Glasgow, Edinburgh, Hamilton, Ayr, Aberdeen and Stirling. Each consultation was designed to address issues raised by UPA congregations within the participating Presbytery and themes ranged from 'Working with Children' to issues around 'Being a Minority Church.'

3.4.5 UPA Working Groups

The UPA Committee's Working Groups have continued to meet throughout the year. The Urban Theology Group produced a paper on 'Working in Partnership' using as a case study the St Andrew's Bellsmyre 'Go for It' Children's Project. The Writers' Group produced 'Rainbow Journey': an All Age Worship Resource, offering a 'rainbow' of worship experiences, including music, song, drama, story and liturgy. The Ministry Group considered the training needs of ministry in UPAs and the Youth Work Group carried out a survey of all 330 UPA congregations, exploring the nature of the Church's engagement with young people. This survey indicated that the church's work with young people in UPAs is becoming increasingly difficult. Traditional youth organisations no longer hold the appeal that they once did, with congregations less able in terms of leadership and resources, to meet the challenges of working with young people in their communities. However it was also evident that the lives of many young people are being enriched through the relationships, opportunities and experiences which UPA congregations are offering to them. There was also a sense that many congregations would like to do more to convey God's love in practical ways and respond creatively to the many complex needs of young people living in areas of poverty. In response to this survey, and in partnership with the Committee on Parish Education, a Day Conference was arranged for those involved in church youth work in UPAs offering the opportunity for sharing information, ideas and resources.

3.5 Rural Committee

3.5.1 During 2000 the Rural Committee has continued to raise the profile of the rural church in Scotland. It has:

- supported a community renewal venture in Shetland
- produced three editions of its publication *The Rural Spirit* and a pamphlet for the Scottish Bible Society
- represented the Church in Scotland at the UK Rural Churches Group
- worked with the Board of Ministry to produce a study leave course for rural ministers
- brought together representatives from banks, unions, rural industry, charitable organisations and churches to discuss supporting rural life
- appointed a working group on mission to the fishing industry; seeking ways in which congregations serving fishing communities can give practical support
- represented the Church of Scotland at the Royal Highland Show

3.5.2 This year the Church of Scotland Stand at the Royal Highland Show was given a high profile through an article in *Life & Work* and by visits to the Stand by both the Princess Royal and the Moderator of the General Assembly, the Right Reverend Andrew McLellan. Both were pleased to discover the presence of the Church at the Show and commended the Rural Committee for its work in organising the Stand. The steady flow of people visiting the Stand all received a special eight-page tabloid newspaper edition of *The Rural Spirit* and a free copy of *Life & Work*.

3.5.3 The Rural Committee continues to engage with the pastoral side of the crisis situation in rural communities. A series of Presbytery events will be held across Scotland to explore the need for pastoral help for agriculture, fishing, forestry, and other areas of difficulty. Consideration is being given to organising a conference in 2002 which will consider the problems of small rural churches. The Committee also hopes that the future will see a more structured approach by the Church to working with all the caring agencies with a concern for rural communities.

3.5.4 As the rural church **travels to the new** much will depend upon congregations giving each other support and encouragement through sharing ideas and resources.

3.6 The Well—Asian Information and Advice Centre

3.6.1 The Well often finds itself dealing with people who have literally **travelled to the new**. 4,100 people visited The Well in 2000, a 33% rise on 1999. This included many more men, a reflection on the developing ministry of Sardar Ghauri, The Well's Faithshare partner. Recent changes in legislation have seen many new people arriving in Glasgow as asylum-seekers. The Well has been involved in lobbying the Scottish Parliament for changes which will improve conditions for those dispersed to Scotland and in supporting parishes where asylum-seekers are housed. The Well was also privileged to be part of a pilot scheme by Strathclyde Police for the third party reporting of racial incidents.

3.6.2 In October 2000 a woman whom The Well had been supporting was granted indefinite leave to remain in the UK after a seven-year wait. The relief of a positive decision has transformed her from a person made ill by fear and uncertainty to a confident, lively woman with everything to live for. She has also been on a spiritual journey. Coming to Scotland has been an opportunity for her to explore the Gospel properly for the first time.

3.6.3 The Community Worker, Catriona Milligan, gained an MSc this year. It is hoped that her dissertation entitled 'The Dilemma of Mission for Christian Community Work in a Multi-faith Context' will be useful to others seeking to do mission among people of other faiths. Catriona is (provided good notice is given!) available to speak to Presbyteries and congregations seeking to engage in mission in this field. Speakers and resources on the work of The Well are also available through the Guild Office as the unit has been selected as a project for support through the 'Strength for Living' initiative.

3.7   Projects in Evangelism

3.7.1   The Projects in Evangelism component of the Mission and Evangelism Resources Committee has responsibility for national support for congregational missions through the Mission's Co-ordinator, for part-time Evangelists recognised by the General Assembly, and for liaison with other projects and enterprises in mission and evangelism undertaken in Scotland.

3.7.2   Among those enterprises in mission followed with interest by the Projects in Evangelism Committee during the year 2000 was the millennium celebration based in Inverness: 'Praise in the Park'. Managed by an ecumenical committee, supported by local Presbyteries and administered by Rev Richard Gibbons, the Board's Highland Adviser, the event saw some four thousand people gathered at Pentecost in the Inverness Caledonian Thistle Stadium. The event included traditional and modern music including a psalm sung in Gaelic by schoolchildren from the Central Primary School in Inverness and the Back and Aridhantuim Primary Schools from Lewis and Harris. Richard Gibbons was the preacher and others involved included Runrig artist Calum MacDonald and Ross County footballer Brian Irvine. The event was recorded and later broadcast nation-wide by Grampian Television. Such praise and celebration

events continue to have an important part both in encouraging small and scattered congregations and in presenting a contemporary Christian challenge. Some 700 requested Christian literature at the conclusion of 'Praise in the Park'.

3.7.3   Based at the Board's Glasgow Office, the Missions Co-ordinator, Rev Paul Beautyman, offers nationally recruited and trained Mission Leaders and teams to support congregational initiatives in mission throughout the year. 2000 was an exciting year for missions in Scotland. As well as the existing summer programme, a new sports-based mission was run in Aboyne. This reached many young people who would not normally attend church events and shared God's love with them in ways relevant to their experience in the world of sport. High School missions were also a continuing development creating bridges between the Churches and High Schools as well as sharing the Christian faith to young people in the high school. During 2000 High School missions were organised in Grangemouth, Dunoon, Aboyne and Gordonstoun.

3.7.4   Resourcing some 30 existing missions and planning new missions is dependent on training Mission Leaders. This important work is done through the Mission Leaders Training Programme; currently nine people are training to lead missions. Another new development is the growth of action groups that are providing impetus for new methods of mission to a new generation. They are 'Dance Music & Drama', 'Multi-Media', 'Prayer', 'Publicity', 'Sports' and 'Worship'. All missions, training programmes and action groups offer new ways for the church to take part in mission to the young people of Scotland. Mission Teams will now come under the title of "Impact". This reflects the wide variety of teams and events working throughout the year.

3.7.5   Since planned missions are sometimes unable to proceed when demand for volunteers exceeds supply, the support of ministers and Kirk Sessions is requested to encourage individuals within their congregations to apply to join mission teams.

3.8 The Netherbow Arts Centre and John Knox House

3.8.1 A dispassionate observer could be forgiven for thinking that AD 2000 witnessed a renaissance in the Christian arts. In addition to major exhibitions such as *Light of the World* (City Arts Centre, Edinburgh), *Seeing Salvation* (National Gallery, London), and *A Poet in Paradise: Lord Lindsay and Christian Art* (National Gallery, Edinburgh), cairns, mosaics, tapestries, stained glass and murals were the focus of local church celebrations. Drama too was prominent with mystery plays, passions, pageants and *'AD'*, a controversial dramatisation of the life of Jesus by Edwin Morgan in Glasgow's Tramway. As Christmas 2000 approached poetry figured with the publication of the first anthology of Scottish Religious Poetry while film made its contribution with *S4C's The Miracle Maker*, an animated life of Jesus based on a novel by Murray Watts.

3.8.2 Much of this activity was not controlled or even generated by the Church but is witness to the activity of God in our wider culture, even when the debate aroused may be a difficult one for Church members. The vocation of Christians is to be interpreters engaged in the life of the world and of the arts, able to influence creative direction. This is the work and purpose of the Netherbow and never was it more in evidence than in the Millennium year.

3.8.3 In addition to supporting and encouraging many local AD 2000 ventures, The Netherbow mounted a national touring exhibition, 'Bible Story', combining seventy new illustrations by Jennifer Stevenson with texts from Christian Focus Publication's 'Little Hands Story Bible'. This large exhibition was supported by the St Margaret's Chapel Guild as a Millennium project. By the end of 2000 'Bible Story' had visited municipal galleries and museums in Falkirk, Edinburgh, Lanark, Greenock and Stirling with an accompanying programme of workshops.

3.8.4 2000 also saw publication of the Scottish Executive's 'Creating Our Future ... Minding Our Past: The National Cultural Strategy'. This document emphasises a distinctive yet diverse Scottish identity, the community arts, traditional arts and arts in education. Throughout the last decade of the 20th century the Netherbow has been campaigning and working in these areas. It is therefore timely that in 2000 The Netherbow Council brought together these themes in a proposed redevelopment of the centre as The Netherbow: Scottish Storytelling Centre. The aim is to reflect Scotland's story and to enable communities everywhere to engage with their own culture and take it forward to the future. The model is one of a 21st century Church actively involved in the cultural future of a politically reshaped Scotland. The operation of the John Knox House Museum will remain integral to this new expanded concept and role. Detailed proposals are provided in section 7.5.

3.9 Prayer, and partnership with others

3.9.1 Encouraging intercessory prayer for the work of mission and evangelism throughout Scotland is co-ordinated through the staff of the Kirkcaldy Office of the Board who issue a regular prayer diary supported by information and requests from a number of Church of Scotland Boards and other organisations. 'Praying Across Scotland' for the General Assembly is similarly resourced. Rev Robin McAlpine, Regional Adviser for the East of Scotland, keeps in touch with Presbytery Prayer Correspondents and occasional conferences are held for these and their congregational Prayer Secretaries.

3.9.2 A concern 'that the people of Scotland in all its parts' may hear and respond to the Gospel of Jesus Christ is shared not only by the Christian denominations but also by a growing number of independent, inter-denominational organisations. The Board, through the Committee on Mission and Evangelism Resources, seeks to keep in touch with potential partners and was pleased during 2000 to offer support to the first Scottish Cell Church Conference which aimed to bring together people interested in how this form of organising congregational life might be adapted to Scottish circumstances and promote Christian discipleship.

3.9.3 During the year the Board was pleased to accredit the ministry of the Church Pastoral Aid Society (CPAS) of their Scottish worker, Rev Richard Higginbottom, who has on a number of occasions worked in association with the Advisers in Mission and Evangelism. Within the Church of Scotland, the Board was pleased to approve an overture from the Board of Parish Education to support the 'Year of the Child'. Work on the issue of Baptism continues through the Joint Working Group led by the Panel on Doctrine and thanks are extended to those congregations and Presbyteries who reported to the Board their conclusions following use of the study guide 'The Impact of Baptism'.

3.10 Society, Religion and Technology Project

3.10.1 SRT at Large
3.10.1.1 The SRT Project's work is mission to the world of science and technology, seeking to be a Christian presence amongst the places where key issues in technology are discussed and decided. SRT's long term and much respected work in the field of biotechnology has now borne fruit with access to places of influence on genetic modification in crops and animals, cloning, stem cells, and related issues. What were once technical questions decided among experts behind closed doors are now public issues, widely debated. In 1992 SRT made a submission to the Government saying that the future of such sensitive areas of science lies in putting the ethical aspects high on the agenda and opening up technology policy to public engagement. Following the BSE crisis, GM food and cloning controversies, a landmark House of Lords' report on science and society indicates the Government's belated recognition of what SRT has been saying for many years. A new climate of openness exists which is giving SRT unparalleled opportunities to engage.

3.10.1.2 The Director has become a member of the Advisory Committee on Public Attitudes of the Biotechnology Research Council. He was an invited Observer to the Global Summit of National Bioethics Commissions and the UNESCO Bioethics Committee, and an invited speaker at international meetings of the OECD, Human Genome Project, the Society for Risk Analysis. At Biovision 2001 Dr Bruce was asked to address a major international gathering of researchers and industry on the ethical dimension of the future of biotechnology, citing SRT as a model. He has also made frequent appearances in national media, including the BBC, STV and Channel 4 news bulletins, Newsnight, the Today Programme, Good Morning Scotland, the Moral Maze and Hypotheticals.

3.10.2 Cloning and Stem cells
SRT became involved in the early development of the cloning issues through its genetic engineering working group and ongoing contacts with the Roslin Institute. This position placed it at the forefront of ethical and political discussion when the applications of cloning and embryonic stem cells became national and international issues. Because of its continuing close engagement with the cloning research community, Government departments and national ethical bodies, SRT has been given many opportunities to give a Christian view to these organisations at the highest levels and was twice invited to address Members of Parliament at the House of Commons. It has earned a rare position of trust and respect, both as to the understanding of the science and the ethics. This impact was seen in the Report of the Chief Medical Officer on Human Stem Cells and Embryonic Cloning published in August 2000,[1] which at several points responds to specific issues highlighted in the joint submission SRT made with the Board of Social Responsibility[2].

3.10.3 Genetic Modification Update
3.10.3.1 A Report to the Assembly on the interface of GM animals and humans is given as Appendix V. Earthscan have asked SRT to produce a second edition of its report on genetic engineering in non-human species "Engineering Genesis" for Autumn 2001. The working group has reconvened to update it to reflect the important

changes on GM food, risk, ecology and Third World aspects since 1998. The Director has chaired a study on GM foods for the Evangelical Alliance which is to be published by Paternoster later in 2001.

3.10.3.2 Genetically modified food trials in Scotland have provoked widely varying local responses. Strong opposition in the Black Isle in August contrasted with more equivocal reactions in Inverurie. In talking to groups around Scotland on GM food, the SRT Director's impression is less of outright opposition as a desire for independent information about GM which people can trust, and make up their own minds. One reason given for the especial Black Isle concern is the perceived damage to the marketing image of "pure" Highland foods. This is a fear largely based on a connotation of "GM", but it is only meaningful *if* there really is some significant health or ecological risk from the particular GMO's. That is what the trials are intended to help show. It is surely more important to get to the truth of the matter, one way or the other. A similar effect was also seen in press and NGO comment on the accidental mixing of GM and non-GM oil seeds in a batch from Canada. It was described with words like contamination, tainted crops and genetic pollution, almost as though the gene was radioactive waste. In contrast English Nature said that the risk that a viable species would result was extremely low. Scottish experts say small amounts of gene flow may occur with some GM crops, but to present this as "pollution" is only valid if it causes an actual, significant ecological harm. This is the reason for holding field trials, albeit they will not answer all the questions. The alternative is to decide no GM risk is tenable, regardless of whether it was genuine.

3.10.4 Climate Change and Fuel Prices : What can your Congregation do?

3.10.4.1 Three events in Autumn 2000 tell an eloquent story about climate change. Record rainfall, floods and storms across Europe brought home the reality that we are indeed changing the climate, but inter-governmental talks in The Hague collapsed. They failed to agree how

to implement even a few percent reductions in carbon dioxide emissions which are almost irrelevant by comparison with the necessary 60% reduction which the Royal Commission on Environmental Pollution earlier in the year eloquently spelt out. One implication is that we are paying far too little for our petrol because the price at the pump fails to include the climatic, pollution and health damage our cars are causing. The Government increased fuel taxes in part to reflect this, but then defaulted on their promises by failing to ring fence the revenues for the environment. The population could not see any benefits accruing from the increased prices and not surprisingly this led to the fuel price revolt, encouraging the worst in our instincts at the very point when the Government could have put down a marker to encourage responsibility and altruism.

3.10.4.2 This is all the more reason for the Churches to take a lead in environmental action, as a witness that faith in God can give people the motivation to go the extra mile to care for His creation. The Eco-Congregation scheme, launched in Scotland on 28th March 2001, now provides congregations with the impetus and the resources to find ways locally to practise what we preach about stewarding the environment. Congregations all over Scotland are urged to join the scheme, make a difference, and have at the heart of worship and life care for God's creation.

[1] Ministry of Health (2000) *Stem Cell Research: Medical Progress with Responsibility*, Report of the Chief Medical Officer's Expert Group (Donaldson Report), HMSO: London

[2] Church of Scotland (1999) *Submission to the Chief Medical Officer's Expert Group on Cloning(CEGC)*, October 1999, Society, Religion and Technology Project and the Board of Social Responsibility, Church of Scotland, Edinburgh.

3.11 Personnel:

3.11.1 During the year the Rev Ian Moir retired after a distinguished ministerial career latterly as Urban Mission Adviser, and Rev Martin Johnstone was appointed Urban Priority Areas Adviser. A limited restructuring of the team of Advisers in Mission and Evangelism was concluded with the appointment of Rev David Curie as Senior Adviser with particular regional responsibility for Edinburgh and Presbyteries in southern Scotland. A prime objective of this restructuring was to give a greater geographical focus to the team. Towards the end of 2000 the Presbytery of Dunoon decided not to continue the externally funded post of Mission Adviser to the Presbytery when the current contract expires in November, the Presbytery will be offered such support as the remaining team can offer.

3.11.2 At the Netherbow, Miss Joanna Bremner (Storytelling Co-ordinator) was re-appointed for a two year term thanks to the availability of full external funding; and at The Well Asian Advice and Information Centre the manager Community Worker, Mrs Catriona Milligan, was re-appointed for a further five years with the Board agreeing to guarantee funding for the post's salary for a second term.

3.11.3 The work of the Committee on Mission and Evangelism Resources depends very largely on the initiatives and vision of its component committees and working groups. Particular thanks are due this year to Mr David H. Maxwell, who stepped down as Convener of the Netherbow Council during 2000, and to Rev John Miller (Glasgow: Castlemilk East) who completed an extended term as Convener of the Urban Priority Areas Committee. The UPA Committee expresses its appreciation of his great contribution to its work in the knowledge that his spiritual leadership will now be experienced more widely in the life of the Church.

4.   Travel to the New ... in Chaplaincy

4.1   The Board's responsibility for the support and development of Chaplaincy is undertaken by three Sub-Committees of the Committee on Chaplaincies.

- Hospitals, Healthcare and Universities
- Church and Industry
- Prison Chaplaincies

4.2   Chaplaincy in Hospitals, Healthcare and Universities

4.2.1   Spiritual Care and Healthcare Chaplaincy Training in the National Health Service

In the past year the Department of Health Gain of the Scottish Executive has set up a Steering Group entitled "Spirituality in the NHS" which has discussed the proposals for the appointment of a whole-time Chaplaincy Training and Development Officer for Scotland prepared by the Sub-Committee and submitted with the agreement of the major denominations by the Scottish Churches Committee on Healthcare Chaplaincy. This Group, which has met twice, is chaired by a member of the Department of Health Gain and consists of representatives of faith groups in Scotland, chaplaincy professional bodies, researchers and others. The Sub-Committee welcomes this development as a positive response by Government to the growing interest in Healthcare Chaplaincy and Spiritual Care. The visit last May by Susan Deacon, MSP, Minister for Health and Community Care, to the Conference for Chaplains at Crieff, at which she made the encouraging statement that she was minded to fund the whole-time post of Training and Development Officer subject to certain conditions was yet another indication of this interest. A firm commitment to funding the post has now been received and the necessary procedures have been put in hand. The Board will continue to fund the part-time appointment of the Rev Fred Coutts, one of the whole-time chaplains at Aberdeen Royal Infirmary, who has agreed to extend his period of sterling service.

4.2.2   Appointing Authority

Since the inception of the National Health Service in 1948, NHS hospital chaplains in Scotland have been appointed by Church authorities with the concurrence of NHS authorities. Recently a few NHS Trusts have decided to make direct appointments themselves; the majority, however, appear to favour the established procedure of Church appointments. It is essential that all chaplains, whole-time and part-time, enjoy the whole-hearted co-operation and support of the NHS staff with whom they will work. The Sub-Committee has encouraged Presbyteries when filling part-time vacancies to ensure that the selection process involves both Church and NHS representatives. A circular regarding the appointment of chaplains is expected to be issued shortly by the Scottish Executive. The Sub-Committee is committed to ensuring that the best appointments are made irrespective of the denomination of the applicants.

4.2.3 Supporting Healthcare Chaplaincy Staff
On 13 June 2000 a day conference was held in the Church Offices attended by the Convener of the Board of National Mission, members of the Sub-Committee and nearly all of the whole-time chaplaincy staff appointed by the Church and NHS Trusts. Issues discussed included the effects of NHS Trust Reconfiguration, the European Working Time Directive, on-call cover, employment of chaplains and chaplains' support. The Sub-Committee continues to fulfil its responsibilities in the selection, appointment, training and support of chaplains who welcomed this further opportunity to meet with the Sub-Committee and address with them these issues. They also welcomed the Sub-Committee's desire to forge even closer links to support all chaplains in their busy, challenging and, at times, stressful ministries

4.2.4 Service of Introduction
For some time the Sub-Committee has felt the need to revise and improve some sections of the present Orders for Ordination, Induction and Introduction to Presbyteries. After careful consideration and, with the help of practising chaplains, the Sub-Committee issued guidelines in November which it believes will assist Presbyteries in their planning of Services of Introduction for whole-time healthcare chaplains.

4.2.5 Review of Chaplaincy Provision in the light of the Community Care Act
At the 1999 General Assembly an addendum was agreed which asked the Sub-Committee to "review chaplaincy provision and responsibility in the light of the Community Care Act". The report of its findings is given as Appendix VI below.

4.2.6 Personnel
This past year has seen the retiral of three long serving hospital chaplains—Rev Melville Schofield, Edinburgh; Rev Robin Rae, Dundee; and the Rev Alan Stoddart, Aberdeen. In addition the following three chaplains' assistants have resigned - Mairi Lovett, in Aberdeen, to begin training for the ministry; Rev Alison Swindells also in Aberdeen, to parish ministry; and Rev Alison Wagstaff in Edinburgh, to hospice chaplaincy. The Sub-Committee warmly acknowledges the faithful and dedicated service given by all these staff and the valuable contribution they made to the well-being of the hospital communities in which they ministered.

The Sub-Committee has welcomed a number of new chaplains in the same period. In Edinburgh, the Rev Alistair Ridland and the Rev Iain Telfer; and in Aberdeen, Muriel Knox and Monica Stewart.

4.2.7 University Chaplaincy
The Department maintains its contact with full-time university chaplains of all denominations and one of their number is represented on the Sub-Committee. It also hosts an annual conference for full-time chaplains. At the most recent conference the chaplain's role in personal relationships in a university setting, the chaplain and the morale of the university, and the stresses they encounter were amongst the topics discussed. Chaplains who attended indicated the conference gave them the opportunity to provide support and genuine care for one another and the sense of belonging to a team. They confirmed that the conference greatly helped to underline the support that the Church of Scotland gives to them all.

During the year the part-time appointment of the Rev Scott Blythe at the Robert Gordon University, Aberdeen was made full-time. At Aberdeen University the Rev Gillean Maclean moved on to parish ministry and was succeeded by the Rev Easter Smart, formerly assistant at St Columba's Pont Street, London. At the University of Edinburgh, following the retirement of the Rev Iain Whyte, the university appointed the Rev Diane Williams formerly Anglican chaplain at Lancaster University.

4.3 Church and Industry

4.3.1 The Church and Industry Committee of the Board acts jointly as the Committee for Scottish Churches Industrial Mission and a Report on SCIM is offered in Appendix VII.

4.3.2 The Board's commitment to Scottish Churches Industrial Mission includes the funding and employment of four Industrial Mission Organisers:

Rev Erik Cramb—Tayside and National Co-ordinator
Rev Alister Goss—West of Scotland
Rev Elisabeth Spence—Glasgow
Mr Lewis Rose, DCS—North of Scotland

4.3.3 The Board acknowledges with appreciation the funding and staffing support given to Scottish Churches Industrial Mission by other denominations and by industry. Particular mention is made of the Industrial Mission Trust through which commerce and industry is invited to contribute to the maintenance and development of the work of Scottish Churches Industrial Mission. Through these wider contributions the following chaplains are supported:

Rev Angus Smith—North East (employed by the Board with funding through the Oil Industry)
Rev Bill Rayne—Edinburgh (Methodist Appointment)
Mr John Hopper—Edinburgh (Edinburgh City Mission Appointment)
Mrs Dorothy Robertson—Gyle Shopping Centre, Edinburgh
Mr William Shirlaw—Buchanan Galleries Shopping Centre, Glasgow

4.3.4 Aware of the development of many new shopping malls around Scotland, the Board has sought to encourage chaplaincy to staff and mission to shoppers. A Retail Chaplaincies Network has been established and a conference is planned.

4.4 Chaplaincy in Prisons
4.4.1 Prison Visits
Members of the Sub-Committee made visits to two Scottish establishments during 2000, in May to HM Prison Edinburgh and in October to HM Prison Peterhead. In the visit to Edinburgh members met with the Chaplaincy Team and toured selected areas of the prison including the recently refurbished Chapel. The Sub-Committee was encouraged by the dedicated work being undertaken by the chaplains especially in the area of pastoral care of prisoners. The visit to Peterhead was an encounter with an institution with an uncertain future. Extensive meetings with Prison Management and chaplains led to the Sub-Committee writing on 31st October 2000 to the Chief Executive of the Scottish Prison Service (SPS) "to endorse the view that it would be no easy matter to replicate the unique culture of Peterhead elsewhere in the SPS estate and that to do so would halt the progress that is being made in the treatment of sex offenders for some considerable period". Peterhead is recognised world-wide as a centre of excellence and the Sub-Committee was concerned that the same standards of work would be maintained in the future.

4.4.2 Moderator's Visits
The Moderator of the General Assembly completed a hectic Autumn schedule of visits to all Scottish Prisons. These visits highlighted prison issues in general and have given the Sub-Committee the opportunity to advance a number of matters pertaining to chaplaincy.

4.4.3 Contracting Out and Full-time Chaplaincy
A particular result of the visits by the Moderator is the beginning of negotiations between the Churches and the SPS which could result in the contracting out of the chaplaincy service from the SPS to the Churches. A full account of these discussions is given in Section 7.7.

4.4.4 Support of and Communication with Chaplains
Minutes of the Sub-Committee are now routinely sent to all Church of Scotland chaplains for their interest with requests for comments as appropriate. Additionally the first of a series of Biennial Conferences for Church of Scotland chaplains has been arranged for 20 March 2001

to which the Moderator has been invited to report and discuss the issues raised during his prison visits. Opportunity will also be given to chaplains to raise their own issues and concerns with the Sub-Committee. It is hoped that the above measures will encourage a two-way flow of communication between the Sub-Committee and chaplains.

4.4.5 Through Care

The Sub-Committee has a concern for the through care of prisoners and is considering ways in which the Church can become more actively involved in offenders' reintegration to society following their release from custody. As a first step plans are being made for a Day Conference to which representatives of those agencies already involved in through care will be invited to describe the work which is currently being undertaken.

4.4.6 The Challenge

The past year has been a challenging time for the Sub-Committee which is keen to respond to the opportunities which have emerged during this period.

5. Travel to the New ... in the Board's Residential Centres

5.1 St Ninian's Centre, Crieff

5.1.1 The work of St Ninian's Centre, Crieff, has since the 2000 General Assembly been under review by a Special Commission. Throughout this period the Board has sought to be supportive to the ongoing work of the Centre and reports that with financial assistance from the Board of Stewardship and Finance work was undertaken at the Centre to obtain Fire Certificates for both the Main Building and Thomson House.

5.2 Badenoch Christian Centre

5.2.1 2000 was a year of consolidation for the Badenoch Christian Centre with a slight increase in use over 1999. Minor improvements have been made to the fabric which also keeps the Centre up to date with health, safety and fire regulations.

5.2.2 As always guests have come from wide geographical, social and spiritual backgrounds; and their programmes have been as varied. The Centre hosted some "choices" breaks of optional activities for older people in the low Autumn season, and the Centre has been marketed more widely than in recent years.

6. Finance and Property and Safety

6.1 Finance

6.1.1 The Board is grateful to all who financially support mission in Scotland. Three sources combine to support mission in Scotland through the Board—the Mission and Aid Fund, interest from the Board's capital reserves, and contributions from agencies such as NHS Trusts and the Oil Industry for the appointment of chaplains.

6.1.2 Despite this income the Board is using reserve capital as well as interest from the capital. In 2000 £549,652 was used which compares with the budgeted deficit of £831,000 on the general fund.

6.1.3 Projected deficits for 2001 and 2002 amount to £1,032,000 and £1,320,000 respectively. But the Board has agreed to a responsible use of its capital to offset these sums until the deficit can be eliminated altogether. A review of investment policy and a continual review of current work are also being undertaken by the Board to control the use of capital.

6.2 Special Mission Trusts

6.2.1 The Trustees of the Special Mission Trusts agreed eleven grants during 2000 and these were awarded to a variety of projects including two large Pentecostal praise events—"Praise in the Park" in Inverness and the Presbytery of Glasgow and Glasgow Churches Together event in Hampden Park.

The annual disbursement of the D.L. Rodger Bequest benefited four projects within the Presbytery of Glasgow. The Asian Advice and Information Centre known as "The Well" was awarded £6,000; the Cambuslang and Rutherglen Reachout Trust was awarded £2,000 to help finance a youth worker; Govan Ecumenical Youth

Association was awarded £1,000 to help finance the Summer programme of activities for young people; and the Mission Strategy Committee of the Presbytery received £4,000 to help fund a mission fund adviser.

6.2.2 The annual disbursement of the MacGregor Trusts benefited twelve projects in Highland and Island Presbyteries including work undertaken by the Scottish Council on Deafness.

6.2.3 The "School's Out" Fund, which gives grants to newly formed out of school care groups, continued to make awards during the year and funds are still available for disbursement.

6.2.4 Information and application forms for any of the above trusts can be obtained from the Secretary to the Trustees at the Department of National Mission Office.

6.3　　Property and Safety

6.3.1　Health and Safety
The Health and Safety Policy of the Board continues to be developed along with a comprehensive Safety Policy now in place. Training for staff and a number of safety issues is ongoing with a view to the Board endeavouring to comply with current and prospective legislation. In 2000 no reportable accidents were recorded. The Board places great emphasis on the health, safety and welfare of its staff, visitors and contractors and continues to develop its health and safety programme accordingly.

6.3.2 As part of this development the Board has resolved to separate the responsibilities of Property and Safety Manager and Secretary of the Committee on New Charge Development. This has allowed Mr Colin Wallace to concentrate on Property and Safety responsibilities with the Rev Willie John Macdonald assuming responsibility for the administration of the Committee on New Charge Development.

6.3.3　Property
In 2000 the Board of National Mission disposed of properties at 47 Millersneuk Drive, Lenzie, Glasgow and 34 Mellerstain Road, Kirkcaldy and two further properties are currently being marketed at 42 Elm Row, Edinburgh and 51 North Berwick Crescent, East Kilbride.

6.3.4　Development
The Board undertook the development of the North Kessock Mission Hall to provide a worship centre on the ground level and a Highland Office for the Board (formerly known as the Inverness Office) on the upper floor.

The Board continues to develop its cyclical and proactive maintenance programme throughout its properties.

6.3.5　Glasgow Lodging House Mission and St Francis in the East Church House
The Board owns two properties in Glasgow which are the bases for the imaginary missionary work at the Glasgow Lodging House Mission and at St Francis in the East Church House. The work carried on in these buildings is managed by local Committees and the Board seeks to be as co-operative as resources permit, not least in the maintenance of the properties. In particular in 2000 the Board engaged in discussions with the Presbytery of Glasgow and other General Assembly Boards on the development of the Glasgow Lodging House Mission.

7.　　Background to Deliverance

7.1　　Revision of Acts IV (1984) and V (1984)
7.1.1 The Committee on Parish Reappraisal has been giving consideration to the possibility of revising Acts IV (1984) and V (1984).

7.1.2 The approval of these two Acts by the Church of Scotland General Assembly in 1984 proved a significant step forward. Until that time on the occasion of a vacancy in a charge readjustment was only raised in some vacancies. The 1984 Act ensured that the question of readjustment was raised in every vacancy bringing a sense of equality throughout the Church.

7.1.3 Until 1990 there were no changes to the Act but throughout the 1990s there have been a number of developments and alterations to suit the needs of the changing Church.

7.1.4 The Committee believes that over the next few years there could be a substantial revision of the whole legislation.

7.1.5 At this General Assembly the Committee offers three particular significant changes for wide discussion in the Church:

(a) The first is to allow Presbyteries the possibility of "fast-tracking" vacancies when decisions taken are in accordance with an Agreed Five Year Plan.

> Throughout the 1990s Presbytery Planning has gained an ever more significant place in the life of the Church and the majority of Presbyteries now have Agreed Plans with the Committee.
>
> As a natural progression of this work, the Committee is now inviting the Church to give consideration to appraisal being considered separately from a vacancy in a charge. If this thought was to be taken forward it would mean adjustment being determined not at the time of a vacancy but rather as part of a more thorough planning process. The proposal before the Church now is that if Presbyteries agree Five Year Rolling Plans with the Committee that decisions on vacancies can be "fast-tracked" with no need for the concurrence of the General Assembly Committee. This could considerably reduce the time between a vacancy being reported and permission being given to call. If however there was no Agreed Plan then the normal procedure as detailed in Act IV (1984) would apply.

(b) The second is to give the possibility for Presbyteries and congregations to "fast-track" each vacancy.

> The Committee believes that the Presbytery process for dealing with vacancies could be streamlined by removing virtually every instance where procedures presently get "held up" for weeks pending the next full Presbytery meeting.

Suggestions are welcome for ways in which such a streamlining could be achieved.

(c) The third is to give consideration to a variety of matters surrounding the role and membership of the Vacancy Committee.

> The Committee would first invite comments on the title "Vacancy Committee". In other areas of life a more common term would be "Search Committee", and the Committee believes that this might be a more accurate and positive way to describe the work that this group has to do on behalf of a congregation. Secondly, thoughts would be welcome on the size and membership of the Vacancy or Search Committee. It is hard to think of any other organisation that places so many people on an appointing group. The sheer size of a Vacancy Committee means that it is hard to conduct focussed interviews, difficult to maintain confidentiality and continuity, and easy to find sub-groups or factions at work. A smaller group working in a more efficient way could achieve significant streamlining of the process. The Committee would be grateful for comments on whether the Church might be ready to trust a smaller number of people (say 6 to 8) to undertake this important work. Comment is also invited on the possibility of Presbytery Assessors having an increased input on this group. Thirdly, there is the question of how this group is appointed. Does this really require a congregational meeting? Could the Kirk Session, for instance, be given the responsibility for finding a balance of people who both represented the spiritual leadership of the congregation and had the requisite skills in interviewing and selection processes?

7.1.6 The Committee believes that it would be of value if these proposals were discussed by Presbyteries and invites responses in terms of the Deliverance of the Board of National Mission by 13th December 2001.

7.1.7 The responses given will greatly assist the

Committee in seeking to determine the ways in which revised legislation should be framed.

7.2   Ministry with Deaf People

7.2.1 The General Assembly of 1997 approved a Scheme of Ministry with Deaf People from 1998 to 2002 in terms of a report from the Committee on Parish Reappraisal.

7.2.2 The scheme involved the appointment of three Ministers under "New Forms of Parish Ministry" with the appointments beginning on 1st January 1998 for five year periods. All salary and related costs and a budget for expenses were to be met. Societies for the Deaf would continue to be invited to provide office accommodation and additional resources where possible.

7.2.3 The detail of these appointments as approved in May 1997 were as follows:

(a) One Minister to be based in Edinburgh with a twin remit of ministering to the congregation at the Albany Deaf Church including deaf people in the Lothians and Fife and also of developing ministry to the Deaf throughout Scotland. The Minister appointed in Edinburgh would be funded for the five year period by funds received from the Committee on the Maintenance of the Ministry and the Board of Stewardship and Finance.

(b) One Minister would be based at the John Ross Memorial Church for the Deaf, Glasgow, with a remit for the Glasgow area and the South West of Scotland including the Ayrshire Mission for the Deaf. This Minister would be funded from the "New Forms of Parish Ministry" budget of the Board of National Mission.

(c) One Minister would be based at St John's Church for the Deaf, Aberdeen, with a remit for Aberdeen and the North of Scotland. The Minister would be funded from the "New Forms of Parish Ministry" budget of the Board of National Mission.

7.2.4 From the outset the Ministers appointed have been designated Community Ministers for Ministry with

Deaf People and since 1998 the following Ministers have served in the appointments:

(a) At the Albany Deaf Church, Edinburgh, the Rev Dr Mary Weir served from 1st April 1998 to 24th April 1999 and from 24th October 1999 the Rev Alistair Kelly has acted as the locum Community Minister.

(b) At the John Ross Memorial Church for the Deaf, Glasgow, the Rev Richard C. Durno has served from 20th June 1998 to the present.

(c) At St John's Church for the Deaf, Aberdeen, the Rev John R. Osbeck has served from 1st January 1998 to the present.

7.2.5 The Committee on Parish Reappraisal appointed a support group consisting of the Executive of the Committee, the Convener and Secretary of the Chaplaincies Committee of the Board of National Mission, and Mr Alex Harrison, Secretary of the Stewart Lochrie Memorial Fund. The support group has met with the three Community Ministers on a quarterly basis and has visited the three churches at which their work is based.

7.2.6 The meetings have included a consideration of reports from the Community Ministers as well as pursuing matters related particularly to Ministry with Deaf People. The group has been encouraged in its work by Canon James Clarke, the Adviser for Ministry with Deaf People of the Church of England, and the Rev Patricia Rogers of "Visible Communications" which seeks to develop video resources for worship and learning within the Deaf Community.

7.2.7 Early in 2000 the support group gave consideration to the workload of the three Community Ministers and recommended to the Committee on Parish Reappraisal that the Minister based in Edinburgh be relieved of the responsibility of "developing ministry to the Deaf throughout Scotland". The understanding was that such national development would become the responsibility of the support group itself.

The Committee on Parish Reappraisal, in noting that

the decision had been taken in full consultation with the three Community Ministers, resolved that the Presbytery responsibilities of the Community Ministers should from that date be as follows:

Community Minister based in Edinburgh:

Edinburgh	West Lothian	Lothian
Melrose and Peebles	Duns	Jedburgh
Falkirk	Stirling	Dunfermline
Kirkcaldy	St Andrews	Dunkeld and Meigle
Perth	Dundee	Angus

Community Minister for Deaf People based in Glasgow:

Annandale and Eskdale	Dumfries and Kirkcudbright	Wigtown and Stranraer
Ayr	Irvine and Kilmarnock	Ardrossan
Lanark	Paisley	Greenock
Glasgow	Hamilton	Dumbarton
South Argyll	Dunoon	Lorn and Mull

Community Minister for Deaf People based in Aberdeen:

Aberdeen	Kincardine and Deeside	Gordon
Buchan	Moray	Abernethy
Inverness	Lochaber	Ross
Sutherland	Caithness	Lochcarron/ Skye
Uist	Lewis	Orkney
Shetland		

7.2.8 Aware of the need to present a Report to the General Assembly of 2001, the Committee on Parish Reappraisal arranged a special meeting of the support group on 29th September 2000 and invited to it representatives of Societies for the Deaf, Congregations for the Deaf, and others with a special interest in ministry with deaf people. At the close of the meeting the following statements were agreed by all present:

- that the meeting affirmed that the Scheme for Ministry among Deaf People should continue; and
- that in the future of the Scheme consideration should be given not only to maintaining the present pattern of ministry among Deaf People but also a consideration should be given to developmental ministry.

7.2.9 When the Committee on Parish Reappraisal received on 17th October 2000 a report of the special meeting of the support group the Committee resolved to propose to the 2001 General Assembly that the Scheme of Ministry with Deaf People becomes an ongoing part of the Ministry and Mission of the Church of Scotland and a Deliverance of the Board of National Mission reflects this decision. The hopes expressed that the Boards of Stewardship and Finance and Ministry would feel able to continue their support for this vital area of work.

7.2.10 During the years when the Scheme has been in place there have been a number of new initiatives in Ministry with Deaf People. One of particular mention is the decision taken by the Albany Deaf Church in Edinburgh to move from the premises of the Society for the Deaf in Edinburgh and the East of Scotland in Albany Street, Edinburgh, to share Greenside Parish Church, Edinburgh, with the congregation. All involved are appreciative of the part played in this process by the Rev Alistair Kelly as locum Community Minister.

7.3 The Presbytery Development Process and a Decade of Evangelism

7.3.1 Background

The 1983 General Assembly instructed *"the Department of Home Mission to prepare a coherent, long-term, Presbytery—centred programme for the evangelisation of the people of Scotland…"* and this programme found expression in a report to the 1985 General Assembly under the title "Presbytery Development Process—the National

Strategy for Evangelism". This report was approved by the Assembly and a special Committee of the Board kept the process under review until it was subsumed into the Mission and Evangelism Resources Committee in 1992. In that year the Board reported: *"The responsibility of ensuring the evangelisation of Scotland has been laid on congregations by the General Assembly. The congregation is the basic missionary unit. However, the Presbytery can encourage that missionary potential by fostering a partnership round a common vision. In order to work in depth to establish mission in the heart of the Presbytery, Presbyteries will be encouraged to enter into a partnership with the advisers in Mission and Evangelism to work for an appropriate period of mission development."*

7.3.2   Presbytery Partnerships

7.3.2.1 Over the years, Presbytery Partnerships were initiated in the Presbyteries of Greenock, Dunkeld and Meigle, Kirkcaldy, Perth, and Ayr. Each Partnership had its own local variation and duration though none were intended to last for more than two years and their basis was a core 'Partnership Committee' working with the Regional Adviser to encourage and coordinate. A Day Conference of the five Partnerships was held in 1997 and by 1999 the Committee on Mission and Evangelism Resources had agreed the following achievements and failures:

7.3.2.2 The achievements of these partnerships were agreed as:

- Initial enthusiasm generated
- Helped to focus both Presbyteries and congregations on a missionary outlook
- Involved both ordained and non-ordained and helped networking
- Produced joint celebration occasions
- Encouraged joint training events
- Involved regional Advisers within the life of Presbyteries

7.3.2.3 The failures of these partnerships were agreed as:

- Enthusiasm was short lived
- Congregations came together to get a 'state of the nation' report and agreed things were dire!
- Take up of training and conference opportunities was limited.
- The Partnership Committees tended to initiate and run programmes themselves instead of enabling the regular Presbytery Committees
- By and large the structures of Presbyteries were left unchanged.

7.3.2.4 No formal Partnerships have in fact been entered into since 1995 though individual Advisers were involved, sometimes deeply, in initiatives taken by the following Presbyteries:

- Presbytery of Glasgow: development of the Presbytery Mission Plan
- Presbyteries of Uist, Lewis and Lochcarron and Skye: provision of training
- Presbytery of Sutherland: 'Mission Sutherland'
- Presbytery of Kincardine and Deeside: restructuring of Presbytery

The concept of developing mission as a focus for Presbytery was latterly pursued by the joint initiative with the Board of Practice and Procedure to encourage Presbyteries to conduct forward-looking quinquennial visitations: particular contact was made with the Presbyteries of Edinburgh, Kirkcaldy, and Irvine and Kilmarnock. This initiative is being taken forward by the Board of Practice and Procedure. Finally, with the creation of the joint Inter-Board on Presbytery Boundaries on which National Mission is represented, this aspect of the Presbytery Development Process may be said to have achieved its objective of rooting forward-looking missionary thinking in the structures of the Kirk.

7.3.3 The National Strategy for Evangelism

Working in a detailed way with particular Presbyteries

was never the whole of the 'National Strategy', best outlined in the report to the 1995 General Assembly (p.390, section 3.1). The Prayer Vision shared then remains at the heart of the Board's work as are the two strategic concepts: "Every congregation a missionary congregation and every Presbytery a missionary Presbytery". The Strategy's "five thrusts", however, (Prayer/People/Partnership/Project Rejoice!/Prophetic Penetration) though their underlying principles remain sound have not achieved widespread understanding as a coherent programme—perhaps because they can too easily be interpreted to suit circumstances—and the Mission and Evangelism Resources Committee has now determined both to abandon use of the 'five Ps' as part of its vision and also to cease to offer formal Presbytery Partnerships on the lines adopted before 1995.

7.3.4 The Decade of Evangelism

7.3.4.1   What has been learnt and achieved during this last decade of the 20th century? The programme 'The Decade of Evangelism' originated with Churches Together in England and a review—'20 from 10'—has recently been published under the auspices of the Churches Together in England Group for Evangelisation, 2000. The main points are as follows and the whole document is available on the internet at: '20 from 10' on *www.evangelism.uk.net*.

"1. In ten years, lots have happened
2. Evangelism is a central activity of the church
3. Evangelism is God's work
4. Evangelism is more effective when ecumenical
5. There is widespread interest in spirituality
6. Most people come to faith gradually
7. Personal relationships are basic in evangelism
8. Good evangelism is an invitation, not a confrontation
9. Evangelism is about sharing Jesus, not about promoting the church
10. A changing culture demands changing approaches
11. Evangelism among children and young people is a major challenge
12. Accessible worship is attractive
13. Good leadership is vital for effective evangelism
14. Local initiatives are best
15. Christian witness in ordinary life is at the heart of effective evangelism
16. Evangelism is part of well-rounded mission
17. Evangelism needs evangelists, but we are all witnesses
18. Personal stories are a powerful tool
19. Evangelism in Britain is a tough challenge
20. The global church continues to grow"

7.3.4.2   In Scotland as in the UK it is clear that we are moving now from the Decade of Evangelism to a real period of transformation for our Church. We must not **travel to the new** aimlessly without dwelling on these lessons already learned. In the past ten years some very positive developments have taken place. Many people have come to faith in Christ or begun a journey to faith through local church evangelism. The Team of Advisers in Mission and Evangelism have been privileged to work alongside congregations in cities, in rural areas, in urban priority areas and in new towns—all engaging in mission in ways relevant to the needs of the communities they are serving. Courses like Alpha, Emmaus and The Y Course have been developed and widely used together with a growing number of local initiatives. Many of the events which were organised during the Decade of Evangelism and more recently those held to mark millennium celebrations were resourced by local churches of all denominations working together.

7.3.4.3   The single most important contribution of the last decade is that Evangelism has been put back at the very heart of what the Church is and does—at local congregational level, at presbytery and at General Assembly. It has been well said: "I thought of mission as an 'optional extra', something to add to the agenda 'when we'd got the basics sorted out'. Now I see the idea of mission not as 'central to the work of the Church' nor that the Church 'exists for mission', but rather that mission is that which characterises the Church. It follows that there cannot be a Church or congregation which is not missionary. There can only be effective missionary congregations and ineffective missionary congregations."

7.3.5 Proposal

7.3.5.1   In 1991 the proposal of the Board of National Mission to create a larger network of Organisers for Evangelism (as the Advisers were previously entitled) was not accepted by the former Assembly Council on the grounds that the emphasis for the immediate future should be *'to concentrate actually on Presbyteries... There has seemed to the Council to be over much concentration in the first few years of the Process on individual congregations'*. It was believed that a smaller number of posts would be needed for a focus on the Presbytery rather than would be needed for congregational support.

7.3.5.2   While not wishing to propose an increase in the number of posts currently funded, the Board believes that it would assist both its overall planning and the daily prioritising of its staff if the Assembly can now agree that the main focus of field staff appointed as Advisers in Mission and Evangelism should be on enabling congregations for mission rather than continuing the Presbytery Development Process.

7.3.5.3   This conclusion is based on the review of Presbytery Partnerships reported above and also on recognition that the provision of trained staff to enable congregational development for mission should now be a priority for the church. The priority of the local is a key conclusion of the 'Decade of Evangelism' and the value of mission enablers to accompany congregations is a recommendation of the ecumenical 'Building Bridges of Hope' programme. This change in emphasis has been urged on the Committee on Mission and Evangelism Resources both by the Team of Advisers and others at various conferences organised by the Committee. Interestingly the Presbytery of Hamilton has in recent years appointed its own Congregational Development Officer.

7.3.5.4   The services of Advisers (however entitled) would continue to be available to support Presbyteries and National Committees as requested. The change in focus as recommended would however recognise what is current practice and also support and encourage the Board as it **travels to the new**.

7.4   Evangelism and Evangelists

7.4.1 Recognising Evangelists

The 1993 General Assembly received a report from the Board identifying *"the New Testament ministry of the evangelist ... one who helps to initiate people into the life of the Kingdom of God, and who goes to meet people where they are."* Noting the Biblical principle that *"the evangelising process of caring, teaching, inviting response and nurturing are rooted in the local community"* the report affirmed the potential of the parish minister in evangelism. Nevertheless, *"the role of the evangelist is not to be subsumed within our current understanding of 'minister'*, there was a place for those with particular gifts to work with and enable local congregations in their mission on a temporary basis. A proposal was made and accepted that an attempt would be made to discover *"two or three people with the gifts identified ... and give them recognition during a period of say eighteen months ... with local agreement ands necessary funding after which there would be a review."*

7.4.2 Rev Albert Bogle

The first part-time Evangelist recognised by the General Assembly was the Rev Albert Bogle. With the agreement of the Presbytery of Falkirk funds were provided over a year between 1998 and 1999 to the Kirk Session of Bo'ness: St Andrew's to allow the congregation to obtain additional support to enable their minister to be released for wider work for a day a week on average. In this way Mr Bogle's gifts in musical and multimedia evangelism were made more widely available. A report of the year was made to the General Assembly of 1999 and the Assembly instructed the Board to "reconsider as a priority a further similar appointment".

7.4.3 While the Board is well aware of numerous Scottish-based evangelists, the logistics of part-time release take time to negotiate. The objective remains to recognise an existing ministry and to provide support to enable the evangelist to be more widely available. The Board does not seek through this scheme to offer direct employment or itself to make an appointment. The short term nature of the recognition is a limitation imposed by the primary employment and calling of the evangelist and in addition the Board would seek over time to assist the Church to recognise a variety of giftings in this field.

7.4.4 Rev James C. Stewart

The Board now invites the General Assembly to recognise Rev James C. Stewart of Perth: Letham St. Mark's as a second part time Evangelist. Mr Stewart's particular strength is as a preacher and he took a key role in the vision for, and planning of, "Festival '99"—the Perth-based Franklin Graham campaign of that year. Of the challenge facing evangelism in Scotland today, Mr Stewart affirms the vital importance of preaching Christ and Him crucified and of adopting a different approach to different audiences.

7.4.5 Proposal

Building on a review of the first such recognition and seeking to **travel to the new** it is proposed to support Mr Stewart as a part time evangelist for a period of two years until May 2003. The longer period is necessary to enable proper consultation, preparation and planning. As before a support group with congregational, Presbytery and National Mission involvement will be sought to help with guidance and co-ordination.

7.4.6 The recognition of Rev Jim Stewart as a second part time evangelist has the support of the Kirk Session of Perth: Letham St Mark's and the Presbytery of Perth. The objective is to make him available as a guest preacher for locally planned missionary and evangelistic events. The beginning and ending must be grounded in the local Church.

7.5 Re-developing the Netherbow as a National Cultural Centre for the Church of Scotland

7.5.1 Background

7.5.1.1 The present Netherbow Arts Centre was opened in 1972 to replace the Gateway Centre which had been gifted to the Home Board in 1946. In 1970 the Board took a strategic decision to retain the Royal Mile site of the Moray-Knox Church for a successor cultural centre. The Moray-Knox Church had been built in the 1850s as part of an integrated development by the Free Church of Scotland of the Netherbow site (beside the Netherbow Port) including restoration of John Knox House as one of Scotland's first public museums. In 1989 the whole site (split at the Union of 1929) was reunited operationally by agreement of the Boards of National Mission (Netherbow Arts Centre) and Stewardship and Finance (John Knox House) enabling major upgrading of John Knox House and linkage with the visitor facilities of the Arts Centre. Soon afterwards the Society, Religion and Technology Project was located in a new office above the John Knox Museum. The short geographic title 'Netherbow' describes the whole site and may be revived as a street name for this section of the Royal Mile halfway between Edinburgh Castle and Holyrood.

7.5.2 Growth

7.5.2.1 When the Netherbow Arts Centre was built in 1970–72 by the former Home Board it was conceived as a small-scale facility for audio-visual production and screenings and church drama groups. The growth of tourism in the late 20th century and the burgeoning Scottish arts scene were not foreseen.

7.5.2.2 The combined facilities of the new Netherbow (John Knox House and the Netherbow Theatre) have proved successful attracting approximately 100,000 visitors per annum (40,000 paying admissions, 60,000 to café, exhibitions and visitor displays). Tourism to Edinburgh, Scotland's Capital, continues to be buoyant with particular interests in cultural and religious heritage.

7.5.2.3 The Netherbow has developed a successful national training and resource centre 'The Scottish

Storytelling Centre', recognised and funded by the Scottish Arts Council and Edinburgh City Council as well as the Board. Usage of the on-site facilities and a national network of storytelling activity are growing rapidly. The storytelling theme contributes to tourism, community arts and education, cultural heritage and Scottish identity, all of which are growth areas, *not least in congregational mission*. Over 140,000 people throughout Scotland took part in a storytelling network event in 1999.

7.5.2.4   With the opening of the Scottish Parliament a new political and cultural spotlight has been placed on historic central Edinburgh with consequent challenges and opportunities regionally, nationally and internationally. The small conference and meeting facilities of the Netherbow are ideally sited to meet such challenges and opportunities on behalf of the whole Church.

7.5.2.5 The needs of this present time are three-fold:
(a) The Netherbow operation has outgrown its present facilities. The 75 seat theatre/conference facility and the 30 ft meeting room are too small for many events and are inadequately equipped. The public facilities (café and foyer) are cramped and badly positioned, not least for children and older people who form two of the principal user groups.
(b) The Netherbow does not conform to the requirements of Disability Discrimination and will lose external public funding after 2004 due to inadequacy of access.
(c) The Board of National Mission has agreed in principle the location of the Scottish Churches Parliamentary Office at The Netherbow.

7.5.2.6   The present Netherbow operates a mixed economy of commercial and subsidised divisions involving an annual turnover of approximately £550,000.
John Knox House Museum—operates at a commercial profit of £10,000+ per annum
Netherbow Café—operates commercially at a break-even position.

Netherbow Arts Centre (on site arts events)—operates on a mixed subsidy (Board of National Mission through staff support, City of Edinburgh Council, Scottish Arts Council) and income generation
Meeting and Conference Facilities—brought up to Health and Safety standards in 1999 and showing income growth in 2000 despite limited promotion.
Outreach and Education—nationwide outreach programme subsidised by Board, Scottish Arts Council and local authorities.

7.5.2.7   Over the decade 1989–1999 the Netherbow has been successful in increasing its income from all sources year-on-year, but further income generation on-site is dependent on capital investment to enlarge and improve core facilities of performance, public welcome, training and conferences.

7.5.3   The Present Study
7.5.3.1   In 1998 the Netherbow Council reviewed the current patterns of growth and the inadequacies of the present building. The option of moving to a new site was considered but rejected on the grounds that the site, including John Knox House, was integral to the public profile and potential of the centre. An outline brief was then drawn up by the Netherbow Council based on the future needs and potential. Preliminary discussions were held with Scottish Storytelling Forum (through whom Scottish Arts Council funding is channeled), Edinburgh City Council and the Scottish Arts Council. All three indicated their willingness in principle to support development at the Netherbow. A staff Steering Group representing the Board of National Mission, the Netherbow Council and the Scottish Storytelling Forum was appointed to liaise with architects (appointed after competition) and oversee the first stage of the development proposals, reporting back to their respective committees.

7.5.3.2   The overall purpose of the brief was to provide the Netherbow site with a clear, modern identity and profile, complementing John Knox House, and emphasising the same missionary linkage between Church and community that is the inheritance of the Gateway and the Netherbow Arts Centre. It was resolved to use the title 'The Netherbow: Scottish Storytelling Centre' and building on the ethos of the past five clear objectives were established.

- To replace the Netherbow basement Theatre with a modern multi-purpose performance/conference/workshop space, looking onto the new Netherbow gardens to the rear.
- To retain and expand the street level public welcome space (remembering the needs of children, families, the elderly and the disabled) with additional provision of a lift upwards.
- To establish a clear visual identity for the performance space at street level and to rationalise routes of access.
- To retain the first floor as the administrative/servicing/managing base of the building and outreach programmes.
- To develop the upper floor meeting, training and office suite for related activity, retaining the meeting and education room as a facility for general building use and providing office space for partner organisations.

7.5.3.3 The designs developed by Malcolm Fraser Architects have fulfilled all these objectives and have maximised the space potential of the site. The reception and public welcome spaces have a potential to be a striking new addition to Edinburgh's High Street and a perfect clearing house for people to access the performance, training, conference and museum facilities offered on site, as well as the national resource network.

7.5.4   Proposal
7.5.4.1 Detailed estimates indicate that redevelopment of the site as a fully equipped and fully accessible modern cultural and educational centre (including the Scottish Churches Parliamentary Office) would cost up to £3.2 million. There is a clear expectation that partnership funding will be available from public bodies, though the Church will have to share a realistic share of the costs of redevelopment.

7.5.4.2   The Board is minded in principle to **travel to the new** with this project and seeks the Assembly's endorsement for its vision of a 21st century national cultural centre, incorporating John Knox House and the Scottish Churches Parliamentary Office. Such a Centre would both serve local communities and congregations through a storytelling and arts network and be a strong expression of the Church's mission in Scotland's story, culturally and politically.

7.5.4.3   The Board's intention, in cooperation with the Board of Stewardship and Finance, is to investigate funding avenues and to establish a practical and feasible level of investment what will secure the Church's presence on this site for the foreseeable future. A full report on the work done so far along with a design scheme, detailed costings and a business plan, are available from the Board.

7.6   Statistics for Mission
7.6.1   2001 is Census Year - and a group has been working to develop a scheme of providing accurate population statistics and trends for all Church of Scotland parishes based on the 1991 and 2001 statistics.

7.6.2   These statistics will be available by 2003 and will include total population figures for both 1991 and 2001 with age, socio-economic, and other breakdowns. They should be invaluable in assisting congregations to understand their parish areas and tailor-make their missionary endeavours and will enable the Committee on Parish Reappraisal to come to decisions about parish staffing with accurate population statistics available.

7.6.3   Already pilot work has been undertaken in the Presbyteries of Dundee and Abernethy and the General Register Office has provided preliminary statistics based on the 1991 Census for the parishes in these Presbyteries. In other words the task is possible.

7.6.4   Most Presbyteries have now appointed a "Statistics for Mission" Co-ordinator and their responsibility is to gather the postcodes for every parish in their Presbytery. Once postcodes are available the General Register Office is able to provide the necessary population statistics.

7.6.5 In order that the database of postcodes is kept completely up to date it would be necessary for changes in parish boundaries to be reported. Many such boundary changes occur through the implementation of Act IV (1984) and are known to the Department but others are not reported. It is the hope of the Board that the General Assembly will approve a procedure for all changes to be recorded.

7.7   The Development of Prison Chaplaincy to meet Changes in Ministry and the Care of Prisoners

7.7.1   For more than a century ministers and priests have served as chaplains in Scottish prisons. Nearly all of them have been parish based and have worked only a few hours each week in prisons. Some aspects of chaplaincy, such as prisoners' education, have been assimilated into other disciplines but while the essential work of chaplains to lead worship and celebrate the sacraments remains unchanged, the volume and official recognition of spiritual care have grown. Prison populations have increased, the number of ministers available has reduced, the social attitude towards prisoners has changed and the Scottish Executive policy on prisons is moving towards a more rehabilitative role, including support to families and to prisoners after release (now called "Throughcare"). These changes have substantial quantitative and qualitative effects on prison chaplaincy. The point has now been reached that in many situations the expectations of the Scottish Prison Service (SPS) and the demands of full-time parish ministry are incompatible. The visits to all Scottish prisons by the Moderator of the General Assembly made possible the constructive exchange of letters between the SPS Chief Executive, Mr Tony Cameron, and the Board of National Mission in December 2000. The SPS seek the development of prison chaplaincy and to receive the service on contract from the two main providing denominations.

7.7.2   To this end the Board has explored the present situation and options as to the future organisation and

employment of chaplains. It has consulted the SPS Specialist Advisers in Chaplaincy, prison governors, staff, chaplains, senior representatives of the Roman Catholic and Episcopal Churches in Scotland and the Joint Faiths Advisory Board on Criminal Justice. All concur that the way forward that will best serve prisoners and their families is to have a mix of full-time chaplains where justified by the size of prisons, part-time chaplains at smaller prisons who have other appointments which are also part-time and which complement prison work, and part-time support chaplains drawn from the parish ministry. (An example of the second category is the proposed combination of two part-time chaplain posts at HMP Low Moss and the Glasgow Lodging House Mission.) The practice whereby the SPS employs chaplains directly would therefore cease and the Board would conclude a contract with the SPS to provide chaplains. All parties agree that this will avoid the otherwise inevitable conflict of interest that arises from having two employers and make possible the better management practice of chaplains being contracted to one employer.

7.7.3 This is a radical and timely change to the employment and organisation of prison chaplains and is fundamental to meeting the challenge of providing specialist ministry in an exceptional setting to members of society with distinctive needs. To ensure the changes achieve this aim the Board will continue to work with the SPS to clarify the terms of the contract, the costs (to be borne by the SPS), the role expected of chaplains, and the way they are deployed throughout Scottish prisons. Conclusion of the last point is dependent upon an imminent SPS review of the prison estate. It is nonetheless foreseen that the planning and organisation of this development will be complete in time for transition to commence in April 2002 after which the employment of chaplains will be adjusted to comply with agreed terms of service.

7.8   Scottish Mission Studies Centre
7.8.1 At the meeting of the Board of National Mission

on 5th April 2000 the Board agreed to establish a "Unit for Mission Studies" to advance the theology and practice of mission and the Minute for that meeting of the Board read as follows:

> *The Board recognised the strategic importance of the missiological research which had been undertaken at St. Ninian's Centre over the years and agreed to the establishment of a Unit for Mission Studies with the following remit:*
>
> - *To enable the Board of National Mission to fulfil its Vision Statement.*
> - *To assist the Board in auditing and evaluating its work.*
> - *To be aware of current missional theology at home and abroad.*
> - *To be abreast of new models of mission.*
> - *To encourage the interchange of ideas and action.*
>
> In establishing the Unit the Board agreed:
>
> - *That the work of the Unit would be directly responsible to the Board of National Mission and would be guided by a Group including representation of the Board and its Constituent Committees, other relevant Boards such as Ministry, World Mission and Parish Education, and representation from other Churches.*
> - *That the Unit be staffed by a full-time Researcher and part-time Assistant Researcher.*
> - *That the Unit be located in co-operation with an academic institution.*
> - *That the Unit from the outset should seek to work in partnership with appropriate other Centres in the UK and around the world.*
> - *That the Unit should be given an assurance of an operational budget to fund research and fieldwork.*
> - *That a commitment be given that the Unit would be functioning by the 2001 General Assembly."*

7.8.2 Despite the decision of the 2000 General Assembly to appoint a Special Commission anent St Ninian's Centre, the Board at its meeting on 7th June 2000 agreed:

> "To give consideration at the September 2000 meeting

of the Board to the establishment of a "Unit for Mission Studies" to advance the theology and practice of mission as defined in the Supplementary Report of the Board to the 2000 General Assembly."

The definition referred to in the Supplementary Report of the Board echoed the wording of the Minute of the Board meeting of 5th April 2000 but removed the commitment to have the Unit functioning by the 2001 General Assembly.

7.8.3 Discussions on the establishment of such a Scottish Mission Studies have continued since then and the Board is convinced of the strategic need for quality missiological research and analysis in the contemporary Scottish context.

7.8.4 The Board has now resolved to await the decision of the 2001 General Assembly concerning St Ninian's Centre, Crieff, before giving further thought to the proposal.

7.9   Project Rejoice!

7.9.1 In its tenth year of operation Project Rejoice! has successfully embraced 21st century technology, presenting not only its customary leaflets and posters for overprinting but also a *Library CD* of images and text for congregations to design their own mission resources. Mindful that not all churches have access to 'high tech' equipment the Project also produced OHP slides and basic guidance notes for leaders, but still with the same aim of stimulating local creativity, not simply providing ready-made materials. The Project was most encouraged to see the successful impact of this philosophy in the widespread use made of its millennium resources through 1999, 2000 and into 2001, and drew lessons from the demand for 'national' resources to tie into major Scottish civic or social events.

7.9.2 In a new venture a fruitful partnership has been established with the National Galleries of Scotland—linking the National Church and the national collection of art—which allowed us to produce 'sell-out' (150,000 items) Christmas and Easter images. Rejoice! also continued to commission new Christian art and offered three paintings for congregational use by Nicholas Mynheer based on Philippians 2 as devotional art images under the theme **Travel to the New**.

7.9.3 Since its inception an ecumenical approach has been intrinsic to the work of Rejoice and the Project fulfilled a request from ACTS to devise visuals for the Ecumenical Assembly in September 2001 on the theme *Breaking New Ground*. All the materials produced are for use across the Scottish Churches and are marketed through ACTS as well as through denomination mailings.

7.9.4 At the end of 2000 Rejoice! conducted a review of its remit and the following points were approved as a basis for future development.

- Future resources should continue to draw for their inspiration on the heart of the Christian Faith and seek to encourage congregations to be confident in their communication of the Faith.

- Rejoice! should continue to support major Christian festivals but the Group should not confine its scope to these.

- In drawing up their programme the Group should listen carefully to the needs of congregations.

- It would not be part of the Group's remit to review and recommend mission materials, visual or otherwise, produced by other organisations.

- In determining its programme the Group should be able to relate to programmes for, or proposed by other Boards of the Church of Scotland, and also ecumenically.

- The Group should continue to be a Working Group of the Board of National Mission itself, if possible convened by one of the Vice-Conveners of the Board; and with the Secretary-Depute (Parish Resourcing) as Secretary. The Group would also be supported by the Board's Congregational Links Administrator and by staff deployed by the Committee on Mission and Evangelism Resources. From this small group, members would be co-opted for their own particular skills rather than on a representative basis.

7.9.5 Project Rejoice! is required to report to this General Assembly and requests that the Project be sustained to continue to develop the use of visual images and text in the mission work of the Scottish Churches. It is clear that a small group of specialists and mission minded Christians can successfully respond to special themes or events in the life of Scotland or its churches and produce powerful visual resources which local churches can further develop for their own needs. The Board now seeks the approval of the General Assembly to advance Project Rejoice! as an exciting and innovative area of work into the 21st century.

8.   Appreciation

8.1   Conveners and Vice-Conveners:

The Board of National Mission appreciate enormously the dedicated commitment of all who serve on the Board, Constituent Committees, and other groups. Particularly appreciation is offered to those who have completed terms of service—

- Rev David J. Randall has completed a three year term as Vice-Convener of the Board. While he has exercised leadership in all areas of the Board's work, David gave a particular lead in the Kirk's celebration of the millennium as documented in Appendix IV.

- Rev Fred Drummond decided in December 2000 to resign from his responsibilities as Vice-Convener of the Committee on New Charge Development in view of other commitments. Mr Drummond's vision for this area of work is exemplified by his willingness to lead his own congregation from their building in central Perth to become a New Charge Development in North Muirton.

- Mrs Nena Dinnes has completed a three year term as Vice-Convener of the Committee on Mission and Evangelism Resources. Coming from the rural south-west, Mrs Dinnes interest has lain particularly in the work of the Rural Committee and she contributed significantly to the development of the presence of the Church at the Royal Highland Show.

- Rev Max Homewood has served for three years as Convener of the Committee on Chaplaincies. The experience in personnel work with the Army prior to entering the ministry has proved invaluable in responding to the many demands of this convenership which embraces chaplaincy in healthcare, hospitals, universities, prisons and industry.

The Board is deeply grateful to these three Ministers and one Elder for their years of service and invites the General Assembly to thank them for their commitment.

8.2   Staff:

Staff retiring or moving on to other spheres of service are thanked at the closing session of the General Assembly. The Board however wishes to place on record its appreciation of the three and half years of service of the Rev Dr Frank D. Bardgett as Secretary-Depute (Parish Resourcing). Dr Bardgett's interest and abilities in research and in administration have proved invaluable—particularly during the Kirk's celebration of the millennium. It was no mean task to ensure that grants were paid and materials delivered on time. Not that this was his only area of responsibility. Servicing the Committee on Mission and Evangelism Resources, the Residential Centres Executive, and the Project Rejoice! Working Group lay at the heart of the responsibilities of the post he held. To all these areas—and to the wider work of the Board—Dr Bardgett brought a commitment to meticulous care. The Board and the whole Church are in his debt.

In the name of the Board

JAMES M GIBSON, *Convener*
DAVID J RANDALL, *Vice-Convener*
FIONA CAMPBELL, *Vice-Convener*
DOUGLAS A O NICOL, *General Secretary*
NORMA HENDERSON, *Secretary-Depute*
FRANK D BARDGETT, *Secretary-Depute*

APPENDIX I

Revision to Constitution of the Board of National Mission

In the Constitution of the Department of National Mission as from 31st May 2001:
In Section 2.3 add "A representative of the Presbytery of Europe"

APPENDIX II

Committee on Parish Reappraisal Tables

TABLE I
NO CHANGE

1	Balerno	Edinburgh
2	Edinburgh: Carrick Knowe	Edinburgh
3	Edinburgh: Duddingston	Edinburgh
4	Edinburgh: Murrayfield	Edinburgh
5	Edinburgh: Stenhouse St Aidan's	Edinburgh
6	The Breich Valley	West Lothian
7	Aberlady linked with Gullane	Lothian
8	Loanhead	Lothian
9	Eddleston linked with Peebles: Old	Melrose and Peebles
10	Dalton, Hightae and St Mungo	Annandale and Eskdale
11	Castle Douglas	Dumfries and Kirkcudbright
12	Darvel	Irvine and Kilmarnock
13	Cairngryffe linked with Symington	Lanark
14	Glencaple linked with Lowther	Lanark
15	Howwood	Paisley
16	Johnstone: High	Paisley
17	Glasgow: Balshagray Victoria Park	Glasgow
18	Glasgow: Baillieston St Andrew's	Glasgow
19	Glasgow: Carmunnock	Glasgow
20	Glasgow: Kirkintilloch St David's	Glasgow
21	Glasgow: Kirkintilloch St Mary's	Glasgow
22	Glasgow: South Carntyne	Glasgow
23	Airdrie: New Wellwynd	Hamilton
24	Bargeddie	Hamilton
25	Blantyre: St Andrew's	Hamilton
26	East Kilbride: Old	Hamilton

27	East Kilbride: West	Hamilton
28	Hamilton: Old	Hamilton
29	New Stevenston: Wrangholm Kirk	Hamilton
30	Newarthill linked with Carfin	Hamilton
31	Strathaven Avendale Old and Drumclog	Hamilton
32	Uddingston: Viewpark	Hamilton
33	Southend	South Argyll
34	Bonnybridge St Helen's	Falkirk
35	Falkirk: Bainsford	Falkirk
36	Grahamston United	Falkirk
37	Stirling: St Columba's	Stirling
38	Tillicoultry	Stirling
39	Beath and Cowdenbeath: North	Dunfermline
40	Rosyth	Dunfermline
41	Perth: Craigie	Perth
42	Broughty Ferry: St Luke's and Queen Street	Dundee
43	Newtonhill	Kincardine and Deeside
44	Foveran	Gordon
45	Insch, Leslie, Premnay and Oyne	Gordon
46	Meldrum and Bourtie	Gordon
47	Acharacle linked with Ardnamurchan	Lochaber
48	Fort Augustus linked with Glengarry	Lochaber
49	Reay linked with Strathy and Halladale	Caithness
50	Wick: Old	Caithness
51	Lochalsh	Lochcarron/Skye
52	Snizort	Lochcarron/Skye
53	North Ronaldsay linked with Sanday	Orkney
54	South Ronaldsay and Burray	Orkney
55	Burra Isle linked with Tingwall (Shetland Arrangements)	Shetland
56	Corby: St Andrew's	England
57	London: Crown Court	England

TERMINABLE TENURE

1	New Cumnock	Ayr
2	Old Cumnock: Crichton West and St Ninian's (united)	Ayr
3	Glasgow: Househillwood St Christopher's	Glasgow
4	Hamilton: West	Hamilton
5	Fetlar linked with Yell	Shetland

REVIEWABLE TENURE

1	Newton	Lothian
2	Bowden linked with Newtown	Melrose and Peebles
3	Stow St Mary of Wedale and Heriot	Melrose and Peebles
4	Penpont, Keir and Tynron	Dumfries and Kirkcudbright
5	Glasgow: Drumchapel St Mark's	Glasgow
6	Glasgow: Linthouse St Kenneth's	Glasgow
7	Glasgow: New Govan	Glasgow
8	Blantyre Livingstone Memorial	Hamilton
9	Overtown	Hamilton
10	Alloa: West	Stirling
11	Aberluthnott/Laurencekirk	Kincardine and Deeside
12	Banchory-Devenick/Maryculter and Cookney	Kincardine and Deeside
13	Cromar	Kincardine and Deeside
14	Kinneff linked with Stonehaven: South	Kincardine and Deeside
15	Stonehaven: Fetteresso	Kincardine and Deeside
16	Daviot and Dunlichity linked with Moy, Dalarossie and Tomatin	Inverness
17	Inverness: Kinmylies (Church Extension)	Inverness
18	Lybster and Bruan	Caithness

AGE RESTRICTION

1	Craigie linked with Symington (not under 50 years)	Ayr

CONTINUED VACANCY

1	Law	Lanark

UNIONS

1	Addiewell, Longridge and Breich and Stoneyburn (The Breich Valley Parish)	15th February 2000
2	Innerleithen, Traquair and Walkerburn	9th November 2000
3	Old Cumnock: Crichton West and Old Cumnock: St Ninian's	31st October 2000
4	Kilmarnock: Laigh and Kilmarnock: West High (Laigh West High)	5th October 2000
5	Auchterderran and Cardenden: St Fothad's	13th August 2000
6	Kirkcaldy: Old and Kirkcaldy: St Brycedale (KIRKCALDY: ST BRYCE KIRK)	5th November 2000
7	Perth: Craigend Moncreiffe and Rhynd (PERTH: MONCREIFFE PARISH CHURCH)	28th February 2001
8	Aberuthven linked with Dunning and Aberdalgie and Dupplin linked with Forteviot (THE STEWARTRY OF STRATHEARN)	7th June 2000
9	Glenisla, Kilry and Lintrathen	28th March 2000
10	Banchory-Devenick and Maryculter/Cookney	19th November 2000
11	Birsay with Harry and Sandwick	30th October 2000

BASIS OF DEFERRED UNION

1	Edinburgh: Cluny and Edinburgh: Morningside Braid
2	Leven: Scoonie and Leven: St Andrew's

LINKINGS

1	Makerstoun and Smailholm, Roxburgh, and Stichill, Hume and Nenthorn	Date of Induction
2	Bellshill: Macdonald Memorial and Bellshill: Orbiston	11th January 2001
3	Cardenden: St Fothad's united with Auchterderran linked with Kinglassie	13th August 2000
4	Dundee: Clepington and Dundee Fairmuir	11th January 2001
5	Glenisla, Kilry and Lintrathen Linked with Airlie, Ruthven and Kingoldrum (The Isla Parishes)	28th March 2000
6	Alvie and Insh and Kingussie	1st November 2000
7	Fearn Abbey and Nigg Chapelhill and Tarbat	27th August 2000

BASIS OF DEFERRED LINKING

1	Applegarth and Sibbaldbie with Johnstone with Lochmaben
2	Kirkpatrick Juxta with Moffat: St Andrew's with Wamphray
3	Auchinleck linked with Catrine
4	Muirkirk linked with Sorn
5	Delting and Northmavine

NEW CHARGE

1	East End of Greenock	Greenock
2	East Kilbride: Stewartfield	Hamilton

DISSOLUTION

1	Glasgow: Townhead Blochairn	22nd December 2000
2	Dunfermline: St Paul's	4th February 2001
3	Aberdeen: Nigg	17th September 2000

CHANGE OF STATUS

1	Stirling: Viewfield (Full Status)	Stirling
2	Dundee: Whitfield (New Charge Development)	Dundee
3	Aberdeen: Bridge of Don Oldmachar (New Charge Development)	Aberdeen
4	Aberdeen: Cove (New Charge Development)	Aberdeen

PART TIME MINISTRY

1	Lochs in Bernera	Lewis

SECESSION

1	Bellshill: St Andrew's	Hamilton

ARTHUR P BARRIE, *Convener*
C NOEL GLEN, *Vice-Convener*
DOUGLAS A O NICOL, *General Secretary*

APPENDIX III
Committee on New Charge Development Statistics

1.1 New Charges
During the year 2000/2001 2 New Charges were created.

1.2 Sites
2.1 At the time of writing, negotiations for the acquisition of several sites at various stages were ongoing. These sites are for the purpose of erecting suitable places of worship.

Glasgow: Gorbals
Glasgow: Robroyston
Dunfermline: Calais Farm
Dunfermline: Bellyeoman
Aberdeen: Cove
Gordon: Blackburn
Inverness: Inshes
Hamilton: Ravenscraig
Dundee: North East

2.2 The Committee has also been invited by the Committee on Parish Reappraisal to enter into discussions to establish the nature of new developments which may require a place of worship in the following areas:

Hamilton: Ravenscraig
Hamilton: East Kilbride: Stewartfield

3. New Buildings
3.1 The Committee is also in the process of constructing new churches in the following locations:

(a) Ardrossan: Kilwinning Mansefield Trinity for a contract sum of approximately £550,000.
(b) Perth: Riverside for the contract sum of £660,000

3.2 Other projects, at the design stage, include;

Glasgow: Gorbals
Dunfermline: Bellyeoman
Inverness: Inshes
Glasgow: Robroyston

4. Acquisition of Buildings
4.1 The Committee has acquired or is in the process of acquiring the following properties:

(a) Property at Glasgow, Robroyston for the purpose of conversion to provide a place of worship.
(b) New manse for Dundee: Whitfield.

5. Repairs
The Committee continues to assist with repairs of existing Extension Charge buildings and is in the process of developing a comprehensive property management system throughout its entire property portfolio, including cyclical maintenance and Health and Safety.

6. Finance
6.1 The Committee is grateful to Murrayfield Parish Church, Edinburgh, for a generous donation of £40,000 towards the work of the New Charge Development at Aberdeen: Cove.

6.2 The surplus for 2000 in the general fund of the Committee on New Charge Development amounted to £88,078.

7. Arbitrations
During the year under review, no Arbitrations took place.

ANDREW RITCHIE, *Convener*
WILLIAM JOHN MACDONALD, *Secretary*

APPENDIX IV

The Church of Scotland Millennium Celebrations

The Church of Scotland Millennium Celebrations —what happened?—a report

1.1   Planning

The Committee on Mission and Evangelism Resources established an AD2000 Working Group in June 1992. The Board reported to the 1993 General Assembly and obtained consent to consult with other Boards and with Presbyteries to ensure that 2000 was 'clearly claimed as a Christian celebration of God's faithfulness in the past and grace for the future'. In retrospect what the Board wrote in 1993 had a visionary thrust:

> 'Whereas often church anniversaries are internal to the church in which it tries to interest others, the distinctive feature of the year 2000 AD is that this is something already in the perception of folk outwith Christian circles, the mode of celebration of which may set the tone of society well into the next century. The missionary potential is considerable.
>
> ... it is vitally important that 2000 AD be seen as a Christian celebration.
>
> A suggested theme would be "Jesus Christ, the same yesterday, today and forever."
>
> ... the fulfilment of the vision of an appropriate Christian celebration, the Board firmly believes, must be rooted in the life of the parishes of our land ...'

Reports to the 1994 and 1995 General Assemblies outlined a campaign from the 1995 Scottish Christian Gathering through to 2001 with a growing emphasis on millennium celebrations as essentially ecumenical and local, underpinned by national themes and resources.

On 26 October 1995 a letter to all Presbyteries laid out six principles for planning:

- Commencement of the Scottish Churches Millennium with activities in 1997 inspired by commemoration of Ninian, Columba and other missionaries.

- Co-ordination with and participation in the planning of local authorities for the period of Christmas 1999/New Year 2000.

- Extended Christian celebration of Christmas at local level, reaching through to a service of rededication and commitment in every church in early January 2000.

- The marking of Easter 2000 as a Season of Evangelism at local and regional levels.

- Evolution of a series of vision-building, national-scale events in key Scottish centres between Easter and Pentecost 2000.

- Active engagement in the debate about values and spirituality in a pluralist society, giving content to the Christian contribution.

By the time of a conference of Church of Scotland Boards in November 1996, the Years of Faith, Hope, Love and Jubilee were in place, together with "Jesus Christ, the same yesterday, today and forever" and (from CCBI) the use of the Lord's Prayer. Further, the Scottish Churches committed themselves to support 'Jubilee 2000' in a campaign for the remission of the debt burden on the world's poorest nations.

One major exercise in consultation was a conference of Presbyteries held in September 1997 where it was agreed that the Scottish Churches should take a leading part in celebrating Easter 2000 to Easter 2001 as a 'Festival of Jesus Christ'. The conference also agreed not to focus on any single national campaign but rather to support the initiatives of Presbyteries and local congregations, according to local choice to hold 'major events' throughout the year, to recognise the ecumenical campaign 'Jubilee 2000', and not to recommend any further single 'national' project.

The concept of 'Jubilee' for AD2000 thus came to be described as …

- Renewal of community in worship and service
- The 'Jubilee 2000' campaign for remission of the debt burden on the world's poorest nations
- Initiatives to end homelessness in Scotland.

From 1996 onwards resources for the celebrations were discussed between the Board and the Board of Stewardship and Finance and in February 1998 a special grant of £200,000 was made available—which sum included a donation of £50,000 from the Royal Bank of Scotland.

2. In the event … National Mission's resourcing of the Church

2.1 Partnership: conversations and finance

The Board sought to co-ordinate Church of Scotland policy in liaison with the appropriate ecumenical and other bodies.

- The Convener of the Board, the Rev Sandy Cairns, represented the Church of Scotland on the Lambeth Group which spoke with the Government on millennium issues.
- Dr Donald Smith, Director of the Netherbow, was seconded to serve as part-time Secretary for the Scotland 2000 Committee of Action of Churches Together in Scotland; and also liaised with the government's agents in Scotland, NMEC [New Millennium Experience Co.]
- National Mission's Rejoice! Working Group co-operated with ACTS to design and promote the Scottish Churches Millennium Symbol, the Scottish Churches Millennium Invitation Card, and the symbol for the first Scottish Ecumenical Assembly, 'Breaking New Ground' (2001).
- Rejoice!'s own membership included representation from the Salvation Army, the Scottish Episcopal Church and the Methodist Church in Scotland.

Financial support was given to a number of the Church of Scotland's other central agencies:

- The resource for schools of the Department of Education—'Perceptions of Jesus'
- The 1999 calendar of the Press Office—'Year of Love'
- The Banner Project of the Guild—'Hold out the Word of Life'

'Life & Work' gave considerable attention to 2000 policy and visual resources and essential co-operation and support was received from the Church's Design Services.

Rejoice! kept close contact with officers of the Board of Social Responsibility.

Mrs Georgina Payne held joint-roadshows with colleagues of the Boards of World Mission and Social Responsibility.

Through membership of the AD2000 Working Group the Board of Practice and Procedure kept successive Moderators of the General Assembly informed of policy and events.

The bulk of financial support—some £150,000—was gifted to regional, area and congregational celebrations and in the main such support was channelled through Presbyteries.

—A sum of £1,500 was allocated and offered to each Presbytery—all but two took up the offer. Most Presbyteries chose to support a large range of congregational activities.

—Congregations were directly offered support for the production of their own external banners.

—Further financial support was offered via Presbyteries in the Autumn of 2000.

—Up to £5,000 was offered to a number of the significantly larger events or where the scope was broader than a single Presbytery. Those selected were—

- 'Christian Witness at Edinburgh's Hogmanay' 1999/00 following the Bogle Band's successful working with and appearance at the 1998/9 Edinburgh Hogmanay which had also supported by the Board.
- Support for a Millennium Resolution signed video resource for deaf people.

- Glasgow Presbytery and Glasgow Churches Together 'Pentecost 2000' Jubilee Festival in Hampden Park. Further substantial support was also given to this—the most ambitious regional event held in Scotland by the Churches in 2000.
- Inverness area: 'Praise in the Park' Pentecost celebration co-ordinated by Rev Richard Gibbons, the Highland Adviser in Mission and Evangelism.
- Presbytery of Irvine and Kilmarnock: regional Pentecost celebration in Rugby Park.
- Key core-funding for the drama group 'Cutting Edge' 2000 tour of Scotland.
- Church of Scotland Mission Projects: sports-based youth mission.
- A rural conference held in August in Unst, Shetland—travel support.
- 3rd Scottish Urban Mission Conference held in Paisley in September.
- 'Deep Impact' Youth Gathering, Inverness: December—travel support.

2.1   Communication

The Board communicated the Scottish Churches Millennium Celebrations strategy via …

- Three editions of 'Millennium Link'—a special newsletter to ministers, Presbyteries, etc.
- 'Link Update'—the Board's own newsletter.
- Articles in 'Life & Work'
- The Press Office
- The Convener of the Board highlighting the theme in Reports to the General Assembly

Attention was given to the plans of para-church and other Christian organisations offering resources and millennium programmes and in particular:

'Jubilee 2000'
'New Start': the programme of CTE' which included the Candle Gift Scheme
'Fanfare 2000'
The National Bible Society of Scotland
Scripture Union—Scotland

The 'Open Book' Project: British and Foreign Bible Society
CPAS
CPO
'JC2000': a government-sponsored arts festival for schools
'Why 2000?' : the 'Jesus Video'
The New Scottish Orchestra
The Bible Story Exhibition
'Cutting Edge' drama company's 2000 tour: 'A Scots Passion'

2.2   Resources

The Netherbow wrote, produced and circulated to schools the free educational pack: 'Light in Darkness' as well as the 1997 resource booklet and pack: 'Celtic Journeys'.

A leaflet on 'The Lord's Prayer' was written and was made available as a free resource. Reprinted seven times: 75,000 copies were distributed by congregations throughout Scotland.

Project Rejoice! resourced the Years of Faith, Hope, Love and Jubilee with sets of specially commissioned posters and leaflets:

1997—the Year of Faith—Celtic theme posters and leaflets reached widely throughout Scotland.
1998—the Year of Hope—photographic posters on themes of Family, Community and Environment with an accompanying resources and ideas booklet
1999—the Year of Love—concentrating on 1 Corinthians, chapter 13, with a Prayer Diary as well as leaflets and posters.
2000—the Year of Jubilee—took the theme 'Jesus in our Community' with a poster and leaflets on 'The Cross' for Easter, emphasised the Scottish Churches Millennium Symbol and promoted resources based on the Beatitudes with posters and a Study Guide.

Some 65,000 Christmas leaflets were purchased in these years; with almost 40,000 at Easter in 1997 and 1999;

and 50,000 at Easter 2000. 137,000 leaflets bearing the Scottish Churches Millennium Symbol were purchased —all these figures indicative of a major effort by congregations to communicate their message.

The Scottish Churches Millennium Symbol bearing the words: 'Jesus Christ—yesterday, today, forever' was designed for Rejoice! by Hannah Frew Paterson at the invitation of ACTS. This was made available free of copyright for local use on the web, on disk, by posters and leaflets. Kits for textile and cross-stitch use were also sold. The furthest-flung reported use of this well-received Symbol was a banner and march organised by the First Presbyterian Church, Auburn, Alabama, USA.

As a greeting from the Churches and containing a personal and group act of contemplation and worship including the Lord's Prayer, the Scottish Churches Millennium Invitation Card was designed by Rejoice! for distribution at Hogmanay 1999/00. In total 700,000 cards were distributed by the Board and, in addition, a significant number of local versions of the Invitation were produced – for example, by Churches Together in Glasgow. Overall at least a million invitations were issued.

£20,000 was made available to assist nearly 250 congregations produce their own banners bearing the Scottish Churches Millennium Symbol for use outdoors throughout the year 2000. Congregations across Scotland also incorporated the Symbol into commemorative pulpit falls, windows, murals, mosaics and in other ways. The distinctive Christian and Scottish design proved successful in expressing what the Churches celebrated in an effective and inspiring way.

3.   In the event … what happened in Scotland

3.1   Jubilee 2000

Backed by the Board of World Mission the 'Jubilee 2000' campaign attracted very substantial support in Scotland—

- Many congregations supported a letter-writing and post-card sending campaign to the Chancellor of the Exchequer, the Prime Minister and the G8.
- Public marches, demonstrations and events calling for debt relief were well supported and these included a

bike ride and a protest attended by the Moderator of the General Assembly at the Japanese Consulate.

3.2   'Homelessness'

The theme was taken up by the Scottish Churches Housing Agency who served as an umbrella resource for a range of practical initiatives. For the Board Rejoice! negotiated donations to SCHA from a range of companies in exchange for access to the Scottish Churches Millennium Symbol. For example, 'Signs Express' donated £1000 from its banner-making income.

The Presbytery of Edinburgh in conjunction with the local Social Work and Housing Departments ran a major practical campaign to assist the homeless: 'Room at the Inn 2000' which is now being carried forward as 'Fresh Start'. Churches in Motherwell also took up this theme.

3.3   Mission: the 'Resolution' and 'Invitation' and other Birthday Gifts

The British Churches agreed to promote CTE's Millennium Resolution, carefully worded to be an attractive expression of Christian ethics and to be widely acceptable in a secular and multi-faith society. To this the Scottish Churches through ACTS Central Council added the specifically Christian Lord's Prayer and commended both together in the Invitation Card for use at and around Hogmanay.

The Community Council of Cranshaws and Duns were so impressed by the inclusive ethics of the Resolution that they commissioned a bronze plaque to hang in their community hall to commemorate their Hogmanay bonfire party—at which the Resolution was affirmed.

The Scottish Churches also accepted as an optional resource the Candle Gift Scheme promoted by CTE for distribution throughout England.

Though the Candle Gift Scheme was not free of difficulty both the Invitation and the Candle resources were widely used in Scotland in what in total was a considerable exercise in local outreach and communication. In addition, congregations also chose to distribute Bibles, Gospels and biblically-based videos to communicate the 2000 message of Jesus' birthday. Examples are:

- In Edinburgh the congregations of St Phillips Joppa, Colinton Mains, Gorgie and Slateford Longstone distributed the Invitation Card. Colinton Mains also used a NBSS leaflet; Slateford Longstone also used the Jesus video and Gorgie also used the Candle Gift Scheme. St David's Broomhouse congregation received financial support for the Candle Gift Scheme and additional publicity.
- In the Presbytery of Duns, the following congregations were jointly involved in the distribution of Gospels: Berwick on Tweed, Bonkyl and Preston, Chirnside, Edrom Allanton, Coldstream, Eccles, Duns, Fogo and Swinton, Ladykirk, Leitholm, Whitsome, Foulden and Mordington, Hutton/Fishwick/Paxton, Gordon: St Michael's, Greenlaw, Legerwood and Westruther.
- The joint Buckie Churches combined a community visitation with gifts of Gospels and the Jesus video and held three celebratory mission concerts.
- The Presbytery of Caithness posted Invitation Cards to every home.
- In the Orkney Islands a major ecumenical initiative involving all denominations active in the islands arranged a visitation of all households with a specially designed local version of the Invitation; and a Christian festival of music was also held in March 2000.

3.4 Mission: Hogmanay 1999–2000

As expected Hogmanay 1999-2000 attracted major public attention. An ecumenical opening to the season in St Giles' Cathedral, Edinburgh, in Advent 1999 received wide television and press coverage. Also in Edinburgh the co-operation forged at Hogmanay 1998 between the Rev Albert Bogle and the Bogle Band and Unique Events—the organiser of the Hogmanay event in Edinburgh— proved fruitful in work undertaken by a group with the title 'Christian Witness at Edinburgh's Hogmanay'. An Edinburgh city church had a very well-attended midnight service; volunteer welfare helpers were on duty; 10,000 copies of a leaflet 'Crossing the Threshold' were distributed together with 100,000 Invitation Cards.

Negotiations throughout Great Britain with the Government and media ensured that public arrangements and broadcast coverage included the Resolution, the Lord's Prayer and the Beatitudes. Part of the nation-wide coverage came from St Margaret's Chapel in Edinburgh Castle and a National Service at St Giles' Cathedral, Edinburgh, was broadcast on the afternoon of 1st January 2000.

East Kilbride, Inverness, Aberdeen and other communities held special joint services in early January and other local events were numerous—for example, congregations in Fort William and in other places arranged floodlighting in association with a special celebration of Christmas 1999.

In London, Edinburgh and Glasgow, major art galleries choose the turn of the year to hold exhibitions of Christian art illustrative of the life and eternal meaning of Jesus with the exhibition in the National Gallery, London, entitled 'Seeing Salvation' becoming the basis of a major BBC2 series. Earlier the Presbytery of Glasgow had sponsored the 'Cornerstone' festival in 1999 as a preparatory event for the Hogmanay celebrations. Active engagement in the debate about values and spirituality in a pluralist society, giving content to the Christian contribution was extraordinarily successful in the very different fields of art, drama and the campaign for release of world debt.

Though other priorities were also visible and sometimes dominant in the media Churches throughout Great Britain were successful in seeing that the significance of AD2000 as an event in 'Christian time' was not overlooked by the public or by the public authorities.

3.5 Mission: A Year of Celebration

Local celebrations throughout 2000 were so widespread and varied that any selection is almost invidious. What is included in this Report is simply an attempt to convey a flavour of a nation-wide endeavour.

In the Presbytery of Gordon, Cluny congregation planted a 'millennium garden'; Campbeltown Churches arranged a fireworks display; in the Presbytery of Ardossan a Presbytery Praise Band Festival and Summer Service was held and at Kilwinning: Abbey a *son et lumiere* presentation was held; the congregations of Ervie Kirkcolm and Leswalt arranged for an illuminated Cross eight metres high that could be seen from Ireland to be in place over the Hogmanay period; the Presbytery of Kirkcaldy sponsored the publication of a specially-collected Book of Children's Prayers; the chaplaincy team at Grangemouth High School arranged an 'It's about time' focus week supported by the Mission's Missions Co-ordinator of the Board, Rev Paul Beautyman.

Youth work and activities have been the chosen focus for some. Among these are - the Presbytery of St Andrews supporting the appointment of a new ecumenical youth worker; the distribution of Gospels to schools in Aberdeen; a special emphasis on youth outreach in the congregations of Glenelg and Kintail, Gairloch and Dundonnell, and Lochcarron in the Presbytery of Lochcarron-Skye.

'World Church' millennium projects included - the Presbytery of Shetland sponsoring a millennium-year Faithshare appointment; the Presbytery of Greenock raising £22,000 for the 'Wells Campaign' for Malawi; 'Partick 2000' in Glasgow raising support for villagers in Peru; the congregation of Forfar: East and Old raising nearly £6,000 for WaterAid to provide water supply, sanitation and health education for villagers in central Nepal.

Apart from Presbytery and congregational activities across Scotland throughout the year there were a significant number of public celebrations at Pentecost. Around 30,000 gathered across the following locations on Sunday 11th June 2000:

East Kilbride
'Praise in the Park' (Calderglen Country Park)

Dunfermline
Family Day (Pittencrieff Park)

Glasgow
'Pentecost 2000' (Hampden Park)

Inverness
'Praise in the Park' (Caley Thistle Stadium)

Irvine and Kilmarnock
Pentecost Festival (Rugby Park)

Kenmay
Pentecost Festival

Perth
Pentecost Festival

Events, special gatherings and projects continued into the Autumn of 2000 bearing testimony that the concept of the Year of Celebration had not been an empty aspiration. ACTS seconded the Rev Rodney Matthews to co-ordinate a pilgrimage entitled 'Pilgrims Crossing' which culminated at Holyrood, Edinburgh, in September as part of a Europe-wide programme of pilgrimages.

The AD2000 Working Group was able to approve 30 grants in the Autumn of 2000 in response to applications from Presbyteries and events and projects supported included the 'Lewis Live' youth event (August), the 'Faith in the Park' event in Aberdeen for youth and young families (September), a multimedia event in Kirkcaldy to mark the end of the year 2000, Advent and Christmas celebrations in Upper Donside, and a 'Last day of the Year' service sponsored by the Churches of Inverness.

4.   Conclusion

Most of the goals set by the Board in October 1995 were in fact achieved—

- Commencement of the Scottish Churches Millennium with activities in 1997 inspired by commemoration of Ninian, Columba and other missionaries
- Co-ordination with, and participation in, the planning of local authorities for the period of Christmas 1999/ New Year 2000
- Extended Christian celebration of Christmas at local level including services of rededication and commitment in every church in January 2000
- The marking of Easter 2000 as a Season of Evangelism at local and regional levels
- Evolution of a series of vision-building, national-scale events in key Scottish centres between Easter and Pentecost 2000

- Active engagement in the debate about values and spirituality in a pluralist society, giving content to the Christian contribution.

There have been some disappointments. On the one hand the least noticeable from a central perspective of goals achieved was the marking of Easter 2000 as a Season of Evangelism at local and regional levels. On the other it is clear that the 1997 decision to avoid very large 'national' scale events was correct with the experience in Glasgow. 10,000 at the ecumenical festival at Hampden Park at Pentecost 2000 was a fine achievement with a lively programme—but the necessary size of the location led to a funding crisis resolved only by the granting of additional financial support by both the Presbytery of Glasgow and the AD2000 Working Group. In some parts there was something of an anticlimax. The Master of Downing College, Cambridge, wrote:

'The Millennium celebrations came and went and we are now left wondering what all the fuss was about. There were lots of parties and fireworks but no Armageddon and no outbreak of the dreaded Y2K computer bug that was predicted would cause aircraft to fall from the skies. And perhaps it was rather meaningless, celebrating a birth date that had been wrongly calculated—and which ought really to have been celebrated a few years ago—and which had little justification beyond being a nice round number. So why then, if the year 2000 had no real meaning, should …' (his college be celebrating a centenary of its own).

Together with continued attention to the logical problem of 'which year anyway?' press and public interest in the financial and other troubles of the millennium symbol of the Government—the Greenwich Dome— also played a part in a downward slide of the image of the word 'millennium'.

Nevertheless this has been a unique episode in mission—carried to fulfilment by an extended and fruitful partnership, often ecumenical, between congregations and Church leaders at all levels, the commitment, skills and time of a range of Church of Scotland executive, office and field staff, and partnership with the Presbyteries and Boards of the Church. An essential point has been the decision to invite and support local initiative:

the fulfilment of the vision of an appropriate Christian celebration, the Board firmly believes, must be rooted in the life of the parishes of our land …'

DAVID RANDALL, *Convener, AD2000 Working Group*
FRANK BARDGETT, *Secretary*

APPENDIX V

GM Animals, Humans and the Future of Genetics

Society, Religion and Technology Project

1. Introduction

While the controversy of GM foods has been so much in the news, the genetic engineering of animals has been comparatively ignored. It was one of the main themes of the SRT Project study "Engineering Genesis", in which context it was mentioned briefly in SRT's 1998 Assembly report as well as in the 1997 National Mission report on Animal and Human Cloning.[1] The recent genetic engineering of a monkey in the USA has now brought to the fore some important issues about the research on animals for human benefits. The dramatic developments in cloning and embryonic human stem cells are raising another basic question of the increasingly blurred borderline between animal and human research. Research done on animals today, like cloned sheep and mouse stem cells, can rapidly become applied for use in humans. Insights from human examples feed back into animal research. In this report, we wish to examine how far we may use and modify animals for human uses, and the relationship between biotechnology in animals and in humans. By way of example, we discuss the latest developments in xenotransplantation, animal models of human disease, and cloning and stem cell technology.

The genetic engineering of animals has stimulated much public discussion, and raises a number of important questions about human intervention in animals. Despite much research, it has not found significant application in animal production for meat, milk, eggs, wool or hides. So far it seems to offer few advantages over conventional breeding and the promising field of genetic marker assisted selection. Genetic engineering in animals has primarily been in novel applications in medicine, and in particular making pharmaceuticals in the milk of farm animals, pig organs in humans, and use of mice and other animals as models of human disease.

2. Theological Reflection on the Human Use of Animals

The universe is created by God. It is not merely "nature". It belongs to God, not human beings. Because God created them, animals have intrinsic value. They exist first of all in relation to God, before any considerations of their value and use to humans. Humans, however, have a special place, being both a part of creation and also over it. Humans are uniquely the bearers of God's image. Two expressions of the relationship are found in the opening chapters of Genesis. For centuries the emphasis was in strong terms of dominion or subduing from Genesis 1.[2] In recent years belated recognition of the environmental damage we have caused has led to a recovery of second picture, in the gentler language of working and caring for a garden.[3]

The relationship of humans to God's creation has been expressed most often in Calvin's notion of the steward. God gives humans a special duty both to develop the natural world—and hence the use of technology - but also to take care of it—which puts limits on our activities. Stewardship means that humankind is answerable not merely to future human generations, but to God, the divine owner, for how we have looked after his estate. Alongside this Ruth Page introduced the notion of companionship, to reflect that we are also fellow creatures in a shared creation.[4] Thus while God puts animals under human subjugation for a wide variety of uses, they are still God's creatures first, and humans will have to give an account to God for their care of them. Old Testament injunctions such as "Do not muzzle an ox when it is treading out the grain", "Do not boil a kid goat in its mother's milk." (Deuteronomy 25:4 and 14:21) imply that wider principles of relationship set restraints on human uses.

This contrasts with historical views of animals as merely there for human purposes,[5] or the view that they are not radically different from us scientifically or morally.[6] Aspects and characteristics which human and animal hold in common, like both being creatures, being "subjects of a life",[7] or being sentient,[8] do not mean that humans cannot eat animals or use them for traction and carriage. The notion of animal "rights" is criticised because in a Christian understanding there are no rights without corresponding responsibilities, and animals do not have responsibilities towards humans it is meaningless to give them rights.[9] Rather we would stress our duties towards them under God.

Commercial animal production by selective breeding would be allowed, but not to every degree possible. Limits are exceeded when this is taken as an end in itself, or if it becomes so dominated by a functional view of the animal under pressures of economic efficiency that wider principles of God's creation are overridden. The case of poultry production has shown that when taken to such degrees that harms, distortions, disablement or impairment of function begin to emerge, a good end would have been taken too far.[10]

3. GM Animals

Genetic engineering opens up an even wider range of technical possibilities. As we have seen most of these relate to medical applications. How far are we justified in manipulating our fellow creatures, or indeed any part of God's creation, even in the cause of human medicine? How do we balance the ethical dilemma which this poses? First we must ask a more fundamental question.

Is genetic engineering inherently wrong, irrespective of its application or its consequences?

Some Christians may consider that to change a single gene in an animal would be attempting to change God's best design, upsetting the wisdom inherent in the natural order by humans who did not know the full extent of the unprecedented changes they were making. Some would say we should not genetically engineer animals in any way we would not do in humans. The SRT report to the 1999 Assembly on genetically modified food and crops established grounds that manipulating genes and transferring them amongst widely varying species did not in itself violate a fundamental limit in the nature of things. The same would apply to animals, but, as with GM crops, there are important caveats. The nature of an animal, like plants and humans, is more than the mere sum of its genes but lies in the wider essence of the creature as a whole. Animals are also in constant genetic variation. To change one or two genes is not like changing a fixed blueprint, which would irretrievably violate the animal, unless the result brought about a severe impairment or suffering to the animal. We must therefore ask whether a particular genetic change poses special problems in relation to the nature of the animal, and also what regard we give to different types of animals, for example, primates, pigs, mice, frogs and midges.

A "No, unless" approach might allow uses where the prime benefit was to the animal, such as increased disease resistance, or in cases where a major human benefit could be achieved with minimal interference in the animal. It would be more critical about increased growth rate in animal production, whether the level or nature of intervention was permissible, and what motives were driving it. It would ask if there were better ways to the same end without manipulating the animal.

4.   Pharmaceuticals in GM Sheep Milk.

The ability to genetically modify animals in order to produce valuable proteins such as pharmaceuticals in their milk has been one of the most innovative applications of the genetic engineering techniques. Pioneered at the Roslin Institute and PPL Therapeutics, it has now been applied to cattle, sheep and goats in order to produce a variety of different proteins. The leading example, now in the last phase of clinical trials, is alpha-1-antitrypsin (AAT) for treating lung diseases emphysema and cystic fibrosis. It is produced in the milk of sheep by adding the human gene which codes for the protein in humans. A related area of research is in genetically modifying poultry to produce pharmaceuticals in the eggs.

The 1997 General Assembly Report on cloning acknowledged that this did not raise undue ethical problems. The use of sheep milk is traditional and therefore to produce a particular protein in the milk would not seem an undue departure from the current situation, particularly since the sheep version of AAT is produced by the animal, albeit in the liver rather than in milk. The intervention in the animal is judged to be small, the human medical need being addressed is considerable, and other routes to the protein are much more difficult. Indeed, it could be argued as a genuine partnership, in which humans give especial husbandry and care of the sheep in exchange for a valuable product in the sheep's milk. No welfare concerns have arisen from this particular example.[11] In general this is an area where we would say "Yes, provided." One such proviso arose in research to produce a more active protein erythropoietin showed unacceptable welfare effects for the animals, which led to the trials rightly being terminated.

5.   GM Pigs for Xenotransplantation

A much more serious intervention in farm animals is xenotransplantation. Various pig organs have potential for transplantation into human beings, including hearts and kidneys. Research in this area has been carried out for many years, prompted by hope that this would meet the shortfall in supply for human organs, where people are currently dying while on the waiting list. There are immense technical problems, however, which in turn pose major issues of ethics.

The first is the rapid rejection by the human immune system of organs from another species. Pigs have to be genetically modified to try to overcome this. Several human genes have to be added to the pig to send "human" signals that would prevent the human immune system not to reject the organ. There are as many as four genes involved. This requires multiple gene changes, something which has never been done before in a large animal, and is hard to achieve even in plants. It also requires knocking out genes in the pig which would trigger the rejection. So far most genetic engineering has only added genes. The nuclear transfer cloning of piglets by PPL in 2000 has opened a potential way to do this, if gene deletion were done *in vitro* in cells, and if pigs could be "grown" from these genetically altered cells. This is uncharted scientific territory. No one knows if this can be done to overcome rejection to a sufficient degree for a viable medical procedure.

The second technical barrier is the remote risk of the transfer of a pig retrovirus to humans, to which humans might not be immune. The concern is less for the patient, who is probably terminally ill anyway, but about the possibility that such a virus might be transmitted to the family and then out into the wider human population. This is an extremely remote risk, in terms of probability, but it could have epidemic consequences were such a chain of events to occur. The origins of HIV and the trans-species aspect of BSE both present scenarios sufficient for the government to have a moratorium on clinical trials. Its advisory body on xenotransplantation has recommended draconian restrictions on the patient and family, were clinical trials ever to begin. The implications and evaluation of this lie beyond the scope of the present report, but it clearly indicates the delicacy and complexity of the animal—human interface.

For the present report our main ethical concern is to review the use of animals in this way. To breed and genetically engineer an animal solely to remove an entire live organ represents a different use of animals from anything humans have done before. It is a large leap from using pig heart valves, which are merely dead tissue with convenient elastic properties. The "yuk reaction", which the idea of xenotransplantation often prompts, suggests that having a complete animal heart inside oneself poses underlying questions beyond mere unfamiliarity. Some respond by contending that if we accept eating pigs, it is even more justified to use them this way to save human life. This purely consequential way of framing the issue is shallow, however. Logically it would justify doing literally anything to a pig in order to save human life. It is at odds with any ethical perspective

based on the notion that animals have intrinsic value, and the implication from the biblical examples that animal use eventually has limits. The landmark Banner Report on animal ethics established that there are some things we should never do to animals, no matter what the reason.[12] This "ham sandwich argument" also side steps other issues. Unlike eating animals, there is no parallel to xenotransplantation in nature. The fact that xenotransplantation is unnatural, in that sense, may not necessarily make it wrong, but it prompts a question whether this is an acceptable extension of human use of animals from traditional suppliers of food, clothing, traction, transport and manure?

For some, even if the genetic change is not an objection, the interspecies mixing of whole organs violates a wisdom in God's natural order, of which the retrovirus risk is a physical indication, indeed a warning that this is quite different from eating pigs. For our working group the majority did not feel they would draw an absolute line here, but expressed some serious reservations. We noted that creating pigs to kill them to obtain transplant organs is different from taking the same organ from someone already dead. It constitutes a serious intervention in highly intelligent animals with some close physiological similarities, and for whom many humans have a special fondness. There are also animal welfare questions about the quality of life for the pigs kept, of necessity, in a highly sterile environment.

We suggested a "no, unless" approach. It would only be justified in exceptional circumstances. Does the mismatch in supply and demand for a surgical procedure which has become resource limited—the "shortage" of transplant organs—might meet the case? A few months of life extension, with immunosuppressant drugs merely delaying the inevitable death would not be reason enough. A long, high quality life might well be, if the technology could work well enough. It is justified to conduct research while this remains a realistic prospect. Given the complexity of the multiple genetic modifications that are now likely to be needed, it is not a foregone conclusion that there will come a point where that ethical balance would be reached for it to become an accepted therapy.

6.   GM Animals as Models of Human Disease

The largest application of transgenic animals by far is the use of mice as models of human disease and tests for potential therapies. The first example was the Harvard oncomouse, with an added human gene which gave it a form of human cancer. The certainty of giving such mice cancer, compared with a statistical probability of a population of mice, was claimed to lead to less mice being needed in research. The opposite has been the case. The applications in mice have increased enormously to the point where GM mice are used in a wide range of experiments.   Once a gene is identified in the human genome project, it has become almost routine to seek to "knock out" the equivalent gene in a mouse and to try and identify the function of the gene.

In "Engineering Genesis" we pointed the anomaly of the vast increase in model mice against the general European trend in animal research of the "3 R's" - reduce, refine and replace.   We suggested that the use had become too automatic, and steps needed to be taken to make researchers think twice before using mice.[13] The fear is that mice have ceased to be seen as animals at all, in this context, and are merely items in a research catalogue.

This poses a deep ethical dilemma for Christians. No one could justify wilfully genetically changing a mouse to give it cancer, or one of a range of fatal and painful human diseases, were it not for the awfulness of those diseases in humans, and the immense difficulties of the medical profession in understanding and treating them. There are almost two cultures, depending on what one's exposure has been to the issue. For the medical research community, the imperative of relieving human suffering is overwhelming in this area of disease. For the animal welfare lobby, there is the sense of outrage at what we are doing to defenceless animals.

Here we reach a generic issue about the use of animals in human medical research. Christians may be torn both ways. There is a deep sense of concern for the human suffering that might be alleviated, but a deep reluctance to treat another of God's creatures merely as a source of spare parts, or to programme them genetically to have dreadful diseases. While we would find it difficult to say an absolute "no" to xenotransplantation or GM mouse models, there would be individual experiments and uses which would not necessarily be justified.

There are also be types of animals whose use might not be justified. It has been suggested that sheep would be a better model for studying cystic fibrosis than mice, because mice do not develop the corresponding symptoms in the lung. For farm animals it is becoming more difficult to justify. To satisfy a "No, unless" policy, it is even more important to ask how necessary would the intervention be and how good the model. In the case of primates, however, utility to human medicine has surely reached a limit.

How do we decide amongst animal species? Most people value large mammals and primates higher than small mammals like mice and rats, because of more human-like characteristics. Primates possess much higher levels of sentience, consciousness and socialisation. The Home Office regulates UK animal research but seldom grants licenses for primate research, requiring "exceptional and specific justification". It is not enough to argue in this case that we need to use monkeys because they model human disease better, because the closer the animal models the disease the more likely the animal is unfortunately to suffer. Whatever animal is used, moreover, a gulf always exists between disease in humans and in another species. It is unlikely that genetically modifying primates would ever provide that one vital difference between a treatment and none. Unless this were so, this use has no justification.

Animals are God's creations and have intrinsic value in themselves, regardless of any human value we attach to them or use we may put to them. While the Bible endorses some use of animals, it also sets restraints. Although there is no hard and fast line across the range of animals, the closer they are to humans, the more this should hold us back from intervening. In 1996 the Nuffield Council on Bioethics questioned the potential use of genetically modified primates as sources of human transplant organs, recommending that non-primates like pigs should be used instead.[14]

While there is undoubtedly a great concern to find treatments for serious human diseases, the ethical imperative for medical research should never be seen as an absolute. Other ethical factors must also be taken into account. These include our respect for higher animals and especially those closest to humans and of high degrees of sentience and consciousness. GM primates should in general be a line we should not cross over. We should be content to use lower animals and accept any limitations this imposes.

7. Cloning and Stem Cells : the Animal—Human Crossover

In 1997, SRT reported to the General Assembly on human and animal cloning. At that point, and since, cloning research was almost entirely confined to animals. The human interest in cloning was in the possibilities that reproductive human cloning might be attempted, despite the declared intention of the UK government never to allow it, and the unlikelihood that this would ever be safe. The persistent question in the media is that somewhere, someone will attempt it in the USA where private sector research is essentially unregulated, or in an "offshore" situation outside any restrictive jurisdiction. It began in animals to help in genetically engineering sheep more effectively to produce pharmaceuticals in their milk, but for some sections of the media, it is still all about who would clone the first human baby, however dangerous and unethical this would be.

In 1998, the isolation of human embryonic stem cells was announced in the USA, extending from many years of work in mouse stem cells. These are special cells in the early embryo before it begins to differentiate. At this point, they can turn into any type of cell in the human body. Two years ago, US scientists found a way to isolate them. Using special chemical treatments, they believe they can direct them into becoming any type of human cell they choose - skin, heart muscle, nerve cells, etc. This opens up a possibility to create replacement cells to inject into patients suffering from a wide range of diseases which cause irreversible cell degeneration, like Parkinson's, some heart conditions and diabetes. In December 2000, the UK Parliament gave its approval to research using these techniques to produce replacement cells for a range of human diseases where cell degeneration is crucial. Thus far, most of the research is however done in animals, for example into the ways in which early embryonic cells go through the strange process of differentiation. Mice have been genetically engineered to induce a form of Parkinson's disease and tests have been done on replacement cells as a possible mimic of a human therapeutic technique. Research in human stem cells will now proceed, but many of the discoveries may also feed back into other mammalian stem cells, and the spiral of development will continue.

8. Cloning for Human Therapeutic Purposes

We welcome the focus away from the cloning of human beings, about which the Church of Scotland was the first to give a clear ethical basis for what is now a near universal rejection. The use of nuclear transfer cloning to create embryos of the right genetic type to produce replacement cells presents further ethical dilemmas, however, in addition to those discussed above for human embryos in general.

The vote in Parliament extended the uses of embryos to include making embryonic stem cells for serious human disease. Most of cells needed would be taken from existing "spare" embryos from IVF treatments. The careless use of the word cloning to describe this caused much confusion, but it does point to an issue of concern. MP's did not have any chance to vote on the cloning of embryos, because it was technically legal due to a loophole in the Act. The present Human Fertilisation and Embryology Act (1990) allows the creation of embryos for limited research purposes, mainly to do with infertility. On these grounds, the creation of cloned embryos has been forbidden, because this would be seen as reproductive cloning. By creating a new legal use for creating embryos for a non-reproductive use - to create stem cells - the Commons vote automatically allowed the cloning of embryos for this purpose, without ever voting on it. The influential European Commission ethical advisory panel reported on these issues in November 2000 and drew an ethical line at cloning embryos, as did a vote in the European Parliament. The UK vote should not be seen as a mandate to allow cloned embryos also, because this has not been put to a proper democratic test. We need early primary legislation on therapeutic as well as reproductive uses of cloning.

Cloned human embryos present several ethical problems. Firstly, it seems illogical to allow the creation of a cloned human embryo knowing full well one would have to destroy it on *ethical* grounds, because it was unethical to allow it to go to term to produce a cloned baby. The second objection is that this involves the deliberate creation of an embryo for other than reproductive purposes, although this is not specific to cloning. The use of "spare" embryos from fertility treatments would be a use of an embryo that would be destroyed anyway.

Thirdly, there is a gradualism argument. Once cloned human embryos were created, it would be much easier for someone misguided enough to go the next step and allow them to be implanted, or for someone rich enough to seek a clandestine "off-shore" treatment. This underlines the need for clear national laws, in those states which do not currently have them, to outlaw the practice of human cloning worldwide.

The creation and use of cloned human embryos should not be allowed as a general therapeutic procedure. We urge, however, that a priority should be put on nuclear transfer research which aims at avoiding use of embryos, by direct programming from one adult body tissue type to another. One could take, perhaps, a blood sample and reprogramme directly into becoming, say, a set of nerve cells. This is of course even more speculative than the methods discussed above, but several routes have recently been suggested. Ethically this would remove most of the above objections.

There is also a further reason. The ethics committee of Roslin's collaborators, the Geron Biomed company, has urged that the technique should have the widest applicability and not be simply a treatment for the rich. It is very unlikely that enough human donor eggs could ever be provided to treat the millions of potential patients across Europe. It would therefore probably be essential to find a method of producing replacement cells without using embryos. On present evidence, however, this would probably be impossible without some human embryo research to work out the method. This poses a deep ethical dilemma whether a very limited and fixed number of experiments should be allowed to obtain the data necessary to avoid any such use of embryos in future. Some would reluctantly argue for very limited research for this sole purpose, but if it seemed unlikely to succeed, then it should stop, and not proceed to use embryos routinely for cell therapies.

Some exaggerated claims have recently been made for alternative sources of stem cells, for example from human adult cells or placental material. While recent advances in these areas are indeed encouraging, scientists are urging great caution over assuming universal therapeutic success with any one method, when these are still very early stages in research. One speculative means to produce stem cells may already be rejected on ethical grounds, however. This is the production of non-viable human embryos within cow's eggs. The idea would be to take a human cell and perform a nuclear transfer into a denucleated cow's egg. Passing an electric current would fuse the two and stimulate the human cell to divide as though it were a human embryo, but one which was not viable. At the blastocyst stage of division, the stem cells would be removed and cultured as human somatic cells. This raises many serious uncertainties and risks, not least whether the use of a cow's egg as a host for the human cell had no adverse effect on the eventual human cell lines. It would raise immense ethical problems. Even though it would avoid the creation of a human embryo, the mixing of human and animal genetic material at such a profound level would raise a major intrinsic ethical objection for many people.

9.   Conclusions

This report has set out several key areas involving genetic engineering in animals for human medical research and examined the complex crossover point, scientifically and ethically. The use of animals by humans is accepted in general, but our duty also to respect them as God's creatures sets limits to what we may do. Animal selective breeding is acceptable, but not where this becomes dominated by a merely functional view of the animal, without regard for any harms caused. Good ends can be pursued too far. GM applications in animals are not seen as wrong in themselves, but require a significant justification. Genetic intervention should not be done to the impairment of the animal without very good reason; some interventions may be unacceptable for any reason. A range of applications was considered in this respect :

- Pharmaceutical production in the milk and eggs of farm animals was acceptable except in cases where it would harm the animal significantly.

- Xenotransplantation is more problematical. Using live pig organs in humans represents a new and serious human intervention in intelligent animals. For some this is fundamentally unacceptable ethically; others have less reservations. A "no, unless" approach is suggested. It would not be justified unless it was realistically likely to deliver substantial human benefit. This is at present uncertain, but it warrants further research.

- The use of GM mouse as disease models poses a serious ethical dilemma between seeking treatments of fatal and painful human disease and the suffering caused in the animal. The great increase in the use of GM mouse models and "knockout mice" arouses concern. The established "3 R's" principle of refining, reducing and replacing animal research use points to the need for greater restraint on the part of medical researchers in GM mouse use.

- The ethical imperative for medical research should not be seen as an absolute. Respect for higher animals suggests that we should not GM primates to model human disease.

The areas of cloning and stem cells illustrate how research begun in animals quickly passes into humans and back again, raising new and complex issues on both sides. The ethical problems of therapeutic applications of human embryo cloning have been briefly reviewed.

Because of a legal loophole, the vote in the UK Parliament to extend the use of embryos to stem cells has automatically allowed the creation of cloned embryos for this purpose. This aspect is proving highly controversial, especially as it is only one step from cloning human beings. It would only be justified under very limited circumstances, if at all. The changes in legislation allow too much latitude on this particular point, and primary legislation is urgently needed. Developments in alternative sources of stem cells without using embryos are encouraging, but at this very early stage in this new science, we should not raise premature expectations by claiming this will necessarily supersede any need for embryonic stem cells. The use of human-animal hybrid embryo constructions are ethically unacceptable.

References

[1] Church of Scotland (1997), "Cloning Animals and Humans", Supplementary Reports to the Church of Scotland General Assembly, May 1997, p. 36/22, and Board of National Mission deliverances 35 and 36, p.16.

[2] Gen. 1:26-28

[3] Gen. 2:15

[4] Page, R. (1986) "The Earth is the Lord's": Responsible Land Use in a Religious Perspective. In *While the Earth Endures*, SRT Project, Edinburgh.

[5] Aquinas, *Summa Contra Gentiles*, Third Book, Pat II, Ch. CXII, (English Translation by the Dominican Fathers, Benzger Brothers 1928, New York)

[6] Farm Animal Welfare Council (1998), *Report on the Implications of Cloning for the Welfare of Cloned Livestock*, PB 4132, Ministry of Agriculture, Fisheries and Food, London.

[7] Regan, T (1988) The Case for Animal Rights, Routledge: London

[8] Singer, P (1990) Animal Liberation, second edition, Cape: London

[9] Barclay, O (1992) Animal Rights: a Critique, Science and Christian Belief, vol 4, no 1, p49

[10] Engineering Genesis, *op.cit.*, p.89ff and p.110ff

[11] Appleby M.C. (1998) Genetic Engineering, Welfare and Accountability. *Journal of Applied Animal Welfare Science*, vol 1, pp 255-273

[12] Banner (1995), *Report of the Committee to Consider the Ethical Implications of Emerging Technologies in the Breeding of Farm Animals* (Banner Report), Ministry of Agriculture, Fisheries and Food, HMSO, London

[13] Engineering Genesis, chapter 5

[14] Nuffield Council on Bioethics (1996), *Animal-to-Human Transplants: the Ethics of Zenotransplantation*, Nuffield Council on Bioethics, London.

APPENDIX VI

Review of Chaplaincy Provision and Responsibility in the light of the Community Care Act

Analysis of a Survey of Healthcare Chaplaincy in Long Stay Units

INTRODUCTION

At the 1999 General Assembly of the Church of Scotland an addendum was agreed which asked the Board of National Mission Hospitals and Universities Sub-Committee "to review chaplaincy provision and responsibility in the light of the Community Care Act".

The National Health Service and Community Care Act 1990 was a far reaching piece of legislation affecting the provision of care of some of the most vulnerable groups in society—those with mental health problems, those who are physically disadvantaged, those with learning difficulties and the elderly. One consequence of the Act has been the transfer of patients in these categories from long stay beds in NHS hospitals to smaller units in the community—supported accommodation, nursing homes, residential homes and other accommodation. The reduction since 1990 in the number of occupied long stay beds in NHS hospitals has had implications for NHS chaplaincy provision and responsibility. It also raised the question of the provision of ministry in community care homes.

Legislation requires Nursing Homes staff to document the religion of all residents in Nursing Homes. This could be interpreted as indicating that residents' religion and spiritual needs do require to be known to the Home and, it is assumed, met.

The Hospitals and Universities Sub-Committee formulated a questionnaire which was sent with a covering letter to all Presbyteries.

Response from Presbyteries

Out of 46 Presbyteries, only 31 returns were received; three offered nil replies, 12 failed to reply at all. This is a disappointing response which it makes it impossible to give an accurate nation-wide picture.

The responses covered 100 hospitals/units. This figure does not include returns from acute hospitals with no long stay beds. It does include hospitals which are due to close but at the time of the survey were still functioning.

Beds and Chaplaincy Sessions

The first two questions sought information about the number of beds and the number of chaplaincy sessions in each unit at 1990 and 1999.

As anticipated there has been a marked reduction in the number of long stay beds especially in larger hospitals. The bed reduction in 20 hospitals with over 100 beds whose bed totals had been reduced by more than 10% was from 7,706 in 1990 to 3,194 in 1999 a reduction of 57.6%. The most dramatic reductions were understandably in those hospitals serving patients with learning difficulties and mental illness earmarked for complete closure. Most smaller hospitals with less than 100 beds have maintained their numbers.

The reduction in chaplaincy sessions has not always kept pace with the reduction in the number of beds. Although information is incomplete, the following observations can be made:

(a) The number of chaplaincy sessions in the larger hospitals has been reduced in line with the reduction in bed occupancy.

(b) Where feasible there has been a move towards whole-time chaplaincy with hospitals previously served by part-time chaplains grouping together to justify a whole-time appointment.

(c) Smaller hospitals have tended not to reduce the number of chaplaincy sessions at all; indeed a few hospitals with reduced numbers have actually increased chaplaincy sessions.

(d) Some hospitals are understaffed chaplaincy-wise e.g. the sessional criteria for the appointment of chaplains is not being properly applied. Where chaplaincy sessions need to be adjusted upwards or downwards, Presbytery should liaise with Trusts and agree the correct level of chaplaincy involvement.

Closure of Long Stay Units and Hospitals

Out of a 100 units for which information was given 41 had lost wards or had been closed all together. Some of these units had been replaced, some had merged and some had moved to new accommodation.

The Responsibilities of Chaplains

The questionnaire asked for information about the change in the responsibilities of chaplains during the period 1990 to 1999. Of 100 replies 41 reported little or no change and two didn't know. Of the rest, the following changes were reported:

(a) More individual patient counselling instead of ward visits; more one to one work.

(b) More work with relatives.

(c) A much quicker turn-over of patients and therefore less continuity in patient contact; more demented patients; a greater concentration of more disabled resident patients; conversation with patients much more difficult; only seriously disabled patients left in the wards; more time spent with patients and staff.

(d) More requests to visit former patients now accommodated in nursing homes and other community care accommodation; more referrals from GPs and consultants; more community referrals; visits requested to rehabilitation units; more visits requested to day hospitals and day bed units.

(e) More work entailed conducting worship in separate units; no services in other units; in yet one other a new monthly service.

(f) Community care staff seek support; more work with staff in hospital is needed; staff facing change and job insecurity require support; the morale of staff has fallen.

(g) More use of volunteers who make an essential contribution to the well-being of patients and residents as visitors, flower arrangers, readers, escorts and offer a host of other services as well.

Ministry to Patients Cared for in the Community

The questionnaire asked for information as to whether chaplains were expected to continue to visit discharged patients in community accommodation. 40 respondents answered 'No'. 17 respondents replied that visits were not expected but requests for them came from patients, relatives and staff.

Chaplaincy Arrangements within Nursing Homes and Supported Accommodation

Pastoral care is often given by parish ministers and ministers of other denominations in the locality. The churches together, local congregations and elders play a part usually on a rota basis. One Presbytery has appointed a chaplain to each home; one Presbytery followed the guidance of the 1990 General Assembly and ensured that each home was given the name of a key minister to contact as required. In some places there were too many nursing homes for any chaplaincy arrangement to be made; for example in one parish there were 8 nursing homes or other places offering supported accommodation.

With one exception all chaplaincy arrangements in supported accommodation units were informal and unpaid.

Comments

Respondents felt the need to establish a system of pastoral care in nursing homes. Many felt that chaplaincy is a key element in long stay units. Some chaplains reported that they enjoyed their ministry. Others were conscious that additional services were required and undertaken; that chaplains were always on-call and that there were many more self-referrals. Some described their ministry as a burden; some as a pleasure.

Implications for Chaplaincy and Recommendations

The Sub-Committee recommends that chaplaincy provision in long stay units should be reviewed regularly by Presbyteries and Trusts.

The work which chaplains undertake in day centres, day bed units and with relatives and members of staff should be acknowledged when sessions are calculated.

Patients who remain in the National Health Service rather than being transferred to care in the community are reported to suffer from much more severe problems and require a lot of time and attention; patients with different kinds of illness are often thrown together and the mix is not always a happy one. This presents doctors, nurses and chaplains with difficulties. Support and training of chaplains would be welcomed by most. There is now an ideal opportunity to find new strategies and models for community based chaplaincy involving a partnership between the Church and the NHS. It is recognised that such development will require funding.

Conversely the private sector is not so well provided as the National Health Service. To our knowledge arrangements in the private sector are informal and unpaid with one exception. Nevertheless local ministers provide a service to most nursing homes and other supported accommodation if invited. Local ministers however and part-time chaplains who have a charge may be overburdened as they are called to work in more and more locations. There is a need for a systematic review of the arrangements and Presbyteries should be invited to undertake this to ensure that ministry from all sources is available in these homes and that responsibilities are shared by all local ministers and churches lest any become over burdened.

Congregations should be encouraged to make welcome in their community those who are discharged from long stay units to live in their midst. It is to be regretted that some local communities have resisted the purchase of accommodation for community care purposes. We would expect the local church to challenge such 'NIMBY' attitudes and offer hospitality in the widest sense.

When patients are transferred from hospital to community care it is important that where appropriate referrals to local congregations are made by the hospital chaplains. A good working relationship between hospital chaplains and local ministers and congregations helps to ensure continuity of care.

APPENDIX VII

Report of Scottish Churches Industrial Mission

"Forestry units from Newfoundland had arrived to undertake urgent work in Speyside, Perthshire and the South and the Home Board reported on the need for an active ministry among them. Church Sisters were appointed as supervisors where girls were employed. They organised their leisure activities and tried to make up for the loss of family life. As a result of this work the Home Board in 1942 appointed a Church Sister to act as a chaplain in a factory where a large number of girls were employed." (from God, It's Monday" by Donald Ross.

Nearly sixty years later, the Rev Elisabeth Spence was the first woman to become a full-time Industrial Missioner in Scotland, when she was inducted on 27th June 2000 in a service that took place in the secular setting of the yard of the former Yarrows Shipbuilders, now BAE Systems, in Scotstoun, Glasgow. In that service we acknowledged the partnership between the churches, the management in industry and commerce and the trades unions that is critical to the working of industrial mission. We recognised too, the long-established, but hugely under-developed partnership between women and men in the work of the Church.

"In its report to the General Assembly in 1942, the Home Board recognised that practically every man and woman not eligible for enlistment in His Majesty's Forces, was working long hours, often at very hard work, and often seven days a week. Many who would worship regularly could not do so. "It is," said the

Report, "the duty of the Church to go to the people if the people are not able to go to church." The Home Board set aside one of its members— part-time—"to promote and develop the work of relating the church to industry and to arrange industrial chaplaincies." (from "God, It's Monday")

This remains the core task of today's industrial missioner.

Sometimes responding to Jesus' call to "follow me" is described as walking into the story of faith and we are able to trace a seamless thread of chaplaincy from our roots with those harvesting the vital raw materials and energy from the forests and hydro schemes in the war and post-war years to those harvesting the oil and gas under the North Sea in modern times; from walking round the shipyards in boom times to joining in the battle for new orders in the lean years of recent times. As the economy and patterns and nature of work has changed, so too the places where industrial missioners are to be found have changed. They are to be found today in retail shopping malls, in call-centres, in local government offices. Among the most significant of new chaplaincies established in the last year have been those to Edinburgh City Council involving an ecumenical team and at the new Braehead Shopping Centre near Glasgow Airport where the new chaplain combines his shopping centre work with other responsibilities in a parish.

We still tell our stories of faith in a Church without walls, incarnate in the workplaces of our land, amidst, very often, chilly winds of adversity, when the word of hope seems a cruel mockery. In an age when the church seems engaged in a desperate struggle for survival, people still respond, and the demand for new chaplaincies continues.

We are very grateful to all the women and men who, as part of their Christian ministry, faithfully serve as voluntary workplace chaplains. So often, far from it being yet another burden in lives already overloaded with responsibility, in workplace visiting they find welcome new stimulation, insight and purpose. Even the "old hands" are constantly invigorated by new experiences.

Rev Angus Smith, the oil industry chaplain tells of a

wedding of a young BP executive and his Norwegian bride. All the Norwegian friends and relatives attending were dressed in their national costume. "A friend of the bride stood beside me on the day and delivered my service phrase by phrase in Norwegian. At the reception, there were many impromptu Norwegian toasts all of which were concluded by a loud basso-profundo "Skol". Afterwards they danced like whirling dervishes to the music of a ceilidh band!". Angus's story also serves as a wee reminder of the global nature of so much of our industry and commerce.

An air of desperation seemed to envelop Britain last autumn. A fuel tax protest all but brought the country to a standstill. Then floods raged devastating peoples' homes and added to the rail chaos that followed the Hatfield disaster.

"Global warming" seemed real, no longer the theory of academics.

It hardly seemed credible that Railtrack knew of the deficiencies in the rails, not just at Hatfield, but on almost every main line in the country. Apparently they did! Almost total disruption of services ensued as emergency work was suddenly deemed necessary, but shareholders were still paid a healthy dividend and those resigning went off with golden six figure handshakes. A sharp contrast with the Biblical demands of responsibility where dangers are well known. (eg the owner of the bull known to be in the habit of attacking people. Exodus 21, 28f.)

Our fleet of nuclear-powered submarines had developed serious faults and polio vaccines were withdrawn because the manufacturers, assuring that there was no possible risk in the process, cut corners and introduced the possibility of CJD contamination. All in the pursuit of maximising profits. The meaning of "corporate responsibility" is now on the agenda in a way that it has not been for more than a generation.

Following all this, could safety in the air be compromised? Air traffic control is being passed into private control. Despite widespread public unease. The government stuck to their public/private partnership plan for National Air Traffic Services, insisting there was no compromise on safety. Perhaps they should heed the proverb, "If you have to choose between a good reputation and great wealth, choose a good reputation." Prov. 22,1.

For the church in Scotland all these difficulties seemed compounded by the sudden death of Duncan McClements, amongst many other commitments, an active voluntary chaplain in Falkirk and a former convener of the Church and Industry Committee. Vital, alive, belligerent, noisy, funny, passionate, compassionate, persistent, always seeking to be the voice of the voiceless, he challenged the Kirk he loved to be better and braver than it is. He was, thank God, a prophet in our day. We cannot doubt the need for the prophetic voice of challenge to continue in the economic and political life of Scotland today.

Jesus challenged, "Would any of you who are fathers give your son a stone when he asks for bread ….. bad as you are, you know how to give good things to your children ….. do for others what you want them to do to you; this is the meaning of the Law of Moses and of the teachings of the prophets."

Are we not the possessors of a treasure chest of truth and wisdom and light indisputably relevant to the world we inhabit?

APPENDIX VIII

Report of the Joint Prison Chaplaincies Board Annual Report 2000

The dissolution of the Board last year brought to an end 11 years of service to chaplaincy in Scottish Prisons. This period has witnessed many alterations in the strategic organisation and operation of the Prison Service in Scotland as it changed from a Department of the Scottish Office to an Executive Agency of the Scottish Office and ultimately of the new Scottish Executive.

The chaplaincy service developed substantially during the 1990s and the Board's initiative in encouraging ecumenical team co-operation in establishments is now the accepted norm.

Two full-time National Chaplains were appointed and these posts have since evolved into the current dual Specialist Advisers in Prison Chaplaincy. The introduction of Prisoners' Week, a time for the Church to commit prayer and reflection to all those affected by the tragedy of crime, was also a worthy milestone.

Thanks are expressed to all from the Church of Scotland, Roman Catholic Church and the Scottish Episcopal Church who gave to the Board their time and energy and provided encouragement, support and oversight to those who served, and continue to serve, in this often difficult, challenging but rewarding ministry.

In the name of the Board

KENNETH MCCAFFREY, *Convener*
JOHN K THOMSON, *Secretary*

APPENDIX IX

Report of the Joint Faiths Advisory Board on Criminal Justice

The Board was established following the initiative by the General Assembly of 2000 with a remit headed by a commitment to:

1 Contribute to the development of criminal justice philosophy, penal reform and the rights of offenders, untried persons and their families.
2 To stimulate the interest and participation of all faiths in ministry within the criminal justice system.

The first meeting was held in October when members explored the many issues the Board might begin to address. One very important task has been to build contacts and relationships with the various institutions, organisations and individuals which form the criminal justice system. As a new entity the Board must quickly establish its credibility to enable it to speak with any authority on crucial issues. It is important for the Board to be able to find among its members the wide-ranging talents, gifts, knowledge and experience to inform its work and to enable its remit to be effectively addressed.

In the name of the Board

BRUCE F NEILL, *Convener*
JOHN K THOMSON, *Secretary*

APPENDIX X

SCOTTISH CHURCHES COMMUNITY TRUST

1.   Formation

1.1   "The establishment of the Scottish Churches Community Trust is a powerful witness that the Church's calling to announce good news to the poor supersedes denominational differences." This was the final sentence in the Report of the Priority Areas Fund to the General Assembly of 2000. The formal incorporation and establishment of the new Trust in June 2000 brought to fruition the vision of the members of the Priority Areas Fund and other like-minded people in other denominations who believed that this work would be done best by the churches working together.

1.2   The denominations co-operating in the Trust are the Baptist Union, Church of Scotland, Congregational Federation, Methodist Church, Religious Society of Friends, Roman Catholic Church, Scottish Episcopal Church and United Free Church. Each of these eight churches has appointed a director to serve on the Board of the Trust. Three co-opted directors with complementary gifts and skills are also serving on the Board.

2.   Launch

2.1   The official launch of the Trust took place on 15th November at the St Matthew's Centre in Possilpark, Glasgow where the Trust has established its office base. It was in a real sense a 'launch' for the Trust had been built over the previous two and a half years by an inter-church Steering Group. All the hard work of obtaining the agreement of the different churches, drawing up the Memorandum of Articles and many other tasks had been undertaken by this group. The new directors literally came 'on board' to take responsibility for an organisation which had been carefully and thoughtfully constructed. The Trust Board would like to pay tribute to the work of the Steering Group and, in particular to its Convener Barbara Kelly and Secretary Iain Johnston.

2.2   Jackie Baillie, MSP, Minister for Social Justice joined church leaders and local people at the launch. Commenting on the inauguration of the Trust Jackie Baillie said: "I have long known that Scotland's churches do make an extremely important and valuable contribution to tackling poverty and disadvantage. By pooling resources the churches will indeed have a greater impact and will be able to deliver more on the ground."

2.3   The Moderator of the General Assembly, Rt Rev Andrew McLellan said: "The launch of the Scottish Churches Community Trust is a pledge to the poorest parts of Scotland that the churches will not walk away, will not refuse to listen, will not stand idly by, but will share in action."

2.4   The President of the Social Care Commission of the Roman Catholic Church in Scotland, Rt Rev John Mone, Bishop of Paisley, explained: "The Trust is about people helping each other to build community. It's a strong message that not only can we 'sing from the same hymn sheet', but also that what we can do together we should do together."

3.   Financial Arrangements

3.1   The Trust is grateful to the Church of Scotland for its contribution of £150,000 for the year 2001 (£100,000 from the Mission and Aid Fund and £50,000 from the Priority Areas Fund). The Trust will take over responsibility for the administration of the payment of grants to the projects already approved by the Priority Areas Fund which are due to run for up to four more years. £350,000 has been given by the Priority Areas Fund to cover these grants. The Trust will also monitor these projects and supervise the use of training allowances of £90,000.

3.2 Each church is free to raise money in its own way. Some denominations will make block-grants like the Church of Scotland. Others have chosen to make a direct appeal to congregations for support. It is hoped that a sum of between £200,000 and £300,000 will be available to be awarded as grants in 2001. The Trust hopes to obtain support from charitable trusts to cover the administration and development costs. A full-time Development Co-ordinator John Dornan and a part-time administrator have been appointed.

4. Grants
4.1 A Grants Sub-Group has been formed to make recommendations to the Board. Two of the directors, along with other people with appropriate skills, serve on this group.

4.2 The Trust will draw on the track record of four separate denominational initiatives involved in funding community development: the Archdiocese of Glasgow Pastoral Care Trust, the Church of Scotland Priority Areas Fund, the Episcopal Church Million for Mission and the Methodist Church Mission Alongside the Poor Programme.

4.3 The Trust will welcome applications for grants from congregations and community groups which are seeking to work together to meet the needs of deprived communities in both urban and rural areas. (For further information telephone 0141 336 3766).

5. Church of Scotland Representation
5.1 The General Assembly appointed Rev Ian Moir, the former Adviser for Urban Priority Areas, as the Church of Scotland's representative on the Board of the Trust. The directors have appointed Ian Moir as the Chair of the Trust. It is recommended that Ian Moir be appointed as the Church of Scotland's representative for a further year.

5.2 Churches often set out to change communities. Experience has shown that communities change churches. The Trust hopes that this will be the experience of many of the churches it will support.

BOARD OF THE IONA COMMUNITY
MAY 2001

PROPOSED DELIVERANCE

The General Assembly

1. Receive the report and thank the Board.

2. Commend the Iona Community in its continuing commitment to the renewal of worship, the promotion of ecumenical understanding and action for social and political change, particularly in the areas of racial justice, social exclusion, nuclear disarmament, and environmental concerns.

3. Encourage the Community in securing its interests in the developing relationship with Historic Scotland on Iona.

4. Express thanks to all the Community's staff at its residential centres on Iona and at Camas, particularly to Rev Brian Woodcock on the completion of his term as Warden in August 2001.

REPORT

General

1 The Board is happy to report that, over the period since the last Assembly, the Iona Community has had another encouraging and busy year. There is continuing evidence of strong interest in the life and concerns of the Community, reflected not only in another very good season on Iona but also in the response to the Community's 'outreach' work (whether through its youth and worship project workers or through events in which Community Members are involved).

Historic Scotland

2 Since the preparation of last year's report, the most notable occurrence has been the transfer to Historic Scotland on 1 April 2000, following careful and demanding discussions over the preceding eighteen months, of the Cathedral Trustees' responsibilities for the management and maintenance of the historic buildings. The experience of the working of the new 'partnership arrangements' over the past year has been broadly satisfactory with a good relationship developing between the Community's staff on Iona and the Historic Scotland staff – mostly local people from Iona and the Ross of Mull.

The admission arrangements to the historic site, and the particular provision for local people, the Community's staff and guests, and holiday-makers on Iona, as against day-visitors, seem to have been generally accepted.

3 One significant result of the changes has been the reduction of the Community's ministry of hospitality and the loss of refreshment facilities and a meeting-place for visitors, staff and guests (through the need to vacate the Community's shop in the Abbey cloisters, so as to accommodate the new Historic Scotland shop, and convert the former coffee-house building into the Community's shop). But the Community is now exploring the possibility of providing space for shop, refreshment facilities, offices and perhaps an interpretation centre either within a new multi-purpose building which would replace the former Coffee House or within other property owned by the Community on Iona.

4 As expected, the relocation of the Community's shop to a less strategically positioned site has resulted in a significant drop in income (over £100000—some £55000 net—comparing 1999 and 2000 figures) and this together with the agreed 'rental' (£15000 at present, rising to

£24000 when the legal processes are completed, and then by ten annual increments to £33000 per year) has affected the Community's overall financial position. The legal processes for the formal transfer of the buildings to Historic Scotland (replacing the present interim management agreement, although even under the new scheme ownership will remain with the Iona Cathedral Trustees) should be initiated shortly when one outstanding point, concerning insurance liability, is resolved.

Membership and Finance

5 Over the past year there have been further increases in the number of Members and Associates who are joining the Community to identify with its mission and share more fully in its work and concerns. Membership now stands at 241, and there are around 1500 Associates and 1200 Friends. 14 new Members were 'hallowed' during Community Week on Iona in August 2000 and, with 15 people starting the first year of the New Members' programme last October, it is at its full capacity of 24, drawn from a range of different denominations and occupations (7 ordained or about to be), covering an age range of early twenties to mid seventies and more or less equally balanced between Scotland and England.

6 With the election of a new Leader, to take over from Norman Shanks in August 2002, due to be held early next year, the Community has decided to embark upon a discernment process which will involve looking not only at the details of the election process but also at policy direction and priorities, and the model or style of leadership needed to achieve these.

7 The Board has also been kept fully informed of the Community's financial situation which has shown some unevenness over recent years, with a surplus in 1996 and substantial deficits in 1997 and 1998. Improvements in the systems of finance management produced a small surplus in 1999. The budget for 2000 was prepared on a break-even basis but the out-turn shows a loss of £5800 (to be covered by legacy reserves), owing largely to both the shop income for the season and MacLeod Centre bookings for the autumn being lower than expected.

Similarly, particularly with the added cost of the 'rent' due to Historic Scotland, it has not been possible to produce a break-even budget for 2001. On the other hand, it is very encouraging to report a steady rise in the contributions by the Community's 'constituency' and in donations (helped considerably in 2000 by the third instalment of the Guild's grant—substantially greater than expected at £22000—under their 'Riches and poverty' project). In order to address the longer-term issues, the Community has set up a fund-raising strategy group to help decide how to approach the situation where the Community can no longer rely, as hitherto, on established sources of funding (trading income, donations etc) but needs more actively to seek support both for 'core-funding' (a difficult task as so many voluntary organisations know) and for specific projects and purposes.

Islands Work

8 For the 2000 season on Iona the overall programme theme was 'Dreams for a new Millennium', and the centres have once again attained encouraging occupancy levels. The programme attracted groups and individuals from a wide range of settings (social, cultural, national), sometimes requiring special efforts by staff to deal with difficult situations and ensure that all were able to share in the communal experience. Among 'outside' programme leaders it was good to welcome back Inderjit Bhogal, not long before the start of his term as President of the Methodist Conference, Ian Bradley, for another highly popular week on Celtic Christianity ('Dreaming dreams and chasing myths'!), and Stan McKay, former Moderator of the United Church of Canada, for a week exploring the significance of 'First Nation' spirituality. The 2000 Youth Festival, catering for a younger age group than previously—14–18, was very successful; and a 'cross-centre' week 'Exploring Iona', run in collaboration with the Iona Heritage Centre, in which several local people were involved, attracted a very enthusiastic response and helped to strengthen relations with the local community. For the first time for several years, the Abbey was open to individual guests over the period up to the Christmas house-party, after which, as usual, it was closed until the start of the 2001 season towards the end of March. The

2001 programme follows the theme '2001—a Faith Odyssey'; and at this stage the level of bookings from groups and individuals compares favourably with previous years.

9   The Board is glad once again to be able to report positively on the staffing situation on Iona. Brian Woodcock as Warden and Jan Sutch Pickard as Deputy Warden have developed an effective style of working, founded on co-operation and consensus. They were successful in the 2000 season in creating a very good staff team who both understood the nature of the common task of witness through hospitality and in their common life embodied the Community's integrated spirituality; and they ensured that the quality of daily worship in the Abbey remains high. Over the past year there were again resident staff and volunteers from many different parts of the world; and for the 2001 season all the vacancies for resident positions, including two key three-year posts—Maintenance Co-ordinator and Domestic Supervisor—were filled in time for the people appointed to take part in the preliminary staff training that precedes the start of the season. Interviews are due to be held in March for a successor to Brian Woodcock who completes his term as Warden at the end of August: he will be returning to a charge in the United Reformed Church and the Board is pleased to record its appreciation of his very significant contribution to the Community's work on Iona and through that to the wider work of the church.

10 The Board has also been pleased to hear that the early evidence is encouraging from the change to the 6-day week in the centres on Iona which, as reported last year, has been introduced as a three-year experiment in an attempt, through reducing the pace and pressure a little, to mitigate or avoid the exhaustion or even break-down that has affected some members of staff previously. And the Board was encouraged too to learn about the Community's decision, on both environmental and financial grounds, to install a solar heating system at the MacLeod Centre. Another worthwhile innovation has been the 'Mac cover' arrangement, whereby a Member comes to the MacLeod Centre each week to provide health and safety cover in the absence of staff and take part in the programme so far as possible.

11 In 2000 the centre at Camas on Mull also had a good season with a committed staff team, led by Rachel McCann the Camas Co-ordinator who will be with the Community for another two seasons. A range of varied groups, mostly from disadvantaged backgrounds, enjoyed the distinctive opportunities and facilities that make Camas so attractive. The transition has been completed towards the creation of a new management structure through which the links with Iona will be maintained, if at a less formal level, but there will be more scope for focussing on the particularities of Camas and pursuing new funding and development possibilities.

12 With both Camas and Iona, the importance of fostering good relations with the local community has been recognised and many new contacts have been established. In the case of Iona the staff are involved in local activities, particularly off-season, the Community is represented on the local community council and the Iona liaison group (drawing together the various public bodies with an interest in Iona), and regular meetings take place with local representatives and Historic Scotland. Over the winter months there have been further discussions also about the route for the weekly Pilgrimage, which was altered for the 2000 season to take account of concern about land erosion in certain places and other issues raised by local people. There is in addition the controversial local issue of the proposed causeway, on which consultants have just completed preliminary consultations prior to a possible feasibility study: while the Community, with a presence on Iona, clearly has an interest in what happens, it has maintained a fairly low-key position, recognising that this is primarily a matter for local residents (who are divided on the matter), and declining to give comments to the press in support of a particular viewpoint.

Mainland Work

13 Since the Community's Youth Development Worker, Helen O'Donnell, with previous experience of working with volunteers in the Roman Catholic church, started

work in March 2000 she has made a considerable impact—through her involvement in the Iona programme and follow-up work on the mainland, through generating fresh enthusiasm among the Community's Youth Associates, and through developing promising and fruitful links with youth networks and within the Community's own structures. The other staff in the Community's administrative offices in the Pearce Institute continue to undertake the everyday tasks involved in maintaining the finances, dealing with the heavy load of correspondence and enquiries, and supporting the committee and membership structures. The staffing complement has been maintained at the previous level; but savings have been made through a shift to part-time work in two cases. It is encouraging that the arrangements for weekly staff worship are being sustained despite the inevitable absences from the office of some people who would otherwise attend regularly.

14   There have been some changes, more of emphasis than direction, within the work of the Wild Goose Resource Group, reflecting changing circumstances within individuals' lives and within the life of the church. The Wild Goose Worship Group, which has met weekly for fifteen years or so, has decided to suspend operations for a year, and Last Night Out, a monthly Sunday evening event in Glasgow to which the Worship Group made a significant contribution, has stopped—both in their prime rather than through any lack of demand or interest. Instead of these the members of the Resource Group are carrying out consultations to assess future needs and possibilities in relation to participative and relevant worship and have mounted a series of events in Glasgow —both training workshops and communal gatherings— over the past few months. In addition, the members of the Resource Group continue to travel widely leading worship workshops and taking part in both local and national conferences throughout Britain and overseas.

15   Over the past year Wild Goose Publications have continued to produce a succession of new titles which have been selling well: a 'sampler' of Wild Goose Worship Group songs—*Rare Species*; two books on healing—

Praying for the Dawn, liturgies and resources for healing services, edited by Kathy Galloway and Ruth Burgess, and *Jesus' Healing Works and Ours* by Ian Cowie; *Advent Readings from Iona* by Brian Woodcock and Jan Sutch Pickard; *My Dinner with Anton*, a book about St Seraphim of Sarov, by Paul Wallis; *The Singing Thing—a case for congregational song* by John Bell; a revised edition of the booklet *What is the Iona Community*; and *The One Loaf* by Joy Mead, a book celebrating and exploring the practical and religious significance of bread. After the completion of this report, but before the General Assembly, it is hoped that the long-awaited new edition of the *Iona Abbey Worship Book* will be available and also the new video, made by Pathway Productions, about the work of the Community—*The Iona Community: Today's Challenge, Tomorrow's Hope*, supplementing the story of the Community's first thirty years told in 1967 in *Sermon in Stone*. Also *One is the Body*, a new collection of songs by the Wild Goose Worship Group, is due to be released in April, in CD and cassette form at this stage with the book to follow shortly.

16   It has always been emphasised that what Members do in their own local situations, through the wide variety of their work and other activities, is as important a part of the life and work of the Community as what staff do and the activities of our centres on Iona and Mull. One of the joys of plenary meetings—the events each year when Members gather together—is the opportunity to catch up with and hear from one another, whether in informal conversation or through the more formal plenary programme. Since last year's Assembly there have been four plenary meetings—the Community's AGM at Glasgow in June, when Committees report, formal business is transacted, and Committee vacancies are filled; Community Week on Iona last summer when, in addition to a series of Members' reports and reflections on the work on Iona and at Camas, the Community was very privileged to have as its guest, and to hear from, Dr Konrad Raiser, General Secretary of the World Council of Churches, and his wife Elisabeth; a meeting at York at the end of October 2000 on the theme of non-violence, reflecting the Community's links with the Scottish Centre for Non-violence at Dunblane and support for the WCC's

forthcoming Decade to Overcome Violence and the UN Year and Decade for the Culture of Peace; and a gathering at YMCA Wiston Lodge, near Biggar in February, reflecting, with the help of Rev Graham Blount, the Scottish Churches Parliamentary Officer, on the work of the Scottish Parliament and themes of social exclusion, culture and identity.

17 It is hoped that some of the Community's social and political concerns will be reflected through the future development of a mainland programme, possibly with a particular focus on aspects of social exclusion, a theme in which is the Community is involved on a number of fronts through contact with the Scottish Churches Social Inclusion Network, connecting with the Scottish Parliament, and Church Action on Poverty among others. On other justice and peace issues, discussion at Community Week pointed to renewed commitment to environmental concerns; concerning nuclear disarmament, there are continuing close links with Trident Ploughshares 2000 and the Community was well represented at the demonstration at Faslane in February; and there has been further work on racial justice matters, through discussion on the future of the Scottish Churches Agency for Racial Justice, the campaign for the reform of Britain's nationality law and local training in racism awareness. Among youth concerns the formulation of an integrated Community child protection policy, building on the practice already in place on Iona, is nearing completion, and discussion is progressing on the revision of the Community's youth policy.

Conclusion

18 Through the wide range of commitments undertaken by staff and members, from local meetings to international conferences, the Community maintains its links with the churches throughout Scotland and much farther afield and seeks to be faithful to its missionary calling. What started as an experiment in ministry and mission, principally within a Scottish context and with a membership for the most part comprising male Church of Scotland ministers, has broadened in scope and grown in size. There are now more lay than ordained members, almost as many women as men, a significant number live in England with a few overseas, and all the main denominations are represented, as is reflected in the Board's own composition (with members from the Church of England, the United Reformed Church and the Society of Friends alongside those appointed by the General Assembly and the Community) and in the Community's formal membership of the ecumenical bodies for Scotland, England and Britain and its strengthening connections with the World Council of Churches. The Board is thus pleased once again to be able to report positively to the Assembly, to thank the Community for its continuing witness and to wish it well for the forthcoming year and beyond.

TOM GORDON *Convener*
JEAN WILLIAMS *Secretary*

COMMITTEE ON THE PRIORITY AREAS FUND

MAY 2001

PROPOSED DELIVERANCE

The General Assembly:

1. Receive the Report.

REPORT

1. INTRODUCTION

1.1 This report is brought to the General Assembly as an administrative review of the work of the Priority Areas Fund during 2000. The Committee's main final report was received by last year's General Assembly, which agreed that the Committee should be dissolved on 31 December 2000 and that the Priority Areas Fund should move on to become part of the newly formed Scottish Churches Community Trust.

1.2 The Scottish Churches Community Trust was set up and launched towards the end of last year and a separate report about this is given with the Report of the Board of National Mission.

1.3 The Committee held its final meeting on 5 December 2000; remaining funds and ongoing responsibility for the support of local projects have now passed to the Scottish Churches Community Trust.

2. REVIEW OF 2000

2.1 During 2000, main grants totalling £197,835 (1999: £213,922) were awarded to local groups. In addition, training allowances totalling approximately £49,000 (1999: £52,000) were allocated. 39 projects were supported covering work with children and young people, community meeting places, family support and childcare and general community support and advice. Approximately 74 per cent of funds were allocated to work in Urban Priority Areas and 26 per cent to rural areas.

Details of all main grants awarded are given in the following paragraphs.

2.2 Presbytery of Edinburgh
2.2.1 *Bosco Youth Association*: £2500 over two years towards the running costs of a youth project in Pilton.
2.2.2 *Drylaw Rainbow Club*: £3000 over one year towards the running costs of a day care centre for older people.

2.3 Presbytery of Dumfries
2.3.1 *Lincluden Church*: £1,000 towards the costs of providing a photocopier.

2.4 Presbytery of Ayr
2.4.1 *Cumnock Parent and Family Support Group*: £12,000 over four years towards the running costs of a centre to provide support to drug users and their families.

2.5 Presbytery of Paisley
2.5.1 *St Mary's Crossover Project, Paisley*: £1500 for one year towards the running costs of this project delivering furniture and related items free of charge to homeless people who have secured new tenancies.
2.5.2 *St Ninian's Eden Project*: £9000 over three years towards the equipment and running costs of a youth and community facility in Ferguslie Park, Paisley.

2.6 Presbytery of Greenock
2.6.1 *Hammy's Out of School Care, Port Glasgow*: £9000 over three years towards running costs of this out

of school care project providing subsidised placements for children in situations of stress.

2.6.2 *Presbytery of Greenock Inverclyde Family Contact Centre*: £7674 over four years towards the running costs of a family contact centre.

2.7   Presbytery of Glasgow

2.7.1 *Caring City*: £2000 towards the running costs of a programme for asylum seekers being housed in the city.

2.7.2 *Cranhill Community Project*: £2000 towards the costs of a feasibility study to create a church community centre.

2.7.3 *Glasgow Association for Mental Health*: £3850 over two years towards the running costs of a drop in centre for people with mental health problems, in partnership with Gorbals Church.

2.7.4 *Govan Ecumenical Youth Association*: £3000 towards the set up and equipment costs of a drop-in centre.

2.7.5 *Groundwork:* £12,000 over four years towards the running costs of an allotment gardening project for people disadvantaged by homelessness, unemployment and poverty.

2.7.6 *Lochwood Church, Easterhouse*: £3000 over four years towards the equipment and running costs of a playgroup.

2.7.7 *St Paul's Provanmill Church*: £3500 over two years towards the running costs of a youth project.

2.7.8 *St Thomas' Gallowgate Church*: £2000 towards the set up costs of a mobile children's project in the east end of Glasgow.

2.7.9 *Spark Initiative, Moodiesburn*: £7000 over four years towards the running costs of a home-support and befriending scheme.

2.7.10 *Starter Packs Glasgow*: £12,000 over four years towards the running costs of a service supporting homeless people in new tenancies.

2.7.11 *Vincentian Volunteers Scotland*: £9000 over three years towards the costs of running a volunteer community in the east end of Glasgow.

2.7.12 *Yoker Old Church*: £12,000 over four years towards the running costs of a community café.

2.8   Presbytery of Hamilton

2.8.1 *St Mary's Church/Women's Royal Voluntary Service, Hamilton*: £3000 towards the capital costs of creating a family contact centre.

2.9   Presbytery of Dumbarton

2.9.1 *Benview Centre*: £7700 over four years towards the running costs of a lunch club for older people.

2.10   Presbytery of Falkirk

2.10.1 *Focus Centre Trust*: £3000 towards the research and development costs of a project to support young homeless people in Denny and surrounding areas.

2.10.2 *Grangemouth Kirk of the Holyrood Church*: £750 towards the equipment costs of a lunch club.

2.11   Presbytery of Dunfermline

2.11.1 *Cowdenbeath District Second Millennium Projects*: £2350 over two years towards the costs of creating a community mural.

2.12   Presbytery of Dunkeld and Meigle

2.12.1 *Kirkmichael, Straloch and Glenshee Church:* £3000 towards the capital costs of a church community centre in Kirkmichael.

2.13   Presbytery of Dundee

2.13.1 *Mains Family Centre Trust*: £12,000 over four years towards the running costs of a family centre.

2.14   Presbytery of Aberdeen

2.14.1 *Mastrick Church, James Tyrell Centre*: £9000 over three years towards the running costs of a day care centre for older people.

2.15   Presbytery of Gordon

2.15.1 *Upper Donside Parish Association*: £3000 towards the costs of a feasibility study to create a church community centre in Lumsden.

2.16   Presbytery of Abernethy

2.16.1 *Badenoch and Strathspey Transport Company:* £6000 over two years towards the running costs of a social car scheme in remote areas.

2.17 Presbytery of Ross

2.17.1 *Strathpeffer Community Association*: £12,000 over four years towards the running costs of a community development project.

2.18 Presbytery of Sutherland

2.18.1 *Assynt Christian Community Youth Project:* £700 towards the costs of a feasibility study to create a youth centre.

2.18.2 *Sutherland Partnership Dial a Bus Service:* £6,000 over two years towards the running costs of a dial a bus service in remote areas.

2.19 Presbytery of Caithness

2.19.1 *Caithness Voluntary Group*: £2000 towards the training costs of a rural transport project.

2.20 Presbytery of Uist

2.20.1 *Leverburgh Village Hall:* £6711 towards equipment and running costs of a community minibus for the south of Harris.

2.21 Presbytery of Lewis

2.21.1 *Pairc Social Club*: £600 towards the running costs of a lunch club for older people.

2.22 Presbytery of Orkney

2.22.1 *Papa Westray Church*: £3000 towards the equipment costs of a parish centre on Papa Westray.

2.23 97 training grants totalling £16,230 (1999: £11,020) were awarded to 34 supported projects covering the following subjects: finance, food hygiene, project management and development, staff development, volunteer development and youth work. Details are given in the following paragraphs.

2.24 Finance

2.24.1 Badenoch/Strathspey Transport Company, £22.00

2.24.2 Bosco Youth Assocation/Old Kirk Church of Scotland, £44.00

2.24.3 Drumchapel Churches Neighbourhood Project, £32.00

2.24.5 Govan Ecumenical Youth Association, £64.00

2.24.6 Groundwork, £22.00

2.24.7 Homelink (Prestonpans), £26.00

2.24.8 Orbiston Neighbourhood Centre (Utheo Ltd), £44.00

2.24.9 St James' Pollok Church of Scotland, £22.00

2.24.10 Trinity Tots Under 5's, £22.00

2.25 Food Hygiene

2.25.1 Aberfeldy Church of Scotland, £20.00

2.25.2 Elutheria Limited, £106.00

2.25.3 Govan Ecumenical Youth Association, £234.00

2.25.4 Mastrick Church of Scotland, £91.13

2.25.5 St Ninian's Eden Project, £120.00

2.25.6 The Oasis Trust, £524.60

2.26 Project Management and Development

2.26.1 Arbroath St Andrews Church of Scotland, £100.00

2.26.2 Badenoch/Strathspey Transport Company, £531.20

2.26.3 Benview Centre, £230.00

2.26.4 Bridging the Gap: Gorbals Ecumenical Project, £155.00

2.26.5 Charleston Neighbour Resource Centre, £200.00

2.26.6 Chryston Church Honeypot Nursery, £350.00

2.26.7 Colston Milton Church of Scotland, £85.00

2.26.8 Drumchapel Churches Neighbourhood Project, £40.00

2.26.9 Elutheria Limited, £60.00

2.26.10 Glasgow Association for Mental Health (Gorbals Drop In), £245.00

2.26.11 Go For It (Bellsmyre Children's Project), £245.00

2.26.12 Govan Ecumenical Youth Association, £160.00

2.26.13 Groundwork, £110.00

2.26.14 Hammy's Out of School Care, £115.00

2.26.15 Inverclyde Family Contact Centre, £100.00

2.26.16 Kidz Count 2, £425.23

2.26.17 Orbiston Neighbourhood Centre (Utheo Ltd), £940.00

2.26.18 Selkirk Dry Bar Association, £25.00

2.26.19 St James' Pollok Church of Scotland, £845.00

2.26.20 St Mary's Crossover Project, £245.00

2.26.21 The Machan Trust, £360.00

2.26.22 Trinity Tots Under 5's, £95.00

2.27   Staff Development

2.27.1 Aberfeldy Church of Scotland, £200.00

2.27.2 Arbroath St Andrews Church of Scotland, £144.60

2.27.3 Bosco Youth Assocation/Old Kirk Church of Scotland, £51.60

2.27.4 Bridging the Gap: Gorbals Ecumenical Project, £43.00

2.27.5 Cairns Counselling Centre, £368.95

2.27.6 Drumchapel Churches Neighbourhood Project, £33.00

2.27.7 Go For It (Bellsmyre Children's Project), £33.00

2.27.8 Govan Ecumenical Youth Association, £620.50

2.27.9 Grangemouth Enterprises Ltd, £352.50

2.27.10 Groundwork, £255.00

2.27.11 Hammy's Out of School Care, £552.00

2.27.12 Homelink (Prestonpans), £140.00

2.27.13 Lochgilphead Church of Scotland, £140.00

2.27.14 Mastrick Church of Scotland, £60.00

2.27.15 Mid Craigie Parish Project, £43.00

2.27.16 St James' Pollok Church of Scotland, £163.00

2.27.17 St Matthew's Centre, £23.00

2.27.18 The Machan Trust, £33.00

2.27.19 The Ripple Project, £753.50

2.27.20 The Spark Initiative, £802.00

2.27.21 West End Churches Key Fund, £33.00

2.28   Volunteer Development

2.28.1 Badenoch/Strathspey Transport Company, £356.40

2.28.2 Drumchapel Churches Neighbourhood Project, £33.22

2.28.3 Fresh Start Edinburgh, £500.00

2.28.4 Homelink (Prestonpans), £120.00

2.28.5 St James' Pollok Church of Scotland, £225.00

2.28.6 Trinity Tots Under 5's, £479.95

2.28.7 Winchburgh Community Initiative, £268.00

2.29   Youth Work

2.29.1 Arbroath St Andrews Church of Scotland, £75.00

2.29.2 Bosco Youth Assocation/Old Kirk Church of Scotland, £600.00

2.29.3 Callander Youth Project, £120.00

2.29.4 Colston Milton Church of Scotland, £530.00

2.29.5 Drumchapel Churches Neighbourhood Project, £121.00

2.29.6 Homelink (Prestonpans), £26.00

2.29.7 Inverness Hilton Church of Scotland, £325.00

2.29.8 Manish Scarista Church of Scotland, £428.60

2.29.9 Vincentian Volunteers Scotland (West), £122.00

2.30   The Committee continued to support and monitor the development of local projects in different ways, reflecting on issues raised in local situations and sharing experience and learning with other groups. Various training and support materials were produced including a video entitled *Building Communities of Hope*, produced by Fiona Brooker, which is now available through the Department of National Mission or the Scottish Churches Community Trust. A project get-together was held in October and the support network for paid staff continued to meet throughout the year.

In the name of the Committee

MARTIN JOHNSTONE, *Convener*
SANDRA CARTER, *Vice-Convener*
IAIN M JOHNSTON, *Development and Training Officer*

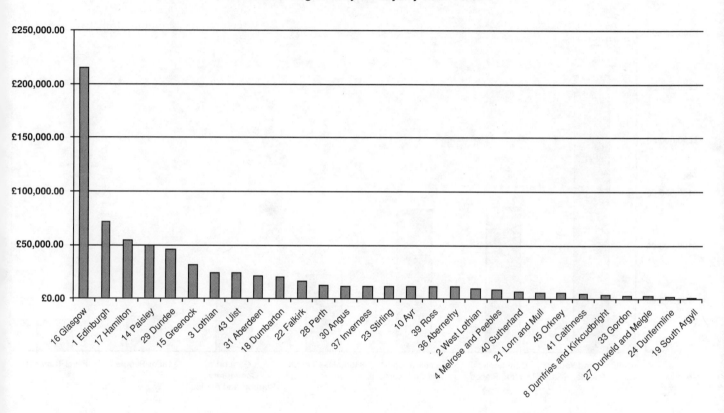

Distribution of grants by Presbytery 1996 - 2000

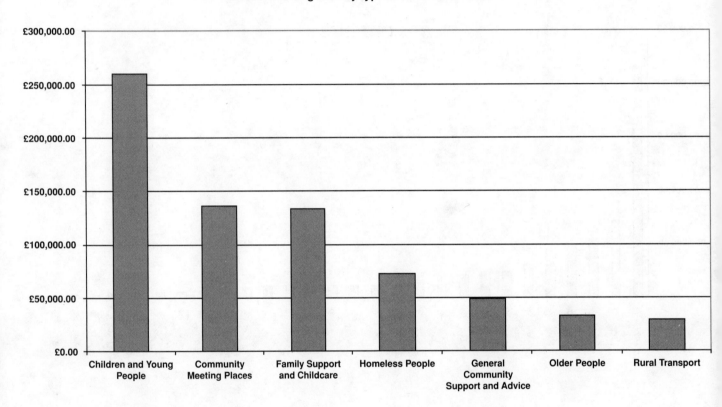

Distribution of grants by type of work 1996 - 2000

CONTENTS

DELIVERANCE

The General Assembly:

1. Receive the Report of the Board and note with appreciation the work of the Convener, Vice-Conveners, Members of the Board and all Staff.

2. Give thanks to God for the foresight and stewardship of previous generations of the Church who developed the work of the Board in Christ's name.

3. Commend the Board for the range of social care delivered to people in need throughout Scotland through the wide variety of services reported upon and for its continuing emphasis on improving the quality of that care.

4. Approve the comments on the issue of begging on the streets and welcome the Board's commitment to exploring new ways of responding.

5. Agree the Board's approach to Human Genetics as follows:

    (i)   Endorse (a) stem-cell research in general, and (b) medical treatment using stem cells derived from the patient concerned or from a consenting donor.

    (ii)   Affirm that IVF treatment may be appropriate treatment for some couples.

    (iii)   Recognise that since God intended human embryos as a means to the end of human reproduction, it may, therefore, be right to use a human embryo in IVF research.

    (iv)   Given that the law allows research on human embryos, welcome the limitation of research to 14 days, and oppose any extension of that limit.

    (v)   Oppose the use of embryos created from human sperm and ova in medical research or treatment, other than that concerned with human reproduction.

    (vi)   Recognise that human embryos created by cell nuclear transfer may be used in medical research and therapy, subject to the 14-day limit.

    (vii)   Recognise that while it may be acceptable to pursue therapeutic cloning, affirm opposition to human reproductive cloning.

    (viii)   Should any babies in future be born from human cell nuclear transfer embryos, affirm they will be fully human, made in the image of God, answerable to God according to their abilities, and our "neighbours" whom God commands us to love.

    (ix)   Welcome research into alternatives to the use of human embryos in medical research or treatment.

6. Request the Principal Clerk to write to the Scottish Executive commending them on:

    (i)   the Scottish Executive's assurances on the acceptance of the recommendations of the Sutherland Report;

    (ii)   the Scottish Executive's positive response to the cost of Police checks;

    (iii)   the proposed legislation under the Regulation of Care (Scotland) Bill.

7. Commend to the Church the Board's publications—*Bio-ethics for the New Millennium* and *The Law and Christian Ethics*; *Social Inclusion—A Study Pack for Churches*; *and HIV/AIDS—a Study Pack for Churches*.

1. Introduction

The report to the General Assembly of the Church of Scotland at the end of the first year of the new millennium is most certainly an occasion to give thanks, to celebrate, to look back and to look forward.

- *To give thanks* for the service offered by so many to so many since the work of the Board first commenced with the formation of the Committee on Christian Life and Work in 1869.
- *To celebrate* the new millennium by seeking to act as a Light in the Darkness in serving others.
- *To look back* and record the variety, range, quality and quantity of work over the last 132 years.
- *To look forward* in faith to deliver Christian social caring services to help and support the people of Scotland in a rapidly changing society.

These thoughts confirm that the fact of the new millennium and the challenges of change, growth and development, come to us within a framework of faith and service to Jesus Christ.

PART ONE: AN OVERVIEW

2. The Work of the Board

Change and development have certainly been evident within the Scottish Parliament since its formal rebirth in 1999 through the formality of the Scotland Act 1998. The Scottish Executive has declared its intention to create an environment in Scotland in which its services and people are integrated and inclusive; everyone should have equal opportunities and the opportunities should be part of an integrated strategy shared with the whole people of Scotland. These are objectives which are supported by the Church and espoused by the Board in its actions over the years. This Report endeavours to show how the Board reflects these ideals.

The **Human Rights Act, 1998** came into force in its entirety in the UK on 2 October 2000, having been applied in part in Scotland under the Scotland Act, 1998. The Act highlighted the need for the Board to scrutinise its employment procedures and practices. Legal advice from specialist employment lawyers has been sought and staff training has been held. Two issues are of major importance to the Board. Firstly to be aware that because the Board receives finance from public bodies (local authorities and health boards and trusts), the Board may be held to be a Public Authority in terms of the Act. It is not anticipated that such an interpretation would have major implications for the Board as its practice is considered to be in compliance with the general terms of the Act. Nevertheless it would be something of which to be aware. Secondly, in the past there have been occasional challenges to the Board around the employment policy of advertising for, and appointing, only workers who have a Christian commitment. There will be some who will hold this practice to be in breach of the Act as it interferes with the right of the individual; the advice which the Board has received is to defend vigorously the Board's right to continue applying the policy. The General Assembly is aware that the Board believes that the policy of appointing only Christian staff who are active in any branch of the Christian churches facilitates the delivery of social caring services in a Christian ethos and atmosphere. It is proposed to maintain this approach. Appendix 1 contains the Board's Christian Employment Policy Statement.

Within the framework of this Act, the Board has also taken the opportunity to consider afresh its approach and practices in the area of *ethnic and gender issues,* the latter in co-operation with the Board of Practice and Procedure. In terms of gender issues, women are well represented at all levels of management in the Department and within the Board, with around 80% of caring and training staff being women. Opportunities for participation in discussion and influencing decision making are equal to both sexes and the Board is aware of the need to ensure that gender issues are given equal weight with other issues. Social work in general terms is an area of work within which political correctness has been of major significance; every effort is made to be aware of this aspect of our work but to retain an acceptable balance. In terms of ethnic awareness a survey done within staff in 2000 revealed that there were staff fluent in 7 ethnic languages and 12 European languages, 16 staff being competent in sign language.

Very much related to the Scottish Executive is the **Sutherland Report,** otherwise known as "With Respect to Old Age: the Royal Commission on Long Term Care"; it has attracted considerable press and media attention and is of significant importance to the Board and its future residential services to older people. The British Government gave their response to the Commission's Report in July 2000 in the form of The National Health Service Plan. The Scottish Executive responded in similar terms in October 2000. The major basis of both responses was that Government accepted the thrust of the recommendations but determined that only nursing care would be free at the point of delivery; Sutherland's recommendation that all care, whether nursing or of a social nature, should be free to the user was rejected. In December the new First Minister, Mr Henry McLeish, intimated that there was to be a review of Scottish Executive policies and this would include a positive re-consideration of the principle of free care for older people. At the time of writing (January 2001) a statement is expected reversing their initial response. The revision is expected to indicate legislation and finance to allow all care, whether nursing or social care, to be delivered free to those who require it. If this does in fact occur, then the Scottish Executive is to be warmly congratulated on accepting recommendations which continue to be rejected for implementation in England and Wales.

The financial position of the Board, which has for too long been one of deficit and anxiety, is in part tied in with the content of the Sutherland Report. No matter how effective financial and other management systems have been applied, monitored and improved, the deficit of the Board has been unacceptably high in financial terms; the frame of reference when acknowledging the care that has been offered makes the deficit acceptable although regrettable. The General Assembly have shown courage and determination in continuing to support the Board and many of Scotland's most needy older people through this very difficult time. As is well known, the major cause of the deficit has been the failure of central and local governments to meet the economic cost of residential care for older people, a position well set out

in the Royal Commission Report. Although we have sought to reduce costs, to date the available solutions have not been acceptable to the Board, namely:

- close all homes to remove the deficit;
- close sufficient homes to reduce the deficit to an acceptable level;
- reduce staff salaries considerably in order to impact on the greatest cost factor in the homes (although in 1997 no annual salary award was made to any staff);
- a combination of these and other cost reducing schemes.

Instead the Board has endeavoured to:

- raise new money to continue the work;
- maximise the occupancy levels in all homes;
- improve the physical conditions within available financial parameters, particularly en-suite single bedroom facilities;
- press both local and central governments for a long term solution to the problem;
- maintain a satisfactory salary and benefits package for staff.

If the Scottish Executive now fulfil their recent statements and make the finance available to meet the cost of residential care of older people who cannot afford to pay for themselves, it is hoped that within an identified timescale the Board can anticipate a real improvement in the financial outlook of the Board. The Board's financial problems may not be then totally resolved but they should be contained within a much more clearly defined limit. Opportunities will continue to be taken to ensure that the services offered by the Board are those which are required in any given geographical area; the possibility of concluding and changing a particular service must always be part of the continuous review of the Board's programme. We are in a time of change and change always brings pain as well as opportunity.

In the second part of this Report reference is made to the reluctance of local authorities to support residential treatment facilities for addiction problems. The Board encourages non-residential facilities when such are appropriate but is strongly of the view that for many people a residential solution offers the best opportunity for recovery. The Board can show specifically through service user comment and experience that residential services appropriately used are positive and successful. It is to be hoped that local authorities will have the courage to support appropriate treatment facilities for individuals rather than pursuing a politically correct solution of care in the community in every case. Residential addiction recovery facilities cannot remain in existence on a 50% occupancy.

Even when financial constraints reduce the opportunities for growth and development it is necessary to look to future possibilities. To this end *the Board has identified some specific services for development when the resources are available.* The Board affirms that the Divisional structure is the correct organisational way forward, that the existing priorities in developing counselling services, the home support service, and using housing stock whenever appropriate, are also correct and should be continued. The Board has also looked at the range of present services and identified those which should be repeated in other parts of the country; for example, the services in Beechwood in Inverness are unique and efforts should be made to develop such services elsewhere. In a similar way the Board will seek to develop more short term care opportunities in line with the Scottish Executive's response to the Sutherland Report, and to develop more family support using local congregations as the base for development.

Alongside the determination for development there is an equal determination to deliver services of quality. *Quality of Service* has always been a hallmark of the Board's service delivery. It is essential that the fine words used by the Convener and the Director, the principles contained in the Board's Development Strategy, the aims and objectives set out in a service user's contract, and the variety of other standards publicised by the Board, are then reflected in the actual services delivered by staff. This can never be guaranteed but the effort to ensure that the "match" is there continues to receive attention

on a daily basis. Some ways of monitoring practice are:

- the Board's procedures and systems are regularly reviewed and revised where and when necessary, such as the new Health and Safety Manual, the implementation of the Financial Procedures Manual and the development of the Tendering Manual to meet Best Standards;
- the application of new systems such as the Quality Assurance System launched in January 2001;
- the statutory inspection of services by outside bodies, and the availability of a widely publicised complaints scheme; it should be noted that the former is completed to an exacting standard and recommendations made are monitored in future reports to ensure compliance;
- the receipt of unsolicited letters of gratitude, thanks and support for services received; and
- the Board's managerial staff are given clear responsibility for monitoring and recording practice and providing personal supervision to staff for whom they are accountable.

Each of these topics could be readily expanded but only two will be addressed, as examples, *the Tendering Manual and the Quality Assurance System.* The Board indicated its Value Base as part of the Strategic Plan placed before the General Assembly in 1999. The Value Base is the first step in ensuring that all services provided by the Board have an effective framework for practice and service delivery which is person-centred, individualised and responsive to the needs and requirements of service users, staff and significant others. Simultaneously, the Government drive towards Best Value means that the Board's services will be open to comparison and competition, producing a significant need to promote standardised practice across the full range of services delivered by the Board.

In response to the requirements of Best Value, local authorities require to ensure that they provide value for money by putting service delivery out to **tender**. The response from the Board was to develop a package for tendering purposes which would meet the requirements of the local authorities, promote the Board's ethos and philosophy and demonstrate endorsement of the principles of Best Value. In essence, the Board provided a two-fold tendering system. The first stage states the Board's policies and procedures, values and standards, indicating a Christian commitment to meeting the needs and requirements of service users and staff. The second stage validates the Board as a service provider defining the particulars of the service tendered for and the essential qualities provided by the Board. This allows the Tender Document to be applicable to each area of service delivery of the Board's work, illustrating its professionalism while ensuring consistency and standardisation in practice and service delivery.

Shaping services individually, responding to needs and requirements while ensuring independence, ownership and continuous improvement, is recognised as essential in an innovative, caring organisation such as the Board. Developing a **Quality Assurance System** confirms a desire by the Board to provide a comprehensive, evaluative system for producing Standards against which the shape and development of practice and service delivery can be compared. This means that the Board should be recognised as a proactive agency verifying that it achieves what it declares it achieves (in an older phrase—it practices what it preaches), or takes steps to redress problems very quickly.

The Board launched the first phase of its Quality Assurance System in January 2001. This phase sets Standards, Outcomes and Requirements while providing service users with information on what they can expect from the Board's services. The Standards Document is also a supervision tool providing scope for training and personal and professional development as well as a basis for measuring performance. The second phase, to be ready by the end of this year, will provide measuring and monitoring systems for internal and external monitoring of practice and service delivery.

While many parts of this Quality Assurance system are in existence within the Department at present, the parts have not been integrated into a system and applied throughout. The Quality Assurance system will provide service users and staff with ownership of services. It will ensure consultation, empowerment, advocacy and communication at a better level than before.

Quality Assurance will confirm the adoption of the principles of Best Value, opening the Board's services to comparison with others. It will ensure that services managed by the Board will meet the expectations of local authorities, customers and consumers. The Tender Document incorporates Quality Assurance and both promote Best Value through Christian commitment.

A final word on tendering. Even when the Board has an opportunity to tender, the option is not always exercised, and even when given an initial positive response, may be stopped at a later stage and before completion.

This year, for example, the Scottish Prison Service indicated that they wished to put a number of social work services to tender. The Board received details and were very keen to respond. However, as a result of official contact with the Prison Service personnel, it became clear that the terms of the projected contract were not suitable to the Board. To reach this stage and to allow an informed decision to be taken Board staff were involved in a considerable amount of work which resulted in a decision not to proceed. It is necessary to ensure that the number of occasions on which the Board conduct such an exercise are limited.

Whatever systems are introduced, good practice requires from staff commitment, hard work and the application of appropriate skills and expertise. The Board continue to place importance on staff training and development, both in the interest of good service delivery and also for personal fulfilment of individual staff. External monitoring of the Board's training programmes for this year has been very complimentary. 49 in-service courses have been held providing training for 1,287 staff. Scottish Vocational Training for care workers resulted in 49 staff completing the Level 3 award and 4 staff completing the higher Level 4. The Board now has trained in excess of 250 staff at Levels 3 and 4, and an additional 135 at a supervisory level. Trained staff regularly leave the Department for promoted posts elsewhere and while this must be accepted, the level of movement must always be monitored to ensure that staff retention is given appropriate attention.

The natural flow of work to the Board means that long before it is necessary to tender for work, we are involved with the Scottish Executive on existing practice development and on new legislation. *Consultation Papers from the Scottish Executive and New Legislation* are a major part of the work of the Board. Responses in the main have been provided direct to the Scottish Executive or through the Scottish Churches Parliamentary Officer. Major responses have been submitted on Supporting Active Communities in Scotland, Adults with Incapacity, the Review of Mental Health, Regulation of Early Education and Child Care, Youth Crime Review, Supporting People, the Scottish Housing Bill, and Scottish Family Law. The major piece of legislation affecting the Board and currently before the Scottish Parliament, is the *Regulation of Care (Scotland) Bill*. This Bill has been presented as a result *inter alia* of the lack of current regulation and the lack of independence of the registration and inspection by local authorities who can also deliver similar services as providers; similar legislation is being processed in Westminster to apply to England and Wales. The legislation will establish two new independent bodies.

- **The Scottish Commission for the Regulation of Care** to regulate care and early education services, using National Care Standards and being completely independent from the previous registering authorities within the health and social services field; and

- **The Scottish Social Services Council** to regulate the workforce, using Codes of Practice and a system of registration for all social services workers. This new Council will assume the current responsibilities of the Central Council for Education and Training in Social Work (CCETSW) and the Training Organisation for the Personal Social Services (TOPSS) in Scotland.

The implications of the Bill for the Board include:

- the duty of registration and inspection of residential homes transferred from local authorities to the new independent Scottish Commission;
- introduction of National Care Standards which should apply evenly to all services throughout Scotland;
- introduction of regulations for the Single Care Home (covering both social and nursing care);
- home care services will, for the first time, be covered by national Regulation and Standards;
- costs for registration and continuation fees are expected to rise by about £10 per bed per year for the next three years (an additional annual cost to the Board of approximately £38,160);
- development of a Register, initially, for social workers and social care workers, to include other workers at later stages;
- employees required to register will be required to pay an annual registration fee, initially expected to be around £20;
- introduction of Codes of Practice for social service workers and employers which will be mandatory and enforceable; and
- the Board is an Approved Training Centre under CCETSW for the award of Scottish Vocational Training Awards; the authority to continue will require to be given by the new Scottish Social Services Council.

Another aspect of legislation recently announced by the Scottish Executive is that the charge for Police Checks of persons who are working with children in a voluntary capacity will be met by the Executive. This is an extremely important decision as it impacts on so many voluntary organisations, including the Church.

Decentralisation and increased local community involvement are themes which the Board has been pursuing for some years. The Board's five Divisional offices are now firmly established and are developing stronger local links with other agencies and with presbyteries and congregations. The data base of congregational service is well used and the circulation of the Board quarterly newspaper—Circle of Care (46,500), the audio tape (1,600) and the prayer letter (9,000)—continue to be well received and well used. These are important vehicles maintaining the profile of the Board within the Church and with outside agencies.

The quality of Board Member input is crucial to the work of the Board. This will be true for all Boards and Committees of the Church; comment is made, however, because the range of knowledge expected from Board members in the area of social care is very wide. The decisions sought regularly require an understanding of complex issues and an acceptance that decisions made will often have an immediate impact on human lives. It is appropriate to record the appreciation of staff for the support and direction given by the Board, its Convener and Vice Conveners.

Planned Millennium Celebrations were intimated to the General Assembly last year; these celebrations were successful and helped to raise the profile of the Board in many quarters. In this Report special emphasis is given to the efforts by staff and service users as they sought to serve the community in which they are located under the theme "Light in the Darkness—Service to Others". This theme reflects the fact that Social Responsibility seeks to bring light into the darkness of people's lives through our service to them. A coloured supplement "Millennium Moments" reflecting the millennium activities was produced and is available to Commissioners.

His Royal Highness Charles Duke of Rothesay on one of his visits to Edinburgh requested a visit to Charis House specifically to meet with the staff "who supported the staff in the Board's homes and centres". This was a highlight for the staff and a recognition that the service delivery arm required the support of central administrative staff. The successful visit took place on 5 October 2000.

Contact with other Boards/Committees and in international arenas continues. The Board's staff co-operate with many of the Church's other Board and Committees; whenever possible the Board adopts a practice of seeking to secure a Church perspective as opposed to only a Board perspective, and where a project can be tackled in a joint manner then this is considered. A similar approach is taken on an ecumenical front and the Scottish Churches Parliamentary Officer and the Secretary to the Committee on Ecumenical Relations have been very helpful. The part played by Friends of the Board and by the many Volunteers who support the work in such a variety of ways is to be acknowledged with grateful thanks. The Board are also aware and supportive of the increasing amount of social caring which is done through local congregations.

On an international level, the Board is active within Eurodiaconia and within the International Christian Federation for the prevention of alcohol and drug abuse; in this latter case it is hoped to participate in a jointly managed conference with the World Council of Churches in Bossey, Switzerland at the end of the year. The Board are also active within Europe within a Staff Exchange Scheme which allows staff to practice in a European country for a period of up to six months, and similarly for the Board to host a staff placement from Europe. This year Mrs Joyce Buchanan, Deputy Director of Social Work had the honour of assisting in the leadership of a conference in Germany on the subject of dementia; this required considerable input from Mrs Buchanan but re-affirmed part of the Board's international network.

The Board is aware of the growing world wide concern regarding **HIV and AIDS** and seek to ensure that the issues of infection and spread of HIV/AIDS are given regular publicity. It is a staggering reality that worldwide 36.1 million people have HIV/AIDS. In Britain the figure is around 30,000, new diagnosis in 1999 being 3,553 the highest level since 1985; 419 people in the UK died of the infection in 1999. Board staff primarily address the issues through the addictions and counselling services and through its women and children work; but also through regular publicity, particularly around World Aids Day on 1 December each year. An education and awareness pack was developed by the Board in the early 1990's and this year it has been completely revised. The new Pack will be available by the summer of 2001.

3. Financial Overview

STATEMENT OF FINANCIAL ACTIVITIES
FOR THE YEAR ENDED 31 MARCH 2000

	Unrestricted Funds £'000	Restricted Funds £'000	Permanent Endowment Funds £'000	Total 2000 £'000	Total 1999 £'000
Income and Expenditure					
Incoming Resources:					
Income from Service Delivery	0	31,140	0	31,140	30,818
Donations	5	1,273	0	1,278	1,027
Legacies	249	1,206	0	1,455	1,746
Gain on sale of assets	0	612	0	612	1,553
Investment Income and Interest Received	298	717	0	1,015	1,062
Less: Deferred Income	0	(529)	0	(529)	(638)
Total Incoming Resources	**552**	**34,419**	**0**	**34,971**	**35,568**
Expended Resources:					
Direct Charitable Expenditure:					
Expenditure on Service Delivery	0	33,633	0	33,633	33,254
Support costs	0	1,817	0	1,817	1,541
Other Expenditure:					
Fundraising & Publicity	0	184	0	184	154
Management & Administration of the Charity	0	295	0	295	285
Total Expended Resources	**0**	**35,929**	**0**	**35,929**	**35,234**
Net Added/(Expended) Resources for the year	**552**	**(1,510)**	**0**	**(958)**	**(334)**

4. Social Interests

4.1 *The Social Interests sector of the Board's work* has been as heavy and sensitive as in past years. Reference is made in Part 2 of this Report to specific topics which have been highlighted by the Press and Media and the attention which they have received from the Board.

At the beginning of the year there was still intense media interest in Clause 28 (or more accurately Section 2A). The decision of the General Assembly 2000 formed the basis of comment by the Board. The Department of Education has continued the Church's commitment by offering a strong response to the Scottish Executive's draft on "Guidance in Sex Education in Scottish Schools".

The Board is delighted to have published "Bio-Ethics for the New Millennium" edited by Professor Iain Torrance. In 1995 the Board produced a report on human genetics and recognised that even in five years, progress and development has been immense. In view of this the Board decided to bring together experts in the fields of scientific research, law, insurance, philosophy, ethics, theology and public policy to address the issues raised by developments in the field of human genetics. The book publishes the papers given at a one day seminar on 12 January 1999 in Aberdeen University. The Board would once again wish to express thanks to Professor Torrance for his contribution to this whole endeavour.

The Scottish Executive issued a consultation document on "Stalking and Harassment" on which the Board took the opportunity to comment. The document was part of the Scottish Executive's pursual of a "secure Scotland where individuals and communities are free from crime and free from the fear of crime". It is pleasing to record that the drive for this result continues with the publication of the Consultation on possibilities for improved communication with, and involvement of, victims of criminal behaviour.

The General Assembly last year was advised of the series of lectures arranged in co-operation with The Centre for Theology and Public Issues at New College, Edinburgh, on the subject of Christian Ethics and The Law. This was an excellent series of stimulating papers which resulted in much discussion and debate. The publication is now with the printers and should be available at the General Assembly.

4.2 The National Lottery

General Assembly has received regular reports on the National Lottery. It may be useful to remind Commissioners of some specific aspects of it.

What is the National Lottery now?

The seven year licence held by Camelot is to be renewed this year. There will be changes in the delivery of the Lottery and these have still to be announced both by Government and by Camelot. It will be necessary to review new arrangements once they are known.

The likelihood is that there will be new games and new regulations concerning the number of winners and the spread of winnings around more of them. At the moment there is the **Main Draw** which allocates a major winner(s), the amount depending on how much is available but always being substantial. There is the **Lottery Extra** which has an accumulating prize money which "rolls over" after each game until it is won. There is the **Thunderball Draw** which can win up to £250,000. Then there are numerous **Instants,** commonly known as **Scratchcards,** winnings being dependent on the type of ticket purchased. At the time of writing some Scratchcard games are Cars & Cash, Moneybags, 3 Times Lucky, 3 Wishes, Stocking Filler, Cracking Christmas, Kitty Cash Doubler, 9s in a Line, Happy Birthday, Blue Spectrum, with Tons of Cash, Lucky Number, and a new £100,000 Rainbow all due to commence in February. The Main Draw, Lottery Extra, and Thunderball are drawn on Saturdays and Wednesdays only, whereas Instants can be played and won at any time. Instants games are £1 each as is one line on the main draws. The Web Pages for the National Lottery (all games) are extensive and packed with statistical information all of which is intended to encourage involvement in the Lottery.

In information terms, figures were provided to the Board in August 2000. A further summary as at 3 January 2001 is provided:

- Sales of Lottery tickets amount to £30.6 billion.

- The "Good Causes" have received grants in excess of £9.3 billion, including £361.1 million from unclaimed prizes.
- Lottery Duty paid to Government is over £3.6 billion.
- Camelot's Charitable donations (separate from the Good Causes) total £23.8 million.
- 1,091 people have won in excess of £1 million.

Additionality

In establishing the National Lottery, Government stated specifically that the proceeds were intended to finance projects which would not be within the normal range of provision through means of national taxation. This issue of 'additionality' has been raised afresh since the introduction of another "Good Cause" fund, the "New Opportunities Fund". The NOF touches on issues of health and education and some have argued that it funds what should be part of the Government's statutory funding.

The priorities of the New Opportunities Fund are to promote social inclusion; improve the quality of life for individuals and communities; encourage community involvement; and complement and enhance relevant national, regional and local strategies and programmes. Its Key Initiatives are:

- **Health**
(a) Healthy living centres, community-led projects and partnership bids are encouraged.
(b) Cancer detection, prevention, treatment and care.

- **Education**
(a) Out of school hours childcare.
(b) Out of school hours learning activities.
(c) Information and Communications Technology training for teachers, school librarians, and public library staff.
(d) Community access to lifelong learning (development of new library network, and community grids for learning and lifelong learning projects).

- **Environment**
Green spaces and sustainable communities; the fund is for the creation, improvement or acquisition of green spaces and sustainable community schemes.

There are others who have argued that the principle of additionality is a nonsense to work and should be scrapped, that the Lottery money should be used where it will do most good, even if it should ideally be done from taxation. At present the Lottery's "New Opportunities Fund" receives only 13% of the benefits from the Lottery. This will increase to 33% next year.

Under-age participation

The following information was taken from research conducted by Sue Fisher, University of Plymouth and John Balding, University of Exeter.

"The respondents showed little preference for the National Lottery draw or scratchcards:

5% had spent their own money on the National Lottery draw during the week prior to the survey.

4% had spent their own money on National Lottery scratch cards during the week prior to the survey.

6% had spent their own money on both products during the week prior to the survey.

Past week expenditure on the National Lottery was significantly associated with age and being male, making 14–15 year old boys the most likely participants:

21% of 14–15 year old boys had spent their own money on the National Lottery during the week prior to the survey.

11% reported illegal transactions.

The children who had spent their own money on the National Lottery during the previous week were significantly more likely than the others to have higher levels of disposable income and to come from households which took popular tabloid newspapers (used as a rough measure of socio-economic group):

28% of the children who received more than £5 a week had spent their own money on the National Lottery during the week prior to the survey compared with 14% who received less than £5.

19% of the children whose households took popular tabloid newspapers had spent their own money on the National Lottery during the week prior to the survey, compared with 17% whose households took tabloids and 12% whose households took broadsheets.

Focus on regular players of National Lottery scratchcards

The study responded to public concern that some children may be frequent, or even problem, players of National Lottery scratchcards by examining the behaviour of regular players. From the total sample of 7,200 12–15 year old boys and girls:

37% (2,601) had played National Lottery scratchcards during the past year.

3% (189) were regular players (played twice a week or more).

34% (2,412) were less regular players (played less than twice a week).

All of the results in this section are based upon responses from these children.

Expenditure

30% of the regular players had spent more than £5 in the past week on National Lottery scratchcards compared with 1% of the less regular players.

26% of the regular players had spent more than £10 in one day on National Lottery scratchcards compared with 2% of the less regular players.

41% of the regular players had spent much more than they planned on National Lottery scratchcards (more than once or twice) compared with 9% of the less regular players.

Potentially addictive behaviours

Regular scratchcard players were also significantly more likely than the other children to be involved in a cluster of other potentially addictive behaviours including regular smoking, regular drinking, regular fruit machine gambling and experimentation with illegal drugs. The following

results are based upon a comparison between the regular scratchcard players and all of the other children.

33% of the regular scratchcard players described themselves as regular smokers compared with 14% of the other children.

44% of the regular scratchcard players had taken alcohol on 3 or more days during the previous week compared with 11% of the other children.

35% of the regular scratchcard players had experimented with illegal drugs compared with 19% of the other children.

46% of the regular scratchcard players played fruit machines at least weekly compared with 6% of the other children.

Future research directions

Under-age access to National Lottery products is a phenomenon that merits further enquiry. The results of this study suggest that the following topics should have priority:

Many of the under-age purchases of National Lottery products were made by parents on behalf of their children. It would be helpful to understand the perceptions parents have about children playing the National Lottery. It would also be helpful to understand the role of families and adolescent peer groups in teaching children about gambling and facilitating their involvement in gambling activities.

This study shows that there is a highly significant relationship between regular playing of National Lottery scratchcards and regular playing of fruit machines. Further research, using more sophisticated analytic techniques is required into the prevalence of all forms of adolescent gambling so that the impact of the National Lottery on adolescent gambling may be more clearly understood.

This study confirms previous findings about the clustering of risk behaviours in adolescents including regular gambling. regular smoking, regular alcohol drinking and experimentation with illegal drugs. There is a need for further research, using multivariate analytic techniques, to explore the relationship between persistent gambling and other risk behaviours in adolescents."

Effect on charitable giving

There is debate on the effect on charitable giving.

On average, almost one-third of households give to charity in a two-week period. Over the last twenty years, the percentage of households giving to charity has fallen by over 5 percentage points although the average donation has risen such that total household donations have gone up in real terms. This greater 'inequality of giving' has a generational aspect.

Other things being equal, the likelihood of being a giver increases with age, income, education and wealth. These factors also affect positively the size of donations.

There is some evidence of misperception regarding the National Lottery. Most households think that a substantial part of the revenue from the Lottery goes to Camelot profits, although in reality much more goes to charity, sports or heritage. Also, almost half think that the Lottery reduces the donations of other households, whereas only 7 per cent think that playing the Lottery reduced their own donations.

Finally, the General Assembly is reminded of the Board's comments in 1996 relative to the other changes in gambling legislation arising directly as a result of the Government ensuring that other forms of gambling can be competitive with the National Lottery. Gambling in the United Kingdom is now much greater than pre-National Lottery.

There is considerable mixed evidence as to whether or not the introduction of the National Lottery has had a negative effect on overall charitable giving. Households that play the Lottery give less to charity than those that do not, but this is not evidence that the Lottery has reduced giving. Rather, they were less likely to give to charity anyway.

4.3 A Christian Response to Begging

The act of begging is not a new one nor is it viewed in the same way throughout the world; in some countries it is accepted as a way of life and little or no official action is taken to stop or reduce it. In Scotland, in the year 2001, it is frowned upon but only occasionally seen as a reason for police action. An example is in Edinburgh during the month of the annual festival of arts when the police do not encourage begging on the main thoroughfares. Equally, begging is not a uniform practice. A student (or, by appearance, a "down-and-out") playing a musical instrument on the streets for monetary reward from passers-by is accepted as a busker; the police would countenance this action as begging unless a licence to busk had been obtained from the local authority. Begging occurs when the same person merely asks for money or even puts out a hat or an empty tin in the hope that money will be given; it is not a reward for effort but a token of good-will to assist someone in need of help.

Homeless people, sleeping rough in shop doorways, may not be beggars insofar as they do not seek financial help from passers-by. Yet they will often be referred to as beggars. Successive Governments have made money available to develop schemes to assist "rough sleepers" but the numbers appear to continue to grow.

All of us will have preconceptions about "who beggars are" and "why" they beg. A recent study in Edinburgh and Glasgow identified the following:

- people's experience of "rough sleeping" almost invariably preceded their involvement in begging;
- almost all those interviewed had experienced severe trauma in their life;
- begging was a "survival strategy" and was overwhelmingly driven by need not greed;
- most of those who begged chose it rather than other unattractive means of securing money because it is seen as a lawful and honest activity;
- the majority of interviewees found begging an embarrassing and degrading experience; and
- the vast majority of those interviewed wanted to move away from begging and homelessness, and aspired to have a "normal life".

It is also clear from much research that nearly 50% of those who beg do so to support an addiction. The alternative for many is direct involvement in crime. It is also known that where the begging provides insufficient money then involvement in crime follows in order that the "habit" can be sustained. It is debatable to argue that not to respond to begging is to encourage criminal activity but it is no doubt one argument that is put forward.

There is evidence that for a minority of beggars the opportunity to seek admission to a hostel or a rehabilitative programme is avoided because of a fear of violence against their person. This might be mythical and with no evidence but is real to the individual and therefore a factor to be borne in mind.

It is against such background knowledge that our response to begging must be considered. When one is approached by someone begging it is necessary to make an immediate decision on how to respond. Say no; shake one's head and keep moving; stop to exchange courtesies but still say no; exchange courtesies and then make a decision to offer small change; offer advice on where help can be given; swerve and walk faster. The range of options is really quite long.

The Lodging House Mission, managed by the Church of Scotland Glasgow Presbytery, has a meal voucher scheme. Anyone can buy a voucher for £1; this can then be given to someone asking for money for a meal. The meal is given in exchange for the voucher (a full breakfast or a three course lunch) when presented at the Centre in the centre of Glasgow.

It should be noted that many of those who do beg will also be receiving services from statutory or voluntary services, such those offered by the Board in areas of homelessness, alcohol and substance abuse, and counselling.

Scriptural Context

Jesus said "the poor you will have with you always" (Matthew 26:11). Our standing before Christ will be judged on how we have dealt with them (Matthew 24). Yet when we see the poor on our streets increasing in number and increasingly younger we can find all kinds of excuses for not helping them:

- they are not really poor;
- the state should help them;
- the problem is too great for my small contribution to make any difference;
- they will just squander what I give them;
- they have already squandered what they had on drink or drugs;
- they should get a job and help themselves;
- why should I give what I have worked for, to beggars;
- giving only encourages laziness and dependence on charity;
- I'd give them work or food but you can't trust them in your home.

Christ came to be a servant. He came to turn upside down the world's accepted way of valuing people according to what they can do. So to look at those who have needs of any kind is surely a huge challenge to us as Christians, saying "what are we going to do about this?". In the eyes of Jesus, who are the meek; the poor in spirit; those who mourn; the hungry and thirsting?

We are saved by grace –

Ephesians. 2:4 But because of his great love for us, God, who is rich in mercy, made us alive with Christ even when we were dead in transgressions—it is by grace you have been saved.

but that grace gives us a responsibility towards others –

Ephesians. 2:10 For we are God's workmanship, created in Christ Jesus to do good works, which God prepared in advance for us to do.

As Christians we are incomplete without a social conscience and without social care… that is being socially responsible. It must extend to all who are in need however we perceive their neediness.

The parable of the Good Samaritan is familiar to most of us. (Luke 10:29–37) Jean Vanier, the founder of L'Arche, who was invited to address the 2000 General Assembly, reflects upon it in this way.

"Time and time again my heart comes back to the gospel of Luke where Jesus responds to the question who is my neighbour and so shows us what it means to love our neighbour (Luke 10). He tells the story of a Jewish man between Jerusalem and Jericho, who is attacked by bandits, beaten and left lying on the road. Two men with important functions in Jewish society pass by, without stopping.

They are frightened. Of what? Of getting their hands dirty? Of being late for an appointment? Of not knowing what to do? Of losing their status? They do not feel that this wounded man is *their* problem, but instead seem to ask the wrong question: what will happen *to me* if I stop?

Then a man from Samaria passes by. The Samaritans were oppressed by the Jewish people at that time. When this Samaritan sees the man on the ground, he is moved by compassion; he stops and takes care of him. He does not say "it is not my problem" or "this man is my enemy, let him die!". His first concern is not where this man comes from or what is his culture or religion; he sees him foremost as *a brother in humanity.* And the "good Samaritan" dresses the man's wounds and takes him to the local inn. He stays with him for the night, pays the innkeeper and asks him to continue to take care of the wounded man, promising to pay for any other expenses incurred.

Three things touch me in this example of the love of our neighbour:

1. **The Samaritan's love is *excessive*.** There are no limits. He does not calculate. He does not do just what is necessary or according to justice, but much more. He spends the night with the wounded man and commits himself to pay for his care.

2. He bridges the gap between the Jewish and the Samaritan peoples. The oppressor or enemy becomes the friend. Our neighbour is not just the members of our own community or those living and working close to us, those who are like us or with whom we feel a certain affinity. Jesus reveals here that our neighbour is the one we encounter on our path, the person in need. The man from Samaria breaks through the barriers of his own culture, religion or ethnic group, barriers that protect him and make him feel that his

group is right, the best, the only one blessed by God. He does not do this in order to convert the other to his religion, but out of love and compassion, trusting that such *love reveals the true face of God* and so calls each person to what is deepest within them.

3. By breaking out from behind his cultural barriers, the Good Samaritan dares to walk the path of insecurity. **What if other Jewish people see him put this man on his donkey?** They might accuse him of being the one who beat him up! What if other Samaritans see him; **they might accuse him of collaborating with the enemy, of being a traitor?** When we accompany broken people there are no set rules and regulations which protect us. We are alone in front of a person in pain. All we have is our good will, our love, our limited skills, ourselves. We do not know where it will lead to—for to love is to risk.

Yet in this story there are two things of which I am sure:

(a) By daring to act out of love and compassion, the Samaritan becomes both poorer and richer. Poorer because he senses he is alone, insecure, even maybe a bit frightened, feeling unprotected. He becomes more vulnerable. This gives him a greater awareness of his need for the help and presence of God. **As soon as we enter into relationship with the poor and the weak, we feel the need for that inner strength that comes from God.**

(b) Both the Samaritan and the Jewish man must have been changed by this experience. Imagine the wounded man opening his eyes and discovering that he has been saved by a man belonging to the group he had despised. Perhaps with tears in his eyes he might say "Thank you!" Never again would he despise a Samaritan. A covenant is born between these two, a covenant of understanding, love and friendship that draws out both from behind their cultural and religious barriers. Something irreversible has happened. Their prejudices have fallen. They have discovered the presence of God in each other. **Whilst they may feel isolated from and rejected by their respective groups, they become a sign of peace and unity."**

Our response to a beggar may be to give what we have which may not always be in money terms or even what the person on the street thinks he needs most.

Acts 3:1 One day Peter and John were going up to the temple at the time of prayer—at three in the afternoon. Now a man crippled from birth was being carried to the temple gate called Beautiful, where he was put every day to beg from those going into the temple courts. When he saw Peter and John about to enter, he asked them for money. Peter looked straight at him, as did John. Then Peter said, "Look at us!" So the man gave them his attention, expecting to get something from them. Then Peter said, **"Silver or gold I do not have, but what I have I give you.** In the name of Jesus Christ of Nazareth, walk." Taking him by the right hand, he helped him up, and instantly the man's feet and ankles became strong.

Conclusion

There are no easy answers to this dilemma; no easy instructions on how to react. Yet Christ's teaching is clear. Therefore, how must we respond?

Perhaps the best for which any of us can aim is to seek to be courteous, to try to be understanding, to develop our own way of showing our love towards all whom we meet, to recognise that sometimes we will give money and on other occasions decide, for us at that given moment, that some other offer of help is more appropriate.

The Board also need to consider new ways of responding and helping Christians to show their love in practical ways, such as more opportunities like the Glasgow Lodging House Mission voucher scheme.

4.4   Human Genetics Group

Over the last few months, much of the Human Genetics Group's work has concerned the "Donaldson" Report and its Recommendations on Stem Cell research.

Why All the Interest in Stem Cells?

All of us began life as a fertilised egg. This divided into two cells, and each of these divided, and this happened again and again until our bodies now contain millions upon millions of cells. All of our cells have the same genes, but they have specialised in different ways to form the different sorts of tissue in our bodies.

Some common diseases (diabetes and Parkinson's for example) happen when one type of cell fails, and could be cured if we could replenish a sufferer's supply of that type of cell. This means getting them from elsewhere, or—much better—persuading some of the sufferer's own cells to change into the type needed.

At the moment we can't make just any cell from our bodies change into another type of cell. However we can do some things with the less-specialised cells called 'stem cells' which specialise in our bodies as required to replace worn-out cells. But even by the time we're born, each of our stem cells has already specialised too far to turn into just any type of cell, and it can be hard to find stem cells of the type and number we need.

The easiest place to find human stem cells is in a human embryo a few days old. These are made up of no more than a few hundred cells, and half of these are completely unspecialised stem cells which can become any other kind of cell in our body. So researchers have been calling for a change in the law to allow cells to be taken from human embryos, to find out how stem cells develop, and perhaps to use in medical treatment until we can use a patient's own cells. These embryos would be made *in vitro* and might be spare ones from IVF treatment (which would otherwise be discarded), or made specially for this research from sperm and ova, or, to preclude rejection by a patient's body, made by 'cell nuclear replacement' ('the Dolly method') from a patient's own cell and a donated human egg.

The Donaldson Recommendations

The Donaldson Report made nine Recommendations about the use of human embryos in stem cell research. These are given below.

1.   Research using embryos (whether created by *in vitro*

fertilisation or cell nuclear replacement) to increase understanding about human disease and disorders and their cell-based treatments should be permitted, subject to the controls in the Human Fertilisation and Embryology Act 1990.

2. In licensing any research using embryos created by cell nuclear replacement, the Human Fertilisation and Embryology Authority should satisfy itself that there are no other means of meeting the objectives of the research.

3. Individuals whose eggs or sperm are used to create the embryos to be used in research should give specific consent indicating whether the resulting embryos could be used in a research project to derive stem cells.

4. Research to increase understanding of, and develop treatments for, mitochondrial diseases using the cell nuclear replacement technique in human eggs, which are subsequently fertilised by human sperm, should be permitted subject to the controls in the Human Fertilisation and Embryology Act 1990.

5. The progress of research involving stem cells which have been derived from embryonic sources should be monitored by an appropriate body to establish whether the research is delivering the anticipated benefits and to identify any concerns which may arise.

6. The mixing of human adult (somatic) cells with the live eggs of any animal species should not be permitted.

7. The transfer of an embryo created by cell nuclear replacement into the uterus of a woman (so called 'reproductive cloning') should remain a criminal offence.

8. The need for legislation to permit the use of embryo-derived cells in treatments developed from this new research should be kept under review.

9. The Research Councils should be encouraged to establish a programme for stem cell research and to consider the feasibility of establishing collections of stem cells for research use.

The Board wholeheartedly endorses Recommendation 6, which opposes the creation of human/animal hybrids, and Recommendation 7 which opposes human "reproductive cloning". Recommendations 2, 3, 5, 8 and 9 seem appropriate given that stem cell research using human embryos is to be permitted. The Board does have difficulty with Recommendation 4, which would authorise research into the treatment of mitochondrial diseases by replacing the embryo's defective mitochondria, treatment which would technically give an embryo three parents. However the research itself raises no issues not raised in Recommendation 1.

So the Board has been mainly concerned with Recommendation 1, and that for two reasons: (a) to take stem cells from a human embryo destroys the embryo, while in 1996 the Assembly affirmed "the sanctity of the embryo from conception"; and (b) to create embryos by cell nuclear replacement is human cloning, to which the Assembly expressed "the strongest possible opposition" in 1997. It appears, then, that previous Assembly Deliverances implicitly—and strongly—oppose stem cell research upon human embryos.

However the matter is not so clear. The 1996 Deliverance did not condemn the use and destruction of human embryos in research, but rather recognised "that IVF treatment may be right for [some] couples"; and if IVF treatment is right, the past and present research using human embryos upon which the success of IVF treatment depends was and is justified.

And with regard to human cloning, the Donaldson Report makes a strong distinction between "therapeutic cloning" (that is, cloning in order to produce human tissue), and "reproductive cloning" (that is, cloning in order to produce whole, mature organisms). It seemed to the Board that the General Assembly opposed the latter in 1997; the Assembly had "Brave New World" in mind, not the production of replacement cells for those who suffer from heart disease or diabetes.

So while the Board clearly had a duty to respond to the Donaldson Recommendations, it could neither oppose nor endorse stem cell research upon human embryos. All it could do, in a letter sent to all Scots MPs, and then in a second letter sent to all UK MPs (a copy of the latter is given in Appendix 2), was call for delay to permit wider public debate and new legislation.

The letters' main argument was that the use of human embryos in stem-cell research raises different ethical issues from those addressed in the Human Fertilisation and Embryology Act of 1990. This only permitted research upon embryos for purposes which are related to the health, or otherwise, of embryos, and arguably are for embryos' collective benefit. The research now permitted is for patients' benefit, not for embryos' benefit. The former respects embryos' biological agenda; the second treats them as resources to be exploited at will.

MPs were not persuaded by the Board's letter, and by objections from other religious groups, but voted by 366 to 174 to accept the Donaldson Recommendations. The Lords also voted to accept them, by 212 to 92, and the research was authorised in principle as of 31st January. But the Board was heartened by the responses from some MPs, who had clearly thought hard about the ethical issues and had come to a conscientious decision, whether for or against the Recommendations.

Since stem cell research and "therapeutic cloning" may produce standard medical treatments, it seems unsatisfactory for the Assembly to have an ambiguous position upon the former, and never to have addressed the latter. The Board believes that the General Assembly ought to take a position upon these matters since this field is developing so rapidly.

Conclusion

1.　The Board aims to help people live the best lives they can. Since the human body repairs injury by generating new cells which are genetically and functionally identical to others which it already possesses, the Board doesn't think it wrong in principle to do this in the laboratory for someone whose body cannot do this for itself. That is, the Board isn't against cloning a person's cells in order to produce "spare parts" or fresh cells of a special type for that human being. Nor does the Board think it wrong in principle for a volunteer to donate cells for use in the medical treatment of another human being. The Board

is therefore in favour of stem cell research as such.

2.　In 1996 the Assembly affirmed "the sanctity of the embryo from conception", and presumably had serious reservations about the use of embryos in research or treatment. But the Assembly also recognised "that the IVF treatment may be right for [some] couples", treatment which depends upon the use of human embryos in IVF research. So notwithstanding the Assembly's high view of the human embryo, the Assembly stopped short of saying that it is always wrong to use human embryos in research.

3.　We can only use human embryos in research if God has not forbidden it. There comes a point in a human embryo's development when we must call it a baby, and we should cherish babies. Christians who accept the use of human embryos in research must, therefore, limit the age up to which embryos may be used. Current legislation forbids researchers to allow embryos to develop *in vitro* beyond their 14th day. At this age the "primitive streak" begins to develop, which is the earliest stage at which it is possible to tell if the embryo will develop as one person, or twins etc., or develop only as a placenta. If human embryos are to be used in research, we may reasonably argue that up to 14 days of age they are still embryos, not babies.

4.　For guidance as to the type of research in which human embryos might properly be used, the Board looks to God's purposes. God created us "to glorify God, and to enjoy him for ever". Our physical development from embryo to adult is part of the process by which God means us to "progress in wisdom and age and favour before God and man". From this it is evident that God intended human embryos, not as an end in themselves, but as a means to the end of human reproduction. The embryos used in IVF research are denied the opportunity to develop, but through their use, other embryos develop which otherwise would not do so, thereby contributing indirectly to human reproduction. So if it is ever permissible to use human embryos in research, it is certainly permissible to use them in IVF research. Conversely, to concede that human embryos may be used in IVF research is not to concede that they may be used in any other type of research.

5. If God intends human embryos as a means of human reproduction, we certainly go *beyond* God's intention if we use them for other purposes. The Board takes the stronger view that we go *against* God's intention if we so use them, and hence opposes their use in medical research or medical treatment.

6. The above 5 points refer to human embryos created from human sperm and (whole) human eggs; but since the creation of "Dolly", it has been clear that human embryos might also be created by cell nuclear replacement. Knowing human nature, it has also been clear that human embryos would be created in this way sooner or later, however much we may regret this. Since Parliament has now given the go-ahead for their creation, we must consider how we ought to treat them.

6.1 We could argue that human embryos should be treated alike however they are created. However the traditional arguments against the indiscriminate use of human embryos apply specifically to embryos created from human eggs and sperm, and can't be applied to human embryos created by cell nuclear replacement.

6.2 The Board argued above against the therapeutic use of human embryos created from human eggs and sperm on the grounds of God's intention for such embryos. This clearly doesn't apply to embryos created in other ways.

6.3 Some argue against the use of embryos created from human eggs and sperm on the grounds that they embody a unique genetic pattern. This clearly doesn't apply to a cloned embryo. A cell nuclear replacement embryo is not a perfect clone of its progenitor, since it acquires its mitochondrial DNA from the denucleated egg rather than its progenitor, but the difference is much, much less than that between full siblings.

6.4 Some argue that since we ought to cherish human babies, and a human baby develops continuously from conception, we should cherish a human embryo as we would a human baby. But we can hardly apply this argument to human cell nuclear replacement embryos

when we do not know for sure—and think it would be wrong to find out—if human babies can develop from them.

6.5 Even if we grant that the embryos which develop into human babies ought to be cherished from conception, it does not follow that all human embryos ought to be cherished. In particular, it does not follow that we should cherish embryos which we know will not develop into human babies (for example, because we mean not to implant them). Those who argue that we ought to cherish all human embryos tacitly assume that, if implanted, human embryos seldom fail to develop into human babies. In fact, this isn't the case. Only something like 50% of "natural" human embryos go to term, and at present, only something like 1 in 100 cell nuclear replacement embryos go to term. If that were the natural success rate for humans, it would never have occurred to us to wonder if we should cherish all embryos. We would not have valued them until late enough in their development for us to be reasonably sure that they would go to term.

6.6 It might be argued that even if 99 embryos out of 100 failed to develop into a human baby, and notwithstanding how much good we might do by using embryos, we should still not use them for the sake of the hundredth. But in life we have to balance the statistical certainty of harm to a few against certain benefit to the many. For example, there will certainly be some miscarriages of justice if we have a criminal justice system, but we continue to accept such a system for the sake of the benefit it offers to society as a whole. We might wonder if the potential benefit from the use of embryos in research or therapy justifies the certain harm to the embryos used; but to judge how much harm we would do, we would have to know these embryos' viability, that is, we would have to try to grow human babies from them, which we believe that it would be wrong to do.

7. Finding the arguments to the contrary uncompelling, the Board is of the opinion that we are free to use human cell nuclear replacement embryos for a good purpose. The Board accepts that stem cell research and therapy are good as such; and hence that human cell nuclear

replacement embryos may be used for them, subject to the 14-day limit.

8.   To create human embryos by cell nuclear transfer is to clone the human being who provided the cell nucleus, and in 1997 the General Assembly categorically opposed human cloning. The Board distinguishes between "human therapeutic cloning" (that is, cloning in order to produce human tissue), and "human reproductive cloning" (that is, cloning in order to produce whole human beings). The Board opposes human reproductive cloning but accepts human therapeutic cloning.

9.   For the avoidance of doubt: while the Board opposes the transfer of human cell nuclear replacement embryos to a womb, whether human or animal, or artificial (should such exist in the future), the Board believes that should this be done, the embryos concerned, and any babies into which they develop, should be cherished exactly as if they were created from human eggs and human sperm.

10. Some types of stem cell can be derived from human placentas after birth, and stem cells taken from animal embryos are already being used in some of the applications for which human embryonic stem-cells are being proposed. There is clearly medical potential in stem cells from sources other than human embryos, and the Board welcomes research in this area.

4.5 Drugs update
In May 1997 the Board presented to the General Assembly its Report on the Decriminalisation of Drugs and a year later commented upon action taken and developments introduced. The range of developments is considerable and it is not intended to produce here an exhaustive list, rather to comment on a number of major developments and trends within which the Church's position can be more easily related and understood.

• Perhaps the most important document is that published by the Scottish Executive in March 1999 entitled "Tackling Drugs in Scotland: Action in Partnership".   This booklet sets out Scotland's drugs strategy against the background of the UK position. The strategy built upon "Planning and Provision of Drug Misuse Services" which had been published in 1994 and widely followed thereafter.   The strategy developed around four key objectives which in simplified terms are:

• To reduce the number of young people using drugs illegally.
• To protect communities from drug related anti-social and criminal behaviour.
• To provide effective treatment to those with drug problems.
• To stifle the availability of illegal drugs on the street.

The Board's Report supported all of those objectives.

• The Scottish Executive expect to receive each December an annual Drug Misuse Review prepared by the Scottish Advisory Committee on Drug Misuse (SACDM).   The major players in planning are the Drug Action Teams which are active in every Health Board area in Scotland.   The contents of the Report for 2000 have not yet been received.

• The Scottish Executive refocused the objectives and funding of Scotland Against Drugs in January 1998, guaranteeing funding of £1 million per year until March 2001.   One result of this for the Board was that the Rainbow Project in Glasgow secured funding from this source in October 2000 to set up an imaginative restoration programme for old buses in co-operation with First Bus. The objective is for residents in Rainbow to work on the restorative programme and if showing a satisfactory application to work and freedom from drub misuse, full time employment will be offered.

• In September 2000 the Scottish Executive announced that additional funding of £100 million would be provided to tackle drugs.   The money was split among the four major objectives of the Scottish Drugs Strategy as identified above. The package proposed confirms a move away from a "Just Say No" approach to a much more effective strategy based on education and rehabilitation. **This was a recommendation in the Board's Report.**

• Diversion from Prosecution schemes have proved effective and the Scottish Executive have now confirmed that they wish to see Diversionary Schemes available throughout Scotland. **This was a major recommendation in the Board's Report**.

• In **1998 the General Assembly** were advised that an inquiry had been set up by the Police Foundation with the backing of The Prince's Trust "to review the effectiveness of the Misuse of Drugs Act 1971". The inquiry, chaired by Viscountess Runciman DBE, reported in the spring of 2000.

The Report is very clearly independent of Government direction and has been very well researched and prepared. There are very detailed comments on the present law, the issues as addressed in other countries, trafficking and non-trafficking offences and enforcement; a particular chapter on cannabis, treatment and the law, and 81 recommendations.

A comment such as this cannot do justice to the detailed thinking and presentation of the Report but comment will be made on only a few issues. The chapter on cannabis sets out very clearly the place of cannabis in the whole abusive drug taking scene. It makes clear that further research must be done in order that changes in use in the future can be monitored, but in the meantime no evidence could be found that the taking of cannabis in small amounts leads on to harder drugs i.e. it is not a "gateway" drug. Secondly, having given serious study to the work of the House of Lords Select Committee and the British Medical Association this Committee concludes "that there is evidence that there are therapeutic benefits from the use of cannabis by people with certain serious illnesses and that these benefits outweigh any potential harm to themselves."

The whole spirit of this section of the Report is in line with the Board's Report.

• **The Scottish Executive has also indicated their intention to set up Drug Courts in Scotland.** The Board was given an opportunity to comment on this possibility and indicated that it would be in favour within the following guidelines:

• The Drug Courts should deal with drug related offences whenever possible, e.g. theft to feed a drug habit.
• That specific judiciary be appointed to this work in order to develop consistency of approach and sentencing.
• That drug offences and offenders be dealt with as soon after charging as possible.

• **Drug Testing Orders**. As a result of the Scottish Executive's programme to tackle drug misuse, Drug Treatment and Testing Orders (DTTOs) have been introduced. This is an alternative to a custodial sentence. There are 2 pilot schemes in Scotland, one in Dundee and one in Glasgow. The orders are sanctioned through the sheriff courts and are usually in place for 12 months with a requirement to attend monthly court hearings where progress is reviewed. Currently there are 41 orders; 6 of which are applied for women, 35 for men. In Glasgow the work is done with a core social work team, linking with areas of Pollok, Easterhouse and Drumchapel. It has a multi-disciplinary approach and is in partnership with the Health Board, Courts and voluntary sector. To be eligible for the programme the criteria applied is:

• lengthy criminal record;
• repeated offending pattern;
• known drug user.

Phoenix House in Glasgow is providing the treatment part of the order, which is an abstinence based 4 day programme. The clients are tested for drug misuse on 3 of these days and live in the community for the rest of the week. The Dick Stewart hostel in Dennistoun is also part of the scheme to provide the accommodation part of the order. The clients admitted on this basis attend the Drugs Problem Survey unit for testing twice per week. The scheme will run for 18 months initially (commenced Oct 2000) and outcomes at this stage are encouraging.

It is satisfying to note that the conclusions of the Board's Report on Decriminalisation of Drugs continue to be very much in line with current serious thinking. The Scottish Executive is addressing some of the issues but there are some which will require a political shift of policy in Westminster.

5.   The Board of Practice and Procedure

As *the Board of Practice and Procedure* indicate in their Report to the General Assembly efforts should be made to reduce the size of Reports in the Blue Book and to make use of Appendices whenever feasible. The Report so far has provided a reasonably full overview of the work of the Board but fails, because of size, to reflect the detailed nature of day-to-day work.   Part 2 of the Report fulfils this objective.   It should be compulsory reading for anyone interested in the Church in action.

6.   Staff

6.1   Employment of ministers in non-parochial work

In accordance with the regulations adopted by the General Assembly in 1949, the Board declares that no minister of the Church of Scotland is employed in its service.

6.2   Thanks to Staff

In responding to people in need, the Board is served by supportive and caring staff. The Board commends staff at all levels and in all areas of work, and gives thanks to God for their service and commitment.

6.3   Employee Attitude Survey

The Board as part of its on-going consultative process was anxious to find a method by which it could consult with staff on a range of issues. Dundee City Council had undertaken two surveys of staff so it was felt appropriate to seek guidance from this Council on the content and methodology of its surveys. Representatives of the Corporate Services Department of Dundee City Council were extremely helpful in providing advice and guidance.

It was decided to undertake a survey and to engage an independent consultant to conduct the analysis of the survey results for the Board. The survey form issued to staff sought information on staff attitude in respect to a range of issues, such as:

- teamworking;
- quality of service;
- management within the workplace;
- communication;
- health & safety; and
- personnel issues.

A Survey Form was sent to 2,000 staff to be returned directly to an independent consultant.

The report received indicated that 616 (31%) staff had returned forms. The level of return is possibly low for an internal survey although it should be recognised that this is the first such survey undertaken. It seems that a number of staff may have been disinclined to respond out of a concern that they could be identified within the organisation. Again it is worth noting that this was a confidential survey and no forms were seen by any representative of the Board.

The majority of respondents, around two-thirds, are agreed that they experience within their workplace and in their wider contact with the Board the sense of being part of a working team, a commitment to quality of service, good management practice, and effective consultation and communication on matters affecting their work.

A smaller group, consistently around one-quarter of respondents, have a negative experience in their work. These indicate that they feel under-valued within their workplace, where senior staff show little respect towards other grades and fail to carry out the responsibilities of management as they should.

The Board can take satisfaction from the indications provided from this exercise that relations within the workplace are generally good, supporting widespread job satisfaction and the promotion of quality. Yet it appears that work remains to be done if all employees are to experience within their workplace a management environment similarly supportive of good practice.

6.4 Staff in the Employ of the Board
at 1st February 2001

	Full-time		Part-time		Total		Full-time Equivalent	
	2001	2000	2001	2000	2001	2000	2001	2000
Operations Staff	783	783	808	798	1591	1581	1254.47	1247.56
Executive, Office & Support Staff	69	70	12	15	81	85	74.48	76.96
					1672*	1666	1328.95	1324.52

*In addition there are an additional 720 people engaged in Sessional, Relief and Home Support work.

7. PART TWO: OPERATIONAL PRACTICE

CONTENTS

7.1 OPERATIONS

7.1.1 Introduction

Although the Board's services are usually described according to their main purpose, many cut across different aspects of need. Examples of this are learning disability services incorporating some dual diagnosis of mental health problems or homelessness or relationship problems. Another would be where children receive individual counselling, but are part of fragmenting families, poor parenting experiences, personal trauma such as abuse or subject to a Children's Panel Order and being accommodated by a local authority.

7.1.2 Child Care

The Board supports work with children and their families through the two residential schools, through residential and respite services for children with profound disabilities, through its Women and Children Projects, through counselling and through working with vulnerable parents and families.

Geilsland in North Ayrshire and Ballikinrain in Balfron continue to explore and readjust the nature of their provision to ensure that they operate as part of a planned programme of care. To this end, major property work, staffing arrangements and review of the day-to-day activity with the young people are all being pursued, in discussion with all relevant agencies. A major effort was undertaken this year to equip all teaching and care staff with a common approach in challenging situations by providing training in Therapeutic Crisis Intervention (TCI). This is a generally proven and accepted method of approaching and defusing difficult behaviour and affords a common understanding and process for staff and for the boys. In addition, work continues to present the efforts of the schools to purchasers of the service in ways which emphasise results and value for money, rather than merely focusing on what is being done, good as that may be. This is in line with the Best Value approach adopted by Central and Local Government across all services.

The Women and Children Project in Dundee continues to offer support and parenting skills in a number of drop-in settings. When HRH The Duke of Rothesay visited Charis House, he met a young mother from that Project who was in the process of coming off drugs. Attendees have differing reasons for using the service, but the main issue is whether or not it works. One mum commented:

"The people at the Group really understand what I'm feeling. They know what it is like to have horrible thoughts and feelings about your son. This helps me to feel less guilty and shows me that I am not abnormal."

An important development has been the establishment of Parents Altogether Lending Support (PALS) in conjunction with Dundee City Council Education Department. This incorporates groups for ethnic minority women of Asian background. Together with a multicultural Health Worker, PALS groups have been held in Urdu/Punjabi and English, with written material also in Urdu. The Board is beginning a similar Parent and Children Project in Glasgow, based at the Renfield St Stephen's Church Centre.

In addition to the above work with children, Number 21 Counselling Service in Edinburgh is developing an increasing focus on counselling for children. The Mallard in Glasgow and Keith Lodge in Stonehaven continue to offer a mix of longer-stay and also respite for children with learning and other disabilities, noting an increasing demand for respite to assist carers. The Mallard also offers a limited Home Support service to help with continuity of care and support. The Post Natal Depression Project (PND) services in and around Edinburgh also assists in child care and family support, as does the Lifestyle Centre in Stornoway with its inclusive approach to rebuilding and maintaining family and peer relationships.

As the Board widens its childcare-related services and increasingly engages with local churches, the need for a mutual understanding and appreciation of the Church's Child Protection Procedures becomes vital, underpinned by common agreement to their full application. For such local engagement, there must be an explicit recognition of need, value and accountability built into these approved procedures. In keeping with the statutory requirements in child care, the Board is also revising its own Child Protection Policy to ensure that it meshes with the Church's approved procedures and the particular needs of children who are being looked after in its various services. The requirement under *Protecting Children: Securing Their Safety* for all people working with children to be subject to a check on previous convictions is referred to within the report of the Joint Boards Group on Child Protection, issued by the Child Protection Unit through the Report by Parish Education. There are major implications in managing this for Board staff and volunteers. The Scottish Executive has now confirmed that there will be no charge to voluntary sector organisations for the Police record check; this decision is warmly welcomed.

7.1.3 Counselling and Support Services

The Tom Allan Centre in Glasgow now has disability access following full refurbishment of the garden flat accommodation to provide an additional group room, two small counselling rooms, a comfortable waiting area, unimpeded access, a general purpose lounge, large kitchen and toilets. These improvements have been welcomed by the 1075 service users, staff and 60 trained volunteer counsellors. The Centre is offering an increasing number of places on Certificate in Counselling Skills course modules validated by the Confederation of Scottish Counselling Agencies (COSCA), with particular emphasis on Board staff being so certificated.

The small Project for Older Persons based at Wallace House in Edinburgh is managed by skilled volunteers, taking as their motto: *"Do not cast me away when I am old. Do not forsake me when my strength is gone."* (Psalm 71). Activities include aroma therapy, reminiscence, exercise, gardening and outings for leisure, pleasure and fun. The Board appreciates the access grant from Edinburgh Council of 50% of the cost of providing access and toilets for disabled persons.

The National Counselling Service continues to extend its service to the people of Scotland, with training schools in 2000 held in Crieff, Fort William, Inverness, Pitlochry and Kyle of Lochalsh in addition to the day-to-day

counselling work in Granton, Dunfermline and Dundee. Planning continues for a new course for the University of the Highlands and Islands—a BA in Theology and Christian Counselling—due to start in September 2001. There is a sympathetic charging policy for counselling services, but funding remains problematic. The Board is grateful to the Gannochy Trust for a generous grant and to the Bank of Scotland and the Newcastle Building Society for grants. Applications for funding have also been lodged with relevant Local Authorities and Health Boards. Additionally, the Board offers praise and thanks for the 70 trained volunteer counsellors, 20 steering group members and 25 volunteer administrators and secretaries taking this work ahead. The Service Manager noticed that some clients were arriving at Wallace House up to 1+ hours early for appointments. Clients responded: *"In this place I have found peace"; "In this place I receive comfort": "In this place I feel understood"* and *"I want to rest here"*. What a privilege when those suffering from loneliness, isolation, emptiness and a sense of meaninglessness can find rest for their souls in drawing alongside what we call our work. Connections, the counselling service based in the St Andrews Day Care Centre in Dunbar and also operating in North Berwick Health Centre, is now managed as part of the National Counselling Service.

Number 21 Counselling Service in Edinburgh, incorporating the Broomhouse Counselling Service and operating with over 60 trained counsellors and therapists, now opens on Saturdays to offer improved availability as a result of increasing demand. The service Manager reports that although this is a well-established and professional service there is an anomaly in that it does not form part of the Edinburgh Community Care local plan, even though many initial referrals are from the statutory services. Each year Number 21 puts on special events during the Edinburgh Festival, in addition to Spring and Autumn conferences, which expands awareness of the work and stimulates new directions of service. Plans are well advanced to work collaboratively with Saheliya, a black and ethnic minority mental health organisation. There is a common thread between all the counselling services regarding the nature of referrals which tend, in descending order, to present as: depression/anxiety/stress; difficulty with relationships/marital partnership problems; sexual abuse/rape; personal growth; financial/work-related; anger/violence; alcohol/gambling and a mixed range of other reasons.

Case Histories

June was a woman in her thirties, who was suffering from bullying at work. She had suffered long-term depression and worked in a sheltered workshop situation. It was her employers who had referred her for counselling. However it was her manager who, in June's opinion, was bullying her. Through a series of counselling sessions, the counsellor explored with June her own sense of self-worth, and the hammering it had taken, suffering from long-term depression. She was able to experience a stronger, survivor side to her personality which in time led her to become more assertive. Eventually she was able to speak to her manager about the sort of pressures she felt she was put under and negotiated a change in her allotted tasks. This has had the knock-on effect that June has begun to feel less depressed and more in charge, to the extent that gradually—and appropriately—she is wondering whether she might prefer in time a job outside of the sheltered workshop situation.

Barry had been a GP for ten years but pressure of work and an unhappy marriage, coupled with a constant questioning about why he had ever chosen to be a doctor, in time led to a quite catastrophic nervous breakdown. When he came for counselling he was unemployed and tentatively trying to put his life back together again. Barry came from a working class family where the pressure on him, as the oldest son, to succeed had been intense. It was a family hope that Barry should become a professional, whereas his passion was working with his hands, particularly carpentry. Through counselling Barry was helped to see the extent to which his family had lived through him, while simultaneously alienating him from them as he moved into an educated, professional world. He was able to understand that the shame he had always felt about his upbringing belonged more to his parents—

that he in fact respected them for wanting so much for him, while recognising they had got it wrong. During counselling he enrolled on a furniture making course and is now on his way to becoming a professional—but a professional craftsman. Miraculously his marriage survived. His wife, as Barry put it, had not married the facade—the GP—but the person he was in the process of becoming.

Jack was, by his own admission, a professional liar. Now in his late fifties and on his third marriage, he left behind him a saga of broken relationships, disappointed and let down children and other unhappiness. He came for counselling because after years of getting himself out of tight corners with a ready excuse he was realising that he had spent his whole life running. Counselling returned again and again to Jack's early childhood. There, subject to the cruel and authoritarian outbursts of a probably manic-depressive father, he had learned that his best protection was to lie. Over a number of sessions Jack was able to face up to some of the mistakes of his life, to the extent of making recompense to his children, offering them an honest view of himself and the possibility of a relationship. He was learning to stop running away.

Post Natal Depression is a most distressing condition. The motto of this Project based at Granton is: *"Weeping may be for a night, but joy comes in the morning"* (Ps 30:5). The service also operates from local church accommodation in Edinburgh city centre, Joppa and Linlithgow, assisted by funding from "Sure Start". This has helped to reduce waiting lists, introduce an infant massage programme and implement a quality assurance questionnaire check with existing and former service users. An encouraging development is the discussion currently in hand with Lothian Health on a collaborative venture to make a video on PND for sufferers and their families. An open day at the Joppa drop-in centre generated considerable local interest, assisted by the publicity which Susan Deacon in her role as local MSP attracted in opening the day. At any one time there are 60 clients using the service and, again, without the able assistance of volunteer trained listeners, counsellors and specific therapists the work would not be able to function.

Some client reflections provide an insight into various benefits of this service:

"I could not cope with my PND if it wasn't for the drop-in centre. They are my life-line at the moment. As soon as I walk through the doors of the Centre I feel as though I'm walking into the only stress-free, friendly, 'normal' place in life. It's great. It has helped me to try and cope with all my fears and anxieties. It has filled me with reassurance and most of all it has made me see that I'm not alone and I'm not going mad. Other people are suffering too. Everyone I have met in the Centre has been so friendly and so genuinely caring. It is such a nice place to be—when you don't want to be at all."

"I have been attending the Post Natal Depression Project for about six months now. It is my time, dedicated to my own needs, purely for me to talk about my feelings and problems. While attending these sessions I have begun to recognise my own feelings and actions and with the help of Angie (my counsellor) learned how to understand myself and cope with issues that have weighed me down and caused depression and repression over the years."

"The crèche is well run, with lots for the children to do and play with and the staff there are wonderful, patient and supportive. The Post Natal Depression Project has been a lifeline to me, giving me hope, understanding, strength and a release. All the staff have been very supportive and helpful and have been there for me even when I didn't have an appointment, to give me someone to talk to in times of need."

7.1.4 Dependencies

Beechwood in Inverness consists of differing but complementary services. The Designated Place offers an alternative to being locked up for being drunk and incapable: it provides 4 immediate access places plus 4 places for a short follow up time. Unfortunately, it is always full, with a worrying rise in under 24-year old and female admissions. Of 984 admissions, 392 were first time referrals. The adjacent 15 place alcohol/drug residential rehabilitation service is recognised for its high standard.

A recent Inspection Report by the external Registration and Inspection Unit stated: *"Staff should be congratulated on their high standard of care provided".* Supported accommodation for up to 12 people is managed by Beechwood staff for those who are temporarily resident while attending the Health Board Osprey day services unit nearby. This has proved to be an effective area of co-operation between the voluntary and statutory sectors for the benefit of individuals with dependence problems and their families. It is indeed a sad reflection on the financial priorities of Local and Central Government that the Board's rehabilitation services for alcohol dependency in particular are under-used. This is despite the fact that alcohol is by far a greater killer and contributor to individual and family relationship breakdown, to work absence and to the cost of health care than drug misuse. It is with relief that the Board observes and welcomes the Scottish Executive initiative in beginning to form a national alcohol strategy and commends those local Drug Action Teams which also incorporate alcohol dependency within their remit. The Beechwood Service Manager comments in her Annual Report Summary to the Board:

"This year has been another roller coaster of emotions. As the statistics show, many people have successfully completed the programme and remain in sobriety. Unfortunately there have also been a number of people who have died this year in the community. These are people who the community of addiction knew well. It is quite shocking when you realise that most of those who died were in their forties or early fifties. The Government has made a huge amount of money available for those who work with drug abusers. While this is obviously commendable, from discussions with our client group over the past two years it would appear that usually an individual's first experience with addiction is with alcohol and/or cigarettes. We need to impact on young people's lives at a very early stage. It's not just money we need to do our work: we need to be proactive in our schools and churches to help change attitudes in society about alcohol and other substances. Children need to be able to grow up in a loving and

caring environment to go on to become loving and caring adults. What we see daily in our work are many broken people who usually have horrific stories and lifestyles of abuse. It's a cycle that we have to find a way of breaking.

We consider that one of the ways we could help is by working in a way that enables whole families to grow, develop and start the business of healing. This holistic approach is the road we feel we should take. We need help and support in order to be able to develop this, if this is the right road to travel.

We will continue to develop and grow in the coming year, making new links into the community. This will be made easier by the growing support of the community at large, of the Presbytery and individual Ministers. We are also fortunate to belong to a Division that is immensely supportive to one another."

This reluctance by local authorities to refer and fund residential alcohol rehabilitation is also reflected in the Board's other services, despite positive Inspection Reports. The Board recognises the need for diversifying services, but in its own experience residential alcohol and drug rehabilitation is an essential life-saver for some people where community-based initiatives have not worked. Deeford in Aberdeen highlights this, with its unusually high success rate on the one hand and recent persistent under-use on the other. Although Aberdeen was not a formal trial area for drug treatment orders, the High Court received reports from Deeford which led to a resident receiving a drug treatment order with a condition of residence at Deeford for six months, as an alternative to a seven year jail sentence. The person successfully completed this six months and was then placed on probation for 2+ years on condition that his contact with Deeford is maintained for up to 12 months. This was a unique and, so far, successful experiment, as it was the first such disposal in Scotland. The 20th Anniversary of Deeford was celebrated at a church service in Ruthrieston South Parish Church and an excellent buffet in the hall. Many former residents attended the anniversary and it was encouraging to staff to meet those whose lives had been changed through being on the

Deeford programme. This service is, however, at risk unless more use is made of it by local authorities. Staff are pursuing this as well as exploring other ways of providing service.

Two statements by former residents indicate benefits of the programme:

"My name is Mike and I am an alcoholic.

I wonder how many times I have said that to myself over the past four years eight months, and yes, I do keep count of the days and months that I have been without an alcoholic drink of any kind.

I came to the conclusion that I was an alcoholic when I could no longer start a day's work without having a drink. I would purchase a half bottle in the morning, illegally from my local corner shop, but I dare say he was quite happy to have my custom, and I would find myself purchasing another half bottle at lunchtime to see me through the afternoon.

I was offered home detoxification that my wife dismissed out of hand and pleaded that I be taken into some kind of residential rehabilitation unit. Because of a lack of beds I was offered the drug Antabuse. I managed in my then very cunning way to conceal the fact that I wasn't taking my drugs, and after a great deal of pain inflicted upon my wife in particular, and other members of my close family, I was found a bed in a residential rehabilitation centre run by the Church of Scotland in Aberdeen.

This changed my life.

I found myself in a caring, well run and enthusiastic environment that gave me the courage and determination to accept the fact that I needed help, and that I couldn't beat the menace I found myself confronted with on my own, and that there were other people with the same problems as myself.

This all took time however, and I was a resident for thirteen weeks in all. We were encouraged to talk about our problems and feelings in daily group meetings, and for myself, to begin with, I found the meetings almost painful because I am not by nature the talkative type. Perhaps this is a male chauvinist trait, I don't know. However things improved and I gained a great deal of strength and understanding from these sessions, and perhaps more importantly from the views and feelings of other alcoholics.

The time I spent in Residential Rehabilitation changed my life dramatically and all for the better. I still have my wife, who through all the hard times has stuck by me. Perhaps now I can begin to repay her for all that I have put her through. I still have my grown-up daughters of whom I am immensely proud. Perhaps now I can give them the support and backing they should have had earlier in life. I still have my life, which I now treasure more than I did before, this might not have been the case had I continued drinking the way I was. These are some of the many plusses that have come about from my stay in Residential Rehabilitation. The alcoholism is still there and will never go away, but I know that if I continue to practice what I learnt during my stay, I can continue my new found life of sobriety and that it will be vastly better than the life I was living before I entered Residential Rehabilitation. It worked for me and I am sure that with the continued dedication and caring of members of staff in places such as the one I attended, they will continue to be a venue of support and help to many more people who have the courage to admit to themselves that they have a problem with alcohol.

I can only hope that my letter may, in some small way, help to keep places like these open and continuing their excellent work."

"I went to Deeford after 4 weeks in Cornhill Hospital down in mind and body and had lost my job after 40 years in the Merchant Navy.

The care I received there helped me to look at my life as alcohol was not the answer. I have not touched alcohol for 18 months.

I believe the Government should give something back after all the tax they take from alcohol

It is far more dangerous than any drug and has no respect for anyone..

Murdo"

The Lifestyle Centre in Stornoway exists to provide one-to-one counselling and support to individuals or families experiencing difficulties because of alcohol or drug abuse. To this end, it offers an alcohol counselling service; a service for partners and family members of those abusing; an offenders support scheme; a "Want to Talk" counselling service for young people, offered jointly with Community Education, and supported accommodation. In addition, the Lewis Street supported accommodation service for people with learning and other disabilities or recovering from a mental health problem while managed on site is also under the aegis of the Lifestyle manager. This service is well placed in the centre of town with partial funding from the Tudor Trust, statutory services and the Board. As part of the millennium celebrations Lifestyle held a very successful day conference on alcohol related matters.

Malta House in Edinburgh works on the basis that to concentrate solely on abstention from abuse without dealing with some of the underlying problems is usually not effective, as the underlying problem will be a main trigger to return to substance abuse. In all dependency work, relapse is a constant possibility. Most people require several attempts at some form of rehabilitation before achieving a successful outcome, a factor not readily appreciated by many funding authorities. Views of present and former residents describe elements of the service and some outcomes.

"A Great Rock of Support (TB)

When I first came to Malta House my first impression was that it was a nice house situated in a quiet part of town. The staff were very friendly, as were the residents. Before I moved in to Malta House my whole world was falling apart and I had no one that understood me. I felt that I was in despair. I have been here for nearly five months now and although facing things that are hard to deal with it has been difficult. I know that I always have the support of the staff team and all us residents try and help each other. If I hadn't come to Malta House I really don't know where I would be now.

The Programme consists of 1–1 sessions with your keyworker, general chores within the house and group therapy. In the groups there is a wide range of topics, some examples are: learning to say no, how your self-esteem is affected by the addiction etc. Malta House also has one afternoon a week for sporting activities such as football, bowling, swimming etc. These too are part of the programme therefore they are compulsory."

"*First Impressions* (AS)

I have been at Malta House for sixteen days since becoming a resident on the 31st October 2000. My first impressions of the set-up are favourable.

All the staff are friendly and approachable and have endeavoured to make me feel welcome and as comfortable as possible.

I have found the other residents willing to help me in understanding the day to day tasks the residents are responsible for. The catering is satisfactory with a varied menu and generous portions.

The various papers that have been discussed at Group Meetings have been both varied and thought provoking, which has started me on a process of self-examination of myself and my actions.

1/1 meetings with my key-worker, although at an early stage, have already raised interesting points and observations, most of which had not occurred to me. This has reinforced the need for self-examination.

I am hopeful that my time spent at Malta House will equip me with the tools to enable me to cope with the outside pressures and allow me to rebuild my life with my family."

"*I'm Learning* (DG)

Since becoming a resident of Malta House 4 months ago, Malta House has given me a chance to build up my self confidence and self esteem again, which was lost when I arrived here. It's given me a chance to fight my addiction with help and support.

It's taught me to stand up for myself again and become more assertive, whereas through my addiction I had lost all of it. I've learned to value myself again and to think rationally. I'm learning to accept criticism and have been trying to motivate myself to change. If I hadn't come to Malta House, I wouldn't have done any of the above.

It's taught me that there are people willing to help me, to be patient, accept my mood swings and that these same people will still support me.

It has made me more broadminded and given me a greater, more intense understanding of my addiction and the troubles it has caused me in my life."

"*At the End of the Day* (SD)

Before I came to Malta House I was struggling to cope with my addiction. Since I've been in I feel I am getting a lot of support with staff and also the residents. I've been in 15 weeks now, but I still have a lot to do.

I'm finding it better than it was—as I can talk to my Keyworker about my past and emotions which is very upsetting. I'm looking forward to getting my own life back when I leave Malta House.

I would honestly recommend Malta House to anyone who has an addiction problem because I know they are helping me, but, at the end of the day—**it's up to yourself**."

"*An ex-Resident's View* (CAD)

My six month Programme ended at a good time for me. I had just worked two weeks full time on a summer play-scheme. This was part of my voluntary placement, which was arranged with my Key-worker. So when I left Malta House I continued this work for another two weeks. By this time I felt part of the 'outside world' again and had made friends with some other volunteers, some from overseas.

I was able to go to pubs with them without feeling tempted to drink. I knew how bad the consequences would be, and I'm under no illusion about being able to 'have one or two'.

That actually really helped me to feel that I was in control of my situation, and that I needn't be excluded from social events. I felt great walking home at night, sober, having only spent a couple of pounds.

The next day at work the others would be nursing headaches and crawling through the day and I felt relieved that I didn't feel like that.

As time passed by and I could go out without even

thinking about drinking, I felt stronger within myself, knowing that I could be around people quite happily without needing a drink.

And soon the romantic notions I had of drinking 'with-friends-in-the-pub' was demystified. As it is now, 4 months later, I very rarely go to pubs as I feel it is a waste of time, I hate the loud music and would much rather socialise somewhere else.

I still have difficult days—but I know drink is not the answer.

The voluntary work I began in Malta House has led to paid work—as a development worker with minority teenagers, with training and prospects for the future that I would not have believed. The placement was so right for me and I've met such good people there. My only limitation now is having enough time!

And I could not overstate how reassuring it was to know that I had a flat waiting for me. I don't believe it is possible to really take control of your life if you don't have a home that you feel happy in.

My Key-worker has referred me on to an art therapy course, which was a good step into another direction of self-development. At the end of the programme at Malta House I think it was necessary for me to move on from alcohol-related counselling. To keep moving forward I suppose.

Day to day things, which seemed so difficult, are now quite simple, and simple things can be enjoyable now. **Life actually keeps getting better!***"*

Ronachan in Argyll has benefited from refurbishment which has met with approval from the Inspection Unit and makes for an improved reflection to clients of the Board's commitment to building a more positive view of themselves. Revenue finance is a major difficulty, with the resource being well recognised for its service quality, but not having sufficient referrals from Social Work Departments to ensure continuing viability. Strenuous efforts are being made to address this. One of the innovations has been a Website which had 80 hits in its first two weeks and elicited placement enquiries from as far south as London. Others are funding for Outreach

Worker posts and assistance with Substance Misuse Road Shows. Almost everyone going to Ronachan for help has been using his or her dependence to solve a problem, rather than just a habit that got out of control. These problems are diverse but unique to the person concerned and include low self esteem; lack of confidence; past trauma that constantly replays; unresolved grief or loss; a mental health problem; physical, emotional or sexual abuse; depression or lack of meaning to life; difficulties in forming and maintaining relationships and negative life experiences that leave a person feeling a failure. The programmes seek to build renewed lives from personal devastation.

The Rankeillor Initiative in Edinburgh is a small but effective range of supports for people recovering from substance abuse or homelessness. This service seeks to sustain people in supported housing or moving into new housing or within their own house or tenancy. Here again the problem is not lack of effectiveness but limited local authority referrals from tight budgets causing stop-go planning and short term thinking in relation to long term problems. Similarly, Victoria View in Glasgow is reviewing its functioning and site to ensure that the service it offers and the quality of the setting meets the evolving policy requirements of funders

While alcohol addiction remains a major issue, rehabilitation for those with drug and mixed dependencies is also undertaken within the various alcohol related services as well as those with a specific drugs focus. Rainbow House in Glasgow, Project Plus in Mid and East Lothian and Simpson House Drugs Counselling and Related Services in Edinburgh have developed new initiatives during the past year. Rainbow is engaged with Scotland Against Drugs (SAD) which provides real work experience for those who have been through the rehabilitation process. This is still at the testing stage but at the time of writing is proving to be a real encouragement to those on the programme. It is being evaluated and may be the beginning of larger initiative by SAD. The Board's Project Plus is a joint agency scheme devised to assist those who have been through drugs programmes in other services to become more securely established in their home area without succumbing once more to the drug culture.

Simpson House continues to offer a valued city centre location with close working links to area services and various prisons. This service continues its own innovative approach to drugs rehabilitation and counselling in developing a range of partnerships to give added value to the service. An Early Intervention Project has been established as a unique resource for young people which resulted in a further visit by Angus McKay, former Deputy Minister for Justice. It is planned to expand this initiative in the coming year in conjunction with National Childrens Homes (NCH Scotland). During the General Assembly the Board was able to outline the range of the work and its results to the Duke of Rothesay as part of his duties as the Lord High Commissioner. The Mound Centre within Simpson House continues to be used well by those involved in the network of drug related services and the premises also hosts an office base for Capital C, a self help group for people affected by Hepatitis C.

7.1.5 Homelessness

In Glasgow, Kirkhaven continues to offer close support to 14 homeless people who have been barred from other resources in the city, despite at the time of writing being established in an area where all other tenants have been relocated. Thenew Housing Association is working with Board staff to identify other more suitable accommodation which would enable this service to move ahead with skill and relevance in a changing homelessness world.

Cunningham House in Edinburgh is a direct access residential resource catering for 23 homeless people in 5 self-contained flatlets. It offers planned emergency accommodation for single, vulnerable, homeless people for a short to medium stay. It is block funded by Edinburgh Council and the DSS Resettlement Agency. A visit by the Moderator of the General Assembly was much appreciated by staff and residents alike. Similarly, Cale House in Inverness continues to offer accommodation and support to homeless people who need some learning time and space to help them move on to more independent living.

7.1.6 General Supported Accommodation

The Lewis Street accommodation with staff support in Stornoway caters mainly for adults with a learning disability moving towards independence. Many referrals come from Grianan, a community day centre nearby, and the service is a good example of a voluntary agency working closely with Health professionals, local voluntary agencies, the Housing Department, Muirneag Housing Association and the local College which also arranges work experience placements. This helps to provide a structure to the day as explained by a service user: *"I now have a structure to my week in that I attend College twice a week and a day centre once a week."*

The Whiteinch Project in Glasgow, established eight years ago in conjunction with the Whiteinch and Scotstoun Housing Association, has been a positive partnership for up to 14 adults with varying difficulties. Enabling total integration of people from different backgrounds back into the community has identified and demonstrated the value, support and learning opportunities each person can experience and share during a stay in this project. Working with such a mixed service user group and the benefit of a good mix of staff add to its uniqueness. As part of the service, one of the flats is managed as 'The Venue' where present and former tenants can meet for social, spiritual or leisure activities. Past and present tenants make their own comments about the service:

"Terrie's Story: I went to the Whiteinch Project in July 1999 after spending 13 months in a rehabilitation centre. I had been abusing drugs for the past 13 years; most of my life was run by drugs. I moved into one of the Whiteinch Project's outside flats in Scotstoun. I was really insecure and needed support and that's exactly what the project offered and gave me.

If I ever needed the staff they were there for me, I just needed to know that someone was there if I hit a "low". I was at the project for 14 months, which I enjoyed, but felt I had to go out and make it in the world on my own. The staff helped me set up a meeting with the housing to get me my own accommodation. They gave me a lot of support in this as it wasn't easy as I wanted to move to the East End of Glasgow, so with a lot of phone calls and a lot of waiting and praying I got a lovely flat in Dennistoun, where I wanted.

My keyworker helped me with my Grant from the DSS and she helped me set up my Gas and Electricity payments for me, as I had never dealt with anything like that before. Moving to my own place has been very scary at times, but it's all paid off in the end and its great now. I know I can phone the Project at any time if I need someone to talk to or if I need anything sorted out. Terrie"

Comments—when asked what do you like or dislike, about staying at the Whiteinch Project, these were some of the responses:

"I like living at the Whiteinch Project because it helps me be more independent. I am learning lots of new things that will help me when I move into my own flat, like paying bills and things like that. I like the people there, all of the residents are nice and so are the keyworkers, most of the time. I enjoy going out with them to different things and I really enjoyed my holiday to the caravan park. I feel a lot more grown up living at the project and it has helped me realise what my responsibilities are when living in the community. Barry G"

"I've lived at the Whiteinch Project for quite a while now and I am moving on in a week or so when I move I will miss all the staff because I like to talk to them about some of my problems, and they help me with my messages and with my tablets too. I'll miss going to the concerts and pictures and all the other nice things we do together with the other residents. I am looking forward to coming back every week to take part in the Wednesday Bible Study Group and I hope I will be able to sometimes come to the breakfast group because Halina makes the best breakfast." Mary C

"The Whiteinch Project is the best in the whole world, it has the best staff. I like when my keyworker, Hamish, takes me out for an all day breakfast. When I feel angry or sad I ask Irene for a private word and then I feel better. I really like taking part in getting organised for
Christmas time. Staff help me with my money and this makes sure I have enough to buy all my Christmas presents for my family and still have some left for me." John B

"I like to have a blether with the staff because it helps me get on better with people. I am hoping to move sometime early in the new year and when I do I will miss everyone, staff too. I'll miss my flat as well. I have learned how to do my shopping better and how important it is to take my tablets at the right time. I hope to come back and visit my keyworker when she is working in the venue at the weekends. I really enjoy going to the Daniel O'Donnell concert and Betty always makes sure that I get to meet him and have my photo taken with him, so I will really miss this when I go." Alex B

"I have only just moved into the project, however, for me it has meant the difference between independent living without support, and therefore aggravating my illness and incurring intense loneliness, to full support and encouragement. Having just left a homeless hostel with a "cell" for a room and sharing amenities with 80 others, to moving into a one bedroomed fully furnished flat will allow me to have privacy, dignity, support but above all independence" Liz.

7.1.7 Learning Disability

The Board manages 13 services for children and adults with a learning disability. One of these is Threshold, a Home Support Service in Hamilton and another is Westhaven in Rutherglen for those where epilepsy is a serious problem to learn to live with. Many of these services are either wholly established, using ordinary houses in local areas, or based on group and individual houses. The Board's small Cairnhill service at Rosshall in Glasgow, which initially catered for 3 young people with autistic behaviour, now comprises 2 houses for a total of 4 people with a learning disability. Although tenants there are expected to remain in the medium to longer term, there is a clearly emerging need for respite. The Board is considering how it could best respond to this need.

Kilpatrick House in Alexandria has been able to offer some limited follow-on housing, courtesy of Dunbritton Housing Association. The main house itself is being re-examined to see how best it could be adapted to offer a greater degree of privacy and lesser dependence in self-contained areas. Some properties do not lend themselves to being flatted and the lessons of Eskmills, Gorgie Park and Saltmarket have been learned that where people can have their own housing with suitable support they flourish. Wolfson House and Dunforth in Edinburgh have started a reprovisioning programme. The process of working with residents to ascertain their wishes is well ahead. However, the process came to a temporary halt when Scottish Homes indicated that residents could not obtain the housing to which they are entitled, because Scottish Homes objected to the Board's policy of only recruiting Christians to work in Christ's Name. At the time of writing, other possible housing options are being explored. An interesting footnote to the Scottish Homes position is that 3.25% of Board staff are from ethnic or minority backgrounds, representing the wider range of Christian culture and experience world-wide. There are 22 different languages spoken within the Board. The Scottish Homes' percentage of ethnic employees is apparently well below the Board's figure.

The Board is a significant provider of accommodation and support for people with learning disabilities with 180 people supported in a variety of house and group settings. Learning disability services managed by the Board adopt models of best contemporary practice collectively referred to as 'Person-centred Planning'. This includes:

- Personal Futures Planning
- Whole Life Planning
- Essential Lifestyles Planning
- Planning Alternative Tomorrows with Hope (PATH)
- Making Action Plans (MAP)

Much of the training in these models is on a partnership basis with other agencies. For example, this is illustrated at Kilpatrick House in Alexandria. Joint training around the values underpinning Person-centred Planning is seen as a foundation for equipping all staff in understanding and practising this approach. This training includes work with Scottish Human Services, a Local Authority Unit Manager, a Clinical Nurse Specialist from the Lomond and Argyll Primary Care NHS Trust and a Practice Teacher from the Board's own Training Section.

Enthusiasm, commitment to best practice and engagement with the task of sensitively supporting the change in service users' circumstances are vital ingredients in developing restructured and revitalised services.

In other supported settings, one tenant who was previously in group care and now enjoys sharing ordinary places said: *"I enjoy going to the library and getting some books and tapes out on my own and I like being independent."* Another said: *"Much of the time I am living at my own home. I am still active around the town. I also go to College twice a week. I love to get out and about and hopefully will be able to travel myself."* There is delight in hearing of such evidence of changed lives and of personal growth in areas which most people would take for granted.

Florentine House in Glasgow, which consists of a number of clustered houses, undertook a major service review to ensure that service users were being assisted to make the most of their own abilities to use ordinary places and do ordinary activities. Person-centred Planning is now fully introduced there and also at Alligan, the Florentine Day Service which is based in a nearby neighbourhood centre. At Gorgie Park in Edinburgh in a number of flats leased from Canmore Housing Association, the level of support varies with the needs of individuals at any given time. Staff there introduced a more flexible staffing arrangement which more closely meets this varying need and at the time of writing this change appears to be successful. For example, one person may just need advice in preparing an evening meal, whilst someone else may require the meal to be prepared. The range of support offered includes: shopping, banking, cooking, housekeeping, care of clothes and finances, social outings and holidays. The range and level of support needed forms part of the individual care plan. Service users and the Inspection Unit comment:

"I'm more independent now and I've got a life. I get

a lot of freedom to do what I want. I can have a coffee when I want and choose what time I eat my meals. I go to the local shops and buy my choice of food after planning my meals. I invite my friends and family to visit when I want company, but I can also be alone when I feel like it."

"When I first came to Gorgie Park I shared a flat and didn't like it. Now I have a flat on my own, so I like living here. I like the fact that the flat is mine and I enjoy living by myself. I enjoy going out too. I attend two clubs, college and church in my spare time. This year I went on an aeroplane for the first time to Spain— it was fine, I like flying. I'm looking forward to Christmas Day, I'm going to have family over to share Christmas dinner."

"I like making toast and honey. I can make it whenever I want with a cup of coffee. I can choose my own food when I go shopping. I like watching television without so many people about, I like peace and quiet. I like having my own things in my own flat. I chose the carpets, they are green, my favourite colour. I like having my own keys so I can lock my front door so my things don't get broken."

"Gorgie Park is the best place I've lived. The staff listen to what I've got to say. I get on well with all the staff. I like being more independent."

"Since I've been here I've started to travel to my Day Centre by myself on the bus, I feel really good about being able to do this. I also pay my own board and lodging into the bank."

Clients were assisted in communicating by a staff member, but where possible their own words were used. An extract from the Edinburgh and Lothian Registration and Inspection Service (ELRIS) Annual Inspection Report 2000/2001 reads as follows:

"Gorgie Park continues to provide a good standard of care to the service users. A discussion with members of staff indicated that high level of commitment was given to achieving the standards of rights, privacy, dignity, choice and independence. This is commendable. Residents enjoy the benefits of good quality accommodation, which is well situated for local services. The atmosphere in the project is warm and friendly with positive relations between staff and tenants. The service users spoken to were satisfied with the level of support they were receiving. This indicates that the duty rotas are now devised in such a way as to give service users access to a level of care which adequately meets their needs."

<u>Threshold Home Support Service in Hamilton</u> was established under contract to South Lanarkshire Council specifically to provide such service to individuals with learning and other disabilities and their families. This service has 10 salaried staff plus a further 34 sessional Home Support Workers, most of whom are looking for stability and a permanent contract, like those in the Board's mainstream Home Support Services. The European Working Time Regulations will increase costs with a resultant reduction in hours available to more vulnerable people. The impact of this is being monitored. This project's motto is from a Christian song: *"God is good, all the time"* and staff praise God for what He is achieving through 850 hours a week of home support and the 24 hour helpline.

7.1.8   Mental Health

Mental Health issues are presented in various forms through the Board's counselling services and through its housing with support services, enabling clients to take charge of their lives as much as possible, particularly where placement follows a hospital stay. A small working group is presently drafting a handbook of resident rights to complement the Board's Policies and Procedures Manual, occupancy agreements and the emerging service agreement. Residents have also been involved in assisting with the interviews for new staff. One commented: *"I found the whole experience nervous but enjoyable and I felt that the interview went well."* At <u>Gaberston in Alloa</u> considerable time has been spent reviewing how the central house and the satellite houses work as a total service; it is proposed in the coming months to concentrate on the satellite houses. The residents/tenants will participate fully in the review. This will now be tackled, with the full participation of residents. The focus on training assists staff in thinking more about the intricate nature of their work, breaking down the use of jargon words rather than seeing them as umbrella terms. The Drop-in Cafe in the centre of Alloa has been reduced to one day a week when the market is on. This helps with the resocialising process and it is heartening to learn of improved contacts with Churches through congregational contacts and the production of a monthly prayer letter. Day Services play an important part in supporting people in their local communities, as is borne out in the work of Morven Day Services in Kilmarnock and Tynepark in Haddington. Various elements of service have been pursued to improve services in East Ayrshire through:

- The Morven Centre—for formal activities and drop-in facilities
- Action for All—volunteer project assisting service users to find creative and supportive work activity
- HIVE—Health in the Valley Enterprise, which includes techno massage, colour therapy and arts and crafts
- Community Guides—helping service users to access local resources.

Excellent links with Presbyteries are maintained and St John's Church at Onthank has assisted in promoting the service. A visit by the Presbytery Moderator was much appreciated by users and staff. The Health Board was particularly supportive by funding an initiative by service users to produce and distribute widely a book of service users' poetry entitled " A Glimmer of Light" to promote confidence, self-esteem, self-worth and a sharing opportunity. Local MP Des Browne led the formal launch of the book, 5,000 copies of which were produced.

Similarly, Tynepark is the basis of a wide range of activity and a listing of some of these would best illustrate the diversity: drop-in area with staff presence; the garden; snack bar; benefits advice; cooking; photography; art and music therapy; badminton; focus groups; outreach; relaxation; aromatherapy; social events and outings; post natal depression; ceramics; crafts; drama; staff/user groups; colour therapy; shiatsu; men's groups; signposts employment support; hospital visits; internet information; Friends of Tynepark; involvement groups; carer's support; newsletter; individual support; salsa dancing and crèche. This prodigious list is ever changing. The external Contract Monitoring which takes place on a regular basis continues to ensure that Tynepark, like other Board services, provides best value.

In summary, the work of the mental health services of the Board can be encapsulated in the vision statement of Allarton in Glasgow, a residential service with linked flats and a Church-based day service:

"Working together with people who experience mental health problems, enabling choice and independence and providing practical support to help each person reach a more positive lifestyle within their own community."

7.1.9 Older People

Despite the continuing restrictions on Board activities over the past 9 years due to the commitment to financially underpin the residential services for older people, the range and nature of this element of work continues at a high level of quality, despite uncertainty about the future. During the year, Morlich and The Elms in Edinburgh were reopened following refurbishment. The Duke of Rothesay, as the Lord High Commissioner, visited Morlich, to the delight of residents. The Elms quickly moved from a renovated building to a fully functional caring home. Prisoners from Saughton Jail participate under the Training of Freedom scheme with supervised work in the gardens. The range and nature of the work and the standard of service is notable. One of the factors which will bear increasingly on services for older people, as well as on other work, is the implementation of *Regulating Care and the Social Services Workforce*. Reference is made elsewhere to this, but suffice to say that its implementation, while onerous, will assist in the best value process and the Board is well placed with its training programme to meet forthcoming qualification levels. The National Care Standards may also make for a more equitable purchasing policy.

All services took some initiative in celebrating the Millennium. Many of the Homes for Older People, such as <u>Devorgilla in Dumfries</u>, held celebration suppers and entertainment throughout the year. In addition, many gave something back to their local communities by planting the Board's millennium rose in key areas, collecting for the Mozambique flood disaster and gifting equipment for District Nurses. <u>Bellfield in Banchory</u> exemplifies the way in which Homes throughout the country celebrated *Age in Scotland* by holding 'Tea on the Water' parties. Having a tea party on a bridge was a great success. Others had boat trips or lunch by the water, making for a fun day out. The *Herald* ran a double page feature on one of the residents who used to be a 'clippie' on the Glasgow trams. The reporter was amazed when the lady produced a copy of *The Glasgow Herald* on the day she was born, 103 years ago, when Axminster carpet was advertised at 3/- (15p) a yard. Discussions are well advanced with the relevant authorities to take forward reprovisioning of <u>Well Hall in Hamilton</u> to provide houses and flats where people can remain in their own house but still have the full benefit of whatever their care and support needs may be. This concept of housing with support is likely to be expanded further, with the Board already having some positive experience of this at <u>Belmont Castle in Meigle</u>.

The <u>Dementia Services</u> continue to offer residential care at <u>St Margaret's, Polmont</u>, <u>Adams House, Elderslie</u>, <u>Williamwood, Glasgow</u> and <u>Cameron House, Inverness</u>. <u>Cumnor Hall in Ayr</u> and <u>Belmont Castle</u> also incorporate smaller dementia flats. Many of the mainstream Homes have numbers of older people with a dementia as well as recognising a greater degree of infirmity in those now moving into residential care. This takes its toll on staff who miss having the level of quality time previously available and who have to be more engaged in direct care. The dementia homes are a lifeline for carers, many of whom have come to the end of their caring reserves, and the standard of care offered in Board services is a real blessing for many who can have peace of mind and the satisfaction of seeing their family member being cared for sensitively and well.

7.1.10   Home Support

The Board's Home Support service is moving up to its fifth year of operation. Finance has not been available to provide adequate "start-up costs" but staff who were given a remit to develop service opportunities have done so with some vigour. The service has been developed where need has been identified. In national terms, this means that the development of service is thriving in some areas, almost static in others, and developing steadily elsewhere. The Board is seeking to identify additional finance that will enable the service to have a specified development strategy as has been successful with the National Counselling Service.

Operational experience shows that to develop a local service it is better to appoint a Home Support Co-ordinator even if there is insufficient identified work at the point of appointment. The task is then to market the service locally, seeking to achieve an identified level of service within an agreed timescale. This has proved successful and the next task is to secure the funding which will allow such a strategy to be applied.

The success of the work that has been developed should not be undersold. The service is presently delivered from 23 locations, providing 2,141 hours of assistance a week to 361 individuals. In care terms this means that many people have been given extra peace of mind, less anxiety and regular planned periods of respite for relatives and carers. It is a service used by older people, by adults with specific care needs and by carers. Home Support offers a flexible response to a wide range of needs and the Board envisages that it will be a service in greater demand from congregations in their local responses to the needs of carers in their community.

7.2   PLANNING AND DEVELOPMENT

The twin themes of "consultation" and "confirmation" have typified the work done in Planning and Development in the past year. In these very uncertain times in social work, it is not any easy task to move forward in providing new or different services for individuals. To try to do so without consultation would be folly. Either staff or service users or both would rightly question why new work was being attempted. Without the support of users and staff no real movement can be made.

Towards the end of 1999, the *National Carers Strategy* was published. This piece of work builds on the government's commitment to help the millions of people who care for relatives and friends and without whose dedicated work the caring task would be far less personal.

In response to this, the Board of Social Responsibility decided to commission a survey of carers attached to local churches. The purpose of this consultative survey was threefold:

(a) to give the opportunity to carers to express their feelings about their task;
(b) to identify opportunities for the Board to provide services which would better meet the needs of the individual;
(c) to identify issues which could be the basis for local church involvement.

It is also proposed to submit the findings to the Scottish Executive to influence its continuing work on its strategy.

As it was anticipated that the findings of the survey would impact on several departments of the church, the Boards of Ministry, Education, Parish Education and National Mission were informed of the Survey and invited to participate in the design of the questionnaire. The Princess Royal Trust for Carers also contributed to the final shape of the questionnaire.

The questionnaire was made available through the Board's congregational contacts system at a series of meetings designed to help contacts understand the purpose of the questionnaire and to encourage them to identify individuals who might benefit from answering it. An interesting spin off has arisen from these meetings. Several contacts have used the questionnaire within their churches to stimulate discussion, not only on how well the church knows the needs of its members and adherents, but also how church members could better support those in caring roles.

The Roman Catholic church, the Free Church, the Scottish Episcopal Church and the Baptist Church were all given the opportunity to use the questionnaire and have it analysed by the researcher. The aim of this offer was to strengthen the report sent to the Scottish Executive and also to pinpoint any issues which could be addressed ecumenically on a local basis. While supporting the idea, for a variety of reasons this offer has not been able to be taken up in any real way.

Following initial analysis of the responses, a series of ten focus groups were set up across the country to explore further the carers' experiences and to identify what help if any they would wish to receive from the church. The findings of this exercise are attached as an appendix.

By offering the focus groups, and following up telephone calls, the exercise has given real insight into the feelings and needs of individual carers, the results of which will help shape some of the future services of the Board both nationally and at a local level.

As the Board seeks to find ways of better meeting the desires and aspirations of its service users, so too do local authorities. They are charged by government to actively demonstrate consultation as part of their Best Value requirement. Each local authority has to be able to show that it is listening to its constituents. As a result of this, different approaches to service delivery are being sought through the tendering process.

When the local authority identifies a service it wants, it will approach providers, the Board being one, to submit a proposal for the work. "Tendering" can be extremely time-consuming as each local authority can ask for information in a slightly different form. The time scale for submission is decided by the purchaser, i.e. the local authority.

During this year, Planning and Development staff have produced standard information which can quickly form the background to any specific tender, thereby enabling the staff who have to produce the detail of the submission more time to customise the service proposal.

This has proved beneficial as it results in a professional, standardised presentation of the Board's work. Each division has the material on disk and can produce the manual to the specific standard. Valuable time is thereby saved and more time given to presenting innovative ways of meeting the service users' needs.

While this may seem a small achievement, it should not be underestimated as it has resulted in staff feeling confirmed in their ability to produce sound work. It has also promoted the standard of the Board's work in general among local authorities and invitations to tender have increased.

The contents of the disk are a result of consultation with staff who have tendered in the past and the church can be confident that the presentation of its work can compare favourably with other providers.

Standards and measuring are a feature of all social work. This has positive and negative elements; it is good to be clear about what has to be done and what has or has not been achieved. This can empower staff and service users—it confirms relationships and methods of working. However if "measuring" cannot take account of nebulous important elements such as feelings, ambience, the experience of the service, then it can become an arid mechanistic task.

With the introduction of the Scottish Commission for the Regulation of Care there will be national standards set with the prime objective of safeguarding vulnerable service users. The inspectors will use these standards to ensure that an even handed approach to inspection will pertain across all providers and indeed across Scotland. At this stage of development, the Board welcomes the initiative. The practical working out of the principles will not be seen until 2002 but this commission linked with the setting up of a national council for registering social care workers should go a long way to confirming the importance of the task of caring for vulnerable people. For too long there has been an undervaluing of the caring task and a lack of recognition of the complexities involved in helping people live to the fullest.

Having a commitment to provide the best for others in Christ's name are the underpinning and overarching values of the Board's work. Quality matters—the quality of the experience of care will only become real as each person involved sees their part in the whole picture and embraces it. Quality is therefore essentially an internal matter which is measured and checked then open to external scrutiny.

In publishing its core standards, the Board has taken ownership of its own quality statement. It is our task to set our standards, to set programmes for review and improvement and to show external bodies through individuals whose lives have been assisted and changed that we are worthy providers of care.

The principle of consultation with staff has been employed throughout the setting and introduction of the standards. A working party drawn from practitioners worked on the initial draft which was then scrutinised and revised by a wider staff group.

Each service will be expected to attain the core standards and can write additional standards which are customised to their specific needs. As a further attempt to ensure that front line staff are involved, they will suggest ways in which measuring tools can be realistically devised.

Lest the service users are forgotten, a new charter has been devised for them which clearly states what they can expect to receive in their service contract. Their involvement in measuring whether or not the service achieves its goals will be crucial. By recognising in a formal way the importance of service users, staff are helped to remain focused on the prime purpose of their work.

The year 2000 has seen the production of several documents designed to assist staff in developing their practice. Planning and Development have carried out a review of operational policies and procedures. This helps break down the Board's major policies into practical application for staff. Again this review was carried out with the help of divisional staff who identified gaps in policies or procedures which needed to be reviewed. Additional policies have been written in the light of operational experience.

In any large organisation, it is easy to become separated from the face to face work. By actively encouraging comment and acting on it, the Board seeks to continue to be relevant to its service users and staff. Such an approach is essential if we are to work out Christ's command to love God and others as ourselves.

7.2.1 Publicity & Public Relations
7.2.1.1 Media enquiries

It was a particularly busy year for press and media enquiries. Between January and December 2000 there were a total of 169 calls to Charis House from newspapers, radio and television stations asking for a quote or 'soundbite' from Social Responsibility on behalf of the Church of Scotland. In addition the Convener received numerous calls at home. This shows a marked increase on the previous year, partly attributable to the media looking for the Kirk's response to debates in the new Scottish Parliament. The subjects on which the Board was asked to comment were extremely wide and varied. Here is a selection:

- The morning after pill
- Paganism in Scotland
- Pre-marital agreements
- Gay superheroes in a new comic
- Couple wanting to choose the sex of their baby
- Square Easter eggs
- Mike Tyson fighting in Scotland
- On-line divorces
- 23 'real sex' films licensed by the B.B.F.C.
- Siamese twins Jodie and Mary being separated
- Compulsory organ transplantation
- Madonna's wedding

Three issues were top of the media agenda: the repeal of Clause 28 (or section 2A as it is known in Scotland); the future of funding of care for older people; human cloning and its implications.

7.2.1.2 Clause 28 (Section 2A)

No subject in the last decade has caused more reaction in the Church community than the proposed repeal of Clause 28. The number of calls, letters and e-mails to the Board of Social Responsibility from individuals, Kirk Sessions and presbyteries was unprecedented. This was in addition to the huge level of media interest throughout the debate; the Board's Communications Officer (Media) logged 44 press enquiries in a four month period in addition to requests for someone to contribute to radio and television programmes. The Board's Convener received numerous letters from Kirk Sessions and Presbyteries supporting Social Responsibility's stance to retain Section 28, typical of which is this one from St. Columba Church of Scotland in Kilmacolm: "It is the earnest belief of our Session that the Bible teaches very clearly that the practice of homosexuality is contrary to a Christian lifestyle. We believe that to allow the promotion of homosexuality as an acceptable alternative to our schoolchildren would be a denial of the clear teaching of God and would be harmful to our children. We would urge you to do all you can to ensure that this legislation is not changed. Far too often we have not had the courage to stand firm on the teachings of the Holy Bible and as a national church we have seen the rewards in terms of our impact and influence on Scottish life. Please therefore urge the Church of Scotland to campaign **publicly** for the retention of Section 28."

7.2.1.3 Future funding for care of older people

The debate about how care of older people should be paid for continued to make press headlines. In March 1999, the Sutherland Report had been handed to the Government with recommendations about funding. However, it was over a year later before the Westminster Parliament gave its response and even longer before the Scottish Parliament voiced its opinion. When it finally did, the Board issued a Press Release on 5th October. It was entitled *"Too little, too late" says Kirk on care funding*:

> *The Church of Scotland has reacted strongly to the statement by the Scottish Executive on the funding for care of older people. The Kirk's Director of Social Work Ian Baillie said: "We broadly welcome the raft of proposals which will improve the quality of life of older people in the community. We are also pleased about the new money to fund nursing care outwith the hospital setting. However I am bitterly disappointed that the major recommendation of the Sutherland report relating to the inequity of underfunding of care in the residential setting has not been addressed by these proposals. It is simply too little, too late." Convener of*

the Kirk's Board of Social Responsibility Ann Allen echoed those views: "Our problem has always been the underfunding by local authorities and central government of residential care for older people who have no personal financial resources. This constitutes the well-publicised 'care gap' which remains an immense financial burden to us. In the last financial year the Board of Social Responsibility has spent £3 million from its own reserves to provide care for hundreds of vulnerable older people in 35 residential homes across Scotland. Therefore we deplore the Scottish Executive's failure to fully implement the major recommendation of the Sutherland report concerning funding of residential care. We will seek to pursue this issue with the minister as a matter of urgency."

The future of residential care and how it should be funded was also in focus when Director of Social Work Ian Baillie wrote an article for the Winter 2000 edition of the Board's newspaper 'Circle of Care':

"I look forward to the new policy statements on care from the Scottish Executive, and although I still have many doubts as to detail, there is no doubt that an acceptance that care costs should be met—no matter what the setting—will make the application of the policy statements easier and much more acceptable. The Board should then be in a position to be much clearer about the future. I have no doubt that the intention of all concerned is to provide good quality care to older people whether they live in their own home or in a group living situation. To achieve this there must be good assessments, effective choices, and proper funding. It would be a great pity if any change in policy is unduly delayed until after 2003."

The Director again emphasised the need for a speedy decision in a feature written for 'Holyrood' magazine in December: "The report by the Health and Community Care Committee published on 28th November highlights the need for Parliament to move towards paying for the personal care needs of older people. It also endorses the objective of retaining people in their own homes whenever possible, an objective fully supported by this Board. When residential care is required then it should be paid for in full, whether the assessed need is of a health or social basis. To this end, the Board has developed its own Home Support Service, encouraged by, but not financially supported by local authorities. The Scottish Executive has an ever-improving record of consultation and action based upon the result of such consultations. It is to be hoped that the remaining fundamental outstanding recommendation of Sutherland (that personal care needs should be provided and paid for from general taxation), is accepted by the Scottish Executive and implemented at an early date. Older people are not a burden on society—from their experience is built our heritage; let us honour them and not make them feel 'past their sell-by date'."

7.2.1.4　Human Cloning

Advances in the field of human cloning have generated much press interest. The Board has set up an ad-hoc group to monitor developments and has issued statements to the media when appropriate. On 16th August a joint release was put out by the Board of Social Responsibility and the Society Religion and Technology Project: 'Kirk welcomes Donaldson Report: Embryos should not be resources':

The Church of Scotland today welcomed the serious consideration of the ethical issues by the Donaldson Report. Dr. Donald Bruce says: "We support research to treat serious diseases by replacement cells, but where embryos are used as the source this poses serious ethical problems, stepping over a new ethical barrier." Rev. Dr. Richard Corbett said: "Until now the embryo has been treated as an entity in itself, used for research which benefits other embryos. To use embryos as a source for body cells would reduce them to a mere resource from which convenient parts could be taken." The Kirk considers that the creation of cloned embryos for routine use as a cell replacement therapy should not be allowed, but nuclear transfer research should focus on avoiding use of embryos, to enable direct programming from one body tissue type to another, as proposed by Roslin and Geron Biomed. Dr. Bruce believes that: *"Since direct reprogramming might be impossible without limited human embryo research, this poses a deep ethical dilemma. Should a very limited number of experiments be allowed to obtain the data necessary to avoid any such use of embryos in the future?"*

When the issue was put to a free vote at Westminster in December, MPs voted by 2 to 1 to allow selective use of embryos. Board member Rev. Dr. Richard Corbett issued this statement:

"We are disturbed by Parliament's decision to allow embryos to be used in medical research. We understand the hopes of the many who suffer, or whose loved ones suffer, from distressing conditions which might be alleviated by treatment based on the stem-cell research using embryos which the Government has authorised. We emphasise that we are not against stem cell research as such, provided that the cells used come from adult volunteers, or from placentas. However since the Church of Scotland 'affirms the sanctity of the embryo from conception' we cannot think it right to use human embryos for even the best of purposes. We are also concerned that by permitting the cloning of human embryos for medical research, Parliament has agreed that humans may, in principle, be cloned. This need not lead to the "Brave New World" of reproductive cloning and of germline engineering which many people fear, but it is a step in that direction."

As can be seen from the above, cloning is undoubtedly going to remain an emotive issue for society and the media for some time to come.

7.2.1.5 Press Releases

During the year 2000, ten press releases were issued by the Media Relations Office at 121 George Street for Social Responsibility. Among the topics were:

- Reaction to the Government's plans for funding of older people
- The Donaldson Report on Human Cloning
- The Queen Mother's 100th birthday
- Planting 'Caring for You' roses on Saint Andrew's Day
- Football tournament for homeless agencies in Edinburgh
- Great Scottish Sleepout 2000 at West Linton

7.2.1.6 'Circle of Care' Newspaper

The Board's free newspaper *'Circle of Care'* continues to increase its print run and circulation with 46,500 copies printed three times a year, distributed primarily via the Board's network of Congregational Contacts. There is also a mailing to 700 church newsletter editors and to the Social Work Directors of Scotland's 32 local authorities. The winter 2000 edition contained a 4-page feature which looked back on the Board's millennium celebrations called 'Millennium Moments'. A new development is that the main stories from each issue are to be reproduced on Social Responsibility's pages of the Church of Scotland website, making them accessible to readers across the globe (www.cofscotland.org.uk).

7.2.1.7 'Circle of Care' Calendar

Twenty years ago in 1981 the first ever 'Circle of Care' calendar had a print run of 6,000 copies. The 20th anniversary edition in 2001 sold almost 20,000 copies and is firmly established as a major publicity and fundraising venture for Social Responsibility. Although sales have dropped in the last couple of years, this is probably due to the gradual changeover from former Guild delegates to Congregational Contacts. There are also fewer Guilds which has led to a reduction in bulk orders. For the first time, adverts for the calendar were placed in *The Scotsman* and *Scottish Daily Mail* which brought in extra telephone orders. The issue of future distribution is being addressed by the Planning & Development team. On the positive side, people who buy the calendar are obviously delighted with it, as can be seen from the letters received, including this one from Agnes MacDougall in Lochgoilhead: "The calendars have arrived and the views are beautiful as usual. My friends will be delighted with them." Regular buyer Rev. James Hannah in Ohio, U.S.A. is also full of praise: "Your excellent calendars are well received here. The 2000 calendar was superb and 'beyond the call of duty'."

7.2.1.8 Christmas Cards

For the second time in four years, the winning design for the Board Christmas card came from The Mallard in Glasgow, which offers residential and respite care to children with learning disabilities. Children from The Mallard joined with local children in Springburn Parish Church in a celebration of the millennium. Workshops explored the theme 'Light in the Darkness' using art, music and drama. Everyone who attended made a contribution by adding their name to a giant candle flame. The final collage, which was over four feet high, was photographed and reproduced as the Board's Christmas card. Over 15,000 cards were sold, mainly at the 'outlets' held across Scotland in October and November.

7.2.1.9 Home Support

In Spring 2000 a Home Support campaign was undertaken in the Inverness area with three different forms of media used to advertise the service. There was a full-page feature in the Inverness Courier followed by four smaller adverts in subsequent issues; two radio commercials ran on Moray Firth Radio (one highlighting the service and another asking for people to apply as workers); and 20 bus backs in the Inverness area had adverts with the new telephone number to call for details—01463 250500. In total, almost £10,000 was spent on this effort to promote the Home Support Service and to recruit Christian workers. The campaign resulted in 120 information packs being sent out, and eight new Home Support workers being appointed and trained.

7.2.1.10 Books and Packs

Following the successful one-day conference at Aberdeen University in January 1999, the nine lectures were published in a book called 'Bio-ethics for the New Millennium' (Saint Andrew Press, £7.95). Professor Iain Torrance from Aberdeen University, who edited the book, expects that it will be a useful resource for anyone interested in genetics and will also be used as a reader in universities and colleges. During Spring 2000, Social Responsibility collaborated with the Centre for Theology and Public Issues at New College in Edinburgh to organise a series of six public lectures on 'The Law and Christian Ethics'. The distinguished speakers included the former Lord Chancellor Lord Mackay of Clashfern and the Principal Clerk of the General Assembly Rev. Dr. Finlay Macdonald. The lectures have been collated into a book of the same name which was published early in 2001 by Saint Andrew Press. At the last General Assembly, the Board presented a report on Social Inclusion which was accepted and '...urged all presbyteries to discuss and take forward the concept of Social Inclusion...' To assist individual congregations and presbyteries to comply with that deliverance, a pack has been produced called 'Social Inclusion—A Study Pack for Churches'. It follows the same format as the Board's successful Marriage PLUS and HIV/AIDS Resource Packs. It is hoped to circulate the Social Inclusion Pack to churches through the Board's Congregational Contacts.

7.2.1.11 Merchandise

The range of Board merchandise continues to expand, and sales are encouraging. In the past year, almost 900 of the 'Light for Christ' (a stained glass candlelight featuring the burning bush and saltire) have been sold. New enamel pin badges have been very popular, with the two designs having to be re-ordered twice to meet demand. Other new additions to the range include a desk tidy and a glass tower clock which is made in Annan and has the Board logo hand painted onto it. The Board's free year planner is now a regular item and is sent to every minister, with requests for extra copies increasing every year.

7.2.1.12 Queen Mother's 100th Birthday

Amongst the thousands of birthday cards the Queen Mother received in August were two from the Board of Social Responsibility. The first card was produced with the help of the Board's congregational contacts who sent in a total of 162 signatures from members of the Church of Scotland who are 100 or over. This unique collection of signatures was then transferred onto the centre pages of a specially designed card. The second card was signed by the 13 centenarians who were living in the Board's residential homes at the time.

7.2.1.13 Prince Charles

Prince Charles was Lord High Commissioner at the General Assembly. In his closing speech, he gave a special mention to the two Social Responsibility projects he had visited during Assembly week: *"In the course of my visits I have met many dedicated and selfless people who have committed their lives to helping others who are in need. Some of them I encountered at Simpson House, run by the Board of Social Responsibility, dedicated to the care, counselling and rehabilitation of people whose lives have been so tragically destroyed by drug abuse. Others I met in a heartwarming example of care for the elderly, also administered by the Board, at Morlich House here in Edinburgh."* During the week, the Prince also expressed a desire to visit the Board's offices at Charis House. So on 5th October HRH The Duke of Rothesay was shown round the former home of the Jenner family which has been the Board's administrative base since 1993. As well as speaking to staff, the Duke also met people from several Board units around Scotland and was shown round a display that included a section on what the Board had done to mark the Millennium. Before he left, he took time for an unscheduled chat with some of the residents from Queen's Bay residential home who had gathered to wave him off.

7.2.1.14 Work with other Boards

There are many occasions when collaboration with other departments is essential. The most frequent is with the various sections of the Board of Communication: the Media Relations Office issues Press Releases and filters media calls; Design Services have worked on a number of Social Responsibility projects including new business cards, Life and Work adverts and a flyer for the *'Caring for You'* rose; Saint Andrew Press print books for us; Pathway Productions are used by the Board as a production house for videos and the *'Circle of Care'* audio tapes. The Board's Communications Officer (Media) is also a member of the Communication Council which brings together representatives from all the Boards to discuss joint publicity issues. Another group which has input from the Board's Communications Officers is the 'Rejoice' Committee of the Board of National Mission. This group was responsible for commissioning the highly successful millennium logo and for the production of associated resource material. The Communications Officer (Congregations) also works with her equivalent from National Mission and World Mission to organise 'roadshows' across the country which inform congregations about the Boards' work.

7.2.2 Congregational Liaison and Development
7.2.2.1 Congregational Contacts – basic statistics and facts

At time of writing there are 1095 Congregational Contacts of which 1075 are in churches across Scotland. There are 1280 charges in the Church of Scotland with 1143 having ministers. Therefore there are approximately 205 charges with out a Congregational Contact informing the congregation and associated clubs and societies of our work (This number is only an approximation as some of our Congregational Contacts receive mailings for more than one church/congregation.). Where there is no congregational contact the only form of communication is via a copy of *'Circle of Care'* in the minister's mailing 3 times each year.

7.2.2.2 Congregational Contact databases and mailing lists

We must not forget that many people in congregations across the world may receive a 'Circle of Care' newspaper or a prayer letter independently of the Contacts system. 'Circle of Care' has a distribution of 46,500 and the prayer letter distribution has recently risen to 9,000. These additional mailing lists reinforce our community links but cannot be seen to replace them where a congregation has no contact person. The team will be looking at the relationship of these mailing lists to the Contacts' database when the entry returns are received. The Communications Officer (Congregations) will then write to all the congregations without Contacts and request that the Kirk Session appoint somebody as soon as possible, explaining the importance of the Contacts system as a way of communication and support for their community projects.

In February 2001 the Planning and Development team are mailing out to all persons with details held on our databases to check information held about them and their congregation.

7.2.2.3   Meetings with Congregational Contacts

During the past year Congregational Contacts have met with representatives of Charis House and of their local divisional office at organised meetings on at least one occasion. Meetings were held in Troon, Paisley, Edinburgh, Glasgow, Inverness, Dundee and Aberdeen. Some divisional offices arranged additional meetings to allow an extra opportunity to share local service updates with Congregational Contacts in their area. These meetings were well received both by Congregational Contacts and by the unit staff who felt that local Churches were genuinely interested in their work.

7.2.2.4   Nationally Organised Meetings in September and October 2000

The Congregational Liaison Officer arranged meetings in September and October to discuss a variety of national issues including the Carer's Questionnaire and the "Caring For You" rose. The meetings also allowed for discussions on the work of the local division and aspects of the Congregational Contact role which were proving to be exciting, demanding, interesting or motivating. Attendance at these meetings was relatively low in comparison to the number of contacts per area however the enthusiasm and motivation of those who attended was overwhelming. One contact expressed that "I come away from these meetings so enthused about the work that is being done around me and I can't help but enthuse others in my church".

7.2.2.5   Suitability of Meetings for Contacts

It is recognised that we may need to look closer at the role of Congregational contacts and continue to review our expectations of their involvement in our work. Many Congregational Contacts work full time and so we need to be aware of this as a factor when organising meetings and information sessions. There is also a need for meetings to be held in smaller geographical area groupings to cut down on long journeys for our contacts and to make the divisional input more specific to the group.

7.2.2.6   How Congregations Provide a Circle of Care

An important aspect of the nationally organised meetings was to reiterate that Church members are the most important part of the "Circle of Care" provided by the Church of Scotland. It is the caring work in the communities of Scotland which is our largest area of service provision. Congregational Contacts provide the vital link between the formal services provided by the Board and the community work and prayers of the local churches and the Board greatly appreciates all the work done by these volunteer champions.

7.2.2.7   The Work of Congregational Contacts

Congregational Contacts undertake work in a variety of ways. They provide current, correct and appropriate information to their Church. They often act as distributors for the 'Circle of Care' newspaper and they act as agents for our calendar, Christmas Card and merchandise sales. In addition, this Autumn, we asked the Contacts to be champions for our Carer's Questionnaire and act as the local distributor for these important forms.

7.2.2.8   Carer's Questionnaire

Copies of the questionnaire were sent to each Congregational Contact along with a suggested article for their newsletter and a poster for their notice board. The Congregational Contact meetings in September and October provided an opportunity to go over the reasoning behind the questionnaire, the importance of the research and the questions we were asking and why. Contacts enjoyed this chance to ask questions about the form and to share distribution methods with other contacts. Some Churches had left piles of questionnaires in the vestibule, others had distributed them via the Elders and some Congregational Contacts had done nothing with them. However, everyone went away with several ideas of how they might ensure that Carers in their Parish might be contacted and asked to fill in the form. Even those Contacts who had already distributed the forms by one method felt motivated to take more and try a different option to ensure that no-one was excluded. Forms have come in from all over Scotland and this is purely due to the efforts of the Congregational Contacts as they were the sole distributors.

7.2.2.9   Creation of Communications Officer (Congregations) Post

In September 2000, a new post was created replacing the Congregational Liaison Officer post with a three-year remit to work with the existing Congregational Contacts structure and assist in devolving the contact with local churches down to local divisional offices.   By keeping congregational contact more local it should ensure that local community groups can be established to identify local needs and that the support, information and advice to these groupings, or to individual churches identifying need will be geographically relevant and community based.

7.2.2.10   Devolution of congregational liaison work

The work surrounding the devolution of congregational liaison to divisional level will involve the preparation of service standards and guidelines for working with Contacts and their congregations to ensure that all congregations receive an equally high standard of support, advice and information independent of the geographical location. Support will also be given to divisional staff to ensure that the devolution of responsibility and communication is done as smoothly as possible and does not place members of staff under undue pressure and appropriate coaching and training is provided where necessary.

7.2.2.11   Marking the Millennium 'Light in the Darkness—Service to Others'

The Communications Officer (Congregations) was involved in collating anecdotes and information from units and homes and preparing a 'Marking the Millennium' display and a supplement for 'Circle of Care' which covered our celebrations to mark the year 2000. Listed below are some examples of how Board members, residents, clients, staff and supporters helped us to mark the millennium.

7.2.2.12   How we Marked the Millennium

Throughout the year 2000, homes and projects were asked to 'mark the millennium' by lighting a specially commissioned Light for Christ, writing prayers for a daily devotions book, providing service to others, granting wishes of service users and residents and planting a *Caring for You*' rose.

7.2.2.13   The Millennium Theme

The Board of Social Responsibility's theme for the Millennium was *Light in the Darkness—Service to others*', reflecting the fact that Social Responsibility seeks to bring light into the darkness of people's lives through our service to them. This theme was reflected in the lighting of candles and the provision of service to others.

7.2.2.14   Millennium Services and Lighting the Lights for Christ

At the start of the year, each unit held a service where their 'Light for Christ' was lit and the whole community could participate in the celebrations. In October 1999 Charis House held a service where it lit its 'Light for Christ' and dedicated the Millennium banner.

7.2.2.15   The Banner

The Board's millennium banner includes hand-embroidered sections from every one of our projects and homes. These sections form the sky of the picture above which hangs a rainbow—a sign of hope. The base of the scene shows the roofscapes of some of our homes—signifying that the Board has room for people who need our care and support.

7.2.2.16   Service to others

Some examples of units giving a 'Service to Others' were:

- Dunselma in Fenwick held a 'Thank you' to the local community in the form of a Garden Party/Fun Day for children.
- Over the summer, residents and staff of The Elms in Edinburgh collected items for the "My Weekly" Helping Hand Appeal 2000 and decorated and filled boxes to be sent to people in need in Romania. They filled 32 boxes which will be distributed in Romania in time for Christmas.
- The residents and staff of Budhmor House on Skye, in conjunction with Portree Woollen Mill, arranged a fashion show of their new Autumn and Winter range. The sum of £300 was raised for a local charity.
- Cunningham House organised a 5-a-side football tournament for agencies in Edinburgh who work with homeless people. The 16 teams were made up of both staff and clients.
- Queen Mary House and Florentine House hosted a Millennium Street Party which provided an opportunity for our neighbours to meet people from the Units and find out more about us and the work we are involved in.
- Clyde View held a Strawberry Cream Tea afternoon for residents and their relatives, to raise money for the Imperial Cancer Research Fund.
- Belmont Castle used the "service to others" theme to think about those people in the community who would be celebrating the Millennium alone. They invited housebound older people to lunch on 6 January and arranged for a volunteer minibus driver to provide a door to door service.
- A small group of stalwarts from Cameron House gathered in Dores Church of Scotland car park to walk from Dores to Elrig (10 miles) in order to raise funds for Drummond School. The school is locally situated and caters solely for children with special needs.

7.2.2.17   Wish Your Wish/Make My Day

Projects were asked to try and fulfil the wishes of their residents, pupils and service users. Here are some examples of how dreams came true:

—The Mallard

During the Millennium year, children and young people from the Mallard in Springburn were given the opportunity to take part in a 'make my day' activity; to buy a special gift with their keyworkers. The keyworkers kept a record of the event in stories, pictures and mementoes to form a part of a special book which was shown at an exhibition evening for parents and friends.

Examples include:

- Helen enjoyed afternoon tea in the company of the Moderator of the Presbytery of Glasgow. Then she visited the St. Enoch Centre where she bought a Charles Rennie Mackintosh style silver necklace. Her day was completed by dinner and a taxi home.
- Hannah had an Italian meal and was entertained by a clown. She bought a 'mother and daughter' Bible.

—Bellfield

Two residents from Bellfield in Banchory went to Balmoral Castle. Mr. Sylvester Buchan had been telephone and postmaster there from 1938-46, and wanted to revisit his former workplace. He was amazed to find that the only change was a modern switchboard! Miss Tibbie Fleming had never been to Balmoral before and wished to see it.

—Clashfarquhar

A resident at Clashfarquhar House in Stonehaven, Mrs Molly McIntosh, went to the Music Hall in Aberdeen with her keyworker and a friend to see her favourite singer Peter Morrison. This was her millennium wish and after the performance she was introduced to him and had several photos taken. Mrs McIntosh could not have asked for a better wish and still talks about it to family and friends.

—Ballikinrain

Pupils from Ballikinrain School near Balfron have enjoyed a year of dreams come true. As well as the obvious wishes—a visit to Ibrox, a visit to Parkhead to meet the teams—other wishes included a trip to Alton Towers, pony rides and go-karting. Some of the more unusual have included Tony's wish to take his granny for a weekend at Haven Leisure. Unfortunately, Tony's granny took cold feet but Tony, one of his pals and his keyworker went and enjoyed themselves. Back at Ballikinrain School, Ronnie's wish was to ride in a stretched limo. He and his friends enjoyed a complimentary ride in the limo to see Robbie Williams at the SECC in Glasgow.

—South Beach House
Charlotte Walker, who is a resident at South Beach became one of the oldest people ever to take to the sea in a powerboat. Mrs Walker has a long standing passion for boats. From her window, Mrs. Walker is able to look out at the various craft headed in and out of the marina everyday. She said she would love to have a go herself to see if a trip on a speedboat lived up to her dreams. Following the adventure Mrs. Walker said that she had a terrific trip and couldn't wait for the next one.

7.2.2.18 Rose Planting
November 30th 2000 was Rose Planting Day across many of the Board's homes and projects. 'Celebrity planters' included actress Eileen McCallum at Charis House; the Scallaway Gala Queen at the Walter and Joan Gray Home in Shetland; entertainer Ronnie Coburn at Belmont Castle in Meigle and radio presenter Alistair Gardener at Oversteps in Dornoch. Rose Planting Day marks the culmination of our millennium celebrations and allows us to come together as staff, resident, client and friends groups to remember those for whom the Board cares and we look forward to enjoying the roses in full bloom in summer 2001. We sold over 1000 roses between August and December 2000. From October 2001 there will be 20,000 roses available.

—About the Rose
"Caring For You" is the Millennium Rose of the Church of Scotland Board of Social Responsibility. It is a special rose that changes colour throughout its life, from vibrant pink at bud stage, through pale pink and peach at the full flower stage to cream at the end of its life. It has a separate and unique beauty at every stage. The Church of Scotland Board of Social Responsibility provides services across Scotland to care for people in all the stages of their lives from young children with learning disabilities through to older people with mental and physical frailty. It is hoped that the rose will raise funds to support this work, as £1.50 from each rose sold comes back to Social Responsibility.

The rose was propagated and grown by James Cocker & Sons of Aberdeen.

—About the rose's name
The name "Caring For You" was chosen in a competition from the many suggestions which came from staff, residents and Board members. The name epitomises what the Board through it's staff does in Christ's name—cares for people who need help and support for a variety of reasons.

7.2.2.19 Write your Prayers
Board members, staff, residents, clients and friends were asked to contribute prayers for a devotions book which could be used in every unit for morning worship. Prayers were collated and each service now has a reading, prayer and thought for each day to assist in preparing morning worship which is proving to be a welcome additional resource.

7.2.2.20 The Website
Another project for the Communications Officers, both Media and Congregations has been the updating of information on the Board's pages of the Church of Scotland web site.

7.2.2.21 Strategic planning regarding the use of the web
We must look strategically at what we want our web presence to do.

- Do we want it to 'sell our services' to funders?
- Do we just want to provide basic information for enquirers and congregations?
- Do we want the site to provide in-depth reports on social interest topics and service provision?
- Do we want to sell merchandise or fundraise over the Internet?

If we want to enthuse, motivate and include all those who want information—be they funders, donors or enquirers both with a physical disability or able-bodied then we need to revise the whole layout and structure of the page. We must make larger click boxes for links, ensure clearer text, add more service provision information and work towards integration of the website with office functions. This would eventually allow on-line donation of money, direct Internet calendar sales, interactive components for young people and search facilities for those seeking information about social interest topics and local services. Over the next 12 months these questions will need to be addressed to ensure that all people can access our site and that the site they access is relevant to them.

7.2.3 Fundraising

The past year has been a fairly good one for Fundraising. While legacy income is down by £291,000, donations have risen by £251,000. The legacy income remains unpredictable but donations are generally the result of fundraising effort and the 24% increase on last year's income of £1,027,000 is significant.

Fundraising income £,000

year	1999	2000	
donations	1027	1278	24%
legacies	1746	1455	-17%
total	2773	2773	-1%

Fundraising income represents 8% of the total income.
Fundraising expenditure represents 0.5% of the total expenditure
The total admin overhead of the Board is 7% of the total expenditure.

7.2.3.1 Legacy paper

This year a **Legacy paper** has been produced with the purpose of encouraging people to appreciate the importance of legacies. This outlines the way forward for legacy fundraising. The plan for implementation includes distribution of a leaflet designed to highlight the advantages of a bequest to Social Responsibility; a video;

advertisements; a pack for volunteers; training for volunteers to help them when they talk to potential donors and supervision of volunteers.

In addition we have collected some historic information—stories of what people think of the services to give insight into the success of projects and to help potential legatees identify areas of need to which they would like to give.

7.2.3.2 'How to' Training manual

More and more, people wish to target their giving at local projects. They are interested in what can be achieved in the services and projects running on their doorstep.

Therefore, one of the major strategies for this year has been to begin training in fundraising for people working in Social Responsibility Units and services. The main elements of this are: a **'How to do it'** pack and a training course for employees. The next stage, which begins in the first half of 2001, is to pilot the training in a small number of projects. This will lead to a revision of the material and a general release of the pack and the training programme.

The 'How to' pack includes topics such as:

- Core values
- Why do people give?
- Legacies
- Trusts
- Committed giving
- Volunteers
- Sponsorship
- Tax

7.2.3.3 Tax and Gift Aid

In March 2000 the Chancellor announced tax changes to benefit charities. The increased scope of Gift Aid along with a relaxing of the rules presents an opportunity to increase donations from individuals. We have been asking each individual donor to sign a Gift Aid Declaration form.

In addition, training and information has gone out to each Project manager so that all gifts that can attract a Gift Aid are made eligible. Some of the projects have a new donation envelope designed as a declaration form to allow small, regular gifts to be treated in this way.

7.2.3.4 Prayer Letter

In the past year the circulation of the **Prayer Letter** has increased to 9,000 copies. This represents a large number of people, mainly in congregations of the Church of Scotland or individuals who are regular donors, regularly remembering our work in prayer. As much as financial gifts we appreciate the time and interest this represents as our supporters join us in grounding our Christian work in our belief that we look for our Heavenly Father's blessing on the work we do in Jesus' name.

7.2.3.5 Ballikinrain

Setting up funds for the provision of a new sports hall and upgrade of bedrooms in the school at Ballikinrain has been one of the major financial tasks of the year. Over £3 million will be required. A local committee has met regularly and decided that the way forward is to enlist the expertise of a consultant. After interviews Dr Allan Webster has been chosen to lead this project. We look forward to working with him in the future.

Meantime the boys and staff have been inventive in setting up a number of initiatives to make maximum use of the resources of their location and facilities in fundraising.

7.2.3.6 Donor Questionnaire

It is our philosophy to treat all people as having worth and to value relationships with them. This applies to fundraising too. We are here to meet the needs of our donors and to use their gifts in the most effective way possible. During the year a researcher was commissioned to compose and analyse a questionnaire to all donors on our current database, individual people—not churches, organisations, businesses or trusts. This is the first time that this has been done.

This survey was sent to all of the 677 individuals who have given financial support to our services. A report on the results was prepared, which was presented to the Board in October.

Highlights of the report (which is still providing useful input to future fundraising strategies):

- 85% of donors are Church of Scotland members
- the majority are women over 60 years of age
- the majority (63%) give for 'Christian' reasons
- most people are interested in work in their local community: 91% want to see that 'the people in their local community have their needs met.'
- The majority of donors are one-off givers
- Not every donor wants or appreciates a prayer letter.

7.2.3.7 Sleepout

We decided to hold the Great Scottish Sleepout this year at the Crossover youth festival in June. (The Crossover report is below.) The reasons for this were that we wanted to find a date, which would catch young people before the summer break (instead of the traditional meeting in September), aim at a wider youth audience and combine the Sleepout with other activities.

While we were able to achieve all our targets in terms of raising our profile and attracting people to think about and discuss the issues around homelessness, the sleepout was not as successful as in the past. Only 66 people took part in the sleepout. Although it raised a lot of interest and raised enough money to cover the expenses of the whole appearance at Crossover, this was nothing like the 300–400 who took part in the past. The reasons were believed to be:

- West Linton was too far out of the city for most of the past participants to come.
- The young people who were attending Crossover were already spending the weekend in tents and so the added excitement of a night under the stars was not enough incentive.

Nevertheless, a man in his seventies joined us, who cycled out from Edinburgh, did the sleepout, and cycled home the next morning. He raised hundreds of pounds. A boy, called Gordon, who celebrated his 13th birthday that day and had never heard of the Sleepout before, took a sponsor form and asked friends and leaders to sponsor him. His enthusiasm encouraged us all. Gordon raised £37 and gained the admiration of all who were there.

7.2.3.8 Crossover

The aim of taking part in the event was:

- To "Sleepout" as homeless people do
- To raise awareness about Social Responsibility
- And to have fun

We were joined by a team of staff and residents from Kirkhaven.

Our standing display featured the 'Beat the Streets' game which was a big success and which most of the Crossover attendees attempted at least once. The game brought players into the environment of people who are homeless and gave them the chance to experience some of the set-backs and frustrations of people on the streets while making decisions about how to seek the best assistance.

Our programme included seminars, discussion, drama, face painting and a finale on Saturday with our own ceilidh and Annie's Soup Kitchen before the Sleepout.

We took one of the worship services and made contact with a large number of teenagers in the context of the Christian response to problems of poverty and homelessness in society today.

7.2.3.9   Beat the Streets Game

This game, mentioned above, was the centrepiece of our display at Crossover. Designed and built by Anna Webber a care worker at Cunningham House, it is a standing interactive game which helps people to think about the issues facing homeless people in Scotland today.

Because of its success we are looking at ways of developing a lighter, portable version which could be used in schools and youth fellowships as a discussion starter. As well as raising awareness it can be seen as a preventative tool to help young people keep off the streets.

7.2.3.10 Football

In October we were able to realise the ambition of some of the staff at Cunningham House to play a 5-a-side football tournament against other services providing for homeless people in Edinburgh.

Eighteen teams took part in an afternoon programme which was exciting and great fun. Ian Baillie as Director of Social Responsibility and the host of the event opened the tournament. The Moderator, the Rt. Rev Andrew McLellan kicked off the first match and 3 hours of fast action followed. Jim Jeffrey (the then manager of Hearts) and Alex McLeish (manager of Hibs) presented the trophy to the winning team—the Cyrenians.

The twin objectives of having a chance to network with other people in similar projects and of having fun were fully met. The cup was sponsored by the Faculty of Advocates and supported by local Council and MSPs.

7.3   CENTRAL SERVICES

7.3.1   Finance & Administration

With the change-over into the new millennium having been successfully negotiated, this last year has seen new staffing structures and personnel settling into their roles—particularly in Technical Section—with a re-appraisal and development of systems, procedures to meet developing and changing demands of legislation and operational requirements of the Board.

The work covers four separate areas—Finance, Information Technology, Health & Safety, and Technical (the latter covering buildings, supplies, and aspects of general administration), with comment also on other aspects of work in addition to the above.

7.3.2   Finance

The revised staffing arrangements introduced in 1999 to facilitate more effective liaison with operational Divisions have been productive, but in the course of the year staff turnover has required us to recruit into 3 posts, including that of Deputy Accountant.

Last year we highlighted concerns about the lack of flexibility in the current computerised Accounting system in the light of changing requirements. Plans are progressing to prepare a new replacement system.

In the meantime further progress has also been made in developing skills of all staff in the Section, particularly in the use of budgeting software, spreadsheets, and electronic forms.

Considerable effort has been put into further refining aspects of financial reporting.

A major specific piece of work in the last year has been the preparation, production, and circulation of a Financial Procedures Manual tailored to the needs of all operational units and projects.

Demands for *ad hoc* financial information for tenders, and feasibility studies, etc continue to increase—as do demands for financial information at regular intervals from Local Authorities involved in the support of specific projects. Negotiations on rates of financial support are particularly time-consuming given the numbers of authorities with whom contact is necessary.

All such considerations, of course, have to be set alongside the ongoing annual cycle of budget preparation, financial monitoring, Final Accounts production, and audits—not forgetting the day-to-day important and mandatory routines of financial receipts, transfers, and payments, bank reconciliations, cash-flow and investments.

7.3.3 Information Technology

A comprehensive review of the structure and staffing needs of the IT function has been carried out, with a view to equipping the Section to meet the fast-growing requirements of the Board for secure and efficient communications, and to take advantage of rapidly developing technology to streamline its administrative functions.

In the meantime further work has been carried out to instal new PCs and develop access to e-mail facilities for Units, more extensive computer virus-protection and other security measures have been introduced, and additional safeguards taken in connection with the licensing of software.

Steps have been taken to decentralise the delivery of IT Training by offering an increasing proportion of training opportunities at Unit level.

Work has been done on the network installation at Charis House to improve its performance and stability, and to extend its capacity by provision of additional cabling and access points. Work has also been done to upgrade networks at the Divisional offices.

In the meantime an ever-increasing support workload is being carried for approximately 300 PCs and 8 networks with associated peripherals at almost 100 different locations.

7.3.4 Health & Safety

This has been the first full year of Health and Safety established as a full-time function and independent of Technical Section.

A new and comprehensive Health & Safety Manual was completed and circulated to all the Board's units and offices. This details policy and practical guidance on all aspects of the subject relevant to the Board's activity. Its contents will be kept under constant review with updates being issued as required.

Attention has also been paid to reviewing the Health & Safety training requirements on such matters as moving & handling, food hygiene, fire, and first-aid. As a result steps are currently being taken to put these key aspects of training out to tender with a view to a completely new structure of Health & Safety training being in place by the beginning of the next financial year.

A cross-branch Health & Safety Group has been established to monitor legislation and its applicability to the Board, to address issues of communication on key issues to Units, to oversee training arrangements, and to resolve any major problems which may need to be dealt with.

Specific input has continued to be provided locally to Units in order to assist them in the important work of Risk Assessments, with the end product having been the subject of favourable comment from more than one local authority's inspection service.

A programme for Unit 'Audits' by the Health & Safety Officer is also being stepped up.

With specially-funded programmes of expenditure having been undertaken on furniture to meet flammability regulations, and on provision of lifting equipment such as hoists for relevant units, attention this year has switched to a major appraisal of lifts themselves with plans now made for an investment programme to meet new standards for safety in operation.

7.3.5   Buildings, Supplies and General Administration

'Best-value' reviews have been carried out in respect of contracts for some of our equipment and services requirements, with new arrangements already made in such areas as maintenance of fire alarms, heating equipment, lifts and the supply of copiers and mobile phones.

The structure of the property database has been streamlined. The database which will provide the basis for energy conservation is now being updated with information from regular returns from Units.

Former garage buildings in the grounds of Charis House have been adapted and extended to provide for the Central Store and its staff to be transferred from its previous Malta House Stable Block which is now available for alternative use.

There is, of course, considerable work to maintain delivery of the capital building and maintenance programmes.

7.3.6   Other Issues

Other matters which have as before taken up much time include providing information about the Board, its structures, its service objectives, its operating standards, its finances, and insurances to local authorities reviewing their Approved Service Provider's Lists.

Similarly in providing specific services to local authorities there is an ongoing flow of paperwork on the detail of Contracts which require discussion, and exchanges of correspondence before agreement is reached. There is no evidence yet of local authorities adopting a standard form of contract.

7.3.7   Training: Practice Assessment

The need to provide continuous development and training opportunities is obvious if the Board is to ensure that staff develop and maintain the necessary care and associated skills necessary to deliver the Board's services. There is a need to prepare and deliver training, to assess practice and to identify future training needs. This year it has also been necessary to balance current requirements with the expected new arrangements for regulating and training social work and social care workers. It is anticipated that National Standards for Practice, and Codes of Practice for both employees and employers, will be introduced under these new regulations; they will have major implications for future in-house training requirements.

Workshops and training courses prepared and run by the Board's Practice Teachers have been well attended and acknowledged as important to the ongoing professional development of Practice Teachers.

The Board continues to be registered as an Approved Assessment Centre for the award of Scottish Vocational Qualifications. The work of staff involved in delivering the SVQ training has been recognised as of high quality and is a credit to the Board. The social work requirements set down by the various regulatory bodies are technical in both detail and delivery and a knowledge of such detail is necessary to fully comprehend the level of commitment required from both the staff who deliver the training and assessment and the staff who seek qualification. The Board's committees receive regular evidence of this area of work.

It is worthy of note that efforts are being made to access European funding to increase the availability of training opportunities.

A major barometer of the success of training is the feedback by participants:

The Training for Trainers Course
"Course was instructive and intense. The small group worked well together, appreciated the time for individuals and feedback."

The Equal Opportunities—Diversity & Rights Course
"I enjoyed both days. The content of the course and group work discussions did give the opportunity to learn where

anti-discriminatory practice improved service delivery."

The Advocacy and Empowerment Course

"Better understanding of advocacy and empowerment in the workplace. How and when to use this for clients. Reinforced needs and options available to them."

The Induction and Refresher Course

"A better understanding of expectations of me as care worker in many aspects."

SVQ Assessor Training

"I found the course to be extremely enlightening and am sure it will prove to be a great asset both in personal and professional life. The course was very helpful and well delivered."

The Senior Staff Induction Course

"Pleasant atmosphere—clearly presented information. Good overview of the work of the Board. Good to meet with others and share experiences. I appreciated the handouts as I think they will be an extremely useful reference in the months to come."

7.3.7.1 Standards Document

The Personnel and Training Manager continues to be a member of the Quality Assurance Group. The Standards document is welcomed by the training staff and will provide a sound framework for future courses. Plans are in hand to provide future training in the Standards and in the forthcoming Quality Assurance system.

7.3.8 Personnel and Payroll Section
7.3.8.1 Recruitment Advertising

Having been with the same company for some years it was decided that a tender document should be issued in relation to the Board's recruitment advertising. A number of agencies expressed interest and were invited to make presentations to Board employees. As a result of the tender exercise it was agreed to change the Board's recruitment agency. Resulting from this change new styles of advertisements have been introduced, the administration for processing advertising has been streamlined and guidelines have been issued to Units and Projects for the first time.

7.3.8.2 Payroll Issues

Payroll staff have continued to deal with legislative changes in payroll processing including the reclaiming of student loans, working families credits and national insurance rebates.

As a result of the development of the health care scheme, payroll staff are now processing payments for a number of employees, there having been an encouraging take up in membership of the scheme.

7.3.8.3 Collaborative Working

A significant amount of work has been carried out in collaboration with the Accounts Section in the past year. The aim of this exercise has been to produce staffing budgetary information in a more useable and accessible form. In particular an exercise has been carried out in relation to Home Support staffing which will enable Home Support costs to be more readily allocated to individual services.

7.3.8.4 Absence Monitoring and Control

Personnel and Payroll staff have produced more detailed information in the past year on the levels of absences in individual Units and Divisions. This has been compared to budgetary information. Work is currently being undertaken on revising the existing absenteeism procedures to ensure that all possible steps are taken to manage and monitor absence in order that it be maintained at the lowest possible level.

7.3.8.5 Job Evaluation

The Board has a well defined grading structure and over the years jobs have been graded in accordance with the criteria. It is however essential that the criteria be reviewed and that a systematic and consistent approach is adopted to determine the gradings of individual posts. A means of undertaking this is to implement a formal job evaluation scheme. A significant amount of work has been carried out over the past year with an external consultant. The consultant has visited a number of units to determine the parameters which might be applied to a job evaluation scheme. Divisional Managers are currently being consulted on the proposals. Once their comments are received steps will be taken to move to further stages in the process with the intention of evaluating all the Board's jobs within a formal job evaluation scheme.

7.3.8.6   Support to Advisory Forum

Personnel and Payroll staff have undertaken a range of remits in support of the Advisory Forum. Examples of the range of issues are identified under the separate section on the work of the Advisory Forum.

7.3.9   External Involvement

Board staff are involved in the following groups:

- Scottish Development and Advisory Group— National Training Organisation for Employment.
- Planning and Management Advisory Group Dementia Services Development Centre.

7.3.10   Advisory Forum

The Advisory Forum has continued as a vehicle whereby Management and Employee elected representatives are able to discuss a wide range of issues relating to the work of the Board. In the past year issues have ranged from Training and Development, Health and Safety, Dress Codes, Use of Internet and E-mail, Family Friendly Policies, Eye Tests, Give As You Earn, Role of Friends Groups at Unit Level, Annual Leave Guidelines, Communication Issues, to Board Standards and Quality Assurance.

In terms of the constitution and due to the fact that the Forum has now been running for three years a number of members have now come to the end of their term of office. It is appropriate to acknowledge the major contribution which these pioneer members have made in the first three years of the Advisory Forum.

in the name of the Board,

ANN ALLEN, *Convener*
JAMES M COWIE, *Vice-Convener*
GILBERT NISBET, *Vice-Convener*
IAN D BAILLIE, *Director of Social Work*

ADDENDUM

RETIRAL OF CONVENER AND VICE-CONVENER

Mrs Ann Allen completes her term of office as Convener of the Board of Social Responsibility at this General Assembly. Mrs Allen first served the Board as a General Assembly nomination in 1986, later as a Vice-Convener and Convener of the Woman's Council and in 1997 as Convener of the Board. In her service to the Board Mrs Allen has shown enthusiasm and commitment in all that she has been asked to do, giving prayerful thought to her actions and contributions.

Mrs Allen has contributed to many study groups which have led to Board publications, particularly Human Transplants, Euthanasia, Human Genetics, Prostitution and Abortion.

During her term as Convener she has been a major commentator to the media and to government, particularly on the contentious and very public debate on 'Section 28'. Mrs Allen has shown grace in many difficult and confronting situations.

The Board records sincere appreciation of Mrs Allen's long service to the Board and gives thanks to God for her commitment and leadership in the service of her Lord and her Church.

Rev James Cowie concludes his term of office as Vice-Convener of the Board and in recording the Board's appreciation of his excellent service, the Board note with satisfaction his willingness to continue service through his acceptance of nomination as Convener of the Board.

In the name of the Board

IAN D BAILLIE, *Director of Social Work*

APPENDIX 1

CHRISTIAN COMMITMENT POLICY STATEMENT

This paper is written as an argument to those who may challenge the Board's Christian Employment Practice under either the Human Rights Act 1998 which will be fully implemented in the UK on 2 October 2000 or the European Equal Treatment Directive (Directive 565) which the UK Government is required to incorporate into UK legislation by 31 December 2002. The Human Rights Act is fact and will be implemented but there is still time to register opposition to the proposed Directive.

THE BACKGROUND AND FACTS

The Board of Social Responsibility is a Board of the Church of Scotland to whom it is accountable for its remit, its practice, and its authority. Accountability is exercised in May each year when the General Assembly of the Church of Scotland calls for the Board to report upon its work for the preceding year and to give notice of any proposed major change in organisation or practice. Only the General Assembly can amend the Board's remit, order a cessation of the work, or instruct the Board in any area of its work or proposals. The Church's work and mission is enacted through many channels, one arm of mission being the delivery of social care through its Board of Social Responsibility.

The Board is committed to the principle of equal opportunities. Within this principle it recognises the right of the Church to expect its mission to be enacted by people who are committed to the Christian life espoused by the Church. The Board's mission statement therefore makes clear that services will be delivered "in Christ's name" and that those who deliver such services are expected to be able to show their Christian commitment through "a live connection with a Christian Church". This seems to be both logical and sensible.

It should be emphasised that the live connection is with any branch of the Christian Church; at the present time staff will have backgrounds in the Church of Scotland,

Methodist, Church of England, Roman Catholic, Baptist, and United Reformed Church, to name only some.

It should also be emphasised that within this requirement, the Board also seeks to fill staff vacancies with the most qualified people for the job advertised; positions are not filled on the basis of Christian commitment only. Indeed in many situations legal requirements would insist that an individual was properly qualified and skilled for the particular post in question, a position which would be fully supported by the Board.

The Board provides services in residential homes, in day centres, in other social and domestic settings, in two specialist schools, and in one-to-one situations. In none of these settings is there any Christian commitment expected from those who receive a service. Service users will be aware that the service is provided by Christians but they will also be aware that their own faith or absence of it will make no impact or difference to the service offered. Where appropriate, for example in a residential setting, arrangements will be made for any person to receive and practice their religious observances in accordance with their individual desire.

SUPPORT OF THE POSITION ADOPTED BY THE BOARD

Primarily, as already stated, it is logical to expect that persons who wish to deliver a service "in Christ's name" and on behalf of a Christian Church have a commitment to Christ in whose name they act. The Christian faith is not a "company philosophy" which can be applied by anyone who accepts employment in a particular company; the Christian faith is a living lifestyle which permeates ones thinking and actions. It is the central fact in life and impacts on how one lives, on relationships, on behaviour, on one's expectations of others.

The Board recognises other faiths and ecumenically works in partnership. Other faiths make a major contribution to today's multi-cultural Scotland and there are numerous examples of the faith communities working together. Working together however does not mean that beliefs are the same. All faiths would accept that they have aspects of their own faith that they would wish to protect and practice unilaterally. There will be positions in all faiths for which commitment to that faith would be a pre-requisite.

It is a widely accepted truth in business management that a company which manages to secure within its workforce a common base from which to develop, has a head start on competition; such a company will find it much easier to secure systems with which all staff can comfortably comply. So it is within the Board. All Staff are motivated by the same desire—to serve Christ. This motivation reveals itself in the practice of staff using prayer together as a part of their daily working.

This common base assists the Board in its extensive commitment to staff training and development. An examination of the requirements for training for social work, and similar requirements for the development of staff through vocational training schemes, will show very clearly that the value base of social work falls easily within the Christian ethos—

- An ability to examine and know oneself.
- Respect and value individuality.
- Respect and value individual human rights.
- To take action against disadvantage.

Board staff can apply these specific aspects of social work easily as individuals and together as a staff group.

Board staff in exercising their duties within a quality assurance system are obliged to give due attention to both the whole person (which includes the spiritual dimension of life) and the "added extra" which refers to anything which the Board offers which a user could not automatically expect in a similar service from another provider; in this latter aspect would fall that ability to offer care in a loving Christian environment.

The Central Council for Education and Training in Social Work published in1997 "Visions of Reality—Religion and Ethnicity in Social Work". The following is a quote from the chapter dealing with the case for religion in social work education:

> "Christianity has supposedly become confined to the privacy of one's home and heart; but have the other religions of Hinduism, Sikhism, Islam, or black and minority Christian communities followed suit? The consensus view would be "no". Yet Jews, Hindus, Buddhists, Sikhs, Muslims and many others are here to stay; they are part of a tapestry that makes up British culture. Often at odds with Christian culture in their ways of thinking and behaving, many people from non-Christian backgrounds interweave their religion into every aspect of daily life. Family occasions are often religious festivals cementing and celebrating family ties. While there have been many changes and compromises made to adjust to the British way of life the old ways are respected and observed. Many would say that this cultural identity is the strength and secret of survival through the crisis and upheavals facing non-Christian families."

Non-Christian faiths, and no faith, are accepted and respected by the Board and that same respect should allow Christians to practise their faith in the daily routine of life.

Over the near 150 years that the Board has given service none of those who have received service and support have made any complaint that the service was provided by a caring Christian organisation and by caring Christians. Government, particularly in Scotland, has developed a good record for consultation on important topics and it may be that they should instigate a very full consultation, including the involvement of existing service users, before coming to a decision on an issue which will have far reaching impact on society.

APPENDIX 2

HUMAN GENETICS GROUP

Letter sent to MPs on 27th November 2000

Dear [MPs name]

THE "DONALDSON" RECOMMENDATIONS

The Donaldson Committee's Report on Stem Cell Research and Cloning is welcome and timely, but its Recommendations raise ethical concerns. We outlined some of these concerns in a letter which we sent to the MPs for Scottish constituencies on the day before Dr. Evan Harris's motion on the Report's Recommendations. In order to respond in the time available, that letter had to be kept short, and the attached paper is an expanded version of its content. We offer it as an aid to reflection before next month's further vote on the Report's Recommendations.

For your information, the Church of Scotland has been at the forefront of national and international ethical debate over cloning and stem-cell technology, through the Society Religion and Technology Project (1) and the Board of Social Responsibility's work on embryology and human genetics (2). The Human Genetics Group advises the Church of Scotland's Board of Social Responsibility. Its members are:

Dr. Donald Bruce, Director of the Church of Scotland's Society, Religion and Technology Project, John Knox House, 45 High Street, Edinburgh

Dr. E. David Cook, Director of the Whitefield Institute, Frewin Court, Oxford

Rev. Dr. Richard Corbett, member of the Board of Social Responsibility

Rev. David Easton, former Vice-Convener of the Board of Social Responsibility

Rev. Dr. David Graham, member of the Board of Social Responsibility

Dr. Susan Holloway, Clinical Scientist

Prof. Peter Howie, Department of Obstetrics & Gynaecology, University of Dundee

Dr. David Short, Emeritus Profesor of Clinical Medicine, Aberdeen

Yours sincerely

(1) "Therapeutic Uses of Cloning and Embryonic Stem—A Discussion Paper" (2000), Church and Society Commission of the Conference of European Churches, Rue des Fosse des Treize, Strasbourg, France,

(2) See, for example, "Human Genetics—A Christian Perspective" (1995), Board of Social Responsibility, Saint Andrew Press, Edinburgh; "Pre-Conceived Ideas—A Christian Perspective of IVF & Embryology" (1996), Board of Social Responsibility, Saint Andrew Press, Edinburgh.

CHURCH OF SCOTLAND BOARD OF SOCIAL RESPONSIBILITY

HUMAN GENETICS GROUP

COMMENTS ON THE "DONALDSON" REPORT

In general, we heartily approve of medical treatment which helps the human body to fulfil its potential. Since the human body repairs injury by cloning stem cells which specialise to take over the function of damaged cells, we do not think it unethical in principle either to clone a patient's cells or to reprogram them into whatever type of cell the patient requires. Nor can we think it unethical for an adult to donate tissue for use in the medical treatment of someone else. We are not, therefore, against stem cell research as such.

However the use in research of cells derived from embryos raises issues of conscience for those who hold that embryos do or may deserve full human status. There are also those who doubt the morality or wisdom of creating human embryos by cell nuclear replacement (the "Dolly method"). In the light of these strong feelings, and since gene technology is already widely distrusted, this research could easily cause major social division. If this research is to be safely undertaken, it must be with the consent of the vast majority of Britons, and it will take time to achieve this consensus.

Accordingly, we do not favour the Donaldson Report's first and most important Recommendation, "Research using embryos (whether created by *in vitro* fertilisation or cell nuclear replacement) to increase understanding about human disease and disorders and their cell-based treatments should be permitted, subject to the controls in the Human Fertilisation and Embryology Act 1990".

The Act itself, as its title makes plain, governs the study of embryos as embryos, while the Donaldson Report recommends the study of embryos as medical resources. We agree that research into degenerative conditions such as Alzheimer's and diabetes is no less worthy than the research into contraception which the Act permits. But the Act treats embryos as entities, while the Donaldson Report recommends breaking embryos up for usable parts. At best the Act does not seem to be an appropriate instrument to govern the latter, and some argue that to use the Act for this purpose would be to deny the "special status" of the embryo safeguarded under the Act.

We are also concerned that, contrary to public expectation, in addressing the Donaldson Recommendations, Parliament will not be addressing the issue of cloned embryos. The first Recommendation includes the granting of permission for research using embryos created by cell nuclear replacement, so that a vote to accept this Recommendation would be a vote to permit, in principle, the creation of embryos by this method. However, as the Donaldson Report points out, the Act does not prevent the creation of embryos by this method, provided that this is done for one of the 5 research purposes which the Act presently permits; so that a vote to reject the first Recommendation would not be a vote against the creation of such embryos in principle. And the creation of such embryos is a matter of widespread concern, since it would raise the possibility of reproductive human cloning and of human germline engineering analogous to that already done with animals. It is true that these things may not happen if we allow the creation of such embryos, but it is equally true that at present they cannot happen unless we allow this.

We do not here argue against the research proposed in the Donaldson Report. Although the Church of Scotland "affirms the sanctity of the embryo from conception", it also "recognises the differences of view which exist on the ethical acceptability of embryo research", and has not yet addressed "therapeutic cloning". But we do believe that if Parliament approves of the research envisaged in the Report, the research should be governed by fresh legislation.

BOARD OF WORLD MISSION
MAY 2001

PROPOSED DELIVERANCE

The General Assembly:

1. Receive the Report, and thank the members and staff of the Board.

2. Give thanks for the life and witness of overseas staff who have died, salute those who have completed their period of service overseas, and uphold in prayer all mission partners who continue to serve overseas.

3. Adopt the new Constitution of the Board of World Mission, as found in Appendix I of the Board's Report; and in consequence agree to delete Standing Order 130.

4. Pass an Act Anent Overseas Charges in terms of Appendix II of the Board's Report.

5. a) Express deep concern, in Christ, for all those affected by the rapid spread of the HIV/AIDS pandemic, particularly partner churches in the worst-affected areas;

    b) recognise that confessing faith in Christ and being part of the body of Christ involves, in today's context, both an active engagement in the battle against the disease and a loving solidarity with those infected; and

    c) instruct the Board of World Mission to consult with other Boards of the Church and concerned agencies in order to develop an appropriate response to the HIV/AIDS pandemic, and report back to the General Assembly of 2002.

6. a) Welcome the formation of Jubilee Scotland and its determination to achieve the goals of Jubilee 2000;

    b) congratulate HMG on the leadership which it has offered in alleviating the crippling burden of unpayable debt borne by many poor countries; and

    c) urge HMG to advocate the cancellation of the debts owed by the poorest countries to the IMF and World Bank, and the establishment of proper mechanisms to ensure its delivery, at the G7 meeting in Genoa in July 2001.

7. Affirm the commitment of the Church of Scotland, in Christ, to her partner churches overseas, especially those facing particular difficulties at this time; and encourage the Board to continue to prioritise the renewal and development of partner church relationships.

REPORT

"Each of you should look not only to your own interests, but also to the interests of others" (Philippians 2:4)

Introduction: A Formative Event

A formative event for the Board of World Mission was its encounter with representatives of 26 partner churches at St Andrews in September 1999. This event brought a powerful affirmation of the commitment to doing mission in partnership which has guided the Board's work since the 1960s:

We are thankful to be sister churches rooted in the Word of God and the Reformed tradition and historically connected with Scotland. We thank God for the movement of his Spirit which has, over the years, brought us to a shared experience of Christ's salvation. We rejoice in the inheritance of trust, of shared understanding, of common purpose which unites us and gives us the capacity to witness together to the coming of God's kingdom in today's world.

This fresh sense of excitement about what can be achieved by the development of cross-cultural inter-church partnerships has encouraged the Board to sustain and renew the bonds which unite the Church of Scotland with partner churches overseas in mission engagement. Old bonds have been affirmed and renewed, faded relationships have been reinvigorated and new possibilities for partnership in mission are being explored.

The St Andrews Consultation was also able to give definition to the points on which partnership would best be concentrated at this time:

1. **Theological Education**—developing ministerial and lay training at appropriate levels in all our churches.

2. **Evangelism**—helping one another to create new models and launch new initiatives to take the Gospel to all people.

3. **Holistic Mission**—enabling one another to respond with Christian compassion to human needs in our rapidly changing societies.

4. **Mission in Pluralistic Societies**—strengthening Christian identity in our multi-religious and multi-cultural societies by supporting one another and sharing our experiences.

5. **Prophetic Ministry**—inspiring one another to discern and speak God's Word in relation to critical issues which arise in our times.

6. **Human and Material Resources**—finding new ways of sharing our resources at all levels of church life.

In the past year the Board has been examining all of its work in light of these partnership priorities. While all of the work is informed and inspired by these six emphases, it is possible to highlight particular initiatives which illustrate the Board's commitment to each. The following overview of the Board's work aims to demonstrate ways in which the Board is actively engaged in addressing the priorities agreed with partner churches worldwide.

1. Theological Education
Jesus said: "I tell you the truth"

The longstanding emphasis of Scottish missions on education is strongly reaffirmed among our partner churches today. In particular, the need for the church to grow in its understanding of the faith is emphasised on all sides. When partner churches were asked to indicate which areas of cooperation they most valued, theological education stood out as the area, above all others, where the role of the Church of Scotland was appreciated. With many of the churches growing at an explosive rate there is a pressing need for new members to be grounded in the faith. Both ministerial formation and training of lay leadership are given highest priority. The Board has responded to this in ways fitted to each context.

Zambia: A Golden Jubilee
The United Church of Zambia celebrated fifty years of service of its Theological College now based at Mindolo in the Copperbelt. Throughout the years of the College's existence the Church of Scotland has been prominent in its support, both in terms of finance and staff, and last year the Moderator of the General Assembly, the Rt Rev Dr Andrew McLellan, himself at one time a member of staff, was able to be present at the celebrations and to play a significant role.

Mozambique: the new Lay Training Centre at Carrupeia
With some 30,000 full members, untold numbers of adherents and only six Ministers, our partner church in Mozambique, the Igreja Evangelica de Christo em Mozambique, is reliant on its laity for both administration and leading the worship of the Church. Until recently there has been little in the way of formal structured training of the membership and "pastras" (elders). With the encouragement and provision of resources from both the Board and various congregations within Scotland, a new ecumenical Lay Training Centre has been constructed at Carrupeia in Nampula and was opened by the Moderator during his visit to Mozambique in July last year.

Malawi: Theological Education by Extension (TEE)
Besides a longstanding involvement in ministerial training in Malawi, the Board contributes to the work of TEEM (Theological Education by Extension in Malawi). TEE is a vital tool of the Church in developing the understanding and knowledge of its people in their faith and large numbers take the opportunity to equip themselves for service in this way.

Kenya: A Roundtable Plans for the Future
The Presbyterian Church of East Africa (PCEA), together with a number of their other overseas partners, requested that the Board participate in discussions concerning the future direction of theological education within the PCEA. Our participation in such discussions is made easier by the fact that we have mission partners very actively involved in theological education. Rev Elaine

McKinnon and Rev Dr Bryson Arthur both play key roles within the PCEA Presbyterian College at Kikuyu. Bryson is quick to point out, however, that Theological Education is not one-way. "I think that Africa is teaching us many things. One of them is that we live significantly, that we live abundantly and the only way to do so is to completely abandon and deny ourselves, even abandon our deepest concerns and worries and trust entirely in Jesus Christ. Love God with all of our heart, soul and mind and truly love and serve one another. That, and not material wealth with its self-sufficiency and self-affirmation, is what truly counts."

Cuba: Resurgence in Seminary Enrolment
When 100,000 people gathered for a Protestant rally attended by President Fidel Castro in 1999, it signalled a new level of hunger to hear the Gospel. Presbyterian and other Protestant churches are filled to overflowing. In this context the Ecumenical Theological Seminary, Matanzas, is experiencing a resurgence in enrolment. Under the inspirational leadership of the Rev Dr Ofelia Ortega, students from widely varying backgrounds are training at the seminary to prepare themselves for ministries to the wider society. The Board assists with provision of books and computers.

A Key Regional Centre: the Near East School of Theology
The Near East School of Theology (NEST) has gone through its ups and downs in the last 20 years. It stands today as an enduring witness to the faith of all those who kept it open during Lebanon's troubled years. Reinvigorated, it is equipping ministers and theological educators from all over the Middle East and beyond. The Rev Dr Mary Mikhael, the first woman President, works tirelessly to raise the profile and funds for NEST. The Board has supported NEST through seconding Mr David Kerry as Librarian to organise and computerise their stocks.

Burma: "South-South" Bursaries
The political and human rights situation in Burma makes relationships with partner churches there extremely

sensitive. Yet the Board continues to offer support and solidarity where possible. Over several years this has involved making it possible for students from Burma to study at Trinity Theological College in Singapore.

Pakistan: Strengthening Key Institutions

The Board provides grants to St Thomas' Theological Seminary, Karachi and to the United Bible Training School, Gujranwala, to support theological education for Christian women and clergy wives as part of a process of supporting empowerment and education of women. The Rev Paul Burgess, mission partner on the staff of Gujranwala Theological Seminary, has been involved in the two significant pieces of work this year: the writing of a new prospectus and curriculum for the college, and also participating in a national survey of theological education in Pakistan by the DOER (Development of Existing Resources) Trust.

Solidarity with Reformed Churches in Eastern and Southern Europe

The Board sustains the longstanding involvement of the Church of Scotland in offering solidarity and support to Reformed churches which witness in predominantly Roman Catholic countries. In the Waldensian Seminary in Italy and the Protestant Theological Faculty of the Charles University in Prague, there are possibilities of exchange visits and study leave opportunities. The Board encourages people to take advantage of exchange visits, of sabbatical leave and study leave. Friendships made and sustained can enrich and enhance the life of the church at home.

Theological Renewal in Romania

In the Protestant Theological Institute in Romania there is a constant need for more books and academic journals to help the students prepare for ministry in the Reformed tradition. The Board has expressed its concern about the lack of access for women to ministerial training and has encouraged the Institute to think about the contribution women can make to the Church in Romania. Mission partner Celia Kenny plays a key role in this initiative.

Bursaries: Equipping the Leaders of Tomorrow

In the academic year 2000-2001, there are 10 bursars studying in Scotland from 10 different churches and countries. They are studying in Aberdeen, Edinburgh, Glasgow and Stirling and each one is linked with a local Church of Scotland congregation. The Bursary Programme is a long-standing feature of the Board's work but just as the work of the Church of Scotland is diverse, so is that of our partner churches. Therefore, our bursars are not only studying theology, pastoral or biblical studies but this year's bursars include students of pharmacy, education management and administration and media management. £100,000-150,000 (3 to 5% of budget) per annum is devoted to meeting the costs of bursaries, in addition to office staff and other costs relating to the programme.

As the needs of our partner churches change over time, so must the Bursary Programme. This year has seen the beginning of a wide ranging review of the Programme. While we have seen many examples of the good that can come of a year of study in a Scottish institution, we have begun to ask the question: Is this the only way? Is this the most useful way to maximise our limited resources? In addition to bursars coming to study in Scotland, are there courses available in their region of the world which will be of equal benefit to them and to their church? As the St Andrews Consultation showed us, we need to be open to hearing about new and meaningful ways of moving forward in partnership, maximising our mutual resources to the furthering of the Kingdom.

Theological Education in Scotland: the Global Dimension

The Board seeks to bring the global dimension into theological education in Scotland. It is grateful to share in conferences for candidates for the ministry and for probationers. The whole church is given the opportunity to sense the excitement of the development of theological education worldwide through the production of such materials as "The Pulpit and the People" – a video arising from the concerns of African churches.

2. Evangelism

Jesus said: "As you go preach this message"

Jesus' command to take the good news to "the ends of the earth" is one which is taken very seriously by many of our partner churches. They urge us to join with them in taking the gospel to communities where it has not been heard before. The Board responds, whenever possible, to emerging opportunities for witness.

A New Ministry among the Karen People in Thailand
Mike and Jane Fucella have taken up a new assignment with our partner church, the Church of Christ in Thailand, to work with the Karen people in Pakh 16 (Presbytery 16) which stretches for 500 miles north to south along the Thai-Burma border. The ministry is focussed on displaced and vulnerable people – refugees, illegal immigrants, and people with no citizenship and few rights who have escaped violence in their homeland in Burma. Mike's initial task is to make a survey of the groups and churches in the entire area and then draw up a proposal of needs and expectations and to develop a lay leadership training programme.

Reaching out to Sudanese Refugees in Cairo
The Joint Relief Ministry in Cairo, to which Dr Keith Russell went to work in the summer of 2000, reaches out holistically to Sudanese refugees who have been forced to flee their homeland and settle in Egypt. While trying to look after their physical needs, the Joint Relief Ministry also addresses the spiritual needs of the refugee population. Because of the continuing civil war in Sudan, the refugee population has soared to 18,000. The medical work continues to be highly valued by the refugees, many of whom are in need of treatment. The programme also encourages the Sudanese refugees with particular medical or other skills to use them to help their fellow refugees; this gives the individuals more responsibility and a sense of worth and helps to reinforce how their faith impacts on their work. As well as medical work, the staff feel called to be involved in deepening the faith of those with whom they work and also sharing faith with those who have never heard the good news of Jesus Christ.

Resourcing the Church's Witness in the Southern Sudan
The civil war in southern Sudan has made it practically impossible for expatriate mission workers to be based there. However, the Board has identified an opportunity to join with a Church Missionary Society team based in Uganda which offers training and capacity-building to the Sudanese church across the border. Because of the political and civil situation, there is great need for indigenous committed Church workers to work under difficult, and often dangerous, conditions to bring the good news to a beleaguered people. The Rev Roderick Campbell has been appointed to offer teaching and training of those willing to undertake this arduous task.

Urban Mission in Europe
When the Rev Robert Calvert was appointed for a second five-year term as minister in Rotterdam, a new feature of the appointment was the provision that part of his time should be spent assessing new models of urban mission and being involved in conferences seeking new ways of practising mission in an urban setting. He has been able to attend consultations in Greece and Budapest. Several of our congregations in continental Europe are strategically placed for outreach to migrant workers and refugees.

Hunger for the Gospel in Cuba
In Cuba, the Church has grown remarkably in the 1990s with many young people taking an active interest for the first time in their lives. Presbyterian churches, abandoned after the revolution when many Presbyterian pastors left the island, are packed to capacity. Most church members welcomed the revolution as bringing Christ's good news to the mass of poor in Cuba in the 1950s. Today, the Church remains supportive of the social infrastructure but critical of some of the excesses of the State mechanisms. Many young people are keen to spend time in study and contemplation of the Bible and in discussion with church leaders and workers to know more about the demands of the Gospel. The Board seeks to assist the church in developing resources to respond to this spiritual hunger.

Jamaica: Institute for Theological Learning and Development

The United Church in Jamaica and the Cayman Islands celebrated the 10th anniversary of its Institute for Theological Learning and Development which offers courses in theology, spirituality, pastoral care and counselling to local communities. The Rev Roy Dodman and the Rev Margaret Fowler are among the tutors. Classes are often full and there is a great hunger from people to learn more about their faith and how it relates to their life. In a society where murder is commonplace and violence endemic, people long for a word of truth from the Gospel.

Africa: Great Zeal for Evangelism

The vast and widespread growth of the Church in sub-Saharan Africa is due, in great part, to the active outreach of its members in bringing people to faith in Christ. Responding to this zeal for evangelism among our partner churches, the Board has supported a number of very successful outreach programmes. Funding has been provided in Malawi, for Livingstonia Synod, which means that each Presbytery in this huge area has been and will continue to be visited by the Synod Evangelism Team. A similar programme has been funded in Mozambique. The Board has also been able to provide core funding for the "Evangelism Desk" of the United Church of Zambia.

3. Holistic Mission

Jesus said: "I am among you as one who serves"

Christlike service to the community has long been a hallmark of Christian mission. Today the Board seeks to work with partner churches as they respond in compassion to the often desperate needs of rapidly changing societies. This is illustrated by the following current pieces of work.

Healthcare in Africa

The desperate shortage of adequate healthcare facilities in Africa has been made even more apparent by the onset of the AIDS epidemic. In this context the Board seeks to work with partner churches in staffing and sustaining hospitals. In 2000, approximately £200,000 (7%) of Board resources were used towards Healthcare in Africa. This paid mainly for our mission partners on placements as nurses and doctors. It also includes grants towards AIDS and Hospital Projects. In addition, many of the donations we receive are designated for the work of our mission partners in Chogoria Hospital, Ekwendeni and other healthcare projects. In addition to financial support, the Board attempts to respond positively to requests for medical staff, and today such appointments make up a large proportion of mission partners working on the continent. Currently our partner churches in Kenya and Malawi are the major beneficiaries of such support but we are always trying to add to these placements.

One very important aspect of having mission partners is the opportunity we have from them to learn in a very direct way the reality of life within the discipline in which they are working. Liz Grant writes from Chogoria Hospital in Kenya, "The hospital is now only a third full, because people simply have no money and the cost of living is increasing. They have no money because they have no crops in their shambas because of the drought. There is nothing in the ground. There is nothing in the store cupboards. There is no money. People, however, are still getting sick. Angus [Angus Grant—mission partner doctor] is devastated at times when he travels to the rural clinics. While we see problems within the hospital, it is outside the hospital gates that poverty really becomes most obvious. There are many in the catchment area who simply do not even consider coming to Chogoria hospital, in the same way that I would not consider buying a Ferrari—utterly unaffordable."

Combating Leprosy

Under a new arrangement with the Nepal Leprosy Trust, Moira and Alasdair Murray have been stationed at the Leprosy Hospital in Lal Gadh, in southern Nepal where the majority of patients are Hindu. The area is one in which intimidation and the threat of violence against Christians is always present. Moira has contributed to the development of nursing and other services at the hospital while Alasdair has made his management expertise available.

Drug Rehabilitation

The Board is working in solidarity with IBTIDA, the drug rehabilitation programme based in Karachi Diocese, Church of Pakistan, enabling new programmes with Christians addicted to heroin in slum villages in the Diocese and also facilitating a training programme for women workers with women addicts. This is a new and essential programme given the cultural sensitivity and restrictions in a Muslim country.

In Jamaica, Margaret Fowler was recently honoured with a national award for her work with substance abusers. Based in her parish at Negril, she continues to offer a wider ministry in drug rehabilitation work.

Reaching out to Sex Workers

The Church of Bangladesh Social Development Programme Office has begun a project working with Destitute Women and Floating Sex Workers. This is an innovative and culturally sensitive project which is supported by the Board and may have an important role in future sex education and HIV/AIDS programmes in Bangladesh.

Relief Work

The Church of Bangladesh Social Welfare Division (CBSWD) is also at the forefront of work in rehabilitation and regeneration in villages throughout the west of the country devastated by floods. This includes a 'cash for work' programme to rebuild roads and homes; nutrition and health programmes; seeds and livestock supply and tree planting to combat soil erosion. The Board supports CBSWD on a regular basis and also through emergency grants when required. Ecumenical mission partner Gillian Rose, in Bollobhpur Hospital, was in the thick of the problem earlier this year when thousands of refugees fled to her area from the floods in neighbouring West Bengal (India). The Church of North India earthquake relief and rehabilitation work in Gujurat Diocese has also been supported by the Board through prayer and emergency grants.

Caring for Refugees

Not only climatic problems but the instability of the post-Cold War era has led to an upsurge in the numbers of refugees worldwide. There is need both to respond to emergency situations and to remember the needs of those who have been refugees for decades. The Middle East Council of Churches works with Palestinian refugees all across the Middle East, bringing relief and aid to people who have been homeless for over 50 years. The work of the Near East Council of Churches in Gaza is important in providing aid as well as work opportunities for refugees who have become permanent fixtures on the political scene. In Lebanon, the Joint Christian Committee of the Middle East Council of Churches works to bring education and relief to refugees who are also marginalised from Lebanese society.

Reconstruction

In the Balkans, the Ecumenical Women's Solidarity Fund continues its sterling work among communities struggling to rebuild themselves in the wake of the years of destruction. From community healthcare to legal advice and small business set-up, the Fund has creatively sought to help women in the Balkans to help their own communities to rebuild and reorganise. The ultimate aim of the Fund is to see each of the grant recipients able to stand on their own two feet and fund their operation. Slowly, step by step, this is being achieved. In Croatia, the Church of Scotland Guild funded the rebuilding of some church buildings and, at the time of writing, the Moderator was scheduled to rededicate the Reformed Church in Tordinci on April 1st. The rebuilding has been of tangible support to the Reformed Church in their witness in Eastern Croatia.

Community Development

The Mel Nathan Institute, an initiative of the United Church in Jamaica and the Cayman Islands, encourages community development, education and skills enhancement. In a society where many young men drop out and many young women need to head the family, the Mel Nathan Institute offers opportunities and hope for their training and a better life.

4. Mission in Pluralistic Societies

Jesus said: "Love your neighbour as yourself"

The process of globalisation has led people in many parts of the world to ask questions about their identity and their relations to "others". Just as this forms a challenge to Christians in situations where Christianity is the majority faith, so it often puts pressure on Christian communities which form a minority within their wider society. Partner churches working in such situations look to the Board for solidarity and support.

Christian-Muslim Relations in India and Pakistan

The minority standing of the Christian church in the Indian subcontinent places the question of relations with other faith communities close to the top of the agenda. Christian-Muslim relations are particularly sensitive and the Board supports both the Christian Study Centre (CSC) in Rawalpindi, Pakistan and the Henry Martin Institute, Hyderabad, India. Both of these institutions are at the forefront of dialogue, education and consciousness-raising on the issues facing Christians and Muslims as they co-exist in differing environments. Both institutions are highly respected and have been called upon by Government departments for information. The Rev Andrew Anderson, Vice-Convener of the Board's Asia Group, used his study leave to serve as Summer Pastor at Murree and to undertake a programme of study on Islam at CSC in Rawalpindi.

Christian-Muslim Relations in Africa

Africa also forms an arena of Christian-Muslim encounter. In some areas, relations are good and positive and much work is being achieved in promoting mutual understanding. However in other areas, notably in Nigeria, considerable tension and mistrust exist between the two communities, sometimes leading to outright violence. The Board supports the work of PROCMURA (Project on Christian Muslim Relations in Africa) and is particularly pleased to have hosted the annual meeting of the European Liaison Committee of PROCMURA at Dunblane earlier this year.

War in Sri Lanka

The Churches (Catholic and Protestant) in Sri Lanka attempt to stand free of the polarisation on cultural, religious and ethnic grounds which has divided the country. Through the National Christian Council and other Christian agencies, Christians are trying to work out a path for dialogue and practical working together as a way to open up a means of reconciliation between ethnic and religious groups at all levels. The Rev Tony McLean-Foreman, working at the Theological College of Lanka in Kandy, has come face to face with the impact of the violence through the experiences of his students—both Tamil and Sinhala. The College is a place of reconciliation and community building.

Jerusalem: a City of Two Peoples and Three Faiths

Jerusalem is a city of two peoples—Israeli and Palestinian —and three faiths—Jewish, Christian and Muslim. The three Abrahamic faiths meet and mingle amidst the complex interaction of the Arab world and the West. The Church of Scotland's work and presence has been a support and a strength to the Christian community. They welcomed the visit of the Moderator of the General Assembly, in Advent 2000, as a tangible expression of the church in the West remembering, supporting and praying for the situation of our brothers and sisters in Christ in Israel and Palestine.

Scotland: a New Context of Religious Pluralism

A religiously plural context is something new to many Scottish Christians and an area where we have much to learn from members of partner churches long familiar with such a situation. Through its Faithshare programme the Board has supported the work of Sardar and Violet Ghauri, from the Church of Pakistan, at The Well, Asian Information and Advice Centre, in Glasgow. For a number of years The Well has done pioneering work amongst the Asian Community, offering an open door to those who live in and around the neighbourhood. The Ghauris are Faithshare Partners for a three-year period, co-funded by the Church Mission Society, London. Their son Shaleem, has also been working hard this year and achieved high grades in his Standard Grades. The Guild has chosen The Well as one of their new projects for 2000–2003 under the title of "Strength for Living".

5. Prophetic Ministry

Jesus said: "He who has ears to hear, let him hear"

At the closing session of the St Andrews Consultation great emphasis was laid on the importance of speaking God's Word to the times in which we live. One of the key features of a strong church-to-church partnership is the capacity to assist one another in discerning the Word of the Lord to our particular context. The Board seeks to enable and equip such contextual ministry.

Role of Continental and Regional Organisations in Africa
An important springboard of prophetic ministry has often been the inspiration gained from interaction and relationship with others, likeminded or otherwise. For many of our partner churches in Africa, principally through lack of resources, it is difficult for them to get together on a regular basis to listen and to learn from each other. Important fora for such meetings are the continental and regional Church organisations which are both directly and indirectly supported by the Board. In addition to the direct funding support, the Board encourages our partner churches to join and participate in the work of continent-wide organisations e.g. the All Africa Conference of Churches, and regional organisations e.g. the Southern Africa Alliance of Reformed Churches and the South Africa Council of Churches. One example of this process was the "Mission in Unity Conference" hosted by SAARC in Johannesburg in October last year, at which the majority of our partner churches in southern Africa were represented, each enabled to be present through funding by the Board.

Centre for Pastoral Studies in Central America (CEDEPCA)
CEDEPCA offers theological training in a local context and helps local people to encounter the key questions in order to bring a sharp theological understanding to life in their own communities. Scottish Churches World Exchange have volunteers placed with CEDEPCA and the Board has given some grant support to its work in encouraging non-theologians to consider the Bible in the context of their own lives.

Christian Conference of Asia (CCA)
The role of the CCA in providing a means for networking, sharing and solidarity for Christians across the region has become more and more essential over the years as conflicts have increased. Programmes for youth; empowerment of women; understanding human rights have all given a vision of a just and equal society to churches in minority situations. CCA is a highly respected organisation in South and South-East Asia and has been able to work to support groups or enable dialogue in situations such as East Timor.

Conference of European Churches: Church and Society Commission (CEC/CSC)
CEC/CSC offers a prophetic witness to the European Institutions and brings the Church's message to the heart of western European political processes. CEC/CSC brings together specialists from churches all over Europe to critique and question civil servants and politicians within the European Institutions. It aims to support greater interaction and co-operation between the nations of the West while not forgetting the other nations of Europe or other parts of the world where European actions have a strong impact.

Sabeel: The Ecumenical Liberation Theology Centre in Jerusalem
Sabeel presses forward a vision for a just and equitable peace and helps both local and international Christians to examine the critical issues of the local and global situation. The Sabeel International Conference,

scheduled for February 2001 in Bethlehem, was to be transformed into "An Alternative Assembly: Speaking Truth, Seeking Justice". Sabeel examines the critical issues of the situation in Palestine and Israel and gives resources and encouragement in pushing for a vision of a just and equitable peace for Israeli and Palestinian, for Christian, Muslim and Jew.

Cry Jubilee: Campaigning for the Cancellation of Debt
The Board has played a full part in the campaign for the cancellation of the unpayable debts of the world's poorest countries, constantly motivated by partner churches' experience of the deprivation which results from the debt burden. The Jubilee 2000 Scottish Coalition ended its work on a high note. It was able to celebrate huge advances in the public profile of the debt issue – the "human chain" around Edinburgh Castle in 1999 was said to be the largest demonstration for an "altruistic" cause to be held in Scotland in recent times. Moreover, significant beginnings have been made in the massive and intricate task of achieving debt cancellation. Nevertheless it had to recognise that the debt which has been cancelled is a small proportion of the total which was targeted. The Board is grateful that the Moderator of the General Assembly, the Rt Rev Dr Andrew McLellan, emphasised how much remains to be done when he met with the Chancellor of the Exchequer in November 2000.

There is need for the campaign to continue and the Board has played an active role in the formation of Jubilee Scotland which carries forward the torch which was lit by Jubilee 2000. It was a motion from the floor at a Local Involvement Conference which led to the Board undertaking "to keep faith with the world-wide commitment to debt remission". "The Debt Effect" and "The Least of God's Children" are two new videos created by the Board to highlight the plight of the world's poor. Together with other members of the Jubilee Scotland coalition, the Board is highlighting the meeting of the G7 in Genoa in July 2001 as a significant opportunity to make substantial progress in the cancellation of poor countries' unpayable debt. The Board has contributed £80,000 to the campaign since 1998 and has committed £20,000 for each of 2001 and 2002 to Jubilee Scotland.

Globalisation: A New Frontier for Mission
The Board has also given close attention to the advent of "Globalisation", particularly its devastating impact on many poor communities. Mission partners contributed to a Board conference on this topic which led to the preparation of an insert in *Life and Work*. It is planned to produce a video and discussion material on the subject to be in circulation by the autumn of 2001. The Bible Studies from the St. Andrews Consultation, published by St Andrew Press under the title *Moving with Christ in Mission*, bring the harsh and diverse realities vividly before us.

6. Human and Material Resources

Jesus said: "It is more blessed to give than to receive"

With what a wonderful range of resources has God blessed the church! Yet what a great challenge it is for the church to deploy all available resources to maximum effect in the mission of Christ. The Board seeks to rise to this challenge as it facilitates the giving and receiving of resources between the Church of Scotland and its partner churches overseas.

Faithshare
Prominent in this enterprise is the Faithshare programme which facilitates the movement of personnel between the churches. This year a further five Faithshare Partners have come to Scotland, including one couple and a young woman from Korea— the first Korean Faithshare Partner. Another five, including one couple, are planned for next year and there continues to be need for more Presbyteries to come forward and take part in this exciting area of the Board's work.

The Rt Rev Jason and Mrs Lydia Dharmaraj from the Church of South India spent three valuable months with the Presbytery of Falkirk. Mrs Mumtaz Gill from Sialkot Diocese of the Church of Pakistan spent four months with the Presbytery of Abernethy. The Rev Lau Makata from Blantyre Synod of the Church of Central Africa

Presbyterian spent six months serving and enthusing with the Presbytery of Shetland. The special witness of the Presbyterian Church in the Republic of Korea became better known to the congregations within the Presbytery of Lanark through the work and energy of Miss Jee Eun Choi.

All these visits have had a far reaching impact on the congregations closely involved and many have responded by planning reciprocal visits. The Faithshare Group is able to assist with these by offering advice and expertise about practical details and the programme planning, as well as limited financial assistance. Prayer always plays a central role in the Faithshare Programme. Members, congregations and Presbyteries often find intercessory prayer more focussed through knowing sisters and brothers in Christ who witness and minister in situations very different from our own. Visits in both directions strengthen tangible links between members of the Church of Scotland and our partner churches. These links have often been expanded to include other denominations participating in the Faithshare Programme. These important links become highly valued by all who deepen their relationship with other Christians through the Programme.

New Forms of Partnership

The St Andrews Consultation has further stimulated the Board to explore with other Churches and Mission Societies new forms of partnership. Meanwhile, congregations and Presbyteries offer examples of lively co-operation.

The Presbytery of Lothian has, after careful research and thorough preparation, entered into a Twinning Agreement with the Diocese of Eastern Himalaya of the Church of North India. It is intended that the Twinning will involve not only mutual prayer and support but also exchange visits. Helping towards such twinning associations is the Rev Anthapurusha, the India Link Facilitator working with the Board and the Scottish Episcopal Church. Anthapurusha has been working extensively throughout the Presbyteries in Scotland to raise awareness and knowledge of the Indian Church. He

returns to his ministry in India in September 2001 and it is hoped that several twinnings of Presbyteries with Dioceses of the Church of North and South India will have been set in place by that time.

In response to a deliverance of last General Assembly, the Board has sought to recognise the work of Church of Scotland members serving with other Churches and Mission Societies. Many have co-operated willingly in supplying such information. The names of those serving are now listed in Prayerlink, the insert to the quarterly magazine, *Insight,* which also includes articles on Mission Societies or some of those serving with them. There is now a shortage of mission partners for the Partner Plan Scheme in some Presbyteries. One, Sutherland, has, with the Board's support, adopted an Overseas Missionary Fellowship couple so that the congregations can have a live link with a part of the World Church.

Mission Partner Appointments: Renewal of Employment Practice

The Board's Personnel Group has been working hard to ensure that the Board is a best practice employer. Policies have been clarified and developed, and procedures streamlined. The Group will continue to review all areas of personnel management to maintain consistency and transparency in all dealings with overseas staff. Areas which the Personnel Group are examining include pastoral care, employing of non-UK nationals, medical insurance, emergency evacuation, interview training, the use of selection schools in recruitment, part-time work and reviewing the Handbook for Overseas Staff and the allowances for mission partners. The Board has agreed a policy on the role of spouses which affirms and supports the role of the spouse while distinguishing the situations where the spouse is an employee in his/her own right as opposed to being in an accompanying role. The review of pastoral care of mission partners was put on hold while awaiting the report of the management consultancy exercise undertaken by McKinsey & Co. It is therefore proposed to report the final results of the review to the General Assembly of 2002. Discussions on training continue and, until a firm programme is constructed, training is tailor-made to each new member of staff. This is working well and the training is evaluated by the mission partner and department. The partner church/institution are also asked for input into the training programme. The new arrangement whereby medical care for overseas staff is provided by the Elphinstone International Health Centre (formerly Care for Mission) has enjoyed a highly successful first year with many staff commending this new provision.

In the past year 16 vacancies overseas have been filled and 12 overseas staff offered new contracts. The Board is responding to requests from partner churches and institutions for personnel but is also being proactive and creative in seeking posts. Ecumenical appointments with other agencies and churches are increasing and it is good to be able to share personnel and resources in this way.

Scottish Churches World Exchange
Co-operating ecumenically within World Exchange the Board has been able to participate in sending volunteers to work with new partner churches and to areas which are no longer appropriate for longer term mission partners. It is particularly pleasing to report that, in response to a question at last year's General Assembly, seven World Exchange volunteers were sent to work in Guatemala. One is working with street children, four are supporting the churches' work with children and young adults, one is working in an orphanage, and one is helping co-ordinate church-based house groups and women's groups. The ages of this group of volunteers in Guatemala range from 18 to 73 years old.

The majority of World Exchange volunteers live and work with partner churches of the Board. This year volunteers have worked in India, Pakistan, Palestine, Lebanon, Egypt, Malawi, Kenya, South Africa, Mauritius, Trinidad, Jamaica and Guatemala. Particular mention must be made of Dr Anne Weatherhead, who adhered to her decision to volunteer at the School for the Visually Handicapped in Beit Jala, Palestine, despite an outbreak of violent unrest only days before her departure. Her presence with the children and the Palestinian staff was an important witness for peace.

Believing an overseas placement to be a tremendous opportunity for those who participate, World Exchange are trying to extend access to include candidates who are not able to raise the required £2,000 towards their placement costs. Working with the Rev Martin Johnstone, UPA Adviser to the Board of National Mission, World Exchange is consulting with Ministers, schools and community organisations in "Social Inclusion Partnership" areas, and with the Scottish Executive, on how to make international experience through the churches a real option for everyone.

St Colm's International House
St Colm's International House has continued to develop, with upgraded conference facilities and the provision of en-suite bedrooms. In the coming year St Colm's will concentrate on providing short courses designed to meet the needs of churches and community organisations in the developing world. This will include three English Language and Management Skills courses, each six weeks long, and a new course for UK-based volunteers wanting to teach English language in a development context.

Scottish Churches China Group
The Board has been pleased to be able to participate in a period of renewal in the work of the Scottish Churches China Group. The newly appointed China Field Officer, the Rev Patricia Johnston, is based in the Board's offices. Under the aegis of the Scottish Churches China Group there are opportunities for short-term service in China, particularly for teachers of English and Theology and for medical clinicians. Amongst those who have come to Scotland from China are two Catholic sisters who enjoyed a successful placement in Edinburgh. The Board extends its thanks to Ms Jill Hughes who served the SCCG for 16 years before relinquishing this responsibility in order to meet the growing demands of the Board's own Asia desk.

Financial Resources: Generosity and Creativity
Congregations and individuals throughout Scotland and further afield continue to share their material resources with our partners overseas. 57% of the Board's £3million

budget comes through the Mission and Aid Fund. A further £200,000 is received in legacies, trusts and donations to general income. Investment income, which makes up the balance of our resources was originally derived from the generosity of individuals. In addition to this budget expenditure, we received over £600,000 of donations in 2000 which were designated for particular uses. Giving in this way allows people to have a very real feeling of sharing and Christian compassion which comes over in the letters we receive along with donations. We are careful to ensure that these donations are remitted to the desired project or mission partner, without any deductions.

In the future, we will be challenged more and more to obtain best value for our expenditure. The current economic climate will bring lower investment returns and globally higher costs. World Mission must meet this challenge through more creative use of income, setting of priorities, and new programmes to share human and material resources.

Communication
Communication is vitally important in maintaining a good and effective relationship with our partner churches and mission partners. At one level this is a fairly obvious statement, but for many of our partners this has been extremely difficult. Over the past year, therefore, the Board has been engaged in improving the means of communication of a number of our partner churches and has provided funds for the purchase of computers and email facilities for the IECM in Mozambique, Blantyre Synod, CCAP in Malawi, the Presbyterian Church in Nigeria and the Theological College of Lanka, Sri Lanka.

This form of communication, while important, cannot be compared with the value of visits to and face to face consultations with our partners. During this past year visits were made to our partner churches throughout all the regions. In Africa visits were made to Mozambique, Malawi, Zambia, Kenya and South Africa. A major visit to Mozambique, Malawi and Zambia was also undertaken by the Moderator, the Rt Rev Dr Andrew McLellan, the highlight of which was his participation in the celebrations by the CCAP in Malawi marking the 125 years since the arrival of the first missionaries from Scotland to that part of Africa. One quite different visit was made by two representatives of the youth constituency of the Church of Scotland. In July and August last year Nicola Parkins and Jonathan de Groot, along with representatives from churches all over the world, attended the Livingstonia Synod Youth Conference in Malawi, the theme of which was "The Rights of a Child".

In Asia, partner churches in South India, Sri Lanka, Nepal and Indonesia were visited, programmes and projects evaluated and plans made for future work and deepening relationships. Two Presbytery World Mission Conveners, the Rev Ian Stirling and the Rev Valerie Allen, together with the Personnel Secretary, Ms Sheila Ballantyne, visited ecumenical mission partners working in Bangladesh and with the United Mission to Nepal in Nepal. In the Middle East, the Moderator visited Israel and Palestine in December. The Project Group of the Israel Centres Committee have made regular visits to Tiberias and Jerusalem while the Rev Alan Greig, the Rev John Renton and the Rev Hugh Kerr represented the Board at the Sabeel Conference in Jerusalem in February 2001. In Europe visits have been made to Turin, Rome, Lisbon, Paris and Malta. The Moderator also visited the Balkans. Within the Caribbean and western Atlantic, the Moderator visited partner churches in Cuba and Jamaica, Christian Aid projects in the Dominican Republic and Haiti, and the overseas charges of Nassau and Freeport in the Bahamas.

Conclusion: Partnership Renewed for the 21st Century

Such visits, together with the indispensable service of those who move to a new country for some time in order to give human expression to church-to-church partnerships, provide the means by which each partnership in mission can be reviewed and renewed. The above report indicates many of the ways in which the Board is seeking to keep faith with the partnership priorities identified by the representatives of our partners churches who came together in St Andrews in 1999. The liveliness of so many of the points of shared work and witness throughout the world offers the promise that partnership in mission will be of strategic importance in the advance of the reign of God in the 21st century. In order to ensure that its structures and operations are well fitted to the task ahead, the Board is undergoing a thorough internal review.

Management Consultancy

As part of its response to the Report of the Special Commission anent the Board of World Mission to the 2000 General Assembly, the Board retained McKinsey & Co, on a *pro bono* basis, to undertake a management consultancy exercise. This took place from October to December 2000 on the basis of wide consultation involving Board members, overseas staff, office staff and other interested parties. The results of the consultancy were presented to the December meeting of the Board which adopted the great majority of McKinsey's recommendations. After further careful work, and some minor adjustments, the remaining recommendations were adopted by the Board early in 2001. As a result, the Board's committee structure has been simplified with a middle tier of committees being removed and a flat structure of working groups reporting to the Board being established. The staff structure is being reformed to improve management efficiency and foster teamworking. Remits and responsibilities for Board members and staff are being defined and clarified. The Board is developing vision and strategy to guide all of its work in the years to come. The benefits of the consultancy exercise are already apparent as secure foundations are laid for the development and management of the work committed to the Board. It is a pleasure to acknowledge with thanks the excellent work done by the consultants from McKinsey & Co, particularly Mr Keith Leslie and Dr Caroline Russell.

Secretariat

The Rev Robert S. Anderson, who had worked for the Board since 1986, transferred in September 2000 to the employment of the Scottish Churches World Exchange Trust. The Board is deeply grateful to Bobby for all that he contributed to its life and work over 14 years, particularly in the pioneering development of the programme which now takes the form of World Exchange. As its Director he will be working very closely with the Board in days to come.

Proposals to the General Assembly

The Board has three proposals to bring to the General Assembly: the adoption of a constitution for the Board, the passing of a new Act anent Overseas Charges, and the development of an initiative to respond to the HIV/AIDS pandemic. Details of each are indicated in Appendix I, II and III of the Report and are reflected in the proposed Deliverance.

In the name of the Board

ALAN MAIN, *Convener*
ALAN GREIG, *Vice-Convener*
ELISABETH CRANFIELD, *Vice-Convener*
KENNETH R. ROSS, *General Secretary*

APPENDIX I

Constitution of the Board of World Mission

At present the Board has no formal constitution. In order to give clarity to Board members and staff as to the constitutional basis of the Board and its responsibility to the General Assembly, it is here proposed that the General Assembly approve the constitution set out in Appendix I of the Report. It had been the Board's intention to present an earlier version of this constitution to the 2000 General Assembly but the proposal was withdrawn when it became clear that the Board would be undertaking a major management consultancy exercise. In the event, the outcome of the consultancy was highly affirmative of the constitution as drafted. Hence only minor amendments were made, e.g. to take account of changes to Standing Orders, before presenting the constitution to the General Assembly for adoption.

In view of the new composition of the Board approved by the General Assembly of 1999 and indicated in the new Constitution, it is proposed that Standing Order 130, which provides for Missionaries and Chaplains on furlough to be Corresponding Members of the Board of World Mission, be deleted. (This would bring the Board into harmony with the practice of all other Boards.) In line with the recommendations of the recent management consultancy, the Board is now enhancing the participation of mission partners in its deliberations by involving them in Board conferences and non-business sessions. Furthermore, the Board has established new guidelines for communicating and consulting with mission partners at home and abroad.

PROPOSED CONSTITUTION OF THE BOARD OF WORLD MISSION

1 Introduction
The Board of World Mission (hereinafter referred to as 'the Board') is a Board constituted by the authority of the General Assembly of the Church of Scotland.

2 Remit of the Board
The General Assembly gives the following remit to the Board:

Give life to the Church of Scotland's understanding that it is part of the Universal Church committed to the advance of the Kingdom of God throughout the world.

Discern priorities and form policies to guide the Church of Scotland's ongoing worldwide participation in God's transforming mission, through the gospel of Jesus Christ.

Develop and maintain mutually enriching relationships with partner churches overseas through consultation and the two-way sharing of human and material resources.

Equip and encourage Church of Scotland members

at local, presbytery and national levels, to enjoy being involved in the life of the world church.

Help the people of Scotland to appreciate the worldwide nature of the Christian faith.

This remit shall be fulfilled in terms of this Constitution.

3 The Board in Relation to the General Assembly
The Board of World Mission shall be accountable to the General Assembly for the work of each of its Constituent Committees and, through its Convener, shall report to the General Assembly on the work of the Board and its Committees. The Reports to the General Assembly shall carry a report of the work of each Constituent Committee and in the General Assembly the Conveners of those Committees, or those appointed for the purpose by the Board, whether or not Commissioners, shall be entitled to respond in person to questions, comments and motions from Commissioners relating to their particular section of the Board's Report.

4 Powers of the Board
The Board shall continue and shall assume the whole responsibilities, rights, functions and interests of all bodies ("the Board's Constituent Bodies") the work or functions of which have from time to time been incorporated within the Board.

Subject always to the direction of the General Assembly and accountable thereto, the Board shall have authority to exercise all powers consistent with its remit and this constitution.

In particular its powers shall include:

- **Finance**
The Board shall receive an annual allocation from the Mission and Aid Fund and it shall be within the power of the Board to allocate, always within the terms of its remit and subject to the direction of the General Assembly, these and its other resources as it judges best. The Board shall assume the whole rights and assets of the Board's Constituent Bodies. Existing Trust Funds and all future donations and legacies received in connection with the

Board's Constituent Bodies or the functions previously remitted to them shall be held and applied by the Board, all according to the terms and conditions applicable to such funds.

- **Employment**

The Board shall appoint such members of staff as it considers necessary and expedient from time to time properly to fulfil its remit. All members of staff of the Board working within the Church Offices in George Street shall be employed by the Personnel Committee, which shall, in consultation with the Board, determine the salaries and conditions of service of such staff. The Board shall be entitled to act as an employing agency of the Church for selected individuals from overseas appointed to serve in Scotland on fixed term contracts of employment under the auspices of Faithshare. The Board shall also act as an employing agency of the Church for its staff serving overseas and shall determine and from time to time review the salaries and conditions of service of such staff.

- **Powers to supply the deficiency of Church Courts**

The Board shall have power, provided it is so directed by the General Assembly, to fulfil the functions of any court of the Church in circumstances of its operations where such court does not exist.

5 Composition of the Board

The Board of World Mission shall have twenty-seven members made up as follows:

1. The Convener and two Vice-Conveners, all appointed by the General Assembly on the Report of the Nomination Committee and holding office in terms of Standing Order 119 of the General Assembly.
2. Twelve members appointed by the General Assembly on the Report of the Nomination Committee.
3. Twelve members appointed by Presbyteries in terms of the rota printed in the appendix to this constitution.

The General Secretary of the Board shall attend the meetings thereof, in terms of Standing Order 117 of the General Assembly.

Notwithstanding the above, the Board shall include four non-voting members appointed by and representing the Board of Ministry, the Board of National Mission, the Church and Nation Committee and the Church of Scotland Guild.

In special circumstances, the Board may approve the temporary co-option of additional non-voting members.

6 Meetings

The Board shall meet at least four times per year and at such meetings receive reports from its Constituent Committees and Groups.

7 Committees and Groups

The Board shall have power to appoint from time to time such committees and working groups as it might determine to be necessary or expedient for the proper fulfilment of its remit. The Board shall have oversight and authority over all such committees and groups.

With the approval of the Board, such committees and working groups shall have power to co-opt additional members with specific expertise to assist their work.

This constitution shall be operative from a date determined by the General Assembly.

APPENDIX
Rota for Presbytery Representation

General Assembly 2000 to General Assembly 2001

		2nd Year	1st Year
Dumfries/Kirkcudbright	Ardrossan	Glasgow	Lothian
Dunfermline	Perth	Kincardine/Deeside	South Argyll
Sutherland	Lewis	Europe	Moray

General Assembly 2001 to General Assembly 2002

	3rd Year	2nd Year	1st Year
Ardrossan	Glasgow	Lothian	Annandale/Eskdale
Perth	Kincardine/Deeside	South Argyll	Stirling
Lewis	Europe	Moray	Ross

General Assembly 2002 to General Assembly 2003

4th Year	3rd Year	2nd Year	1st Year
Glasgow	Lothian	Annandale/Eskdale	Irvine/Kilmarnock
Kincardine/Deeside	South Argyll	Stirling	Dunkeld/Meigle
Europe	Moray	Ross	Uist

General Assembly 2003 to General Assembly 2004

4th Year	3rd Year	2nd Year	1st Year
Lothian	Annandale/Eskdale	Irvine/Kilmarnock	Greenock
South Argyll	Stirling	Dunkeld/Meigle	Aberdeen
Moray	Ross	Uist	England

General Assembly 2004 to General Assembly 2005

4th Year	3rd Year	2nd Year	1st Year
Annandale/Eskdale	Irvine/Kilmarnock	Greenock	West Lothian
Stirling	Dunkeld/Meigle	Aberdeen	Dumbarton
Ross	Uist	England	Buchan

General Assembly 2005 to General Assembly 2006

4th Year	3rd Year	2nd Year	1st Year
Irvine/Kilmarnock	Greenock	West Lothian	Jedburgh
Dunkeld/Meigle	Aberdeen	Dumbarton	Falkirk
Uist	England	Buchan	Lochaber

General Assembly 2006 to General Assembly 2007

4th Year	3rd Year	2nd Year	1st Year
Greenock	West Lothian	Jedburgh	Ayr
Aberdeen	Dumbarton	Falkirk	St Andrews
England	Buchan	Lochaber	Lochcarron

General Assembly 2007 to General Assembly 2008

4th Year	3rd Year	2nd Year	1st Year
West Lothian	Jedburgh	Ayr	Paisley
Dumbarton	Falkirk	St Andrews	Angus
Buchan	Lochaber	Lochcarron	Shetland

General Assembly 2008 to General Assembly 2009

4th Year	3rd Year	2nd Year	1st Year
Jedburgh	Ayr	Paisley	Edinburgh
Falkirk	St Andrews	Angus	Hamilton
Lochaber	Lochcarron	Shetland	Gordon

General Assembly 2009 to General Assembly 2010

4th Year	3rd Year	2nd Year	1st Year
Ayr	Paisley	Edinburgh	Duns
St Andrews	Angus	Hamilton	Lorn/Mull
Lochcarron	Shetland	Gordon	Inverness

General Assembly 2010 to General Assembly 2011

4th Year	3rd Year	2nd Year	1st Year
Paisley	Edinburgh	Duns	Wigtown/Stranraer
Angus	Hamilton	Lorn/Mull	Kirkcaldy
Shetland	Gordon	Inverness	Caithness

General Assembly 2011 to General Assembly 2012

4th Year	3rd Year	2nd Year	1st Year
Edinburgh	Duns	Wigtown/Stranraer	Lanark
Hamilton	Lorn/Mull	Kirkcaldy	Dundee
Gordon	Inverness	Caithness	Orkney

General Assembly 2012 to General Assembly 2013

4th Year	3rd Year	2nd Year	1st Year
Duns	Wigtown/Stranraer	Lanark	Dumfries/Kirkcudbright
Lorn/Mull	Kirkcaldy	Dundee	Dunfermline
Inverness	Caithness	Orkney	Sutherland

APPENDIX II
Proposed Act anent Overseas Charges

Over the last few decades the Board has been involved in the reorganisation of the Church's charges overseas. The guiding policy has been to incorporate the charges into the Presbyterian or Reformed church indigenous to the context in which the congregation was set. Some other charges have been organised into Presbyteries of the Church as in Jerusalem and more recently Europe. However there are a number of charges where it has not been possible to put either of those processes in place. Some of these charges have become independent Reformed congregations with mixed results of sustainability, while others have remained with the Church of Scotland, developing a series of *ad hoc* relationships with the structures of the Church.

The aim of the Act is to recognise the status of these remaining congregations as charges of the Church and to bring them formally into the care and supervision of the General Assembly with the Board of World Mission providing such Presbyterial functions as may be required. The Act therefore sets out the rights and responsibilities of the Church acting through the Board, and of the congregations, as charges under the care and authority of the Assembly. The Act, however, has a flexibility to deal with the differing contexts of the charges.

All the charges listed in Schedule A have been visited by Board representatives prior to the drafting of the Act, and some after the drafting. While each context is different and there are different hopes for the future, each congregation was clear in its desire to clarify and formalise its relationship with the Church. There has been a feeling of isolation and lack of concern and they look forward to a more positive relationship in the future.

From the Board's perspective, we have been impressed by the quality of leadership exercised by many ministers, elders and members of our overseas charges, not only within the congregations but also within their respective nations. We hope that the Act will be the basis for their increased participation within the life of the Church of Scotland.

New Act on Overseas Charges

The General Assembly enact and ordain as follows:—

1. For the purposes of this Act the following terms shall be deemed to have the meanings hereby assigned to them:

(a) A "charge" shall mean a sphere of pastoral duty to which a minister is or ministers are inducted.

(b) For the purposes of this act only a "congregation" shall mean a company of persons associated together whose names are on the Communion Roll or other register approved by the Board of World Mission and who are under the pastoral oversight of a minister or ministers and a Kirk Session, for Christian worship, fellowship, instruction, mission and service.

(c) A "Financial Board" shall mean the body responsible for managing the finances and heritable properties of a congregation e.g. Congregational Board, Deacons' Court, Committee of Management.

(d) The "Board" shall mean the Board of World Mission of the General Assembly, or any successor body assuming the responsibilities, functions, and interests of the said Board.

2. The overseas charges of the Church of Scotland shall be as specified in Schedule A annexed hereto provided that the General Assembly may amend Schedule A without references to Presbyteries under the Barrier Act.

Appointment of Ministers

3. The appointment of ministers to overseas charges shall be in accordance with the general practice of the Board; provided that new appointments made after the passing of this Act, and in terms of Schedule C, hereof shall be subject to the provisions of Section 13 of Act V 1984 and to the provisions of Act III 1995.

Relation to General Assembly

4. Overseas charges shall not belong to any Presbytery. The Board will fulfil the relevant functions of Presbytery in respect of each individual congregation subject to the powers and responsibilities conferred on it by the General

Assembly. In particular the Board shall be responsible for the following:—

(a) Superintendence, including regular visitation of the congregation and inspection of its records, at a frequency to be determined by the Board.

(b) Vacancy procedures in terms of Schedule C of this Act including the appointment of an Interim Moderator, the sustaining of a call and the introduction of a minister; ordination of ministers shall be reserved to Presbyteries.

5. Each Overseas Charge shall be entitled to send its minister and an elder as commissioners to the General Assembly once in every four years. It shall be for the Board to determine the rota that shall apply. In the event that a minister who is not a minister of the Church of Scotland serves as a commissioner to the General Assembly, he or she shall not be entitled to vote.

6. Appeals against decisions of the Kirk Session or of the Board shall be competent to the General Assembly, the Judicial Commission or the Commission of Assembly as appropriate.

Constitution

7. Each overseas charge shall operate in terms of a Constitution approved by the Board.

8. The Financial Board of the congregation shall be responsible for the property and finance of the congregation, and the property shall be held in terms of the regulations in Schedule B.

9. Each overseas charge shall be assessed for the cost of ministry using criteria determined by the Board in individual consultation with each charge. Each charge shall be expected to make a contribution, through the Board, to the Mission and Aid Fund of the Church of Scotland.

10. The law and practice of the Church shall apply to overseas charges in so far as not inconsistent with this Act, and in any question of interpretation this Act shall

prevail, provided that the charges shall not be bound to perform any function which by reason of the difference between conditions overseas and conditions in Scotland is clearly not applicable to it, and in the event of any question arising as to the application of any law of the Church to these charges such questions shall be referred to the Board of Practice and Procedure which shall decide the question and whose decision shall stand unless and until the General Assembly shall decide otherwise. The Board of Practice and Procedure shall report all such decisions to the General Assembly.

11. Nothing in this Act shall affect the relation in which mission partners and ministers of the Church of Scotland stand at present with the Board.

SCHEDULE A

Overseas Charges

Christchurch, Warwick, Bermuda
Greyfriars St Ann's linked with Arouca and Sangre Grande, Trinidad and Tobago
Lucaya Kirk, Freeport, Bahamas
St Andrew's Presbyterian Kirk, Nassau, Bahamas
St Andrew's Colombo, Sri Lanka

SCHEDULE B
Regulations Anent Heritable Property

1. The heritable property pertaining to an overseas charge ("the property") shall be held by the Financial Board and the Trustees in whom title to it is vested for the use of and occupation by the overseas charge concerned.

2. Matters relating to the day to day management of the property shall be dealt with by the Financial Board of the overseas charge. It shall be the duty of the Financial Board to maintain the fabric of the property in proper order and repair and fully insured against loss or damage by fire and also against loss or damage by such other risks or perils as is from time to time deemed appropriate by the Financial Board.

3. Without the consent of the Board previously obtained, it shall not be lawful nor in the power of the Financial Board or the Trustees in whom title is vested to make any extensive alterations to the property nor to sell or demise, grant, convey, exchange or otherwise dispose of and deal with same nor to give and execute mortgages, charges, pledges or other securities over the property, it being declared that the consent of the Board to any of the foregoing acts shall be sufficiently evidenced only by (a) an Extract Minute of the Board signed by the General Secretary thereof or (b) in the event of the Board having by resolution thereof delegated its powers hereunder to one of its Committees or another body an extract Minute of that Committee or body signed by the Secretary thereof. Any decision made by or on behalf of the Board in terms of this Regulation shall be reported to the General Assembly. For the purposes of these regulations "extensive alterations" shall have such meaning as shall from time to time be determined by the Board.

4. The Financial Board and the Trustees in whom title to the property is vested shall each year submit a joint written report to the Board concerning the property which shall include details of their management and maintenance thereof and summarise the details of the insurance cover in force with respect to the property.

SCHEDULE C
Regulations Anent Appointments to Sanctioned Overseas Charges of the Church of Scotland.

1. Ministers shall be appointed by the Board for a fixed term contract not exceeding five years subject to the normal retirement age for ministers as determined from time to time by the General Assembly. The Board may delegate its powers of appointment to an appropriate committee.

2. On the occurrence of a vacancy within an Overseas Charge the following procedures shall apply:

2.1 The Board shall appoint an Interim Moderator who shall be available to advise the congregation, normally through the Kirk Session, in regard to vacancy procedures.

2.2 The Interim Moderator and the congregational representatives referred to in subsection (2.4) below shall receive all relevant papers in respect of those who, in due course, are being considered by the Board as candidates in the vacancy.

2.3 The Interim Moderator shall be entitled to be present at the expense of the Board when interviews to fill the vacancy are taking place. He or she shall be entitled to be heard but not to vote.

2.4 The interview panel shall consist of two representatives appointed by the Board and up to two representatives of the congregation. The representative(s) of the congregation shall be entitled to be heard and to vote. Where the congregation's financial situation does not allow any representative of the congregation to be present, the congregation shall be entitled to make application to the Board for such financial assistance as would allow the maximum of two representatives of the congregation to be present.

2.5 The member(s) of Staff of the Board with responsibility for the Overseas Charges and for personnel should normally be present but without the right to vote.

2.6 Not later than twelve months before an appointment to an Overseas Charge is due to end, the Board shall ascertain, in confidence, from the minister concerned whether he or she wishes to discuss the possibility of a new contract.

2.7 Where a minister expresses a wish for a new contract, the Board shall take steps to initiate the necessary review and inform in writing the minister and the congregation of this fact, complete the review not later than six months before the existing contract is due to end and thereafter inform in writing the minister and the congregation of the outcome of the review.

3. If the Board do not offer a new contract to a minister, his or her rights to use of the church and manse and to the emoluments pertaining to this appointment shall cease: provided always that if the minister concerned does not acquiesce in the decision not to offer a new contract, an appeal shall be competent to the Commission of Assembly in terms of s.5(b) of Act VI, 1997.

4. The General Assembly reserve to themselves the right to raise at any time the question of the continuance of any Overseas Charge: and their decision to dissolve an Overseas Charge shall *ipso facto* terminate the appointment of the minister as if his or her term of appointment had expired.

APPENDIX III

Confessing Faith in Christ in the Context of the HIV/AIDS Pandemic

AIDS, an acronym which has now entered many languages, stands for Acquired Immune Deficiency Syndrome. It is spread by the Human Immunodeficiency Virus, known as HIV, which steadily weakens the immune system so that its victims fall prey to a whole variety of infections and ailments which they are not able to resist. Victims are susceptible to opportunistic infections, such as pneumonia and certain cancers, which invariably lead, in the end, to death, although remission can be achieved by expensive antiretroviral treatment. The virus is spread by the transfer of body fluids, most often by sexual contact but also by the use of dirty needles in drug abuse and occasionally by blood transfusions. This is one of the highly distinctive features of the disease—it spreads not at random but according to patterns of human behaviour which can be clearly identified. The global scale and wide-ranging effects of the pandemic mean that it constitutes a crisis not just for those most acutely affected but for everyone living at this time. Nevertheless, to put the problem in its proper perspective, it is necessary to consider how it affects families where the disease takes hold.

Mission partners tell of people they have known:

Keith Russell, mission partner in Cairo tells us the story of Liza, a refugee from southern Sudan. Liza was in her early thirties. Her husband died of HIV when the family were still living in Sudan. Her three children were aged about 9–13 at the time when, because she had lost the breadwinner from her family, and because of the precarious political situation in her part of the country, Liza fled southern Sudan and made the exhausting journey by rail and steamer from her home in a mud hut to the metropolis of Cairo. She had some family who had made the journey earlier and were already in the city.

However, she soon fell ill. She contracted resistant TB and grew worse, despite careful treatment. She then developed ovarian cancer. At last, a reluctant Egyptian doctor tested her for HIV. The result was kept confidential because if the authorities found out that her results were positive she would be immediately deported in a truck by the police back over the border into north Sudan. So she was sent home to die.

She lived with her mother and three children in a two-roomed flat on the 7th floor of a Cairo tower block. Folk from the church visited her and her family weekly. They sang with her, read the Bible together and took her food and a little money to buy rice and bread. She died three months after the HIV diagnosis was made. The local church scraped together enough funds to buy her a small plot in the local cemetery, where she was buried. Her three children are now being looked after by an aged grandmother. No-one dares check the children for HIV. If they are infected it means instant deportation to a hostile part of the country they originally came from as refugees.

Carol Finlay, mission partner at Ekwendeni in Malawi, tells the story of Mercy, now a student nurse. Mercy was orphaned by HIV/AIDS at the age of 15 and she became the sole carer for her young brothers and sisters. Luckily for her, her uncle continued to pay her school fees which enabled her to complete her schooling and gain a place at the nursing school. Her young brothers and sisters live at home, alone, many miles from the nursing school. Mercy did not go home to her family last holiday as she did not have the bus fares. Mercy writes: "HIV to me means death, orphans and bereaved parents. It also means a long illness in hospital, at home and in the community at large. It has affected me in a number of ways. I am very concerned at the break-up of families. Parents are dying, leaving children who are not independent. Those children lack parental care, advice, support and love. In the end many become thieves, prostitutes and drug abusers because there is no-one to advise them on good behaviour. Many do not proceed with their education because they have no-one to support them materially and financially. This leads to a miserable life, since they do not have any means of earning a living. Not only children are affected. In many cases, parents are left alone because their children have died of AIDS and therefore do not have anyone to look after them when they get old. I am also concerned to see how many people are being admitted into the hospitals. Many are dying while they are still young, which is a loss to the family and to the nation itself. The youths are the future leaders of the nation and if they are dying who will take over from the present leaders? Also the development of the nation is not improving because people have no time to work which will develop the nation. Most of the time is spent nursing the sick. If HIV will continue infecting people day by day, who will look after one another in future?"

Jane and Mike Fucella, mission partners in Thailand, through the friendship of their daughter, Rachel, with Ann, got to know Ann's family, her parents and her older sister May, very well. Sadly, just before her 3rd birthday, May died of AIDS. Children under three are not given any funeral rites in the Buddhist/Animist community and so the family felt really comforted when Jane was able to help practically with collecting her body from the hospital, helping to lay her out and bury her. During this time many from the Christian community visited and prayed for the family. Combined with the loving care May had received before she died, this concern from the Christian community drew the family into the Church and they became Christians. Mot, Ann's father, died in November 1999 and although Dockmy, Ann's mother, and Ann herself are both healthy at this time, they are both HIV positive.

Three family tragedies caused by HIV/AIDS and a desperate view of life in the midst of the AIDS pandemic—such tragic stories are being repeated countlessly and daily around the world. Last year the General Assembly recognised the massive and "pending threat" to human life posed by HIV/AIDS. No longer is HIV/AIDS a "pending threat", it is now a reality with horrendous implications for many. The facts speak for themselves:

Current estimated number of adults and children with HIV/AIDS:

a) in sub-Saharan Africa	25.3 m
b) in Eastern Europe and Asia	7.1 m
c) in Latin America and the Caribbean	1.8 m
d) in rest of world	1.9 m
Total worldwide	36.1 m

India provides an alarming example of the rapid spread of HIV/AIDS. National AIDS Control Organisation (NACO) estimates 3.9 million people to be currently infected with HIV in India. This is about a tenth of all people living with HIV/AIDS in the world. A realistic estimate is that 0.5% of the one billion in India are HIV positive, but since detection and reporting is still at its initial stages this could be a gross underestimate. Surveillance data has revealed high prevalence (1–3% among antenatal women, 10–30% among STD clinic attendees) mainly among heterosexuals in South India (Maharastra, Andhra Pradesh, Tamil Nadu and Karnataka). High prevalence among IV-drug users is evident in the north-eastern states of the country in Manipur (49% among IV-drug users), Mizoram and Nagaland.

Although HIV has been detected to be at higher levels in urban areas, it is rapidly spreading to rural areas too, where it often goes undetected. Several international organisations are involved in helping India to tackle the situation. They operate through the National AIDS

Control Organisation and Non-Governmental Organisations. Thus several programmes have been implemented to educate communities at risk. However, they seem grossly inadequate when one meets HIV patients, who even after some months of being detected to be positive, are struggling with lack of information or support. The urban poor and the rural people are the ones who are the hardest hit when they find themselves positive. The general attitude to HIV is "it does not concern me", and thus it causes greater shock when detected to be positive. There is a great deal that needs to be done in India, and soon, in order to prevent it from reaching the proportions it has attained in sub-Saharan Africa.

Speaking at the International AIDS Conference in Durban last year the former South African President, Nelson Mandela, described the AIDS pandemic as "one of the greatest threats humankind has faced. Let us not equivocate: a tragedy of unprecedented proportions is unfolding in Africa". UN epidemiologists predicted in 1991 that by the end of the decade nine million people in sub-Saharan Africa would carry the HIV virus, the cause of AIDS. Current figures are 2-times that number. Experts fear that in four years' time, 2005, fifty million people worldwide could be living with HIV, and this may well be an underestimate.

Since the start of the pandemic, 55 million people have contracted HIV (36 million in sub-Saharan Africa) and to date 19 million have died of AIDS (12 million in sub-Saharan Africa). 5,500 people die of AIDS in sub-Saharan Africa every day and by 2010 it is expected that about 13,000 will die daily.

In contrast to many other illnesses, it is not the very old or the very young who are most directly affected. It is young adults who are most at risk. Commonly those who die of AIDS are people in their 30s, losing their lives just at the point when normally they would be taking most responsibility for the raising of children and the care of the elderly. When the middle generation in a community is decimated by such a disease, everyone suffers. One elderly woman in Malawi, responsible for the care of seven grandchildren, commented: "I have been bringing up children for fifty years and I am so tired now. My husband is old and cannot do anything."

Not only are families put under unbearable pressure, but the whole society is plunged into crisis. In Zambia, in the first ten months of 1998, 1300 teachers died, the vast majority from AIDS. In the same country, deaths of health care workers have increased 13-fold. In this context, no one should be surprised when they hear of social services crumbling. Industry and commerce likewise reel under the impact. One of the major companies in Kenya has reported a ten-fold increase in the incidence of illness and a five-fold increase in funerals among employees between 1989 and 1997.

AIDS has created over 13 million orphans, 95% of whom, over 12 million, live in sub-Saharan Africa. By 2010 UNAIDS estimates that, because of AIDS, there may be 42 million orphans in the world.

Life expectancy, already cut by AIDS in many sub-Saharan countries is expected to fall further by 2010:

Namibia	life expectancy without AIDS	70 years
	life expectancy with AIDS	39
Botswana	life expectancy without AIDS	67
	life expectancy with AIDS	38
Zambia	life expectancy without AIDS	60
	life expectancy with AIDS	38
Malawi	life expectancy without AIDS	57
	life expectancy with AIDS	35

In 16 countries in sub-Saharan Africa, more than 1 in 10 adults is infected with HIV. In 7 of these nations 1 in 5 carries the virus. Rates of infection have been recorded as follows:

Malawi	16.0%
South Africa	19.9%
Zambia	20.0%
Botswana	35.8%

In Botswana, where more than one-third of the adult population has been infected, President Mogae spoke recently of his people facing the possibility of extinction if the epidemic were to continue to spread unchecked.

AIDS has become the leading cause of death in sub-

Saharan Africa and 1,700 people are newly infected in South Africa alone every day—globally the figure is 15,000. The main cause of death:

in the world

1.	heart disease	12.7%
2.	Cerebrovascular disease	9.9%
3.	Respiratory infection	7.1%
4.	**HIV/AIDS**	**4.8%**
5.	Pulmonary disease	4.8%

in sub-Saharan Africa

1.	**HIV/AIDS**	**20.6%**
2.	Malaria	9.1%
3.	Diarrhoeal diseases	7.3%
4.	Respiratory infection	7.1%
5.	Perinatal conditions	5.9%

In some countries, particularly in southern Africa, patients with AIDS and AIDS related diseases occupy over 30% of hospital beds.

The good news is that the trend *can be* reversed. In Uganda, where the government, churches and community organisations have worked together in strong prevention campaigns, the prevalence rate has fallen from 14% in the early 1990s to 8% today. There is still a long, hard road ahead but the evidence suggests that, in Uganda, the tide may have been turned.

Nevertheless, examination of the statistics makes clear the major impact HIV has, and will continue to have, within the developing countries and regions of the world. As we know, HIV/AIDS does exist in Western Europe, North America and other areas of the "developed" world. While the numbers of infections are proportionately lower than in the rest of the world, it is important to consider the factors which make the difference in reducing the impact of the disease on our society. While high levels of education and communication contribute significantly to the low impact of HIV/AIDS in our society, the major reason for the differential is the wealth which allows those with HIV to be treated with expensive drugs. For example, in the United States drugs to fight HIV, known as antiretrovirals, began to slow the increase in AIDS related

deaths with the introduction of AZT in 1987. That year, 16,000 died in the US while 150,000 died in sub-Saharan Africa. As the costly drugs became more effective, the death curve flattened and then plunged in the US and in other Western countries where patients and society could afford the drugs. By 1995, effective combination therapies brought an absolute decline in the number of American lives lost to AIDS. However, in sub-Saharan Africa, where very few can afford the treatment, the yearly total kept soaring, so that in 1999 just over 10,000 victims died of AIDS in the USA and 2.4 million died in sub-Saharan Africa.

At today's market prices, treating HIV/AIDS patients with antiretroviral medicines would cost more than the healthcare budgets of many developing countries. For some, including Uganda and Zimbabwe, the cost would dwarf the size of their national economies. At a cost of £8,000 per year per patient for the three-drug combination therapy, the comparison is startling:

		Switzerland	Uganda	Zimbabwe
a)	Population	7 million	21 m	12 m
b)	People with HIV	12,000	930,000	1.5 m
c)	Cost of treatment	£96 million	£7.4 billion	£12 billion
d)	Cost as % of GNP	0.06%	172%	265%
e)	Total healthcare spending as % of GNP	7.1%	1.8%	3.1%

It is in the midst of this reality that under-resourced national governments and world bodies are attempting to stem the flow of the disease on the one hand and on the other care for the victims, their families, communities and infrastructures which are crumbling around them. It would seem that dealing effectively with the factors that fuel the pandemic, because of their variety and inter-relatedness, is beyond the reach of most authorities. A major issue preventing adequate HIV prevention is the stigma attached to HIV/AIDS in many cultures. Stigma often leads to a deadly form of denial that paralyses prevention efforts. In Malawi, for example, no-one "dies of AIDS". Malawians die of a "short illness". Since 1994, 29 of Malawi's 177 members of parliament have died from "short illnesses". In addition to stigma, other factors which contribute to the spread of HIV include cultural practices, including initiation rites and multiple sexual partners, male sexual domination, the inequality of women, violence, risk taking, lack of availability and use of condoms, and injecting drug use. Within societies as a whole, poverty, lack of education, isolation and poor communication, rapid urbanisation, civil unrest, migration and inadequate health services also fuel the epidemic.

Since the disease is spread predominantly by sexual contact, there is clearly an important moral dimension to the crisis. But we should not make the false equation that everyone infected by HIV has been behaving immorally. Some have been the victims of rape, others have been infected through the unfaithfulness of a spouse, some have been accidentally infected in the course of medical treatment, others again have been forced into risky lifestyles through no choice of their own. The moral dimension is very important but it is *not* a matter of simply equating HIV infection with immorality.

There *is* need for change at the level of individual behaviour. People saying "no" to promiscuity is the single biggest factor which can arrest the spread of the disease. Use of condoms by those at risk has also been shown to have a positive impact in reducing infection rates. But there is also the wider challenge of overcoming poverty, offering educational opportunity, giving people a chance to believe in themselves—when progress is made on these fronts then the conditions in which AIDS flourishes can be reversed. Here it is necessary to appreciate that none of us are immune from AIDS in the sense that we have all played a part in creating the conditions in which it spreads and we can all play a part in reversing such conditions.

National governments, international bodies, and many non-governmental organisations are seeking to address the crisis caused by the AIDS pandemic. Education programmes and palliative care are being developed by many agencies. Is there a particular role for the church? Since the behaviour which leads to the spread of AIDS rests upon profound questions of personal and communal identity, it cannot but be a religious question. The way people understand God, and themselves in relation to

God, is one of the primary springs of the character and conduct which is determinative in the spread of HIV/AIDS. Hence there is an inescapable spiritual dimension to the crisis which the church must address, besides any contribution which it might make to medical care or sex education. Not only does this call for a place in the regular teaching and catechesis of the church but there is need for special initiatives, such as peer groups where young people can have fun together and build self-esteem without feeling that they have to prove themselves by having sex; or working to provide a better quality of care for those who are suffering as a result of the disease.

In his important book *God in AIDS* (London: SCM, 1996), Ronald Nicolson observes that "every now and then something comes along which changes the way we think about everything" and suggests that the AIDS pandemic is in this category (p. 1). The scale of the suffering which it causes and the inability of currently available resources to resist it, poses a challenge not only to social and medical science but also to theology and spirituality. "We cannot deal with AIDS without taking the spiritual dimension of life into account, and we cannot continue in a spirituality which leaves AIDS off the agenda."(p. 21) There are certainly acute questions of theodicy which must be faced: can the terrible suffering apparent in the spread of the AIDS pandemic be reconciled with belief in a gracious God with loving purposes? The "why question" is especially sharp for those who confess Christian faith. Yet Nicolson wisely leads us on from a question to which there is no accessible answer and suggests that "The right question is not 'Why?' but 'What now?' What is God doing about AIDS? What does God want us to do about AIDS?" (p. 51)

In Mark 1, we read of Jesus' encounter with a man suffering from leprosy. Here was someone who suffered from a desperate illness and who was excluded from society as a result. Not only did he have to endure the physical suffering caused by the leprosy. He was also subject to the Old Testament provision: "The person with such an infectious disease must wear torn clothes, let his hair be unkempt, cover the lower part of his face and cry out "Unclean, unclean!' As long as he has the infection he remains unclean. He must live alone; he must live outside the camp." (Leviticus 13:45–46) It was this ritual uncleanness and separation which would have been uppermost in the mind of Jesus' contemporaries when they encountered a leper. For them the remarkable thing in this incident was not only the physical healing but especially the restoration to full membership in Israel. That is why Jesus laid emphasis on the completion of the ritual sacrifice which marked the leper's renewed membership of the people of God. Those suffering from AIDS face a very similar twofold catastrophe—their physical health is crumbling and at the same time they very often face abandonment and exclusion from the wider society.

Jesus broke through all the expectations of his time when he reached out his hand and touched the man suffering from leprosy. He did so because he was filled with compassion. Throughout his ministry, he made a particular point of reaching out to those who are most vulnerable—the sick, the despised, those regarded as unclean. Can we doubt that in today's world those suffering from AIDS are a particular focus for Christ's compassion. What will the church do to give expression to that compassion?

Already, quite a number of our mission partners are involved, as doctors, nurses or community workers, in the care and treatment of AIDS patients in mission hospitals and in their communities. They put themselves at risk in order to demonstrate the love of Christ to those afflicted by the disease. Especially those who are involved in surgery know that, while they take maximum care to protect themselves, still they face a small but real risk of infection. They take that risk because they are convinced that it is the way of Christ. Following the one who was filled with compassion and who reached out to touch the man with leprosy, they lay themselves on the line in Christ's name. For the church, it is not enough to speak—there is the need to go, the need to be there, the need to be the eyes and the hands and the love of Christ to the victims of the AIDS epidemic. "Then I heard the voice of the Lord saying, 'Whom shall I send? And who will go for us?'"

Not all of us can go and offer that costly service. But we all can take this crisis to heart, we all can pray for those who are infected and those who are at risk of infection, we can all support those who go in Christ's name to offer care and education and healing. We can all make the AIDS pandemic *our problem*. Following a Lord and Saviour, who was filled with compassion and who reached out to touch the sufferer when he was confronted by disease, can we do anything less? "I tell you the truth," said Jesus, "whatever you did for one of the least of these, you did for me." What shall we in the Church of Scotland do for those who are afflicted by HIV/AIDS?

In the context of the AIDS pandemic, it is important to reassert the Christian conviction that every human being, without exception, is created in the image of God and is loved by God so much that he sent the Son into the world. Those who are stigmatised on account of their HIV-positive status may hear the good news of a Saviour who has taken away our stigma by taking it on himself. None of the ravages of AIDS can ever cancel out the image of God in the sufferers nor do they ever go beyond the reach of God's love. In the last stages of their illness AIDS sufferers are often blind, incontinent and demented yet the love of God, Creator and Redeemer, is strong enough to be with them in that dark valley. Even in torment and abandonment we can find comfort and hope through the crucified Christ who "loved us and gave himself for us". The church which bears witness to God's love in Christ has a special duty to demonstrate care and compassion towards those who are dying of AIDS in our time.

To belong to the church of Jesus Christ, is to be part of a body where "if one part suffers, every part suffers with it; if one part is honoured, every part rejoices with it." What a source of strength this is in time of need! At the same time, it lays upon each of us a responsibility "not to look only to our own interests but also to the interests of others". In the context of the HIV/AIDS epidemic, it means that no member of the church can be unaffected as so many brothers and sisters are infected with the virus. If one has AIDS, we all have AIDS. The virus has infected our body. It is a crisis which involves the whole membership of the church. "Bear one another's burdens and so fulfil the law of Christ."

In practical terms, for the Church of Scotland, this means not only reaching out to those near at hand who are directly affected but also finding meaningful ways to stand alongside partner churches in areas where the pandemic is most heavily concentrated in order to join with them in combating the spread of the disease and in caring for those who are suffering. Such involvement and action is already underway. Through the support that the Board of World Mission gives to our Partner Churches throughout the world in their anti-HIV/AIDS programmes, the Board has gained a considerable insight into the concerns and difficulties faced by the Churches and national governments in this war. Through the Guild's funding of the Livingstonia Synod AIDS Programme in Malawi (LISAP), many church members have also been able to sense a little of what the world is experiencing in the face of this pandemic. Several of our partner churches are based in countries where the AIDS pandemic is taking its heaviest toll. South Africa, Zambia and Malawi are in the eye of the storm. Thailand, India and Jamaica are also heavily affected. In their hour of need partner churches in such countries look to the Church of Scotland to stand with them and to offer succour. The Board has received requests from many of its Partner Churches for assistance in one form or another e.g. financial assistance for South Africa and Malawi for ongoing programmes, training of personnel from Ghana, funding for the establishment of new HIV/AIDS awareness programmes and the production of teaching aids for Zambia.

For the Church of Scotland to have integrity in its profession of partnership with churches in the desperate circumstances of large-scale HIV infection will mean committed and sacrificial action for the foreseeable future. It is time to develop a strategy which will engage every congregation in meaningful participation in the struggle to roll back the advance of the epidemic. There are many opportunities through which we can help to make a difference and these need to be fully explored, for example, through the production of HIV/AIDS discussion material for Kirk Sessions, Guilds, Youth Groups, Bible Study Groups etc (as has been pioneered by the Board of Social Responsibility), encouraging congregations to become actively involved with HIV/AIDS organisations at the local level and also, through the Board, supporting our Partner Churches throughout the world in their fight against the disease. Many are the contexts where it falls to the church to take the lead both in care for the sick and dying and in action to protect the vulnerable from the risk of infection. The development of concrete initiatives will enable the Church to offer at least some answer to cries like this one:

What about the little ones. The children.
Your little Angels and Saints.
Do you see their suffering Lord?
Did you see Solomon, Priscilla and James?
What about Sarah and Najjuma?
And do you remember Brenda?
She followed her mum only five months later.
What do you think about this suffering Lord?
It has not spared the innocent and weak.
Lord we have waited too long.

Now we hear in Europe and America there is
*   medication.*
It is called HAART or ARV. They swallow it free of
*   charge.*
But in Africa where we are dying in big numbers
We don't see this medication. We can't swallow it for
*   free.*
One would need about $1000 a month.
Lord you know that we don't have the dollars.
As we wait, some lives seem more important than
*   others.*
Yet you said in your eyes we are all equal.
Lord we have lost too many.

We have waited for long…., Beatrice Were

Sources:
a   Statistics: United Nation AIDS Programme.
b   Ronald Nicolson, *God in AIDS* (London: SCM, 1996).
c) "We have waited for long……, by Beatrice Were"
     BBC, The Orphaned Continent.

APPENDIX IV

Staff Selected and Preparing to take up Appointment
from 1 January 2000 to 31 December 2000

Rev Roderick Campbell
Dr Alexander Maclean
Rev Robert Mackenzie
Rev Ian Manson
Mr Michael Nolan
Miss Jane Petty

APPENDIX V

Staff Taking up Appointment between
1 January 2000 and 31 December 2000

Mr Martin Harrison, Accountant, United Church of Zambia, Zambia (ecumenical appointment)

Mr John Jaap, Locum Teacher, Tabeetha School, Jaffa, Israel

Miss Lynda Keen, Teacher, Tabeetha School, Jaffa, Israel

Rev Clarence Musgrave, Minister, St. Andrew's Church, Jerusalem, Israel

Dr Keith Russell, Medical Administrator/Co-ordinator, Joint Relief Ministry, Cairo, Egypt

Miss Helen Scott, Teacher, Ekwendeni Girls' Secondary School, Church of Central Africa Presbyterian, Malawi

New Contracts Offered between
1 January 2000 and 31 December 2000

Mrs Karen Anderson, Teacher, Tabeetha School, Jaffa, Israel

Rev Robert Calvert, Minister, The Scots International Church, Rotterdam, Netherlands

Rev John Cowie, Minister, The English Reformed Church, Amsterdam, Netherlands

Mrs Jane Fucella, Church Development Worker, Church of Christ in Thailand, Thailand

Rev Michael Fucella, Church Development Worker, Church of Christ in Thailand, Thailand

Rev Colin Johnston, Minister, Trinity United Church in Zambia, Lusaka, Zambia

Mrs Elizabeth McKee, Teacher, Murree Christian School, Pakistan

Rev Anthony McLean-Foreman, Lecturer, Theological College of Lanka, Sri Lanka

Mr John Ross, Pharmacist, United Mission to Nepal, Patan Hospital, Nepal

Miss Christine Stone, Educationalist, United Mission to Nepal, Nepal

Rev Eileen Thompson, Communication Consultant, Church of South India, Madras, India (ecumenical appointment)

Miss Irene Wilson, Teacher, Tabeetha School, Jaffa, Israel

APPENDIX VI

Staff and family members overseas
during 2000

ASIA

Church of Bangladesh

Miss Gillian Rose, Midwifery Manager, Bollobhpur Hospital (ecumenical appointment)

Rev Andrew Symonds, Theology Teacher, St Andrew's Theological Seminary, Dhaka (ecumenical appointment)

Mrs Rosemary Symonds, Dhaka Development Office (ecumenical appointment)

Rev John Bennett, Minister, Church of Bangladesh (ecumenical appointment)

Mrs Rita Bennett, Administrative Assistant, Dhaka Diocese (ecumenical appointment)

Miss Ann Tuesley, Nursing Tutor, Rajshahi (ecumenical appointment)

Church of South India

Rev Eileen Thompson, Communication Consultant, Church of South India Diocesan Office, Madras (ecumenical appointment)

United Mission to Nepal

Miss Christine Stone, Educationalist, Kathmandu
Mr John Ross, Pharmacist, Patan Hospital, Patan

Nepal Leprosy Trust

Mrs Moira Murray, Nurse, Lalgadh Hospital, Lalgadh
Mr Alasdair Murray

Church of Pakistan

Rev Paul Burgess, Lecturer, Gujranwala Theological Seminary, Gujranwala
Mrs Catherine Burgess
Mrs Elizabeth McKee, House-Parent and Teacher, Murree Christian School
Miss Helen McMillan (study leave), Teacher, United Bible Training Centre, Gujranwala
Mr Ian Murray, Teacher, Murree Christian School
Mrs Isabel Murray, PA to Director, Murree Christian School
Miss Catherine Nicol, Religious Educationalist, St Columba Christian Girls' Religious Training College, Sialkot
Mr William Seaman, Teacher, Murree Christian School
Mrs Catherine Seaman
Mr Alexander Sneddon, Diocesan Development Officer, Peshawar Diocese
Mrs Marie Sneddon, Alison, Duncan and Andrew

Sri Lanka

Rev Anthony McLean-Foreman, Lecturer, Theological College of Lanka

The Church of Christ in Thailand

Mrs Jane Fucella, Church Development Worker, Sangklaburi
Rev Michael Fucella (study leave), Church Development Worker, Sangklaburi
Rachel and Aylie

CARIBBEAN, CENTRAL AND SOUTH AMERICA

Rev Dr James Berger, Minister, Nassau
Mrs Patricia Ann Berger
Rev Douglas Jenkins, Minister, Freeport
Rev Jan Jenkins, Minister, Freeport

Bermuda

Rev Alan Garrity, Minister, Church of Scotland, Christ Church, Warwick
Mrs Elizabeth Garrity

The United Church of Jamaica and the Cayman Islands

Miss Maureen Burke, Staff Associate, Mel Nathan Institute, Kingston
Mrs Jane Dodman, Research and Training Officer, Mel Nathan Institute, Kingston
Rev Roy Dodman, Minister, Shortwood United Church, Kingston
Rev Margaret Fowler, Minister, Negril United Church, Montego Bay

Trinidad

Rev Harold Sitahal, Minister, Church of Scotland Greyfriars—St Ann's and Sangre Grande, Port of Spain
Mrs Ruth Sitahal, Richard and Roxanne

MAINLAND AND CONTINENTAL EUROPE

Belgium

Rev Stewart Lamont, Executive Secretary, Church and Society Commission, Conference of European Churches
Mrs Larisa Lamont
Rev Thomas Pitkeathly, Minister, St Andrew's Church, Brussels

France

Rev William Reid, Minister, The Scots Kirk, Paris
Mrs Esther Reid

Gibraltar and the Costa del Sol
Rev John Page, Minister, St Andrew's Church, Gibraltar and the Costa del Sol
Mrs Janet Page

Hungary
Rev Bertalan Tamas, Ecumenical Officer, Hungarian Reformed Church, Budapest
Mrs Elizabeth Tamas
Rev Kenneth MacKenzie, Minister, St Columba's Church, Budapest and Mission Partner to the Hungarian Reformed Church
Mrs Jayne MacKenzie, Mairi, Catriona, Ruaridh and Kirsty

Italy
Rev David Huie, Minister, St Andrew's Church, Rome
Mrs Margaret Huie

Malta
Rev Colin Westmarland, Minister, St Andrew's Church, Valetta

Netherlands
Rev Robert Calvert, Minister, The Scots International Church, Rotterdam
Mrs Lesley-Ann Calvert, Simeon, Zoe, Benjamin, Daniel
Rev John Cowie, Minister, The English Reformed Church, Amsterdam
Mrs Gillian Cowie, Matthew, Sarah, Ruth

Portugal
Rev Gordon Oliver, Minister, St Andrew's Church, Lisbon
Mrs Jenny Oliver

Romania
Rev Celia Kenny, Lecturer, Protestant Theological College, Cluj

Switzerland
Rev James McLeod, Minister, Calvin's Auditorium, Geneva
Mrs Marjorie McLeod

Rev Douglas Murray, Minister, The Scots Kirk, Lausanne
Mrs Sheila Murray
Rev Paraic Reamonn, World Alliance of Reformed Churches, Geneva
Mrs Rowena Reamonn

MIDDLE EAST & NORTH AFRICA

Egypt
Dr Keith Russell, Medical Administrator/Co-ordinator, Joint Relief Ministry, Cairo
Dr Lai Fun Russell, Mhairi and Katharine

Israel, Church of Scotland
in Partnership with the Diocese of Jerusalem and Middle East
Mr James Aitken, Pilgrim Co-ordinator, Jerusalem
Mrs Karen Anderson, Teacher, Tabeetha School, Jaffa
Rev Maxwell Craig, Locum Minister, St Andrew's, Jerusalem
Mrs Janet Craig
Mrs Moira Cubie, Acting Head Teacher, Tabeetha School, Jaffa
Rev John Cubie
Miss Emma Given, Manager, St. Andrew's Hospice, Jerusalem
Rev Frederick Hibbert, Minister and Director, Sea of Galilee Centre, Tiberias
Mrs Diana Hibbert
Mr John Jaap, Locum Teacher, Tabeetha School, Jaffa
Mrs Muriel Jaap
Miss Lynda Keen, Teacher, Tabeetha School, Jaffa
Mr Christopher Mottershead, Head Teacher, Tabeetha School, Jaffa
Mrs Susan Mottershead
Rev Clarence Musgrave, Minister, St. Andrew's Church, Jerusalem
Mrs Joan Musgrave
Mr Michael Nolan, Teacher, Tabeetha School, Jaffa
Mrs Margaret Nolan
Miss Irene Wilson, Teacher, Tabeetha School, Jaffa

Lebanon
Mr David Kerry, Librarian, Near East School of Theology, Beirut

SUB-SAHARAN AFRICA

Presbyterian Church of East Africa, Kenya
Rev Dr James Bryson Arthur, Theological Lecturer, Nairobi
Mrs May Arthur
Dr Elizabeth Borlase (nee Bevan), Doctor, Kikuyu Hospital
Mr Kevin Borlase
Dr Angus Grant, Doctor, Chogoria Hospital
Dr Elizabeth Grant, Rebecca and Catriona
Rev Elaine McKinnon, Lecturer, Pastoral Institute, Kikuyu
Dr Alison Wilkinson, Obstetrician/Gynaecologist, Chogoria Hospital

Church of Central Africa Presbyterian, Malawi
Mrs Lesley Balaj, Sister Tutor, Ekwendeni Hospital
Mr Nelu (Ioan) Balaj
Miss Anne Dawson, Head Teacher, Ekwendeni Girls' Secondary School
Miss Margaret Duncan, Midwifery Tutor, Ekwendeni Hospital
Miss Carol Finlay, Sister Tutor, Ekwendeni Hospital
Dr Andrew Gaston, Doctor, Ekwendeni Hospital
Mrs Felicity Gaston and Katy
Miss Helen Scott, Teacher, Ekwendeni Girls' Secondary School

The Evangelical Church of Christ in Mozambique
Rev Iain Forbes, Church Development Adviser, Nampula
Mrs Ruth Forbes
Rev Dr Leslie Milton, Lecturer, Ricatla Theological Seminary, Maputo
Miss Aileen Reid, Women and Youth Worker, Nampula

United Church of Zambia
Mr Martin Harrison, Accountant (ecumenical appointment)
Ms Bridget Kellett and Reuben
Rev Colin Johnston, Minister, Lusaka

South Africa
Rev Graham Duncan, Lecturer, Fort Hare University
Mrs Sandra Duncan, Faculty Secretary/Administrator, Fort Hare University

APPENDIX VII

Staff—Retired or Not Returning Overseas between 1 January 2000 and 31 December 2000

Pakistan
Mr Ian Murray, Teacher, Murree Christian School
Mrs Isabel Murray, PA to Director, Murree Christian School
Miss Catherine Nicol, Religious Educationalist, Sialkot

**Mainland and Continental Europe
Switzerland**
Rev James McLeod, Minister, Geneva (died 25 January 2001)

**Middle East and North Africa
Israel, Church of Scotland**
Mr James Aitken, Pilgrim Co-ordinator, Jerusalem
Rev Maxwell Craig, Locum Minister, St Andrew's Jerusalem
Mrs Moira Cubie, Acting Head Teacher, Tabeetha School, Jaffa

**Sub-Saharan Africa
Church of Central Africa Presbyterian, Malawi**
Miss Anne Dawson, Head Teacher, Ekwendeni Girls' Secondary School
Miss Margaret Duncan, Midwifery Tutor, Ekwendeni Hospital

The Evangelical Church of Christ in Mozambique
Rev Iain Forbes, Church Development Adviser, Nampula
Rev Dr Leslie Milton, Lecturer, Ricatla Theological
Seminary, Maputo
Miss Aileen Reid, Women and Youth Worker, Nampula

APPENDIX VIII

In Memoriam

	2000
Rev Thomas S Colvin, Malawi	24 February
Mr Alistair James Gordon, India	February
Rev George Buchanan, Buenos Aires, India and Bermuda	13 April
Rev James McGregor Couper, India	19 May
Miss Frances Cameron, India	27 June
Rev John Campbell Becke, India	30 June
Miss Alexa Scott, India	10 October
	2001
Rev James W McLeod, Switzerland	25 January

APPENDIX IX

Appointments

Ministers	16
Other church workers	3
(religious, education, consultancy)	
Teachers, lecturers, educationalists	20
Doctors	4
Nurses	3
Pharmacists	1
Administration	3
Community Development Workers	6
Ecumenical Appointments	7
Spouses	27
Children	22
Total Appointments	63
Total Overseas	112

APPENDIX X
Faithshare Partners 2000/2001

Rev Gabriel K Akorli, Evangelical Presbyterian Church, Ghana, parish work in the Presbytery of Perth, September 2000 to March 2001

Ms Jee Eun Choi, Presbyterian Church in the Republic of Korea, community work in the Presbytery of Lanark, September 2000 to March 2001

Rt Rev Jason S and Mrs Lydia Dharmaraj, Church of South India, Tirunelveli Diocese, parish work in the Presbytery of Falkirk, April to July 2000

Rev Sardar and Mrs Violet Ghauri, Church of Pakistan, Peshawar Diocese, Assistant Community Worker at the 'The Well' Asian Information and Advice Centre in the Presbytery of Glasgow, 1999 to 2001

Mrs Mumtaz E Gill, Church of Pakistan, Sialkot Diocese, community work in the Presbytery of Abernethy, April to August 2000

Rev Lau J Makata, Church of Central Africa Presbyterian, Blantyre Synod, parish work in the Presbytery of Shetland, August 2000 to February 2001

APPENDIX XI
Bursars 2000/2001

Dr Ladislav Benes, Evangelical Presbyterian Church of the Czech Brethren, three month intensive English Language Course, St Colm's, Edinburgh

Mrs Beatrice Boateng, Presbyterian Church of Ghana, MSc in Education, Management/Administration, University of Edinburgh

Mrs Huai Man Cing, Myanmar Council of Churches, MTh in Biblical Studies, University of Glasgow

Rev Dave Hazle, United Church of Jamaica and the Cayman Islands, 2nd year of a PhD in Christian Ethics and Practical Theology, New College, Edinburgh

Mrs Grace Kusu-Orkar, NKST – Nigeria, nominated by the WCC, MSc in Clinical Pharmacy, University of Strathclyde

Mr David Mondal, Church of Bangladesh, English and Computer studies, Telford College, Edinburgh

Rev Sylvia Kasapatu Mukuka, United Church of Zambia, Postgraduate Diploma in Pastoral Studies, University of Aberdeen

Miss Gretel Qumsieh, Roman Catholic Church in Bethlehem, PhD in Tourism, University of Strathclyde

Rev Gabriel Gai Riam, Presbyterian Church of Sudan (A), MTh/Diploma in Theology, Culture and Development, New College, Edinburgh

Rev Granmar Ignatius Sheri, Anglican Church of Kenya, nominated by the WCC, MTh/Diploma in Theology, Culture and Development, New College, Edinburgh

Ms Hung-Ni Wang, Presbyterian Church of Taiwan, MSc in Media Management, University of Stirling

Pastorally supported
Mr Joo-Seop Keum, Presbyterian Church of Korea, PhD in Third World Theology and Ecumenism, New College, Edinburgh

Rev Gin Khan Khual, Zomi Baptist Convention of Myanmar, PhD in Liberation Theology and Biblical Interpretation, University of Glasgow

APPENDIX XII
Teachers in China with the Amity Foundation

Long Term Teachers
Anne and Mick Kavanagh, Nanping Teachers' College, Guanshatian 45, Nanping, Fujian Province 353000

1998 – 2000
David Conkey, Tai'an Teachers' College, Tai'an, Shandong 271000

1998 – 2001
Richard Brunt, Shangrao Teachers' College, Shangrao, Jiangxi Province 334001

1999 – 2001
Valerie King, Juijiang Teachers' College, Juijiang, Jiangxi Province 332000

Jason Waller, Fuzhou Teachers' College, Fuzhou, Fujian Province 350011

1999 – 2002
Sarah Ker, Juijiang Teachers' College, Juijiang, Jiangxi Province 332000

Mark McLeister, Changwei Teachers' College, 65 Shangli East Road, Weifang, Shandong Province 261043

APPENDIX XIII
Scottish Churches World Exchange Volunteers starting or extending in 2001

Caroline Burdon, India
Helen Brogan, India
Lyndsay Brown, India
Martha Chester, Mauritius
Helen Curren, Malawi
Angela Dodds, Lebanon
Rosalind Elliot, Guatemala
Susan Finlayson, India
Norma Forbes, India
Jessica Gordon, Guatemala
Nicola Hardy, Guatemala
James Hudson, India
Claire Hunt, Guatemala
Nicola Jones, Malawi
Mary Kirke, Egypt
Sheila Lothian, Kenya
Mhairi Millar, India
Laura Moschini, India

Helene McLeod, Guatemala
Seumas McQuaker, Kenya
Judith Plastow, India
Elizabeth Ringhofer, Guatemala
David Roberton, India
Hamish Shepherd, India
Claudia Smitherman, India
John Martin Smith, Kenya
Nichola Souter, India
Marianne Stephen, India
Ina Stephenson, Malawi
George Stephenson, Malawi
Jean Stott, Pakistan
Gayle Sweeney, India
Clare Whiteford, Malawi
Alimay Wilson, Malawi
Alison Wraight, Guatemala
Heather Young, India

COMMITTEE ON ECUMENICAL RELATIONS

MAY 2001

PROPOSED DELIVERANCE

The General Assembly:

1. Receive the Report and thank the Convener, Vice-Convener and Committee members for their work.

2. Encourage Presbyteries to promote the new Ecumenical Relations video and study booklet entitled 'Patterns of Partnership'. (par. 1.1)

3. Approve the appointment of Rev Marjory Maclean to the talks on Church Union (3.4.1)

4. Commend the possibility of twinning with Church of Norway congregations as a means of strengthening ties within the Leuenberg Fellowship of Churches. (4.10)

5. Commend that the WCC's Decade to Overcome Violence should become part of all agendas within the Church. (4.11)

6. Approve the appointment of delegates to other churches' assemblies, synods and conferences as listed in Appendix I.

7. Approve the appointment of representatives to Ecumenical Bodies listed in Appendix II.

8. Approve the membership contributions to Ecumenical Bodies for 2002 as detailed in Appendix III.

REPORT
PATTERNS OF PARTNERSHIP

1. Local Partnerships

"We have discovered, through experience, that we can actually achieve more together than we can individually. But more than that, it is not just that we can achieve more—we can actually achieve it better." (St Andrew's, Carlisle)

1.1. Planning for the Millennium provided an incentive for local congregations to discover that they could work more effectively together. The Committee on Ecumenical Relations was delighted to be able to produce its first video together with a study booklet—**Patterns of Partnership**. Six stories of ecumenical good practice have been used as the basis of five studies, each exploring different aspects of ecumenism and showing the wide variety of partnerships that are possible. Urban and rural, urban priority area and settled community, hospitality, co-

operation and union—all feature in the video and raise their own set of questions while conveying the excitement of those involved in grass roots ecumenism. It is planned that the video will be distributed free of charge through ecumenical and education contacts in Presbyteries and Presbyterial Councils and to every congregation in order that it will be widely used.

1.2 Visits to groups of Presbyteries continue as the Committee seeks both to support ecumenical officers and ecumenical presbytery contacts and to gather a clearer picture of the diversity of local ecumenism. In many places there has been a move away from restricting ecumenical contact to a few well-worn events during the year to more regular contact and, sometimes, local projects. The presbytery ecumenical officers and contacts play a vital role in ecumenical thinking and practice at local level and in ensuring that stories are told as widely as possible for the encouragement and inspiration of all. At their annual conference the ecumenical officers and contacts agreed to submit an annual report. This will enable the Committee to keep abreast of ecumenical developments across the country and assist it in its work of sharing stories and information.

"If the churches can't work together it is very hard to say that we can work with anybody else." (Drumchapel)

1.3   Rural ecumenism is deservedly emerging into the limelight. The conversations recorded in Colonsay and Lochaline for the video are just two examples of the growing number of stories that have been told from places as far apart as the Presbyteries of the south west (Ayr, Annandale & Eskdale, Dumfries & Galloway and Wigtown & Stranraer), the north east (Buchan and Gordon) and the west (Dunoon and South Argyll). The offering of the gift of ecumenical hospitality is proving an increasingly exciting way of breaking down the barriers and learning about each other's traditions.

"One would hope to maintain one's religion. And in the absence of a priest or (the) Mass, one would still wish to worship." (Colonsay)

1.4   New initiatives are being explored, also in different parts of the country, and old ones are being reviewed to take into account new developments in housing. In the former category, Barrhead Churches used the year 2000 to move slowly and carefully towards the setting up of a shadow joint structure which, if it proves workable and acceptable to the churches, will become a prototype maxi-parish as outlined in the Scottish Church Initiative for Union *Interim Report*. Of the more established ecumenical partnerships, Livingston Ecumenical Parish is being reviewed. The Sponsors' Council is among those who are taking part in a consultation initiated by the Board of National Mission. For a number of years now Mid Craigie Parish Church and St Ninian's Episcopal Church in Dundee have been seeking to have their relationship on the ground confirmed through legislation. Unfortunately, despite much effort, this has not proved

possible. The Sponsors' Council continues to work with the congregations, offering encouragement and support.

"… feeling part of the one Church of God … is something that some people are born with because of their background, and other people learn …" (St Andrew's)

2. National Partnerships

2.1   Though there are no grounds for complacency, the amount of work being done with ecumenical intent and conviction is undoubtedly increasing. Consultation with other Boards and Committees shows an increasing amount of work being done with ecumenical sensitivity. The Committee also welcomed initiatives that have involved genuinely ecumenical appointments, where representatives of other churches are equal partners throughout the process. In the past year National Mission, World Mission, Parish Education, Doctrine, Worship & Artistic Matters, Education and the Guild each presented papers and shared discussion with the Committee's Liaison Team about aspects of their work.

2.2   The Committee has also been invited to be part of other consultations. In the past year, we have been consulted by the Special Commission anent Review and Reform, the Assembly Council, the Board of Ministry's Admissions and Readmissions Committee, the Inter Board Committee on Presbytery Boundaries, Parish Education's Youth Ministry Development Worker and contributions have been made to the Co-ordinating Forum.

2.3   The launch of the Scottish Churches Community Trust provided an excellent stage to show the Church of Scotland in partnership with other Churches in Scotland working together to make a difference amongst Scotland's poorest people.

2.4   The centenary of the Edinburgh World Missionary Conference in 1910 is now less than a decade away. While events will be planned in different parts of the world, and many will concentrate on world mission today, the interest of Ecumenical Relations has been registered. The

1910 Conference was a significant step along the way of the emerging modern ecumenical movement and it is important that this dimension is not neglected as plans are set for the decade ahead.

3. Patterns of Inter Church Partnerships

3.1 **Reformed Churches in Britain & Ireland.** Plans were laid for a consultation between the Presbyterian Church in Ireland, the Presbyterian Church of Wales, the Church of Scotland and the United Reformed Church who hosted the event in March 2001. The consultation allowed four churches of very different size, history and ecumenical conviction to explore matters of common interest.

3.2 **The Church of England.** Plans for a bilateral meeting in 2001 had to be postponed, once again, because of difficulty in finding suitable dates. In the meantime, an invitation was received from the Church of England's Council for Christian Unity to hold exploratory talks to see if it would be possible to draw up a doctrinal agreement along similar lines to that of the Reuilly Common Statement between the Anglican Churches in Britain and Ireland and the French Lutheran and Reformed Churches. The Reuilly Common Statement is based on fundamental agreement in faith, a common understanding of the nature and purpose of the Church, and convergence on the apostolicity of the church and its ministry. It builds on a former Agreement, the Meissen Agreement of 1988, between the Church of England and the Evangelical Church in Germany, which contains Lutheran, Reformed and United Churches. With a growing number of Agreements established between Anglicans and our partners in the Reformed Churches, it is only right that we look at the possibility of squaring the circle. The Committee on Ecumenical Relations and the Panel on Doctrine are to be part of the initial consultation. In accepting the invitation, we have made it clear to the Church of England that, should we decide to draw up such a document, both the Scottish Episcopal Church and the United Reformed Church should be partners in the process.

3.3 **The Roman Catholic Church.** The first meeting of the new Joint Commission on Doctrine met in September. It was agreed to focus on two areas in the next two years—Baptism and Christian Initiation, and Christian Anthropology. Both topics pick up on the current agenda of the Joint Working Group between the World Council of Churches (WCC) and the Roman Catholic Church. In the first topic, the relationship between baptism and church membership will be explored. This will be done at a meeting in 2001. Papers are being commissioned from both churches for an exploration of Christian Anthropology for a more extended consultation in 2002. The Joint Commission afforded us useful space to discuss with the Roman Catholic representatives the publication of the controversial document from the Congregation of the Doctrine of the Faith, *Dominus Iesus*.

3.4 **Scottish Church Initiative for Union.** The SCIFU Group as a whole and the Church of Scotland representatives in particular were shocked by the sudden death of Duncan McClements in September. In his inimitable style Duncan had won the respect and affection of all those engaged in the discussions. His sharpness of mind, deep knowledge and understanding of the Church he loved and seemingly boundless energy helped to drive the discussions, keeping the momentum going towards the envisaged goal. He is sorely missed as the negotiations continue.

3.4.1 The Committee on Ecumenical Relations gave consideration to restoring the Church of Scotland delegation to its complement of four members. At this stage in the negotiations it was felt necessary to include someone who had specific knowledge and expertise in the history of the Church of Scotland at the beginning of the twentieth century in relation to the formation of the Articles Declaratory and who also had an overview of current practice within the Church, including the possibility of changes. The Committee is pleased to nominate Rev Marjory Maclean, Depute Principal Clerk.

3.4.2 The SCIFU Group has undertaken a thorough

revision of Appendices I–III published with the *Second Interim Report*. The three original appendices were examples of working papers before the SCIFU Group. These revisions took into account responses to the *First Interim Report* and advice from our own Reflection Panel. As these texts have been agreed by the SCIFU Group, they have been circulated to ecumenical officers and contacts in presbyteries for their information and use. Representatives from both the SCIFU Group and the Reflection Panel have taken part in local discussions of the *Second Interim Report*.

3.4.3 The Reflection Panel has continued to give advice and guidance to the Church of Scotland representatives on the SCIFU Group. The Panel is clear that SCIFU is not fundamentally about structures but about mission. Along with other Committees and Commissions, it addresses the question of what kind of Church would best suit Scotland. The Panel expressed concern about the difficulties of different groups addressing similar questions with perhaps insufficient collaboration between them. It strongly encouraged a continuation and intensifying of internal collaboration between groups so that an integrated picture could be painted through reports to the General Assembly. The Church resembles a jigsaw of many pieces, each in its own way of vital importance to the whole picture. The Reflection Panel felt that in this conversation, if the SCIFU piece were to be taken away, an important part of the wider process in which the Church is engaged would be missing.

4. Partners in Ecumenical Bodies

4.1 **Action of Churches Together in Scotland (ACTS).** A growing sense of dissatisfaction with the way the Commissions and Committees of ACTS work led first to a calling together of all those who represent the Church of Scotland on these Commissions and Committees. They shared their feelings and frustrations with Kevin Franz, the General Secretary of ACTS, and Lesley Macdonald, one of the Associate Secretaries. This was part of a wider process of questioning the extent to which ACTS was failing to realise its potential. The Central Council took up the issue in its October meeting and appointed a small group to bring forward specific proposals about the core work of ACTS, its location and its staffing.

4.2 Plans have progressed for the first **Scottish Ecumenical Assembly**, which will take place in Edinburgh in September 2001. A small, but enthusiastic implementation group was set up to flesh out the vision and the churches have been invited to make nominations. The Church of Scotland has been allocated 90 places. The theme: *Breaking New Ground* will be explored in seven sub-themes. Every effort has been made to ensure the widest possible representation from all areas of church life. We have also submitted suggestions for agencies and people who might be identified as 'Partners and Communities in the Nation'. The expectation is that by next year the fruits of the Assembly will constitute a visible part of the on-going work of the Church of Scotland as it takes forward a common agenda for the churches' mission in Scotland in future years, based on ecumenical priorities identified at the Ecumenical Assembly.

4.3 **Churches Together in Britain & Ireland (CTBI).** The Church Representatives' Meeting (CRM) met for the first time outside London when it came to Glasgow in April 2000. This provided an opportunity for the Scottish Churches, co-ordinated by ACTS, to share something of our context and our ecumenical journeying. This more in-depth opportunity, drawing in people outside the membership of the CRM, created a greater interest and more informed discussion. The commitment is that the spring meeting of the CRM should be in a different part of Britain and Ireland so that we get a genuine feel for the diversity of our nations. The meeting in spring 2001 was in Wales.

4.4 **Churches Together in England (CTE).** Contacts with CTE continue to be sustained through the Presbytery of England. The millennium work throughout the year 2000 gave CTE a higher profile than it has had thus far. There are now questions about how the experience gained can be followed through to keep the momentum alive. It is hoped that liturgical material will be produced for use throughout England for celebrations of the Queen's Golden Jubilee.

4.5 Throughout the year too, CTE has been in negotiation with the Free Churches Council about entering into 'a collaborative agreement'. A 'Free Churches Group' will continue the work of the Council which brings together both large and small 'free' Churches in England and also a small number in Wales. It also allows space for those churches which are members of the Free Churches Council and not of CTE. Following acceptance of the *Proposed Mode of Implementation* by both bodies, a Joint Operating Agreement will be drawn up, describing in greater detail the intended ways of working. It is planned that CTE will move into the offices of the Free Churches Council.

4.6 Conference of European Churches (CEC). CEC continues its work, despite immense financial difficulties. The *Charta Oecumenica*, an ecumenical charter requested at the Second European Ecumenical Assembly in Graz in 1997, ran into difficulties. The Orthodox Churches were not happy with the text and many Protestant Churches expressed unease in the wake of the publication of *Dominus Iesus*. A revised document was then prepared by the Committee. It was agreed that the revised document would be sent out to member churches with a letter explaining that 'the Charta is being transmitted to the churches for their reception, study, implementation and, if necessary, adaptation to their particular national and local contexts.' The letter would be jointly signed by the Presidents of CEC and the Council of European Episcopal Conferences (CCEE) of the Roman Catholic Church at a special Ecumenical Encounter in April 2001. The Ecumenical Encounter would bring together in Strasbourg the CEC Central Committee, other European Church leaders and one hundred young people from across the continent. The Church of Scotland was invited to send a young person.

4.7 The next CEC Assembly is to take place in Trondheim, Norway from 3–9 September 2003, provided the money for it is in place. The theme will be *Jesus Christ Heals and Reconciles: Our Witness in Europe.*

4.8 The World Alliance of Reformed Churches (WARC). A particular focus for WARC in 2000 was the unrest in Indonesia, particularly the Moluccas. The new General Secretary, Setri Nyomi, has settled into his position. The date for the next General Council was fixed for 2004 in Accra, Ghana, with the theme *That all have life in fullness*. Attempts to run a parallel meeting with the Lutheran World Federation failed, as did a suggestion that Confessional bodies like WARC might form a part of the next General Assembly of the WCC. WARC hopes that all member churches will participate in preparation for the General Council so that it is not simply an event for those who attend when the time comes. More information is expected during this year. In the meantime, plans for the next European Area Council are being progressed. A request to run the Area Council in some kind of association with the next CEC Assembly proved too difficult. However, the financial pressure on the churches in the face of so many ecumenical assemblies is such that the European Area Committee has agreed to hold a reduced-number Area Council i.e. two representatives per member Church. The Area Council will take place in Romania in September 2002.

4.9 The European Area Committee continues to look at the role of minority churches, particularly in relation to the state. Theological reflection continues on the particular contribution to ecumenical debate of reformed theology.

4.10 The Leuenberg Fellowship of Churches. The Convener represented the Church of Scotland in Molde, Norway, when the Church of Norway signed the Leuenberg Concordat, the first Nordic Lutheran Church to do so. This gives the Church of Scotland the opportunity to strengthen the links that already exist with the Church of Norway. A request has been made in particular for increased twinning arrangements between congregations. The Committee on Ecumenical Relations is happy to commend this to the Church. It is anticipated that the Church of Denmark will sign the Concordat later in 2001.

4.11 World Council of Churches (WCC). The Church of Scotland continues to be involved in the work of the Council through the Central Committee and representatives on Advisory Groups and Commissions. Boards and Committees of the Church were asked to respond to a preliminary paper from the World Council aimed at mapping what work churches are already engaged in that in some way confronts violence or seeks to build a culture of peace. The responses are printed in Appendix IV. The WCC's **Decade to Overcome Violence** was launched in February 2001 at the meeting of the Central Committee in Potsdam, Germany. The Church of Scotland is involved in initiatives to co-ordinate work in ACTS and CTBI. It is hoped that throughout the Decade the work of the Church at local and national level will be done against the constant backdrop of the commitment of the churches to work together to overcome violence.

4.12 In December 2000, the WCC hosted the launch of the **Advocacy Alliance**. The Alliance is wider than the WCC and includes Regional Ecumenical Organisations like CEC, Confessional bodies like WARC and some international Aid agencies. The request to set up such an Alliance came from churches in the wake of the successful campaigns to Ban Landmines and Jubilee 2000. Churches were asked to say whether or not they supported the proposal and to suggest areas of priority where concerted action by churches and their partner organisations could make a difference. The Board of World Mission and the Committee on Church and Nation were consulted and a response prepared. The problem of globalism and its effect on trade was the one aspect the Church of Scotland chose to highlight. We were clearly not alone. When the Alliance was launched two primary issues were identified: Global Economic Justice with a focus on global trade and the Ethics of Life with a specific focus on HIV/AIDS. Peace and conflict resolution was identified as urgent concerns for all, but it was felt that the WCC Decade to Overcome Violence will allow many of these issues to be addressed.

5. Patterns of Partnership with Other Faith Communities

The Committee on Ecumenical Relations holds a co-ordinating role for inter faith relations in the Church of Scotland. It hosts an interdepartmental *Inter Faith Forum* to reflect on the Church's work in an increasingly inter faith context. The Forum agreed to the setting up of a project which would be done in partnership with the Churches Agency for Inter-Faith Relations in Scotland and the Department of Christianity in the Non-Western World at New College. Funding is being sought in order to gather stories of the experiences of ministers in relation to people of other faith communities. It is clear that more and more questions are being asked as we become more and more a multi-faith society. Many ministers feel isolated in their work: through the hearing and sharing of stories it is hoped to show both the positive and less positive sides to living with other faith communities, and through this to help create a network of people who are working in similar situations.

6. As we commit ourselves to a Decade to Overcome Violence, it is perhaps time to reflect on the words of Hans Küng:

"Ecumenical dialogue is today anything but the speciality of a few starry-eyed religious peaceniks. For the first time in history, it has now taken on the character of an urgent desideratum for world politics. It can help to make our earth more liveable, by making it more peaceful and more reconciled.

There will be no peace among the peoples of this world without peace among the world religions.

There will be no peace among world religions without peace among the Christian churches.

The community of the Church is an integral part of the world community.

Ecumenism ad intra, concentrated on the Christian world, and ecumenism ad extra, orientated toward the whole inhabited earth, are interdependent. Peace is indivisible: it begins with us."

(Hans Küng, *Christianity and the World Religions* (Collins, Londond, 1985), p. 443)

In the name of the Committee

THOMAS MACINTYRE, *Convener*
SUSAN BROWN, *Vice-Convener*
SHEILAGH M KESTING, *Secretary*

ADDENDUM

The Committee notes that Rev Susan Brown completes her term as Vice-Convener of the Committee. The Committee is grateful to her for the freshness and vitality she brought to its work. The Committee recognises that this was given cheerfully at a time when the challenge of a new charge was making heavy demands on her time, yet she ably supported the Convener and shared in opportunities to represent the interests of the Committee both within the Church of Scotland and beyond. She also encouraged the staff in their work. Her enthusiasm and quick wit will be missed by all involved in Ecumenical Relations.

In the name of the Committee

THOMAS MACINTYRE, *Convener*
SHEILAGH M KESTING, *Secretary*

APPENDIX I

DELEGATES TO OTHER CHURCHES

The following have been appointed as delegates to the Assemblies, Synods and or Conferences of other Churches:-

Presbyterian Church in Ireland –
  The Moderator, Chaplain and Elder
Presbyterian Church of Wales –
  Rev S Kesting

United Reformed Church –
  The Moderator, Chaplain and Rev T Macintyre
Church of England –
  Rev H Davidson
United Reformed Church Scotland Synod –
  Rev S Blythe
Scottish Episcopal Church –
  Dr A Elliot
Methodist Synod –
  Rev R Mitchell
United Free Church of Scotland –
  Rev P Graham
Baptist Union of Scotland –
  Rev D Lunan

APPENDIX II

ECUMENICAL BODIES

The following serve on assemblies and committees of the ecumenical bodies of which the Church is a member:-

World Council of Churches
Eighth Assembly (September 1998)
  Rev G Elliot, Rev N Shanks, Mrs C Tait, Mrs V Ott, Rev Dr R Page
Central Committee
  Rev N Shanks
Faith and Order Commission
  Rev Dr P H Donald

World Alliance of Reformed Churches
23rd General Council (August 1997)
  Rev S Cowell, Miss J Martin, Mr C Miller, Rev M Miller, Rev Prof G Newlands
Europe Committee
  Rev S M Kesting, Mr C Miller

Conference of European Churches
Eleventh Assembly and Second European
  Dr W Blair, Dr A Elliot,
Ecumenical Assembly (June 1997)
  Rev S M Kesting, Rev B Robertson

Central Committee
Dr A Elliot
Church and Society Commission
Dr A Elliot

Churches Together in Britain and Ireland
Assembly
Rev D B Anderson, Rev P Beautyman, Rev D Brown, Rev W Brown, Rev M Cuthbertson, Mrs Margaret Foggie, Mrs K Galloway, Rev J Gibson, Mrs F S Gordon, Mrs H Hughes, Mrs E Kerr, Rev S Kesting, Rev M Macaskill, Rev Dr F A J Macdonald, Rev T Macintyre, Rev G Maclean, Rev F Marshall, Rev M Millar, Rev S Mitchell, Mrs A Newell, Rev D A O Nicol, Rev K Petrie, Rev J Purves, Rev Prof K Ross, Rev M Scott, Rev D Shaw, Rev F M Stewart, Mrs P Stewart, Mrs A Twaddle, Mrs L Wright, Mrs J Young
Church Representatives Meeting
(Vacancy), Rev S M Kesting, Rev Dr F A J Macdonald
Steering Committee
Rev Dr F A J Macdonald
Finance Committee
Mr F Marsh

Action of Churches Together in Scotland
Central Council
Rev W Brown, Dr A Elliot (vice-convener), Miss H Hughes, Rev S M Kesting, Rev Dr F A J Macdonald, Rev T Macintyre, Rev F Marshall, Rev S Mitchell, Rev D A O Nicol, Rev D Shaw, Mrs P Stewart, Mrs A Twaddle
Commission on Unity, Faith and Order
Rev Dr I R Boyd, Rev Dr P H Donald, Rev M MacLean, Rev Dr J L McPake, Mrs E Templeton, (vacancy)
Commission on Mission, Evangelism and Education
Rev J H Brown, Rev E Cranfield, Mrs N Dinnes, Rev A Greig, Rev C Sinclair, Mr I Whyte
Commission on Justice, Peace, Social and Moral Issues
Rev Y Atkins, Dr D Bruce, Rev E Cramb, Miss M Donaldson, Rev A McDonald, Rev Dr D Sinclair

Committee on Communication
Mr R J Williamson
Finance Committee
Mrs V Dickson
Committee on Local and Regional Unity
Miss M Cameron, Mrs N Summers (vacancy)
Network of Ecumenical Women in Scotland
Rev V Allen, Mrs E McVie
Committee on Scottish Churches House
Rev A A Moore (vacancy)
Youth Action
Mr R Hunter, Mr S Mallon

Churches Commission on Mission
Mrs F Campbell, Rev E Cranfield, Rev Prof A Main, Rev K L Petrie, Rev D A O Nicol, Rev Prof K Ross

Joint Liturgical Group
The Very Rev G I Macmillan, Rev D Galbraith

APPENDIX III

CONTRIBUTIONS TO ECUMENICAL BODIES

	2001	2002
	£	£
Action of Churches Together in Scotland	130,303	134,212
Churches Together in Britain and Ireland	57,953	59,692
World Council of Churches	38,192	39,338
World Alliance of Reformed Churches	19,176	19,751
Conference of European Churches	16,968	17,477
Churches Together in England	290	299
	262,882	270,769

APPENDIX IV

DECADE TO OVERCOME VIOLENCE

A response to the WCC from the Church of Scotland

The initiative of the WCC in launching the Decade is welcomed, particularly in the breadth of its scope. From the point of view of our Church's woman's organisation, The Guild, there is appreciation that the horizons have been widened beyond the narrow focus of violence against women.

1. **What issues of overcoming violence does your church need to address?**

We wish first to acknowledge those areas that are currently being addressed or have been addressed in the recent past.

- Local churches provide places to meet for coffee, discussion & action, which provide safety away from violent or potentially violent (domestic) situations.
- The Board of National Mission encourages the role of the local church in providing pastoral care for victims of violence, sometimes taking the role of mediator, and sometimes participating in community groups and councils.
- The Church of Scotland encourages inter-faith co-operation in order to lessen racial violence. Its Board of National Mission set up an advice centre for people in the Asian community in Glasgow called The Well. In the next three years The Guild is to be promoting six projects, some of which will have a reconciliation aspect to them, including support for the Well.
- Building bridges within the community for religious tolerance through different Christian traditions working together. Scotland is wrestling with a nascent sectarianism which surfaces from time to time, particularly in the West.
- The Board of National Mission ensures the provision of chaplains, drawn from various church traditions, in prisons. In this way the Gospel of Jesus Christ is shared with those who have offended against society.
- Through its Church & Nation Committee, the Church of Scotland continues to voice and demonstrate its opposition to nuclear weapons in general and Trident in particular. This Committee is involved in trying to set up a seminar with military personnel and politicians with the churches, in the spring of 2001, on alternatives to spending on weapons of mass destruction.
- The Committee on Church & Nation has under review the development of the death penalty worldwide.
- The General Assembly of the Church of Scotland has welcomed the work done by Vashti, Scottish Christian Women against Violence, which is supported by the Guild and others within the Church with a concern about the levels of domestic violence in Scottish society both within and outside the Church.
- The Church & Nation Committee is involved in work on economic violence. This is done through the Scottish Churches Social Inclusion Network and the WTO Alliance. Attention has been focused on the need to eradicate poverty as a necessary part of overcoming violence. The Board of World Mission has also done work in this area and has helped to keep the issues before the Church. It is expected that the World Alliance of Reformed Churches' study of the *Professus Confessionis* on economic justice will also become part of our on-going thinking in this area.
- The Board of Social Responsibility, the Department of Education and the Church & Nation Committee will be considering a response to a consultation document of the Scottish Executive of the Scottish Parliament on the physical punishment of children.
- The Church & Nation Committee has responded positively to a request to nominate someone to be a member of the Management Committee of the Scottish Centre for Nonviolence.
- The Church & Nation Committee continues to study the effect of NATO bombing on the Balkans, attempting to build links of understanding with other groups closer to that area.
- A number of Boards and Committees of the Church work together under the general leadership of the Church & Nation Committee to ensure that matters of racial justice are kept before the Church.

It is accepted that the Church itself must acknowledge its part in these situations. For too long the Church has turned a blind eye to the pervasiveness of domestic violence in society at large and has failed to speak out against it in public. By saying nothing the Church is seen to condone. The Gender Attitude Project (GAP - see below) recognises that violence, both physical and emotional, is sadly a common feature of our society and, to our shame, it is be found within church families and communities as well. GAP hopes to raise awareness within the Church and to ensure that the issue becomes something, which the Church will continue to address with energy and commitment.

Areas where the Church of Scotland could be doing more are:

- Encouraging study groups to look at the whole paradigm of violence and its many manifestations, locally, nationally and culturally and how these affect the total consciousness and lifestyle of those involved.
- Affirming the importance of seeking to reflect the grace and love of God in attitude, actions and lifestyles.
- The Church of Scotland has a Gender Attitude Project (GAP) which was set up to keep before the Church issues relating to the community of women and men. The Group tries to encourage people within the Church to look at practices, structures and underlying attitudes, which prevent all people from playing a full part in the service of the Church according to their abilities and desires. There is plenty of evidence that tradition, habit and established and unchallenged attitudes are still present as far as the roles of women and men are concerned.
- GAP also seeks to encourage more discussion about issues of violence against women and children until the Church is in a position to take a lead in making such painful matters unacceptable either in our own society or in other parts of the world.
- Gap is commissioning research about the climate in the Church in regard to gender roles, sexist attitudes, awareness of the powerlessness of women and so on.

2. **What efforts, resources, opportunities would your church like to contribute to the Decade to Overcome Violence?**

- The Church of Scotland's Society, Religion and technology Project encourages members to undertake an environmental audit and as a result perhaps reduce violence against creation. This same project is taking an interest in genetically modified food and crops.
- The Netherbow Arts Centre which is run by the Church of Scotland, is a community, national and international project. The use of media, including story-telling could highlight to the need for reconciliation and peace.
- Work done in encouraging people in Urban Priority Areas to live their lives as a witness of God's love. In these areas the community is subjected to violence on a wide variety of levels, some of which is a direct result of policy decisions taken outside those communities.
- There is the promotion of partnerships and events between different types of congregations throughout the country e.g. rural, Urban Priority Area, suburban. These help people of faith to begin to understand the reality behind the stories of violence.
- There are attempts to increase understanding of various peace movements. The Guild looks certain to have a Discussion Topic for 2001-2002, which will revolve around peace and peace-making.
- GAP has worked over the past few years to raise awareness of sexism within the Church, running workshops, producing a leaflet inviting churches to seek more information or help, requesting gender specific statistics to be produced with regard or ministers and office-bearers. It is now beginning to hold discussions with the Boards and Committees of the Church on these issues.

The Guild discussion topic is designed to involve members in discussion of an issue importance and with a view to some local action being taken where a need can be identified. It is possible that there will be opportunities to include some of the questions raised by the WCC in the Topic Guidelines.

3. **What do you hope will be achieved by the decade to Overcome Violence?**

- Biblical reflection on the theme of *shalom* in which people learn from each other and show the preference for peace, reconciliation and conflict resolution, implying a rejection of violence and hate. (A Project on the 'Peace Line' in Northern Ireland is instanced as an example)
- The creation of a desire to overcome barriers and cross boundaries by bringing different groups of people together to improve communication, develop dialogue, engage in listening, solve problems by negotiation, despite difficulties involved.
- The encouragement of a preference for community fellowship and working together rather than a competitive individualism: a faith that together we can achieve change.
- A seeking to create a consciousness, platform and forum where new and healthier attitudes can be embraced.
- Promotion of study, exchange visits, cross-cultural communication but always endeavouring to take it to a local level.
- A hope that people will feel less isolated if victims and more tolerant if perpetrators, of violence.

The Church of Scotland's Board of National Mission supports all peace-making efforts and re-affirms its belief in the life-changing power of Jesus Christ as the ultimate answer to violence in the human heart. But it does make a caveat that there should not be an overreaction to the issues involved. For example, it singles out the suggestion that there should be a challenge to educational systems that promote competition between children. It suggests that it is one thing to oppose violence and another to oppose innocent competition.

DEPARTMENT OF EDUCATION

MAY 2001

PROPOSED DELIVERANCE

The General Assembly

1. Receive the report.

2. Concerned at the continuing problem of disruptive behaviour in the classroom encourage the Committee to continue to monitor the situation. **(2.1)**

3. Encourage the Education Committee to seek to ensure the continuing place of Religious Education in the school curriculum and in consultation with teachers to produce resources on Christianity and on the Church of Scotland appropriate for different levels. **(2.2)**

4. Urge the Committee to continue conversations with members of the Scottish Executive responsible for Health and Sex Education in order to press for:

   a) the production of good exemplars which illustrate how parents can work in partnership with schools. **(10.2)**

   b) the inclusion in any school curriculum of an appreciation of the value of commitment in relationships and partnerships, the responsibilities of parenthood and the value placed on marriage by religious groups and others in Scottish society. **(10.3)**

5. Instruct the Committee:

   a) to make representations to the review of Initial Teacher Education.

   b) to monitor the funding of teacher education courses by the Scottish Higher Education Funding Council (SHEFC). **(7.1)**

6. Encourage the Committee to continue to seek ways of supporting chaplaincy in Scottish Colleges. **(8)**

REPORT

1. Introduction

In 1824 the General Assembly " *...unanimously agreed that a Committee be appointed to enquire, and to Report to next Assembly, as to an advisable plan for the Church to adopt, for increasing the means of Education and of Religious Instruction throughout Scotland in general, where it may be needed, but particularly in the Highlands and Islands, and in large and populous Cities and Towns; and, that the Committee be instructed, after collecting, and digesting the relative facts, to take what proper and prudent measures may be in their power to learn, for the information and direction of the ensuing Assembly, what degree of co-operation may reasonably be expected from Heritors and others in the different districts of the country; and whether also, and in what manner, Government may be disposed to give public aid .... ".* Since then the Committee has sought through resourcing and by critical appraisal to advance education and religious education in schools in Scotland. With the passing of the years methods and rationales may have changed but the concerns remain the same. The main thrust of the Committee's work continues to focus on ensuring that the Church's voice is heard both at local and at national level by Church and Government alike. Some 177 years on it is interesting to note that certain issues do not change - the needs of all children, the provision of sufficient funding, religious education, the moral standards of the nation, the training of teachers, the education of pupils for active and responsible citizenship and the equipping of young people for life, all concerns of the Church in these early days, remain some of the main issues today as will be seen from the examples of the work covered by the Committee this year. (See also APPENDIX B)

2. Correspondence with Local Authorities and the Scottish Executive

2.1 Disruptive Pupils and Exclusion

2.1.1   Aware that the continuing difficulties teachers are facing in handling disruptive pupils and the effect these pupils have on the education of other pupils remain a matter of concern, the General Assembly last year instructed its Education Committee to call on Local Authorities to ensure that their policies with regard to indiscipline and disruptive behaviour were fully implemented and to take the necessary appropriate steps to deal with and eradicate incidents of violence, physical and verbal. In the light of this all Directors of Education in Scotland were written to seeking assurance that their policies with regard to indiscipline and disruptive behaviour were being fully implemented and expressing the desire that they should take the necessary appropriate steps to deal with and eradicate incidents of violence, physical and verbal.
A similar letter on behaviour in the classroom was also sent to the Minister responsible for school education at that time, Mr Sam Galbraith.

2.1.2   Responses to date from Local Authorities express an awareness of the seriousness of disruptive behaviour in the classroom and a continuing commitment to eradicating the problem and to making appropriate provision for pupils with emotional and behavioural difficulties. Many have set up support services (such as Inclusions Support Co-ordinators and extra Classroom Assistants) to create alternatives to exclusion strategies. However it is evident that disruptive behaviour is still a pressing issue in many areas and the Scottish Executive have made it clear that they intend to take further steps. In the meantime the Committee intends to visit a number of schools to find out what the position is in local situations.

2.2 Religious and Moral Education in the Curriculum

2.2.1   In the same letter Directors were asked to give assurances that with the introduction of Health Education and Personal and Social Development into the same curricular area as Religious and Moral Education in the 5 – 14 programme the time presently allocated to Religious and Moral Education as stated in Circular 6/91 would be protected. Replies received so far indicate that most authorities do not foresee any erosion of the recommended curricular time however the Committee will continue to monitor the issue. It may be that the new approach will allow a degree of flexibility which will enhance the delivery of all subjects.

2.2.2   The very full and comprehensive reply from the minister covering both Classroom Behaviour and the time allocation for Religious and Moral Education is attached to the report as Appendix A.

3. Training Meetings for School Chaplains

A number of successful conferences has been held throughout the year. These have included those involved in Primary and/or Secondary sectors. The Committee would like to express its appreciation of the co-operation of Presbyteries and Local Authorities in helping to arrange these. In most cases school staff, often headteachers, have attended and the discussions which have taken place between staff and chaplains have contributed greatly to the usefulness of the conferences.

4. Church Representation on Local Authority Committees with Responsibility for Education

The Committee continues to regard the work done by its representatives as of great importance able as they are to speak for the Church and to the Church on educational issues. Nineteen out of thirty two church representatives met with members of the Assembly's Education Committee at Scottish Churches House, Dunblane on Monday 18th September for a two-day residential conference. This was the second time that such an extended meeting for church representatives had been held and the whole concept was well received by all who attended. One of the most important topics discussed was the reorganisation of local authorities following recommendations of the McIntosh Commission. While up until now representatives are being allocated places on whatever new committees have been appointed to deal with education matters it is important that the Assembly's Education Committee continues to monitor the situation to ensure that there is no threat to the statutory position of church representatives. Last August all Presbytery Clerks were written to asking them to advise the Committee of any changes taking place in the structure of the authorities within their bounds. This letter was acknowledged by five Presbytery Clerks. In the meantime in co-operation with the Catholic Education Commission it is planned to hold a conference this year to which Church of Scotland, Catholic and also the third category of church representatives will be invited.

5. Catholic Education Commission

Meetings with the Commission continue to be held on a regular basis. Both Churches find the sharing of ideas and concerns very helpful. A joint letter was sent to the First Minister Mr Henry McLeish, MSP last November expressing confusion about the different initiatives taking place in the field of sex education and seeking clarification on the *Healthy Respect* project which had been launched by Health Minister Susan Deacon and about who was actually taking responsibility for Health Education in schools. The response from the First Minister is now being studied and it is likely that some issues will be re-visited when representatives meet with Mr McLeish or Ms Deacon.

6. Scottish Qualifications Authority

During the problems with the Scottish Qualifications Authority and the failure of SQA to provide secure, reliable and fair examination results for all candidates, the Committee wrote to the then Minister for Children and Education, Mr Sam Galbraith MP, MSP, to Ms Mary Mulligan Convener of the Committee on Education, Culture and Sport, and to Mr John Swinney, MSP, Convener of the Committee on Enterprise and Lifelong Learning.

The letter, written while matters were still uncertain and under investigation, paid tribute to the efforts of the vast majority of Scottish young people who had been presented as candidates for public examinations in the year 2000 and affirmed confidence in the overwhelming majority of Scottish teachers who, in schools and colleges, prepared and provided teaching and encouragement for the students who had been presented and who felt let down by a system which promised much. These teachers have had to face the business of standing by young people trying to come to terms with the confusion and anxiety generated in them by the failure of the SQA to provide reliable and trustworthy results. The Committee also wished that there should be an acknowledgement of the efforts of those of the staff of SQA who had diligently tried to do their best despite the apparent problems of management and the failures of the operations of computer systems and expressed its fears that unless urgent steps were taken immediately the SQA might not be in a position to manage the internal assessment data and the diet of examinations in 2001.

7. Universities

7.1 Funding Teacher Education

7.1.1 The department has written to both of the Scottish Executive ministers with responsibility for education to express concerns about the proposals of the Scottish Higher Education Funding Council (SHEFC) outlined in a current consultation paper.

SHEFC is proposing to rationalise the existing funding categories from some 20 or more to 6 broad categories. However, the proposed funding allocations attached to the new categories have implications for the funding of teacher education courses. The B.Ed (Primary) would see a severe reduction in funding and the PGCE would enjoy an increase. The B.Ed is an honours degree held in high regard by the primary sector of school education. It provides a professional training over 4 years, meeting the needs of school leavers and others entering higher education already committed to a career in primary teaching. The PGCE course is the one year course for graduates. The majority of new primary teachers are graduates of B.Ed courses, currently the ratio is 60 B.Ed students to 40 PGCE students. The proposed funding allocations will reduce overall funding to faculties of education. Increases in PGCE funding will not off-set the huge loss of B.Ed funding. Reductions in funding have implications for staffing and quality assurance. Universities offering the B.Ed courses facing a sizeable reduction in income might be inclined to favour the post-graduate route into primary education. Therefore there would be implications for the proportions of new primary teachers entering the profession by these two routes.

7.1.2 The teachers' settlement following the McCrone report requires the addition of some 4,000 primary teachers in the next four years. To achieve this and to maintain recruitment into primary teaching it is necessary to maintain both routes into primary teaching. The teachers' settlement also envisages a review of initial teacher education and the SHEFC proposals would seem to pre-empt this by proposing to devalue what is currently the major route into primary teaching.

7.1.3 If the SHEFC funding proposals go through reductions in funding allocations to other subject areas in Universities could make problems for the recruitment of secondary school teachers of Art, Home Economics and Business Studies.

7.2 Graduate Endowment and Student Support (Scotland) Bill

Student support and student poverty remain concerns and the Committee awaits the outcome of the Scottish Executive's deliberations on the matter.

8. Chaplaincy in Scottish Colleges

A group has been formed to support chaplaincy in Scottish Colleges.

The group includes an assistant principal, a representative of the Association of Scottish Colleges, a student services manager, college chaplains, a representative from the School of Further Education, a member of a college board of management and members of the Education Committee.

After a successful initial meeting the group is exploring various ways of offering support including the possibility of holding a consultation for chaplains and appropriate college staff.

9. National Priorities for Scottish Education

9.1 In August last year the Committee responded to a Scottish Executive Consultation Paper on National Priorities for Schools Education in Scotland. We welcomed many of the proposals set out in the document and in particular:

- the objective of identifying National Priorities and the intention to take into consideration the views of teachers, parents, pupils and the wider community:

- the inclusion in the Standards in Scotland's Schools etc Bill of the duty of local authorities to secure that education is directed to "the development of the personality, talents and mental and physical abilities of the child or young person to their fullest potential":

- the engagement of parents in their children's learning and development and the emphasis on the social skills which children learn from parents, families and in daily life and the recognition of the need for motivated and highly skilled teachers and other staff to work in partnership with parents in the promotion of positive behaviour and values:

- the attention being paid to the physical environment of teachers and pupils and the promise of increased resources for school buildings:

- the recognition that any use of targets to improve performance must take into account the fact that social and economic factors can and do affect performance levels in schools:

- the assurance that an inclusive system will make the highest quality provision for children with special educational needs and that any target setting in mainstream schools will take account of their provision for such children including those with emotional and behavioural difficulties:

- the focus on a broad range of skills which include personal and social skills.

9.2 In addition the Committee asked that there should be:

- a recognition of the importance of values in education through the delivery of a broad, balanced and flexible curriculum that would enable young people to develop a sense of meaning and purpose and help them to develop abilities which would equip them for living:

- a commitment to provide the training and the time and the funding to produce motivated and highly skilled teachers and other staff who would work in partnership with parents:

- a focus on aesthetic subjects that develop creativity, imagination and the appreciation of cultural diversity:

- a recognition of the importance of the skills which would help young people build and maintain good relationships and concern and respect for others:

- the acknowledgement that in some circumstances mainstream provision may not be in the best interests of many children with special needs and the need to ensure that alternative provision continues to be available:

- the provision of alternatives to exclusion for pupils with emotional and behavioural difficulties.

9.3 The Committee is happy to acknowledge that many of the above suggestions have been included in the new proposed National Priorities. These National Priorities seek to recognise the important role parents play in the development and education of their children. While reflecting the importance of academic achievement they also take into account the importance of life skills and the need for pupils to learn respect for themselves and others. The Committee has also noted the priority given to supporting teachers and enhancing school environments. The Committee looks forward to seeing how local authorities and schools work out and apply these Priorities in their individual Development Plans. Will, for example, a stated priority such as "the self-discipline of pupils" prove to be an adequate directive to ensure that more effective ways of dealing with indiscipline are put in place? The spirit of the National Priorities is meant to ensure action will be taken on issues like the appropriate provision for all children with special needs, a commitment to provide the training and the time and the funding for continuing staff development, and the engagement of parents in their children's learning and development, but it remains to be seen how all this will be accomplished.

10. Sex Education in Scottish Schools

10.1 In December the Committee responded to the Scottish Executive's Consultation Documents on Sex Education. What follows is a summary of that response. The Church of Scotland Education Committee continues to support the provision of good sex education taught within the context of Health Education, Personal and Social Education and Religious and Moral Education. We do so because we believe that information and facts should also be given in the context of beliefs about self-respect, forming relationships and moral values. In terms of aims and content much of what is here is good and helpful but we believe that this document as it stands is inadequate if it is to achieve the desired ends. Here we draw attention to a number of matters requiring attention.

10.2 Ideally parents and carers of young people should ensure that their children are given positive attitudes and values about sex as they grow up, which will help them cope and become confident and responsible adults. We therefore welcome the encouragement to schools to develop partnerships with parents and carers when developing their programmes of sex education for children. We trust that such partnerships will not end at the planning stage but also include liaison with parents as the programmes are being implemented so that they can share in this educational process for the benefit of the young people.

- We have asked the Scottish Executive to produce good exemplars which illustrate how parents can work in partnership with schools.

- We have also asked that schools be advised of the practical steps they could take to help parents play their part.

10.3 Where the documents suggest that pupils should be encouraged to appreciate the value of stable family life we have suggested that this should include an appreciation of the value of commitment in relationships and partnerships, the responsibilities of parenthood and the value placed on marriage by religious groups and others in Scottish society.

10.4 We are concerned to note that no questions or advice about to how to identify and deal with sexual abuse are offered in the documents.

10.5 The documents state that "sex education should contribute to the physical, emotional, moral and spiritual development of all young people within the context of today's society… it should reflect cultural, ethnic and religious influences…". We agree with this but would have liked some illustrations as to how this can be done given the reluctance of schools to tackle an area like "spiritual development" and given that there seems to be no explicit reference to sex education in the present Religious Education curriculum.

10.6 It is apparent that sex education will be dealt with in a number of subject areas. There is a need for help and guidance for teachers and parents where so much cross-curricular and cross-referencing is expected. In too many places the documents (particularly the Guide for Parents and Carers) lack the explicit reference to sex education (and how that draws from and contributes to other curriculum areas) that is currently needed. Exactly where and when sex education is to be delivered by schools will need to be clarified by the school if parents are to understand how sex education is being dealt with and whom to approach.

11. Citizenship and International Education

11.1 Earlier this year the Committee was invited to respond to a consultation paper on Education for Citizenship in Scotland.

In general the Committee welcomed the document. Aspects of good citizenship have always featured in a balanced and well-structured curriculum in Scottish schools.

However while acknowledging that schools have a key role to play in educating young people for active and responsible citizenship we would maintain that it is equally important that society itself reflects, in all its human activity, the best of such responsible citizenship.

11.2 While it is important to learn what it means to be what the paper describes as a "global citizen" it is surely necessary that there should be prior appreciation of what a "community" is and of what is meant by the school and the family as a communities? We need to break down the kind of individualism which emphasises rights at the expense of responsibilities. It is important that young people see what they can contribute as individuals to the community. This means also highlighting our interdependence and the importance of co-operation in the school setting where competition often predominates. It is in this context of community and co-operation that informed choices and decision-making should be discussed.

11.3 We have also expressed our opinion that there should be some reference in this context to family life which is not mentioned. What about the family as a community in which respect and care and responsibilities are all important? Is family life not a microcosm of society where it is also important be a good citizen?

11.4 In its response the Committee also expressed its regret that a number of significant issues reflecting important aspects of life in Scotland had not been raised or discussed. For example:

1. The social forces antagonistic to democracy and shared responsibility. The Committee believed that the Scottish Executive should clearly state its willingness to face up to and overcome racist and sectarian divisions in our society and express an appreciation of the contribution which all cultures, faiths and ethnic groups make to the community.

2. The feelings of alienation and indifference on the part of those who feel disenfranchised by deprivation, unemployment, poverty and the inequality of life. There has to be the recognition of and the desire to tackle the effect of poverty and deprivation.

3. The apathy of the younger generation and the feeling of powerlessness which many feel in spite of the Scottish Parliament's attempts at more open participative government. An effort needs to be made to establish attitudes of enthusiasm amongst young people so that they see meaning, value and purpose in the activities they are being pressed to address.

4. The concept of patriotism in the context of citizenship. There is a need to define Scottish identity positively by emphasising what we are rather than by describing what we are not.

Attention should be given to the place on the curriculum for the study of Scottish literature and history which we believe are equally necessary to our understanding of citizenship. Perhaps use could be made of a recent Scottish Executive publication dealing with Scotland's Culture - *"Creating Our Future: Minding Our Past, the National Cultural Strategy"*.

5. At the same time we believe that the document needs to point to international citizenship as something which people should welcome in today's world. Apart from one or two references to "globalisation" and "responsibilities as global citizens" there seems to have been little attempt to expand on this and work out the implications for education for citizenship in Scotland.

A previous Scottish Executive consultation on the International Dimension of Education has already highlighted this desire that young people should see themselves as global citizens. In its response to that paper the Committee sought to emphasise the important part Religious and Moral Education could play here. If, as stated, the aim of International Education is to help pupils develop a world view and appreciate the social groupings and the social needs of other people then surely it must encompasses some understanding of the impact of religion and faith on national cultures and moral attitudes and of how living faiths and religious customs influence the politics and social structures, the internal conflicts and the international policies, of societies all over the world.

12. Special Educational Needs and dilemmas of inclusive education / social integration

12.1 In response to a Government enquiry into *The diversity of provision across Scotland in special needs education* the Committee supported in principle the ideal of inclusion of all children in mainstream schooling and reaffirmed its belief that education for children with special educational needs, as for all pupils, is not only about academic outcomes but also about their personal and social development. For children with special educational needs this means not only having the opportunity to play a full part in society but also the opportunity to have contact with other children who have similar difficulties. This includes the provision for all children with low incidence disabilities. For the larger authorities, where there is a concentration of population, this is sometimes possible as the numbers of children with low incidence disabilities means that there can be groupings of children with similar needs. This can be either specialist or mainstream provision. For smaller authorities however where the numbers of pupils with low incidence disabilities can be very small it may not be possible to meet all the academic and social needs of these children.

From information gleaned through several sources the Committee is aware of areas of good practice in the inclusion of children in the mainstream of education.

However, for true inclusion to be effected there is a need for greater understanding of the full meaning of inclusion. It should mean that everyone is entitled to equal access to the same opportunities and no barriers are put in the way of this.

Among other things the Committee asked the Government to give consideration to:

- Undertaking a national audit of the number of pupils in individual authorities with low incidence disabilities and how authorities are providing for these pupils.

- The recognition of the need for specialist centres to meet the needs of children with low incidence disabilities.

- The value of the provision made by voluntary organisations and the need for continuing support for the contribution of the voluntary sector.

- Ensuring that local authorities offer a range of special educational needs provision to allow children and parents to have a choice.

- Recognise that, in order to offer this choice, authorities will require additional funding to maintain present provision and develop new provision.

- More emphasis on the meaning of inclusion in teacher pre-service training.

- A much greater input in pre-service training on meeting the needs of children with special educational needs in the classroom.

- Changes in funding to resource schools in terms of human resources and appropriate adaptation and equipment.

- The need for Health agencies to become more involved. There is a need for therapy input and medical advice. This will ensure that the needs of children with physical or medical needs are fully met and education staff understand and are confident in meeting these needs. The Government should examine how funding for therapy delivery for children is allocated.

- The formation of a Children's Services Department where all agencies work together thus perhaps lessening budgetary constraints and artificial divisions of responsibility instead of separate agencies with separate funding.

12.2   The length of school week for pupils in special schools and units has been under consideration recently. It is the opinion of the Committee that SEN pupils must not be disadvantaged in any way by a shorter school week and should have adequate teaching time to cover a curriculum appropriate for their abilities and needs.

However given the complexity of Special Needs we believe that it will be necessary to make many exceptions and that the length of the school week, like the curriculum, will need to be tailored to suit if the needs of all children are to be met. Any lengthening of the school week would meet with a number of practical difficulties and would perhaps require a staffing increase. The starting point should be the needs of the pupils and these should determine what organisational structures are required to be in place to ensure that these needs are met.

13. The Scottish Joint Committee on Religious and Moral Education

During the year there have been discussions with the Educational Institute of Scotland regarding the future servicing of the SJCRME. Historically joint secretaries have been appointed from the EIS and the Church's Education Committee. It has been agreed that this practice should continue with both bodies sharing responsibility for the administration and servicing relating to meetings of the Full Committee and of the Executive.

Any labour costs relating to meetings of the Full Committee and of the Executive Committee (as incurred by the Joint Secretaries) would be met by the Church of Scotland and the EIS. Material costs relating to preparation, duplication and circulation of papers would be met by the SJCRME from it own funds as would the payment for travel costs for meetings of the Executive and Standing Committees.

The EIS have appointed Lachlan Bradley as Joint Secretary (EIS) and the Church of Scotland Education Committee has agreed that the Secretary of the Committee should continue to be the Joint Secretary (Churches) and consequently has appointed the Rev John Stevenson meantime.

14. European Connections

14.1 Connections with those involved in Religious Education in Europe continue to be built up.
The European Forum for Teachers of Religious Education (EFTRE) is planning a European Conference to be held in Pollock Halls, Edinburgh from the 30th August to 2nd September this year. The Convener and Secretary represent the Committee on the Scottish Planning Group for this Conference and the Department is assisting with administrative arrangements. The theme of the Conference is "Handling Truth Claims in the RE Classrooms of Europe". Members of the Religious Education Movement (Scotland) (formerly C.E.M.) are helping to raise funding to bring a number of RE Teachers from Eastern European countries.

14.2 Last June the Convener and Secretary attended a conference in Trondheim, Norway, organised by the Intereuropean Commission on Church and School (ICCS). Discussion at this conference centred on opportunities for co-operation between church and school in a pluralistic European society.

15. Staffing Note

The General Secretary, the Rev John Stevenson, retired at the end of November last year. However in view of the inquiry being carried out by the Special Commission anent the Department of Education the Committee, following the decision of the General Assembly, agreed to invite him to take up a short-term contract as Secretary to the Department. This will terminate at the end of August 2001. The Committee would like to express its thanks to Mr Stevenson for agreeing to undertake this role.

In the name of the Department

JOHN J LAIDLAW *Convener*
WILLIAM T WEATHERSPOON *Vice-Convener*
JOHN STEVENSON *Secretary*

APPENDIX A

October 2000

SCOTTISH EXECUTIVE
Sam Galbraith MSP
Minister for Children and Education
Victoria Quay Edinburgh EH6 6QQ

Dear John
Thank you for your letter of 11 August enclosing the Deliverance of the Education Committee. I am grateful for the support shown by the Church of Scotland to the Scottish Executive in the field of Education. You raise four specific areas of concern to which I will respond in the same order that they arise in your letter.

Time allocation for Religious and Moral Education

There are no proposals to alter the time allocated to Religious and Moral Education in the 5–14 curriculum programme by SCCC (now Learning and Teaching Scotland). The time for Religious Education is set out in Circular 6/91 and stands at 10% and the revised guidelines makes explicit reference to the circular.

What is proposed is that in primary schools, for the purposes of time allocation and planning, the areas of religious and moral education, personal and social development and health education are allocated a minimum of 15% of available teaching time. In a primary school this amounts to approximately 3.5 hours per week. The proposal is not intended to reduce or damage the importance of religious education, but it is also important that it is not seen in isolation and that there are opportunities for making clear connections with aspects of personal and social development and health education.

Inclusion into mainstream schooling of children with special educational needs

You refer to the recent decision by the Scottish Executive to strengthen the right of children to be included in mainstream schooling. The new Standards in Scotland's Schools etc. (Scotland) Act 2000 does include a provision which requires education authorities to provide for the education of all children in mainstream schools, unless certain conditions apply. The rationale underlying this new duty is that most children with special educational needs will benefit from being educated alongside their peers in mainstream schools; that their inclusion has a positive impact on schools; and can help them to develop a positive ethos to the benefit of all pupils.

However, the new provision includes specific exceptions under which an education authority may refuse to provide education for a child in mainstream. One of these exceptions is where inclusion would be incompatible with the provision of efficient education for the children with whom the child would be educated. This acknowledges that for inclusion to work the needs of all children in the class must be taken into account.

I recognise that for inclusion to be achieved local authorities and staff need to be supported. For this reason, the Scottish Executive is providing funding of £5 million to local authorities for Special Educational Needs in-service staff development and training. In addition, a further £12 million over 2 years is available to assist local authorities to include children with special educational needs in mainstream provision either by physical adaptations to premises or measures to access the curriculum.

I am also aware of the important contribution that special schools and units can play in ensuring that children receive a quality educational experience appropriate to their needs. Special schools and units enable a range of provision which allows parents (and children) an element of choice. This is particularly important for children whose needs are complex or severe and who require support from a range of specialist services.

The overriding principle is that children and young people experience an education which meets their needs. Sometimes pupils in special schools have a more inclusive educational experience than some of those in mainstream schools. Mainstream schools can therefore learn from best practice in special schools.

Behaviour in the classroom and exclusion policies

You express concern about the difficulties experienced by teachers in dealing with indiscipline and disruptive behaviour in the classroom and the effect such behaviour has on other pupils. I agree that good discipline is essential to creating a purposeful educational environment and the Scottish Executive is taking several measures to improve discipline in schools.

The Scottish Schools Ethos Network was set up in 1995 and now has over 1000 members from all 32 education authority areas. It is sponsored jointly by Moray House Institute of Education and the Audit Unit of HM Inspectors of Schools. The Network's activities include: running national seminars on aspects of ethos in education; publicising case studies to share successful initiatives in particular schools; and involvement in conferences and making presentations to groups of interested individuals. Previous case studies have included good practice in managing discipline, improving attendance and tackling bullying. It offers an Ethos Award to schools each year.

The 'Promoting Positive Discipline in Scottish Schools' programme was set up in November 1996. The programme enabled schools and education authorities to share good practice and supported them in instituting practical school-based developments. It brought schools together to share experiences and promote positive approaches to establishing good discipline and relationships, including, for example, peer mediation and circle time. Work in this area will be continued this year with the development of a CD-ROM to assist teachers in dealing with difficult behaviour.

Following concerns from teaching unions about indiscipline and violence in the classroom, a guidance Circular of June 1997 was issued to local authorities, schools, School Boards and other bodies on reporting, recording and monitoring incidents of violence against school staff. Monitoring the incidence of violence enables schools and education authorities to assess the problem and monitor the effectiveness of strategies to reduce violence.

Exclusion from school is an important sanction which ought to be available to local authorities, but should only be used as a last resort in response to serious breaches of discipline or criminal behaviour. Being excluded from school means missing out on learning, and once pupils miss time it can be difficult to catch up. In these circumstances there is a risk of young people disengaging from learning altogether.

'Alternatives to Exclusion' is a Government initiative to help authorities develop radical alternatives to exclusion. The national objective is to support authorities in making provision for pupils at risk of exclusion and thereby assist them achieve the national objective of reducing exclusion by 30%, and to ensure that full time education is provided for all excluded pupils. Projects include in and out of school support units serving a particular school or a group of schools, programmes of personal and social development, enhanced staffing in schools and in support of schools, vocational schemes involving work placements, behaviour support systems and outreach services into schools. Most involve multi-agency work, including education, social work and voluntary organisations. Grants totalling £23 million over 3 years are made to authorities for this initiative from the Core Programme of Excellence Fund for Schools. A more recent initiative is Section 40 of the Standards In Scotland's Schools etc. (Scotland) Act 2000, which places a duty on education authorities to make special arrangements for the continued education of excluded pupils outwith school.

Schools as a community resource

At present funding for New Community Schools is in place for 3 years with each pilot project being eligible for up to £200,000 per annum over a 3 year period. Some projects will receive their first allocation of funding during the year 2001–2002 and this will continue until March 2004. No decisions have been made at this stage as to funding beyond that period.

I agree that a meeting would provide a useful forum in which to discuss these issues.

APPENDIX B

The Role and Work of the Committee

Rationale

The General Assembly Education Committee (The 'Committee') is concerned with educational matters at every level, including pre-school, nursery, primary, secondary and special education as well as further and tertiary education.

The *Committee* draws upon appropriate expertise within its membership in order to:

- **respond** promptly to any educational initiative at national or local level.
- **maintain**, defend or make known the Church's interests in matters of education.
- **co-opt** and consult with such experts outside the *Committee* as will enable it to produce reports or papers on matters falling within its remit.

Religious Education

One of the main tasks of the *Committee* is to ensure the continuing place of RE in the school curriculum and to offer advice on appropriate ways for the teaching of Christianity.

Resources

The *Committee* seeks to support teachers in schools with appropriate resources. Recent publications include a video on *Work and Worship in the Church of Scotland* and a resource pack entitled *Perceptions of Jesus*.

School Chaplains

The *Committee* offers training for school chaplains in association with Local Authorities and publishes a Bulletin for Schools and Chaplains from time to time.

Church Representatives

In accordance with the statutory provision the *Committee* nominates one representative to each of the 32 local authorities. Representatives serve on committees dealing with education and are supported in their work by the *Committee*.

General Teaching Council

The *Committee* has a statutory right to nominate a person to serve on the General Teaching Council for Scotland.

The Scottish Parliament

The Scottish Parliament presents a new and developing situation for the Church and unique opportunities for the *Committee* to promote the Church's educational concerns. This the *Committee* seeks to do through:

- **maintaining** a working relationship with the **Scottish Executive** and the two Parliamentary Committees that include educational matters within their remit.

- **submitting** considered responses to all relevant consultation documents issued by (i) the Scottish Executive Education Department or by (ii) Learning and Teaching Scotland.

- **liaising** with HM Inspector of Schools – the HMI responsible for Religious and Moral Education attends *Committee* meetings as an invited observer.

- **representation** on the Church of Scotland Parliamentary Users' Group convened by the Church's Parliamentary Officer.

Other Bodies

The *Committee* co-operates with other bodies including:

- Scottish Joint Committee on Religious and Moral Education (SJCRME)
- Association for the Teaching of Religious Education in Scotland (ATRES)
- Religious Education Movement (Scotland) (REMS)
- Scottish Forum on Education
- Catholic Education Commission
- European Forum of Teachers of Religious Education
- Inter European Commission on Church and School

PARISH EDUCATION
MAY 2001

PROPOSED DELIVERANCE

The General Assembly

1. Receive the Report

2. Welcome the development of Regional education posts to provide localised provision of services alongside national elements   (1.3)

3. Affirm the Year of the Child process and encourage Presbyteries and Congregations to become involved in this concept   (2.1.1)

4. Instruct the Board to consider the implications of the findings of research carried out into work with children and young people and to report to the Assembly of 2002   (2.1.4 and Appendix 1)

5. Warmly urge Presbyteries to consider ways in which they might show their appreciation of the service of Elders   (2.4.2)

6. Recognising the increased recruitment to the office of Reader, commend this ministry to the wider Church. (2.5)

7. Commend the developing work of Church Advocacy for Learning Difficulties and note that the team of advisers can offer advice and support to congregations that are anxious to include those with learning difficulties in the life of the Church.   (2.7)

REPORT

1. Introduction

The past year has seen many changes in the work of the Board of Parish Education and we are now set on a course that we believe will offer the Church a new approach to its educational life that can greatly enhance all that we do.

At a senior staff meeting in the late summer of last year, those present were asked to say what they thought was the main purpose of their work.

It was agreed unanimously that this should not be the provision of courses, the publishing of resources or the staging of major events.

Rather it was to help local churches develop confidence in themselves so that they might better undertake the opportunities that lie before them as the Church in their area.

This idea has been taken forward significantly in the past few months.

The Board of Parish Education has been long aware of the fact that a number of groups within the Church have been looking at ways in which we can operate more effectively and allow the potential of our institution and its individual members to be released, to the benefit of all concerned.

The Board has decided, therefore, to offer a number of new initiatives to reflect the needs of local situations and of particular groups in the development of its services, whilst maintaining a national service to allow the wider Church to benefit from the strengths of its national resources.

1.2 Offices

In 2000 the Board of Parish Education reported the establishment of its West of Scotland base. Over a year into this concept, it is working well.

The staff in the Glasgow base have made it known as a place where visitors are welcome and where resources of the Board of Parish Education can be accessed.

The Board would also want to record its on-going positive relationship with the Presbytery of Glasgow, with whom it shares the premises. The co-operation of the Clerk, the Treasurer and the Youth Office staff have been instrumental in this and we look forward to that continuing into the future.

Meanwhile, the Board has also been considering the matter of its offices in Edinburgh, with regard to practicality, efficiency, accessibility and so on.

Furthermore, the work of the Scottish Churches' Open College and its developing strategy as a resource for Higher Education within the Scottish Churches has had a major part to play in these considerations.

At the time of writing, discussions were on-going regarding a number of options.

1.3 Regional Education Project

Central Boards of the Church are often regarded as having a national agenda that takes inadequate account of the local situation.

Much of the work of the Board of Parish Education has, over the past several years, been aimed at addressing this concern.

1.3.1 Changes in our publication policy, research undertaken and reported later in this report into the experience of young people in the Church, youth work, the Year of the Child which is about to begin; all of these give some image of the desire of the Board of Parish Education to decentralise its work and to form an agenda which has been informed both from the wide circles of national and international experience and from the local insights that so many bring to us.

This year we have gone a major step further.

The Board has decided to appoint four people, for a period of three years in the first instance, to promote and develop education as an integral part of the life of local congregations.

1.3.2 These people will be employed to work with local people to identify the educational and training needs within the different locations and to find ways of providing for those needs, be that through services available within the Church or from elsewhere.

The Regional workers will have a working budget at their disposal and the spending of that budget will be overseen by the Board. In addition, the local staff will have access to advice and support from their colleagues with specialist remits operating within the Board at a national level.

This project is an attempt by the Board of Parish Education to reflect much of the thinking being done within the Board and other groups in the Church regarding the sharing of decision making and prioritisation between national and local structures.

It is a beginning and no more than that, but we hope that the Church will find this a positive development and that ways can be found of sustaining it in the longer term.

1.3.3 Furthermore, it is innovative in that it will allow an educational agenda to be set to a very great extent according to local need and will offer the chance for the wider Church to assess what it means by education, what priority is placed on it and what implications there are for the whole culture of the Church.

The project is aimed at the delivery of our services and of our enthusiasm for the value of education to be transmitted to others. We believe it reflects much of the thinking that has taken place in other Committees and Commissions.

2. Denominational Work

2.1 Children's Ministry

2.1.1 Year of the Child

Announced officially in December 2000, the process of consultation which will culminate in the Year of the Child has already begun well, with over 100 children's forums now meeting in churches around Scotland. The actual year begins in Advent 2001 and aims to encourage every church in the Church of Scotland to rethink the way it works with and relates to children.

Central to this is the idea that:

- Children are people with their own needs, views and contribution to the work of the Church

- Children deserve the very best environment we can offer them

- Children can bring us insight and experience which informs the work of the whole Church and goes far beyond the traditional models with which we have worked for so long

The emerging Children's Forums and the growth of concepts such as advocacy and children's roles in the decision making processes of our Church add weight to the principle of the integration of safety issues within the wider educational remit of the Board of Parish Education.

The Year of the Child has the support of the Boards and Committees of the church as well as some key external agencies. More churches are coming on board every week. An exciting ecumenical flavour to the project is also emerging.

The concept of the Year of the Child should be seen as much more than a one-off project. Rather, it is the beginning of a whole new approach to the work of Children's Ministry that will allow us to explore worship, education, decision-making and all other aspects of our Church life.

Indeed it would difficult to over-estimate the potential of such a process, or to limit the scope of its effects.

2.1.1.2 Internet Project

As part of the Year of the Child process it is hoped to bring together younger teenagers in the Church through an Internet project. The Board is keen to see how this medium can be harnessed to complement its work at all ages and in particular amongst the young.

2.1.2 Children's Ministry Adviserate & National Training Course

The Adviserate continues to add a local dimension to the Board's work. Presbytery based, the Advisers are primarily offering the National Training Course in Children's Ministry with healthy numbers of children's workers taking up this opportunity. In the context of the Board's plans and desire to allow for a greater level of local initiatives and in the light of the findings of the surveys

carried out on its behalf by Christian Research, there is now a need to look at how best to work with Presbyteries and the Board looks forward to discussion and innovation in this area.

2.1.3 CHOK

The children's ministry newsletter, Children of the Kirk (CHOK), was launched in December 2000. There has been an overwhelmingly positive response to this publication, which aims to resource, inform, support and network children's workers in the Church of Scotland.

2.1.4 Christian Research

During the year 2000, the Board commissioned the research organisation, Christian Research to conduct two surveys into the situation regarding those in the Church aged between 10 and 14.

The first of the surveys was conducted using a questionnaire that was sent to all congregations in the Church of Scotland and used to establish quantitative information regarding work with this group.

A total of 635 returns were received, some 56% of those sent out and from this an in-depth report was produced and presented to the Board in February of 2001.

The second report was based on interviews with a series of "focus groups" drawn from Ministers, Youth Leaders, Youth Workers, Parents and Young People.

The content of the reports goes into too great detail to be reproduced in full here, but the following points arise to which the Board seeks to make constructive responses. Indeed, it is heartening for the Board that many of the recommendations (see Appendix 1) are in keeping with policy decisions and plans of the Board that are already in place or planned.

Points to note:

- There is cause for optimism in terms of the numbers of young people involved with our Churches in Scotland.

- There is a great deal of contact being made with young folk both from families with Church connections and those without such a connection

- The continued success of uniformed organisations is clear

- The importance of building relationships with young people is fundamental to the success of such work
- The problems and successes in children's and youth work are uniform across the country and in different types of congregations

However:

- It is clear that the importance of and the vision for youth work in general must be made priorities for the Church of Scotland
- The loss of people in their late teen years may well reflect on the experience they have at the 10-14 age-range
- Problems with regard to attendance and participation that typically arose in the past at the ages of 14-17 are happening earlier. In other words we have to rethink what we mean by children and young people
- Ministers and members who do not have direct involvement with young people should be encouraged to learn more about this work and to experience it more fully
- Resources must be found to prioritise children's and youth work

2.1.5 Follow-up to the Reports

The Board has already begun to respond to these reports in a number of ways, many of which are reported in other sections. In general, we react in these ways:

- By looking to raise the profile of Children's Ministry beyond the traditional models of Sunday School and in particular through the Year of the Child and its attendant initiatives
- By developing the work of the National Training Course, through improved access to and quality of leadership training
- By working with elders and ministers to look more closely at how we work with the young people in and around our churches

2.1.6 Child Protection
2.1.6.1 Training and Advice

The Child Protection Unit continues to work closely with congregations and with other groups to promote its training and advice service.

The number of people who have undertaken training in recent years gives some indication both of the continuing level of response to this area of work across the Church of Scotland and the level of commitment and effort being put in by staff members and volunteer trainers.

Numbers trained over the period to February of 2001 are as follows:

Volunteers 18 275

Co-ordinators 1 356

Ministers 1 142

Readers 120, with most others of the 355 in total registered for training.

In terms of training, the Unit is now looking at ways in which the momentum of the past few years can be maintained and how follow-up and update training can best be offered in ways that are flexible and local, and yet retain a high level of consistency and quality.

The feeling that the Unit had achieved high levels of success both in its services and in its support systems was recognised by the report of the Internal Auditor of the Church which commended the work and the way in which it was being done.

Further information regarding the work of the Child Protection Unit can be found in the report of the Joint Boards Group for Child Protection.

2.1.6.2 Child Protection Handbook

In the last year, Sue Wheatley, in conjunction with the Child Protection Committee has written and produced a Child Protection Handbook, which has proved a popular and valuable resource, bringing together all of the regulations, guidance and support ideas that the Unit has been communicating and refining.

The book, published by the Board in loose-leaf format to allow it to be readily updated, has attracted attention from outside the Church of Scotland as well as being well received within it, and the Board looks forward to its continuing importance as an aid to congregations and individuals.

2.1.6.3 Child Protection and Children's Ministry

An exciting and positive development in child protection work has been the developing co-operation between the Unit and the work of Children's Ministry in general.

It has long been the vision of the Board that Child Protection work should be seen as more than a legal requirement and that integration of the principles of protection and safety with the nurture and education of our young people as well as others in the Church is essential.

Consequently, the Unit has become closely involved in the development of the Church of Scotland Year of the Child, of which much will be heard in the next several months and is reported more fully elsewhere.

2.1.6.4 Staffing

In October, Sue Wheatley left the employ of the Board. In early 2001, it is hoped that a new Training Officer will be employed to work with the Unit on the maintenance and development of the training programme. The Board acknowledges the assistance of the Personnel Department in the creation of this post, in particular with regard to the flexibility offered by the conditions of the appointment.

2.1.6.5 In conclusion, therefore, the Board is happy to report that the Child Protection Unit has continued to be a valued and creative element within its work and we look forward to the future as new issues and new responses to the safety of children unfold.

2.2 Youth Ministries

2.2.1 Assembly Youth Night 2001

This event takes place in the Usher Hall on Saturday 26 May, the day after the General Assembly's business is formally concluded. Young people from all over Scotland will gather for the event, which will include a wide variety of performances and participation.

This event, a combination of worship, fellowship, learning and fun is a major opportunity for young people of the Church to join together and to celebrate their part in our Church.

2.2.2 Youth work training

The National Training Course in Youth Ministry course is being redeveloped following the findings of the Christian Research study (see above, 2.1.5). It will be available again in autumn 2001 in settings around Scotland.

2.2.3 Employed Youth Workers

The Board seeks to help local churches employing youth or children's workers to be the best employers they can be. The Board published the book, The Works, last year to assist local congregations in working through the issues surrounding such appointments. It is hoped that this will prove a major help to all.

In another model, Board staff were invited to undertake a review of the Youth Project run by the two Church of Scotland congregations in Banchory last autumn. Staff worked alongside members of the congregations and the staff and young people of the project and produced a report, which was well received by the project's management group. The Board is always ready to offer this kind of support to local churches and projects that need an external view to assist them in working out how they should proceed in their work.

2.3 Adult Education

The work of the Board in terms of Adult Education is very wide in its nature. Much of what is done is in the name of the Scottish Churches Open College, but adult education also appears in much of our training of leaders, Elders and Readers.

In addition, there is a field of informal adult education, which continues to draw our attention and much is being done to establish what the content and format of such education should be.

Furthermore, we need to recognise that much of our work in the Youth Assembly and with Youth representatives to the General Assembly is also part of the heading of adult education, as the people involved are young adults.

2.3.1 Youth Assembly

This took place in the West Park Centre, in Dundee from 6-9 April. It was good to move away from the Central

Belt for the event and the Board is grateful to the Presbytery of Dundee and Dundee City Council for their hospitality. This was the first of the annual National Youth Assemblies that had to be organised in a very short space of time by staff who were still in recovery from the 2000 event. It is clear that this is now one of the church's permanent fixtures and that it is valued and appreciated by many individuals and congregations in the church. Many young people who have taken part in the Youth Assembly have gone on to offer themselves for Christian ministry here at home and also overseas.

The Board of Parish Education welcomes the decisions of the Co-ordinating Forum and of the Board of Stewardship and Finance to support the National Youth Assembly with permanent funding. Such decisions can only reflect a high degree of trust in our young people and a desire to help them find a voice within the wider Church community.

2.3.2 Daniel Project
This project, involving young adults leading small bible study and discussion groups around the country, has taken more time to develop than was anticipated. It was re-launched at the Youth Assembly in April with a new name, style and approach. It is hoped that there will be many more groups of young people meeting together in this way by this time next year.

2.3.3 General Assembly Youth Representatives
This has now become an established part of the Board's work with an average of 40 or so young people taking part in the General Assembly each year. The majority of young people stay together in a residential centre and work through the process of the Assembly in a community context. This offers real scope for discussion, sharing of ideas, arguments and just spending time with people of their own age. Young people seem to really enjoy the experience, and go away with a very positive view of the Assembly. The Board welcomes the increased powers given to the Youth Representatives and looks forward to the day when they will be given full voting rights.

2.3.4 Crossover
Crossover Christian Youth Festival continues to grow in quality and in attendance. This partnership with the Boy's Brigade, Girl's Brigade, Frontier Youth Trust, Christian Aid and the Boards of National Mission and Social Responsibility has proved to be a valuable addition providing a residential experience for a variety of youth groups. This year's Crossover takes place at the Broomlee Centre, West Linton on 16th to 18th June 2001.

2.3.5 Ecumenical Youth Ministry
Last year saw an unprecedented level of ecumenical activity by the Board's youth service. First of all youth staff from the Roman Catholic Church were involved in parts of the programme of the Youth Assembly and around 30% of the young people who took part were young people from other churches in Scotland, the UK and Zimbabwe.

In August 2000, 20 young people and staff took part in the World Youth Day celebrations in Rome, having been invited to take part by the Archdiocese of Glasgow. This proved to be an arduous but incredibly worthwhile experience for our young people as they learned a great deal about what it is to be young Presbyterians while standing in a field with 2 million Roman Catholics. The event provided our young people with opportunities to see how the Christian story had developed from Rome to what we see of it now.

In 2000 Steve Mallon, the Department's National Youth Adviser and Depute Director, became co-Convenor of Youth Action, the body within Acts with responsibility for youth work issues. Steve has been increasingly involved in the work of Youth Action and much of this work will culminate in the 24 hour event, Naked, to be held in George Square, Glasgow. This will be the first event for Scotland's young people which is genuinely ecumenically organised across the board. It is anticipated that young people from all over Scotland will gather together to engage in an unusual encounter which might begin to change the shape of Scotland. Steve also contributed to the publication, Breaking New Ground, which was published by Acts for the lent season.

This ecumenical commitment will continue in 2001 with a planned pilgrimage to the Taize community in July and continued involvement of other denominations in the Youth Assembly process.

2.3.6 Informal Adult Christian Education

The Board is undertaking research into what is going on at the present moment in churches in terms of adult education. The Board is convinced that if the Church is to proceed confidently, it needs a well-equipped and confident membership. It is anticipated that there will be a number of positive developments to report in this area of work next year.

The Board also wishes to record its thanks to the Guild Educational Representatives, who continue to be a source of support, and fine promoters of the idea of education in our Congregations.

2.3.7 Rediscovering Faith: explorations in Christian belief

This book of individual and group material for those who are enquiring about the Christian faith was published in August 2000 and is being used in adult learning groups around the country. It is hoped that more material of this nature will be made available in the coming months.

2.4 Elder Training

2.4.1 Elder Trainers

At present there are 39 Elder Trainers in 26 Presbyteries, with 4 more in training. There are 4 United Free Church Elder Trainers. Five Trainers resigned during the year and we wish to record our thanks for their work. Keith Deighton, one of our trainers in Glasgow, died in November and we have in him lost a valued colleague. Working alongside our Elder Trainers in Hamilton Presbytery we have an adult education team of four under the guidance of David Geddes, Congregational Development Adviser.

2.4.2 Participation in Training

In the year 2000, 3176 people participated in at least one session led by an Elder Trainer.

Over 300 Session Clerks have attended either a residential or one day Presbytery conference. In Uist, a joint elder and session clerk conference was held, and in Glasgow and Perth joint minister and session clerks conferences.

Elder Trainers are regularly impressed by the commitment of time and talent to the church shown by the elders with whom they come in contact. We would warmly recommend that Presbyteries consider ways of showing their appreciation for the service of elders. This might take the form of, for example, a Service of Celebration, a designated Elder Sunday, the introduction of new elders to the Moderator. These kinds of events would encourage a sense of worth and identity in the Eldership.

2.5 Readership

2.5.1 The encouraging trend in enquiries about Readership and the subsequent significant rise in applications has continued this year. Currently there are fifty-one candidates in training. Increasingly, Presbyteries are encouraging recruitment to the Readership, which is a continuing recognition of the contribution Readers make to the life and worship of the Church at local and national level. There are now two hundred and seventy-one Readers, many of whom are attached to congregations. Readers are also increasingly being asked to act as locums during vacancies and extended study leave and to undertake chaplaincy work in hospitals, hospices, homes for the elderly and prisons.

2.5.2 The programme of training approved by General Assemblies and offered in conjunction with Scottish Churches' Open College (SCOC) continues to provide a unique and valued preparation for the Readership. From September 2001, candidates for the Readership will follow the new "Living Worship" Cert.H.E. course offered by SCOC and validated by Napier University. The standards set by the Church and the quality of training offered by SCOC have established an invaluable model for training.

2.5.3 Child Protection Training

Child Protection Training for Readers is well underway. There has been an excellent uptake. Readers are to be commended for their positive response. It is anticipated that the programme of training will be completed by June 2002.

2.5.4 In-service Training

As required by the regulations, Readers continue to take advantage of the in-service training programme. The three in-service training weekends are heavily subscribed, demonstrating the enthusiasm of Readers for personal growth and professional development. It should be noted that the demand for these courses and the increased demand anticipated with the increase in candidates will put pressure on the current funding provision.

2.5.5 Ordination Working Party

The Vice Convenor, Rev Sally Foster-Fulton, and the Secretary of the Readership Committee, Revd Dr Donald Macaskill, have played a full part in the discussions of the Ordination Working Party. The Committee believes that the work undertaken by this group and the awareness of the needs expressed in its Report for the creation of a new working party to consider the relationship between the Readership and Auxiliary Ministry to be fundamental at this time. Those who are increasingly offering themselves for the ministry of the Readership, together with the Committee, are eager for a resolution to some of the obvious pastoral, theological and procedural concerns evident in the Working Party's Report, published elsewhere in the volume of reports.

2.5.6 The office of Readership has served the Church well throughout its history. The availability of Readers has ensured that worship is maintained in areas where there may be few ministers. The expanding role of Readers in collaborative ministry is enabling many congregations to expand and develop their worship, mission and service. The Church extends its thanks to those who serve as Readers for their continuing commitment and service. The office of Readership is commended to the Church as a living partner in the ministry of the whole Church.

2.6 Parish Education Publications

2.6.1 Marketing and Publicity

The Publications arm of the Board of Parish Education has been increasingly involved in the raising of awareness of the services of the Board in general as well as the resources that it publishes and promotes.

This has meant a presence at Church of Scotland events and external events such as Crossover festival, work with Christian Aid and Alternativity and other church publishing events, and participation in bookfairs and exhibitions in a variety of locations.

The increasing circulation of the Board's newsletter, PEN, is a further indication of the success of this area of work.

2.6.2 Co-operative working arrangements for publications.

This recently developed area of publishing has been operating particularly well. We have strengthened the range and level of resources available through external sources with our bought-in external projects provoking interest, enthusiasm and increased sales interest. Our first ever co-publishing venture of a children's bible, (In the Beginning), done in conjunction with Dutch and German religious houses, was a particular success. Likewise through the experiment of stocking in other Church of Scotland resource material in our catalogue, we have been able to place our contacts at the disposal of other Departments, and the results so far have been very pleasing for all concerned.

In addition, this arrangement works in both directions; our own PEP publications are in their turn now being stocked and distributed by other Christian publishing houses.

2.6.3 Our place in the wider field of Christian publishing.

Besides participating in a number of resource forums in the UK, both staff members and committee personnel have this year travelled by invitation to North America to assist in consultative meetings with religious resource providers. Sharing the costs of such ventures with our overseas colleagues results in an approach to publication which is both exciting and cost-effective compared to the development of in-house products such as major curricular materials.

The changeover has thus been made from curriculum development to project resource development; from large-scale and often unwieldy book series to issues of regular, targeted, cost-effective single projects that stand or fall by their own merits. This necessary evolution has been made to the increased success and recognition of our publications range and to the increased strength of our financial position.

2.6.4 Staffing
The appointment of a Publicity, Information and Marketing Officer, Janet deVigne, has already had a demonstrable effect on the work of the Board in terms of publicity and marketing.

2.6.5 New Publications
PEP has produced these new resources in the past year:

PEP projects, internally generated:

Teen material:	*Get A Grip: hands on Christianity*
	The Millennium Challenge
Adult work:	*Interpreting Scripture*
	Re-discovering Faith: explorations in Christian belief
Children's/youth work:	
	The Works – Guidelines for workers in children's and Youth ministry
Musical:	*Sing me a Song of Christmas*

Co-editions published as PEP stock:

In the beginning – a bible for young people

Publications sourced from outside PEP:

UPA materials
Alternativity resources
Department of Education resources
Nimbus Press dramatic books
Health Education Board of Scotland materials
Pastoral books from Woodlake/Northstone
Books from Australian Council for Educational Research

2.6.6 Visible success
This year saw sales figures reflect both the best monthly sales total on record (of more than double the previous best monthly take) and also in total the best year on record; and recognition of the appeal of new PEP products to a widening market came with our first books being sold into mainstream bookshops such as Thins and Waterstones. Recognition from others in the field and same market was also much more in evidence through reviews in peer journals, broadsheet coverage and radio reporting.

The presentation of a copy of *In the Beginning* to HM, Queen Mother on the occasion of her 100th Birthday also brought recognition in the press.

2.7 Learning Difficulties
"Some people are even more unluckier, they can't even talk". That was the assessment of a severely disabled child when asked about her condition.

The last several months have seen significant progress as we seek to re-engage the work of the Board of Parish Education in the whole area of special needs.

A conference involving a range of people with an interest in this area of work was held to look at how best to progress the work. It was agreed that we should move on from the idea of the network of volunteers that make up the Church Advocacy for Learning Difficulties as being advisers, but rather as facilitators who can meet local difficulties, discuss and then perhaps offer solutions to local problems and challenges.

2.7.1 The Challenge
The challenge that faces us in this area is in working with people who have been excluded from the beginning of their lives and who face life-long exclusion from the Church and from society. Furthermore, we have to recognise that difference is normal and that all people are of equal value in a community that claims to be a family.

2.7.2 The Commitment
As part of its response to the challenge, the Board of Parish Education offers this commitment:

To offer friendship that values lives, following Jesus' example

To work ecumenically in the area of Learning Difficulties

To ensure that those for whom we have a concern are at the heart of every initiative so that each individual's needs are met

To drop labels and actively seek integration

To work to create an environment where worship is accessible and available

To be flexible and to identify special needs at an early stage so that progress benefits everyone

2.7.3 The Task
From this, we identify our task as being:

To be available to meet with ministers, elders and others to help find solutions to local dilemmas

To ensure that individual needs are met in realistic and genuine ways.

3 Ecumenical Work

3.1 Scottish Churches' Open College
The Board of Parish Education continues to play a very significant role in the work of the College, in terms of staffing, accommodation and resources. The Board sees the College not as a separate entity, but as a major element within the spectrum of its provision.

3.1.1 President
At the end of last year, Very Rev Professor Robert Davidson retired from the position of President of the College. All in the Board who worked with Professor Davidson in this role would thank him for his work and wish him well for the future.

The Board would also want to offer good wishes to his successor, Rev Norman Shanks.

The past year has seen the College take significant decisions regarding its prospectus and developing a plan to deliver an innovative programme of opportunities under the heading "Living Theology". This new programme, including both the Certificate in Higher Education in Working with People in the Church and Community and a BA degree will join the College's Counselling Programme and its Spirituality programme as a main plank of the prospectus in the next year.

Details of the work of the College are available in the annual report and from staff at Annie Small House.

3.2 Other Ecumenical Involvement
The Board is well represented in a number of ways in the ecumenical world. Representation exists in groups relating to Children's Work at UK and European levels; to Adult Theological Education groups in the same way; to ACTS and its constituent groups; involvement in SCIFU negotiations; with the Ecumenical Spirituality Network; work with Partners in Learning and the Church Publishers Association and many others.

Furthermore, involvement of other denominations and groups in our events and projects is encouraged as reported elsewhere in this report.

4 Finance

The financial performance of the Board is reported elsewhere in the volume of reports. However, the Board reports that the year 2000 saw its finances affected by some unforeseen factors related to building repairs and staff expenses that largely accounted for a deficit in its revenue accounts.

5 Staffing

The Board employs the following ministers in non-parochial appointments:

Rev Dr Donald Macaskill; Rev Ian Walker; Rev Alison Newell

REV G STEWART SMITH, *Convener*
MRS LORNA PATERSON, *Vice-Convener*
MR IAIN W WHYTE, *General Secretary*

Appendix 1

Christian Research Reports

At the General Assembly of 2000, the Board of Parish Education undertook to commission research into the attendance and participation of young people in the Church. This was achieved by contracting the organisation Christian Research to produce two reports, one statistical and one qualitative.

The first of these involved the issuing of a questionnaire to all churches aimed at discovering the numbers, ages and involvement of young people. This report was carried out by Dr Peter Brierley.

The second took evidence from a series of focus groups involving ministers, youth workers, parents and young people. This report was carried out by Ms Heather Wraight.

Copies of these reports can be obtained from the Board of Parish Education, at a cost which covers printing and postage.

The Board intends to make extensive use of the findings of the reports in informing its agenda and in the support of those leaders within the Church who work with our young people. It is worth noting, however, that the researchers were greatly encouraged by why what they found, in terms of the numbers of young people associated with our congregations, their commitment and the quality of the experience that many of them have. There is always room for improvement and that is what we can develop in the light of these reports.

The Board was also encouraged by the fact that much of what was discovered chimes closely with the plans and services of the Board, particularly with regard to relational approaches to children's and youth work.

A Statistical Report Recommendations

1. More Leaders' training is required

Much work is being undertaken by churches with young people in Scotland, some of it successful. A substantial proportion of people in most congregations are involved with Sunday School, Holiday Club or other activities. As congregations age and youth work becomes less easy, it is essential that more training be given, especially to smaller churches or to those in the more difficult areas, e.g. in UPA's or rural areas.

2. Encourage salaried Youth Workers

Churches seem by and large to be coping with younger children, (under 11), who come in good numbers. However, they are less successful with older children, as the proportion of those 11 to 14 and especially those aged 15-18 is smaller than the comparative proportion in the general population. A specialist youth worker is seen as the answer to this problem and already almost a third of churches in the survey have one or access to one. More than half the churches would employ a salaried youth worker if they had the finance. Finding a way to give financial support to these churches is the most important recommendation to arise from this study. It is especially important for churches in UPA, housing scheme and rural areas.

3. Encourage communication about youth work

Many churches undertake special events once or twice a year, some times with attention catching titles! If a church wishes to expand its youth programme, what are the best ways to do this? Which activities work best? How can they learn form others? What training courses are available? Where are the stories of best practice? Who is doing what and where? How do you hire a youth worker? What is their job description? Is there an alternative to a disco, camp or holiday club? What material does, say, SU publish? How best does working in schools operate? Such information is not readily available. The answer is not a magazine, but a web site dedicated to youth work in Church of Scotland churches, if such does not already exist, and accompanying publicity as to its availability.

4. Offer special events

If special events work so well for those who already do them, how can more churches be encouraged to run them? Should reasonably regular events be organised centrally and taken on tour, not to big venues, but to local churches? Could such a tour be combined with providing training?

5. Youth work works!

This survey shows that many churches are effectively reaching out to young people in their area through their midweek youth activities. A fifth of those who come are not from church families. How can they best capitalise on the opportunities this presents?

6. BB Link?

Consider a strategic alliance with the BB. Both this quantitative survey and the Focus Groups found that BB is of significant value in churches that have a company. Can more churches be encouraged to develop a viable Brigade?

7. Essential to encourage more youth leaders and Elders

The number of young people under 35 in leadership positions in their churches is small…three fifths of churches don't have even one, Elder or non-Elder! Even where there are some, the proportion of them is only half that of he general proportion they have in the congregation. The image of not having such leaders, the lack of future development of such young people and the consequential missing of an opportunity for changing the church to meet more of the demands if the post-moderns 21st century all require urgent change. This is probably the second most important finding from this survey.

8. More facilities

A minority of churches are hindered by not having modern facilities and resources for youth work. Can some kind of one-off help be offered?

9. Lack of Vision

In some churches there appears to be a lack of vision of the potential of youth work. Whilst sometimes that is because parents discourage and sometimes the congregation discourages, sometimes it is because the minister lacks vision, time or energy. Could training in vision building be given, perhaps helping ministers, leaders and elders to understand their key gifts, so that they can work more effectively and efficiently together?

10. Uniformity of findings

There is one in interesting facet of this study. The variation in the answers given are remarkably uniform. We have statistically tested them against the different control factors…size of church, type of community, location and so on and there is much less variation than is usual in a survey of this size. That adds to the importance of the answers given above. While, of course, there is some variation some if it is naturally linked. Large churches have more elders, more activities etc, but the main variation where it occurs at all is in type of community, rather than in size as such.

Dr Peter Brierley,
Executive Director
Christian Research, January 2001

B Focus Group Survey

1. Adults who do not regularly have contact with 11–14 year olds need to be helped to understand hat they are likely to be somewhat different in their attitudes and level of maturity to what they were at the same age. This could be done in a variety of ways, some suggestions of which are:

"twinning" an older person with a young person who is not a member of their family. They could for example agree to pray for one another, work together on such activities as are within the capacities of this age group (serving tea and coffee after services, welcoming new comers, collating newsletters, etc). having social events that appeal to all ages, e.g. barbecues encouraging this age group to lead a service from time to time, e.g. quarterly

2. Ways must be found of enabling especially ministers and youth workers to come to a measure of mutual understanding of their particular perspectives of work with this age group. Could ministers be encouraged to spend some time working as part of the young people's leadership team, not only visiting it, in order to gain a truer understanding of the realities of youth work today?

And can youth workers be helped to see more clearly the wider church issues?

3. Youth worship for older young people may not meet the needs of 11–14's, so it may be either in an individual church or perhaps jointly by several churches in a locality.

4. Sunday morning is not seen as a good time for youth activities. Should such activities be offered at a more appropriate time? E.g. Does Bible class have to be held during Sunday morning service, or could it be held during the Sunday evening service where one exists?

5. Choice of leaders for work with this age group is very important. They must be able to:

• build relationships with young people

• understand their perspective on life

• be willing to put time and effort into the ministry

• work well as part of a team

Perhaps a Code of Good Practice for selecting and training youth workers could be developed by the Board of Parish Education.

6. Leadership of this age group is very demanding, but long-term relationships with young people are essential in order to develop trust, empathy, etc. Therefore, leaders need to know their work is valued and seen to be important by others in the church. They may need a support system to keep them going.

7. The kind of programme put on for them is important, though secondary. The following factors are worth noting and ways need to be found to disseminate them:

• Sunday morning may not be the best time to run anything for this age-group

• Mid-week activities are preferred because of the freedom and choice involved

• the facilities available are less important than what is done with them

• young people want to be consulted in planning what happens

• they do not want a scaled down version of the adult programme, but something relevant to their needs, likes and dislikes

8. The attitude of the rest of the church is more important than they probably realise. If it is not supportive it is very disheartening for leaders and can be a factor in young people leaving. Addressing this issue really means a change in church culture to not only give lip service to the church being made up of all ages, but to find positive ways of working that out in practice. Young people of this age are not as antagonistic to older church members as is often made out, but they do want to be valued, listened to and treated as individuals.

9. Among the youth workers interviewed there was some discussion about the Youth Assembly. They would like to see it as part of a nation-wide church structure as the General Assembly is. They would also like it to have real power.

Heather Wraight,
Christian Research
January 2001

Appendix 2

Rev G Stewart Smith

Stewart Smith retires as Convener of the Board at this Assembly. He has been closely involved with the educational work of the Church of Scotland since before the inception of the Board of Parish Education in 1993. As a member of the Board; Convener of the Eldership Working Party and Convener of the Board, he has made a major contribution to many of the changes that have taken place in our work. He has been Convener as we have seen the development of the Youth Assembly, the presence of Youth Representatives at the General Assembly, the inception of the Year of the Child and has Convened the Joint Boards Group on Child Protection.

Both staff and Board members are indebted to Stewart for his commitment, insight and valued support throughout his period of office and we all wish him well for the future.

BOARD OF COMMUNICATION

MAY 2001

PROPOSED DELIVERANCE

The General Assembly:

1. Receive the Report

REPORT

1. Business and Service Planning

1.1 This year, the Board's principal challenge has been to oversee the development and implementation of a business and service planning process. In December the Board unanimously approved a forward-looking and ambitious package of measures. When fully implemented, this initiative will represent a significant investment aimed at developing and improving Church of Scotland communication services. This planned approach is designed to set out a clear course of action for translating the Board's strategic aims, endorsed by last year's Assembly, into effect.

1.2 The Board's six-member planning and development task group worked in close co-operation with the director and section heads to draft the plans. Operational plans are now in place to take forward the development of all services including key areas such as Internet services, Saint Andrew Press, Pathway Productions and Life & Work.

1.3 Having detailed operational plans means that Board, management and staff will all be working towards the same goals. The plans complement the Church's staff development scheme, which enables operational targets and results to be used to set and monitor individual goals and training requirements for the director, section heads and staff.

1.4 The introduction of business and service planning is important for the Board of Communication which depends mainly on generating income by selling goods and services within the Church and in the market place. An approach based on business and service planning offers a range of benefits:

1.4.1 Providing operational plans that are specific, measurable, achievable, realistic and within agreed time-scales;

1.4.2 Offering customers an effective, efficient range of communication services that responds sensitively to their needs;

1.4.3 Enabling the best possible stewardship of available resources and providing a sustainable future for services;

1.4.4 Achieving improved levels of accountability of all involved in the Board's work in the fulfilment of their respective remits;

1.4.5 Creating a more informed budgeting process and a clearer sense of service value;

1.4.6 Giving the Board, management and staff the clearest possible picture of what is being aimed for and how effectively and efficiently this is being achieved;

1.4.7 Offering staff and Board members a stimulating and enriching environment within which to work;

1.4.8 Providing performance information on Board of Communication services to assist the wider Church organisation in making informed choices.

2. Implementing the Strategy

2.1 Last year's Assembly endorsed the Board's communication strategy. This report will relate the business and service plans and other operational initiatives to the strategy.

Strategic aim 1: Improve dialogue between the Church and the wider community

2.2 Objective: Continue to explore/develop an active media relations service aimed at promoting dialogue with the wider community:

2.2.1 Satisfaction levels with the Board's media relations service are high at present and the intention is to build on this positive foundation.

2.2.2 While maintaining the present high level of commitment to media relations at national level, the focus for the year ahead will be on enabling greater Church interaction with local media throughout Scotland. Staff from the Board's Media Relations Unit aim to strengthen and, where appropriate, encourage the establishment of Presbytery press contacts who can interact with local media. This will be achieved through direct contact with Presbyteries including visits aimed at offering media relations training to Presbytery contacts. It is hoped that this will help to fulfil the aim of promoting the widest possible dialogue This move acknowledges the current discussions on the possibility of an organisational tilt towards the local level of Church government.

2.3 Objective: Develop the Church presence within the broadcast media:

2.3.1 The Board has identified new, revised and enhanced roles for Pathway Productions, the Church's broadcast unit. Pathway is now gearing itself to new broadcast opportunities and platforms such as webcasting – broadcasting visuals and audio via the Internet - digital television and other multi-media approaches. At this point in its development, the Internet represents what is effectively an open access broadcasting opportunity. The Board hopes that Pathway can be adapted to enable the Church of Scotland to take advantage of this opportunity.

Pathway is producing the webcast of this year's Assembly on the Church's website (www.churchofscotland.org.uk).

2.3.2 At the same time, Pathway remains committed to clearly identifying and maintaining core services such as video/audio production, which are important to established clients.

2.3.3 In order to fund this new initiative, the Board is exploring several options for reducing Pathway's overheads by moving to new premises. A move of this kind could save an estimated £45,000 per year to provide resources for developing new approaches. This would also pay for new equipment and would help to create the opportunity to experiment that is vital at this point in a highly volatile and rapidly evolving broadcast communications environment.

2.3.4 The redeployment of a former Pathway staff member to a role elsewhere in the Department also helpfully contributed to lowering Pathway's overheads.

2.3.5 Pathway is also looking seriously at a change of underlying approach in the proposed move - away from a facilities-led approach to managing a flexible mix of internal and external resources. The key feature of this approach would be greater reliance on buying in skills and services as required for specific jobs.

2.3.6 Pathway provides the technical support for the Media Relations Unit's regular audio press releases that are broadcast on independent local radio stations throughout Scotland.

2.3.7 Working in partnership with external agencies, Pathway is beginning to explore the scope for originating and developing broadcast opportunities.

2.3.8 The Board retains the services of the Rev Alan Sorensen as the Church of Scotland's Advisor on Local Broadcasting. Amongst other duties, Mr Sorensen represents the Church of Scotland at the

Churches Advisory Council on Local Broadcasting (CACLB), an important forum for exchange on broadcasting related matters. CACLB has been involved in the revision of the code of advertising with the Independent Television Commission. Following representations from interested parties, the BBC now features religion on its website. In his annual report to the Board this year, Mr Sorensen highlights the development of radio as a broadcasting medium and the use of digital radio by the majority of commercial radio stations. He also highlights the BBC plans for 5 radio and 4 television digital stations.

2.3.9 The Internet is becoming an increasingly important method of broadcasting locally, nationally and globally. As an example of this Mr Sorensen cites that the BBC has a website link from their main website for every programme that they produce and broadcast. As a result the BBC now has the largest website in Europe.

2.3.10 Mr Sorensen emphasises the immense rapidity of change and development across all broadcasting platforms. This presents the Church with both an opportunity and a tremendous challenge to use this media explosion to communicate the Gospel and the values of the Kingdom and to promote the Church's interests and viewpoint. The Board of Communication is keenly aware of these developments and is seeking to rise to this challenge on behalf of the Church of Scotland.

2.3.11 The Board is very grateful to Mr Sorensen for his very effective representation of the Church's interests in this complex and volatile area.

2.4   Objective: Develop/expand the Church presence on the Internet:

2.4.1 This is the area of most rapid growth in the Board's range of communication services for the Church of Scotland. Since the launch of the new site last year, the monthly user statistics for the new website have been consistently and significantly five-six times greater than previous figures. Projecting on the basis of current patterns, the site will have registered somewhere between 1.5 to 2 million hits over its first year. Around half of those visiting the site come from overseas, and the Board is actively exploring the potential that this wide range of visitors represents for marketing Christian books, videos, CDs and other products.

2.4.2 The Board is developing Internet services in two principal ways. Firstly, by training existing staff thereby helping the Communication Department to move towards the ultimate operational goal of technical self-sufficiency. Secondly, by buying in the skills and experience of an Internet specialist to advise the Board on policy and practical development of the service. This twin approach is working well and should provide a solid foundation on which to build, while offering a degree of flexibility in responding to changing needs.

2.4.3 Alison Buckley, formerly depute editor of Life & Work, has taken up the new role of website editor within the Media Relations Unit, and this has greatly strengthened service delivery.

2.4.4 Design Services staff have been trained to provide an in-house web design service and Allan Ross, internet/media relations officer, has been trained in technical support.

2.4.5 Development of the website is one of the six projects adopted by the Guild for their financial support in the period 2000-2003.

2.5 Objective: Work with the Moderator's office and Assembly Conveners to maximise positive publicity for the Church:

2.5.1 This is an established element of the work of the Media Relations Unit and has been very successful in gaining publicity for the work and views of the Church of Scotland. There is close co-operation between the Moderator, his support staff and the Unit in ensuring that news items, statements, features and itineraries are readily available. The Moderator's visit to Scottish prisons is one of many examples of a story that generated large amounts of media coverage and the Church's website has carried regular items relating to the Moderator's activities and statements. Conveners and senior officials of Boards and Committees are also co-operating in helping to achieve this objective.

2.6 Objective: Consolidate/develop publishing services for the Church:

2.6.1   Saint Andrew Press is in the process of a radical redevelopment. The proposals in the business plan are aimed at developing Saint Andrew Press into a more significant force within religious publishing. Within this transition, the essential ethos of service to the Church will be retained. The aim is to improve sales by adopting realistic commissioning, new imprints, strengthened infrastructure, increased reliance on outsourcing of key services, targeted marketing and promotion.

2.6.2   There is also scope for improvements to service publishing for the Church through the production of a handbook, clearly laying out processes and time-scales and this is in the process of being prepared.

2.6.3   Identifying measurable value will be an important element of Saint Andrew Press's future operations to ensure that service work is properly credited and not simply seen as a cost.

2.6.4   An important part of Saint Andrew Press's resurgence is the commitment to publish a revised version of the internationally best selling *William Barclay Daily Study Bible Series* with accompanying videos. This project is progressing well with all parties strongly committed to ensuring its success when it is launched in Autumn of this year.

2.6.5   The Board has identified a potential fee-earning market to provide warehousing and distribution services to internal and external customers along

the lines of the present arrangements with Wild Goose Resource Group. Discussions are taking place with a number of possible customers both within and outwith the organisation at the time of writing.

2.6.6   Alison Fleming, formerly of Pathway, is now the marketing and publicity officer for all sections and her presence has been particularly helpful in raising the profile of Saint Andrew Press and its products. This was especially the case for the launch in November 2000 of *Scottish Religious Poetry*, which garnered exceptional pre-launch publicity including very positive coverage of both the book and Saint Andrew Press from Scottish Television's religious affairs programme *Eikon*. Prominent literary and religious figures also responded very positively to *Scottish Religious Poetry*, the first ever anthology of its kind. *Inspector Rebus* author, Ian Rankin called it 'the first great Scottish work of letters of the twenty first century', sentiments echoed by A.L. Kennedy, Alastair Gray, the Right Reverend Dr Andrew McLellan, Archbishop George Carey, Cardinal Thomas Winning and Bishop Richard Holloway. The Board is also exploring the potential for capitalising on international interest in Saint Andrew Press books via the website and e-commerce.

2.6.7   The Rev Ronald Blakey was appointed by the Board as the editor of the Church of Scotland Year Book. The Board appreciated the publication of the Year Book in early October 2000.

Strategic Aim 2: Improve dialogue between the Boards and the wider Church

2.7 Objective: Continue to explore/develop a strategy for Life & Work:

2.7.1   The Board is committed to continuing its investment in the editorial and design quality of the magazine and to aim over the next year or so to stabilise sales at present levels by attracting new and lapsed subscribers via a national marketing and promotional campaign. Achieving this will involve utilising the knowledge of those who work within the Church along with external specialist input.

2.7.2 The new editorial stance and re-design, initiated by new editor, Rosemary Goring, has sought to retain the best of what has gone before while taking the magazine forward. Reaction to these changes has been positive and a System 3 survey carried out last year yielded very illuminating results indeed. Survey results showed that Life & Work has a committed and loyal readership but also clearly identified a large potential readership. For example, one in every ten Church goers sampled did not know that Life & Work existed.

2.7.3 There has been no previous attempt at marketing or promotion on this scale. Professional advice from System 3 and other marketing specialists has taken a very positive view of the opportunities for attracting new and lapsed readers from within the Church of Scotland and beyond.

2.7.4 The Board is looking at several marketing agencies on a competitive basis with a view to employing one of them to assist in the marketing and promotional campaign for the magazine. It is likely that the marketing approach will be piloted in a specific area within Scotland and then rolled out over the next year or two.

2.7.5 If successful, the Board hopes that the marketing initiative will become self-financing as the initial investment is translated into higher sales figures. At this stage, the Board is making this investment in the quality of the magazine and in marketing and promotion without raising the cover price of Life & Work.

2.7.6 Quite apart from its principal role as the Church's main channel of internal communication, Life & Work has for many years helped to underwrite the Board's other activities. If this is to continue, investment is essential to maintain and develop this important source of income.

2.8 Objective: Develop Board of Communication contact with Presbyteries:

2.8.1 As mentioned earlier (paragraph 2.2.2.), the Media Relations Unit is planning to undertake a programme of Presbytery visits and other contacts aimed at building and training a network of contacts dealing with local media in an effective way.

2.8.2 The Board's Design Services Unit will be approaching Presbyteries with a view to ascertaining the level of potential demand for the professional print media and web design services that they supply. It is hoped in this way to extend the benefits of this high-quality service to the Church organisation at local level.

2.8.3 Immediately following last year's Assembly the Presbytery of Dumfries and Kirkcudbright hosted another in the highly successful series of Church Alive events. These events are designed to inform people in the wider Church about what is being done by the Boards and Committees in their name. Attendance at the Dumfries and Kirkcudbright event exceeded the expectations of the Presbytery organisers and the entire event continued the successful run enjoyed by the *Church Alive* initiative to date.

2.9 Objective: Improve Board of Communication publicity services and the provision of resources:

2.9.1 As noted in section 2.6.6. above, the Board now has the services of a full-time marketing and publicity officer and this has greatly enhanced the ability to maximise opportunities to promote products and services for the Board.

2.9.2 This new post will enable the Board to offer some level of marketing and promotional service to other Church clients for the first time. The marketing and publicity officer will also assist in the planning and execution of co-ordinated publicity initiatives involving all Boards and Committees.

2.9.3 The Board is examining the logistics of providing a 'one stop shop' for all Church of Scotland resources in liaison with Saint Andrew Press's warehousing and distribution facilities. This has become a more pressing priority with the success of the new website, which is perceived by many users as a 'one door' point of entry when seeking goods or services from the Church organisation.

2.9.4 The Board offers a limited service in making available multi-media projectors for presentations and display materials for exhibitions.

2.9.5 Once again, Pathway is deeply involved in the provision of technical support for the Assembly and was responsible for the technical resourcing of the Guild's annual gathering in August of last year.

2.9.6 Last year's Assembly gave a joint remit to the Board of Communication and the Panel on Worship to examine multi-media worship, with a view to the possible provision of resources to support this area of the Church's life. The Board has taken the remit given to it seriously and has taken the initiative in establishing a working party, together with the Panel on Worship. It is not possible to move forward on this rather complex matter without knowing what is currently available within the parishes of the Church. Accordingly, a survey has been sent out and the Board is grateful to the ministers and office-bearers who took the trouble to respond to it. As expected, this has shown that there is a considerable variety of interpretations and practice of what might be described as 'multi-media worship'. At the time of writing, the Board is looking carefully at the results of the survey and this will help to inform

the decision on how best to move forward on this matter.

Strategic Aim 3: Improve internal communication between the Board of Communication and other Boards

2.10 **Objective:** Extend/improve Board of Communication consultation with other boards:

2.10.1 This objective lies at the heart of much of the Board's work in servicing the Church organisation and is an important value in the work that we do for all our service users and customers.

2.10.2 In order to formalise its communication with other boards and committees and make it as open and effective as possible, the Board has set up a new Communication Council. The Board intends that the Council, chaired by a Board member and serviced by Communication Department managers, will be an effective vehicle for discussing communication matters of significance to all Boards and Committees. The Council is also intended to help the Board and the Communication Department to remain aware of the requirements of their internal customers and service users. The Communication Council has three key roles:

    i.   To receive customer and service user feedback on Board of Communication services;

   ii.   To co-ordinate inter-departmental publicity initiatives such as *Church Alive* events, the Scottish Christian Resources Exhibition and involvement in the General Assembly;

  iii.   To receive suggestions for communication initiatives to be considered by the Board of Communication.

2.11 **Objective:** Extend/improve use of in-house communication facilities:

2.11.1 Following a staff survey, the Media Relations Unit

re-launched the staff magazine under the new name *One-to-One News* (changed from its former title of *121 News* to make it more inclusive for staff in other sites), a move which has been welcomed. The magazine is used to update staff on significant news within the workplace.

3. Finance

3.1 In the context of the planning and development process there have also been developments to departmental systems which will enable the Board to account more accurately for the amount of time devoted to service provision (i.e. work which is not directly paid for by the recipient, such as technical support for the General Assembly). These systems will come on stream in 2001 and will enable a more appropriate assessment of the value offered by each service to the Church, as opposed to the ability to generate fee income from other sources.

3.2 Along with other Boards and Committees, the Board of Communication had to accept a moratorium on its Mission and Aid for the years 2000 and 2001. Prepared to use its reserves to further the Church's aims, the Board had planned for a deficit of £34,955 in 2000. In the event the actual deficit was £48,607. £40,000 of this was the result of expenditure necessitated by recruitment and the need to pay for long-term cover of staff on extended sick absence. These costs were unbudgeted.

3.3 The current year will be a further challenge financially with a budget deficit of £266,804 anticipated. Of this approximately £150,000 will be investment in strategy initiatives. As these are fed into the planning process they will require short to medium term support to ensure they can reach fruition. The balance of the deficit, £116,000, is the result of an underlying trend arising from a pattern of reducing income and increasing costs and expenditure. The Board receives £466,000 from Mission & Aid, generates £889,000 through fee earning and trading activities and will use £266,000 of its reserves in this year.

3.4 The decision to invest at this time has been driven by the business and service plans with their key objective of implementing in practice the strategic aims endorsed by last year's Assembly. At the same time the Board is concerned, during this time of change, to safeguard the future provision of its core services.

3.5 This utilisation of reserves will allow investment in the editorial resources of Life & Work and Saint Andrew Press. It will enable the Board to implement the marketing and promotional initiative aimed at stabilising the readership numbers for Life & Work. It will add expertise to the development of the web strategy and the exploration of the potential for webcasting.

3.6 The Board recognises that this level of deficit is significant and is concerned to demonstrate that all its expenditure is translated into value for the Church. A value for money audit of all services will be undertaken by Scott Moncrieff, an outside agency skilled in carrying out such a task (clients include local government and the National Health Service). Scott Moncrieff are also retained as the internal auditors for the Church organisation. This audit will allow the Board to make a critical assessment of the use of all resources and will also inform the Board's decision making when planning the allocation of its resources.

4. Staff Changes

4.1 In June of last year Ann Crawford took up her post of Head of Publishing for Saint Andrew Press. Ann, who comes from a blue chip publishing background, has lectured in publishing as well as being a professional practitioner. The Board wishes to thank Derek Auld, who has many years' experience within Saint Andrew Press, for ably fulfilling the role of Interim Publishing Manager until Ann started.

4.2 In July of last year Rosemary Goring, formerly a senior editor with *Scotland on Sunday*, took up her post as new editor of Life & Work. Muriel Armstrong, who served as part-time features writer on the editorial staff for many years, very effectively acted as Interim Editor until Rosemary began. Muriel is now working full-time for the magazine in the new role of assistant to the editor.

4.3 Three members of staff have been successfully redeployed within the past year. Alison Buckley, formerly depute editor of Life & Work is now working as website editor. Alison Fleming, formerly Pathway's marketing officer, is now occupying the role of marketing and publicity officer for the whole Communication Department and Derek Auld, formerly production and operations manager for Saint Andrew Press, is the Department's new customer services manager.

4.4 After thorough investigation and consultation with the Personnel Manager, the Board has identified 1.5 full-time equivalent posts that are surplus to requirements within the finance and administrative support area. To accommodate this, the present staff of three full-time positions needs to reduce to one full-time and one part-time post. However, in anticipation of a retirement due in June 2001, the need for a part-time post (in Saint Andrew Press warehouse) has been identified. This could be covered by the existing staffing; therefore only one full-time post would actually be surplus. Whilst every attempt is being made at the time of writing to redeploy or retrain, this could result in one member of staff being made redundant.

4.5 Very sadly, Betty Cruickshank who worked for almost seven years as Pathway's part-time administrator died suddenly just before Christmas. Betty's premature death came as a great shock to her colleagues who held her in high regard. The Board and staff extend their sympathy to Betty's family and friends, particularly to her son Lindsay.

5. Thanks

5.1 The Board would like to thank staff for their work in the past year.

6. Personnel Statistics

6.1 In the past year the Department of Communication employed 31 full time members of staff. There are, at present, no ministers on the staff.

In the name and by the authority of the Board

JEAN MONTGOMERIE, *Convener*
PETER GRAHAM, *Vice-Convener*
BRIAN MCGLYNN, *Secretary and Director*

Joint Report of the Boards of Parish Education, National Mission, Social Responsibility, Practice and Procedure, Ministry and Stewardship and Finance on the Protection of Children and Young People in the Church

MAY 2001

PROPOSED DELIVERANCE

The General Assembly

1 Receive the report

2 Instruct the Principal Clerk to write to the Deputy First Minister to express the Church's appreciation of the Scottish Executive's decision to provide free criminal record checks in terms of Part V of the Police Act 1997 for volunteers working with children in the voluntary sector. (4.1–4.6)

3 Determine the following:
   a) that such checks for volunteers working at congregational level should be carried out only via the Church's Child Protection Unit
   b) that the Joint Boards Group are authorised to take all necessary steps to effect registration on behalf of the Church with the proposed central registered body
   c) that Child Protection Unit will institute suitable procedures for the processing of applications for checks and the results thereof. (4.1–4.6)

4 Remind Presbyteries of their responsibilities in terms of superintendence of congregations, instructions of previous General Assemblies and general responsibilities as outlined in section 2. (2.3–2.4)

REPORT

1. Introduction

Operating on behalf of the General Assembly, The Joint Boards Group is responsible for the creation and monitoring of policy with regard to matters of Child Protection.

The success of the Child Protection Unit over the past three years bears testimony to the co-operative work within the Joint Boards Group which has seen the Boards of Parish Education, National Mission, Ministry, Social Responsibility, Stewardship and Finance and Practice and Procedure work along with the Law Department to ensure the strategic interests of the Church are kept in mind as we put good practice and consistent standards of delivery in place.

2. Effective Execution of Policy

2.1 One of the biggest challenges that the Joint Boards Group have faced is the communication of policy from the Assembly to local areas. It is inevitable that there will be matters that require to be subjected to evaluation and monitoring in an area of work that involves practical, relational and legal concerns.

The Child Protection Unit strives to be as supportive and flexible as it can within its remit, while recognising the need for standards of provision and processes for the delivery of that provision. Indeed, this can become more difficult through time as familiarity and complacency become risks to the continued implementation of policy and guidelines.

2.2 However, there is a general impression that the response of the Church to the whole issue of Child Protection has been extremely positive and conscientious and the Joint Boards Group welcomes that as a support to its work and a factor that eases the difficulty of that work.

2.3 Against this background, the Group is keen to support Presbyteries as they seek to fulfil their role within the process of monitoring and maintaining practice and would take this opportunity to remind Presbyteries of their responsibility to monitor Child Protection matters within congregations; Presbytery visits being of particular importance. Further guidance relating to this matter is contained within the paper issued by the Board of Practice and Procedure, outlining the basis for discussion between a Presbytery and congregation.

Clearly, there is a need to go beyond a basic review of the existence of systems within Congregations to the demonstration of good practice in the out working of such systems.

2.4 In addition, the Group would encourage Presbyteries to seek advice on the actions open to them should they become aware that difficulties may exist in Congregations, be they in terms of process or of practice.

3. Beyond Child Protection

3.1 The Group has begun to address issues that take its work beyond the basic system of the Guidelines for the Protection of Children and the Code of Good Practice. Much Research and development work in other places has been undertaken into the ways in which Churches can deal with both the victims of child abuse and how they might react towards the perpetrators of abuse.

3.2 Indeed, the whole country has been made aware of the problem of what to do with the abuser through media coverage of public reaction to the proposed introduction of a so-called Sarah's Law, following the tragic case of Sarah Payne last year.

3.3 There is much that is difficult about this, but the Church must consider its response to the problem of the abuser and the abused if it is to have a clear idea about how to deal with the aftermath of abuse cases in their entirety.

3.3.1 The Joint Boards Group expects to look further at this area and report to a future General Assembly.

4. Police Checks in terms of Part V of the Police Act 1997.

4.1 As reported to previous General Assemblies, the above legislation contains powers to enable Scottish Criminal Record Office checks to be carried out on people volunteering to undertake work with children for Voluntary Organisations. The Joint Board's Group has been much concerned about the implications for the Church of the costs of such checks (previously estimated at £10–£15 each) and following upon the matter being raised in the Scottish Parliament, a Review Group was set up chaired by Ms Jackie Baillie, Minister for Social Justice on which the Scottish Churches Committee was represented. Following upon the submission of the Group's Report to the Deputy First Minister, the Scottish Executive, towards the end of last year, announced that checks on those volunteering to work with organisations within the voluntary sector in Scotland would receive a 100% subsidy. It was also announced that that the Executive would further establish and meet the funding for a new central registered body which would process applications from voluntary bodies and also provide guidance and advice.

4.2 This represents an extremely welcome development. Indeed, it is a development, which at the time of writing sets Scotland apart from the rest of the country, where it is still expected that charges will be levied.

4.3 Given that the cost to the Church of Scotland could have reached six-figures in the first year alone, it is clear that this is a very significant announcement, not only in terms of cost, but also in terms of the likely commitment to the use of the checking system and therefore to the continuing standard of our child protection work.

4.4 At the time of writing, the details of the process, the posts which would require checks, how long these would last and so on, are still being developed by the Scottish Executive which has undertaken to do so in consultation with the Voluntary Sector. The current expectation is that the checks will become available from October 2001 but there is a possibility that this start date may require to be delayed.

4.5 The Joint Boards Group recommends that the Church of Scotland's process for dealing with applications for SCRO checks should be administered nationally by the Child Protection Unit, rather than locally, with these benefits

- A central register of volunteers checked removes some of the stresses associated with local gathering of such information

- The economies of scale make the task more practical and the standards more consistent

- The need to keep track of people and to co-ordinate processes between the Church and other Organisations is more easily met, thereby making it less likely that a volunteer will be required to have repeated checks done for more than one organisation

- The individual who gives consent for these checks to be carried out can be reassured that sensitive conviction information is not held locally, so the risk of a breach of confidentiality is removed.

- The decision of whether an offence is relevant to the person's suitability to work with children will be taken at a national level, thus removing the chance for disagreement or dispute within the local congregation.

4.6 The Child Protection Unit will be monitoring developments very closely and will keep the Church up to date as they happen.

5 Management of the Unit

The Joint Boards Group recognises the work of the Board of Parish Education in the day to day management, support and accommodation of the Unit. Further information regarding the role of child protection within the work of Parish Education is contained within the report of the Board of Parish Education.

The name of the Joint Boards:

REV G STEWART SMITH
Convener of the Joint Boards Group
Convener of the Board of Parish Education

REV DAVID LACY
Convener of the Board of Practice and Procedure

MR LEON MARSHALL
Convener of the Board of Stewardship and Finance

PROFESSOR WILLIAM STORRAR
Convener of the Board of Ministry

REV JAMES GIBSON
Convener of the Board of National Mission

MRS ANN ALLEN
Convener of the Board of Social Responsibility

MS GILLIAN SCOTT
Secretary of the Joint Boards Group

DELEGATION OF THE GENERAL ASSEMBLY
MAY 2001

PROPOSED DELIVERANCE

The General Assembly:

1. Receive the Report of the Delegation of General Assembly and thank it for its work.
2. Continue the appointment of the Delegation with the same powers as hitherto - the Principal Clerk of the General Assembly to be Chairman and the Depute Clerk of the General Assembly to be Vice-Chairman.

REPORT

The Delegation has to report that during 2000 it granted, in virtue of the powers conferred upon it by the General Assembly, eighteen additional Model Deeds of Constitution.

The present amended Model Deed of Constitution was approved and adopted by the General Assembly on 21 May 1994 for issue to each Congregation whose temporal affairs were then administered by a Congregational Board under the Model Deed and for granting to each Congregation thereafter adopting it. The total number of Congregations to which Model Deeds have been issued or granted up to the end of 2000 is now 1,188, of which 134 relate to new Parishes.

In the name and on behalf of the Delegation

FINLAY A J MACDONALD, Chairman

RETURNS TO OVERTURES

MAY 2001

PROPOSED DELIVERANCE

The General Assembly:

1. Receive the Report.
2. Convert into a Standing Law of the Church the Overture Anent Discipline of Ministers, Licentiates, Graduate Candidates and Deacons, as revised and printed in Appendix II.
3. Convert into a Standing Law of the Church the Overture Anent Ministers and Deacons in Public Office, as revised and printed in Appendix III.

REPORT

As will be seen from the returns detailed in Appendix I both Overtures sent to Presbyteries by last year's General Assembly have received overwhelming support. Many Presbyteries offered comments and the Committee has given careful consideration to these. The Committee has also been guided by the Procurator on a number of matters, including human rights legislation, the required standard of proof and the basis of appeals.

I. Overture Anent Discipline of Ministers, Licentiates, Graduate Candidates and Deacons

This Overture was a substantial and complex piece of work, and the Committee appreciates the many suggestions from Presbyteries that assist the clarity and effectiveness of the provisions of the scheme. Most of these improvements require no explanation and are consequently not narrated in this Report. The Committee believes they constitute textual improvements or very minor adjustments of process, and do not require further Barrier Act procedure. Commissioners should therefore read the Overture, as printed in Appendix II, with awareness that a number of these adjustments appear there.

The Committee does, however, make the following observations in respect of suggestions made by Presbyteries.

s.1(1) (d) and (f) One or two Presbyteries suggested that the Committee of Presbytery should be five persons not three, and/or that the Presbyterial Commission be seven persons not five. The Committee takes no view on the merits of this substantive change. Whilst it would not require Barrier Act procedure, the appropriate way to advance these suggestions would be by motion before the General Assembly.

ss.4 and 5 These sections have been redrafted and now reflect a concern expressed by a number of Presbyteries that, as originally drafted, there was a risk that a potential case might be discussed on the floor of the Presbytery before going to the Investigating Committee. The original s. 5(1)(d), about speaking to the press, appears in a redrafted form as a new s.3(3).

s.11 In order to accommodate the possibility of a challenge to competency or relevancy which can be disposed of only after proof, an amendment has been suggested and incorporated into s.11(2) with consequential amendments to ss.11(3) and 11(4). S.11(5) has been amended to allow for a plea in mitigation.

s.12 One Presbytery raised the possibility of hearings being in private.

The issue is that Article 6(1) of European Convention on Human Rights requires as a norm a "public hearing" when a person's civil rights are being determined. The

Article allows the exclusion of the press and the public from all or part of the proceedings "in the interests of morals, public order or national security in a democratic society, where the interests of juveniles or the protection of the private life of the parties so require, or to the extent strictly necessary in the opinion of the court in special circumstances where publicity would prejudice the interests of justice."

The public character of the hearing is a fundamental principle and is designed to protect litigants by allowing public scrutiny of the administration of justice. The norm therefore requires to be a public hearing. But a private hearing (in whole or in part – eg. the evidence of a particular witness) may be justified in cases involving sexual offences (particularly against children), cases analogous to divorce where the privacy of the Respondent or of witnesses might be seriously compromised and cases where publicity could prejudice the administration of justice.

As the right to a public hearing is in substance that of the Respondent it may be prudent to provide that the Committee of Presbytery should show cause why the hearing should be in private. Similarly, as a public hearing is the norm and there may be an important public interest in allowing the presence of the public which should override a Respondent's wishes, it is not unreasonable to require the Respondent to show cause why he waives his right to a public hearing.

In light of this the Committee has amended the opening words of section 12 as follows:

"The first diet and proof shall take place in public except (a) where either the Committee of Presbytery or the Respondent request that, and show cause why, the hearing or part thereof be held in private…"

s.14 One Presbytery raised the possibility of the standard of proof being raised to the criminal, not civil, standard. This appears in only a single return, and the Committee is not persuaded that there is a case for changing from the present standard of "balance of probabilities", (See Weatherhead, "The Constitution and Laws of the Church of Scotland", page. 71, for a discussion of this point.)

s.19(1) Commissioners should note that the ground of appeal is an appeal on a point of law. Several Presbyteries suggested that there should be an appeal against a finding of fact. If the right of appeal is confined to a point of law, there will not be scope for a general review of the evidence and for arguments that the Presbyterial Commission misunderstood the balance of the evidence or that it should have preferred the evidence of one witness over that of another. An appeal on a point of law against a finding would be confined to arguments such as that the evidence led did not justify the Presbyterial Commission in making a particular finding. However, the Committee was reassured that an appeal on a point of law would also cover unfair procedure, the legality of a finding on the merits and the sentence and believes that this is adequate.

s.20(2) One Presbytery suggested a right of appeal against this part of the process. The Committee believes that this section completes a sequence of actions taken at an earlier stage, and the taking of an appeal belongs at an earlier point in the proceedings.

s.25 There is some concern about the effect on a case if the subsequent General Assembly did not confirm rules adopted during the case. The Committee believes this would not automatically invalidate the outcome of the case, and the Presbyterial Commission should not be prevented from acting with discretion and in the interests of justice during the course of a case.

s.26 has been adjusted to render it consistent with s.19.

II. Overture Anent Ministers and Deacons in Public Office
The Committee has adopted exactly the same procedure in respect of the Overture revised and set out in Appendix III, which should therefore be read with the same *caveat*.

The Committee makes the following particular observations.

s.1(1)(a) Comments on the specification of hours ranged from a request for more exact specification to a concern about the arbitrariness of specifying an amount. In light of the range of comments, the Committee proposes not to alter this section.

s.1(3) One Presbytery wished the congregation to be consulted about their willingness to have their minister or deacon so serve. Whilst the Committee believes such consultation would be the good practice of any Presbytery, the impression should not be given that the congregation would make this decision or have a veto over it, especially in the case of a deacon who may not be its employee in any case. The Committee therefore believes there is no need or justification for altering the text in this regard.

s.3(1) Commissioners should note that the restriction to time-commitment has been removed from this section, because one Presbytery pointed out that other characteristics of the appointment may cause concern to the Presbytery, and time may not be the only relevant criterion.

s.3(1)(b)(ii) The alteration of 'imposed' to 'created' should facilitate a suggestion by one Presbytery that a part-time reviewable appointment may in some cases prove a flexible solution. One comment suggested a provision to deal with the eventuality where the General Assembly's Committee on Parish Re-appraisal failed to concur with such a suggestion. The reporting Committee believes that the existing mechanism of reference to the Commission of Assembly is the appropriate one, and whilst acknowledging that it may require a period of administrative suspension whilst the matter is resolved, this is preferable to an automatic vacancy or termination of another church appointment.

In light of comments received the Committee has added new sections 4 and 5 to provide for the situation where the holder of a public office wishes to take up an ecclesiastical appointment.

One Presbytery wished to see a mechanism for congregations to initiate concerns in this area where no-one in Presbytery raised the matter. The Committee believes the existing mechanisms of superintendence are adequate in this respect, and does not propose to amend the Overture.

In the name and by the authority of the Committee

FINLAY A J MACDONALD, *Convener*

APPENDIX I

Abstracts of Returns from Presbyteries Under Barrier Act Procedure

Overture anent Discipline of Ministers, Licentiates, Graduate Candidates and Deacons

No of Presbyteries		Members voting for	
Approving	*Disapproving*	*Approval*	*Disapproval*
45	3	2,509	97

Overture anent Ministers and Deacons in Public Office

No of Presbyteries		Members voting for	
Approving	*Disapproving*	*Approval*	*Disapproval*
46	2	2,460	161

APPENDIX II

I. Overture anent Ministers and Deacons in Public Office

Edinburgh, May 20, 2000 Sess. 1

The General Assembly adopt the Overture, the tenor whereof follows, and transmit the same to Presbyteries for their consideration under the Barrier Act, directing that returns be sent to the Principal Clerk not later than 31 December 2000.

Part 1 Introduction

1. (1) For the purposes of this Act:

   (a) "disciplinary offence" shall mean

(i) conduct which is declared censurable by the Word of God, Act of the General Assembly or established custom of the Church or

(ii) a breach of a lawful order of any court of the Church.

(b) "investigatory proceedings" shall mean those proceedings carried out in accordance with the provisions of Part 2 of this Act in respect of any disciplinary offence alleged to have been committed by a Minister, Licentiate, Graduate Candidate or Deacon.

(c) "disciplinary proceedings" shall mean those proceedings carried out in accordance with the provisions of Part 3 of this Act in respect of any disciplinary offence alleged to have been committed by a Minister, Licentiate, Graduate Candidate or Deacon.

(d) "Committee of Presbytery" shall mean a Committee of Presbytery of three persons, of whom at least one will be a minister and one an elder.

(e) "Presbyterial Panel" shall mean a list of ministers, elders or deacons submitted by Presbyteries in accordance with the following procedure. Every Presbytery, with the exception of the Presbytery of Jerusalem, shall be entitled to appoint one person in respect of every one hundred members, or part thereof, of the Presbytery, to form the Presbyterial Panel. Such appointments shall be made annually with effect from 1 July, shall subsist for one year and shall be intimated in advance to the Principal Clerk. Persons may be re-appointed up to a maximum of three times. Elders so appointed need not be members of the Presbytery, but shall be members of Kirk Sessions within the bounds of the Presbytery. Ministers or deacons so appointed shall be in full membership of the Presbytery.

(f) "Presbyterial Commission" shall mean a body of five persons, three of whom shall be selected from the Presbyterial Panel randomly as provided for in terms of s.10(2), together with a Convener and Vice-Convener appointed by the General Assembly on the Report of the Nomination Committee, such convenership and vice-convenership being so arranged that one office is held by a minister and the other by an elder qualified to practise as a lawyer. An alternate Convener and Vice-Convener shall be appointed at the same time, but if for any case a further alternate shall be required, the Secretary to the Commission shall consult with the Convener of the Nomination Committee for a further appointment. The Solicitor of the Church shall normally serve as Secretary to Presbyterial Commissions, but may appoint a Depute to act in his or her place in any particular case. The Secretary shall not be a member of the Commission.

(g) "Respondent" shall for the purposes of this Act only mean the Minister, Licentiate, Graduate Candidate or Deacon (i.e. member of the Diaconate), as described in paragraphs (b) and (c).

(h) "censure" shall mean one or more of:
(i) reprimand, which shall be an expression of disapproval of particular behaviour with counsel regarding future conduct;

(ii) suspension of status, either for a fixed period or without limit of time, subject to restoration by the Presbytery upon the expiry of the term or upon petition by the individual;

(iii) removal of status, subject to restoration only by petition to the General Assembly.

(i) "administrative suspension" shall mean an instruction by a Presbytery to an individual under its jurisdiction to abstain from the exercise of all the functions of his or her office as minister or deacon until proceedings under this Act are finally disposed of; it shall not constitute a form of censure.

(2) Throughout this Act the singular shall include the plural where applicable.

(3) For the avoidance of doubt it is declared that any proceedings under this Act are part of the exclusive jurisdiction of the Church and in accordance with the Articles Declaratory of the Constitution of the Church of Scotland in matters spiritual, as hereby interpreted by the Church.

2. (1) All investigatory proceedings shall be initiated by the Presbytery having jurisdiction in terms of this section.

(2) Ministers and Deacons shall be subject to the jurisdiction of the Presbytery of which they are members and that notwithstanding that they may reside beyond the bounds.

(3) Ministers and Deacons who are not members of any Presbytery shall be subject to the jurisdiction of the Presbytery within whose bounds they normally reside.

(4) Licentiates shall be subject to the jurisdiction of the Presbytery which licensed them or to which they have been regularly transferred.

(5) A Graduate Candidate shall be subject to the jurisdiction of the Presbytery in whose bounds is situated the congregation of which he or she is a communicant member in terms of section 27(a) of Act V, 1998 as amended.

3. (1) A Presbytery may initiate investigatory proceedings whenever there come to the notice of the Presbytery circumstances indicating that a disciplinary offence may have been committed.

(2) Should circumstances indicating a possible disciplinary offence come to the notice of a Presbytery other than that having jurisdiction in terms of section 2, it shall communicate the same to the Presbytery having jurisdiction together with all information pertaining thereto in its possession.

(3) It shall be a disciplinary offence for any member of Presbytery to issue press statements or otherwise talk to the media about an alleged disciplinary offence after the Presbytery receives notice of an alleged offence until the conclusion of any disciplinary proceedings and any appeals relating thereto.

Part 2 Investigatory Proceedings

4. (1) On receiving notice of circumstances indicating that a disciplinary offence may have been committed, a Presbytery shall appoint a Committee of Presbytery to consider the circumstances, and, if appropriate, to investigate and prosecute the case. In the exercise of any of its functions in terms of this Act, the Committee of Presbytery shall have all the powers of Presbytery. Except insofar as provided herein, the Presbytery shall have no further part in the proceedings.

(2) In considering whether to carry out an investigation the Committee of Presbytery shall have regard to all the relevant facts, and in particular:
(a) the bona fides of any person making an allegation that a disciplinary offence may have been committed;
(b) any representation made by the person who is the subject of the allegation; and
(c) the gravity of the alleged offence.

(3) Before deciding whether to carry out an investigation the Committee of Presbytery shall intimate in writing to the person who is the subject of the allegation ("the Respondent") the nature of the offence alleged and the nature of the evidence purported to exist in support of the allegation and shall offer him or her the opportunity to make any answer thereto, provided that he or she shall not be obliged to answer.

(4) If the Committee of Presbytery decides that it is not appropriate to carry out an investigation in respect of all or any of the allegations made, the Committee of Presbytery shall report that decision to the Presbytery. Without prejudice to its existing powers of superintendence the Presbytery may issue an instruction to the Respondent regarding his or her conduct. Any disobedience of that instruction may be treated as a disciplinary offence.

5. (1) If the Committee of Presbytery decides to initiate investigatory proceedings it shall:

(a) give notice to the Respondent of the decision to investigate the case and of the allegation or allegations which are to be investigated;

(b) to give notice to the Presbytery of that decision and of the allegation or allegations which are to be investigated: and

(c) give notice to the Board of Practice and Procedure, which shall appoint a legally qualified assessor to advise the Committee of Presbytery on matters of law and procedure.

(2) On receipt of the notice referred to in section 5 (1) (b), the Presbytery shall:

(a) make such arrangements as appear to it appropriate for the provision of pastoral support for the Respondent and his or her family, for the person or persons who made the allegation and for any witnesses within the bounds of the Presbytery; and

(b) be entitled at its discretion to suspend the Respondent immediately from carrying out the functions of his or her office, which suspension shall be administrative only, and where appropriate to appoint an Interim Moderator to the Respondent's charge.

6. (1) The Committee of Presbytery shall carry out such investigations as it deems necessary to determine whether a disciplinary offence may have been committed.

(2) In all cases under this Act the Presbytery shall keep a Record Apart of the investigatory proceedings. The Record Apart shall comprise all evidence obtained by the Committee of Presbytery including witness statements, and a transcript or recording of the evidence given at any hearing.

7. Before reaching any conclusion on whether a disciplinary offence may have been committed, the Committee of Presbytery shall make known to the person against whom the allegation has been made the substance of the complaint made against him or her and the nature of the evidence existing in support of the allegation and shall offer him or her the opportunity to make any answer thereto; provided that he or she shall not be obliged to answer.

8. Upon consideration of the allegations and evidence submitted and of any answers given, the Committee shall be entitled to resolve that no further investigation shall be carried out if there is no *prima facie* case to answer. In that event, it shall report to the Presbytery which shall recall any administrative suspension imposed in terms of section 5(2)(b).

9. (1) In the event that the Committee of Presbytery decides to initiate disciplinary proceedings it shall prepare (a) a Notice of Complaint setting forth the alleged disciplinary offence or offences (hereinafter referred to as "charge" or "charges") in respect of which it is proposed that disciplinary proceedings should be commenced and (b) a summary of the evidence, whether from witnesses, documents or otherwise, that is considered to support the charge or charges made.

(2) The Notice of Complaint will run in the name of the Committee of Presbytery and will be in such form that, in respect of each offence, there is set out the time and place of the disciplinary offence and the facts necessary to constitute the disciplinary offence.

Part 3 Disciplinary Proceedings

10. (1) The Committee of Presbytery shall initiate disciplinary proceedings by lodging with the Solicitor of the Church:
    (a) a Notice of Complaint setting forth one or more charges;
    (b) a list of the names and addresses of the witnesses to be adduced by the Committee of Presbytery;
    (c) a list of the productions to be put in evidence by the Committee of Presbytery; and
    (d) a request to appoint a first diet and to grant a warrant to the Committee of Presbytery for service of the Notice of Complaint and to cite the Respondent to attend the first diet.

(2) The Solicitor of the Church shall notify the Convener and Vice-Convener of the Board of Practice and Procedure and arrange for the selection of a Presbyterial Commission in terms

of section 1(f) and shall, thereafter, in the name of the Commission, pronounce an Order -

(a) fixing a date for the first diet, being a date not earlier than fourteen days after the expiry of the period specified for intimation and service; and

(b) granting warrant for service of the Notice of Complaint on, and intimation of the first diet and a list of the names of those selected to serve on the Presbyterial Commission to, the Respondent within such period as he or she shall appoint.

(3) The Committee of Presbytery shall, within the period fixed for intimation and service, intimate to the Respondent the date fixed for the first diet and shall serve upon him or her by recorded delivery post or personally by means of a Sheriff Officer-

(a) the Notice of Complaint and lists of witnesses and productions; and

(b) a summary of the evidence specified in section 9(1)(b).

(4) In the event that service of the Notice of Complaint has not been timeously or regularly effected the Solicitor shall as aforesaid

(a) grant warrant for the re-service of the Notice of Complaint as above; and

(b) fix a fresh date for the first diet, being a date not earlier than fourteen days after the expiry of the period specified for the fresh intimation and service.

11. (1) The first diet will be held before the Presbyterial Commission .

(2) At the first diet the Respondent may challenge-

(a) the competency or relevancy of the Notice of Complaint; or

(b) the constitution of the Presbyterial Commission:

provided that in respect of any challenge to the competency or relevancy of the Notice of Complaint intimation of the ground of such challenge must be given to the Committee of Presbytery and the Presbyterial Commission not later than 24 hours before the diet is due to be held and any challenge made in terms of this sub-section shall ordinarily be disposed of immediately unless the Presbyterial Commission considers that the matter cannot be decided without proof.

(3) The Presbyterial Commission may—

(a) adjourn the first diet for whatever reason;

(b) allow the Notice of Complaint to be amended by deletion, alteration or addition so as to cure any error or defect in it or meet any objection to it, on such conditions as it thinks fit;

(c) sustain or repel any challenge to the competency or relevancy of the Notice of Complaint in whole or in part.

(d) defer consideration of such challenge until after proof.

(4) After disposal or deferment of any challenge referred to in sub-section (2) above, the Respondent shall be required to state whether he or she admits or denies each of such individual charges, if any, which remain on the Notice of Complaint.

(5) Where the Respondent admits all the individual charges brought the Presbyterial Commission shall, after hearing and considering any statement by, or on behalf of the Respondent, in mitigation, pass such censure upon the Respondent as appears to it appropriate or discharge the Respondent and shall record their decision in a document signed by the Convener.

(6) Where the Respondent denies some or all of the charges brought, the Presbyterial Commission will appoint a date for the proof of those charges which are denied and defer consideration of the question of censure in respect of any charges which are admitted until close of the proof; provided that the Committee of Presbytery may—

(a) accept any denial of any individual charge; or

(b) accept an admission of an individual charge in part;

in which case the proof will be confined to those charges which are denied and which denial is not accepted by the Committee of Presbytery.

(7) The date appointed for proof shall be not less than 28 days nor more than 56 days after the first diet or any adjournment thereof, but the Presbyterial Commission shall have power, upon cause shown by either party to fix a date outwith that period, or to adjourn the proof diet.

(8) Where the Presbyterial Commission has appointed a date for proof, it may make an Order requiring the Respondent to intimate to the Presbyterial Commission and to the Committee of Presbytery within such period as it shall specify a list of the names and addresses of the witnesses to be adduced and a list with copies of the productions to be put in evidence by him or her.

(9) Where a) the Respondent has intimated in writing to the Committee of Presbytery and to

the Presbyterial Commission i) that there is no challenge in terms of sub-section 2 hereof and ii) that the charge or charges on the Notice of Complaint are all denied and b) both the Committee of Presbytery and the Respondent intimate in writing to the Commission that there are no other matters which they wish to raise at the First Diet, it shall not be necessary to hold a First Diet and instead the Convener, Vice-Convener and Secretary of the Commission shall appoint a date for the proof of the charge or charges and make any order in terms of sub-section 8 hereof.

12. The first diet and proof shall take place in public except a) where either the Committee of Presbytery or the Respondent request that, and show cause why, the hearing, or part thereof, be held in private or b) where the hearing of evidence from any person, or narration of facts thereof, in the opinion of the Presbyterial Commission is likely to prejudice morals or public order, to affect adversely the interests of justice or the private life of the parties or in any other special circumstances where publicity would prejudice the interests of justice, provided that in any event the Presbyterial Commission shall restrict publicity only to the extent strictly necessary.

13. If a party fails to attend or be represented at the time and place fixed for the proof, the Presbyterial Commission may a) adjourn the proof to a later date; b) if that party is the Committee of Presbytery, dismiss the Notice of Complaint; or c) if that party is the Respondent, proceed to hear the proof in his or her absence, to reach a decision thereon and if appropriate to pass censure.

14. (1) The rules of civil evidence in Scots law shall apply and the standard of proof shall be the balance of probabilities. Witnesses shall be required by the Convener to take the oath or to affirm prior to giving evidence.

(2) The proceedings at the proof shall be recorded. The shorthand writer or technician shall be sworn by the Convener prior to the commencement of the hearing.

(3) In subsection 2 "The proceedings at the proof" shall, unless the Presbyterial Commission shall direct otherwise, mean the whole proceedings to the close of the proof, including, without prejudice to that generality a) discussions on all matters arising in the course of the proof and the decision of the Presbyterial Commission on any such matter, b) the evidence led at the proof and c) the speeches of the parties or their counsel or solicitors on their behalf.

15. Each party shall be entitled to give evidence, to call witnesses, to question any witness and to address the Presbyterial Commission, provided that the Respondent shall have the right to speak last.

16. Subject to sections 14 and 15, the conduct of the proof shall be in such manner as the Presbyterial Commission considers most appropriate for the determination of the issues before it and to the just handling of the proceedings.

17. (1) No proof shall fail or the ends of justice be allowed to be defeated by reason only of any discrepancy between the Notice of Complaint and the evidence.

(2) It shall be competent at any time prior to the decision of the Presbyterial Commission, unless the Presbyterial Commission see just cause to the contrary, to amend the Notice of Complaint by deletion, alteration or addition, so as to—

a) cure any error or defect in it;

b) meet any objection to it; or

c) cure any discrepancy or variance between the Notice of Complaint and the evidence.

(3) Nothing in this section shall authorise an amendment which changes the character of the charge or charges, and, if it appears to the Presbyterial Commission that the Respondent may in any way be prejudiced in his or her defence on the merits of the charges by any amendment made under this section, the Presbyterial Commission shall grant such remedy to the Respondent by adjournment or otherwise as appears to the Presbyterial Commission to be just.

18. (1) At the close of the proof the Presbyterial Commission shall give its decision on whether and if so to what extent each charge on the Notice of Complaint has been established and the decision shall be recorded in a document signed by the Convener, provided that the Presbyterial Commission may take time to consider its decision and adjourn the diet of proof to a later date for that purpose.

(2) Upon giving its decision and, in the event of any charge being found to be established or admitted (including, without prejudice to that generality, those charges admitted and deferred in terms of section 11(6)), after hearing the Respondent in mitigation, the Presbyterial Commission shall pass such censure if any upon the Respondent as appears to it appropriate according to the circumstances of each charge.

(3) After giving its decision in terms of sub-section (1), the Presbyterial Commission shall set forth in a document a) those findings in fact which it has made and b) the censure if any which it has imposed, giving reasons for both elements of its decision. The Presbyterial Commission shall also record the majority by which its decision in respect of i) each charge and ii) censure or absolute discharge was reached.

(4) The Secretary of the Presbyterial Commission shall send the documents referred to in sub-sections (1) and (3) to each of the parties, the Presbytery Clerk and the Principal Clerk of the General Assembly and shall make them available for public inspection.

Part 4 Appeals

19. (1) Subject to the provisions of sub-sections (2) and (3), if either the Committee of Presbytery or the Respondent is dissatisfied with any decision of the Presbyterial Commission they may appeal to the Judicial Commission on a point of law at the conclusion of the proceedings. No right of appeal or dissent and complaint shall be allowed in respect of any act or decision done or taken in terms of this Act, otherwise than in accordance with the provisions of this Act.

(2) Any appeal taken in terms of sub-section (1) which relates to matters of doctrine shall be to the General Assembly in terms of Act II, 1988 section 3 as amended.

(3) For the purposes of this Act, an appeal on part of a case or on a procedural point shall not sist procedure except with the leave of the Presbyterial Commission. Failure to obtain such leave does not reduce the right to appeal, but such appeal shall be included when an appeal is taken at the conclusion of the proceedings in terms of sub-section (1).

(4) Any appeal in terms of this section shall be by way of Note of Appeal lodged with the Principal Clerk of the General Assembly within 21 days of the date on which the appellant receives intimation of the written decision of the Presbyterial Commission and shall consist of brief specific numbered propositions stating the grounds on which it is proposed to submit that the appeal should be allowed.

(5) Appeals to the Judicial Commission shall be heard within 56 days of their being lodged, or within such further period as the Judicial Commission shall on special cause allow, by the Judicial Commission, but excluding any member a) who has or has had any connection whatever with the case, b) who is a member of the Presbytery, or a congregation within its bounds, which has initiated the proceedings which are the subject of appeal or c) who is objected to for cause shown by any party to the appeal and whose objection is sustained by the Judicial Commission.

(6) The judgement of the Judicial Commission shall be final and shall be sent in writing to each of the parties and reported to the General Assembly in the form of a minute of its findings.

Part 5 Subsequent Process

20. The Presbytery shall meet within not less than twenty-one and not more than thirty-five days after receiving intimation of the written decision of the Presbyterial Commission or, in the event of an appeal being taken, after receiving intimation of the judgement of the Judicial Commission or the General Assembly and—

(1) In the event that the decision has not involved suspension or removal from office, it shall

a) lift the administrative suspension upon the person;

b) relieve the interim moderator of duty;

c) undertake such steps of discipline against other individuals and superintendence of its members and congregations as it finds necessary.

(2) In the event that the decision involved (i) a suspension of such length that, in the judgement of the Presbytery, the pastoral tie requires to be terminated, or (ii) the removal of the status of the Respondent

a) any parish of which the person was minister shall be deemed to have become vacant on the date of the meeting of Presbytery and any other ordained appointment which he or she occupied shall terminate on that date;

b) the appointment of an interim Moderator shall be confirmed or a new appointment made;

c) the Presbytery shall undertake such steps of discipline against other individuals and superintendence of its members and congregations as it finds necessary.

(3) In the event that the decision involved a suspension which is not of such a length that the pastoral tie is to be terminated

a) the appointment of an interim Moderator shall be confirmed or a new appointment made;

b) the Presbytery shall undertake such steps of discipline against other individuals and superintendence of its members and congregations as it finds necessary.

(4) This section shall apply *mutatis mutandis* to Deacons.

Part 6 Miscellaneous

21. The Committee of Presbytery and the Respondent may be represented by counsel or solicitor at any stage of the investigatory proceedings, disciplinary proceedings or appeal.

22 The expenses of the Committee of Presbytery and the Respondent in the conduct of disciplinary proceedings and any appeal following thereon, and

the necessary expenses of witnesses, as the same may be taxed by the Auditor of the Court of Session, shall be met from the central funds of the Church.

23   The Presbyterial Commission may relieve a party from the consequences of a failure to comply with a provision of this Act shown to be due to mistake, oversight or such other excusable cause on such conditions as the Commission thinks fit.

24.   The Presbyterial Commission shall have power to make regulations to regulate and prescribe the practice and procedure to be followed in any proceedings brought before it in terms of this Act, provided that such regulations shall be laid before and be subject to alteration, revocation, amendment or modification by the General Assembly.

25.   No member of the Presbyterial Commission shall participate in any proceedings brought by a Presbytery of which he or she is a member or within the bounds of which there is a congregation of which he or she is a communicant member. This section shall not apply to the Solicitor of the Church.

26.   Act II, 1988 anent the Judicial Commission is amended as follows:—

Amend section 3 to read as follows:—

In terms of Section 1 above, the Judicial Commission shall hear Appeals on points of law against the decisions of Presbyterial Commissions in cases relating to discipline of Ministers, Licentiates, Graduate Candidates and Deacons except in matters of doctrine.

The findings and final judgement of the Judicial Commission in Appeals in terms of this Section shall be incorporated in a written Report to the General Assembly, but shall not be subject to review by the General Assembly.

Amend the Rules of Procedure rule 2 as follows:—

After "Inferior Court" add "or Presbyterial Commission".

Amend Rules of Procedure rule 3 as follows:—

Add at the end the words ", except as excluded by the Act Anent Discipline of Ministers, Licentiates, Graduate Candidates and Deacons".

Amend the first sentence of Rules of Procedure rule 4 to read:—

"In Appeals arising under the Act Anent Discipline of Ministers, Licentiates, Graduate Candidates and Deacons the Secretary of the Presbyterial Commission shall within fourteen days of the receipt of the written statement of Appeal transmit to the Clerks of the Judicial Commission the written statement of Appeal, the Notice of Complaint, Notice of Special Defence, if any, productions, transcript of evidence, and the whole record of proceedings".

Amend Rules of Procedure rule 8 as follows:—

In the second sentence delete the first occurrence of the word "The" and substitute "An".

Amend Rules of Procedure rule 10 as follows:—

After "the Inferior Court" add ", the Presbyterial Commission".

27.   Act VII, 1935 anent Trials by Libel is hereby repealed. Act XIX, 1889 shall not apply in relation to proceedings under this Act.

APPENDIX III

I. Overture anent Ministers and Deacons in Public Office

Edinburgh, May 20, 2000 Sess. 1

The General Assembly adopt the Overture, the tenor whereof follows, and transmit the same to Presbyteries for their consideration under the Barrier Act, directing that returns be sent to the Principal Clerk not later than 31 December 2000.

1.   (1) A minister or deacon in a charge or appointment of the Church who wishes to stand for:

      (a) any elected public office where the performance of duties could involve more than an average of five hours per week or

      (b) any office specified in Section 50 (2) of the Employment Rights Act 1996 c.18 as originally enacted (see the Appendix)

      shall inform the Presbytery of which he or she is a member of his or her intention before so standing.

  (2) A minister or deacon in such charge or appointment who is offered appointment to any public office which may affect the ability to discharge his or her ecclesiastical responsibilities shall inform the Presbytery of the offer.

  (3) A Presbytery shall have the right to commence process in terms of this Act on its own initiative.

2.   (1) A minister or deacon elected as a Member of Parliament, a Member of the Scottish Parliament or a Member of the European Parliament or elected or appointed to any other full-time public office will be held to have demitted his or her charge or resigned his or her appointment immediately upon election or upon the date such other appointment becomes effective.

  (2) It shall not be necessary for such a minister to make formal application to demit in terms of Act V, 1984 section 27, but the Presbytery shall allow the demission unless there be special ground to refuse to do so, issue a Practising Certificate unless there be special ground for withholding it, and appoint an Interim Moderator in terms of the said Act V, 1984.

3.   (1) When a minister or deacon in a charge or appointment of the Church stands for election as a local councillor or other part-time public office, or is offered, and does not decline to accept, any office referred to in section 1 (1) (b) or 1(2), the Presbytery shall judge whether it believes the bearing of such public office would be compatible with the exercise of the present ministry of the minister or deacon, and shall either

      (a) give permission for him or her to remain in post whilst bearing the said public office, or

      (b) in the event that the Presbytery judges that the public office sought or offered, if subsequently accepted, is not compatible with the proper fulfilment of the said ministry, it shall confer with the minister or deacon and with the office-bearers of the charge and determine either:

      (i) that, if the minister or deacon is elected or accepts the public office, a special and reviewable arrangement of ministerial staffing and financing, to allow the minister or deacon to remain in post, should be created by the Presbytery subject to the approval of the General Assembly's Committee on Parish Reappraisal, or

    (ii)   that the charge should be declared vacant, or other appointment terminated, in terms of section 2.

(2)   Any decision made in terms of this section shall be subject to review by the Presbytery at any time during the duration of the period of the office held.

4.   Before a call to any Member of Parliament, Member of the Scottish Parliament or Member of the European Parliament or holder of any other full-time public office to any charge is sustained, or before he or she enters as a minister or deacon upon any appointment in the Church, he or she must have demitted such public office. Such a person may, if otherwise qualified, be nominated and elected to a charge on undertaking so to demit.

5.   If a local councillor or the holder of another part-time public office or any office referred to in section 1(1)(b) wishes to hold, along with that office, any charge or appointment as a minister or deacon in the Church he or she must apply to the Presbytery, which shall deal with the matter in a similar way to that laid down by section 3, and shall make a determination in terms similar to those laid down by section 3(1) or 3(1)(a), or shall determine that the applicant may not hold the charge or church appointment while holding the public office.

6.   For the avoidance of doubt:

(1)   It shall not be necessary for a minister or deacon who demits office or appointment in terms of this Act to demit status.

(2)   It shall not be competent for a Presbytery or employer to grant to a minister or deacon indefinite, fixed-term or sabbatical leave or any comparable arrangement in order to bear office as defined in this Act.

APPENDIX

Section 50 (2) (a)–(g) of the Employment Rights Act 1996 c. 18 as originally enacted

(a)   A Local Authority,

(b)   A Statutory Tribunal,

(c)   A Police Authority,

(d)   A Board of Prison Visitors or a Prison Visiting Committee,

(e)   A relevant Health Body,

(f)   A relevant Education Body, or

(g)   The Environment Agency or the Scottish Environment Protection Agency.

OFFICE MANAGEMENT COMMITTEE
MAY 2001

PROPOSED DELIVERANCE

The General Assembly
1. Receive the Report.

REPORT

Office Manager and Buildings Officer

Mr Robert G. Simpson, who had served as Office Manager and Buildings Officer since 1991, retired in December 2000. Mr Simpson had contributed enormously to office life over his years of service and had encouraged the creation of welcoming meeting rooms, open plan office areas and the development of catering facilities that greatly enhanced the quality of life in the Offices for both staff and Board and Committee members.

The Office Management Committee has appointed Mrs Dorothy H. Woodhouse as Mr Simpson's successor. As an Affiliate to the British Institute of Facilities Management, Mrs Woodhouse brings to her new post considerable experience in office management and the contribution which she has made to office life particularly in the area of health and safety since her appointment in January 2001 has been greatly appreciated.

Security at the George Street Offices

As reported to the 2000 General Assembly thought has been given over recent years to finding the best and safest access to the George Street Offices. With this in mind a secure entry system has been installed and in the Spring of 2001 will become operational. The purpose of the new entry procedure is to protect both the staff who work in the Offices and those who attend meetings in the building and the greater sense of security will be of value to all.

Information Technology

The Information Technology Department is responsible for the provision and maintenance of IT hardware and software in the George Street Offices, to Presbytery Clerks through the Presbytery Clerks Project and at a number of offices and centres of the Board of National Mission.

To assist the staff of the Department in the development of their work, the Office Management Committee has employed a Consultant from the University of Strathclyde and the Report to be offered in the Spring of 2001 will give guidance on future staffing needs in this strategic area of modern administration.

Central Co-ordinating Committee

The Committee was represented on the Joint Working Party which is bringing proposals to the General Assembly for the establishment of the Central Co-ordinating Committee.

The Committee believes that the establishment of the Central Co-ordinating Committee is a positive development in the effective management of the Church and fully endorses the proposals to be considered by the General Assembly.

In the name of the Committee

DOUGLAS A O NICOL, *Convener*
DOUGLAS GALBRAITH, *Vice-Convener*
DOROTHY H WOODHOUSE, *Secretary*

JOINT WORKING PARTY
MAY 2001

PROPOSED DELIVERANCE

The General Assembly

1. Receive the Report

2. Establish the Central Co-ordinating Committee in terms of the Report with effect from 1 September 2001 at the same time discharging the Personnel Committee and the Office Management Committee.

3. Agree that the Central Co-ordinating Committee should appoint a corresponding member to the General Assembly in terms of Standing Order 32.

4. Agree that the Central Co-ordinating Committee should be represented on the Co-ordinating Forum by its Convener and the Personnel Manager.

5. Transfer ownership of the Offices at 117–123 George Street from the Board of Stewardship and Finance to the Central Co-ordinating Committee

6. Discharge the Joint Working Party.

REPORT

1. Background and Composition of Joint Working Party

The Working Party was set up by the General Assembly of 1999 on the recommendation of the Special Commission on the Board of Communication. The membership of the Working Party is drawn from the Board of Practice and Procedure, the Office Management Committee and the Personnel Committee. The original remit proposed by the Commission asked that the Working Party investigate the idea of a Chief Executive for the Church Offices, issues of staff development and representation and the establishment of induction procedures for new Board members. However, the General Assembly withdrew the first of these.

Last year's Assembly received and approved a report on the remaining three areas and resolved to continue the Working Party for another year, instructing it "to bring proposals with regard to the management of the Church's central administration to the General Assembly of 2001". This we now do.

2. Present Arrangements

A number of different elements presently characterise the Church's central administration:

*   the Office Management Committee which oversees the maintenance of the George Street Offices. This includes all the Secretaries together with the General Treasurer, the Solicitor of the Church, the Information Technology Manager and the Office Manager who acts as Secretary to the Committee. This body oversees the Information Technology (IT) Department which services the central administration (excluding Charis House), a number of Church centres throughout the country and Presbytery Clerks;

*   the Personnel Committee which is the employing agency for the majority of those who work in the central administration;

*   the further employing agencies, namely the Boards of Social Responsibility, National Mission, World

Mission and Ministry, which employ various specialist staff;

- the various Boards and Committees which oversee the work of their own departments and which are accountable directly to the General Assembly;

- the Co-ordinating Forum which brings together the Conveners and Secretaries of all Boards and Committees to advise the Board of Stewardship and Finance on relative priorities in the preparation of the Church's budget;

- the Board of Stewardship and Finance which has responsibility for preparing the budget and seeking its adoption by the General Assembly and also for internal audit. In addition the Board owns the George Street Offices;

- the Law Department which provides legal services to the various agencies of the Church both at central and local level;

- the General Treasurer's Department which provides financial services to the various agencies of the Church both at central and local level.

3. The Working Party's Proposals

In considering the present arrangements the Working Party came to a view, widely felt within the Church, that while the various elements all played their part, there is lacking any effective co-ordinating body. This inevitably resulted in a piecemeal approach, breakdowns in communication, overlap and a failure to achieve maximum cost efficiency benefits. Accordingly, the Working Party proposes the establishment of a new Central Co-ordinating Committee in terms of the Constitution set out in Appendix 1. This Committee would have a dual role.

Firstly, it would assume responsibility for matters currently within the remit of the Office Management Committee and the Personnel Committees (both of which would, as currently constituted, cease to exist). The Committee would thus be the employing agency for staff currently in the employ of the Personnel Committee. It would further oversee other "central services" namely the functions performed by the General Treasurer's and Law Departments and would have a new role in setting up a central purchasing and travel unit and a centralised insurance function. The latter facilities would hopefully result in individual departments saving both time and money in regard to the purchase of such goods and services. Responsibility for internal audit would also pass to the Committee as would ownership of the buildings at 117–123 George Street.

Secondly, the Committee would operate as a "sounding Board" in cases where any of the "Central bodies" ie. the General Assembly Boards, Statutory Corporations and Committees planned substantial re-organisation or other changes with personnel implications. The Central body would have to consult with the Committee which would thereafter issue its recommendations in writing. These would not be binding but the Central body would require to re-consider its proposals in the light of the Committee's recommendations. Should it decide not to follow them, it would be bound to report its decision and its reasons for reaching it to the following Assembly. The Committee would also be entitled to call two or more of the Central bodies together to discuss re-organisation proposals and to comment on proposed senior staff appointments in cases where the Committee would be the employing agency of the proposed employee. Again recommendations from the Committee would not be binding but failure to follow them would mean that the Central body would have to justify its decision at the following Assembly.

The Committee would consist of seven Assembly appointees from whom the Convener and Vice-Convener would be drawn together with four *ex officiis* members, namely the Principal Clerk, the Solicitor, the General Treasurer and the Personnel Manager and would be serviced by an Administrative Secretary who would not be a member. The *ex officiis* members would not have voting rights.

It is envisaged that the Committee's work in regard to the first part of its remit would be largely delegated to its proposed sub-committees namely the Executive, Internal Audit and Personnel Committees.

It is the Working Party's hope that the new Committee would stimulate additional cost saving efficiencies through the integration of specialist functions, eg. purchasing, which are at present administered on a department by department basis. Additionally, its consultative role would assist in avoiding in the future the difficulties identified by the Special Commission.

The draft Constitution is an endeavour to formulate these proposals and the Working Party warmly commends them to the General Assembly.

4. Corresponding Membership of General Assembly and Representation on the Co-ordinating Forum

As with other Standing Committees it is recommended that the Committee would be entitled to appoint a corresponding member to the General Assembly and participate in the Co-ordinating Forum. In connection with the latter it is proposed that the Convener of the Committee and the Personnel Manager should be members of the Co-ordinating Forum.

DAVID W LACY, *Convener*
FINLAY A J MACDONALD, Secretary

APPENDIX I

Draft Constitution of
The Central Co-ordinating Committee

The Central Co-ordinating Committee ("The Committee") shall be a standing committee of the General Assembly, it shall be directly accountable to the Assembly and shall report to the Assembly through its Convener.

Membership

The Committee shall comprise eleven members as follows:-

1. A Convener and Vice-Convener, appointed by the General Assembly through the Nomination Committee in terms of Standing Order 119;

2. five Assembly appointed members; and

3. the Principal Clerk, the Solicitor of the Church, the General Treasurer, and the Personnel Manager as members *ex officiis*. The *ex officiis* members shall be full members but without voting rights.

In addition, the Committee may from time to time as may be required co-opt to it or its Sub-Committees for a maximum period of twelve months up to two persons to be non-voting members, such persons to have relevant experience in regard to the particular issue in respect of which he, she or they are co-opted.

The Office Manager and the Information Technology Manager shall be in attendance at meetings (or for specific items of business) of the Committee and its Sub-Committees as required by the Convener of the Committee or Sub-Committee as the case may be.

The Committee shall be serviced by an Administrative Secretary, who shall not be a member of the Committee but who shall be in attendance at all Committee meetings and shall carry out all necessary correspondence and administrative work for it, including, in consultation with the respective Convener of the Committee and its Sub-Committees, the preparation of agenda for meetings and the Minutes thereof.

Remit

The remit of the Committee shall be:-

1. (a) To be responsible for the proper maintenance and insurance of the Church Offices at 117–123 George Street, Edinburgh ("the George Street Offices");

(b) To be responsible for matters relating to Health and Safety within the George Street Offices;

(c) To be responsible for matters relating to Data Protection within the George Street Offices and with respect to the General Assembly Boards and Committees based elsewhere;

(d) To be responsible for the allocation of accommodation within the George Street Offices and the annual determination of rental charges to the Boards, Committees and other parties accommodated therein ;

(e) To oversee the delivery of central services to departments within the George Street Offices and to the General Assembly Boards and Committees based elsewhere namely:—

(i) Those facilities directly managed by the Office Manager;

(ii) Information Technology (including the provision of support services to Presbytery Clerks);

(iii) Insurance;

(iv) Purchasing and Travel;

(v) Personnel Services;

(vi) Financial Services (as delivered by the General Treasurer's Department);

(vii) Legal Services (as delivered by the Law Department and subject to such oversight not infringing principles of "client/solicitor" confidentiality); and

(f) To provide an Internal Audit function to the General Assembly Boards, Statutory Corporations and Committees (other than the Board of Social Responsibility).

2. (a) The Committee shall act as one of the five employing agencies of the Church and shall, except in so far as specifically herein provided, assume and exercise the whole rights, functions and responsibilities of the Personnel Committee.

(b) Whilst the Committee shall *inter alia* have responsibility for determining the terms and conditions of the staff for which it is the employing agency, any staff who are members of the Committee or who are appointed directly by the General Assembly shall not be present when matters solely relating to their own personal terms and conditions of employment/office are under consideration.

3. The Committee shall act as a consultative and advisory body to the General Assembly Boards, Statutory Corporations and Committees ("the Central bodies").

Any Central body proposing to implement any substantial re-organisation, or other changes in the manner in which it undertakes its remit which have personnel implications, shall be bound, at the outset, to intimate such proposals to the Committee in order that the Committee may assess their impact on the work of the wider church. The Central body shall subsequently provide to the Committee full co-operation and any information which the Committee may require to enable it to assess the proposals and give advice in connection with them. The Committee shall invite the Convener and General Secretary (or equivalent post-holders) of the Central body concerned to be present at all meetings when the proposals are being discussed and the Committee's recommendations are being formulated.

The Committee shall thereafter provide its recommendations in writing to the Central body with respect to the proposals, setting out, in particular, any difficulties which it perceives may arise as a result of the proposals being implemented, including those in respect of staff employed by any of the Church's employing agencies and having regard to Church and employment law as well as any other relevant factors.

The Committee shall have the right to call a meeting as between any two or more of the Central bodies in situations where it perceives there is a need to discuss proposals involving re-organisation of the work undertaken by one or more of the bodies concerned and to make recommendations to the said bodies in the light of any matters raised in any such meeting.

Any Central body whilst implementing any re-organisation shall require to keep the Committee fully informed as matters progress and to consult with it should any unanticipated difficulties arise.

Similarly, all the Central bodies shall require to intimate to the Committee, in cases where the Committee would be the employing agency for the prospective employee concerned, any proposal to replace a Head of

Department or other senior staff member or to create a new senior post and the Committee shall be entitled to examine and make recommendations to the Central body concerned in respect of such proposal. This provision shall not apply to personnel appointed directly by the General Assembly.

The Central body receiving recommendations in respect of any of the above matters shall require to consider revising its proposals to take account of the Committee's recommendations. Whilst the Committee shall have no power to require the Central body to accept its recommendations, should the Central body decide not to do so, it shall require to report its decision and its reasons for reaching it to the General Assembly immediately following.

Meetings

The Committee shall normally meet three times in the year in the months of June, October and February and shall meet at other times as shall be required.

Structure

The Committee shall appoint an Executive Committee which shall comprise the Convener of the Committee together with the Convener(s) of the Personnel and Internal Audit Committees aftermentioned and of any other Sub-Committee established by the Committee and the *ex officio* members of the Committee.

The Convener of the Committee shall be the Convener of the Executive Committee.

The Executive Committee shall meet at least twice per annum with the Staff Association and separately with the departmental heads of the Central bodies at least once per annum.

The Executive Committee shall in all matters be subject to the authority and direction of the Committee. Between meetings the Executive Committee shall act as the Committee in relation to all matters referred to it.

The Committee shall further appoint a Personnel Committee which shall comprise three of the Assembly appointed members together with the *ex officiis* members of the Committee. One of the Assembly appointed members shall act as Convener of the Personnel Committee.

The Committee shall further appoint an Internal Audit Committee which shall comprise three of the Assembly appointed members together with the Convener of the Finance Committee of the Board of Stewardship and Finance *ex officio*. One of the Assembly appointed members shall act as Convener of the Internal Audit Committee which shall be entitled to report directly to the General Assembly, should it consider it appropriate and necessary so to do.

The Committee shall be entitled to set up other Sub-Committees as it considers to be necessary to facilitate the implementation of its remit.

Finance

The Committee shall assume the whole rights and assets of the Office Management Committee and the Personnel Committee. The Committee shall assume ownership of the George Street Offices from the Board of Stewardship and Finance and title thereto shall be held by the Church of Scotland General Trustees for behoof of the Committee.

The Committee shall work within the budget allocated to it by the Board of Stewardship and Finance and the other income received by it.

Adoption of Constitution

This Constitution shall take effect from 1 September 2001.

APPENDIX II
Membership of Joint Working Party

Board of Practice and Procedure
Rev David W Lacy, *Convener of the Joint Working Party*
Mr W Alexander MacNiven
Mrs Ann I McCarter
Mr David Thomson

Office Management Committee
Mr Ian D Baillie
Very Rev Dr Alexander McDonald
Rev Douglas A O Nicol

Personnel Committee
Mr Graham Charters
Mr George B B Eadie
Mr David Fotheringham

Solicitor of the Church
Mrs Janette S Wilson

General Treasurer
Mr Donald F Ross

Principal Clerk
Rev Dr Finlay A J Macdonald, *Secretary of the Joint Working Party*

At Edinburgh, and within St Andrew's and St George's Parish Church, the 12th day of September 2000 years at 11.00 am, which day the Commission of Assembly appointed by the last General Assembly in terms of Act VI 1997, being met, was constituted with prayer.

In terms of Section 5 of Act VI 1997 and in the absence of the Rt Rev Andrew R C McLellan, the Commission appointed the Very Rev Dr James Harkness as their Moderator for the meeting.

Dissent and Complaint: Rev Alice Kirkpatrick

The Commission of Assembly took up consideration of the Dissent and Complaint of Rev Alice Kirkpatrick against a decision of the Presbytery of Shetland of 2 May 2000.

The Principal Clerk read the relevant part of SO 72.

The Commission received a request from Miss Kirkpatrick in her absence for the consideration of her Dissent and Complaint to be postponed until mid-November 2000, a medical certificate from Miss Kirkpatrick's General Practitioner and a Protestation from the Presbytery of Shetland in the following terms:

I Charles H M Greig for the Presbytery of Shetland hereby take protestation that the Dissent and Complaint of the Rev Alice H Kirkpatrick against a deliverance of the Presbytery given on 2 May 2000 has been fallen from and that the said judgement has become final; and I take instruments and crave extracts.

Parties were called.

The Rev Charles Greig Convener of the Presbytery Parish Reappraisal Committee appeared for the Presbytery of Shetland. Mr Andrew Nicolson and Mrs Marion Jamieson appeared for the Parish of Northmavine.

Mr Bob McGregor and the Rev Winnie Munson appeared for the Parish of Delting.

The Rev Arthur Barrie, Convener, Mr Noel Glen, Vice Convener and the Rev Douglas Nicol, Secretary appeared for the General Assembly's Committee on Parish Reappraisal.

The Very Rev Alexander McDonald, General Secretary appeared for the Board of Ministry.

The Commission received the Report of the Investigating Committee appointed by the Board of Practice and Procedure in terms of Section 5 (d) (iii) which was given in by the Rev Valerie Watson, Convener.

Parties were heard.

Questions were asked.

Parties were removed.

It was moved and seconded:-

That the Commission grant the Protestation of the Presbytery of Shetland.

It was moved and seconded as a counter-motion:—

That the Commission postpone consideration of the Dissent and Complaint of Miss Kirkpatrick to a later date.

The Principal Clerk read the relevant part of SO 72.

There voted for the motion 49 and for the counter-motion 23 and the Commission of Assembly resolved accordingly.

Parties were recalled and judgement was intimated.

Petition: Mr Donald Michael MacInnes

The Commission of Assembly took up consideration of the Petition of Mr Donald Michael MacInnes.

Parties were called.

Mr Donald Michael MacInnes appeared for himself.

The Rev Ian Taylor, Convener of the Committee on Education and Training, the Rev Professor William Storrar, Convener of the Board, the Rev Nigel Robb, Director of Educational Services, the Rev Dr Christine Goldie, Convener of the Committee on Vocational Guidance and the Rev Dr Douglas Murray, Principal of Trinity College Glasgow appeared for the Board of Ministry.

The Rev Tom Sinclair, Presbytery Clerk, Dr John Hay, Convener of the Committee on Ministry, and Mr Ewan McKinnon appeared for the Presbytery Lewis.

The Principal Clerk read the relevant part of SO 72.

It was moved, seconded and agreed:—

The Commission of Assembly take the Petition as read.

It was moved, seconded and agreed:—

The Commission of Assembly receive the Petition.

The Commission agreed that questions, when relevant, would be put by the Court and not by Parties.

The Commission received the Report of an Investigating Committee appointed by the Board of Practice and Procedure in terms of Section 5 (d) (iii) and with the consent of the Parties, part of which was given in by the Rev Grant Barclay, Convener.

The Commission addressed the question of fact; whether the Petitioner had satisfactorily completed his prescribed course within the meaning of Act V 1985.

Parties were heard.

In the course of the Petitioner's addressing the Commission on this question, the Commission declined to hear him on the question of the agreements made or offered by the Board and the Presbytery of Lewis. The Petitioner entered his Dissent.

Questions were asked.

Parties were removed.

The Principal Clerk read the relevant part of SO 72.

The question of fact was put to the Commission.

There voted For the proposition 59 and Against 6 and the Commission of Assembly resolved accordingly.

Parties were recalled and judgement was intimated.

The Commission suspended from 1.05 pm until 2.00 pm.

The Commission addressed the question of law; whether the Board of Ministry had no legal right, in terms of Act V 1985 Section 46 to withhold an Exit Certificate from the Presbytery of Lewis upon the completion of the Petitioner's training in terms of Sections 43 and 44 of the Act. Mr Barclay, Convener of the Investigating Committee was heard.

Parties were heard.

Questions were asked.

Parties were removed.

The Principal Clerk read the relevant part of SO 72.

The question of law was put to the Commission.

There voted For the proposition 65 and Against 0 and the Commission resolved accordingly.

Parties were recalled and judgement was intimated.

Parties were removed.

It was moved and seconded:—

The Commission, without making any judgement on Mr MacInnes' continuing fitness for the ministry, find that he has satisfactorily completed his prescribed course as required by Act V 1985, find further that, in view of this the Board of Ministry had no authority in terms of the Act to withhold an Exit Certificate, and accordingly grant the crave of his Petition to the following extent:

1. *Instruct the Board of Ministry to issue an Exit Certificate to the Presbytery of Lewis in respect of Mr MacInnes' candidacy;*

2. *Instruct the Presbytery of Lewis in consultation with the Board of Ministry to take steps to satisfy itself as to Mr MacInnes' continuing fitness as a candidate in terms of Section 23 of Act V 1998 and, only if satisfied, to consider the question of his licensing.*

The Principal Clerk read the relevant part of SO 72.

On a vote being taken For or Against there voted For 66 and Against 0 and the Commission of Assembly resolved accordingly.

Parties were recalled and judgement was intimated.

This being all the business, the Sederunt was closed with prayer at 3.40 pm.

St Andrew's and St George's Parish Church
Edinburgh, 12th September 2000

The General Assembly of the Church of Scotland
The Report of the Special Commission anent Review and Reform

A Church without Walls

Contents

Appendices

Website

www.churchwithoutwalls.org.uk

The General Assembly of the Church of Scotland
The Report of the Special Commission anent Review and Reform

PROPOSED DELIVERANCE

The General Assembly:

A. Receive the Report.

B. Reaffirm as primary purposes of the Church the calls to the Church:

1. to follow Jesus Christ as Lord.
2. to share in Christ's mission in the world.
3. to turn back to God and neighbour.

C. As a process of continuing reform towards reshaping the Church locally, regionally and centrally:

The Shape of the Local Church

1. Urge congregations to choose to study, reflect on and live by one Gospel for one year in the first instance, and let Jesus shape the life and structure of the congregation.

2. Urge congregations to reflect on the cycle of grace and what it means to live out that grace in our life together.

3. Urge congregations to undertake a community review at least once every ten years to reflect on the issues, changes and missionary opportunities in the community, in collaboration with others, wherever appropriate.

4. Urge Kirk Sessions to undertake a review of the worship of the existing congregation and assess potential for developments within and beyond the congregation.

5. Urge congregations to consider how the cell, congregation and celebration dimensions of being the church might be applied locally.

6. Urge congregations to determine to integrate children and young people into the life of the congregation; or to offer the resources to plant a church for a new generation alongside the current congregation.

7. Urge congregations to form paths for the spiritual journey to help people become Christian disciples in today's world.

8. Instruct Kirk Sessions to review the leadership structure, consider what ministry team is needed for current needs and determine how it might be developed in the next five years.

9. Urge congregations to form groupings according to their natural communities to explore shared mission and mutual ministry, with other churches in the area.

10. Urge congregations to establish links with other congregations in a different social context as a partnership of mutual ministry.

11. Urge congregations to research an area of the world church and establish a personal partnership with a congregation or project.

12. Urge congregations to explore ways of being more environmentally aware and responsible as a witness to the Christian care of God's creation.

13. Urge Kirk Sessions to identify the spiritual gifts of the people and grow the church around the people we have rather than deploy people to support existing church structures.

14. Instruct Presbyteries to develop a coordinated strategy to equip congregations to sustain worship, pastoral care and mission with the appropriate staffing, and monitor progress through the Quinquennial/Presbytery visits.

15. Instruct Kirk Sessions to offer an opportunity for all elders who have not undertaken training in the past three years to share the current vision of the role and expectations of an elder in the Church of Scotland.

16. Urge Kirk Sessions to develop appropriate open styles of meeting and processes of communication.

17. Instruct the Board of Practice and Procedure to examine whether the present "model constitution" represents the best and most flexible way of managing a local congregation.

18. Instruct the Board of Ministry, in consultation with the Board of National Mission and the Board of Parish Education, to develop a coordinated process of recruiting and training people with missionary gifts which are vital for service within and beyond the constraints of a parish context.

19. Instruct the Board of Ministry, in consultation with the Board of National Mission and the Board of Parish Education, to develop a database with the current Curricula Vitae of all ministers, auxiliary ministers, Deacons and Readers to assist in the strategic deployment of personnel.

20. Instruct the Board of Ministry and the Board of Parish Education to develop working patterns of active collaboration to equip the whole people of God for Christian service.

21. Encourage the Panel on Worship in the review of services of ordination, induction and commissioning, in order to celebrate imaginatively the ministry of all God's people within them.

The Shape of the Church: Regional and Central

22. Remit sections on "The Shape of the Regional Church" and "The Shape of the Central Church" to the Board of Practice and Procedure and the Assembly Council.

23. Instruct the Board of Practice and Procedure to review the culture and timing of the General Assembly in order to increase the quality of reporting, participation and decision-making.

Proposals for Continuing Reform

24. Urge Kirk Sessions to identify ways of deepening the prayer life of their congregations individually and together.

25. Urge the leadership in every area of church life to institute the discipline of a period of retreat, rest and reflection to allow space for God to change us.

26. Urge congregations to take risks, to try new ways so that faith may grow.

27. Instruct Kirk Sessions and Presbyteries to study the report as a stimulus to identifying the levers for change and the limits to growth in the local situation; Kirk Sessions to establish a "local needs" plan and Presbytery to establish a "regional needs" plan of support, with special reference to recommendations 1–16 and 24–28; and to apply, where appropriate, to the Community and Parish Development Fund.

28. Urge congregational leadership teams to form networks focused on a shared context or a shared concern in order to build trusting relationships as the basis of future cooperation.

29. Urge the Coordinating Forum to develop its role of capturing the larger vision within which people are operating.

30. Resolve to appoint a planning group of seven persons including a Convener and Vice-Convener to prepare a "Stakeholders' Conference" in 2005 as a point of National Celebration and a milestone of progress and instruct the Selection Committee to bring names to a future sederunt.

31. Resolve to establish a Board of Community and Parish Development as described in Appendix 8, and accordingly instruct the Board of Stewardship and Finance

    a) to set up a Parish Development Fund of £7.5 million over 5 years in terms of Appendix 8 and report to the General Assembly of 2002;
    b) to appoint and manage two field directors until the Board of Community and Parish Development comes into being;
       and instruct the Nomination Committee to nominate 12 people for the Board of Community and Parish Development and report to the General Assembly of 2002.

32. Instruct the Assembly Council, through the Coordinating Forum, to establish overall priorities for the work of the Church in the light of the emerging shape of the Church and to convey these to the Board of Stewardship and Finance, so that these priorities can be incorporated into the Co-ordinated Budget proposals which the Board will be bringing to the General Assembly in 2002 and subsequent years, with appropriate amendments to the Constitution of the Coordinating Forum and the Board of Stewardship and Finance.

33. Instruct the General Trustees, in consultation with the Board of Ministry and the Board of National Mission, to monitor changing patterns of ministry and building requirements, and report on how best to fund the needs of the emerging church and report to the General Assembly of 2003.

34: Instruct the General Trustees to examine the Consolidated Stipend Fund and bring proposals to the General Assembly of 2002 that would allow congregations more flexibility of investment.

35: Instruct the General Trustees to examine the Consolidated Fabric Fund and bring proposals to the General Assembly of 2002 that would allow congregations more flexibility of investment.

36. Instruct the General Trustees, in consultation with the Board of National Mission, to examine the application of the proceeds of the sale of buildings following readjustment, and report to the General Assembly of 2002.

37. Instruct the Panel on Doctrine to undertake a study on the theology of power and report to a future General Assembly.

38. Instruct all Kirk Sessions, Presbyteries, Boards and agencies of the Church to study the Report, take appropriate action and establish the necessary accountability for progress by 2005; and instruct the Assembly Council to monitor developments through its ongoing consultations and assessments in 2002–3 and 2004–5.

39. Instruct the Board of Practice and Procedure to facilitate the study of the Report throughout the Church.

D. Thank and discharge the Special Commission anent Review and Reform.

The Remit of the Commission

In 1999 the General Assembly appointed a Special Commission

> *"to re-examine in depth the primary purposes of the Church and the shape of the Church of Scotland as we enter into the next Millennium; to formulate proposals for a process of continuing reform; to consult on such matters with other Scottish Churches; and to report to the General Assembly of 2001."*

At the same time the Assembly Council was given a renewed remit which involved consultation, assessment, identifying priorities and developing appropriate strategies for the future. While there was an obvious overlap in issues and concerns, it was agreed from the outset that there be open communication between the two bodies, collaboration wherever possible and the avoidance of unnecessary duplication, especially when consulting with others.

The Commission acknowledges a debt to the careful research and the open consultative processes of the Assembly Council. The Council's consultation on "Change or Decay?" has raised the issue of change around the church. We believe that the outcome of our partnership has been a strengthened witness to the issues being faced by the Church and pointers to the future. We trust that this is symptomatic of a greater sense of openness and trust within the Church at large.

The experience of the last few months has been daunting and humbling. The cooperation of many people has allowed us to listen to many perspectives. The range of experience put at our disposal and the debt owed to so many is recorded in **Appendix 1**.

The Commission offers its findings as one contribution among many at a time when many prayerfully reflect on God's call to be the Church of Jesus Christ in our times.

A Summary of the Report

The Report of the Special Commission anent Review and Reform encourages the Church to return the ministry of the Gospel to the people of God. The aim is to give them the tools and the trust to shape a vision for the church in their own area.

> *The Church 'works' where people join together, building relationships with each other and the community to which they belong. It is through these relationships that the Gospel is spread. In each place the church is different. There is no one model that fits all. We rejoice in the diversity within the Church. We celebrate and encourage it.*

This is achieved best by allowing congregations the space and opportunity to develop their own patterns of ministry, mission, worship and leadership that best suits the people and situations where they are.

Structures require to be flexible, not rigid. It means that nationally and as Presbytery we require to listen to the local voice and to serve the local church. This may mean a U-turn, so that the local church dictates the agenda and is served by Presbytery and '121'. At present many perceive things to be the other way round.

Churches—within new-sized Presbyteries—will plan together the best way forward for their location and be supported by the Presbytery.

We believe that it is important that the local church is allowed to flourish and grow in its own unique way with all possible resources at its disposal. The Commission therefore believes it is vital that we trust our congregations to be good stewards of their resources and to give them increased flexibility of choice on funds held centrally for their benefit, while challenging them to increased stewardship of local giving.

In order to help and support new ideas, where local resources are not available, we propose the creation of a

Community and Parish Development Fund. This fund will give financial backing to new and imaginative forms of ministry and mission.

To enable and encourage these proposals, the report outlines a process of change that will assist the church on this road. The Commission is well aware that Church is not changed by recommendations or deliverances. The Commission is not placing into the hands of any one group or Committee the responsibility for implementing these recommendations. Rather, we place them into the hands of everyone who has any responsibility and concern for the future welfare of the church.

We place into the hands of God's people the opportunity to live out our faith, each according to our uniqueness, made in the image of God. It is our hope and prayer that the report, together with the many other initiatives within the Church at present, will stimulate the Church to face the future in faith and hope.

SECTION I:

The Primary Purposes of the Church

1. The Core Calling of the Church

> **Jesus said, "Follow me."**

"Follow me". These two words of Jesus Christ offer us the purpose, shape and process of continuous reform of the Church at the beginning of a new Millennium and at any other time. The Commission has joked about making these two words the report to the General Assembly. The Church of Jesus Christ is about nothing more and nothing less than this. Like a computer icon, the words "Follow me" carry within them the complex and comprehensive processes of being God's people in God's world.

That core calling takes us back behind the secondary

> **"The most important single thing about the people of God is that they are there."**

identities of denomination or tradition and calls us to turn again to be people with Jesus at the centre, travelling wherever Jesus takes us. It is so simple we cannot miss it. It is so profound we can never exhaust it. This calling invites us to risk the way of Jesus.

The calling is *personal.* Jesus calls people personally by name. When he calls us out of our individualism, he affirms our individuality. The church is shaped by our personal faith and obedience. The aim of the Guild captures well the spirit of our core calling: to invite, encourage and enable people to be disciples of Jesus Christ.

That calling is *local* rather than general. As Jesus came into the world at a particular time in history to a particular place and culture, our purpose is to follow Jesus in our place in our time, in the concrete situations of Stranraer or Lewis, Drumchapel or Drumnadrochit.

That calling is *relational* rather than institutional. Jesus leads us into love for God and love for our neighbour, expressed in communities of worship and mission. We are to be disciples before we can make disciples. Those who are learning the Way will accompany contemporary searchers in the Way. We are to be communities of the Way.

The calling is *sacrificial.* "Take up your cross and follow me." It is a costly calling. We cannot save and be safe at the same time. The love of security is addictive. It will take courage and commitment to break that addiction. The sacrificial service of Christians, past and present, in Scotland and around the world, challenges patterns of church life that settle for comfortable options. The only way to Resurrection is by way of the Cross.

That calling is *radical.* A prominent Hindu once said that he would believe in the Christian Saviour, if Christians looked more saved. The Sermon of the Mount challenges us to ask if our congregational life supports us in living out street-level examples of God's Kingdom. When Jesus challenged the establishment of his day, he highlighted the priorities of justice, mercy and faith. "What does it mean for the pastor to have as his/her job description, not the sustenance of a service club within a generally Christian culture, but the survival of a colony within an alien society?" (Stanley Hauerwas)

That calling is *global* in its scope, sending us to make disciples of all nations. Matthew's Gospel begins with representatives of the Gentiles coming to the Messiah and ends with the representatives of the Messiah going to the Gentiles. The local church shares in an international partnership of mission. We rejoice that we are part of a global movement of God's people that makes up one third of the world's population. While our local experience of the past fifty years has been of decline, we recall that we are living in a time when the advance of the Church of Jesus Christ around the world is unprecedented.

That calling is *eschatological*. God's Kingdom is breaking in on us and is coming. The church is a sign and pointer. It is never the end in itself. The church looks for God's presence breaking into the world and waits for Christ's coming with prayerful expectancy. The Church invests its talents and resources generously and serves Christ unselfconsciously in "the least of these".

The church shaped by the Coming Kingdom will live less by historical precedent and more by the future expectation of becoming part of God's new creation. We participate in God's mission for a redeemed planet and people, and the church is created on the way. It is not that the church 'has' a mission, but the very reverse: the mission of Christ creates his own church.

The eschatological perspective challenges our obsession with buildings and money, releases us from our "structural fundamentalism" to sit lightly to inherited structures. It frees us from anxiety about our changing place in society. According to J.L. Segundo, "it is the situation of Christendom that represents a distortion, or at least an abnormal condition, in the understanding of the church's role in history. The normal condition and the one that is coming back into focus today is that of a creative minority dedicated to the service of the vast majority."

> **The church exists by the grace of God and for the glory of God.**

That calling is *doxological*. The church exists by the grace of God and for the glory of God. People worship in response to God's grace. We love because he first loved us. Congregations need to know that they are loved by God—and their minister. Ministers need to know that they are loved by God—and by their congregation. A worshipping church is a church soaked in the grace of God.

"The pastor must not fail to understand the congregation just as it is, as a historical community brought into being warts and all, by God; and must not fail to be grateful for it, just as it is, warts and all, to God.

"The most important single thing about the people of God is that they are *there*. They *exist*. They *are*, not because of favourable conditions......, not because of certain perceived needs for which the church can provide a market, but because God called them out of nothing and made them his people (Hosea 1:10)." (Eugene Peterson)

This reminder of the church's continued existence by grace alone—a divinely given fact in any cultural context—challenges us to do as the Jews did in Exile, to rebuild God-honouring community in an alien environment, but to do it non-anxiously.

The purpose and shape of the Church of Scotland at the beginning of a new Millennium arises out of that calling of grace. Our sole purpose is the glorification of God. Only when the people of Scotland and other nations are released into worship of the God of grace is that purpose fulfilled. That calling is eternal.

Steve Bruce, Professor of Sociology at Aberdeen University, writes: "*the only area of life where the church can compete with any secular institution or social practice and win is in the glorification of God.*"(unpublished letter to the Commission)

Our prayer as a Commission is that the Church of Scotland recovers the sense of doxology, of glorifying God and enjoying God for ever.

Call 1: The Church is called to follow Jesus Christ as Lord.

Jesus said, "Follow me."

2. The Constitutional Calling of the Church of Scotland

The Church of Scotland as an historical entity does have a declared constitutional purpose. That is expressed in the Third Declaratory Article of 1921:

"As a National Church, representative of the Christian Faith of the Scottish people, it acknowledges its distinctive call and duty to bring the ordinances of religion to the people in every parish of Scotland through a territorial ministry".

The assumptions behind this statement of purpose need to be examined and questioned at the beginning of the 21st Century when Church and society have changed. **(See Appendix 2: Church and State: The Declaratory Articles)**

"The only area of life where the church can compete with any secular institution or social practice and win is in the glorification of God" (unpublished letter to the Commission)

Assumption 1. The Christian Faith is the "Christian Faith *of* the Scottish people", assuming that the majority of the population hold to that allegiance.

When the Scottish Census of Church Attendance in 1994 revealed that only 14% of the population were in church on that Sunday, and only 5% of the adult population were in any Church of Scotland church, the assumption no longer holds. This is one measure of the secularisation of Scotland throughout the 20th century.

While there is more goodwill towards the Kirk than these statistics would suggest, Robin Gill's recent research shows that loss of Church attendance does lead to the erosion of Christian belief in society. There is no solace in attributing Christian belief to a nation that worships at other altars.

The Church of Scotland must take her place alongside other churches in being a "representative of the Christian faith among the Scottish people.'

Being Christian in today's Scotland is different from being Christian in 1921. Scotland is multicultural and has welcomed new Scots of other faiths. The statement is heard in a new political context that is conscious of the dynamics of majority/minority interests.

Assumption 2. The Church was held to be "representative of" that majority faith. It was claiming to be the voice *of* the people rather than a voice *to* the people.

The Church of Scotland must take her place alongside other churches in being a "representative of the Christian faith *among* the Scottish people." The context is now overtly missionary with the collapse of the Christendom canopy. Pastoral presence, creative communication, and patient persuasion require a more proactive role for the Church of Scotland in the 21st century.

Assumption 3. The "ordinances of religion" were to be offered on a supply and demand basis.

The opportunities for pastoral presence are still our privilege at the crucial points of life relating to birth, marriage and death—as well as other points of intervention such as divorce and remarriage. The congregation that is able to be alongside people and accompany them on the journey of life, will not lack opportunity to share the Good News of Jesus Christ in appropriate and life-changing ways.

While demand for baptisms and marriages decreases, the demand for funerals remains high, requiring a massive time commitment from ministers. This commitment alone highlights the need to be part of a team ministering in the area, if pastoral leadership is to remain fresh, and bereavement care is to be appropriately offered. Teams will be different in different places.

Assumption 4. The "territorial ministry" is taken as a norm assuming social stability and cohesion. Today we recognise the many sector ministries that have emerged in the past 50 years in industry, hospitals, universities, technology and the arts.

Society is such that everybody lives in a parish, but nobody lives in a parish. People belong to networks of friendship, work and leisure pursuits, or associate with the "flow cultures" of transient groups of people. Apart from rural communities, the virtual community of the docu-soaps or the Internet may be more real than the neighbour next door.

The future lies in sharing partnerships with neighbouring congregations of various traditions, and tapping into the sector specialisms designed to connect with people in their work, leisure, or crisis moments. Trust and openness will create grassroots "matrix ministry".

The parish structure may become a problem when it is used as a base for power or possessiveness. When put at the service of the Gospel and the whole church, it can still be a catalyst to mission. As we learn how to work together as one Church in Scotland, the Church of Scotland parish church is still perceived as the strong partner with a unique power base in the community. Christ-formed relationships will reflect the mind of Christ who laid aside the place of power to take the way of the servant.

Partner churches have spoken of the generosity of the Church of Scotland in many ecumenical ventures, and the "charism of the big heart". Where that spirit is shown locally, the potential for partnership in mission is immense.

Assumption 5. The basic assumption is that the people are Christians and we offer a national spiritual health service on demand. The result is a deep frustration and cynicism among office-bearers who will still speak of people not being "Kirk hungry". They lost their appetite a long time ago for church, but there are many signs of a spiritual quest that is passing our doors.

The changed situation is an opportunity, not a threat.

Often people feel ill-equipped to meet that challenge, which requires a capacity for deep listening, a new spirituality and a focus on Christian discipleship rather than church membership.

In times past, faith has been passed from one generation to another. Today that "chain of memory" has been broken. People are mobile, families are fragmented and society is less stable. All these factors erode long-term memory in our culture. How does the Church nurture long-term disciples in a short-term culture?

> *In times past, faith has been passed from one generation to another. Today that "chain of memory" has been broken.*

Assumption 6. The final observation lies in the issue of identity. If the Church of Scotland defines itself as a National Church only by statute, it will have at its heart a legalistic flaw. The only rationale for the Church of Scotland is to declare its identity, purpose and calling to be by the grace of God in Jesus Christ. To live *in* the grace of God means to live *out* the grace of God. The parish system is a sign that the grace of God is offered to every person in the land, in all its parts and sectors. Grace means travelling with God across inherited boundaries to be part of the networks of society and understand the many sub-cultures around us.

If the Church of Scotland assumes that it exists by legal right and by claims of social influence and power, it will lose its life. If it lives by grace and gives away power by grace in order to make known the Gospel of grace, then, in partnership with the whole Body of Christ, we will share in making Christ known in our land.

If we were to restate the purpose of the Church of Scotland in our context, it might include:

As part of the world Church, we are committed to the spiritual welfare of the whole Scottish nation and to share in God's mission across the world.

Along with other branches of Christ's Church, we seek humbly to represent the Christian Faith among the Scottish people.

Together, we acknowledge our distinctive call and duty to bring the Gospel of Jesus Christ to every person in every part of Scotland.

We recognise the call, through a shared ministry of pastoral and prophetic evangelism, to serve people in all the communities and sectors of their lives.

As part of the world church we celebrate the privilege of partnership in the Gospel of Jesus Christ.

As the Church of the Way, we sit loose to every pattern of organisation, ready to respond to the call of the Spirit in our times.

As part of the whole church we are called to share the whole Gospel with the whole nation—and the whole world.

> **Call 2: The Church is called to share in Christ's mission in the world.**

3. The Hidden Calling of the Church: Shaped by God and for God.

The purpose of the Church is to be shaped within history by God and for God. The seductive danger of our managerial culture is to imagine that we are involved in the re-engineering of an organisation.

We come at the task with a deep sense of mystery for our task is to discern the deeper purposes of God with his people in our times. One moment of insight that sparked the imagination was to see our situation through the lens of the call of the prophet Jeremiah.

Many voices claim that the Exile is a lens for seeing God's hand on the church today. The forces of change are seldom crises. Consequences are not easily connected to causes. They are usually slow moving processes that have a long time lapse between the cause and the outcome. The purposes of God are hidden in the slow moving processes of our culture and the slow learning processes of a reluctant people. The critical moment of the fall of Jerusalem was only a datable moment of visibility. In the same way we look behind this critical

> *the core issue is the erosion of belief: the lack of plausibility of faith for many people.*

moment in the church's life to the hidden processes.

This prophet was brought up within the establishment of his day, lived through the structural and organisational reforms of Josiah, but saw that surface reform was not enough. The time was coming when God would work a reformation that would be deeper and more durable, but more costly. That reform is captured in the vivid imagery of land-clearance and replanting, or demolition and rebuilding: *See I appoint you over nations and kingdoms to uproot and tear down, to destroy and overthrow, to build and to plant. (Jeremiah 1:10)*

Who does this? It is not Jeremiah, but God working through the social, cultural and political forces of his time. The process will involve exile, cultural dislocation that will expose God's people to God in a new way. It takes time.

Why does the exile happen? The people have turned their backs on God and committed spiritual adultery by putting others gods in place of the true God. There are always competitors for God's place. The people of God require constantly to turn back to God.

What is the outcome? God forms a new covenant relationship with his people, and exposes them to new ways of expressing that relationship in an alien culture.

"Uproot and Tear Down": What cultural forces of erosion have uprooted the church?

Professor Steve Bruce highlights that the core issue is the erosion of belief: the lack of plausibility of faith for many people. This has undermined the confidence of many Christian people, and made communication more complex as we have become immersed in the televisual culture. The social basis of the church has been eroded as the church has become disconnected from local community, through social fragmentation and congregational isolation. The "chain of memory" between the generations has been broken, cutting the church off from the rising generation. The political significance of the church has changed as Scotland has become multicultural and many-voiced.

After 40 years of erosion of youth statistics, the impact is felt on leadership. Without discipleship there can be no leadership. The leadership basis of the church is changing as 211 ministers retire in the next five years and candidates for ministry come forward at the rate of 20–25 a year. Shifts in population, informal patterns of relating and interactive styles of communication mean that the physical buildings of the church are often the wrong size, in the wrong style or in the wrong place. The General Trustees estimate that the Church of Scotland needs only 1700 of its current 2500 buildings.

The cultural appropriateness of much church life is sadly out of tune with the times. We live in a "sonic" culture where people pick up subconsciously the way we do things. That intuitive signal speaks of a cultural gap. Membership is alien to people who see life as a journey, or who want a real challenge. Church membership seems too static for the searchers and tamely passive for the adventurers. They are looking for looser patterns of belonging and activities that make a real difference to the world.

"Destroy and Overthrow": What areas of church life are to be actively demolished?

The Church of Scotland mission strategy is based on the 19th Century mission model: one minister in one building in one parish. All the resources of the uniting church of 1929 were harnessed to servicing this strategy.

As we enter the 21st Century, the emerging pattern for mission strategy must be much more diverse to permeate the fragmented nature or our society: ministry teams operating in a variety of community bases to be incarnate in a network of communities. Instead of occasional variations to the assumed 19th Century norm, it is time to recognize the new components of the new strategy and resource it accordingly.

> *The Church of Scotland structure is perceived by most people to be overly centralized. Presbyteries are places where people do their Presbyterian duty, but gain little inspiration or support. Local congregations with the desire for vision and change sense a culture of inhibition that limits initiative for all except the boldest.*

As we enter the 21st Century we believe the shape of the church needs to turned upside down: to affirm local responsibility, offer regional support and supervision and release the central administration to offer its skills in servicing the system.

The Church of Scotland has a long and honourable legacy as a National Church taking its place in the life of Scotland over the centuries. Today we have a new Scotland and a new globalised world, which call for a redefining of a new national and global identity.

We take our place in Scotland as evangelist and servant, and as partner and prophet: bearers of the Good News of Jesus Christ and sharers in mission of God for the greater good of our nation. Our continuing role in education, social care and influencing public policy is vital for the spiritual and moral health of the nation.

We lift our eyes beyond our small church and join the massive movement of Christian people across the world where the church grows as never before. As partners in the world church we are humble but hopeful.

"Plant and Build": What is emerging of God's purposes?

The purposes of God are hidden and mysterious. The gift of Jeremiah's prophecy is to disclose what is hidden. The cultural dislocation of Exile will lead to spiritual reorientation of God's people. We believe that there are signs of that reorientation today.

We celebrate the creative work with children to build church from the crèche up, and the range of youth initiatives from the Youth Assembly to partnerships with other youth agencies. If the church will permit innovation and work at integration, the face of the church would be different in ten years' time. We see the potential of the Third Agers (over 50's), who have much to offer the church locally, nationally and overseas.

We celebrate new patterns of community work in Urban and Rural Priority Areas. We see committed church members working alongside people in the community, both working to God's agenda. They are less anxious about numbers and less guilty about the nominal or lapsed members who once made vows, but have slipped their moorings. When the church seeks first the Kingdom of God and is less concerned about her own survival, God is at work.

We celebrate the increasing shift from membership to discipleship. The *Alpha* courses, Emmaus Courses and locally devised schemes are drawing members into a renewed faith in Christ. For many the way to faith is through sharing in adventurous projects at home and overseas. Being part of the Church in action leads to a deeper desire to be a disciple of Christ. People want to belong to a God who does not want children to die because of international debt, or to see homeless people go hungry and cold.

We celebrate the shift from running a congregation to building communities of faith in Christ. The Cell Church movement has given some the handle on building church relationally and organically. The Celtic renaissance has offered some a new lens for seeing church and mission in our culture: nurturing the heart for God, offering a home to the stranger and becoming a hub for mission to resource people in daily life.

We celebrate new patterns of leadership. New elders are being given a new vision for the role. Readers are being trained and deployed to congregations. Ministry teams are operating well and creatively.

We celebrate the openness to consider new structures and ways of working. On all sides we have found an openness to change. The test lies in our readiness to

> **The cultural dislocation of Exile will lead to spiritual reorientation of God's people. We believe that there are signs of that reorientation today**

explore specific changes, which may be costly to ourselves. Practitioners are already pointing the way. It will require the authorizing decisionmakers—local, Presbyterial and National—to support them.

We celebrate those who have been like Jeremiah and "bought a field at Anathoth" as a sign of hope. We encourage people not to wait for a reconstruction of the Church of Scotland, but to act in faith and in hope that God is already planting and building. *I will rejoice in doing them good and will assuredly plant them in this land with all my heart. (Jeremiah 32:41)*

We celebrate the God of grace who works in the dark times to call us back to the light, and believe that it is God who is at work in the untidiness of the building site of demolition and reconstruction.

In the name of this God of grace we call on all God's people to turn back to love the God and Father of our Lord Jesus Christ, with all our heart and soul and mind and strength, and to love our neighbours as ourselves.

> **Call 3: The Church is called to turn back to God and our neighbour.**

SECTION II:
The Shape of the Church

> *Jesus said, "Follow me."*

Guiding Principles

The Purpose: Follow me
The Focus: Local and Relational
The Shape: Upside Down
The Foundations: Trust, Responsibility and Resources
The Ethos: Interdependence
The Barriers: Fear and Power

"Follow me" is a call to travel "down" with Jesus and to live at the "edge". The spatial metaphors are worth debating, but they do convey something of the spirit of following Jesus in a church which is perceived to operate "top down" and to be overly "centralised".

While challenging the existing structures, we have become aware of the hurt caused by the breakdown of trust between the Church locally and centrally. We have found that some of the greatest frustration with the current system of church is to be found among those who operate "at the centre". There is a passion to serve the local church, but our mental models have created false expectations and often paralysis of action.

The current mental model assumes a top down pattern of governance—from centre to Presbytery to local congregation. We recommend that the shape of the church be turned upside down to affirm the primacy of the local Christian community, supported appropriately by Presbytery and central administration.

Local church is the focus of action—the place of initiative, questions and vision. Our vision is of local churches discovering their vision of what God is doing and joining in.

Regional church is the focus of support—the place of oversight, encouragement and appropriate accountability. The role of Presbytery needs to be radically revisited.

Central church is the focus of essential servicing and national role—the place of ensuring equity and fostering links with national and international institutions. The role of the centre needs to be revamped in the light of the new roles of Presbyteries.

Instead of the hierarchical model, the Biblical imagery of the Body encourages us to see the whole as relationships of interdependence, with Christ as the Head. As we all own Jesus as Lord and live in openness to the Spirit, we make our contribution as we are able, and trust others to make theirs.

> **Guiding Principles**
> **Purpose:** Follow me
> **Focus:** Local and Relational
> **Shape:** Upside Down
> **Foundations:** Responsibility and Resources
> **Ethos:** Interdependence
> **Barriers:** Fear and Power

We need a radically increased amount of flexibility within the institutional church. The radical move is not to destroy the current institution, but to make it flexible and open, generous and accommodating, encouraging and enabling, so that new things can safely and happily emerge within—and, when they emerge outwith the system, to be easily acknowledged.

"Follow me" is an act of trust in Jesus and trust by Jesus that these ordinary people may "fish for people". When he sent out the 70 (Luke 10), he trusted them to fulfil their mission, gave them specific responsibilities and limited (yet unlimited!) resources.

We believe that the church will flourish where trust, responsibility and resources are present.

Trust. We are all on the same side. We all love the Church and long to see her strong. We will have different dreams, perhaps different visions of a strong Church, but there is only one Lord, one gospel, one Church, one Spirit. We need to trust the Lord to build his Church. We need to trust one another that we will all, separately and together, seek his will for his Church.

> **Presbyterianism has become a form of institutionalised distrust**

At present our shape displays a culture of inhibition and little trust. Presbyterianism has become a form of institutionalised distrust. It rightly takes seriously our fallenness and is designed to check any personalised power trips, but tends to legalism. If we believe that by creation and redemption, grace is prior to and greater than our sin, then a culture of trust follows. Even mistakes will be redeemed. The issue at the heart is a choice between a spirituality of grace or law.

Responsibility. To those we trust we give responsibility. Responsibility encourages action. Distrust and lack of responsibility inhibit and restrict. It is important to challenge the cynicism about "the structures" which is rife in the church. We believe that those who serve centrally serve by the call of God as do others in the service of the church and are to be appreciated and trusted with that calling.

We believe that the core issue of the reshaping of the church is trusting local people to find their own vision under the guidance of the Spirit. In the true spirit of Presbyterianism, that will involve each taking responsibility for others in our Presbyterian fellowship. A relational church will be a responsible church inspired by our criteria of "justice, mercy and faith" in the use of our resources.

Resources. Trust and responsibility without resources will discourage and frustrate. We display our trust by allocating our resources and assets, by giving to those we trust. People will believe they have responsibility when they are resourced; when finance is allocated, when time is made available and when talents are focused.

The Church of Jesus Christ operates on trust. This involves risk. What if we never learn to trust one another? This is a risk worth taking. For such a shape to work and such trust to be engendered we need responsibility and resources to be given and received.

To affirm our trust in the local church, we recommend the formation of a Community and Parish Development Fund, which will allow congregations to pursue local visions of renewal for mission with the assurance of substantial support. **(See Proposals for Continuing Reform No 6: Modelling Change and Appendix 8)** This will be a sign of trust, responsibility and resources being given to those who have a vision for following Jesus into his world today. To fund local initiative is one way of following the Spirit who alone can reshape the Church for the purposes of God.

> *From the outset the Commission has heard the plea for changes in structure, but has remained convinced that changing structures without changing mindsets achieves little.*

A. The Shape of the Local Church

A.1. Shaped by the Gospel

A.1.1. Living out the Story of Jesus

"Follow me". The Church of Jesus Christ will want to be shaped by the Gospel of Jesus Christ to be a community that expresses the life and love of Jesus Christ. That shape is not about structures. It is about the lives of individuals and congregations being shaped by the "mind of Christ."

From the outset the Commission has heard the plea for changes in structure, but has remained convinced that changing structures without changing mindsets achieves little. John Tiller writes:

> "The Gospel community relates to church structures as a new building to the scaffolding which surrounds it. Reforming the structures is like reorganising the scaffolding: it may be necessary but it does not in itself alter the building. Creating alternative new structures is like replacing the scaffolding: it may be useful, but then it may be a waste of time." (The Gospel Community, p 51)

Jesus' imagery of new wine in new wineskins has often been used to refer to new church structures, but Jesus first used the illustration to address the "structures of the mind". The inherited mindsets of the Jewish leaders could not accommodate the life of the Kingdom of God. The subversive ministry of Jesus was hidden and deep. The Temple became redundant, but he did not lift a finger to its physical structure. In time a "Temple of living stones" was to replace it.

The shape of the church in each village, town and city of Scotland will emerge as we take time to "follow Jesus" through a saturation in the Gospel stories. We recommend that each congregation choose one of the Gospel writers as their pastor for the coming year and let them teach us about following Jesus.

Matthew will speak well to those who value order and history, and sow subversive seeds of the Kingdom. The outcome will be to turn the congregation inside out and from past to future. Mark will suit the activists. Here is a manual for active discipleship, introducing us to the way of the Cross. And if, despite the reality of the resurrection, we are still afraid, we find ourselves in good company. Doctor Luke is for those who value the call of the Spirit to prayer and to mission, but watch out for the challenges about wealth and poverty. John is for the reflective ones who want to learn how to be a contemplative community around Jesus. He makes sure that our words about loving God are earthed in loving each other. The challenge is for a congregation to live the reality of all four Gospels and so reflect the full glory of Christ's presence.

Imagine every congregation choosing to follow Jesus in the company of one of these pastors. Imagine little clusters of people meeting to read the story together. They are challenged by the truth they find and hold each other accountable for living by that truth for the coming week. Imagine the preaching and worship unpacking the story in fresh ways. Imagine pastoral projects designed around the Good Samaritan, the woman taken in adultery, the parable of the talents. Imagine a finance committee studying Luke's accounts of Jesus' teaching on wealth and poverty. Imagine a church that decided to live for a year in "silent witness" on the instruction of Jesus: "By this shall the world know that you are my disciples because you love one another."

Imagine the impact on a society where "you tell me your truth and I tell you mine", if Christian people lived the difference by "doing the truth" with compassion, courtesy and courage.

We have reflected on the marks of a healthy church shaped by Jesus at the core and offer that for reflection in our situation. (**Appendix 4: The Marks of the Healthy Church**)

> **Recommendation 1: That congregations study, reflect on and live by one Gospel for one year in the first instance, and let Jesus shape the life and structure of the congregation.**

A.1.2. Living out the Spirituality of Grace

We re-affirm the Reformation doctrine of "justification by grace through faith". We believe that the rediscovery of that fundamental truth of the Gospel will liberate the people of God into the mission of God. A lived spirituality of grace will overflow into all relationships as Christian communities, and shape our patterns of ministry and mission. Too often our relationships are marked by a need to achieve and measure up in order to prove ourselves to one another and, ultimately, to God. We pray for a grace-soaked, grace motivated Church.

Frank Lake, the clinical psychologist, speaks of living in the "cycle of grace". In his desire to understand healthy human development, he drew on the account of Jesus' baptism. He saw in the words of the Father profound acceptance ("You are beloved Son. With you I am well pleased."). In the gift of the Spirit he recognised the sustaining strength of God for life in its most testing times.

The purpose of the baptism was to set Jesus upon his public ministry as the suffering servant Messiah. The outcome was the achievement of that ministry, culminating in the Cross and Resurrection. Achievement is not the same as success. Grace puts failure into the hands of God and waits for God to do what only God can do.

Lake's insights can be expressed diagrammatically:

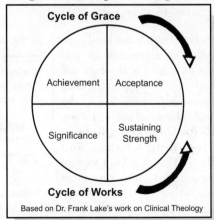

Based on Dr. Frank Lake's work on Clinical Theology

Where we live in a "clockwise" direction

(acceptance>strength>significance>achievement), our personal and congregational lives grow as Christ grew. That is the cycle of grace. Where we live in the "anti-clockwise" direction(achievement>significance>strength>acceptance), we are driven by unhealthy motives of achievement and failure. That is the cycle of works.

Individuals, congregations and our denominations are constantly trapped in the wrong cycle. Congregations become busier and busier, and feel the pressure of external criteria of money and membership. It is the gift of the Gospel of grace that liberates us to live as Christ lived. The fundamental shift of mindset for the whole culture of the church is towards living out the cycle of grace in every relationship. Living out that spirituality of grace lies at the heart of the core calling to "Follow me."

> **Recommendation 2: That congregations reflect on the cycle of grace and what it means to live out that grace in our life together.**

A.2. Shaped by the Locality

The primary expression of church is local. The Incarnation is our mandate and our model for being local. "The word became a human being and moved into the neighbourhood" (The Message). The parish system at its best is one way of expressing that belief in the God who is as down to earth as that. Incarnational theology is in the DNA of the Church of Scotland.

A.2.1. Local means identity. The local congregation stands as sign of God's commitment to that place. The local congregation is a community of God's people, gathering to worship Him, encouraging one another to grow in knowing God in Jesus Christ, serving in Christ's name and going to all peoples to make disciples of the Lord Jesus Christ.

The congregation brings distinct gifts to the wider

> *The local congregation stands as sign of God's commitment to that place.*

> *It is vital that congregations look at and listen to their locality.*

community by being distinctive itself. This distinctiveness arises from gathering to worship around the Story of the Gospel that transforms lives in word, sacraments, example and dialogue. The local congregation is the space where Christian life is nurtured in practical discipleship, earthed in the concrete realities of local life. The congregation shows the way by serving alongside the community and inviting others to become followers of Christ.

For reasons of theology and missionary strategy, we affirm the local Christian congregation as the primary expression of the church. However, that does not mean more of the same! A congregation may avoid the challenge of becoming a missionary congregation. A congregation may develop a fortress mentality of isolation that is no longer a servant of the Kingdom of God.

A.2.2. Local means diversity. We have heard from rural communities and the Highlands, from City Centre and towns, and from Urban Priority Areas. (**Appendix 4: The Church in Context**) Contexts vary and our vision is that every congregation discovers its own vision of being a worshipping, witnessing community.

It is vital that congregations look at and listen to their locality. We recommend that congregations undertake a community review every ten years in the wake of the National Census. We welcome the initiative of National Mission to make available to Presbyteries and congregations relevant information from the 2001 Census, and commend their resources to undertake such a survey in partnership with others in the area.

We have already acknowledged that people live in networks of communities. In the days when people lived, worked and worshipped in the same place, worship was the gathering of an already existing community. In a time when life is fragmented, congregations need to work more creatively at being real communities of faith. Without a Gospel community, there is no communication of the Gospel.

The priority for the Church is the renewing, refocusing, relocating and planting of local worshipping congregations for mission across Scotland.

A.2.3. Local means interdependency. In the mind of the Commission the words "local" and "relational" have been inextricably linked. The God of the Incarnation is the God of the Trinity and God's people will reflect God's nature. A primary theme of the Body of Christ is interdependency, a mark of all mature relationships. Congregations that are independent to the point of isolation deprive themselves and others in the Body of Christ.

We have observed the way in which the Urban Priority Areas and projects supported by the Priority Areas Fund have developed support networks to help them face their demanding missionary challenges. Over the years they have been meeting in areas to tell stories, identify issues and develop mutual resources. Their example is to be commended for other groups of congregations. These groups may live in the same area or they may share similar contexts (e.g. Rural, City Centre or Suburban) or be developing similar initiatives (e.g. children's ministry, worship, community development, evangelism, workplace ministry). The important thing is to move beyond isolation to interdependency.

> *"The storm is so serious, I believe that it marks the end of 'business as usual' for the churches and marks the need for us to begin again building the church from the ground up."*

Recommendation 3: That congregations undertake a community review at least once every ten years to reflect on the issues, changes and missionary opportunities in the community, in collaboration with others, wherever appropriate.

A.2.4. Local means creative flexibility. Every area of Scotland has "people groups" that are not touched by the church. They may be an age group that we never see around our church. They may be a social group who feel unwelcome. They may be those who find their experience of belonging and transcendence in other kind of clubs—night clubs or football clubs. In the spirit of Jesus, we challenge each congregation to identify its "no go area" and go there.

We are in an era where planting new kinds of churches for our generation will be essential if some people are to have any experience of Christian community. We recommend worship with a variety of menu in a variety of venue to be accessible to different groups of people.

Loren Mead of the Alban Institute challenges us to be radical here:

> "The storm buffeting the churches is very serious indeed. Much more serious than we have admitted to ourselves, and much more serious than our leaders have yet comprehended...The storm is so serious, I believe that it marks the end of 'business as usual' for the churches and marks the need for us to begin again building the church from the ground up." (Transforming Congregations for the Future, p ix)

The resources of the Panel of Worship, Parish Education and the New Charge Development Committee offer support and advice for congregations willing to explore new ways of being church. The experience of those who have learned from Willowcreek Community Church and the Cell Church Movement are invaluable, as is the experience of some of our World Mission staff, who can help with facing the cross cultural challenges. Congregations will benefit from sending groups to visit other places and learning from other people.

Recommendation 4: That Kirk Sessions undertake a review of the worship of the existing congregation and assess potential for developments within and beyond the congregation.

A.2.5. Local means cultural sensitivity. The

Western world is undergoing a culture shift of a magnitude that is experienced only every few hundred years. There are philosophical, historical, sociological and technological causes and effects of this change. Every local community is living in this mega-cultural environment. (**Appendix 5: The Church in a Changing World**)

Our changing social context can be symbolised by the microchip, the Internet, shopping malls or the mobile phone. Changing social relationships are seen in the attitudes to sexuality, marriage, racial equality and gender roles. Changes in political dynamics may be seen in the Scottish Parliament, the implications of the European Convention of Human Rights, or the shifts of power through globalisation from nation states to trans-national companies. Changing cultural values may be described as post modern or hypermodern, but the underlying core value is that individual choice is the only absolute. The right to choose is the one inviolate principle for shopping, politics, relationships, genetics or religion.

Every one of these factors will affect the shape of the church: our pastoral care, our patterns of belonging, our communication, our understanding of the Gospel, our evangelism and our discipleship. We are called to live "in" the world but not "of" the world as Jesus did, fully engaged, yet distinctive (John 17).

A.2.6. Local means visionary possibility. As the local church gains in confidence, we envisage local worship centres, which create opportunities to build a local team to lead the various church ministries. They will recognise the untapped resources—the many gifts in a local congregation—and understand the evangelical attraction of informal partnerships with other agencies. They will develop a vision that is local and global, while being confident that the local congregation is the national face of the church for our communities. They will recognise that Information Technology means the "centre" can be local. They will link in partnerships with other congregations, and learn to network with congregations who share common goals.

As we engage with the diversity of being worshipping communities, we will see emerging:

a menu of worship with a variety of times and styles, including a range of music;

communication of the highest quality – personal, creative and imaginative;

a philosophy of community that is interactive in style;

an organisation that understands communication-internal and external;

adequate and creative administration with church office staff;

creative use of finance;

partnerships with churches at home and abroad;

partnerships with other agencies in multiple projects.

This calls for building a leadership team to lead the various church ministries:

that takes time for regular retreat and reflection;

that has a bias to action and can react flexibly;

that is continually updating skills;

that is contextualising the message in the culture.

A.3. *Shaped by Friendship*

"Local and relational" has been a catch phrase in the Commission. As we have tried to reach behind the complaints about "the structures", we have seldom discovered legal obstacles to action. Instead, it has usually been a frustration that our church environment does little to encourage relationships—with God or with each other.

> *We recommend that the church recover the lost art of Christian friendship. This lost art is not about being a "friendly church", but being a church that makes friends beyond "those that salute you".*

In a culture that is increasingly at ease with the language of spirituality, it is strange that conversations about our spiritual development are avoided by many church members, elders and even ministers. One issue for us in these times of spiritual openness is how much God actually matters to us. Belief in God is common. Belief that God matters is distinctive.

Kirk Sessions can be formal and formidable.

Presbyteries have become administrative units for servicing the system of committees and regulations rather than a fellowship of mutual encouragement and inspiration. The Central

> *As we have tried to reach behind the complaints about "the structures", we have seldom discovered legal obstacles to action. Instead, it has usually been a frustration that our church environment does little to encourage relationships— with God.*

Committees are viewed with suspicion from the parishes and are often impersonal for those who attend. The General Assembly has its moments, but is hardly the best forum for major decision-making.

There are many Christian people who are still committed to following Jesus, but they will not or cannot express that commitment within the context of the local church. This is not the fall out of individualism and consumerism. Quite the opposite is true. These are people in search of authentic community.

We recommend that the church recover the lost art of Christian friendship. This lost art is not about being a "friendly church", but being a church that makes friends beyond "those that salute you". Once again our thinking is shaped as we follow Jesus into the Upper Room and reflect on his words: "I no longer call you servants but friends " (John 15:15). Here friendship is about commitment to each other ("No one has greater love than this, to lay down one's life for one's friends") and openness with each other ("I have called you friends, because I have made known to you everything I have heard from my Father").

If we follow Jesus in that kind of friendship, it will transform our approach to children and young people, our relationships as church members, our understanding of team ministry, our mission in our communities, our inter-church relationships and our international viewpoint.

Think of each of these areas as areas to share friendship

as Jesus describes it: in covenant commitment and transparent openness. They are no longer the issues of the few enthusiasts. They are the responsibility of all and within the competence of every Christian.

A.3.1. Friendship with fellow members. Do we have a best friend at church? How would we assess the spirit of hospitality in the congregation? How well do we handle conflict? In a society that is riddled with conflict, is the local church known as the model of mediation – friends of the crucified Mediator? Grand schemes of church renewal fail at the simplest level of an ungracious word, a dismissive look or an unforgiving heart. (**Appendix 6: The Church of the Beatitudes**)

Human nature seems to require different dimensions of belonging: the small group for support and intimacy, the medium sized group to share in tasks, and larger gatherings for inspiration and celebration. Some of the church growth literature describes these as:

cell + congregation + celebration.

The typical Church of Scotland way has been to focus on the congregation as the basic unit: often to the exclusion of cell and celebration. The research of the German Institute of Church Development among 1000 growing churches across the world discovered that the one factor, which stood out among all others, was the "multiplication of small groups".

The insights of the Cell Church movement have shown that when we begin small and go deep with a few, then, in time the Gospel spreads. It follows Jesus' own pattern of investment in the Twelve.

> *Human nature seems to require different dimensions of belonging: the small group for support and intimacy, the medium sized group to share in tasks, and larger gatherings for inspiration and celebration.*

The Commission has noted significant developments based on this intensive investment, both in Whiteinch, where a New Charge has been grown from a small, focused approach to discipleship; and in Gillespie Memorial: Dunfermline, where a group of twelve have been nurtured to lead worship, support pastoral care and encourage the wider ministry of the congregation in mission.

Likewise, as a Church, we often fail to offer occasions of celebration and inspiration. Congregations would be encouraged by regular shared gatherings. The tradition of the Highland Communion Season was a time of families and friends gathering from around the area, to be called afresh to worship God and receive the grace of the Lord Jesus Christ. Many rural congregations would benefit from the reinvention of that tradition for the 21st century.

Recommendation 5: That congregations consider how the cell, congregation and celebration dimensions of being the Church might be applied locally.

A.3.2. Friendship with the next generation. We are a covenant community. By baptism we welcome children into that covenant community, but too often our congregations fail to be covenanting community needed for children and families to flourish in faith and life. Within the Commission, members have celebrated the birth of four children. We dedicate this task of reshaping of the church to them.

The current emphasis on the role of children through Parish Education will offer congregations opportunities to build friendships with our children and their families. Community is built on names. The friendships will begin when every member can name some of the children in the Sunday School or the youth club.

Young people are crying out for the church to recover the relational quality and integrity characterised by the grace and truth of Jesus. In the "Friends" generation, young people are finding new places of community and belonging. The church culture of formality, regulations, expectations and conformity sends out a corporate "vibe" than makes today's generation instinctively uncomfortable.

A Church that can trace 40 years of declining youth statistics must ask if all the excellent youth work of two generations has been frozen out of church life because we have failed to build relationships of friendship across the generations. We have been caught in the mythology of the generation gap instead of being pioneering mythbusters.

Communication with the next generation will require many creative youth work skills and pioneering work to develop new patterns of church, but communication without community will be sterile. Every person brings gifts to the community that create the space for young people to feel they belong and that they matter. With Jean Vanier we celebrate the "gift of the grandmother" in building community.

> *Young people are crying out for the church to recover the relational quality and integrity characterised by the grace and truth of Jesus.*

Recommendation 6: That congregations determine to integrate children and young people into the life of the congregation; or to offering the resources to plant a church for a new generation alongside the current congregation.

A.3.3. Friendship with the searcher. The title of a recent conference on evangelism was "communicating with absent friends". Celtic motifs of pilgrimage and celebrating the good in our culture, Ignatian retreats on spirituality and faith accompaniment, business themes of mentoring have alerted us to a pattern of evangelism that comes alongside and travels the journey as a friend. We follow the Christ of the Emmaus Road who walked, listened, explained, intrigued and was welcomed as a Friend.

Amidst all the discussions about the shifts in our culture, there are certain recurring constants about our humanity, which take on cultural clothing. Those constants ("these three remain") are faith, hope and love. Every human being yearns for trust in the beyond, needs a sense of purpose and meaning, and wants to belong. It has been shown that people "belong before they believe". The received wisdom was that people behaved well, believed correctly and then belonged fully. That is the way of legalism.

> *The way of grace (and the way of our relational culture) is to give people a place of belonging, leading to opportunities of believing and then exploring patterns of Christian behaving—not churchy behaviour, but Christ-like behaviour.*

The way of grace (and the way of our relational culture) is to give people a place of belonging, leading to opportunities of believing and then exploring patterns of Christian behaving—not churchy behaviour, but Christ-like behaviour. The success of courses like *Alpha* lies in the social focus of food and friendship as the context for discovering faith. We recommend that congregations explore the right discipleship path for their situation.

> **Recommendation 7: That congregations form paths for the spiritual journey to help people become Christian disciples in today's world.**

A.3.4. Friendship with the community. Partnerships are blossoming around the country as the church in its mission comes alongside the community for the common good of everyone. The church has moved from being the centre of the community with certain rights in local politics, through a time of being ignored and marginalized, to a time when the church is welcomed as a partner in community welfare, education, health and politics. Partnership and friendship are the models of relationship.

> *Elders have written pleading for more teamwork between elders and ministers. Ministers speak of isolation and overload.*

One community worker indicated that she gave 70% of her time to the community and 30% to the congregation. If every congregation in the land budgeted 70% of its time and efforts on being in and for the community, the church would begin to find her role again. These relationships are the foundation of authentic worship and witness of the Incarnate Christ among his people.

A.3.5. Friendship with fellow leaders. Elders have written pleading for more teamwork between elders and ministers. Ministers speak of isolation and overload. To follow Jesus is to work closely with other leaders – investing intensively in few over a period of time to build the team. "Jesus worked with 12 Jews for three years in order to win all Americans"!

There are numerous examples of ministry teams around the country: elders' teams, pastoral teams, teams of ministers with deacons or readers or youth workers, and occasional teams from different denominations. We recommend that congregations work towards breaking the isolation of the "one person ministry" by forming ministry teams according to their needs and resources. Breaking the mould of the "one person ministry" eases isolation and releases a synergy of creativity.

> **Focus: Local and Relational**

> **Recommendation 8: That Kirk Sessions review the current leadership structure, consider what ministry team is needed for current needs and determine how it might be developed in the next five years.**

A.3.6. Friendship with other churches. People have knee-jerk reactions to ecumenism—for it or against it. Perhaps it is time to forget the word and learn the art of friendship—building trust and transparency. In some communities the church is a scandal to the Gospel because of the inability of Christian congregations to be friends together. Such situations are a counter sign of the Kingdom. Planned cooperation among groups of churches would release great potential for the Kingdom.

The Commission is aware of the ecumenical debates around the proposals of the Scottish Churches Initiative for Union, and has not taken a view on the issue of future Union. This debate has its own forum and process for discussion and ultimate decision. However, we welcome the many local initiatives, and the examples of cooperation in the areas of worship, education mission and national consultations.

In recommending increased local cooperation we have heard of partnerships in Barrhead, Carluke, Drumchapel and Paisley, to name a few. We repeat our concern that the Church of Scotland live up to the "charism of the big heart" and be sensitive to needs and gifts of other churches in the area. The effectiveness of such cooperation may be helped by the appointment of a person whose role is, in part at least, to facilitate these partnerships.

Recommendation 9: That congregations form groupings according to their natural communities to explore shared mission and mutual ministry with other churches in the area.

A.3.7. Friendship with rich and poor. We stand accountable to the poorest people of the land. If our reshaping of the church does not give our God of love and justice a local face, then we have not touched the heart of God's covenant love. The prophetic voices of Scripture used the care of the poor as a touchstone by which to judge the religious establishment. The Reformation missionary mandate explicitly included the care of the poor. In our consultations with the Urban Priority Areas, we were reminded, "Public policy is to be judged by its effectiveness at the point of delivery of service."

That is a test for every policy of the church beginning with the poorest in the local parish.

Jesus challenged his contemporaries to align their priorities about resources around the core issues of "justice mercy and faith" (Matthew 23:23). Many congregations in our poorest areas have to struggle against immense odds with minimal resources. And yet these congregations have often by necessity faced hard issues of mission, worship and leadership styles ahead of the rest of the church.

> *We stand accountable to the poorest people of the land. "Public policy is to be judged by its effectiveness at the point of delivery of service.'*

The Church is called by God to care for the poor, to address the causes of poverty and learn more of Christ from being alongside the poor. The "Jubilee 2000" campaign to release the world's poorest countries from international debt is one example of the political complexity of dealing with these issues. The church is called to more than occasional charity. We are called to a determined stance. That determination is not yet reflected across the Church, and we need to help each other sustain our obedience.

> **Ethos: Interdependence**

We recommend partnerships and friendships that will allow an exchange of resources between congregations of different social backgrounds. Examples of these partnerships reveal relationships that are mutually enriching: one congregation offering people, skills and financial support, the other offering new insights into worship, mission, spirituality and much more.

Recommendation 10: That congregations establish links with other congregations in a different social context as a partnership of mutual ministry.

A.3.8. Friendship with the World Church. In our globalised world, where 51% of the world church is now in the South and only 3% of the world church is Presbyterian, we take a humbler role in the world and accept the gifts of "reverse mission". Environmental concerns and economic imbalances link us and challenge us to make new lifestyle choices in a global context.

In the culture of the "World-Wide Web" we are only too aware of globalisation in communication, economics and politics. The Church is in a position to lead the way as a global family. When the effects of globalisation are likely to depersonalise and marginalize, the church can stay local globally by establishing living links with churches in other parts of the world. We recommend that local congregations explore with World Mission how they might establish such partnerships.

> **Recommendation 11: That congregations research an area of the world church and establish a personal partnership with a congregation or project.**

A.3.9. Friendship with God's Creation. The relational church recognises our interdependence in the weave of creation, and our call to be an example as good stewards of God's creation. We recognise the angst among younger people about the future of the planet and recommend that churches review their policies on energy and consumer goods, and raise awareness of those aspects of contemporary society that will hurt or heal the environment. We commend the resources of the Society, Religion and Technology Project and the calls to earlier General Assemblies for congregations to conduct an environmental audit.

> **Recommendation 12: That congregations explore ways of being more environmentally aware and responsible as a witness to the Christian care of God's creation.**

The theme of friendship could be developed further. It may be the key to many locked doors.

A.4. Shaped by the Gifts of God's People
A.4.1. Recognising the Gifts of God's People

> *Jesus said, "Follow me."*

"Follow me" means every disciple following Jesus is to share in his ministry through his Body, the church. Each person is a gift from God to the Church, to be celebrated and nurtured. Every disciple is a servant-friend of our Lord and is gifted in many ways, or as Ephesians 4:7 says, "to each one of us grace has been given as Christ apportioned it". The word "celebrated" is used deliberately because it emphasises the joyful generosity which is needed to give freedom to people, so that they can grow and become fruitful. Each congregation is to be a living college, where people learn to exercise their gifts in an environment of grace characterised by encouragement, humility and cooperation.

The arena of service will be primarily in the world: in

> *Each person is a gift from God to the Church, to be celebrated and nurtured. Every disciple is a servant friend of our Lord and is gifted in many ways.*

family, work or community. The service of the church is where the church is present as salt and light through people being church. When the church is gathered for worship and shared service, care needs to be taken to discover, develop and deploy the gifts of God's people. A church of grace will offer space to succeed or fail, and learn and grow. We recommend that congregations follow the processes and courses available to help people identify their passion and serve according to the gift of grace apportioned to them. Kirk Sessions should lead the way and ensure that the team is playing to its strengths.

> *The arena of service will be primarily in the world.*

> **Recommendation 13: That Kirk Sessions identify the spiritual gifts of the people and grow the church around the people we have rather than deploy people to support existing church structures.**

A.4.2. Releasing the Gifts of God's People
Current structures are often too rigid. Rather than give

relational space, they crush creativity. However, there are signs of change. 80 Readers are being trained each year and are deployed strategically within Presbyteries. In the past 15 years around 1000 people have graduated from the Scottish Churches Open College and a wide range of training is offered to elders.

We trust that developments in the Board of Ministry will keep faith with the affirmations about the ministry of the whole people of God. In practical terms, we recommend close collaboration with the Board of Parish Education, especially in the well-developed work in training elders for new roles.

The new regulations for New Charges create the open space for new patterns to emerge. The example of non-stipendiary in the Episcopal Church should encourage us forward. That may be one of the more strategic gifts of ecumenical cooperation.

> *We need leadership. We need elders with vision and flexibility ... there needs to be an honest appraisal of the gifts and callings of our elders.*

We have the resources across the Church to equip any congregation to lead worship, engage in pastoral care or to sustain mission and evangelism with the appropriate staffing. We are aware that for many working people time and energy are in short supply and a staff team may be desirable. The aim of any ministry team will be to release the gifts of the people of God.

We recommend that Presbyteries set a five-year goal to ensure that every congregation is working towards this capacity. We believe this would release an immense amount to energy and creativity among members and ministers alike. Tragically, there has been little coordinated planning to encourage this kind of development. The result has been a patchy evolution where there is the enthusiasm or where the necessity of an extended vacancy or a multiple linkage has demanded it.

Recommendation 14: That Presbyteries develop a coordinated strategy to equip congregations to sustain worship, pastoral care and mission with the appropriate staffing, and monitor progress through the Quinqennial/Presbytery visits.

A.4.3. Affirming the Gifts of Leadership: (1) Eldership Refocused

We need leadership. We need elders with vision and flexibility. In our Presbyterian church the role of elders is crucial. In the role of the elder the "one size fits all" pattern of districts is prevalent, but that does not give room for variety of abilities to be exercised. There needs to be an honest appraisal of the gifts and callings of our elders, and to recognise that not all elders are gifted in leadership, nor are all gifted in pastoral care. We recommend that all elders who have not undertaken training in the past three years be required to attend a short course on the current role and expectations of an elder in the Church of Scotland.

If younger people are to be elders, then "whole life" commitment may be an impediment. This does not mean that their commitment will not be genuine, but that shorter term commitments will allow them to decide priorities and focus their energy.

At a time when elders have increasing demands on time, and when the church needs to be flexible and responsive to changing situations, we encourage Kirk Sessions to develop a pattern of "terms of service" (each Session can determine the appropriate length of the term) with regular sabbaticals. These will be times for elders to step back and see things from a new angle, taking advantage of the in-service courses so freely accessible in the church today.

Recommendation 15: That Kirk Sessions offer an opportunity for all elders who have not undertaken training in the past three years to share the current vision of the role and expectations of an elder in the Church of Scotland.

In some congregations, the Kirk Session is perceived as remote from the congregation. There is little access to the decision-making and the business is not communicated to the congregation clearly or regularly. As Presbytery is a public meeting unless it needs to meet in private, we recommend that the Kirk Session makes its meetings as open as possible, and develops ways of maintaining good communication links between Session and congregation. This is in line with the recommendations of the Board of Practice and Procedure on freedom of information.

Recommendation 16: That Kirk Sessions develop appropriate open styles of meeting and processes of communication.

As congregations explore different ways of releasing the gifts of their members, they may come to realise that the "model constitution" (which requires a two-tier decision-making process) is too cumbersome and inflexible, and often ties people into administrative structures and meetings rather than releasing them for active service.

Recommendation 17: That the Board of Practice and Procedure examine whether the present "model constitution" represents the best and most flexible way of managing a local congregation.

A.4.4. Affirming the Gifts of Leadership: (2) Ministry Teams

**Foundations:
Trust, Responsibility and resources**

We need a strong ministry team. We welcome the review of the enquiry and selection processes by the Board of Ministry. We affirm the emerging patterns of training and support: local responsibility in selection, greater emphasis on continuous practical development in training, early challenges towards teamwork, pro-active professional development, new thinking on the total independence which we call tenure. We look forward to their proposals on some notion of appraisal.

The term "ministry of word and sacrament" remains our description of "the ordained minister". That role means keeping the people of God truly centred on Jesus Christ as revealed in the Scriptures and the sacraments. The role of Christian leadership is to keep Christ central and all other competitors for that position secondary.

Purpose: follow me

However there is a limitation of using the time-honoured description. It represents an unquestioned assumption that sticks with the role of pastor-teacher as the primary model of leadership. The Biblical description of leadership in Ephesians 4:12 includes also the apostle, the prophet and the evangelist, along with the pastor and the teacher. According to that passage it takes all five leadership roles to express the "ministry of Christ". This is a time to recover and reaffirm these other roles of leadership and break out of the reductionism of the pastor-teacher model.

The "word and sacrament"/"pastor-teacher" emphasis belongs to the Christendom context, with the re-emphasis on these roles in the Reformation to offset the ignorance and superstition of the day. The context of the 21st century is undoubtedly missionary and post-Christendom. The assumptions that ride on the terminology will not be adequate for the future.

The church will require the pioneering gifts of the apostle ("sent out"), the building and dismantling gifts of the prophets, and the frontier-friendly gifts of the evangelist. The pastor and the teacher are no less important, but their monopoly on the term "ministry" needs to be broken. We recommend that in our time, we recognise, recruit, select and train evangelists who can help others share the Gospel with others. The same is required for those with "apostolic" (perhaps a church planting capacity) and "prophetic" gifts (perhaps an ability to encourage the church or a capacity to address the public arena in the name of Christ).

The collaborative nature of ministry begins by reclaiming these gifts as essential to the full development of the church to be the church of Christ in our times. It will mean taking account of these gifts in the selection and recruitment process and offering the necessary specialist training rather than the omnibus version that assumes that everybody will be a parish minister.

> **Recommendation 18: That the Board of Ministry, in consultation with the Board of National Mission and the Board of Parish Education, develop a coordinated process of recruiting and training people with missionary gifts which are vital for service within and beyond the constraints of a parish context.**

Ordained ministry is a demanding role and there are subtle influences that erode or limit the development of the gifts of those in ordained ministry. The sacred cows of security of tenure and the right of congregational call deserve attention. While not wishing to create unnecessary insecurity, there are situations where the movement of a minister would create new possibilities for all parties. Interim Ministers and ministers in other appointments already surrender their tenure voluntarily, and put themselves at the disposal of the Church.

We recognise the effects of the "short term contract" culture in business and the caring agencies– often leading to cynicism, insecurity and lack of loyalty. On the other hand, an appointment to a situation for fixed term with a specific remit can focus the mind creatively.

We recognise the distinction between long-term pastoring of people and the short-term focus of a project.

> *The issue is how to achieve the flexibility necessary for a changing situation, and the stability necessary for the spiritual development of people.*

We also recognise the different personalities whose gifts will be different. There will be limiting factors on movement. The issue is how to achieve the flexibility necessary for a changing situation, and the stability

necessary for the spiritual development of people. This would be met by making the "ministry team" the norm with people employed on different terms.

We recommend the creation of a database of aptitudes and needs by the Department of Ministry. Congregations, Presbyteries and Departments would have access to this pool for the normal processes of filling posts. There would then need to be a process of matching requirements to gifts and deploying people after due consultation.

> **Recommendation 19: That the Board of Ministry, in consultation with the Board of National Mission and the Board of Parish Education, develop a data-base of all ministers, auxiliary ministers, Deacons and Readers to assist in the strategic deployment of personnel.**

A.4.5. Developing the Gifts of Leadership

We welcome the Board of Ministry's emphasis on collaborative ministry. To encourage this ethos, we believe that the Board can give a lead in two ways: by developing active partnerships with the Board of Parish Education, and by encouraging training that brings candidates for ministry alongside other ministries who are in training e.g. Readers, Deacons or Overseas Bursars.

Since the primary ministry is the ministry of Christ through the whole Body of Christ, the Board of Ministry can offer a lead in affirming the development of elders, youth workers, children's ministries and much more. At present there is limited collaboration and that is to the detriment of all parties. We recommend that both Boards establish working patterns that will offer mutual enrichment.

The name of the "Board of Ministry" reinforces old perceptions of the omni-competent ordained minister. We await changes in reorganisation as a new Presbytery style emerges. Our hope would be that the other facets of authorised leadership might come under a board of ministries as recognition of diversity.

> *Ethos: Interdependence*

Recommendation 20: That the Board of Ministry and the Board of Parish Education develop working patterns of active collaboration to equip the whole people of God for Christian service.

A.4.6. Celebrating the Gifts of all God's People

The mindset of the church will be reshaped by our liturgy. We recommend that services of ordination of ministers and elders, and services of induction be revisited to reflect the new realities of theology and practice in relation to ministry and eldership. Our Episcopal neighbours have rich liturgies that affirm the whole people of God, and in practice are much less priestly than many Church of Scotland ministers.

> **The mindset of the church will be reshaped by our liturgy.**

Recommendation 21: That the Panel on Worship review services of ordination, induction and commissioning, in order to celebrate imaginatively the ministry of all God's people within them.

B. The Shape of the Regional Church

B.1. The Presbytery Revisited

The Presbytery is the characteristic expression of the Church of Scotland as a member of the family of Presbyterian churches. Before embarking on further discussion, it is worth setting our Presbyterial constitution in the context of the world church. Presbyterians have inherited a sense of our Scottishness being identified with the adjective Presbyterian. That connection is challenged by the ecumenical climate of 21st century Scotland, but it is both humbling and encouraging to step outside our inherited focus and see the world perspective.

According to Peter Brierley's *Future Church: a Global Analysis of the Christian Community to the year 2010*, Monarch/Christian Research Association, 1998:

> "In 1995 there were 48 million Presbyterians worldwide. This was 3% of Christendom and 1% of the world's population. These proportions were the same in 1960 and will remain so by the year 2010 if present trends continue, showing that the Presbyterian church is keeping pace with world trends but neither beating them, nor losing to them. This means that they will grow from 30 million in 1960 to 52 million in 2010." (p 109)

Brierley goes on to show that Presbyterianism is growing mainly in Asia where in 50 years the Presbyterian Church has grown fourfold, mainly in South Korea and Indonesia. The factors to which he attributes growth are (pp 114-9):

1. *A high profile focus and commitment to prayer;*
2. *Clear vision, thoroughly owned by the people;*
3. *A large amount of missionary involvement as witnessed by the number of Korean missionaries sent overseas;*
4. *Continuous ongoing evangelism and thorough integration of converts into small cell groups;*
5. *Publicly affirmed integrity of Christian people through their behaviour in wartime and since.*

Returning to the role of the Presbytery in Scotland, it is a matter of significance and concern that this chief characteristic is not considered to be the source of inspiration and support for the worship and witness of local congregations. The perception of many congregations is of a Presbytery as a necessary irrelevance—necessary for maintaining the system as we have it, but irrelevant to congregations unless in the case of a vacancy or readjustment.

The origins of Presbytery lie in the "weekly exercises" for ministers to find spiritual support for their pastoral and evangelistic callings. The erosion of that relational heart is of vital concern if we are to pursue two key values in the shape of the church—to affirm the local and strengthen the relational.

Our history and contemporary missiological research encourage us to revisit the Presbytery as a focus of area/regional support and inspiration to local congregations. This will include excellent administration, for "good administration is good pastoral care".

> **The erosion of that relational heart is of vital concern if we are to pursue two key values in the shape of the church—to affirm the local and strengthen the regional**

B.2. Towards a Theology of Presbytery

How can Presbytery be a fellowship of Christian leaders sharing a vision for the Kingdom within a given part of Scotland? In what way can Presbytery function as a Gospel community? What would Presbytery look like shaped by the Gospel rather than by legal procedure or managerial function?

If the Church exists by the grace of God and for the glory of God, then, as matter of integrity, this characteristic forum of our church will be shaped by worship and mission.

> **Purpose: Follow me**

If the Church is formed by participating in the mission of God to see the new creation in Christ, then Presbytery will be shaped by future challenges and possibilities rather than past precedent.

If the Church is formed around Jesus Christ in the fellowship of the Father, Son and Spirit, then the Presbytery will be a community shaped by the mutual honouring of persons rather than the static notion of equality or parity.

If the Church is to follow Jesus on the way of grace in the Incarnation, then its primary question is what aspect of the Word of God is to be made flesh in this place at this time, not a legal question of administrative functions.

If the Church is the community of the Cross and resurrection, then Presbytery decision making will be marked by humility and integrity which will call on all our courage, compassion and companionship to dare to follow Christ together.

If the Church is the community of the Spirit, then we will be alert to the charisms of the Holy Spirit in individuals and in congregations and learn to function as the Body of Christ together in our part of Scotland, enjoying unity within diversity, including other neighbours of other denominations.

If the Church is the community of the New Creation, then Presbytery will be a sign to a divided and broken world of how to mediate in conflict and to thrive on the chaos of change as God beckons us into tomorrow.

Such a redefinition of Presbytery around the Gospel acts as a touchstone for future practical discussions on functions. It takes us further in our deconstruction before aiming at reconstruction.

Presbytery is shaped currently by a vision of God as stability, continuity and sameness. This owes more to Platonic ideas than to the God of the Hebrews who kept his people on the move and the God of Jesus who neither "possessed nor was possessed", but released the wind and fire of God on waiting disciples.

> **If the regional leadership of the church is to be an inspiration to the local church, then it must reflect the life of God in Christ as an example—a community of communities with Jesus at the centre.**

B.3. The Shape of Presbytery
B.3.1. The 3-D Presbytery as Regional Support

We have kept open communication with the Committee

on Presbytery Boundaries and discovered that the logic of our "upside down" church has led us to similar conclusions. The Commission offers its thinking as part of the consideration of future "shape", but our recommendation will be to invite the General Assembly to remit this section of the Report for wider consultation through the future work of the Presbytery Boundaries Committee.

Shape: Upside Down

The future shape of the Regional Church will have three functions: relational support for local strategy, regional centres of worship and inspiration and regions for more comprehensive oversight and allocation of resources.

We favour the formation of *local area groupings* for mutual support and missionary partnerships. Where appropriate, these districts may be ecumenical to foster the relational bonds of trust. Local and relational are the underlying principles.

We also favour the smaller number of *larger groupings* (more like the original Synod) with the strategic responsibilities, staff and financial resources to offer the local support needed to the congregations. Attention must be given to ensure ecumenical membership and regular collaboration.

Notes of caution have been sounded There is concern about duplication of effort and about the devolution of old mindsets. The success of these moves will depend on how far the new groupings create an environment where local initiative can thrive, and decisions are taken on the principle of subsidiarity.

The third dimension might be called the *"Presbyterial Cathedral"*. This is a plea to place worship and Christian community at the heart of our life together. In times past Cathedrals offered inspiration, celebration and pastoral encouragement to local congregations. We see centres of excellence being developed to encourage renewal in worship, fellowship, leadership, mission and spirituality—regional bases that offer a lead by example.

As we look around the world we see the inspiration of churches like Willowcreek Community Church, Chicago, or Hills Church, Australia, which have taken on the role of global cathedrals. They have offered many people an example of worship, evangelism, discipleship, community work and servant-leadership. While we are not advocating these churches as examples for all, we see that they offer a starting point and practical teaching resources that flow from the integrity of a worshipping, witnessing community.

In Scotland, there are many who would see Iona Abbey as a similar example of inspiration for over 60 years. We believe that there are churches around Scotland where that same inspirational leadership might be offered to others. Our Scottish reluctance to affirm or recognize others may deprive us of good news and good practice to help us all move forward.

> *The future shape of the Regional Church will have three functions: relational support for local strategy, rregional centres of worship and inspiration and regions for more comprehensive oversight and allocation of resources*

These centres may be a grouping or network of congregations, charged by the Presbytery to pioneer new aspects of our calling, and to share these insights with the wider church. Too much good work goes unsupported or unreported. This would ensure down to earth pilot plants to inspire and encourage others.

Part of the "example" would be their capacity to collaborate with each other in the true Presbyterial spirit. The network would necessarily change with time as different initiatives were affirmed as offering the lead direction for the moment.

B.3.2. The Style of Presbytery as a Gathering

Much of the frustration of Presbytery lies in its style of operating. It has been suggested that it move from "courtroom" to "courtyard" – a pattern of dialogue rather than debate, and conference rather than confrontation. There are times when formal rules of debate are essential for good decision-making, and appropriate procedures when meeting as a "court", but much more time could be given to letting other voices be heard. Even competent speakers can be intimidated in the context of Presbytery meetings. This is about tone and style rather than legal necessity.

Again future consultations on Presbyteries will bring specific proposals for the change of style. Our concern is that the relational dimension of the districts be carried into the larger gatherings through story, worship, small group discussion and the use of better group facilitation. It is open to any Presbytery at any time to make the first steps towards expressing that relational style. Pilot schemes will feed the future process of consultation.

B.3.3. The Leadership Role of Presbytery

Presbyteries will require people who can function as area leaders. While the church is well served by many fine elders, in practice Presbyteries are often peopled by elders who are retired or who have been seconded for a year as a "link person" for the Kirk Session.

Elders' ordination vows need to be made more explicit and include the commitment to the wider church. Those who are seconded to Presbytery work should be released from some areas of local service. The role of the Presbytery elder should be seen as a real job of work.

> *Much of the frustration of Presbytery lies in its style of operating. It has been suggested that it move from "courtroom" to "courtyard" — a pattern of dialogue rather than debate.*

There were discussions some years ago about the training of Presbytery elders in the ways of Presbytery. That was given scant attention, but did include visionary elements as well as nuts and bolts about the system. Such training can be made available for the new roles in the new Presbyteries.

> **Ethos: Interdependence**

There are ministers who contribute little to Presbytery—often through lack of confidence in Presbytery itself. Ministers might be encouraged to 'tithe' their time to the wider work of the church (Presbytery and National Committees) in a way that is recognised at the time of induction by minister and congregation alike. This might protect the overly 'committee-ed' and draw in those gifted people who are shy of the system. If nomination committees adopted the principle of "one person – one job", energy would be better focused and more widely harnessed.

Leadership in the augmented Presbyteries will include issues of staffing and the role of "regional moderators" or "superintendents" for an extended period of time to offer pastoral and missionary encouragement to the districts and congregations.

> *The key will lie in creating a culture of trust and local responsibility to find and share resources. Relationships of grace are once again the key.*

B.3.4. Resources at the Disposal of Presbytery

Resources of people and money will be decentralised. Resource people for National Mission, Parish Education, Social Responsibility and Stewardship will be locally accessible and budgets will be locally controlled. There remains a question of how far existing investments are tied to existing Boards and Committees.

Staffing of the Regions will again be a matter for consultation. Already central Boards have regionalised their staff and this will continue. The team for administration and mission will be shaped by the local challenges and gifts.

In the interest of justice there will need to be an overview of distribution to avoid the inevitable outcome of the free market where the rich-poor gap widens. There is a genuine concern that Presbyterial bureaucracy may not be any cheaper than centralised bureaucracy. Resources held more locally are not by definition stewarded better or worse. The key will lie in creating a culture of trust and local responsibility to find and share resources. Relationships of grace are once again the key.

The future process will carry significant implications

for the current central administration. While the Commission has given consideration to the shape of life at the centre, everything must depend on the decisions relating to the newly developed Presbyterial structure.

C. The Shape of the Central Church

C.1. Where Committees Began

> **"Presbyterianism as a form of Church government was designed for the administration of an organisation the whole of whose activities were confined within its parishes, each of which was more or less self-contained and enjoyed a large measure of autonomy. Its initiatives almost all came from the perimeter, and its objective was that the ordinances of religion should be available to the people in every corner of Scotland completely free of any charge. For that purpose the design was both adequate and admirable...."**

"It was in the latter half of the nineteenth century that the Church first began—not without many grace misgivings and much hesitation—to feel a sense of wider responsibility—for overseas mission, for example. This was something which had not been tackled by the Church as a whole, for obviously it could not be administered at parish level. The parishes had their part to play in furnishing the necessary funds, creating interest, in maintaining enthusiasm, but the whole administration had to be centralised. And so the Assembly appointed a Committee of their own number to do this job, always under their own direction and control. With the passing of the years the number of such 'outside' interests grew, with a consequent steady increase in the number of Committees. The Committee system had come to stay. The Year book for 1950 records no fewer than 65 Committees all reporting directly to the Assembly—25 Standing and 40 Special Committees."

To these comments of Dr Andrew Herron, authority on church law, we add these words of Dr Douglas Murray, the Church historian:

"Regarding Herron's comments on the origins of Boards and Committees. What he says happened in the late 19th century is that the Church took on greater responsibility in certain areas and this involved an increase in administration and in the work of certain committees, such as those dealing with foreign missions. Committees of the Assembly existed before that (e.g. the Accommodation or Church Extension Committee chaired by Chalmers in the 1830s), but it was in the later 19th century that there was an increase in the centralised bureaucracy of the Kirk. The Free Church in particular had to raise its own funds and this led to a more centralised structure and power tending towards the Assembly Committees and their Conveners. The '121' syndrome is very much a Free Church phenomenon. In addition congregations became more autonomous since it was they who raised the money. The result, in my view, was that presbyteries became squeezed between the centre and the localities, a situation which has remained."

The last sentences in Dr Herron's reference indicate something of the recent past. Boards and Committees have been wedged together e.g. the former Board of World Mission and Unity. No doubt this was done for good reason, e.g. the old Union and Readjustments committee became the Parish Reappraisal committee, a constituent committee of the Board of National Mission, intending to give reappraisal work a missionary focus.

C.2. The Evolving Future

The shape of the new centre will depend on the shape of the new regions.

While the Commission has give considerable thought to possible realignments within the central administration, it has become clear that any suggestions would be premature, and indeed unhelpful, in the light of the proposals about new styles of Presbytery, a direction which we have already endorsed.

> **Foundations:**
> **Trust, Responsibility and resources**

With this in mind, it is recommended that the thinking of

the Commission be carried forward by whatever group is charged with the ongoing consultation and implementation of the Presbyterial plan. In this way we trust that the work of the Commission will be integrated into one of the significant streams of reform to encourage future development of thinking.

C.3. Questions for Future Consideration

Future consultations on the shape or regional and national aspects of the Church may have to take up questions that have not been resolved within the limited timescale of the Commission.

C.3.1. What are the implications of the emerging role of the Assembly Council?

Tribute has already been paid to the cooperative spirit between the Commission and the Assembly Council. The role and remit of the Council is about consultation, assessment of priorities and developing strategies for the future. The ethos of the Council has been to develop an ongoing role of listening to the Church locally, regionally and centrally.

This process offers a uniquely new way of communicating opinions within an interdependent Church. It offers a "safe space" for different voices to be heard and represented across the interfaces of the Church's life. We commend that as an expression of the "relational" church, and we wait with interest to see how this style will be applied in assisting the church decide priorities in a way that avoids old-style confrontation.

It is our hope that future discussions will find an acceptable way for some body to fulfil an Executive Function among the Boards and Committees. The Commission is aware of the history of former Assembly

> *The issue is not that the church should speak with "one voice" to suit the convenience of the media. The honesty of debate is not to be stifled. The issue is rather that there be a consistent interaction of ideas through an umbrella Board of Church and Society.*

Councils and the attempts to perform this function. Much depends on the evolving shape of the centre, but the General Assembly requires a focus for its Executive Function in setting priorities among the Boards and Committees in line with agreed strategy.

C.3.2. Where is the Voice of the Church?

Between General Assemblies, there is confusion about the "voice of the Kirk". In a devolved church, many issues could be addressed from the Regions. However, there may be the need for a coordinated setting for engagement with national policy issues: politics, education and social practice. Currently, these are handled by the Church and Nation Committee, the Department of Education and the Board of Social Responsibility. National Mission and World Mission have aspects of their work which have a political impact, and will feed into debates of Church and Nation as required.

The issue is not that the church should speak with "one voice" to suit the convenience of the media. The honesty of debate is not to be stifled. The issue is rather that there be a consistent interaction of ideas through an umbrella Board of Church and Society. Umbrellas do not assume agreement, but at least people are close enough to listen to each other and talk together.

While the Board of Communication, through its Press Office, copes with immense pressures from the media, it might help them in their difficult role of being "cultural translators" between the agenda of the journalist and the confusing culture of the Church.

For all that, the official voice is not necessarily the prophetic voice. For that authentic voice of wisdom, we need to learn to listen to the edges and the people whose obedience has taken them the humble way of the Cross. Amidst the media-saturated noise, we still need to listen for the still small voice of the Spirit, and let that voice be heard. That is a subtle discernment.

C.3.3. Where is the Leadership within the Central Administration?

The Church is operating with two cultures: the Presbyterian ethos that resists personal leadership, and a business organisation at the heart of its administration, which requires executive powers. The proposals from the Joint Working Party to introduce a Central Coordinating Committee may address that issue.

However, as well as a strong appeal for some kind of body being proposed, many senior staff would value the appointment of a Chief Executive to oversee the central organisation. It could be argued that the proposals for reshaping regional and central organisation make it essential to have a person in the central offices who can help steer that part of the organisation through the changes. It seems inadequate that such a responsibility should lie with a Convener who has another full-time occupation far away from the workplace, or, by default, with other senior officials within the offices, whose responsibilities are onerous enough.

> *The Church is operating with two cultures: the Presbyterian ethos that resists personal leadership, and a business organisation at the heart of its administration, which requires executive powers.*

> *As well as a strong appeal for some kind of body being proposed, many senior staff would value the appointment of a Chief Executive to oversea the central organisation.*

C.3.4. What about the role and style of the General Assembly?

The General Assembly exercises legislative, judicial and executive functions. In a church of courts it is the Supreme Court of appeal. Today much of that intricate work is delegated to the Commission of Assembly because the processes of the Assembly have proved cumbersome for issues that require a more subtle context for decision-making.

If more people are to have a voice, then new *styles of decision-making* will be essential. While Moderators and business conveners are always helpful to new Commissioners, and the Assembly is always kind to a new voice struggling with procedures, there is still a need to change the ethos, so that the power does not lie only with those who know the system.

In recent years, we have seen changes in styles of dress, worship and involvement. In pursuit of our concern for a more relational church to affirm and release the gifts of the people, we recommend the Assembly take a lead from patterns of the Youth Assembly: holding area consultations for Commissioners in advance of the Assembly so that the key issues are aired in advance; and ensuring the time is divided between conference style and decision style.

In the current context, many Boards and Committees could function adequately on a *two or three yearly reporting system*, with the opportunity to bring essential decisions to the intervening Assembly. This would avoid the undue time pressures to produce annual reports on everything. The major reports would set the policy direction for the next two-three years, leaving space for short annual progress reports as required.

The Executive Function of the Assembly currently focuses on reports from Boards and Committees, creating the impression of the Annual General Meeting of the Central Administration rather than a reflection on the life of the Church as a whole. There is a tension between the desire to offer a point of visibility to celebrate the local and global life of the Church, and the need to make policy decisions for the good of all.

In a decentralised context, the reporting processes may be different. There may be more direct access of Presbyteries to the Assembly, both to bring forward issues of substance, and to contribute to the *celebratory aspects* of the Assembly—each year featuring one Region in rotation. These occasions would inspire and challenge the Commissioners and the whole church, if the media reported them well. The Assembly has the potential to be a time of national celebration and inspiration for the Church and the nation.

With the changed nature of Central Boards and Committees, the role of *General Secretaries* might change. They might be appointed to be directly accountable to the General Assembly, with the support of smaller Advisory Boards. They could have direct access to speak to the Assembly as the people called and entrusted with the Assembly's policy. They would enjoy high trust and high accountability.

The *timing of the General Assembly* could be more efficient. The present date in May means a substantial loss of time for those who have to report to the Assembly: the summer gap, six months to prepare reports for the printer in February and then a Spring gap before the next Assembly. A September Assembly would give a full church year for committee work and the summer months for printing and immediate preparation for Assembly arrangements.

> **Recommendation 22: That the sections on "The Shape of the Regional Church" and "The Shape of the Central Church" be remitted to the Board of Practice and Procedure and the Assembly Council.**

> **Recommendation 23: That the Board of Practice and Procedure review the culture and timing of the General Assembly in order to increase the quality of reporting, participation and decision-making**

SECTION III:

Proposals for Continuing Reform

1. Praying through Change

> **Jesus said, "Follow me."**

"Follow me" is a call to change. The history of the church is an account of our failure to respond to that call, and Christ's faithfulness in recalling us again and again to the Way. The call to change is not a threat, but an invitation at the heart of the Gospel.

From the outset, we have recognised that the core issue of change in the church is not about structures. It is about mindsets. It is about creating an environment in which our relationship with God and our neighbour may flourish.

We have looked at the current phase of church history through the lens of the Exile. The people of God—now as then—are cut off from familiar routines and patterns of life as they struggle to live the life of faith in a culture stripped of the symbols that sustain faith. Is the time of exile about to end and the people return to God? Or have we yet to learn the true lessons of the Exile?

When Jeremiah spoke of the Exile, he warned against the false prophets who saw it coming to a quick conclusion. Jeremiah spoke of the exile lasting for 70 years. In that time, the people were to settle in Babylon, pray for the welfare of the city and go about life faithfully before God in their new environment. In his vision of the baskets of figs (Chapter 24), he compared the basket of good figs to those who went into Babylon and promised that the experience would lead to new heart for God. (24:5-7)

Whatever the experience of God's people in our time of cultural dislocation, it is a time when God addresses us with hope: *"For I know the plans I have for you, plans to prosper and not to harm you, plans to give you a hope and a future. Then you will call upon me and come and pray to me and I will listen to you. You will seek me and find me when you seek me with all your heart. I will be found by you," says the Lord.* (Jeremiah 29:11-13)

> **The heart of reform is the reform of the heart. The first proposal for reform is a call to prayer.**

The heart of reform is the reform of the heart. The first proposal for reform is a call to prayer. People at prayer will be people who learn to live within the purposes of God with patient hope. If God be long in coming, so be it. If God comes quickly, we will be the more ready to welcome him and the future he brings.

Praying people recognise our daily dependence on the

Holy Spirit. A call to prayer is a call to praise, confession, repentance, meditation, intercession and to decisive redemptive action. A call to prayer is a call to live with God. A call to prayer begins with the leadership of the church, that those who lead may be open to being led by the Spirit. A call to prayer rests on every Christian person: in the privacy of the home, in the melee of the working day, in public worship or committed prayer groups. The ways are many. The call is one. Let us pray.

We recommend that congregations explore how they might deepen their life of prayer to be more open to the renewing Spirit of God. We will not settle for reform that changes structures and leaves lives untouched by Christ. *I will give them a heart to know me that I am the Lord. (Jeremiah 24:7)*

> *Sabbath is a time of realising that we do not run the world. It is a time to recover the rythms of grace as we trust in God the Creator. It is a time to realise our responsibilities to the poor and the lost as we look around us. We recommend a Sabbath rest for the people of God.*

God in Jesus Christ. At the end of the time (between Easter and Pentecost?), allow time to share whatever God may have revealed. Choose one area of review of congregational life to look, listen, reflect and act. Repeat the process each year over the next five years.

We recommend that *Presbyteries* build in spaces for retreat together over the next five years. Changes will come, but the changes must not become ends in themselves. They are only valid as they lead us closer to God and to each other and to our neighbours.

We recommend that in anticipation of a major movement for structural change from 2002-5, *Boards and Committees* review programmes to be less proactive. As far as is practical, we urge a disciplined moratorium on new initiatives from the centre, to allow congregations and new-forming Presbyteries to discover their direction and take up responsibilities.

Sabbath is a time of realising that we do not run the world. It is a time to recover the rhythms of grace as we trust in God the Creator. It is a time to realise our responsibilities to the poor and the lost as we look around us. We recommend a Sabbath rest for the people of God.

> **Recommendation 24: That Kirk Sessions identify ways of deepening the prayer life of their congregations individually and together.**

2. Creating Space for Change

It is difficult to change direction. The old routines, requirements and habits are instinctive. We often need to stop, stand back and reflect before we can reset our priorities. We recommend this for *individuals* in any position of leadership in the church, that they set time for spiritual retreat within the course of the year. Spiritual leadership is about keeping the essentials central. We lead by the light we shed or the shadow we cast. Solitude with God is essential for every one in any leadership role.

We recommend that *Kirk Sessions* choose a time in the near future to give the congregation a sabbatical from activity. It may be a good exercise for Lent 2002 and 2003 to agree that usual church activities are suspended for six weeks. Set people free to meet as friends without an agenda. Offer spaces for retreat, reflection and prayer at home or at a retreat centre. Plan times for the leadership to step back from the routine and rediscover the grace of

> **Recommendation 25: That the leadership in every area of church life institute the discipline of a period of retreat, rest and reflection to allow space for God to change us.**

3. Giving Permission to Change

In any change process, there are those who initiate change and those who authorise change. We are confident that the initiative for change is local and specific. There can be no diktat of Assembly that ushers in a new Reformation, but there can be permission to change.

> **Barriers: Fear and Power**

We affirm that the Church of Scotland offers more freedom for change and innovation than most people believe. Among the many suggestions for change, the majority require no legal or procedural change. What we must address is rather the culture of inhibition and distrust, which creates a fear of change. Most of the changes that are needed can already happen, and can be richly supported, if people make the decision to make the change. We trust you. Take the responsibility. Take the risk.

Our response is simply to declare the Gospel of grace to a paralysed church: "By the grace of God you are free! Get up and walk!" Most people have to walk a very long way before they find any structural impediment to change. It is a matter of mindset and faith. Go for it!

> **Most people have to walk a very long way before they find any structural impediment to change. It is a matter of mindset and faith. Go for it!**

Recommendation 26: That congregations take risks and try new ways so that faith may grow.

4. Looking for Levers for Change and Limits to Growth

In every situation there are levers for change and limits to change. On some estimates, the levers for change may

> **Change in the church will not be the result of people following through a long list of recommendations. Change will come where people take the time to discover the one area that might make a difference for them and then they do it.**

be found in "the 15% rule": 15% effort in the right place produces 85% of the results.

Change in the church will not be the result of people following through a long list of recommendations. Change

will come where people take the time to discover the one area that might make a difference for them and then they do it. We are part of a complex system of relationships and structures. We have suggested issues that may give you a handle on a lever for change. Find your lever and pull it.

There are limits to growth. In *The Fifth Discipline: The Art and Practice of the Learning Organisation,* Peter Senge claims that in our complex world we need to practice the art of being a "learning organisation". If we keep pushing at the good idea, it will eventually slow down or burn out because it triggers the "balancing system" of resistance. Behind the resistance is a "limiting factor". Once we discover the "limiting factor", we release the good for growth. Once again, we have suggested some limiting factors. We pray that people may find the relevant one and have the courage to address it.

We do not claim to have identified more than a few potential levers and limits, but we offer them as potential leads to those that matter in the local situation.

Presbyteries can assist here. They can build this into a process of one to one visits or Quinquennial Visits to identify areas for growth or limits to growth. The Presbytery then builds up a "gap analysis" identifying where congregations need resources of people, training or finance. From that they create a "regional needs plan" to meet it. Presbytery will then be keyed into supporting the local congregation on its way to becoming a worshipping community sharing in Christ's mission.

Recommendation 27: That Kirk Sessions and Presbyteries study the report as a stimulus to identifying the levers for change and the limits to growth in the local situation; that Kirk Sessions establish an "local needs" plan and Presbytery establish a "regional needs" plan of support, with special reference to recommendations 1-16 and 24-28; and apply, where appropriate to the Community and Parish Development Fund.

5. *Supporting One Another through Change*

We are aware that many people find change daunting. We would encourage people to see it as exciting. Anxiety and excitement are both a kind of fear. One expects a negative outcome and the other expects a positive outcome. As people of the Resurrection, we face change with hope, not fear.

However, we are aware that there is often low morale among congregations and among ministers. We believe that the way to face change is in the company of others who can travel with us through change. We commend the wisdom and experience of the many advisers and consultants in the employ of the Church e.g. in Parish Education, National Mission, Social Responsibility, and Stewardship and Finance.

The heart of the "local and relational" theme is to be worked out in the formation of local groupings. We recommend the formation of networks of common interest or common context to share struggles and ideas. Around the church there are churches that are strugglers, survivors, searchers and signposts. We encourage joining hands to move across the pain threshold of change. It is only as friendships form and trust builds that other decisions of cooperation may follow.

> *"Though it was the common task which brought us together, what made us a community were the personal relationships which were quickly established on each occasion. These relationships were not incidental but integral to the work in which we were engaged."*
>
> From Appendix 7 A Narrative of the Special Commission

The story of the Commission has been recorded in **Appendix 7**. This story emphasises the journey of trust that has been travelled together. It takes time. It takes commitment and openness. It is our conviction that the renewal of the church will begin when leaders of local congregations take time out together in retreat, to reflect prayerfully and honestly on the Gospel and our mission. Only communities of trust will sustain the process of local reform that emerges.

The experience of the Commission cannot be passed on. The process of the Commission can be offered as one way of creating the new environment of trust.

> **Recommendation 28: That congregational leadership teams form networks focused on a shared context or a shared concern in order to build trusting relationships as the basis of future cooperation.**

Interdependence is key to our future. That applies in every area of the church. We welcome the development of new relationships among Boards and Committees through the Coordinating Forum, but recognise the imbalance of power based on budgets. It is essential that the larger Boards do not develop a "Premier League" that leaves the low budget committees in second place. The Gospel principle of the strong being at the service of the weak applies in this dynamic.

We recognise the importance of people fulfilling the remits of their area of work, but that creates its own tunnel vision. We recommend that the Coordinating Forum, representing all Boards and Committees, continue to develop their residential times to ensure that the constituent parts are set within a vision of the bigger picture.

> **Recommendation 29: That the Coordinating Forum develop its role of capturing the larger vision within which people are operating.**

Celebration is one dimension of inspiring one another for the future. As the church moves into a new shape in the coming years, we recommend that celebration be built into these movements as milestones on the way. We recommend that a "stakeholders' conference" be planned for 2005 as a national celebration, representing the churches around Scotland and partners from across the world, and with representation from various areas of national life.

This will be an opportunity to celebrate our faith and life together, a point of accountability of progress and a time to pledge ourselves to moving forward together into God's future

> **Recommendation 30: That the General Assembly appoint a planning group to prepare a "Stakeholders' Conference" in 2005 as a point of National Celebration and a milestone of progress.**

6. Modelling Change: The Community and Parish Development Fund

We need examples of new models of the Church for our time to encourage us to face the future together. Innovative new beginnings are already emerging around the country. It is essential to fund those visions in such a way that they may be able to flourish and share their insights with the wider church.

> *There are many congregations around the country who have a big vision, but limited resources. We believe that one way to encourage growth is by making significant funds available*

There are many congregations around the country who have a big vision, but limited resources. We believe that one way to encourage growth is by making significant funds available.

We recommend the formation of a Community and Parish Development Fund of £7.5 million over 5 years. **(Appendix 8: Community and Parish Development Fund)** It would be the preferred option to give out substantial grants to congregations and local groupings allowing them to put together funding packages that would attract other funders. Making grants of up to £30,000 per annum over a five-year period would mean that congregations could begin to bring on board a variety of people to work in ministry teams. Many of those brought on might be youth workers or worship leaders or local church administrators.

The aim would be to facilitate congregations to become vibrant worship centres. On this basis we could support around 50 congregations over a 5-year period. The money would be fast tracked, going directly from the centre to

the congregation. The administration of this project would mirror the flexible management approach of the Rank Foundation. In essence they keep their management of the projects to a minimum. They seek to supply support where required by linking in other agencies to deliver the service. We would recommend that two field workers be employed to develop the use of the Fund to the fullest advantage.

We would invite major funding agencies to help us formulate the most effective way of administering this Fund. We would also negotiate with these trust and others ways in which they too could partner us in these huge community investment projects. The principle would work on the three Rs adopted by Rank Foundation. These are, to help projects develop in **Relation** to each other, to be prepared to take **Risks** with local congregations and local groupings, to find additional **Resources** to reward success. (At present up to 50% of Rank's projects in Scotland have a Christian basis to them.)

To ensure that the money is spent equitably and effectively, certain criteria would be established to include partnerships with other churches and an intentional process of sharing the fruits of the development with others. In this way the money of the whole church will be invested in some churches for the benefit of the whole church.

> *On this basis we could support around 50 congregations over a five-year period. The money would be fast tracked, going directly from the centre to the congregation.*

Recommendation 31: That there be established a Board of Community and Parish Development as described in Appendix 8, that the Board of Stewardship and Finance

a) **set up a Parish Development Fund of £7.5 million over 5 years in terms of Appendix 8 and report to the General Assembly of 2002;**

b) **appoint and manage two field directors until the Board of Community and Parish Development comes into being;**

and that the Nomination Committee nominate 12 people for the Board of Community and Parish Development and report to the General Assembly of 2002.

7. Investing in Change: Reviewing our Financial Strategy
Change means funding the vision. Change in shape and priorities will mean a change in investment to support those changes. Investing in change means reviewing our financial strategy. While the main issues and recommendations are represented here, the detailed arguments for reviewing our financial strategy are set out in **Appendix 9: Reviewing our Financial Strategy**.

The Church of Scotland centrally has an approximate annual income of £100 million and around £300 million in invested funds. Over £40 million of the annual income comes by way of congregational contributions to Ministry Funds and the Mission and Aid Fund. While the sources and uses of this money can be described in terms of what is and what has been, the danger is that we continue to think along existing tramlines and simply move small amounts among the existing jam jars.

One of the fatal flaws in our system, which goes to the heart of future development, is the governance of the Church in relation to finance. There is currently no mechanism to establish priorities across the Church. The General Assembly is an impossible mechanism for such work and each Board has its own commitments to fulfil and corner to defend.

> *One of the fatal flaws in our system, which goes to the heart of future development, is the governance of the Church in relation to finance. There is currently no mechanism to establish priorities across the Church.*

The Church's priorities continue to be shaped by inherited assumptions and patterns of funding. New patterns are emerging which will require a reallocation of resources. Without that substantial reallocation, financial restrictions will limit future movement.

Recommendation 32: That the Assembly Council, through the Coordinating Forum, establish overall priorities for the work of the Church in the light of the emerging shape of the Church and to convey these to the Board of Stewardship and Finance, so that these priorities can be incorporated into the Co-ordinated Budget proposals which the Board will be bringing to the General Assembly in 2002 and subsequent years, with appropriate amendments to the Constitution of the Coordinating Forum and the Board of Stewardship and Finance.

> *As we enter the Third Millennium, it is important to steward the resources of an emerging church for the missionary purposes of the Church of Scotland. In the emerging church, the nature of ministry will be more varied than "ministers of word and sacrament", places of worship and mission may be temporary bases in the community rather than fixed buildings for generations and the context of mission may be to enter some of the "flow cultures" of our society rather than the immediate geographical area around a church building.*

The strategic shift will include moves
from parish + building + minister
to networks of communities + multiple bases/venues + ministry teams.

Since the General Trustees steward a Consolidated Stipend Fund of £59 million for the benefit of 1400 congregations and a Consolidated Fabric Fund of £33 million for the benefit of 700 congregations, there are very considerable resources tied up in a historically inherited structure of 19th century mission models.

In 1995, an Act of Parliament removed a key obstacle to flexibility and ensured that the funds held by the General Trustees are under the sole jurisdiction of the General Assembly. If the purposes and shape of the church are redefined, then the funds may be used as the General Assembly decides for the benefit of congregations.

Recommendation 33: That the General Trustees, in consultation with the Board of Ministry and the Board of National Mission, monitor changing patterns of ministry and building requirements, and report on how best to fund the needs of the emerging church and report to the General Assembly of 2003.

Flexibility will be essential for the future of the church, a factor which affects the work of the General Trustees:

1. Congregations with large sums invested may wish to use these funds for another area of mission development, but that choice is not open to them.

2. Congregations have no choice on how funds may be invested between the growth of income and the growth of capital. The range of options is Stipend >Fabric>Minimum Stipend Fund or Fabric>Stipend>Central Fabric Fund.

3. Congregations do, however, have the choice to be generous with their Fabric Funds within the Presbytery, as befits a Presbyterian Church.

> *Flexibility will be essential for the future of the church, a factor which affects the work of the General Trustees.*

4. The choices may be extended in the case of the Consolidated Fabric Fund to include "or other purposes as agreed by Presbytery". This allows a more strategic view to be taken of the missionary needs of the area and avoid tying money unnecessarily to buildings.

5. Uniting congregations should be more creative in the use of funds derived from the sale of properties.

Recommendation 34: That the General Trustees examine the Consolidated Stipend Fund and bring proposals to the General Assembly of 2002 that would allow congregations more flexibility of investment.

Recommendation 35: That the General Trustees examine the Consolidated Fabric Fund and bring proposals to the General Assembly of 2002 that would allow congregations more flexibility of investment.

Recommendation 36: That the General Trustees, in consultation with the Board of National Mission, examine the application of the proceeds of the sale of buildings following readjustment, and report to the General Assembly of 2002.

8. *Moving through Barriers to Change*

Throughout the report we have emphasised the grace of God at work in the church. Change occurs when we release what is good, by removing the barriers to change. We have reported on the openness to change around the church, but in our consultations we have been warned never to underestimate the resistance to change. One look at our history tempers our optimism.

We need only track back through the attempts in the 20th Century to introduce change to the Church of Scotland. Suggestions of community parishes, team ministries, lay witness, missionary congregations, cell-style churches, redesigned Presbyteries and calls for spiritual renewal can be traced through the Committee of Forty in the 70's, the Tell Scotland movement of the 50's, the Baillie Commission of the 40's and right back to the writings of John White prior to the formation of the present Church of Scotland in the 1920's!

At the risk of raising a cynical sigh of weariness, let John White speak into a new century:

> "Have we been using our great united forces for the winning of Scotland? The Church is not infiltrating through the Community as it can and as it ought....We are all to blame. Too many of our good respectable Church folks still think of their own church as if it were a private religious club. They miss the main function of Church life and worship—to go out to their brothers and sisters and compel them to come in."

We listen to the passionate plea and say that it is time to throw off the burden of our history, and take responsibility for obeying the call of Christ in a culture that is seen as a totally new era of human history.

> **Two barriers to change lie deep in our nature: the twins of fear and power.**

Two barriers to change lie deep in our nature: the twins of fear and power.

Fear. Fear has many faces. Some fear the mess of change, others fear the effect on people we serve. Some fear admitting our failure or taking the risk of failing. Some fear stepping outside the safety of the regulations or the tradition. Some fear the pain of the unknown. Some fear the exposure of weakness or the exposure to conflict.

We have no answer to that except the call of Jesus: Follow me. He calls us into faith, hope and love—each one an antidote to fear.

Power. Power is an issue that is very difficult to identify in our system. The resistance to power focused on individuals leads to circuits of power that operate in hidden ways, from passive aggression to outright manipulation. While we are familiar with the famous phrase that power corrupts and absolute power corrupts absolutely, it has also been said that what really corrupts is the fear of the loss of power. That may be the most sinister barrier to change of all. The power of money is equally crucial. We recommend that the Panel on Doctrine undertake a study of the Christian use and abuse of power.

If we are to follow Christ, we will be led to the place where we release our power into the hands of God, put

> **The Commission considered different ways of ensuring that its proposals might be carried forward. In the end, the decision was made to offer these reflections and directions to the prayerful and committed attention of the Church.**

power at the service of others, and face the future with a trusting powerlessness.

> **Recommendation 37: That the Panel on Doctrine undertake a study on the theology of power and report to a future General Assembly.**

9. Trusting God's Spirit through Change

The Commission has become convinced of a mood for change across the Church. That mood has the potential to become a movement. The prayers of many people are being answered as the Spirit of God calls us onwards. We believe that we need to trust the Spirit and trust the people of God to listen and follow in the way of Jesus Christ in the place where we are set.

The Commission considered different ways of ensuring that its proposals might be carried forward. In the end, the decision was made to offer these reflections and directions to the prayerful and committed attention of the Church.

> **That is a matter of trust. The responsibility belongs there. The resources are available in the grace of God and the people of God. There is no other plan.**

While changes to Presbyteries and Central Administration will require careful consultation and management as they unfold, that process will be in good hands. The main emphasis of the report has been on the "local and relational" aspects of Church life. What that means for local Christian communities is for these communities to discern and determine.

That is a matter of trust. The responsibility belongs there. The resources are available in the grace of God and the people of God. There is no other plan.

We end as we began.

The purpose, shape and process of continuing reform lie in these timeless words of Jesus: "Follow me."

> **Jesus said, "Follow me."**

Recommendation 38: That all Kirk Sessions, Presbyteries, Boards and agencies of the Church study the report, take appropriate action and establish the necessary accountability for progress by 2005; and that the Assembly Council monitor developments through its ongoing consultations and assessments in 2002-3 and 2004-5.

Recommendation 39: That the Board of Practice and Procedure facilitate the study of the Report throughout the Church.

The Grace of the Lord Jesus Christ be with us all.

APPENDIX 1:

Listening to Many Voices

Listening, reflecting, discerning and deciding. These have been the task of the Commission. The first stage of listening has meant taking account of many voices.

1. The Commission

We listened to ourselves. We began here, not because we knew better than others, but in the belief that God's dreams and our human frustrations are woven together into our experience of life. We told of our passions and our frustrations and shared our journeys of faith. From the beginning we recognised the need to discover the meaning of faith for a new generation and the community to embody it. Worship and daily spirituality were high on our list of concerns, as was our desire to see God's gifts released into God's service as the Church in the world.

2. Boards and Committees

Every General Secretary was interviewed to gather an overview of the work of the church and the issues as they saw them. Among the many visions and dreams being expressed by so many, there was a frustration that our current structures did not serve the purpose of the Gospel reaching the whole nation.

There was a desire for more relational qualities of trust and communication. There was no real forum for deciding overall priorities. Church issues needed to be set in the context of the nation and beyond that in the global setting of a vast movement of Christian people across the world. There was an openness to change, but a concern that the change be properly paced and owned by all who were involved.

An early draft of the Commission's ideas was circulated and discussed with Conveners and Secretaries of all Boards and Committees. The wide-ranging responses have been taken into account in the final report.

3. The Urban Priority Areas

Visits to urban priority areas and the priority areas fund (for urban and rural projects) opened up the need for vulnerability and the inspiration from Luke 10 of doing more with less, as Jesus sends us out with little. In a sector of society that assumes that the church is not for the likes of us, they wanted to be the church that likes to say 'yes'.

We heard a tale of two churches: despite the massive support being given to UPAs in many ways, there was a feeling that the "other church" did not understand the massively complex challenges being faced by fragile communities of Christians. The gauntlet was thrown down to the Commission to deliver something that will make a difference—the litmus test of "policy at the point of delivery of service."

4. The Highlands

A survey was undertaken of congregations in Sutherland. We recognised the rich spiritual tradition of this part of the church, but saw how the treasure was locked into prison houses of traditionalism. Some of the best and the worst of the Reformed heritage is to be found here: the rich emphasis on the Word of God and prayer, but the constant fear of stepping out of line from the conventional inherited patterns.

The "temple template" of the holiness tradition assumes an inward pull of the Spirit and constrains the missionary movement to go where people are. The scandal of divided Presbyterianism is a cause for deep concern and repentance. Remote communities looked for a decentralisation of power and responsibility.

5. Rural Areas

Rural means different things to different people: from Buchan to Ayrshire, or Angus to Newcastleton. Commissioners carried with them rural experience in touch with the rural crises in farming and housing, the pressures of multiple linkages and the good news stories of ministry teams to sustain worship and witness in the various communities. Heartfelt cries for a "ministry of truth" were heard from places where the system was breaking down and needed to start again.

6. Towns and Cities

In our towns and cities where church was operating as a focus for community life and family support, we heard stories of congregations building long term from the crèche up, and reshaping buildings to serve the community.

The aspirations for the ministry of the people of God were often frustrated by the time constraints on people: fragmented families divide loyalties and demanding business pressures rob communities and churches of the people's time.

In the complexity of city life, it was impossible to go it alone. We heard of partnerships of churches and "matrix ministries" between sector and parish or centre and suburbs. In our postmodern society city ministry operates in an archipelago of mini-cultures each requiring its own pattern of church.

7. Elders

In an attempt to listen to elders, we gathered comments from a number of focus groups of elders around the country, though not so often as we intended in the beginning. The readiness for our core leadership to face change was challenging and encouraging. Here is a sample of their concerns:

Prayer—developing personal spirituality and corporate prayer

Church in the Community—engaging in evangelism and social justice

Recruitment and retention of members—winning, keeping and building disciples

Life-long learning—deepening faith and living faith in the everyday world

Communication—harnessing new technology for new generation

Parish System— working a team system

Ecumenism—working towards greater cooperation

Patterns of worship—offering a variety of options

Participation—increasing the range of involvement in worship and other activities

Ministers and elders—developing better teamwork

Ministers and elders—reviewing and encouraging training

Radical Change—managing change carefully

These comments highlight the key areas of discontent, and discontent is the precursor of change. Looking at this list, the question that stands out is: What is stopping the change? What is needed to release people?

8. Thenew

"Thenew", named after the mother of St Mungo is dedicated to identifying and eliminating violence and abuse towards women in church and society. A lively conversation with one group alerted us to the ways in which women today feel excluded from an institution that has been created by men, and sensitised us to the pain felt by abused women in our use of language and in the assumed styles of organising and decision-making.

9. Chaplains

Reports from some chaplains reminded us of those who are daily immersed in the places where people face the greatest stresses and strains of life. Here was incarnational ministry seeking to be where people are, connect the Christian Gospel with the life issues and bear witness to Christ beyond the safety zones of our churches, bother pastorally and prophetically.

There was feeling that many of the patterns of ministry being worked out by these specialists offered clues to the parish ministry today. There needed to be a closer link between these specialists and congregational life. If the UPAs reflect a tale of two churches, the chaplaincies reflect a tale of two ministries that have not been recognised as mutual and complementary.

10. Journalists

We set out to meet with people who could give an outsider's view of the Church. Among them we heard from journalists who spoke of the need for the church to relate to the new identity of the Scottish nation, and to address the loss of trust in society. There was still a massive respect for the church as an institution, but a growing lack of "insider knowledge" among journalists. The need for some clearer system of a "church voice" was raised.

11. The Video: A Church without Walls

Around 100 congregations responded to the video, "A Church without Walls", distributed in the summer of 2000, focusing on the themes of relationships, resources and risk. While there was some criticism of the video's lack of rural context and its sweeping statements on church finance, the responses were substantially positive about the key themes. There was strong affirmation of ecumenical partnerships, decentralisation, the need for ministry appraisal and the recognition of the need for two churches to run side by side.

People were concerned about the missing generations, "central-beltism" and the need for a focus on discipleship, new patterns of ministerial training and a readiness to challenge injustices. All responses were analysed and discussed by the Commission.

12. The Scottish Churches

At an early stage we invited Kevin Franz, Secretary of Action of Churches Together in Scotland, to spend time with the Commission. This gave us insights into the variety of contexts in Scotland and affirmed the Church of Scotland as having "the charism of a big heart".

At a later stage we had the benefit of responses from Sr Maire Gallagher, Convener of ACTS. Other churches were given drafts of the report and invited to comment. Conversations with our own Ecumenical Relations Committee helped sustain our awareness of our neighbouring churches.

13. Finance

The financial expertise of the General Treasurer has been freely offered as we have wrestled with the complexities of a financial system comprising of over 4000 separate funds, and the inherited allegiances which they represent.

We have received challenging advice from Professor Ewan Brown, Investment Banker, and Sir David Tweedie, past chairman of the Accounting Standards Board, both of whom are serving elders of the Church. They have helped us separate strategic issues from the technical detail of day to day financial management. Amidst the range of opinions and emotions generated by money, we have tried to hold to the theology of grace and faith: faithful to the God who in Jesus Christ gives generously and invites us to trust unreservedly.

Listening has taken many forms. Through the courtesy of World Mission, National Mission, Ecumenical Relations, Ministry, Parish Education, former Moderators, the Coordinating Forum, the Assembly Council, the Priority Areas Fund, The Scottish Youth Focus, the National Youth Assembly, the Committee on Presbytery Boundaries and various Presbytery groupings, we have been involved in fruitful conversations about the future of the Church.

Through personal conversations with individuals including theologians, sociologists, business people and others with a concern for the future of the church, ideas and opinions have been shaped and moulded.

How well the Commission has listened, reflected, discerned and distilled the wisdom of these people is for others to decide. For our part, we thank each and all for their time and wisdom freely and generously given.

APPENDIX 2:

The Church and The State:
The Declaratory Articles

There are various ways in which a national Church can relate constitutionally to the political environment in which it is set. One model, uncommon nowadays, is for the Church to rule all aspects of the life of the community with no separate secular authority (or one that is subordinated to the ultimate religious authority). A second model, pejoratively termed 'Erastian' after an early Swiss example, gives the secular power all ultimate authority, with the Church subject to that worldly jurisdiction. The third model avoids either of the above tendencies, either by separating the jurisdictions of

Church and State so that each has its area of rule, or else by encouraging the Church to be a completely conventional voluntary organisation within society subject to the jurisdiction of civil law - so far as civil law can appropriately regulate the Church's affairs.

Scottish History

There is little trace in Scottish history of the first model of power, though there is evidence of the influence of the Papacy in political history.

The turbulent history of the post-Reformation Church in its relations with the Stuart Dynasty represented the resistance of the Reformers and their successors to an Erastian connection with the emerging British nation-state. The tendency of interference by those kings (e.g. the Black Acts of 1583, the Articles of Perth in 1618, Laud's Liturgy introduced in 1637) took several generations to dismiss.

After the settlement of the House of Orange in 1690, a different ethos prevailed, and there developed a sense of parallel jurisdictions being the civil powers in secular matters and the Church's courts in ecclesiastical matters. This was a recognition by the state of an ancient, fundamental and inherent property of the Church, and not as something devolved or conceded by the State.

Establishment

The theory of Establishment, put simply, is the belief that the State has a responsibility to provide, fund and/or protect the existence of a national religion. It is the articulation of a spiritual duty on the part of the civil power, and therefore differs from the issue discussed above of secular interference in the Church's internal affairs.

However, the two issues, the State's right to interfere and its responsibility to protect, have often been confusing, and never more so than in reading the history of the nineteenth century. In the Ten Years' Conflict immediately before the Disruption, the Court of Session regarded the Establishment of the Church as justification for extensive civil interference in its affairs. When Thomas Chalmers led the Disruption in 1843, he made it clear that he was not criticising the theory of Establishment, but only necessarily leaving the Established Church on the principle of religious freedom. When elements in the Free Church switched their allegiance to the (unsuccessful) Disestablishment campaign of the 1880s, it was in the recognition that there was no disentangling spiritual independence from disestablishment, and pursuing the former principle necessitated supporting the latter. So the mid-nineteenth century witnessed the Free Church supporting Establishment with spiritual freedom and the United Presbyterian (formerly Secession) Church insisting on the same spiritual freedom but with the Voluntary principle of financial self-maintenance. Only with the change in the Free Church's position could the union of those Churches proceed in 1900, to form the UF Church.

The Articles Declaratory

The Articles Declaratory presented a new self-understanding of the Church of Scotland and took a minutely precise course through the differences of principle of the Established and United Free Churches. All the precious spiritual demands of both sides were to be met, in a Church that would be national but free, related to the state but not Established in the old sense, territorial but not subject to external authority. They were a remarkable accomplishment, overcoming differences that many people thought were insuperable.

In terms of the distinctions made at the beginning of this appendix, this was a settlement which continued down the route of separate jurisdictions. In the areas of doctrine, worship, government and discipline the Church has its independent spiritual jurisdiction, and has proved successful in fending off attempts at civil actions in those types of case.

Current critique of the settlement as it pertains today would include the following difficulties.

Power or Love. The trouble with taking a legal jurisdiction and dividing it between the secular and Church courts on the basis of subject matter, is that it assumes that the kind of authority the Church has (or seeks) is a worldly kind of power. Ecclesiology like Ruth Page's distinguishes models of 'power from above' from the gospel paradigm of love, attraction and service. The exercise, by the courts of the Church, of a legal power of command or punishment is not convincingly founded in theology. The gospel virtues of service and humility do not sit well with the dignity of a self-contained legal system in the Church. **The Church should be uncomfortable with any top-down power.**

Privilege and the Church. Other Churches in Scotland have the constitutional status of voluntary organisations, and the civil law largely leaves them to govern their own affairs internally, provided they do so justly. The Church of Scotland bases its claims to spiritual independence on a legislative provision that only we have. **The Church should not be a guardian of privilege, and one branch of it should not rejoice to have privileges others do not share, unless particular good can come of it.**

European Convention on Human Rights. The ECHR, now directly accessible in the Scottish Courts, provides protection in Article 9 for freedom of religious expression. Since the vast bulk of our debate and internal case-law about doctrine, worship, government and discipline does not hold the slightest interest for the civil law or courts, the general protection afforded to all religious organisations by this Article probably secures a liberty of internal regulation for the Church of Scotland which will scarcely differ in substance and effect from the specific privilege of the 1921 Act. **The Special Commission rejoices that religious liberty is still regarded as a fundamental human right, and the Church benefits from this international recognition.**

APPENDIX No. 3:

A Healthy Church

Integrity
means:

Jesus is at the core,
He is the beginning, middle and end of our story
We remember our Church's experience covers
thousands of years.
What we say is consistent with what we do.

Body and Soul
means:

We strive for a lasting face to face encounter with God
We involve the whole person and the whole people of
God
The quality of our worship and devotion are vital
The whole of life is our concern

Open House
means:

We welcome all with open doors
and open arms
We go out to find the uninvited
We make our home among need
We listen and we speak

Growth
means:

We are trainees learning skills
We are followers on the road
Seeds have to be nurtured before they will bear fruit
God adds to our number

Local
means:

The global good news needs to be spoken in a local
accent
We choose to be real rather than virtual
We value every locality

Love and Care

means:

Our Community will only be satisfied with
Christ-like relationships
We put our hands to work

How can these characteristics be cultivated in 21st
Century soil?
Where do we see them being well cultivated today?
What about other characteristics?
They may be beautiful, efficient and sensible, but are
they necessary?

APPENDIX 4:

The Church in Context

THE CHURCH IN THE HIGHLANDS

Factors of Geography
The Highland Church has many distinctive features, not least its geography and scattered population. In 1999, the roll of the whole Presbytery of Sutherland was 1096. While being fully aware of the number of adherents who are more active than most Lowland members, we must set these numbers against the fact that the small congregations are scattered around hundreds of miles of the coast of Sutherland.

The Highland life is rich in its natural network of community, but isolation and distance can also lead to insularity. The traditional community is being changed as "new Highlanders" migrate from the South, enriching the community in many ways, but sometimes skewing the local economy by buying up houses for holiday homes at prices locals could never afford.

These factors of geography affect the whole community: the range of educational opportunities from single pupil schools to Dingwall Academy of 1300 pupils,

with pupils having to travel large distances and often boarding out during the week. The same is true for health where services are focused in Inverness, a two and and half hour drive from Wick. A trip to the cinema from Scourie may mean an overnight stay in Inverness.

Factors of History
The Highland Church is very distinctive. Its history is marked by the strength of diverse Presbyterianism, remnants of Episcopalianism and pockets of Roman Catholicism overlaid on centuries of clan loyalties created by our geography of mountains, glens, lochs and islands. At the same time it is not unusual for the Highland church to be home to people of many different traditions. Other denominations have to stretch their resources very widely: the non-stipendiary Episcopal priest in Lairg cares for four congregations, while being the local chemist.

Factors of Spirituality
The inheritance is a mix of affirmations and challenges. We affirm the deep prayer and quiet spirituality of the people which is an inspiration to many - a unique contribution to the renewal church in faithful prayer. We affirm the place of the church in the community where it will have a central role even for those who may not be actively committed. The role of elders and Readers in preaching and leading worship is an example to other parts of the church of local leadership.

We affirm the creative and inspiring responses to being the church today. Consider the youth outreach at Bayhead in Stornoway, with young people from all the churches reaching out at night to the vulnerable young folk on the streets. Travel to Benbecula and the attempts to be the church in the community or Barra with its lively congregation living peaceably with the Roman Catholic majority. Gairloch has shown the way in quietly developing the people of God in ministry as has Killearnan and Dornoch. Radical new approaches to worship, discipleship and outreach are being implemented at Hilton, and Tongue has made use of modern technology to make worship lively and breathe with the mood of today. There are many other stories to tell—from different denominations and different areas.

Factors of Identity

The issues that challenge the Highland church are primarily issues of identity. At one level that is about a negative identity based on inherited criteria of doctrine and practice adopted as acceptable conventions, usually to mark groups out from each other. The divisiveness in one village of several little churches based on secondary identities other than Jesus Christ is a scandal to the Gospel in many places. There needs to be the rediscovery of our positive identity in Christ that set us free to cross old barriers.

Identity lies at the heart of the recurring adherents issue. Who are we? Who belongs here? Who is in and who is out? How do we pass through this "buffer zone", "ecclesiastical no-man's-land"? Church is defined by boundaries rather than by the centre in Jesus Christ. Instead of the image of Jesus bringing sheep within the walls of the sheep-fold, perhaps we need to think of Jesus in the midst of the crowd. People who are physically close to him may be in opposition to him, while those at the edge of the crowd are straining to hear and follow.

The identity of the Church must change because the identity of the Highlands is changing. It is one of the romantic myths about Scotland that because the mountains and glens are measured in millennia that the people are not themselves subject to change or initiators of change. The history of the highlands is one of dramatic social change, and recent patterns of life are affected by improved transport links, information technology, population migration and the all-pervasive media-saturated culture. The pace of change may be more measured, but the fact of change is a given of life.

Factors of Theology

The Highland church must change if it is to follow Jesus more obediently. Like the church at large needs to revisit its roots in the Gospels, going behind the inherited shibboleths of Disruption and Reformation and redefine its identity as the people of God for the emerging generation of highland children. There is a crucial theological issue of being the church for all or the church for some—limited atonement means limited church.

Open church does not mean an easy universalism, but it does mean an inclusiveness to share the journey that will reveal Christ on the road.

One underlyng spiritual issue for the whole church is the issue of fear—fear of change, fear of stepping out of line, fear of failing or being seen to fail. It may be that the Highland tradition of tough independence of mind can be sanctified for the renewal of the church. Instead of being hi-jacked as a reactionary mindset to affirm Highland identity over against central-beltism, it might be baptised into Christ as a readiness to turn sterile conservatism into a dynamic radicalism—a return to the Word of God and to prayer and the community of faith as primarily about relationships not religious observance. That radicalism would be a gift to the wider church.

Factors of "Temple Christianity"

The main challenge to the Highland concept of church lies in the fact that many churches operate with a kind of "Temple Christianity". This mindset lies behind the recurring refrain that "I am not good enough" to be a member or an elder. The way of grace is the way of release from that way of guilt and unworthiness. That involves breaking the "temple template" that lies embedded in the religious psyche.

The Temple operated with an outer court for the Gentiles, and inner court for the people of Israel, a priestly court and then the Holy of Holies for the High Priest. Highland churches have the same gradations of access, which have been socialised as the "adherents" (God-fearing Gentiles), the people of Israel (members), the court of the priests (the elders) and the High Priest (the minister). The model means that law is the core, not grace. When Jesus died, the Holy of holies was burst open, a new priesthood was released among the people and the boundary wall of Jew and Gentile was broken down. The legal model operates from the outside in. The grace model operates from the centre out, removing the barriers and opening the doors.

The text for Highland renewal may be the Letter to the Hebrews—an extraordinarily subversive letter. In it the writer uses the imagery of Temple, priesthood and sacrifice to explain the ministry of Jesus Christ in a way that shows that all three are now fulfilled in him. The Temple model has been superseded. As we move to the end of the letter, the static imagery of Temple is overtaken by the mobile procession of the people of God who are to keep their eyes on Jesus, and we are taken back behind the Temple in the City to worship in the wilderness, and end by meeting Jesus "outside the camp".

Factors of Mission Strategy

It follows from this image of Jesus "outside the camp" that we are no longer to wait for people to come to us - an image reinforced by centuries of singing Psalms about the nations coming to Zion. The missionary muscle of the Highland church has withered under that imagery. It is time for the Christian people of the church to go and meet Jesus "outside the camp" and to meet Christ's absent friends. Jesus' way of holiness was not worked out in separation from people. He was separated to God, but he was totally involved with people. So much so that they called him the "friends of tax collectors and sinners." If we made up our minds that "any friend of Jesus is a friend of mine", our lifestyles would be turned inside out and we would become the "church without walls."

A Reformation that put Jesus Christ above every religious convention, deconstructed the ecclesiastical pecking order and turned a static-gathered church into a mobile scattered church who began to find Jesus beyond our walls in strangely "unholy" places—now that would be a Reformation worthy of the name.

THE CHURCH IN RURAL AREAS

Rural Variations

Almost 50% of Church of Scotland congregations are in rural areas. "Rural" covers many different contexts. The Borders are different from Buchan. The Western Isles are different from the Northern Isles. Angus is different from Argyll. Rural ministry begins with respect for locality, a "knack for here" (Wendell Berry).

Rural life feels the threat of a succession of farming crises, fuel costs and limited transport. Housing prices are affected by the arrival of people from wealthier areas, or the extension of villages into commuter areas for cities and towns. The pace of life will vary from area to area and within the one community. The tension of different expectations between the traditional families and the incomers can be an issue in community life and in congregational life. Community life is sacrosanct. Feelings are usually private. The quality of life is valued, and there are deep motivations to conservation and conservatism.

Size

Rural church is usually small – the family sized church, where leadership lies with key people rather than official leadership. Young people move out for jobs and education. Leadership can sometimes be limited in numbers, but at their best elders are well-informed and personally concerned. Names are more important than numbers. Certain areas such as Angus and Buchan still have conventional pulls to membership, but attendance is low. Nominalism is endemic.

Linkages

The strains on rural church life lie in the multiple linkages, making massive drains on finances and time. This feature of rural church life more than any other, makes rural church and ministry distinctive. Add a vacancy or two in a rural Presbytery and it becomes unmanageable. The cost of maintaining buildings takes more money than can be justified in terms of the advancement of the Kingdom.

In some situations, it is time for the common sense that offers transport to a central point and the benefit of an enthusiastic worshipping congregation rather than three demoralized groups of die-hards. By contrast, where churches have developed local worship teams, such as Upper Tweeddale, worship has been sustained in local communities by local people, with the support of the minister.

On the other hand, in Orkney, the children asked why they went to one school but had to attend different churches. The outcome was united worship for the good of everybody. In some linkages, more could be done to affirm the distinctives, and let different churches develop different ministries and styles of worship. Instead of a reactionary defensiveness, it could be a proactive strategy to have a youth congregation or reflective worship or a "peace and justice" centre. Celebrate positive difference.

Denominational Allegiance

The potential for ecumenical cooperation varies from area to area. In some parts of Scotland, the Church of Scotland is the only church for miles, with the challenge of offering a spiritual home to people from many different traditions. This is both enriching and demanding, depending on attitudes and expectations. Membership rules need to be loosened to allow the gifts of people from other backgrounds to share in the governance of the congregation without requiring a change in denominational allegiance.

Patterns of Leadership

A General Kirk Session in a linked charge can allow the elders to come together around issues of strategy or to consider wider matters of church, nation or world concern. The individual Kirk Sessions can deal with the day-to-day issues of the local congregation and community. Finding elders can be difficult for reasons that are as much cultural as spiritual, and looser patterns of organization are needed to let the natural leadership be expressed without the full weight of officialdom.

One minister pleads for a "ministry of truth" about situations where the old ways are just not working. The numbers are so low that morale has gone. The leadership is tired. The church has cut itself off from the community and lost the simple art of communication and basic courtesy. Presbytery is often too close to the situation to challenge the issues.

Team ministry is essential for linked charges over wide areas. Gairloch developed a team of preaching elders to sustain worship in the different communities. Aberfeldy has employed a youth worker (formerly a dentist) to work in the schools, and develop new patterns of worship. Readers are being appointed to linked charges and given pastoral responsibilities to develop a true pastor-teacher relationship instead of being the occasional preacher.

Teams from within, or by employment, or through collaboration with other denominations are essential for the future of the rural church. Preparing the churches for multiple ministries might be the single priority of rural Presbyteries in the foreseeable future.

Church and Community

The rural church is usually immersed in the local community as the leaven in the dough. Church and community are not marked off by clear boundaries. Evangelism is best done when shaped by the human life cycle or the cycle of Christian year – the times when community attends church and are part of the faith community. One church offers the theme of pilgrimage and marks out milestones for each year – a journey to travel together. Another prays for all the children on the cradle roll. Another invites the families of all baptised children to a special service once a year.

Spirituality

The faith of the rural church is seldom vocal. Some people have found inspiration in the Celtic renaissance, where life and faith are gently woven together. Worship in small numbers requires thought and creativity on the part of the person leading the worship, and a different degree of involvement for the congregation. In some places, where the old ways are sustained for no better reason than that we have always done it this way, worship can be more exhausting than inspiring. In other places, like the Western Isles, a deep and quiet spirituality permeates the most traditional of gatherings.

Presbytery

The formation of the Committee on Presbytery Boundaries was largely due to the concerns about rural Presbyteries that had become too small to be sustainable. There is a deep frustration about trying to service central demands, and mirror General Assembly structures, with limited personnel.

Whatever the final outcome of Presbytery changes, these rural areas need "upside down" church, which takes its agenda from the local congregations and offers support, encouragement and inspiration to the small churches in the area. Rural church will find much to affirm and challenge in the twin themes of "local and relational".

The Report was completed before the outbreak of foot and mouth disease.

THE CHURCH IN URBAN PRIORITY AREAS

Through the able assistance of the Rev Ian Moir, then Urban Adviser, members of the Commission were invited to meet people working in parishes in the North of Glasgow and in an ecumenical partnership in the Inner East End of Glasgow. The Rev John Miller, then Convener of the UPA Committee, joined the Commission for a debriefing on the experience. The Commission expresses appreciation for the time and effort put into the preparations and presentations.

Starting at the End

From the experience, the Commission highlighted important signs for the Church:

—The flexibility to respond to community needs with openness and hospitality.
—The call to be the Church that likes to say "Yes" to people who assume rejection.
—The readiness to go empty-handed, like the disciples described in Luke chapter 10.
—The commitment to focus 70% of congregational time in the community.
—The cooperation between the churches of different traditions.
—The creative use of volunteers and their gifts.
—The need to go beyond the usual statistics to find alternative measures of a healthy church.
—The fragility of these situations, highlighting a church divided over resources.
—The dispersal of poverty throughout cities means it is less visible than it once was.
—The drain of the same people seeking funding from a limited range of sources.
—The mixed blessing of buildings - signs in the community, but a drain on time and money.
—The principle that "public policy is to be judged by effectiveness at the point of delivery."

The Commission was left with uncomfortable questions about the divided church where resources need to be reallocated. Why should these congregations on the edge of mission have to spend so much time and energy seeking funding from sources beyond the church? Is the Gospel really perceived as good news for the poor in Scotland?

From the Beginning.....

An Urban Priority Area is so designated by indicators from the Scottish Office and the National Census. There are 330 parishes in Scotland containing at least 10% of the worst 20% of the most deprived population. Of the 330 parishes, 100 are within the Presbytery of Glasgow.

Much has been written about work in these areas, but, the Commission records is visits to parishes in Ruchill, Colston Milton and Possilpark, all of which over 90% UPA status.

Ruchill

The minister of Ruchill described three structural barriers to being the church in his area:

—buildings take up 60% of the income;
—ministers are trained to be suburban;
—doctrine gets in the way of valuing people first.

The Youth and Family worker is working in the community with children, who in turn bring teenage brothers and sisters, and finally the wider family. The key is to be 70% in the community and to build friendships with the young people where they are.

The convener of the Community Council valued the church's involvement in the whole area in collaboration with other churches. She has been deeply affected by the local **Alpha** course, but challenged us to live with the realities of life, not the sham.

Summary of Key Issues
1. Be where the people are.
2. Invest in friendships around the real issues of life.
3. Find funding without having to go so far afield.
4. Consider the barriers of buildings, training of ministers and doctrine that excludes people.

Possilpark

Resources are a challenge on two fronts: the lack of money (the sectors of the church are disconnected) and the lack of members who live in the parish (the sectors of our lives are disconnected). Liberation theology thrived when the priests were on the ground and kept close to the community.

The parish is much reduced in size and a new building has given a new base for mission. The most significant development has been the Abigail Project, a cafe for drug users, involving banner-making, talks, family support groups and visits to Iona. What is emerging is a "parallel church". It is fragile.

They are determined to be the church that likes to say "Yes" to people who assume "No".

Summary of Key Issues

1. The cultural divide of congregation and community— and the time to be in the community.
2. The spirit of hospitality—say yes!
3. The emergence of the parallel church in the Abigail project.
4. The need for collaboration between congregations and with the wider community.
5. The funding priorities.

Colston Milton

We heard the story of the area over the forty years from being a thriving area for families to the ageing and decline of the community The result has been the draining of resources and the loss of children. The community is now becoming more responsive.

The changes in the church are: first of all, the renovation of the building to be more usable by the community; and secondly the breaking of the "ministerial mould" as lay workers lead breakfast clubs and take school assemblies.

A strategic development has been the arts project that has attracted 80-90 young people in the worst section of the community.

Summary of Key Issues

1. Stay with the community and move with it through the generations.
2. Let the "weakness" of the few be the power to break the ministerial mould.
3. Use the building for the community.
4. Develop the arts as the way of reaching communities.

Glasgow Inner East End Churches Together

Inner East End Churches Together (IEECT) consists of Barrowfield Franciscan Friary, Bridgeton St Francis in the East (C of S), Church House (C of S), Calton Parkhead (C of S), The Episcopal East End Team, St Luke's and St Andrew's (C of S) and St Thomas', Gallowgate (C of S).

Their mission statement reads:

IEECT represents congregations from the Church of Scotland and the Episcopal Church working as a team in an open and collaborative way, identifying common concerns and problems within our communities, and discovering the present and future reality of the Kingdom of God.

We want to do this by the way we work, pray, study together, celebrating our diversity, sharing hospitality, our faith, experience, energy, love, care and concerns, not forgetting our vulnerabilities as individuals and churches together.

This mission statement is given "teeth" in a team contract based on values of respect, affirmation, safety risk and mutual care, and practical commitments to 8 meetings with specific components of worship, agenda setting, decision-making and a rotating chairperson. An annual review with an external facilitator is built into the contract.

When the Presbytery of Glasgow invited areas to develop a Mission Plan in 1998, this was done together.

The Area

A video provided a vivid insight into the area's history, decline and current changes: closed shops, the HQ of the Orange Lodge, the Barras, the hostels for homeless people, "the grieving and hoping" as 63 new houses are built and Merchant City encroaches on the area. The population was 35,882 in 1997 - in some wards an increase of 45% since 1991. This is a growing area.

The Inner East End has some of the worst multiple deprivation enumeration districts in Europe despite years of social planning:

> 75% of the population are dependent on welfare of state benefits/pensions.
> 70% of school children are receiving clothing/footwear grants.
> 71% of households are in receipt of housing benefits.
> 6% of the population has some form of Higher or Further Education qualification.

The people of the area speak of lack of facilities, drug abuse, territorial rights and a low level of involvement

In the Mission Plan, the churches mention several responses to this situation, but called for a "skills exchange" from churches around the city to meet the needs; and for funding for a skilled Project Worker to work alongside the four churches and seek wider funding.

The Church

"We are all struggling".

One minister spoke of 100 funerals per year, while 300 people pass through Church House each week. There has been a 45% increase in population, but congregations are small. Five members live in the parish. Five members are in full-time work and three are part-time. Drug abuse is a constant pastoral challenge. The renovation of buildings to be usable costs hundreds of thousands of pounds.

The struggle goes on, but the journey of IEECT has begun to offer support and hope for the strugglers. The staff meets for regular lunches, and there is a programme of events for congregations and team. The minister of St Thomas' Gallowgate is appointed with 25% of her time as facilitator for the team. Snippets of hope in the struggle.

Summary of Key Issues

1. The commitment of the church to stay with the community through the painful changes.
2. The contractual, practical nature of the commitment made by members of the team and congregations.
3. The creative appointment of one minister with 25% time allocated to ecumenical coordination.
4. The need for wider church in the Presbytery to commit people and resources to support the initiatives.

Final Comments

1. An Injustice.

   It is wrong that areas of massive need and limited resources have to go in search of financial support to sustain innovative projects. While recognising the existing commitment of the church in terms of staff, buildings and national support structures, there is still much to be done to foster stronger Presbyterial partnerships of shared resources.

2. A Pointer

   If every congregation in the land budgeted 70% of its time and efforts on being in and for the community, the church would begin to find her role again. These relationships are the foundation of authentic worship and witness of the Incarnate Christ among his people.

3. A Model

   The formal structure of collaboration in the East End deserves reduplication around the country, noting the fact that one of the ministers allocates 25% of her time to facilitating this teamwork.

4. An Image

   The image used was of a "building site" where work is in progress, but the outcomes are unclear. We live with hope amidst the confusion and trust that God is not only uprooting and destroying, but building and planting.

5. A Question

    What would give greatest encouragement to the Christian congregations of these areas? A strong affirmation that the church was backing them for the long haul, without feeling that they had to prove themselves or be judged as failures. They do not ask to be beyond accountability, but that the criteria be less about the measurables of money and membership, and more about faithfulness to the Way of Jesus.

THE CHURCH IN THE CITY

The Church in the city is a kaleidoscope of patterns covering city centre, suburbia, areas of deprivation and sector ministries in shops, industry, hospitals, universities and prisons. City life brings is own challenges to the church to think "outside the box".

Residents: The Mobile Generation

Cities are places of transience. Resident populations in city centres are often short term, and in areas like Garnethill may be multiethnic. The culture is fluid and the church in the city requires to be flexible and sensitive to keep in touch with the changing needs of the changing community.

The environment of the city is highly stimulating, with global connections. The church in the city is uniquely placed to represent the international dimensions of the Gospel, through partnerships and celebrating the church of the nations. The globalisation of the local church is essential here, but we do not yet have multiethnic teams to develop that international and multicultural focus of the church in a global world.

Churches in the city centre are usually gathered congregations, drawn together by family history or for a distinctive approach to worship: places noted for a preaching or teaching ministry, or churches which offer particular music or liturgical styles. There is scope in the cities to offer a range of worship and to be innovative: encouraging interaction, imaginative experience and spiritual search through services that reflect different traditions and styles. That potential is offset by the observation that our readiness for change is often in inverse proportion to the distance we travel to church. Our travelling is an investment in our chosen pattern of church. Our choice makes us resistant to change.

Business: The Stressed out Generation

Our cities are centres of commerce. People may work in the centre and live in the suburbs. A number of city centre church buildings have been restyled to be open to the business communities: notably Renfield: St Stephen's in Glasgow and the current refurbishment in St George's West, Edinburgh. Café and the chapel stand side by side.

Stress in the workplace is recognised as a modern day plague. Pastoral support is offered through chaplaincies to shopping centres and businesses. Beyond that, Christian people are looking for more connections between worship and the workplace in their worship, or through congregational groups to support them as they face real life-issues.

In every city we have specialists—chaplains to industry, hospital, university and prison—whose expertise is seldom integrated into the life of congregations to develop local ministries to these groupings in the city. We need "matrix ministries" to let different insights inform and inspire us.

Church life can often become another source of stress. Many people in business require the service of stillness and sanctuary for the journey. That may be one of the unique gifts of the church in the city to a stressed out generation.

The Weekenders: The Playful Generation

Cities are places of leisure and entertainment. The church has not been good at either sharing in the carnival or being in touch with the lament that runs through that sector. Cinemas have been described as cathedrals of image and the place where we are must likely to encounter public religious discourse. One church paid for its youth group to view several films and then meet in a café to talk about them. A group of young adults meets as an informal film club and find it leads into discussing deep issues of spirituality and our times.

It has been said that the Reformation was talked about in the coffee houses of Europe. In our café culture churches would often find better quality conversations meeting "off site" in the ordinary meeting places of the city—the pubs and clubs which are the nodes of community in a fragmented society. Christians in Sport can point the way to tapping into the fitness market.

Homeless People: The Vulnerable Generation

The city attracts the nomads, and contributes to the increasing numbers of people without a home to call their own. The factors are many, but usually significant relationships have broken down. The call of the church is to offer friendship to people who are often ignored in the impersonal bustle of the street.

City churches are often the places where vulnerable people can find healing community through hospitality: from lunches or support groups to care shelters throughout the winter months. The Churches' Millennium Project in Edinburgh resulted in a partnership of churches, banks and commercial enterprise to establish Fresh Start, a registered charity to help people moving into their first homes after a period of homelessness. The Churches support initiatives to address the underlying social and political dimensions of homelessness.

The homeless people on the streets and at the door are a practical challenge for the Church in the city to follow the "downward way" of Christ: to meet God among the poor, and to be open to being evangelized by the poor.

Shoppers: The Consumer Generation

For many the city means shopping—the Mecca of the consumer generation. In practical terms, that presents a challenge to the churches in the centre, such as the Steeple or St Mary's in Dundee. Where the retail parks are expanding, the church finds remarkable openness to chaplains, but has yet to rise to the challenge of the "Ikea Church" which might offer access to the Gospel to people who are accustomed to visiting cathedrals of consumerism designed around chapels of choice.

The more subtle influence is the consumer mentality.

People will "shop around" for the church of their choice. More subtly, we have carried over the shopping mall mentality into our spirituality. There is a serious challenge to transform pick and mix spirituality into Christian discipleship. While that is a facet of our wider culture, it is a distinctive aspect of being a city church.

Decision-makers: The Political Generation

Cities are centres of power and political influence. City churches have a legacy of being chaplains to the powerful, colluding or colliding with the powers that be. As the forces of secularisation pushed the Church to the margins of influence, so the forces of post-modernity have opened up a new marketplace of opportunity for debate. Churches which are willing to build relationships with councillors and policy makers, ready to be well informed and pray for the welfare of the city, will be find political allies as partners in seeking the common good. They will also be better placed, when necessary, to be prophets that challenge the systems that are oppressive. City churches do well to equip members in active citizenship in a participative democracy, and to sustain the preaching that recognises the Gospel as public truth for the city—"Christ in whom all things hold together" (Col 1:17).

Ray Bakke, a specialist in urban mission, once said that the person who "loves Jesus, the church and the city is a rare bird". Nurturing that passionate public spirituality is a peculiar challenge of being the church in the city.

APPENDIX No 5:

The Church in a Changing World

To say that the world is changing faster than ever before is to say something trite but true. Technological, social and "existential" changes impact upon our lives in complex and inter-connected ways. Causal links between our environment, our genes and our experience are up for discussion in ways we could not have imagined only a few years ago. Society and the individual within it are bound together: their experiences of the shifting sands of post-modernity may be diverse, but there is no escape from its influence, whether for better or worse. The Church as an institution and as a collection of individuals cannot fail to be affected by this climate of change.

A Changing World

The recent Board of Ministry's Report "Changing Scotland" highlights some of the cultural, social and economic shifts that have taken place in Scotland. During the period we call "modern", roughly from 1850 to 1950, Scotland was firmly part of the industrial society within the United Kingdom. Class, employment, Trade Unions and religion offered some measure of security and identity. Within the family, the roles of women and men, and of the young and the old, were fairly well-defined. Of course, the impetus for change was already to be found within this period, and included the massive upheaval caused by two World Wars. The process of change has accelerated the past forty years, as Scotland has evolved into a thoroughly post-modern society.

The economic shift from an industrial to a post-industrial society is obvious. Tourism rather than manufacturing is now the biggest industry in Scotland. More than 70% of the workforce are now employed in the service industry, where flexible working patterns are the norm. The number of women in the workplace continues to grow, and now there are more women in the workplace than men. Trade Unions have no longer the influence they once had. Workers are expected to take responsibility for their own career development, where the opportunities for employment exist. In a global economy, economic Scotland owes its allegiance to Europe and the world rather than to the imperial state that was the UK.

The home life of Scots has undergone a similarly momentous change. Just over a quarter of households are made up of traditional family units. 27% are made up of pensioners, and a surprisingly high number of people of all ages (28% of households) now live on their own. There is more economic and geographical mobility than ever before, and the extended family unit may stretch over long distances and over several class boundaries. In his paper to the Board of Ministry, "Changing Scotland: A Commentary", ProfessorDavid McCrone comments that "this is a 'privatised' family pattern in the main, as households are thrown back on their own social resources, rather than locking into kin networks which have been left behind in time and place". There may be greater prosperity in the population as a whole, but among a minority of Scottish households, for example those who are single parents, endemic poverty is concentrated. The gulf between the elderly who are comfortably off and those who struggle to get by has also widened.

Who are We in this Changing World?

Without making value judgements about the nature of these changes (who could deny that some are positive while some are negative?), it is possible to note some of the cultural shifts that have arisen alongside or out of them. Individual identity is no longer bestowed by an accident of birth, but personally chosen in so far as circumstances allow. The values of one class or religion are no longer accepted in their entirety, but are selected from according to the needs of the moment. The roles of women and men are negotiable within relationships, and these might change through time. There is a complexity and fragmentation about the culture of today, demonstrated most clearly in the experiences of young people.

Kenda Creasy Dean's paper "X-Files and Unknown Gods: The search for truth of post-modern adolescents" offers fascinating insights into the inner lives of American teenagers, surely not so distant from the experiences of Scottish teenagers. She comments:

Today's adolescents take for granted a world where microchips become obsolete every eighteen months, information is instantaneous, and parents change on weekends. Indeed, the one constant in their young lives is upheaval. In such a world truth is fluid, generic, self-constructed—and so are they. (p.1)

Adolescents scarcely have to take on board the nuances of post-modern literary theory to be affected by the pressures and realities of post-modern society. The older generations, who tend to make up our church congregations, may be affected less acutely, but are unlikely to remain completely untouched by the world around them. Some may have felt the effect of our post-modern society in terms of changing patterns of employment and a loss of job security. Others may have felt its effect in shifting family relationships, whether their own or their children's.

Few are unaffected, and yet to many in the older generations, post-modern society is an alien culture, a world to be viewed with suspicion. Will Storrar's thesis is that congregations and the modern world exist as two separate worlds, sometimes overlapping and yet still clinging to their own perspectives. In a world where the big pictures are no longer viewed as adequate in themselves as patterns for living, the church is tempted to retreat into the big picture it inherited from previous centuries. In a world where structures are fluid and dynamic, the church is drawn to the rigid ways that suited past generations. In a world where change is accepted and even welcomed in the name of technological advance, the church resists and is threatened by change on many different levels.

Throughout the work of the Commission, in response to these tensions, we have sensed the need for initiatives to be local and relational, and we have seen examples of places where the post-modern world and congregations have interacted fruitfully on that basis. Sometimes in consultations we have heard pleas for movement forward in a way which takes account of the society we live in. But we have also heard stories of disappointments and fears and an impatience with a world which seems disinterested in the church and its message.

The Church in a Postmodern World
In a changing world, what hope does the church have? What can our response be to the changes in society around us and within us and what resources are available to us? For Dominic Smart in his paper "Postmodernism, the Bible and the Church", post-modernism, and deconstruction specifically, are ultimately dead-ends for the Christian faith:

> Personally, I cannot see a more complete cultural reversal of the life of faith as Luther described it. No longer, on this line, are we *excurvatus ex se*—turned outwards from ourselves. Now we are inescapably returned to that fallen condition of being *incurvatus in se*—turned in upon ourselves, God's grace is replaced by our narcissism. (p7)

For Smart, the truth of God's word can and will prevail over this dangerous intellectual fashion, and a return to the big picture provided by Christianity will be possible. The point is debatable, but here we have to distinguish between post-modernism, the theoretical movement which has spawned deconstruction and other literary and philosophical theories, and post-modernity, which charts the trends and changes in our culture over the past 40 years or so. "Post-modernity" is the name for where we, as a society and as individuals, are today. Few people are directly influenced by post-modernism in its pure form; but no-one can escape the influence of post-modernity, although attitudes towards it may vary. The hallmarks of post-modernity have already been sketched, and of course can never be divorced entirely from its more theoretically rigorous offshoot. We are dealing with rapid change, loss of established identity markers, a reluctance to commit wholesale to a ready-made system of belief or ideology. Radical scepticism and true relativism are not (as yet) features of most people's consciousness. Nevertheless, the challenges facing the Church from post-modernity itself are severe, although as Christians we want to affirm that there is no cultural shift which is beyond the grace of God. Wherever society is, God offers the resources to meet its needs.

Dean's paper offers some clues that might point the way forward for the church. Her comments about adolescents' search for truth would no doubt ring true for many people under 40 today:

The postmodern adolescent's view of truth echoes the word's etymology, from the Old English term for 'fidelity' or 'faithful', and connotes authenticity of action and congruence of character. Today's youth refuse to abstract truth from experience or reduce it to empirical data. Truth for them is neither hard-boiled fact nor universal principle; rather it embraces doubt and ambiguity. To postmodern youth, truth is event-personal, passionate, transcendent. They unapologetically up-end Descartes: "I experience, therefore I know". (p5)

Dean argues for a recovery of a Christian faith which would meet the needs of these post-modern young people, a Christian truth which is "inherently dynamic, personal, transcendent, and passionate, and as such … can exercise extraordinary influence on the construction of self" (p20). Belief in God is not the issue (as David McCrone's analysis highlighted, far more people admit to being somewhat religious than go to church on a regular basis). Believing God *matters* is what is important.

The Church where God Matters

If the Church is called, in this postmodern age, to proclaim that God matters, then its worship and the relationships it fosters are key areas of concern. For those caught up in the postmodern maelstrom, truth must happen in worship, and it must involve the whole person:

As event, truth assumes a kind of dynamic ambiguity, best caught not by creeds or confessions but by immediate sacred experience, ambiguously captured in sacrament, icon, and community practices in which God 'happens' in the here and now. (p12)

For Dean, the truth of God "happens" in the primary experiences of community belonging and participation in worship. If postmodernism has taught us anything, it has reminded us sharply that words and systems are created by us, not God given. At the heart of the mystery of faith there is an inescapable act of trust in the possibility of God. But the secondary aspects of faith: its language, its organisation and ethics- are provisional and revisable.

This creates a fruitful though painful tension in the Christian life between trust in God and detachment from the structures we create to express and define that trust. Christianity invites us to a generous and open-hearted commitment to God, though not necessarily to the words we use to talk about God, or the systems we develop to respond to God. We load these words and systems with theological meaning, and we cling onto them as certainties. But all we do in the process is alienate those who cannot subscribe, and force ourselves into positions we find it harder and harder to justify. By creating idols out of words and systems, we create refugees who have been wounded and excluded by our oppressive certainties. People on the edge of Christianity who feel there is no place for them in the church because of their lifestyle or their intellectual difficulties with the way Christianity is officially expounded. But in worship, the truth of an experience of God may be explored, if language, music and image are used in ways which are culturally sensitive and conscious of their own provisionality.

Since 1997, St Andrew's Bo'ness has been experimenting with worship using video and computer imaging, linked with contemporary music, lighting and a variety of liturgical innovations. Essentially lay-led, although with back-up from the ministry team, these monthly worship events explore contemporary issues within a Christian framework using all aspects of the technologies available and familiar to people of the twenty-first century. TGI multi media worship may not be the future for all congregations, but it offers an insight into the possible for many.

We need to be alert to other examples of ways the Church might respond and is responding to the changing society of which it is a part (apart?). Resources are already available to the Church as it tries to move from one world into another. Our post-modern world need not be a threat to faith, but a place of opportunity and creativity, in which diversity may be celebrated.

APPENDIX 6:

The Church of the Beatitudes

Our calling is to live in the Kingdom of God in response to the blessing of God in the grace of Jesus Christ. The blessings of the Beatitudes precede the radical call to discipleship in the Sermon on the Mount. Only in the confidence of that blessing of grace, will we be free to rise up and follow Christ in the radical agenda of the community of salt and light.

Blessed are the poor in spirit... Blessed are those that mourn....

Blessed is every individual and congregation that is open to God's present and future activity, because we are aware of our own weakness and failure. We know that we cannot renew ourselves. We feel a deep sense of loss that we are not closer to God and closer to one another. We feel the pain of our broken culture and long to be a touching place for Christ. We will not run away from the pain. We will run to God and meet his Kingdom coming towards us.

Jesus says: *Blessed are you.....*

Blessed are the meek.....Blessed are those who hunger and thirst after righteousness....

Blessed is the person and congregation that has been humbled by the experiences of life. The Church in Scotland is being humbled by the Spirit. We know that the old ways will not work. We are ready to be led by the Spirit into new ways of being Jesus' people. We have a growing passion to see wrong put right—in global poverty or personal relationships. We ache for the right relationships marked by justice and shalom, reconciliation with God and each other.

Jesus says: *Blessed are you....*

Blessed are the merciful......Blessed are the pure in heart.....

Blessed is the person or congregation that is reckless in generosity and forgiveness. We do not give in to cynicism or shut people out. We see the good and seek the best. Holiness has taken on a new attraction. Amidst all our stumbling, there is a magnetic pull to single-minded obedience to Jesus Christ.

Jesus says: *Blessed are you.....*

Blessed are the peacemakers...Blessed are those who are persecuted....

Blessed is the person or congregation who so loves their enemies that they are not afraid to make them.
We face up to our differences and work them through. We are found in the places of conflict as agents of reconciliation, and are crucified for our trouble. We are determined to be salt that makes a difference in the everyday world. We laugh a lot, for we know who has the last laugh.

Jesus says: *Blessed are you.....*

Jesus says: *You are the salt of the earth. You are the light of the world......Blessed are you.....*

APPENDIX 7:

A Narrative of the Special Commission

When the Special Commission on Review and Reform in the Church was set up by the General Assembly of 1999, all of those who had been appointed to it knew that the task that had been entrusted to the Commission was not only exciting and challenging but also in many respects impossible.

We were under no illusions that the task could actually be *completed* by ourselves, but we were excited by the prospect that we might able to make some kind of meaningful contribution to the current debate about the state of the Church, and perhaps even add some impetus and sense of urgency to the mood for change that we all recognised was growing in the Church. We were also very much aware, however, that this desire for change was being inhibited by inertia and fear.

Among the first issues that had to be addressed were the methodology and working patterns that we should adopt as a Commission and the prioritisation of the various tasks that would emerge. There was an acute awareness of the short time-scale and of the limited resources available to the Commission.

Three particular decisions were made at the outset:

- Normal meetings of the Commission would be *residential* (lasting at least 24 hours). This would enable us to tackle issues in reasonable depth, but, more importantly, it would allow us to get to know each other personally and give us sufficient time to build up trusting relationships with each other. Only in this way would be able to deal constructively with the fact that we were all very different people each with his or her own different theological bias and agenda, not to mention personality.

- We would aim to be as *open* as possible and communicate with the whole Church so that there would be few, if any, surprises when the Commissions final submissions were made. We realised that this communication process would have to be two-way, requiring us both to listen to and also speak to various constituencies. In particular, we hoped that we might be able to use a Website to facilitate this dialogue although at the beginning this proved to be more difficult to achieve.

- We would also listen to each other's *personal* faith-stories and experiences of church, not only to help us understand one another but also as an attempt to discern common threads. Again, we were not naïve enough to imagine that in a Commission of only 15 members we would encompass the whole breadth of the Church of Scotland, but equally we felt it would be wrong to ignore altogether who we were and what each of us had already experienced in the Church.

We believe that each of these decisions, taken at that very early stage, turned out to be quite crucial, and became in themselves significant pointers for the some of the ways forward for the whole Church. In fact as soon as we defined the Church as a *community* of faith rather than as an *institution* we quickly realised that we could in some respects regard the Commission itself as a microcosm of the Church and use it as a test-bed for any of our theories and ideas.

If our ideas didn't work *among* us, could we expect them to work *beyond* us?

Of course there would be questions of scale and we would have to take into account the special nature and focus of the Commission together with the fact that each of us in the Commission was already to some degree convinced of the need for change, and this might not be the case in the Church as a whole.

The Commission as Community

Each time we gathered in a locality—whether it was Dunblane, Carberry, Pitlochry, or wherever—we became a community again. Though subtly different on each occasion (for one thing not every member of the Commission could be present at each meeting) there was a continuity derived from shared experience, shared memory and shared faith. Though it was the common *task* which brought us together, and provided our focus, what made us a community were the *personal relationships* with each other which were quickly re-established on each occasion through time spent together informally and in shared worship. These relationships were not incidental but *integral* to the work in which we were engaged, for they affected the way we thought, discussed and decided matters. They enabled us to respect one another, listen to one another, learn from one another, disagree creatively with one another and therefore to "think out of our boxes".

The sense of trust that we gradually built up with each other also meant that listening to others became more than a policy decision, it became the *mindset* of the group.

Most of the members of the Commission already had experience of serving on Church Boards and Committees where, for a variety of reasons, there was not the same emphasis on inter-personal relationships and the focus was almost entirely on the business to hand. All agreed that it would have been significantly harder for us to have addressed the issues as thoroughly as we did had the Commission operated in that way.

Out of this group-dynamic two key concepts began to emerge which we soon realised may be of some significance for the Church as a whole and this was increasingly confirmed in all our consultations with groups and individuals.

The two key words were *LOCAL* and *RELATIONAL*.

The significance of the RELATIONAL:

Our present church structures, patterns of worship and church life evolved during times when people lived, worked, relaxed and worshipped in the same geographical location. Those who came together on a Sunday to worship were *already* a community, often with a shared history, and certainly with an already existing network of inter-personal relationships. This is hardly ever the case now. It is far more likely today that a person will live in one town or village, work in another, shop in some large out-of-town retail park and enjoy various leisure pursuits in many different locations among many different groups of people. We no longer live in one community: we participate in many different communities, including, for some, the Internet-community which transcends geographical location.

If any contemporary worshipping congregation is to become a welcoming community, then opportunities for relationship-building have to be deliberately *created*. A sense of belonging has to be generated through the creation of collective experiences and the sharing of personal stories. The *vertical* relationship to God is, of course, foundational, but the *horizontal* relationships to each other are also crucial.

The very first item of business at the initial meeting of the Commission (Crieff, June 1999) was to allow each member of the Commission to share with the others her or his church experience and particular issues of interest. As we discovered in the Commission, a willingness to open ourselves up to one another, also made it possible for us

to become much more open to others.

The first test of this openness came at the second meeting of the Commission in Scottish Churches House, Dunblane (August 1999) where we discovered that another group (THENEW*) was meeting at the same time. We invited the participants in the THENEW meeting to come and share their story with us.

This dialogue not only exposed the Commission to an area of concern that might not otherwise have been identified but also enabled the Commission to recognise how significant in the life of the Church were the effects of fear, and the distribution and use of power—themes which were to re-emerge in subsequent consultations. It was the first of many "voices from the margins" to which we would listen.

The significance of the LOCAL:

In the telling of our own stories to each other we quickly recognised the diversity of our experiences and of the situations from which we had come. It also became clear that the local setting often determined what was effective and what was not. It was clear that the "one size fits all" approach often adopted by centralised Boards and Committees was quite inappropriate to the kind of Church which the Church of Scotland is and the kind of country in which we serve. This meant, of course, that there could be no "blueprint" or single plan of action for the renewal and reform of the Church and our report would have to deal with underlying principles and broad themes rather than detailed prescriptions, though "models of good practice" might be provided as illustrative of the principles.

Realising the significance of the local we decided, for example, that in order to consult with the Church in Urban Priority Areas we would have to visit and see for ourselves the particular challenges of such situations.

In that setting we were impressed by the creative use of limited resources but also with another theme that began to re-emerge in other situations—that often local congregations felt themselves hindered rather than enabled or supported by central bureaucracy and legislation. Sometimes this was no more than a perception and other initiatives proved that much more is possible within the system than many local congregations realise. Were the examples of "good practice" more widely publicised and shared among churches some of those misconceptions might be corrected. (The local often has global significance.)

Communication

From the outset it was decided that, as far as possible, the Commission would utilise e-mail facilities to allow individual members to share their own reflections and contributions with the rest of the Commission and do work in their own time. Some members were comfortable with this approach, others preferred the creative sparking of ideas that occurred during meetings (in itself a recognition of differing gifts and differing styles of working.)

Far more important, in terms of communication, was our discussion on the importance of the language and vocabulary which we used. We recognised that so many of the words and phrases which we so readily adopted in our conversations came loaded with associations which were not always helpful, or which meant different things to different groups of people. Using words like "ministry", for example, may well prevent people from thinking "out of the box" and even when used in phrases like "ministry of the whole people of God" may carry presuppositions that are based on previous experience of the ordained Ministry of Word and Sacrament.

We recognised the need to find a new vocabulary that would not carry with it unwanted associations but would communicate clearly. This is no easy task.

One discussion with Dr. Ruth Page, however, gave us a useful distinction between "power as clout" and "power as attraction" and we recognised that a process of re-definition was needed for many of the words we used.

Worship:

Worship was an integral part of the life of the Commission and not merely a formality.

Members of the Commission took it in turn to lead worship, prayer and celebration of the Sacrament and in this way the diversity of people's gifts was expressed. The more we became a community, the more important and more meaningful our worship became.

Worship, in fact, because an expression of our common life. We learned to appreciate the distinctive gifts and insights that each individual brought to the whole but found that together we 'owned' the worship, whatever shape it took—and the shape of our worship did vary. We followed set liturgies, specially written liturgies or relatively spontaneous orders of worship depending on who was leading. We listened to stories from each other, some drawn from personal experience, others from a variety of sources. We used a variety of kinds of music, with or without accompaniment, depending on who was present. We met in a variety of settings, sometimes in places specially set aside for worship (like the chapels at Dunblane or Carberry) or simply in the room where we had been meeting. Where possible we invited others around to participate with us. There was greater use of silence and symbolism than is often experienced in the average Church of Scotland service. For example, on one occasion the Convener made the highly significant and appropriate gesture of laying his diary upon the Table beside the Communion elements to represent a sacrificial offering of his time for the work of the Commission, an action with which we all identified. A simple act, but in its context powerfully symbolic and effective.

When worship becomes a formality, or a formula, as it often seems to do in the committees and courts of the Church, and sometimes even in congregations, (no matter how sincerely offered) it frequently becomes disconnected from the business at hand or from everyday life.

In contrast, perhaps the most significant feature of the Commission's shared worship (and it is one which is often recognised when people make space to live together in Christian community, even for a short time) was the way in which business, worship and relaxation became integrated into an almost seamless whole rather than being kept apart in separate compartments. So, for example, there were worshipful moments during complex discussions, especially if one of the group articulated a new insight; and friendships nurtured in mealtimes and shared leisure activities (e.g. a late-night visit to the Cinema on one occasion) spilled over into worship as well as work.

What made the difference seems to have been something to do with the time allowed for genuine meaningful relationships to be built up. We believe that, although this is a simple point, it is one that is not sufficiently taken account of in the way in which the structures of the Church normally operate.

If no serious attempt is made to build up a common life, truly communal worship becomes impossible.

* THENEW is a group aiming to articulate a Christian response to violence and abuse against women and concerned with the historical failings of the Church in this respect. It is associated with the VASHTI movement in Scotland and the European DAPHNE initiative.

APPENDIX 8:

The Proposed Community and Parish Development Fund

Why create another Board when many are thinking about a decentralised structure?

This will be a different type of Board from the other Boards of the Church. It should be viewed more as a Board of Directors or Trustees acting as the funders of initiatives which will be based within a parish or local community.

This new Board will represent the interests of local congregations and will also seek to integrate and affirm the work of other Boards of the Church by giving grants to projects and initiatives that seek to promote collaboration between the Boards and the parishes of the Church.

The Board of Community and Parish Development will be given a seat at the regular budgeting meetings along with the other Boards in the Co-ordinating Forum and will be able to bid annually within the allocation system for funds. **The Board of Community and Parish Development will act primarily as a fast track funding mechanism to get money out to the local congregations willing to explore partnership projects that reflect the ethos of the SCARR Report.** It may turn out to be an important holding mechanism which will allow creative development to continue to be funded during a period of decentralisation.

How will this Board relate to the work of the other Boards of the church?

This Board will act as the broker between other Boards allowing them to channel their resources and expertise in a collaborative and interdependent way into the life of local congregations. Community and Parish Development will act as the contact through which Boards and congregations meet in partnership with each other and with the wider community. In a decentralised church some Presbyteries may choose to have a Board such as Community and Parish Development to continue this work or develop its remit.

What will the Community & Parish Development Fund be used for?

At present most of the resources which are directed at local level support the model of the single ministerial practitioner. This fund will be an essential part of the ongoing strategy of reform outlined in our report. We believe it will create levers for change in the mindset of the church over the next five years. The fund will signal to local congregations that the General Assembly is willing to invest substantial amounts of money in local communities and parishes to create multi-skilled team ministry. One way to establish such a team is by funding congregations to work interdependently with each other across geographical boundaries, changing mindsets in the process. We believe the Boards of Parish Education, Ministry, National Mission and World Mission and others will continue to have much to contribute to this ongoing process.

We recognise that, compared to other denominations, the Church of Scotland has a poor track record when it comes to developing and sustaining successful teams within parishes. This lack of success may say more about our historic style of training for leadership rather than the concept of working together in teams, which has become the recognised training policy of our existing Board of Ministry. Like the Board of Ministry we, too, believe multi-skilled team ministries to be essential for the future life and health of both congregations and ministers.

The Boards of National Mission, Parish Education, Social Responsibility and World Mission endorse this view and are currently endeavouring as individual Boards to further this philosophy. We believe that the creation of a new Development Fund will allow some of the work and current thinking of the existing Boards to come together and be expressed in a practical way by funding local initiatives and creating new models of multi-skilled team ministry.

It will be essential that these initiatives and teams have a recognised pattern of leadership, but we believe this will vary in style in different places. The experience of the existing Boards in their various disciplines will be invaluable in training the leadership of multi-skilled ministry teams. Ongoing training in leadership will be encouraged via the various current opportunities within the Church's own resources.

To create an environment in which multi-skilled ministry teams within congregations and other community groups can flourish, the Church of Scotland will take the lead through funding projects and initiatives which have a built-in bias for interdependency. It will be essential that leadership and accountability be agreed before funds are invested in local initiatives. It will also be essential that these teams seek to promote aspects of the primary purposes of the church as set out in the report.

How much will be invested in the Fund?

Over a five-year period we would propose to spend £7.5

million out of resources held centrally. We believe that an equal amount could be raised through match-funding from one or two major trusts. Beginning with an investment of £1.5 million per annum, we could prime the pump for a minimum of 50 multi-skilled team ministry projects or initiatives of differing emphases to come into being over a five-year period.

When will it commence?

Preparations for a pilot group will commence in the year 2002. This will include putting into place the appropriate field staff. We recognise that it may take time for projects to come on-line, but we are convinced that the incentive of financial help will encourage congregations and Boards to think creatively, stimulating the implementers of change at the centre and the grassroots.

During 2002 we will invite Boards (especially those who intend to invest in the fund) to nominate a project which could become a collaborative, interdependent model for multi-skilled team ministry. This approach will continue to cement partnerships between the centre and the local. and give the Development Fund a good basis for success.

How will the Development Fund be established?

To help establish the Fund in 2002 we will request Stewardship and Finance to make a special grant of £1.5 million for the first year from the accumulated credit balance in the Mission and Aid Fund. (This has benefited from substantial unrestricted legacies in recent years.)

The Boards and the General Trustees of the Church of Scotland will be encouraged by the Commission to consider the merits of this proposal and work together to bring about a collective investment of £1 million per annum from their reserves during the four year period from 2003–2006. This will be a practical opportunity for the Boards to affirm their commitment to the priority of the local church's witness. Some Boards might be able to cash in some reserves while others may opt to take a lesser share of the Mission and Aid Allocation choosing to tithe their share back to the congregations. (Note the fund will be up and running for a period of 18 months before the first joint grant from the Boards is required.)

If reserves were used, the cost in lost revenue to the Boards would be approximately £40,000 per annum in year one (2003) rising to approx. £160,000.per annum by the year 2006. However, the amount of money being levered back into the church through matched funding from other sources will make this a highly profitable investment.

In addition, the Board of Stewardship and Finance will be asked to provide a further £0.5 million per annum over the four year period by way of special grants from the Mission and Aid Fund. (This will be dependent on the continued receipt of unallocated legacies). By this means, it will be possible to establish a £7.5 million fund with limited disruption to present investment structures over a five year period. The exciting and creative side of all this is that we know of two major funds who have expressed genuine interest in being involved with the new Development Fund once it is up and running.

The Commission intends, therefore, to invite the General Assembly in May 2001 to instruct the General Trustees, and Boards of Mission, Ministry, Parish Education, Social Responsibility and World Mission to consider the potential of this fund. Thereafter to bring to the Assembly of 2002 the financial plan which will allow an initial, collective investment of one million per annum to be paid over into the Community and Parish Development Fund for the four year period between 2003-2006. It may be that a formula will be devised to ensure that Boards pay pro rata according to their wealth.

Why will the Boards wish to put some of their reserves into such a fund?

The Boards will recognise this as a long-term investment in their own work. We are confident that the Boards are already beginning to recognise their own interdependence on one another and especially on local congregations. Indeed, the sustained spending power of Boards depends on having strong, financially secure congregational units.

How sustainable is this idea?

The action of all the Boards in putting money in the Community and Parish Development Fund will be the first act of serious decentralisation for the church for many years. If the pilot scheme were successful it will be our intention to grow the scheme to include many more congregations. This model will still be sustainable if our governance is decentralised to the regions.

How will it function?

Using the Rank Foundation's funding principles as a guiding example the Board of Community and Parish Development will function as an independent, grant awarding body working in close collaboration with the other Boards of the Church. It will help facilitate their local policies. The Board will be directly responsible to the General Assembly. It will be primarily concerned with obtaining and dispensing funds to enable congregations and groups of congregations to create and develop relevant forms of ministry for the 21st century. It would encourage congregations to tap into the collective wisdom and resources of the existing Boards of the Church.

Who will be responsible for the creation of the Board ?

The Board of Stewardship and Finance will be requested to:

a. Write the constitution for the Board of Community and Parish Development.
b. Select twelve appropriate people to serve on the Board and bring nominations to the General Assembly of 2002 via the Nominations Committee
c. Appoint and manage two field directors until the Board of Community and Parish Development comes into being. The field directors will eventually be responsible to the Board of Community and Parish Development when it is established in 2002.

It will be important that members of the Board of Community and Parish Development have the relevant qualifications and experience to facilitate the aims and objectives of the fund.

Who will bring the projects to the Board?

The Development Fund will employ the two full time field directors who will have a proven track record in management and experience in Community and Parish Development. The field directors will be the key to the success of the venture. They will seek to discover the best initiatives by helping congregations articulate their vision. This will involve on-site visits including assistance in obtaining third party support. In consultation with Board Members, the field directors will bring forward the projects that in their estimation will work. The Board will then decide which to support, defer or reject. The field directors will be in constant contact with the applicants helping them to formulate their projects. Two field directors could bring on board 25 projects each and sustain them over the five-year period. The field directors would be involved in bringing the projects and initiatives together from time to time for mutual support.

How much could each project receive?

Grants could be made of up to £150,000 over a five-year period. Those applying for help will have a better chance of success if they can also match fund part of the project. As a rule, we would expect a minimum of 25% of the total funding to be raised locally in addition to monies from other trust funds. We anticipate that there may be occasions where local parties might struggle to qualify under these conditions. It would seem right to us that if the project or initiative had a rare quality or merit, the Board would have liberty to suspend the rules.

How much would it cost to run the fund?

The cost would be the salaries of two highly experienced field directors and secretarial back up. The field directors would be answerable to the Board. This would mean that they would have to be self-starters with a bias for action. The cost of servicing such a fund with this kind of staff would be in the region of £100,000 per annum. Board members would act in a voluntary capacity. Job descriptions for the field directors and their secretarial support would be agreed with the Personnel Department.

APPENDIX 9:

Reviewing our Financial Strategy

The Church of Scotland centrally has an approximate annual income of £100 million and £300 million in invested funds. Over £40 million of the annual income comes by way of congregational contributions to Ministry Funds and the Mission and Aid Fund. While the sources and uses of this money can be described in terms of what is and what has been, the danger is that we continue to think along existing tramlines and simply move small amounts among the existing jam jars[1].

One of the fatal flaws in our system, which goes to the heart of future development, is the governance of the Church in relation to finance. There is currently no mechanism to establish priorities across the Church. The General Assembly is an impossible mechanism for such work and each Board has its own commitments to fulfil and corner to defend.

What are we here for? The core business of the Church is making disciples of Jesus Christ who will love God and love our neighbour as Jesus did. As the Church of Scotland our core purpose is to ensure the possibility of every person in every community of Scotland having access to the Gospel through a local church.

We are clearly failing in that core business, losing 3% of our membership per annum. The challenge is to recover the ability to win new generations of people to faith in Jesus Christ and to share in God's mission to transform the world.

When we deal with money we deal with a deeply charged subject, emotionally and spiritually. Psychotherapist David Krueger writes in *The Last Taboo,*

> *"Money is probably the most emotionally meaningful object in contemporary life; only food and sex are close competitors as common carriers of such strong and diverse feelings, significances and strivings."*[2]

Inherited Priorities of Invested Funds

If the priorities of the Church are set in terms of current invested funds of the Boards[3] then our inherited priorities at 31 December 2000 are reflected as follows:

	£m
Ministry of Word and Sacrament	55
World Mission	39
National Mission	36
Social Responsibility	31
Parish Education	2
Mission and Aid Fund	5

One conclusion from these figures is that the Church's 1200 professional ministers are the key to the mission of the Church. At best, this may be so. At times a minister, like any other person, may be a block to mission. What is clear is that the ministry of all God's people must be enhanced and supported. This will require a priority investment if there are to be communities of faith nourished by worship, pastoral care and mission. Even taking into account the role of the minister to equip the people, this historical allocation of resources does not recognise the support needed for the many elders and members who would like to pursue opportunities to develop their faith and service through the support of other agencies of the church. That would suggest more resources for the work of Parish Education or for some future Board of Parish Development.

If the renewal of worship is a priority, then more support needs to be given to ministers and congregations who are struggling to respond to the variety of worship styles that will be part of our post-modern church. This would suggest strengthening the role of the Panel on Worship.

If we see a need for the fostering of ecumenical partnerships on the ground, and working out patterns of partnership organically rather than structurally, then there is an argument for more resources for Ecumenical Relations to support these developments.

The Church's priorities continue to be shaped by inherited assumptions and patterns of funding. New patterns are emerging which will require a reallocation of resources. Without that substantial reallocation, financial restrictions will limit future movement.

Refocusing Priorities: Shapes and Money

So far, we have simply assumed the existing structures to illustrate the messages that go out from our current deployment of finance. If we now assume the redistribution of priorities according to the emerging thinking of the Special Commission and the Committee on Presbytery Boundaries, then the structures will change significantly:

1. *The Local Church is the primary focus for worship, pastoral care and mission to Scotland in all its parts – the communities, sectors and mini-cultures that make up our fluid society.*

2. The Regional Support will be focused in newly formed Presbyteries with a three dimensional life: a) networks of congregations for mutual support in shared mission; b) centres of inspiration to set worship and mission as the renewing heart of the Presbytery; and c) a base for strategy, oversight and support with staff and finance at the disposal of the emerging strategy for the area.

3. The Central Servicing will be a much reduced administration that will offer professional services, facilitate networking among the Presbyteries while ensuring equity of policy across Presbyteries on issues such as salaries and employment policy for all staff, not only ministers. Attention must be given to the cost and dangers of duplication, and the scheme be subject to regular review.

On this model, the jam jars are smashed and tramlines are torn up. Local groupings will determine local strategies and priorities. Regional support units will have control of financial resources to meet these strategic developments. Some overseas work might be regionalised with each Presbytery hosting a World Mission desk and adopting an area of the world e.g. Borders Presbytery relates to Africa. The aim of this would be to increase the local involvement in overseas work and to advance the internationalising of local congregations. Appropriate central coordination would be essential to ensure common issues of policy and a national face to international missionary bodies.

It is hoped that funds held by General Assembly Boards and Committees might travel outwards and, where legally possible, restrictions be lifted on usage so that local and regional priorities can be assessed. A process of assessment and allocation will need to be worked out, but in a way that "keeps it evergreen"[4].

The new shape of the church will include: focusing on discipleship ("follow me") that supports people in family, work or leisure, offering worship as "a variety of menu and a variety of venue", nurturing a new generation of children through to maturity in life and faith, creating ministry teams with a diversity of roles and skills, building partnerships with other congregations, traditions and community groups, facilitating international connections that will bridge the local-global dimensions of everyday living, and applying Jesus' criteria of "justice, mercy and faith"[5] to our common life and common purse.

These ideas need to be quantified in terms of who is already mandated with these tasks and what resources they have their disposal.

Recommendation: That the Assembly Council, through the Coordinating Forum, establish overall priorities for the work of the Church in the light of the emerging shape of the Church and convey these to the Board of Stewardship and Finance, so that these priorities can be incorporated into the Co-ordinated Budget proposals which the Board will be bringing to the General Assembly in 2002 and subsequent years, with appropriate amendments to the Constitution of the Coordinating Forum and the Board of Stewardship and Finance.

Revisiting the Roots of our Tradition

It is essential that we revisit the roots of our own financial traditions to ask if they meet these criteria and will resource the emerging shape of the church. The General Trustees were established by Act of Parliament in 1921 to hold heritable properties and in 1925 to steward the patrimony of the Church of Scotland. In this way the resources of the pre-Union Church of Scotland were held in trust for the purposes of the Church of Scotland. In the terms of 1929 that was understood as providing the

"ordinances of religion" by supplying a minister and a building within a territorial parish. That was the missionary strategy.

As we enter the Third Millennium, it is equally important to steward the resources of an emerging church for the missionary purposes of the Church of Scotland. In the emerging church, the nature of ministry will be more varied than "ministers of word and sacrament", places of worship and mission may be temporary bases in the community rather than fixed buildings for generations and the context of mission may be to enter some of the "flow cultures" of our society rather than the immediate geographical area around a church building.

The strategic shift will include moves

from parish + building + minister
to networks of communities + multiple bases/ venues + ministry teams.

Since the General Trustees steward a Consolidated Stipend Fund of £59 million on behalf of 1400 congregations and a Consolidated Fabric Fund of £33 million for the benefit of 700 congregations, there are very considerable resources tied up in a historically inherited structure of 19th century mission models.

In 1995, an Act of Parliament removed a key obstacle to flexibility and ensured that the funds held by the General Trustees are under the sole jurisdiction of the General Assembly. If the purpose and shape of the church are redefined, then the funds may be used as the General Assembly decides for the benefit of congregations.

If the General Assembly agrees to the norm of "ministry teams" and a range of "ministries" for differing contexts, then the term "stipend" will not apply exclusively to "the parish minister", but to supporting whatever ministry is agreed as necessary for that area. Otherwise £59 million will be tied to paying fewer parish ministers, albeit with better salaries.

It is not widely appreciated that "Fabric" can apply to the premises necessary for the mission of Christ in a given area. That may include shop fronts and community buildings as well as permanent church buildings. The needs of the church in a fluid missionary situation are changing. It is wrong to commit a substantial part of the Church's income to sustaining 1700 ecclesiastical buildings, of which at least one third are estimated by the General Trustees to be in the wrong place or unsuitable for contemporary use. That Gordian knot must be cut.

Past attempts at overall rationalisation have been resisted fiercely. In the spirit of this report, the responsibility for that lies locally, for the church to make hard decisions about buildings that are essential for the mission of Christ in the area. We are a church possessed by our possessions. There may be no more direct application of the Gospel call than for some local churches to let go of inappropriate buildings for the sake of the Kingdom.

Recommendation: That the General Trustees, in consultation with the Board of Ministry and the Board of National Mission, monitor changing patterns of ministry and building requirements, and report on how best to fund the needs of the emerging church and report in 2003.

Who has Control of the Money?

The Consolidated Stipend Fund and the Consolidated Fabric Fund are made up of funds that are held by the General Trustees for the benefit of local congregations. The bulk of the Funds derive from the patrimony of the heritors, made over to the General Trustees in 1925. Technically, that has never "belonged" to congregations.

Nonetheless, it is recognised that money from the locality is for the benefit of the church in that locality. A major concern is that, the congregations have no control on how it may be used or invested.

1. Congregations with large sums invested may wish to use these funds for another area of mission development, but that choice is not open to them. If £100,000 is in the Consolidated Stipend Fund from the sale of a glebe 20 years ago, it may produce £4000 towards stipend. If the congregation wants to use that £100,000 to create a new base for mission in the community, and work at raising the £4000 per annum, they are not free to make that choice.

2. Congregations have no choice on how funds may be invested between the growth of income and the growth of capital. The range of options is Stipend >Fabric>Minimum Stipend Fund or Fabric>Stipend>Central Fabric Fund.

3. Congregations do, however, have the choice to be generous with their Fabric Funds, as befits a Presbyterian Church. A well-endowed congregation may choose to make a surplus in the Fabric Fund available to a "linked partner" or to another congregation in the Presbytery. These options are publicised through the Treasurer's Handbook and by a leaflet issued to congregations by the General Trustees whenever a new fund is established. The take up on this opportunity has been disappointing.

4. The choices may be extended in the case of the Consolidated Fabric Fund to include "or other purposes as agreed by Presbytery". This allows a more strategic view to be taken of the missionary needs of the area and avoid tying money unnecessarily to buildings.

Recommendation: That the General Trustees examine the Consolidated Stipend Fund and bring proposals the General Assembly of 2002 that would allow congregations more flexibility of investment.

Recommendation: That the General Trustees examine the Consolidated Fabric Fund and bring proposals to the General Assembly of 2002 that would allow congregations more flexibility of investment.

There is an earlier stage at which strategic thinking is required before the proceeds of the sale of local properties. When a union or linking of congregations takes place, the Basis of Union or Linking often commits the proceeds of sale to fabric funds on the assumption that property from the past helps pay for property in the future. That process has become a matter of "use and wont", but is not a legal necessity.

We recommend that congregations be creative in their approach to these opportunities and consider if funds may support some new initiative in the area rather than be committed to bricks and mortar forever.

Recommendation: That the General Trustees, in consultation with the Board of National Mission, examine the application of the proceeds of the sale of buildings following readjustment, and report to the General Assembly of 2002.

The Theology of Grace

The theology that underpins our consideration of all our financial considerations is simply grace and faith: grace that gives freely to release people from poverty of opportunity into new potential; and faith that encourages risk and movement into new territory for the sake of the Gospel.

In all our conversations we are aware that the general level of giving across the church is far below its potential for the cause of the Kingdom. Stewardship must become a way of life for Christian people if we are not to be possessed by our possessions.

We believe that those who hold national roles in the church must offer a lead by making the first move (grace) and taking the first risk of release (faith) as an example to the church at large. We believe that if the visions are funded, then the grace of giving and the releasing of resources by faith will rise among the people of God across the land.

The current policies may be defended as saving the church for a future generation. We believe that such a "rainy day" mentality locally or centrally is counter to the Spirit of Christ who calls us to lose our lives in order to save it.

[1] Images used by Sir David Tweedie, past chairman of the Accounting Standards Board, at the meeting of the Special Commission, 25 November 2000. The image highlights the fact much of our money is aligned to inherited priorities and is not easily moved from one place to another. There is no implication of lack of professionalism in the administration of the Funds as they stand.

[2] Quoted in *Credit Care*, article by Antonia Swinson in *Life and Work*, December, 2000.

[3] "Briefing Paper on Church of Scotland Funds" prepared by the General Treasurer for the Board of Stewardship and Finance, February 2001.

[4] A phrase used by Walter Williamson, management consultant, about any process of change. We seem to work out models and apply them beyond their sell-by date. It will take a total reshaping of the environment to stimulate a new pattern of thinking which Peter Senge calls "The Fifth Discipline" – the art of being a learning organisation.

[5] Matthew 23:23 – Jesus comment to the Establishment of his day who had their financial priorities wrong, following the "hand-me-down" patterns of tradition rather than the radical re-rethink from their roots in the nature of God who is righteous, compassionate and faithful.

APPENDIX 10:

Members of the Special Commission anent Review and Reform

Members:
Fyfe Blair
Albert Bogle
Ian Boyd (resigned March 2000)
Susan Brown
Susan Clark
Iain Cunningham (Vice-Convener and Representative on the Assembly Council)
Richard Fraser (resigned June 2000)
Peter Gardner
Alison Jack
Gordon Kennedy
Michael Lyall
Alan Miller
Pat Munro
Peter Neilson (Convener)
Ramsay Shields

Associated:
David Denniston (Representative from the Assembly Council)
Marjory MacLean (Secretary, Depute Clerk)

REPORT OF THE SPECIAL COMMISSION
ANENT ST NINIAN'S CRIEFF
MAY 2001

PROPOSED DELIVERANCE

The General Assembly:

1. Receive the Report.

2. Approve the recommendations of the Special Commission.

3. Instruct the Board of National Mission, the Board of Practice and Procedure, the Board of Stewardship and Finance and other Boards and Committees referred to in the Report to implement the recommendations in full.

4. Thank and discharge the Special Commission.

"For everything its season, and for every activity under Heaven its time"
(**Ecclesiastes 3.1**)

APPENDICES

I. INTRODUCTION AND METHODOLOGY

In terms of the crave of a Petition by the Rev Bruce Ritchie and others, anent the closure of St Ninian's Centre, Crieff, to the General Assembly of 2000, a Special Commission was appointed *"to review the management, purpose and future of St Ninian's Centre, to consult widely, and to report to the General Assembly of 2001."* (See Appendix 6).

The General Assembly appointed the following members of the Special Commission:

Very Rev Dr William Macmillan (Convener)
Mrs Elspeth Burnett
Mr Robert Hynd
Rev Alan Macgregor
Rev Gordon Palmer
Rev Tony Stephen.

Not all those nominated by the Selection Committee and appointed by the General Assembly proved able to serve, and, on the nomination of the Convener of the Nomination Committee, a seventh individual was approached and agreed to serve. For professional and personal reasons it proved impossible for him to attend meetings, and by the time this became apparent it was too late to replace him on the Commission. Accordingly this Report is in the name of the six remaining Commission Members. The Rev Marjory A MacLean, Depute Secretary to the Board of Practice and Procedure, was appointed Clerk to the Special Commission.

At its initial meeting in July 2000, the Special Commission duly agreed that the need for St Ninian's Centre in Crieff, its purpose and its future, was the prior question. It was however incumbent upon the Commission to examine also the background of the Centre and to study issues implicit in the Petition relating to the running of the Centre, the scope of its ministry, questions of its management (locally and by the Board), the costing of its development, the oversight of its properties, the funding for any redevelopment, and the future possibilities for its work and ministry. Accordingly all the Board's files relating to St Ninian's were requested

for examination along with property reports, the valuation of these properties, the Director's job description (Appendix 5), the Youth Worker's service contract and other contracts of employment. There was also the question of Income and Expenditure, especially over the years 1996–99. Relevant minutes of the Board of National Mission and its sub-committees including the Residential Centres' Executive, the Director's plan for the future of St Ninian's, plans for the proposed Mission Unit and other documents also required to be examined.

A video recording of the debate on the Petition and Answers at the General Assembly on 24th May 2000 was studied by each of the Commissioners.

The Special Commission visited the Centre and stayed overnight in order to see the place and the properties concerned and to meet with some of those who were using and running the Centre.

In the interest of achieving the widest possible consultation it was agreed also to issue a questionnaire to congregations in the September 2000 "Ministers' Mailing", and to insert a paragraph in the edition of "Life & Work" of September 2000 giving information about the Questionnaire and its use by the Commission (see Appendix 3).

In the course of its deliberations the Commission also received a considerable number of submissions from interested parties. A separate written submission was received from the staff at St Ninian's apart from that submitted by the Director. The Commission invited the staff to send representatives for interview, but that offer was declined, as they believed their submission was sufficient.

The Commission resolved to devote the entire second week of November to interviews with relevant individuals involved with St Ninian's Centre, both past and present. (Appendix 2)

The Commission has no hesitation therefore in declaring that its work in fulfilment of its remit has been extensive, comprehensive and thorough. Each of the individual Commissioners has taken part in something of a personal voyage of discovery in relation to the fulfilment of the Commission's remit. It is both interesting and affirming to relate that the various components of that voyage have been the same for each member and have been specifically related to particular periods in their deliberations. Each has come, first separately and then collectively, to the same conclusions, and it is therefore with more than usual force that the Commission is able to say that the views expressed in this Report represent its unanimous opinion as a Special Commission of the General Assembly.

II. THE ORIGINAL PURPOSE OF ST NINIAN'S CENTRE, CRIEFF

St Ninian's Centre in Crieff was conceived as a Project by the late Rev D P Thomson, sometime Home Board Organiser for Evangelism. It was to be a Centre for the training of Missionary Teams, Conferences and Youth Work. In 1958 it became a reality with the transfer to local Trustees (explained more fully below) of the redundant West Church of Crieff. The original concept is concisely described in his submission to the Special Commission by the current Director, Rev Dr Adrian Varwell, entitled "The Vision of D P Thomson"

"The purpose of St Ninian's was to create a *"permanent headquarters which would be a base for the planning and carrying out of training of workers for future outreach in Scotland."* [*Fire in His Bones; Biography of D P Thomson by W H Frame, c1991*] Thomson himself saw St Ninian's as a *"Shining Light in a Darkening World"* [ibid.]. In one of his reports, Thomson described the Centre as catering for:

- *"men and women seeking guidance as to the most effective service they can render Christ and the Church"*,
- *"men and women anxious to equip themselves better for the work in which they are already engaged for Christ and the Church"*,
- *"men and women eager to equip themselves for new forms of service in the Church"*, and
- *"Groups anxious to enrich their corporate life and fellowship, to extend and widen the horizons of their*

thinking, and to fit themselves better for work and witness".

"Thomson saw the Centre for groups *"with a staff set apart for the work, and with a knowledge of the sort of conditions that are conducive to [a] traffic of mind with mind and heart with heart"*, and identified three objectives in working with them:

- giving the opportunity for sharing in a way not possible in weekly or monthly meetings,
- providing a distinctive environment in which the particular need, situation and potentialities of the group might be met, and
- receiving from each group a contribution to enrich the outlook, experience and corporate life of the Centre's staff.

"Furthermore, Thomson stated that the contribution of the Centre to each group was to:

1. *"widen their horizons—to enable them to see aspects of Christian life, experience and service they have not seen before, and to enable them to see their corporate life, work and witness in a wider context than they have hitherto seen it, and with a greater relevancy to the world situation as a whole"*,

2. *"deepen the level of their corporate fellowship"*,

3. *"make their corporate witness and their service more effective"*.

"Above all, the Centre sought to achieve these ends through a Christian family atmosphere, the sharing of domestic duties, and corporate Christian fellowship of worship, Bible study and training.

[The Basic Principles of Group Training (at St Ninian's, Crieff): D P Thomson, 1962]"

In its earlier days St Ninian's provided a stimulus to evangelism and mission. It also made a significant contribution to thinking about evangelism and mission, largely through reflection upon practice. Over the period St Ninian's was able to draw on instances and examples of good practice, to identify trends and provide researched information. This work of being a locus for thinking and strategising continued, albeit in different forms as the years passed, and as different people came to be involved in leading the work. It would be true to say that the contribution of St Ninian's was, at some times, very influential

As aspects of the work of the Board of National Mission have become geographically more devolved and so less tied to St Ninian's, it has been found to be more difficult to identify clearly what the precise role of the Centre is and how integral is that role to the Board's overall mission.

Training at the St Ninian's Centre

One of the original reasons for the establishment of the St Ninian's Centre was as a Centre for lay training. With responsibility for lay training now resting with the Board of Parish Education, the role of the Board of National Mission and therefore of the St Ninian's Centre, as presently established, in this field is at an end. The Commission understands that other Boards of the Church feel that the present arrangements which they make for their own training programmes—and which do not involve a role for the St Ninian's Centre—are more suited to their purposes.

1. **The Commission therefore cannot recommend any resumption of lay training as a role for the St Ninian's Centre in the future.**

III.   THE LEGAL HISTORY OF THE CENTRE

In order to be fair to all parties the Special Commission has followed a path along which it has been able to examine many essential facts which it has endeavoured to put in order.

Title to Heritable Property

The building which is now the St Ninian's Centre in Crieff was, originally, the West Church of Crieff. Title to the property was vested in the Church of Scotland General Trustees until 6th June 1958 when it was transferred to "Trustees for St Ninian's Centre, Crieff". As part of the title arrangements made then, a Minute of Waiver was

granted by the Superior, the Earl of Ancaster, allowing the building to be used for a purpose other than that of a functioning place of worship which had been a requirement of the original grant of the site by one of his ancestors. Originally that Minute of Waiver was to be granted to "Trustees for the Work and Witness Movement" but that was altered in the final version of the Minute of Waiver to "Trustees for St Ninian's, Crieff". Recent memoranda circulating within the Law Department of the Church suggest that the St Ninian's Centre was, in fact, established as a formal (possibly public) Trust. That may be the case, but no evidence has been produced to the Commission to suggest that such a formal Trust was ever established. The Centre did, however, have a Constitution (see below) but, in the absence of evidence to the contrary, it appears that the Trustees for the St Ninian's Centre, Crieff were merely *ex officio* holders of particular offices, who had, as a result of such office, held the title to the St Ninian's Centre from its 1958 conveyance to them by the General Trustees, much as local Trustees do in certain congregations of the Church today. Support for that view, which the Commission has adopted, is provided in the first version of the Constitution of St Ninian's, Crieff dated 7th June 1958. Clause 5 of that Constitution states:

> "All property belonging to, or connected with, St Ninian's, Crieff whether in the form of lands, buildings or moveable subjects, shall be vested in the Trustees who shall be the Chairman, Vice-Chairman, Warden, Secretary and Treasurer *ex officio* with the proviso that the said Trustees shall not have the power to purchase, sell, rent or mortgage the property without the authority of the Board of Management …".

The "Trustees of St Ninian's Crieff" are therefore specifically characterised in that Constitution as representatives of another body and were not, as would be the case in an effectively established Trust, able to make decisions, such as those indicated above, regarding the property on their own initiative.

As such trustees, the Trustees for St Ninian's held the

title until the retirement of the Rev Dr D P Thomson in 1966. On his retirement, it was agreed that the Home Board would assume the whole responsibility for the running of the Centre and that title to the heritable properties would be vested again in the General Trustees but for behoof of the Home Board. The Commission, having read and evaluated Minutes of the Home Board and its sub-committees, correspondence and other documentation surrounding that event, has come to the conclusion that it was, undoubtedly, the intention of both the Board of Management of the St Ninian's Centre and the Home Board, approved in a Minute of a Meeting of the Home Board on 16th February 1966 that:

> "The Title Deeds of the property of St Ninian's should be vested in the General Trustees for behoof of the Home Board"

Unfortunately, the heritable property, comprising the St Ninian's Centre, had not, as a matter of fact, been transferred to the Church of Scotland General Trustees at the time the Commission began its deliberations. This fact was only discovered by the Law Department as a result of their research into the title position in relation to the Centre in 1999 when its possible closure was being considered by the Board of National Mission. Whatever the reasons for this omission, it is certainly the Commission's view that there is sufficient, continuing and overwhelming evidence of agreement over the period from early 1966 to date, with regard to the intention that the title to the heritable property, forming the St Ninian's Centre at Crieff, should be transferred from the Trustees for St Ninian's to the Church of Scotland General Trustees.

2. **Given the overwhelming weight of evidence, from 1966 to the present day, that the title to the St Ninian's Centre, the former West Church in Crieff, should have been transferred to the Church of Scotland General Trustees, the Special Commission at its meeting on 13 November 2000 made a preliminary recommendation to the Law Department that** **that instruction be implemented by way of an appropriate Disposition in favour of the General Trustees. Whatever the outcome of the deliberations of the Commission and the decision of the General Assembly thereon, undoubtedly the conveyancing title to the St Ninian's Centre requires to be regularised without further delay.**

The Constitution of the St Ninian's Centre

Until its final minuted meeting on 24 September 1998, the Board of Management of the St Ninian's Centre had operated, since 1966, under no fewer than five constitutions which progressively increased the bias of its membership away from the original management which included the "Work and Witness Movement" (which the Commission believes now no longer exists) and the Presbytery of Auchterarder, and its successor the Presbytery of Perth, towards the Home Board of the Church and the Board of National Mission as its successor. Following its assumption of its continuing responsibility for the St Ninian's Centre in 1966, the Home Board set up a committee structure which included a Home Mission Committee (of up to 60 members) which had a specific sub-committee relating to St Ninian's, Crieff consisting of six members plus unlimited co-options. The minute of the Home Board establishing the sub-committee relating to St Ninian's, Crieff does not make any reference to the constitution of the Board of Management of St Ninian's and it may have been that, at this time, this sub-committee was, in fact, intended to be the Board of Management. The revised constitution of 12th June 1980 (the second in the series), would tend to suggest that it was not so intended (whether by accident or design) since 20 representatives of various bodies are named in that version of the Constitution, including the Work and Witness Movement, the Presbytery of Perth and the Church's departments of Home Mission and Education together with two of the staff of the St Ninian's Centre, and up to a further 14 co-options with the Committee "not to exceed 34 in all". The 1980 Constitution goes on to state, unequivocally, that "St Ninian's Crieff, is under *the control of the Church of Scotland department of Home Mission … administrated* (sic) *by a Board of Management …"*. On the basis of that Constitution, the Commission has concluded that that sub-committee could only have served in an advisory capacity to the Board of Management of the St Ninian's Centre.

Clause 7 of the 1980 Constitution states *"all property belonging to, or connected with, St Ninian's, Crieff, whether in the form of land, buildings or moveable subjects, shall be vested in the Department of Home Mission of the Church of Scotland"*. This is in accordance with the decision of the Home Board at its meeting of 16 February 1966, quoted above, but is in sharp contrast to the position in 1958 when the title to the West Church in Crieff was transferred to the Trustees of St Ninian's who were, as mentioned above, representatives of the then Board of Management of the St Ninian's Centre.

In all versions of the Constitution of the Board of Management of the St Ninian's Centre, including the last one approved on 27th February 1997, the relevant Clause allowing for the alteration of the Constitution permits the Constitution to be altered by a simple majority of the Board of Management. In this Constitution, as in its predecessors, there are provisions regarding the giving of precise notice of the change proposed to be made and the fact that such changes can only be made at the Annual General Meeting of the Board of Management which seems to have been customarily held in May of each year. From the evidence before the Commission, or indeed in some cases the lack of evidence, it is clear that not all changes to the Constitution of the Board of Management of St Ninian's were, in fact, properly and formally approved at Annual General Meetings of the Board of Management. That said, despite these irregularities, compounded on several occasions throughout the history of the St Ninian's Centre, no objection appears to have been taken to them by any member of the Board of Management of St Ninian's at any time. Given the effluxion of time, the Commission is satisfied that these changes have been homologated by subsequent actings or failures to act of all of the parties involved. The Commission has not seen any evidence from Minutes or any other documentation of the Board of National Mission or its predecessor, the Home Board, to the effect that any effort has been made to ratify such irregularities either by the Board of National Mission, or its predecessor, or by the Board of Management of the St Ninian's Centre. Indeed, the evidence available to the Commission would tend to suggest, at best, a disregard for the niceties of the formal constitutional position of the Board of Management of the St Ninian's Centre after the responsibility for the Centre passed to the then Home Board on 1st November 1966, up to and including the creation of the Residential Centres' Executive in 1998 by the Board of National Mission. This, effectively, brought the purpose of the Board of Management of the St Ninian's Centre to an end. Sometimes, the Commission would suggest, disregard for the Constitution of the Board of Management of the St Ninian's Centre has been overt and, indeed, cavalier or, if not, amounting to such by way of default or ignorance, particularly on the part of the Executive of the Board of National Mission and its predecessors.

3. **Whilst the Commission has concluded that the various changes in the Constitution of the St Ninian's Centre during its history have been validly made, whether as a result of homologation by, or actings or lack of actings on the part of the Board of Management of the St Ninian's Centre or otherwise, the Commission recommends that the Board of National Mission and other Boards or their equivalents within the Church should review the particular Constitutions of all bodies such as the former Board of Management for the St Ninian's Centre reporting to them, to ensure that at all times such bodies, and the Boards of the Church to which they report, operate in accordance with such Constitutions and, without prejudice to that generality, particularly in relation to the alteration of such Constitutions.**

The creation of the Residential Centres' Executive by the Board of National Mission in 1998 brought to an end the function of the Board of Management of St Ninian's Centre. It is with this more recent period, from 1996 to date, that the main work of the Commission has been concerned.

IV.   DIRECTORSHIP

The Founder of the St Ninian's Centre, the late the Rev Dr D P Thomson, styled himself as "Warden" and created a unique role for himself comprising much more than that title implied.

The Commission does not doubt the sincerity with which the views and opinions, particularly in relation to the late Dr Thomson's "vision", are held by individuals, and has taken due account of the history and past work of the Centre. It would be surprising, at this remove in time, if there were amongst those corresponding with, or giving evidence to, the Commission, unanimous agreement as to the nature and content of the late Dr Thomson's "vision" and its relevance for today and the future. By concentrating on the present purpose and potential for the future of the St Ninian's Centre, the Commission does not decry the importance of Dr Thomson's work. Rather the Commission seeks a practical outworking of his intentions in the present day.

After Dr Thomson's retirement in 1966 the Rev William Shannon took over as Warden at St Ninian's until 1974, when he was succeeded by the Rev Peter Bissett who continued in that role until his retirement in 1992.

Mr Bissett's successor, the Rev Peter Neilson, was appointed in 1992, not only as Director of St Ninian's but also as the National Adviser in Evangelism for the Church of Scotland. Whilst this put the Centre at the heart of thinking on mission and evangelism in the Church of Scotland, Mr Neilson felt he did not do the part of the job specifically relating to the Directorship at Crieff as well as another person might and found himself divided between the two parts of the job. He submitted his resignation in September 1996 and left the post in the summer of 1997.

As a result of Mr Neilson being overstretched between the two parts of the job, the Board of National Mission, in the view of the Commission, took a perfectly proper strategic decision at that time to separate the two roles. Thereafter the Director of St Ninian's would not have an advisory role in mission nor be an Adviser on that subject in the wider Church. Unfortunately, the Board did not follow through on that strategic decision by involving Mr Neilson in discussions as to how the role of Director of the Centre itself should be cast. Indeed, it is evident from his interview before the Commission (supported by evidence provided by the former Convener of the Board, the Rev Sandy Cairns and the General Secretary of the Board, the Rev Douglas Nicol), that although the Board was clearly reviewing the role of the Director of the Centre, Mr Neilson was not involved in that review. The opportunity was not taken at that time of major change to undertake what would have been a coherent strategic process of reviewing the role and purpose of the St Ninian's Centre.

The Commission was told by Mr Cairns and Mr Nicol and also by the Rev Dr Frank Bardgett, Depute Secretary to the Board of National Mission until December 2000, that the post of Director did not prove easy to fill. Indeed, by the frank admission of Mr Cairns in evidence before the Commission, supported by further evidence from Mr Nicol, with the reflection available from hindsight, the Board should perhaps have thought more about the role of the Director of St Ninian's and the qualities required of the individual who might fill it at that time.

The Board however set about identifying suitable candidates and approached them directly with a view to their applying for the post. It was at this stage that Dr Varwell was invited to apply for the post and was thereafter interviewed for the position. After careful examination of this process the Commission is satisfied that Dr Varwell was not individually head-hunted for the position or enticed to apply.

Dr Varwell took up the post of Director with effect from 1st October 1997 on a seven year contract, employed through the Personnel Committee of the Church by the Board of National Mission. The description of the role, its responsibilities, the qualities and experience required for it, in terms of which Dr Varwell was appointed, form Appendix 5 to this Report. One of the unwritten roles Dr Varwell was to fulfil was effectively to be that of consultant to the Board during his seven year contract.

Mr Neilson gave early indication to the General Secretary of the Board of his wish to leave office, and lengthy notice from September 1996 of his intention to resign in the summer of 1997. Over a year elapsed between formal intimation of that resignation and the appointment of Dr Varwell as Director of the Centre. The Commission finds it difficult to understand why the Board of National Mission could not during that period of time have given due, proper and full consideration to the nature, scope and responsibilities of the role of Director of the St Ninian's Centre and the qualities and experience required of the individual to fulfil it. This loss of time and the difficulties which the Board encountered in filling the position should have indicated that it was insufficient to "make it up as [they] went along", a phrase used in conversation by two interviewees. Whilst the Commission can accept that every talented individual brings to an appointment new dimensions which cannot be foreseen by those interviewing them at the outset, to be in a position where the view of the employer as to the nature, scope and responsibilities of the role is so inchoate as to regard the individual appointed to it as little more than a consultant on a seven year contract should certainly have alerted the Board and its Executive to the possibility that there was a need for a greater review of the St Ninian's Centre between September 1996 and October 1997 than merely that afforded by the appointment process of a new Director.

Whilst it is clear that the Personnel Department of the Church was involved at a later stage in the process of the appointment of the Director, the professional advice available to the Church from that Department was not sought at a stage early enough to focus the Board's thinking on the nature, scope and responsibilities of the role of Director of St Ninian's Centre and the qualities and experience required of the individual who might fill it.

4. **The Commission therefore recommends that the Board of Practice and Procedure should review the procedure whereby the Personnel Department of the Church is involved in the making of senior appointments by Boards and other employing bodies within the Church, with a view to ensuring that the professional advice which the Personnel Department can provide is made available at an early stage in the process of making new appointments.**

5. **The Commission also supports the recommendations made by the Special Commission Anent the Board of World Mission, which reported to the General Assembly in May 2000 in its particular recommendations as follows:**

   "That contracts of employment should embrace the complete range of rights and obligations of both the Board and the jobholders…"

   "That job descriptions should be clear and unambiguous. They should state the long-term objectives and the main tasks to be undertaken. They should specify the responsibilities and degree of authority delegated to the jobholder".

The Commission is convinced that had this been the practice of the Church before September 1996, this would have given rise to a more thorough review of the management, purpose and future of the St Ninian's Centre at that time.

The Rev Dr Adrian Varwell—Director of the St Ninian's Centre

Dr Varwell prepared a lengthy Submission to the Commission which consisted in large part of a paper which he informed the Commission had been agreed by his staff.

The Commission interviewed Dr Varwell at some length and indeed recalled him to clarify certain matters following upon the Commission's interviews with the Assistant Director and the Youth Worker at the Centre.

Given the totality of the job description, responsibilities, qualities and experience required of the new Director in terms of Appendix 5, the Commission was somewhat surprised to find that Dr Varwell, despite close and persistent questioning by each Commissioner, did not give a personal view as to what his ideal scenario for the future of the St Ninian's Centre at Crieff would be. Instead, he proffered the suggestion that the Church as a whole must decide what it wanted of St Ninian's. In the light of the consultancy role expected of Dr Varwell by the Board of National Mission, the Commission found this somewhat perplexing, since it had hoped for assistance from him with regard to the fulfilment of its remit. Similar enquiries by individual Commissioners regarding Dr Varwell's understanding of "mission" also met with a lack of clarity. The Director stated that he wished to see St Ninian's at the centre of the work of the Board of National Mission and its new developments, and truly a Resource Centre for Mission. To do that he said that he required to be involved with the Advisers on Mission employed by the Board of National Mission. In Dr Varwell's view, this meant that the policy of the St Ninian's Centre had to be driven by the policy of the Board of National Mission and that this should allow him to be more involved in the latest thinking on mission, and to know who the latest innovators in mission were. He had a feeling of personal isolation from all of these sources.

The Commission reluctantly concluded that this feeling on the part of Dr Varwell was not so much a negative mindset which had grown as a result of the uncertainties over the future of the St Ninian's Centre (which had existed for a year or more prior to the General Assembly of 2000), but more indicative of his style of management and approach to his work. In later evidence given to the Commission by the Rev Colin Sinclair, now Convener of the Mission and Evangelism Resources Committee, it became apparent that the Advisers in Mission met relatively frequently at the St Ninian's Centre, and it was always open to Dr Varwell to attend meetings of these Advisers. The fact that Dr Varwell has not availed himself more frequently of such opportunities to be more at the centre of the thinking of the Board of National Mission, in accordance with his express desire, is therefore disappointing.

The Commission noted that no new writing on Mission or indeed on any aspect of Practical Theology has emanated from St Ninian's during Dr Varwell's tenure as Director. During his interview, Dr Varwell advised that his necessary commitment to the Centre, particularly for evening duties as a result of staff shortages or perceived inadequacies of training or contractual obligation of staff, have meant that he was left with little time for such work or the preparation of courses for those attending the Centre, whether bespoke or of general interest. He also stated that he has had to concentrate on the "hotel management" side of his role rather than on a "marketing" role, throughout and furth of Scotland, bringing the work of the Centre to the attention of those who might be expected to make use of its facilities. Evidence provided by both the Assistant Director, and in the written submission of the other staff to the Commission, indicates that the hotel management side of the role seems to be more than adequately covered by other staff. If Dr Varwell is, in fact, involved in that side of the business of the St Ninian's Centre, this is to duplicate responsibilities being adequately undertaken by others. His lack of appreciation of the situation and the evidence gleaned from the interviews with the Assistant Director, the Youth Worker and the written submission on behalf of the other staff of the Centre, lead the Commission to believe that communication with others, on whatever level, is somehow difficult for Dr Varwell. If anything, he admitted that he saw his role more as one of being a representative of the staff at the Centre in relation to the Board of National Mission and the wider Church, including the Special Commission, and not that of agent for the Board of National Mission at the St Ninian's Centre. The latter was one of the roles which the Board of National Mission, as confirmed by its immediate past Convener and its General Secretary, expected him to fulfil at the Centre. Clearly, at least on this important particular, communication between the Board and the Director is not even a one-way process. Even basic management practice would suggest that it ought to be a reciprocal experience.

It did become clear to the Commission that the

reporting line between the Director and the Assistant Director was one on one and that it was through the Assistant Director that the Director managed, or communicated with, all of the other staff at the Centre. This is always a wasteful and duplicative management structure; but the fact that it could and did exist and was made to work is indicative of the management strengths and skills of the Assistant Director. Had Dr Varwell so chosen, this would have allowed him the freedom and time to market the Centre; to become involved, as he desires, at the centre of the Board of National Mission's policy and thinking on mission; to take part in meetings of the Advisers in Mission; to have written and published work for broader dissemination, under the name of the St Ninian's Centre. His failure to do this is most unfortunate, but this is not entirely his responsibility since, of course, the greater responsibility in the making of any appointment always falls on the employer, in this case the Board of National Mission, and not on the appointee.

Throughout his interview before the Commission, Dr Varwell, if he expressed any preference, seemed to want to fulfil a job description for the Director more akin to the joint post originally held by the Rev Peter Neilson, which had never been on offer to him from the Board of National Mission. Given the overall experience of the Commissioners with Dr Varwell, both at Crieff and in interview, the Commission is reluctantly drawn to the conclusion that the appointment of Dr Varwell to the role of Director of the St Ninian's Centre by the Board of National Mission in 1997 was not exactly what was required at this stage in the history of the Centre.

Miss Pauline Greenaway—Assistant Director of the St Ninian's Centre
The Commission was indebted to Miss Greenaway for attending interview soon after a road accident. She was, however, keen to assist. She had joined the staff of St Ninian's on 1 April 1999 and very quickly had to make her mark on the domestic, or hotel management, side of the Centre rather than on the role which had been envisaged for her in her job description, which had encompassed business management, administration,

human resources and marketing. At her interview with representatives of the Board of National Mission and the Director, it had been more or less promised to her that no-one would expect her to do all of these things. She had rather fallen into the domestic role out of necessity because her previous experience of a similar role fitted her well to provide management cover in more domestic areas. The promised training in finance and accounting and assistance with marketing had not materialised. That said, she had been so busy on the domestic side that even if the training had become available, it would have been difficult for her to have found the time to take it up. She is clearly a self-starting, creative individual who has been able to develop her own role at St Ninian's and has not allowed initial suspicion from the existing members of the staff community, lack of support from those senior to her or other drawbacks to stop her fulfilling an important management role.

Unfortunately, she was given no induction to the role by the Director, nor was she formally introduced to the other staff by him. The only introduction she had to the other staff was that the Director had left her job description (ie the one which she had *not* been expected to fulfil) on the desks of other members of staff.

It became clear to the Commission, during the interview and in the light of other evidence, that the Centre would have great difficulty functioning as a residential centre were it not for Miss Greenaway's abilities and flexibility together with her commitment both to the Centre and to the staff, including the Director. It is unfortunate that an opportunity which she saw for broadening her experience by moving into the areas of responsibility which were set out in her job description, did not prove possible to fulfil. This is clearly a matter which the Executive of the Board of National Mission ought to have monitored at an earlier stage and discussed with her, to assure her of continuing support and of training opportunities. This lack of appraisal and monitoring of her position by the Board, particularly in the light of the uncertainty over the future of the Centre, is a significant omission on the part of the Board. The Commission noted with disappointment that Miss

Greenaway had not had any formal appraisal of her performance in her role since her appointment on 1 April 1999.

In substance, the written submission by other staff members affirms the evidence given by Miss Greenaway.

6. **The Commission recommends that relevant Boards of the Church introduce at any such residential centres for which they are responsible a system of regular staff review and appraisal on at least an annual basis.**

V.   YOUTH WORK

When examining the history of the St Ninian's Centre, its present purpose and its possible future, the Commission could not fail to be impressed with the evidence, drawn to its attention by several correspondents, and added to by the knowledge and experience represented in the Commission, of the quality and value of the youth work based at the St Ninian's Centre during its history. The current Project Worker, Mr Ian McDonald, is a very gifted and committed individual, who exercises a valuable ministry to young people and others both at St Ninian's and at Crieff Parish Church. The St Ninian's Centre has historically been associated with high quality teaching weekends and previously with the Summer Mission programme.

The number of residential centres available for use by Christian youth groups has increased in recent years. Many offer opportunities and instruction for outdoor and physical pursuits, a high level of multi-media facilities or a range of accommodation and meeting options, eg the Badenoch Centre, operated by the Church through the Board of National Mission, the Compass Christian Centre near Glenshee, the Abernethy Trust Centres at Nethybridge and Ardeonaig and Scripture Union Centres such as Altnacriche and Lendrick Muir. Many other centres operate throughout the country. These centres are well equipped and well managed and they offer Youth Groups a range of options that can be tailored to suit the needs of each particular group. The St Ninian's Centre

has neither the location nor the dedicated facilities to compete with such Centres.

There has been a move in Christian youth work in Scotland away from attending centralised gathered events and towards supporting locally relevant Christian youth work and in particular relational work with young people in their local Christian community. The work of the Board of Parish Education in resourcing and training individuals for such work is highlighted in their recent publication "The Works – Guidelines for Working in Children's and Youth Ministry in the Church of Scotland". This kind of work can most effectively be done in a range of different venues throughout the country, where local needs can be met. The fruits of this kind of work have been represented at the successful National Youth Assembly, and in the youth representation at the General Assembly.

Mr McDonald has a contract until July 2001 which is shared between the Board of National Mission and Crieff Parish Church. He impressed the Commission as a dynamic and gifted individual with clear ideas about the role of Youth Work in the Church and an impressive record of service both at the St Ninian's Centre and to the Parish Church in Crieff where he is also involved as a Family Worker. He is a real asset both to the Centre and to the Parish Church in Crieff and the Commission was not surprised to hear that both bodies would be sorry when Mr McDonald's contract came to an end. Indeed, even if Mr McDonald or a successor Youth Worker were available for a similar position from July, the Commission was informed by the Rev Bruce Ritchie, the minister of Crieff Parish, that the Church could not continue to use the Trust Funds previously allocated to fund its share of Mr McDonald's employment costs owing to a commitment to major refurbishment over at least the next four years. The courts of Crieff Parish Church have decided, after taking professional advice, that these funds will be devoted towards that refurbishment.

Mr McDonald's commitment to his position has been such that his own leisure time must have been at a premium. It appears that he has sole responsibility for planning, publicising and running all the Youth Weekends offered at St Ninian's and, indeed, he has devoted his own assets, including the use of his stereo and sports and other equipment, to the job. When asked by the Commission why he had had to devote his own personal property to the fulfilment of his job, Mr McDonald had not seen any difficulty in doing this. To the surprise of the Commission, when questioned further, he advised that there was no budget within the St Ninian's Centre for Youth Work and, whilst the lack of a stereo and other equipment had been mentioned at senior management meetings, he had not been given any encouragement by the Director to seek such assistance from the funds administered by the Director at the Centre or, directly, from the Board of National Mission.

The Commission was so disturbed by this information, particularly in light of the Church of Scotland's own guidelines for working in children's and youth ministry (mentioned earlier) which clearly recommend budget provision for workers themselves and for the actual work in ministry, that the Commission sought confirmation of it from both the Assistant Director and the Director when the Commission recalled him to give further evidence. Indeed, the position was worse. There were no budgets for any purpose whatsoever prepared at the St Ninian's Centre and the whole Centre has worked for some time, and continues to work, on the basis of what amounts to a deficit financing arrangement by the Board of National Mission. Subsequent questioning of Miss Liz Orr, the Accountant to the Board of National Mission, has satisfied the Commission that it has been a combination of the circumstances of illness of a key member of staff at the Centre, only recently permanently resolved, and other priorities for Miss Orr's time, that have prevented the evolution of a budget for the Centre. Surprisingly, there has been no request or desire expressed by the Director for such a budget to be created. The Commission was also satisfied by Miss Orr that the lack of a budget did not imply any lack of record-keeping or the non-availability of prime accounting or book-keeping records, either at Crieff or in the Board of National Mission's office. The Church's auditors have confirmed this to the Board in their communications with Miss Orr. The Commission also ascertained from Miss Orr that the particular pieces of equipment which Mr McDonald was using from his own resources in the fulfilment of his Youth Work at the Centre, for example stereo equipment, would have been equipment which could, quite justifiably, have been bought from St Ninian's funds or from funds of the Board of National Mission. Miss Orr would have been quite happy to recommend that this be done had she been asked. Similarly, a multi-media projector which the Director would have liked to have at the Centre and a desktop publishing software package which the Assistant Director would have liked to have for marketing purposes for the Centre, would also have been approved. Neither Miss Orr nor, as far as she was aware, any other member of the Executive of the Board of National Mission had had any such requests from anyone at the Centre. Whatever the reason for this lack of communication of reasonable requests from Crieff to Edinburgh, the Commission regards it as primarily the Director's function to initiate such requests. Moreover, the Director should ensure that no members of the staff who report to him have to use their own personal equipment in the fulfilment of their role.

7. **The Commission therefore recommends that, without delay, formal budgets be introduced for the operation of all Centres within the accounting and financial reporting structures of the Board of National Mission: that the monthly management accounts produced by the Board of National Mission be reformatted to report against that budget, and that this procedure should continue for as long as such Centres remain administered by the Board of National Mission or by any other Board of the Church.**

With regard to Youth Work, the inspiring nature of Mr McDonald's fulfilment of his role at the Centre, and the reputation built by his predecessors, despite the limitations of the venue, emphasise beyond doubt that the key to the success of Youth Work at the St Ninian's Centre, in the past as at the moment, is very much down to the individual Youth Worker involved. Without Mr McDonald or an individual of similar calibre, the St Ninian's Centre has no particular attributes of geographical location or facility which uniquely lend themselves to youth work.

In the Church of Scotland, responsibility for the Christian education of youth is primarily that of the Board of Parish Education.

8. **The Commission therefore recommends that, unless seen as an integral part of any future purpose for St Ninian's Centre, the role of Youth Worker and the provision of facilities for youth work, including residential facilities for youth work, at the St Ninian's Centre, should be discontinued with effect from the end of Mr Ian McDonald's contract with the Board of National Mission and Crieff Parish Church in July 2001.**

VI.   RESIDENTIAL ACCOMMODATION

1.   Health and Safety Matters

In the course of its investigations the Commission came by degrees to some appreciation of the responsibilities, even obligations, towards staff as well as residents, which the law in the last three decades has placed on those who own or manage any kind of residential facility. Since the Health and Safety at Work Etc Act 1974 was introduced the law has been updated regularly and new regulations have been brought into effect, particularly throughout the 1990s. These regulations cover every aspect of the running of a residential establishment from fire precaution measures to the serving and handling of food: from first aid training to the cleaning of floors and refrigerators. They require constant vigilance on the part of management, regular training of staff and the upkeep and recording of testing procedures. The penalties for non-compliance are severe. To meet these requirements, the Board of National Mission has introduced a more professional approach to the running of the properties for which it is legally responsible. Since 1997 the Board has employed a Health and Safety Officer, developed its Health and Safety Policy and a related Handbook and introduced a system of centralised procurement to ensure that the purchasing of goods and services complies with legislation.

The Special Commission commends the policy of the Board of National Mission with regard to Health and Safety. The attention paid to this by the Board through Mr Colin Wallace, its Property and Safety Manager, and his insistence on enforcement of the highest standards of safety is exemplary.

It may be a matter for regret that the "good old days" and simpler, more informal, ways of operating are in the past. It may well have become a matter of frustration when individual housekeeping departments felt constrained by regulations and a distant and perhaps not clearly articulated central procurement policy. The world has changed since the Rev Dr D P Thomson became based in Crieff nearly half a century ago. Modern science has led to a much greater understanding of the hazards within the domestic arena and the consumer has come to expect much higher standards. When something goes wrong, there is less likelihood that this is accepted as an "accident".

It became apparent to the Commission that communication between the Director and Assistant Director on the subject of Health and Safety was not always good and Mr Wallace indicated in evidence that he felt that the subject was not taken seriously enough by members of staff deployed by the Board. On one occasion he found that the Assistant Director appeared not to know where the Fire Risk Assessment and Fire Engineering Logbook were kept. He became aware too that while the logbook was regularly marked up, no faults were recorded—this despite training sessions with the handyman to whom the task was devolved.

The difficulties involved in not having a Fire Certificate, thereby limiting marketing of accommodation from 1999, illustrate the circular arguments surrounding St Ninian's, when authorisation of expenditure was kept on hold pending resolution of the ongoing search for the purpose for which the Centre might be developed in the future. £41,000 was spent in May 2000 in an attempt to improve the bednight situation in the current financial year.

It seems to the Commission that these factors place a burden, both legal and financial, on a Board which does not regard the running of residential accommodation as an integral part of its remit and add further to the sense that there has developed an over-concentration on the day-to-day running of the St Ninian's Centre itself, at the expense of creative research work.

9. **The Commission recommends that the Board review its emergency procedures in the light of recent experience at the St Ninian's Centre with a view to improving the clarity and integrity of the decision-making process in emergencies.**

2. **Residential Experience**

In evidence provided by the Director, the Assistant Director and those previously associated with the St Ninian's Centre, the significance of the residential experience for Christian groups was underlined. As individuals, Commission members can also attest to that. The importance of one community, a semi-permanent community of staff at a location welcoming another transient community eg, a kirk session or youth group, allowing that transient community to realise things together which they might not otherwise have done, was emphasised.

The Commission affirms the importance of the residential experience, but is aware that the St Ninian's Centre is not the only centre in Scotland to offer such an experience. Other centres offer similar, if not better, facilities than those currently offered by the St Ninian's Centre. Its user base clearly does not define it as a national centre for the Church of Scotland or the Church in Scotland.

Successive General Assemblies have encouraged Boards, Departments and Courts of the Church, both based at 121 George Street and locally in parishes, to use the Centre. However, as its mix of residential accommodation is presently configured and as it is presently managed, its ratio of bednight use remains too low for it to break even in financial terms. On behalf of the Petitioners, the Rev Bruce Ritchie, minister of the Parish Church in Crieff, strongly suggested that, in addition to the General Assembly encouraging the Church and those associated with it to use the St Ninian's Centre, the General Assembly should in fact go further and explicitly instruct agencies of the Church to use St Ninian's. This flies in the face of both the statistics for the use of the Centre over the last few years and the preference of committees and Boards of the Church to use accommodation, including the St Ninian's Centre, considered by them to be most apposite to the conference or event which they have arranged. The Commission believes that to ask the General Assembly to support such a dogmatic instruction as that proposed by Mr Ritchie would be counter-productive. Residential centres must attract groups and individuals to use them on their own merits and in competition with other facilities.

The Commission noted from the Director's paper attempts to establish a programme of Retreats at the Centre, which has not been pursued further. There are various reasons for this, including economics and staff changes.

VII. THE QUESTIONNAIRE

In the name of the Special Commission a Questionnaire was distributed to charges, mainly through the Ministers' Monthly Mailing of September 2000. This was done to assess more generally the views of the Church at large since it was deemed insufficient to have consulted only Boards and committees as was done at a consultation held on 13 April 1999 by the Residential Centres' Executive. Through that consultation the view was expressed, amongst others, that "St Ninian's appealed to its own constituency whose traditional ethos did not commend itself for general use or by National Boards" (see page 46 of the Order of Proceedings, 2000).

Approximately 1300 questionnaires were sent out, of which 381 were returned and of these 375 were received in time to be included in the analysis. The Questionnaire did not seek to elicit any response to using St Ninian's as a Day Centre, since this is not seen as the Centre's primary function, and in any case inhibits by distance the range of congregations who might be able to use it for a Day Conference or some such event. It was designed rather to obtain responses in two main areas, namely past experience and future intentions.

Some 245 of those who replied had held a Congregational, Kirk Session or Youth Group event in the past five years. Of these 132 had had a residential event, and of this number 87 had used St Ninian's and had found it satisfactory. Only 4 congregations who had held a residential event were unaware of its existence. This seems to suggest that ignorance of its facilities due to lack of publicity is not the barrier to usage which some had suggested. In fact it raises the question whether increased publicity would significantly affect use of St Ninian's.

As to future intentions, 370 congregations indicated that they were likely to hold a Congregational, Kirk Session or Youth Group event in the next 2 years. A higher response as compared with past experience may indicate an increased awareness of the benefits of holding such events, or it may merely reflect good intentions that are more readily expressed than realised.

Of those who intended to hold such an event, 282 were considering a residential one. If these are realised it would negate the view that congregations are moving away from residential to single-day events.

The proportion who might consider use of St Ninian's in the future was roughly comparable with the proportion that had used it in the past. This would suggest that the eventual uptake of future usage would probably be no greater than in the past. The overall impression gained from the survey is that there exists within the Church a limited but loyal constituency of congregations who have used and might be likely to use St Ninian's as a Centre for residential gathering.

In addition to the returned questionnaires the Commission received a number of submissions from individuals for whom St Ninian's has a special place in their experience. The Commission appreciates not just nostalgic affection for the Centre because of the inspiration found there, but the fact that for not a few it is something of a spiritual home.

The fact that only 370 out of 1300 charges responded to the questionnaire, however, does not mean that the overwhelming proportion of congregations have no intention of holding a residential event of any kind. On the contrary, it has been frequently suggested to the Commission that a variety of groups from churches do have such arrangements but most probably in venues at more convenient locations.

VIII. "KEEPING OUR OPTIONS OPEN"

The Commission then addressed the Board of National Mission's responsibility for strategic thinking and planning in relation to St Ninian's. During the mid 1990s it had become clear to the Board that the St Ninian's Centre would have to be encouraged to move forward, and consideration was given to the purchase of the sanctuary of the former South Church in Crieff, near to the site of the St Ninian's Centre itself, for use in connection with the Centre. Early in 1996, the Board of National Mission resolved to accept the advice of professional advisers and its own Property and Safety Manager not to pursue that purchase. Given the nature of the South Church building and the potential for continuing, extensive and expensive maintenance costs, not to say the costs of alteration and conversion to use for the Centre, this was a wise decision.

The Warehouse Site at Milnab Terrace, Crieff

At about that time, a former warehouse owned by the Strathearn Lighting Company in Milnab Terrace, close to the Director of the Centre's home in "Barnoak" and the staff accommodation adjacent thereto at 41A and 41B Milnab Terrace, became available. A bargain was concluded for its purchase at £41,000 (valued in November 1999 with outline planning permission for development at £20,000) (see Appendix 4). There was, apparently, an idea that this site might be used for the building of further staff accommodation to replace outdated accommodation in the houses known as "Stanleybank" and "Greenbank" which might thereafter be sold or, alternatively, that a Youth Centre facility could be built. Such a facility, over half a mile from the Centre, across two busy public roads and some way along a narrow, ill-lit street might be thought to be of questionable utility, particularly in terms of the functional integrity of St Ninian's as a whole and in the best interests of child protection. Both the former Convener of the Board of National Mission and its General Secretary were at pains to deny before the Commission that this was a speculative purchase (although the Commission can see no other reasonable way to describe it) following the decision not to pursue the purchase of the former South Church building in Crieff. Mr Cairns and Mr Nicol both confirmed to the Commission that the Board of National Mission did not indulge in speculative property purchases, except in relation to certain areas of land bought some time ago for anticipated mission purposes. In other words, a purpose such as anticipated New Charge Development is a special, legitimate form of speculative activity. Even such a description for the purchase of the warehouse site in Milnab Terrace would be better than that of the site having been bought to broaden their options, as the Convener of the Board said at the debate on the Petition before the General Assembly on 24 May 2000 and confirmed to the Commission. Mr Cairns and Mr Nicol specifically denied that the warehouse site was a property purchase for the purposes of financial investment. Given that nothing other than the vaguest possible purposes were discerned for the purchase at the time, it is hard to see how the purchase of the former warehouse site in Milnab Terrace, Crieff, can be described as anything other than "speculative".

10. **The Special Commission therefore recommends that no Board or central Department of the Church should be allowed to purchase or lease any heritable property without a specific purpose in mind for the property concerned.**

Knox House

In January 1998, shortly after his appointment as Director of the St Ninian's Centre in October 1997, Dr Varwell was contacted by the Rector of Morrison's Academy in Crieff to advise him that Knox House, immediately to the east of the main Centre building in Comrie Road, Crieff, was being discontinued in use by the School Governors and would therefore become available for sale. Dr Varwell has explained to the Commission, in detail in writing and orally, as indeed he explained to the then local Board of Management of the St Ninian's Centre and the Mission and Evangelism Resources Committee of the Board of National Mission, the possible purposes to which Knox House might have been put for use in association with the St Ninian's Centre. During their visits to Crieff, Dr Varwell showed members of the Commission round Knox House, which had clearly been specifically adapted for educational use and which had suffered from inappropriate and poor quality extensions in the 1960s. The Commission was advised by Mr Colin Wallace, the Board's Property and Safety Manager, that a survey of the buildings was carried out by a national professional firm of Chartered Surveyors, a report on the property and its valuation obtained and thereafter negotiations conducted between the Board of National Mission (represented by the Law Department) and the School Governors for the purchase of Knox House at a price of £225,000 with entry at September 1998. The Commission was advised by the immediate past Convener of the Board, its General Secretary and its Property and Safety Manager that, so far as they were aware, there was no element of enhancement of the purchase price owing to the fact that the Board of National Mission as *de facto* holder of the title to the adjacent St Ninian's Centre, might be seen as a "special purchaser" of Knox House. Notwithstanding that belief on the part of these individuals, a subsequent valuation of Knox House in November 1999 by a more local firm of Chartered Surveyors, gives a market value for the premises of £125,000 (see Appendix 4), representing £100,000 of a loss in value over a maximum 14 month period. Whilst the Commission is aware that valuation is not an exact science, a difference in value of $44\frac{1}{2}$ % over a 14 month period may be felt to be worthy of investigation. The Commission knows, from his interview, that the Property and Safety Manager of the

Board is also concerned by this diminution in value.

11. The Commission therefore recommends that the Board of National Mission through its Property and Safety Manager, pursue with the firm of chartered surveyors who prepared the original Report Valuation of Knox House in 1998, its apparent diminution in value between September 1998 and November 1999 and ask for a satisfactory reason for such diminution. If no satisfactory reason is provided by that firm, the Commission recommends that the Board of National Mission, through the Law Department, take such action as the Law Department may consider appropriate to pursue a claim against the professional firm involved for possible professional negligence in the provision of the original Valuation on which the purchase for Knox House in September 1998 was based.

The Commission questioned closely the Director of the Centre, the Assistant Director, the Convener of the Board at the time, the General Secretary of the Board and the Depute Secretary with responsibility for the St Ninian's Centre, the Rev Dr Frank Bardgett, with regard to Dr Varwell's proposals for Knox House. The Commission pressed them regarding why no properly formulated Business Plan and no definitive use for Knox House was produced to and approved by the Board of National Mission during the eight month period between the availability of Knox House becoming known to the Director and its purchase by the Board of National Mission. Where reasons have been put forward for this omission, they have been given as lack of time. A more sophisticated variant of this reason has been lack of time in relation to the cycle of the meetings of the Board of Management of the St Ninian's Centre and the Board of National Mission. Indeed this is true, but only because the decision-making process was becoming increasingly, and needlessly, complex. Therefore neither version of the given reason will suffice. In any reasonable estimation, eight months is more than sufficient time to devise and take forward a Business Plan/Project Plan for an investment in the region of £250,000. Not to provide such a Plan and detailed costings for its requirements is, at best, bad stewardship and, at worst, a dereliction of duty on the part of the Board of National Mission in relation to its resources, being its capital reserves from which the purchase price of Knox House was provided. The Convener of the Board of National Mission, at the General Assembly debate on 24 May 2000 stated that the reason for purchasing Knox House at a time of review by the Board of National Mission of the future and purpose of St Ninian's Centre was "to keep their options open". Few organisations, commercial or otherwise, have the resources so to do. Those who do would not choose to spend such a sum of money without conducting a full feasibility study into the purchase of the asset involved, its future use and contribution to the organisation and all of the costs associated with bringing it into operation before any commitment to the purchase of the asset were made. The Commission finds it hard to understand why any other criteria or process should be applied to the purchase of an asset at such a price on behalf of the Church. Indeed the Commission believes the standard required of those choosing to spend sums, especially of this magnitude, on behalf of the Church ought to be higher than that required in a commercial organisation. A commercial organisation is using its own resources, raised from its shareholders or retained from the profits of its enterprise. The Church, far less one of the Boards of the Church, was here seeking to use financial resources provided by members of the Church with less consideration than that required of a congregation by its Presbytery in relation to the spending of in excess of £15,000 in a given financial year. The Commission does not find sufficient the reason given by the former Convener that the purchase was *"to keep our options open"* and that the Board, having the capital resources available for the purchase could, indeed, therefore go ahead to make the purchase. Indeed, the Commission finds the entire conduct of the Board surrounding the acquisition of Knox House—the research, negotiations and the purchase—to be lacking in the basic essentials of good stewardship; and the Commission unreservedly condemns the decision of the Board to go ahead with the purchase of Knox House in such circumstances.

Even if the result of proper evaluation and approval of such a purchase (which need not with reasonable efficiency take over long) were that the opportunity to purchase the asset in question were lost, that would be a better outcome than the reckless spending of other people's money, simply because a Board of the National Church had such a sum within its capital reserves.

12. **The Special Commission further recommends that the Board of Stewardship and Finance should be advised in advance of the proposed purchase of any heritable property or other asset valued in excess of £50,000 by a Board or central Department of the Church, and should approve such purchase, if need be through powers delegated to the Convener and other designated office-bearers to act between formal meetings.**

The Auditors

The Auditors to the Board of Management of the St Ninian's Centre, a sub-committee of the Board of National Mission, wrote a letter on 2 July 1997 to the Board of Management as follows:—

"*Centre Development*
We note from the minutes of the Board of Management meetings that the Centre is considering upgrading existing facilities and the construction of a new hall on a nearby site as a Millennium Project. This is at a time when demand for Centre facilities is changing, and room occupancy rates are decreasing.

The risk arises that, without careful management, capital expenditure would impose significant cash liquidity problems on the Centre, and that the facilities constructed would not attract more visitors.

We recommend that the Centre carries out research on the demand for new facilities and carries out detailed costing of all proposed developments. This will allow

the Board of Management to assess which development options are likely to give the best return on the expenditure required."

Whilst such a Management Letter does not form part of the Auditor's Report on the Accounts, it is a careful warning to the management of any organisation to abide by its terms. If, presumably for good reason, the organisation finds itself not able to abide by the terms of such a letter, the reasons for going outwith them should be explained.

Miss Liz Orr, the Accountant to the Board of National Mission, received this letter through the Board of Management of the St Ninian's Centre and was aware of its terms. In evidence before the Commission, she was able to prove to its satisfaction from her own notes of the occasion, that she had brought the terms of the Management Letter to the attention of the General Secretary of the Board of National Mission and presumed that he would have brought the terms of the letter to the attention of members of the Board. The General Secretary of the Board admitted that he had had this letter drawn to his attention and whilst the Convener of the Board "could not recall" whether or not such a letter had been drawn to his attention, he did not deny it as a possibility. Miss Orr made the distinction, in her evidence before the Commission, between the resources of the Centre itself and the resources of the Board of National Mission. She contended that because the resources provided to purchase both the site in Milnab Terrace and Knox House came from the Board of National Mission, that Board in providing these was not in breach of the terms of a Management Letter addressed to the Board of Management. The Commission appreciates her reasoned argument here, but feels, particularly in the light of a decision to abolish the separate Board of Management of the St Ninian's Centre within a year of the date of the Management Letter—and the fact of the Management Letter itself—that specific, minuted consideration of the Auditors' Management Letter should have been given by the Board, particularly in relation to its decision to purchase Knox House. Whilst, for the reasons given above, the Commission would not have considered the purchase of Knox House to be so sufficiently justified as to have allowed the Board of National Mission to go ahead in the face of the wording of the Auditors' Management Letter, the fact of its consideration ought to have been minuted by the Board of National Mission and the reason why the Board decided not to follow the Auditors' advice in this matter should also have been minuted. There is no mention whatsoever of this Auditors' Letter in the minutes of the Board. The General Secretary explained that he regarded minutes as lists of decisions. In most cases, this is a defensible manner in which to draft minutes. It is not, the Commission would submit, a defensible or sufficient manner in which to draft minutes in relation to the purchase of a building, on a private basis, from another institution at a purchase price in the region of £250,000 without a fully formed Business Plan or Project Plan for its use simply *"to keep [the Board's] options open"*.

Overall, the Commission was disturbed by the relative lack of importance which was attached by the Executive and the former Convener of the Board to this Auditors' Management Letter. As might be expected, the Accountant to the Board of National Mission was well aware of its purpose and adequately drew it to the attention of her superior. The fact that nothing further was done to recognise the importance of this letter is not her responsibility.

13. **The Commission therefore recommends that, as a matter of policy, the Board of Stewardship and Finance should lay down guidelines for boards, central departments of the Church and, if it considers it necessary, presbyteries and congregations in relation to the importance of Auditors' Management Letters, Reports, Certificates and the like. These should be drawn to the attention of the members of the Board, Department or Court concerned. The fact of their having been so drawn to their attention should be minuted at a relevant meeting. In particular, the Board of Stewardship and Finance should make it clear that, if the recipient of the advice given by the Auditors wishes to carry out a considered course of action contrary, or apparently contrary, to that advice, their reasons for pursuing such a course of action should be adequately explained in the minute, in particular with regard to how any adverse financial consequences, highlighted by the Auditors in their advice, will be avoided.**

IX.   THE REVIEW PROCESS

The Commission has discussed above the process whereby a new Director of the St Ninian's Centre was appointed in October 1997 and the opportunities which were lost, despite various signals during the period between September 1996 and October 1997, for a further review of the buildings, purpose and future of the St Ninian's Centre to be carried out. Indeed, the Commission has mentioned that the Board of National Mission envisaged the appointee to the role of Director as being their consultant for the purpose of thinking out the future of the St Ninian's Centre. That opportunity having being lost, Dr Varwell as new Director embarked upon his own review in November 1997. That was followed by a review instigated by the Board of National Mission through a Review Group established by the Board in April 1998. Dr Varwell was invited to join the Review Group and, presumably, the idea was that his review would then become part of the overall review instigated by the Board of National Mission. The Review Group was intended to review the management, structure, purpose and future of both the St Ninian's Centre and the Badenoch Centre near Kincraig. It is clear from the minutes of the Board of National Mission and of the Review Group that the Review Group was established with the intent of supporting the development of both Centres. Indeed, as much was said by the Board and by the Review Group and publicised.

In June 1998, the Review Group reported to the Board of National Mission that a new body to be known as a "Residential Centres' Executive" should be set up to replace the local Boards of Management for both Centres. The recommendation of the Review Group was somewhat inchoate in that the full remit of the Residential Centres' Executive was not brought before the Board, nor was an exhaustive list of those who should be represented or be members of it produced. Nonetheless the Board accepted the recommendations of the Review Group and went ahead to form the Residential Centres' Executive. The Board attempted to make up for the deficiencies in the Review Group's recommendations with regard to the purpose and membership of the Residential Centres' Executive.

Whilst the Commission does not imply any desire on the part of the former Convener to bulldoze his preferred structure for the management of the Badenoch and St Ninian's Centres through the Board of National Mission, and indeed accepted from him in evidence that it was because of the importance which he and the Board placed upon the review that he became Convener of the Review Group, the Commission thinks it unfortunate that he should have been at one and the same time the Convener of a Group set up for the purpose of a major review of the management of the St Ninian's and Badenoch Centres, and Convener of the Board itself. At the same time, he also became Convener of the Policy Group expressly established to look at broader matters of policy within the Board. Inevitably, where such roles are combined, opportunities for objectivity and new thinking are lost and the accusation of conflict of interests can be easily, if not justifiably, made.

14. The Commission therefore recommends that, in future, should any Board of the Church be undertaking a review of policy in any area of the Church's work for which it is responsible, the Convener of any Review Group, Working Party, Sub-Committee or the like should not also be Convener of the Board.

The intention of the Residential Centres' Executive was to bring a greater degree of professional management to the two Centres at Badenoch and Crieff. From the evidence of the former Convener of the Residential Centres' Executive, (the Rev James Gibson), the former Convener of the Board, the Depute General Secretary (who acted as Clerk to Residential Centres' Executive) and the Board's Property and Safety Manager, clearly the Residential Centres' Executive achieved some success in this task. It was, however, unfortunate that perhaps the nature of its role and the reason for its coming into being was not effectively communicated to the relevant staff at the St Ninian's Centre. As a consequence, acceptance of its role, which the Commission appreciates as necessary in a world of increased regulation, particularly in relation to Health and Safety, Food Management, Property Licensing and the like, was made all the harder, and an opportunity to persuade people of the very real benefits to be obtained from its creation was lost. Instead, the impression gained by the staff of St Ninian's is of more remote management, indulging in over-centralisation of activities, including purchasing, to no apparent end. In fact what is being done and achieved is the provision of more professional management to both Centres, the purchase of materials consistent with required regulations for Health, Safety and Food Management and, in time, a better overall standard of management for both Centres. This has resulted in a centralised list of contractors and suppliers to fulfil these obligations of the Board and also to meet new Inland Revenue regulations. It is therefore unfortunate that none of these substantial reasons for the existence of the Residential Centres' Executive appear to have been effectively communicated to local management.

15. The Commission therefore recommends that the Residential Centres' Executive, or any successor thereto, should produce an attractively designed and printed memorandum for all staff at the Residential Centres which it manages, explaining the reason for its existence, its role in the management of the Centres and an explanation of how it supports the efficient local operation of the Centre. In particular, the reasons for centralised purchasing and a limited

list of contractors should be explained in the memorandum which should be cast in easy to understand, user-friendly language.

This positive note of support continued in relation to the St Ninian's Centre and its future, and was endorsed by the Board of National Mission in its Report to the General Assembly in 1999.

> *"The Board of National Mission looks forward to reporting to future General Assemblies the progress of its Residential Centres' Executive, convened by the Rev James Gibson, in securing and developing the further wellbeing of our Centres at Badenoch and St Ninian's, Crieff. Our prayer is that the Centres may be able to flourish in their service both to the Church in Scotland and to those beyond".* (From Board of National Mission Report, Volume of Reports 1999, page 20/10.)

In 1998 the General Assembly decided that all Boards and agencies of the Church should exercise good stewardship in the use of their resources and live within their budgets and means. But not until well after the publication of the Board of National Mission's Report of the following year was adequate thought given as to the purpose and future of the St Ninian's Centre. This may be thought to have been somewhat late in the day following the appointment of a new Director, the purchase of property at an aggregate purchase price of £261,000 and the conduct of a review by the new Director and by the Review Group specifically set up for that purpose by the Board. At about this time this review process was hampered by the absence of key personnel through illness, army service and geographical location.

Although it was denied by the immediate past Convener of the Board and its General Secretary, the Commission has come to the conclusion from the particular Minute of the Board which approved the purchase of Knox House, mentioned above, that there came to be, as described by the Depute General Secretary, two strands of thought on the Board with regard to the future of St Ninian's. The one which might be said to be articulated by the Rev James Gibson, sought a further review of the purpose and future of the Centre before the purchase of Knox House, not just on financial grounds. The other was one of continued support, perhaps based more on St Ninian's past reputation than on its present role or future potential.

However, in early 2000 there was a sudden shift of the balance of opinion on the Board towards closure. This was achieved even in the absence of Mr Gibson, and it involved a change of heart by a Board which who had been previously inclined to support the St Ninian's Centre at all costs, and, as has been described above, at some cost to the principles of good stewardship. Others, it seems, would have preferred to argue the case for closure of St Ninian's on the grounds of its lack of present and future purpose, and for financial reasons, in a report to the General Assembly of 2001, rather than have a rushed proposal for closure before the General Assembly of 2000 by way of a Supplementary Report.

It is doubly unfortunate that the immediate past Convener of the Board again chose to carry out more than one role at this stage. This time he acted both as Convener of the Board of National Mission and as Interim Convener of the Residential Centres' Executive during the absence of Mr Gibson. It has been made clear by the General Secretary of the Board that this had to happen because of the fact that, given the nature of Mr Gibson's service, he was not contactable by the Board and had, to all intents and purposes, to be regarded by the Board as not being available for consultation. Whilst Mr Gibson accepts that there would have been difficulties in contacting him in Bosnia and that, for all practical purposes, the General Secretary is accurate in his recollection of the circumstances surrounding his posting there, the fact is that he clearly feels (although forbore to spell it out during his interview before the Commission) that it was unfortunate that a decision as important as the closure of the St Ninian's Centre could not have been discussed with him. Undoubtedly Mr Gibson would have preferred a fully argued and reasoned Report to have been presented, by way of the main Report of the Board of National Mission, to the General Assembly of 2001. Again, the Commission cannot help but feel that, notwithstanding the importance which Mr Cairns as

Convener of the Board clearly gave to the role of Convener of the Residential Centres' Executive at this time of discussion of the future of St Ninian's, the fact that he took this role upon himself removed a degree of objectivity from deliberation on a decision which could well have done with the maximum possible objectivity and time taken in its consideration (perhaps even extending to the timing of the Supplementary Report recommending the closure of the Centre to the General Assembly in 2000). It is for this reason that the Commission makes the above recommendation (14).

16. The Commission recommends that, where a Board of the Church is considering a major change in its policy with regard to an area of its activity, there should be consultation, at the very least, with the Convener of the Sub-Committee of the Board most closely associated with that area of policy; where this proves impossible, a final decision on the matter should be delayed until such time as that individual can be consulted by the Convener of the Board and the General Secretary. The Commission recommends that this principle be adopted by all Boards and Committees of the Church.

X. SUPPLEMENTARY REPORT OF THE BOARD OF NATIONAL MISSION (MAY 2000)

This Report turns now to the Supplementary Report included in the Order of Proceedings document issued in early May 2000.

The Commission has been advised by both the past Convener of the Board of National Mission and its General Secretary that at the time the Board's Report for inclusion in the volume of Reports to the General Assembly of 2000 had been prepared, the Board "genuinely remained open-minded on the future of the St Ninian's Centre" and it was not known until the meeting held on 5 April 2000 what the outcome of the Board's deliberations with regard to the future of St Ninian's would

be. Neither the then Convener of the Board nor its General Secretary acknowledged that there were two strands of thought on the Board in this regard. Whilst this may be understandable in the case of the then Convener, acting as both Convener of the Board and Interim Convener of the Residential Centres' Executive, the difference of opinion on the Board, which was not brought to a vote, caused an extended period of indecision. The curious mixture of haste and delay with regard to the review of the St Ninian's Centre's future, illustrated by the chronology of events in Appendix 1, continued and, in the end, the decision to close the Centre by the Board of National Mission related in the Supplementary Report appears to have been made quite suddenly. If it was genuinely not decided until the meeting on 5 April 2000 that the St Ninian's Centre should close, rumour at St Ninian's and throughout the Church in late 1999, fed further by the brevity of reference to the Centre in the Board's main Report to the General Assembly of 2000, seems puzzling.

Situations that give rise to decisions like the one to close the St Ninian's Centre develop over a reasonable period of time. If such decisions are communicated by means of Supplementary Report, this implies a lack of proper deliberation on a situation and the General Assembly is not able to give such decisions the mature consideration which they require. The Board of National Mission therefore made a serious error of judgement in communicating its decision to close the St Ninian's Centre to the General Assembly by way of Supplementary Report.

The reason given for the late date on which the decision to close the Centre was made, and the need to put this in a Supplementary Report to the General Assembly of 2000, was stated by Mr Cairns, Mr Nicol and Dr Bardgett, to be in order to minimise the period of uncertainty for staff at the Centre. The result of the General Assembly's acceptance of the Crave of the Petition giving rise to the appointment of the Commission has achieved the opposite of this intention. There is no doubt that whatever good intentions the Board of National Mission may have had in presenting its decision to close the St Ninian's

Centre to the General Assembly of 2000 by way of a Supplementary Report, it gave rise to an understandable feeling among Commissioners that the Board was attempting to *"bounce"* the General Assembly into a decision to close the Centre. If proof were needed of that feeling, reference need only be made to the content of the debate on the Petition on 24 May 2000.

17. The Commission therefore recommends that, except in the case of manifest emergency proved to the satisfaction of the Convener of the Board of Practice and Procedure and the Principal Clerk, Boards and Committees should not bring major issues before the General Assembly by way of a Supplementary Report.

XI. THE PRESENT PURPOSE AND THE FUTURE OF THE ST NINIAN'S CENTRE

The Special Commission was required to consider *"the purpose... and future of St Ninian's Centre"*. Throughout the earlier part of its history, St Ninian's had a clear, if sometimes varied, purpose. One by one these purposes had come to an end or been transferred elsewhere. The reasons for these decisions being made were sufficient for their time on an individual basis. It was perhaps not understood, nor could it have been, what would be the aggregate effect of all these decisions on the purpose and future of the Centre.

The Commission heard evidence from interviewees, clearly supportive of what the St Ninian's Centre had once been, who looked back with great affection on their visits to the Centre, but nonetheless agreed that the Centre had no present purpose within the Church of Scotland or, indeed, within the wider Church in Scotland. It was said by those interviewees that were it not for the fact of the buildings and "plant" existing at Crieff, there would be no reason to build or purchase them today. The Commission agrees. Buildings need a purpose and their mere existence should not in itself drive a search for a purpose. Buildings, in a Church context, are but tools for the advancement of the Kingdom. A tool without a

purpose is simply a burden, using resources which might be better used elsewhere. Regrettably, when considering the present purpose of the St Ninian's Centre, the Commission could find none which was not catered for and indeed catered for better in other locations and buildings.

From its earliest days, St Ninian's was a stimulus to evangelism and mission. Some of that work continues, although no longer based in Crieff. As aspects of its work have become less tied to, and identified with St Ninian's, the Board of National Mission has found it more difficult to identify how integral is the Centre to the Board's overall work. The Board believes that it is the contribution to research and field practice that was and is the Centre's main contribution. The Board is keen to retain this aspect as part of its work, although it sees no reason why that needs to be tied to the Centre or to Crieff. The Board has started exploratory discussions to establish a mission studies unit, probably tied to an existing academic institution.

The Commission agrees that this is vital work that the Board should pursue as seems best to it. However, whatever the worth of the Board's preference to link up with an academic institution, the Commission believes that this will provide something quite different from what St Ninian's contributed. Consequently, the Board's proposal should not be presented as the retention of what was best from St Ninian's. Nor is the Board thereby continuing any aspect of the Centre's work which is not being pursued elsewhere.

During its deliberations, the Commission spent a great deal of time considering whether it might be possible to suggest to the General Assembly that there might be a demand for a Centre such as the St Ninian's Centre for a particular constituency in the wider Church in Scotland, which constituency is not restricted to the Church of Scotland. In accordance therefore with the conclusion that it is not appropriate that the Board of National Mission (or any other Board or Committee or Department of the Church) should be involved in the ownership, maintenance and running of such a Centre, the Commission explored in detail the possibility of transferring the title to the heritable property forming the St Ninian's Centre at Crieff (and for reasons of economy and market size of the niche constituency to which such a Centre might appeal, the St Ninian's Centre itself only) to a Trust or to a Company Limited by Guarantee, the Trustees or Directors of which might include members of the Board of National Mission, other denominations of the wider Church in Scotland and other co-opted individuals. When the Commission canvassed this decision before interviewees, it received varying degrees of support, including strong support from the Rev Bruce Ritchie, minister of the Parish Church in Crieff.

Had the Commission thought that there was a purpose and future for the St Ninian's Centre not available elsewhere in Scotland, it would have had no hesitation in recommending such a solution to the General Assembly. Having carefully reviewed the work required to be done to the St Ninian's Centre itself, even to bring the quality of the accommodation up to the minimum standard required by modern conference-goers, the Commission has come to the conclusion that a minimum of £500,000 would require to be spent in capital terms and that any such Trust or Company Limited by Guarantee would require to be certain of continuing deficit-financing on its revenue account for an indefinite period of time for it to succeed. After careful deliberation the Commission has come to the conclusion that to transfer the St Ninian's Centre, even to the limited extent of only the Centre building itself, to such a Trust or Company, would be tantamount to dumping a problem created during the ownership of the Church of Scotland on to others. The Commission considers this neither honest nor proper.

The Commission would have been prepared to recommend to the General Assembly any clearly expressed and fully justified proposal which might have resulted in the prolonging of the useful life of the St Ninian's Centre in Crieff. Regrettably, the potential solution of transferring the Centre to a more locally managed Trust or Company, no matter whether it continued to be supported to some extent by the Church of Scotland, would in the Commission's view—far from prolonging the useful life of the St Ninian's Centre—have simply prolonged its death. That is not a responsibility which the Commission could recommend to the General Assembly.

As mentioned above, the preparation of this Report has been the result of a voyage of discovery made by each member of the Special Commission. It is the Commission's developing understanding that has led it to determine the conclusion it recommends to the General Assembly.

As will have been seen from this Report, the Commission has many criticisms of the management, failure to manage and maladministration by the Board of National Mission in relation to the St Ninian's Centre since 1996. However, in broad substance, the Commission agrees with the content and conclusions as set out in the Supplementary Report of the Board of National Mission of May 2000 to the General Assembly of that year. The Commission has therefore come to the conclusion that it is not within the remit of the Board of National Mission nor indeed that of the Church of Scotland to continue to offer the facilities at the St Ninian's Centre in Crieff.

Whatever its aspirations may once have been, the overwhelming weight of evidence shows that the St Ninian's Centre does not operate as a national centre for the Church of Scotland. Despite the encouragement of successive General Assemblies for organisations and individuals in the Church to use the St Ninian's Centre, this has not happened in numbers sufficient to provide the income necessary to support the continuance of the Centre and, moreover, to justify a programme of refurbishment and upgrading such as might be expected to have significant impact on the usage of the Centre by the Church and other groups.

If it were simply a question of finance then this Report could end here. That it is not has been made clear from the documentation examined by the Commission and the evidence from the interviewees listed in Appendix 2 to this Report. The remit requires the Commission to review the management. This it has done and found it wanting in the Secretariat and Executive of the Board of National Mission and also in the Director of the Centre.

In coming to this conclusion the Commission is acutely conscious that any decision to close the St Ninian's Centre in Crieff is not just about buildings. It has consequences for each and every individual member of staff at the Centre in terms of loss of their livelihood and in unwanted career change. The staff will particularly require the pastoral care of the Church, nationally and locally, and the prayerful support of all.

XII. CONCLUSION

18. The Commission therefore recommends that the Board of National Mission withdraw from the St Ninian's Centre at Crieff in the following manner:

(a) That the St Ninian's Centre in Crieff be closed with effect from 30 September 2001;

(b) That the employment contracts of all staff at the St Ninian's Centre be terminated from and after the same date;

(c) That the contract of Mr Ian McDonald, the Youth Worker based at the St Ninian's Centre, Crieff, in partnership with Crieff Parish Church, continue until its expiry in July 2001;

(d) That, to allow time for relocation and resettlement, the accommodation arrangements for all staff utilising staff accommodation at the St Ninian's Centre be progressively terminated by 31 March 2002;

(e) That the Board of National Mission ensure that each of the staff of the St Ninian's Centre be offered as much pastoral care and practical assistance as is possible with regard to their preparation for their future life. The Church is deeply indebted to each one of them and, in particular, owes them a debt of gratitude for continuing to give service at St Ninian's during a period of manifest uncertainty over the last two years.

(f) That the heritable properties listed in Appendix 4 be offered for sale on the open market for the best possible price over a period not exceeding three years from the date of the acceptance by the General Assembly of this recommendation, and the proceeds directed towards the capital resources of the Board of National Mission or any successor Board or substitute body or bodies within the Church of Scotland as the General Assembly may direct;

(g) That from and after the date of the closure of the St Ninian's Centre the Board of National Mission be directed to wind up the present Residential Centres' Executive of the Board and replace it with an Executive Committee for the management and oversight of the Badenoch Centre, which Executive Committee should be a sub-committee of the Mission and Evangelism Resources Committee of the Board of National Mission, reporting to that Board through that committee.

The views expressed in this report represent the unanimous opinion and conclusions of the Commission in respect of the remit provided by the Crave of the Petition accepted by the General Assembly on 24 May 2000.

WILLIAM MACMILLAN (*Convener*)
ELSPETH BURNETT
ROBERT HYND
ALAN MACGREGOR
GORDON PALMER
TONY STEPHEN

The Special Commission wishes to record its grateful and enduring thanks to its Clerk, Rev Marjory MacLean, for her thoughtful administration of all of their deliberations and in particular for her compliance with their requests for information from others and her organisation of the series of interviews of those named in Appendix 2 to this Report. Her attention to the detail of matters within the remit and her advice on the fulfilment of that remit within the practice and procedure of the Church has been as meticulous as it is invaluable.

APPENDIX 1

CHRONOLOGY OF RELEVANT EVENTS

2 July 1997
Management Letter to the Board of Management of the St Ninian's Centre from Messrs Scott-Moncrieff, Chartered Accountants, their Auditors.

September 1997
Purchase of Milnab Terrace site at a purchase price of £41,000, concluded.

November 1997
Dr Adrian Varwell appointed as Director of the St Ninian's Centre on a contract of seven years' duration.

March 1998
Establishment of Residential Centres' Review Group by the Board of National Mission.

May 1998
Residential Centres' Review Group offers support to both the St Ninian's Centre and the Badenoch Centre.

June 1998
Establishment of Residential Centres' Executive.

24 September 1998
Last formal meeting of the Board of Management of the St Ninian's Centre.

September 1998
Date of entry and completion of the purchase of Knox House at a purchase price of £225,000 from the Governors of Morrison's Academy, Crieff.

February 1999
Report of Board of National Mission to the General Assembly 1999 in which the work of the St Ninian's Centre, is supported.

May 2000
Supplementary Report of the Board of National Mission recommending closure of the St Ninian's Centre.

24 May 2000
Hearing of Petition of Bruce Ritchie and Others at the General Assembly 2000 and the granting of the Crave of that Petition by the General Assembly.

APPENDIX 2

INTERVIEWEES : 13TH TO 17TH NOVEMBER 2000

Rev Dr Adrian Varwell – Director, St Ninian's Centre.

Miss Pauline Greenaway – Assistant Director, St Ninian's Centre.

Mr Ian McDonald – Youth Worker, St Ninian's Centre and Crieff Parish Church.

Rev Douglas Nicol – General Secretary, Board of National Mission.

Rev Dr Frank Bardgett – Depute Secretary, Board of National Mission (until December 2000).

Rev Bruce Ritchie – Minister at Crieff.

Rev Sandy Cairns – Convener, Board of National Mission 1996 – 2000.

Rev Mary Morrison – Convener, Board of Management of the St Ninian's Centre until 1998.

Rev Peter Neilson – Associate Minister, St Cuthbert's Parish Church Edinburgh (Former Director of the St Ninian's Centre).

Rev James Gibson – Convener, Board of National Mission (and former Convener Residential Centres' Executive).

Rev Colin Sinclair – Convener, Mission and Evangelism Resource Committee.

Mr Colin Wallace – Property, Facilities and Safety Manager, Board of National Mission.

Miss Liz Orr – Accountant, Board of National Mission.

Rev Elinor Gordon – Minister, Trinity Gask and Kinkell linked with Muthill (Presbytery of Perth)

Rev David Denniston – Minister, Perth: North (Presbytery of Perth).

APPENDIX 3

QUESTIONNAIRE ISSUED BY THE SPECIAL COMMISSION TO ALL CHARGES IN THE CHURCH OF SCOTLAND AS PART OF THE MINISTERS' MAILING OF SEPTEMBER 2000

St. Ninian's, Crieff

Congregational Usage & Awareness Survey

[Please circle the appropriate response/s in **bold type** response]

Congregation: ....

1. Has your Congregation/Kirk Session/Youth Group had a group event in the last five years? **Yes/No**

    If "no", go to Question 2, otherwise continue below:

    (a) If "yes", was it a residential event? **Yes/No**

    If "no", go to Question 2, otherwise continue below:

    (b) If "yes" did you use St. Ninian's, Crieff? **Yes/No**

    If "no", go to (d), otherwise continue below:

    (c) If "yes", how would you rate your group's experience?

    Highly satisfactory/Satisfactory/Unsatisfactory

    Go to Question 2

    (d) If "no", did you consider using St. Ninian's, Crieff? **Yes/No**

    (e) If "no", were you aware of St. Ninian's, Crieff and its facilities? **Yes/No**

    (f) If "no", go to Question 2, otherwise continue below:

    (g) If you considered using St. Ninian's, Crieff but did not finally use it, what factors influenced your decision?

    Cost/Distance/Facilities/Accessibility/Other (please specify)

2. Is your Congregation/Kirk Session/Youth Group likely to hold a group event in the next two years? **Yes/No**

    (a) If "yes", is it likely to be a residential event? **Yes/No**

    (b) If "yes" would you consider using St. Ninian's, Crieff **Yes/No**

    (c) If "no", why not? Cost/Distance/Facilities/Accessibility/Other (please specify)

APPENDIX 4

HERITABLE PROPERTIES IN THE OWNERSHIP OF THE CHURCH OF SCOTLAND IN CRIEFF

	Market Value November 1999	Purchase Price (where relevant)
St Ninian's Centre, Comrie Road, Crieff.	£70,000.00	
Knox House, Coldwells Road, Crieff.	£125,000.00	£225,000.00
Thomson House, 56 Comrie Street, Crieff.	£90,000.00	
Stanleybank, Comrie Road, Crieff.	£67,500.00	
Glenview, Comrie Road, Crieff.	£70,000.00	
St Ninian's Lodge, Lodge Street, Crieff.	£55,000.00	
Westridge, 1A Burrell Street Crieff.	£45,000.00	
Warehouse Site, Milnab Terrace, Crieff.	£20,000.00	£41,000.00
Barnoak, 39 Milnab Street, Crieff.	£160,000.00	
41A Milnab Street, Crieff.	£72,500.00	
41B Milnab Street, Crieff.	£72,500.00	

APPENDIX 5

JOB DESCRIPTION OF THE DIRECTOR OF THE ST NINIAN'S CENTRE, CRIEFF – 1997 (EXCERPT)

Responsibilities:

(a) To accept overall responsibility for St Ninian's Centre, Crieff.

(b) To ensure the availability of appropriate courses for all ages to meet the needs of the Church for her mission and the renewal of her life in Christ; and to respond to the specific requests of congregations and groups.

(c) To co-operate with the Board of National Mission, the St Ninian's Board of Management, and staff in the development of the Centre for the advancement of the Church's mission and the renewal of its life into the new Millennium.

(d) To undertake whatever work is reasonably requested by the Department of National Mission.

Qualities and Experience:

- Appropriate theological training and Church experience.
- To be highly motivated with an ability to motivate others.
- An ability to work in a Team and to delegate responsibilities.
- A willingness to learn through experience and training.
- An awareness of the culture of the different areas of Scotland.
- An experience of congregational development.
- Experience in training and presenting.
- An understanding of Christian youth work.
- An understanding of the need for pastoral care.
- An understanding of publicity and marketing strategy.
- Proven administrative and management experience.
- To be computer literate.

APPENDIX 6

A

PETITION
THE REV BRUCE RITCHIE AND OTHERS

Unto the Venerable the General Assembly of the Church of Scotland –

The Petition of Bruce Ritchie, Alexander Gunn, Robert McNab, Peter Neilson, William Shannon and Michael Shewan

Humbly sheweth –

Whereas

1. the Board of National Mission has failed to give the staff of St Ninian's the means to fulfil the visions the Board affirmed at recent General Assemblies, thereby restraining (a) the day to day running of the Centre, (b) the scope of its ministry, and (c) the promotion of its work.

2. the Board of National Mission has not given serious consideration to, nor properly costed, all the relevant proposals for development of St Ninian's Centre laid before it.

3. the Board of National Mission has not properly managed its properties in Crieff, failing by default to develop the potential of the properties through undue delay, and failing to dispose of those surplus to its requirements.

4. the Board of National Mission has not given due consideration to creative funding for the redevelopment and future work and ministry of St Ninian's Centre.

5. the Church of Scotland has need of a national Centre where Christians of all ages, from different areas, parishes and background can meet for encouragement, training and renewal.

6. St Ninian's Centre was created, gifted, and accepted as an Interdenominational Centre for the benefit of the whole Church in Scotland, any decision on its future should be made with time and means for the whole Church, locally and nationally, to respond.

May it therefore please your Venerable Court—

1. To recall the decision of the Board of National Mission to close St Ninian's Centre, Crieff.

2. To appoint a Special Commission of seven persons to review the management, purpose and future of St Ninian's Centre, to consult widely, and to report to the General Assembly of 2001.

3. To continue St Ninian's Centre in operation pending the report of the Special Commission.

4. To remit to the Selection Committee to bring forward names of persons to serve on the Special Commission to a later sederunt of this General Assembly.

Or to do otherwise as your Venerable Court may seem good.

And your Petitioners will every pray.

B

MINUTE OF THE PETITION TO THE GENERAL ASSEMBLY OF 2000

PETITION – REV BRUCE RITCHIE AND OTHERS

The General Assembly took up consideration of a Petition in the name of Rev Bruce Ritchie and Others.

Parties were called.

The Rev Bruce Ritchie, the Rev Peter Neilson, Mr R McNab and the Rev Michael Shewan appeared.

It was moved, seconded and agreed-

The General Assembly take the Petition as read.

It was moved, seconded and agreed—

The General Assembly receive the Petition and resolve to treat any motion that the crave of the Petition be granted, as a counter-motion to Section 2 of the Proposed Deliverance of the Supplementary Report of the Board of National Mission.

Parties were heard.

Questions were asked.

Parties were removed.

It was moved and seconded as a counter-motion to Section 2 of the Deliverance of the Supplementary Report of the Board of National Mission:—

The General Assembly grant the crave of the Petition.

On a vote being taken between the motion and the counter-motion the counter-motion carried and the General Assembly resolved accordingly.

Parties were recalled and judgement was intimated.

REPORT OF THE SPECIAL COMMISSION ANENT THE DEPARTMENT OF EDUCATION
MAY 2001

PROPOSED DELIVERANCE

The General Assembly:

1. Receive the Report.

2. Approve the recommendations set out in Section 8 in the following terms:-
   (1) Recognising education as a central concern of government and a continuing concern of the Church, reaffirm the responsibility of the Committee on Education to represent the Church in all matters concerning education in schools, colleges and universities.
   (2) Taking account of changes which have affected the Department of Education in recent years, resolve to abolish it and in its place constitute the Committee on Education as a free-standing committee reporting directly to the General Assembly, without prejudice to any future inclusion within a new administrative arrangement.
   (3) Recognising the need for continuity within the Secretariat of the Committee, authorise the Personnel Department to proceed with the appointment of a successor to the Rev John Stevenson, such an appointee to be designated Secretary to the Committee on Education.

3. Thank and discharge the Special Commission.

REPORT

The Special Commission anent the Department of Education was appointed by the General Assembly of 2000 as the result of a counter-motion to the Department's Deliverance intimating their intention to make a new appointment in succession to the retiring General Secretary, the Rev John Stevenson. The Assembly decided that any such appointment should be postponed pending a full review of all the implications of such a proposal and appointed _a Special Commission of seven persons to conduct such a review and, in particular_ :-

(a) *to enquire into changes since the appointment of the current General Secretary with a view to determining the responsibilities and workload of the Department;*

(b) *to examine how the work of the Department might best be delivered within the current organisational structures of the Church;*

(c) *to consult with the Personnel Department concerning the proposed workload and terms and conditions of service, in particular the appropriate level of remuneration;*

(d) *to clarify the division of responsibility between Convener and Secretary in representative roles on inter-church and inter-agency committees and bodies.*

The Assembly instructed the Special Commission to bring its report to the Assembly of 2001. Meantime a temporary appointment as Secretary was authorised for a period of up to nine months from the date of retirement of the present General Secretary.

It is important to state that at no time was there any criticism either stated or implied regarding the work of the retiring General Secretary, whose outstanding service to the cause of education in Scotland had recently been recognised with the award of the FEIS.

The members of the Special Commission and the method of their working are noted in an Appendix to this report.

1. Background

1.1 The remit of the Committee on Education, the longest-serving Committee of the General Assembly (est. 1824), is to act for the General Assembly on all matters concerning education in schools, colleges or universities. Its interface being with state education the Committee's sphere of operation is to be distinguished from that of the Board of Parish Education which is church-orientated.

1.2 The Department of Education, constituted in1992 to include the Committee on Education and the Committee on Education for the Ministry, was subject to a radical restructuring during 1997-98 as a result of which it was left with the Committee on Education as its sole remaining constituent. Arrangements were made for the Rev John Stevenson to continue in post as departmental General Secretary until his due retiral date of December 2000, at which point it was understood by all concerned that the appointment would have been reviewed. (*Assembly Reports* 1997 31/3.4). Recognition of this requirement was contained in the Department's Report to the General Assembly of 1999 when it was stated that a small review body had been set up by the Committee "to look at its future work, staffing and required funding". A Report on these matters was promised for the General Assembly of 2000 (*Assembly Reports* 1999 27/15).

1.3 In the event no report of such a review was made to the 2000 Assembly.

1.4 Some weeks prior to the meeting of the 2000 Assembly the Committee on Education approached the Personnel Department to set in motion a process for filling the impending vacancy. The post was advertised as that of General Secretary to the Department of Education and applications were already being received at the time the Assembly met. As a result of the appointment of the Special Commission, all proceedings in connection with an appointment were sisted.

2. The Departmental Review 1999

2.1 From the outset of their enquiries it became apparent to the Commission that the question of the adequacy or otherwise of the review undertaken by the Department of Education during 1999 was a key issue. Not only did the non-appearance of the promised report arouse uneasiness on the floor of the 2000 Assembly but the quality of the review itself had raised earlier concern in certain quarters e.g. amongst those with allocation responsibilities in Stewardship and Finance.

2.2 The issue of the funding of the Committee on Education beyond the year 2000 had not been ignored by the departmental review body. Historically the Committee had subsisted on income from trusts and investments without recourse to the central funds of the Church but after the re-organisation of the Department in 1998 involving the removal of the Committee on Education for the Ministry an arrangement was made that the projected deficits arising between then and Mr Stevenson's retiral in 2000 would be covered by an interim funding package arranged through Stewardship and Finance but without reference to the Mission and Aid Fund (*Assembly Reports* 1998 35/8). Looking to the matter of funding beyond the year 2000, the Committee took their case to the Co-ordinating Forum in September 1999 where, on the basis of a plan of future work, a claim was tabled for admission to the Mission and Aid Fund in the figure of £60,000.

Questions were raised in the Forum regarding staffing and structures but no powers lay with the Forum beyond advising on priorities for financial allocation. In a situation of severe financial restriction, where to give to one agency was to deny another, the Forum decided by a majority vote to affirm the importance of the work of the Committee on Education by admitting it to the Mission and Aid Fund. Discussion favoured a figure of £30,000 for 2001 in view of the general financial stringency, a suggestion accepted by the Committee's representatives. In the event, Stewardship and Finance admitted the Committee to the Mission and Aid Fund but at the reduced figure of £5,000, advising that any shortfall be made up from the capital reserves of the Committee which were estimated at something approaching £1m. This latter advice reflected a new policy on the use of capital resources introduced by the Board of Stewardship and Finance at the 2000 Assembly.

2.3 Evidence from the Board of Stewardship and Finance presented to the Commission made clear that in their deliberations on the funding of the Committee on Education they were not satisfied that the review procedure on the part of the Committee had been as thorough or as objective as they might have hoped. Testimony differed between the Committee and the Board as to whether a new appointment to replace Mr Stevenson had been specifically mentioned at the Co-ordinating Forum. What was clear to the Commission was that neither the question of departmental status nor that of the Secretariat had been rigorously addressed under the Committee's review. While it is true that no objective review body presently exists in the Church's structures to which such questions might have been referred, the Commission considers that the Committee could have used their "in-house" review to better effect by a more thorough attention to these key matters. It is fair to record that the Convener of the Committee accepts that a report of the departmental review should have been placed before the General Assembly of 2000.

3. The Responsibilities and Workload of the Department

3.1 The Department of Education in the year 2000 was a considerably different entity from that to which Mr Stevenson was appointed General Secretary in 1992. At the outset it had consisted of two substantial committees, Education and Education for the Ministry, serviced at the executive level by a General Secretary whose responsibility included not only departmental administration but also the Education remit, and by an Assistant Secretary whose duties lay with Education for the Ministry. In 1998, however, with the transfer of Education for the Ministry to the Board of Ministry, the Committee on Education remained the sole constituent

of the Department. The General Secretary continued in post as the sole executive officer, the departmental staff falling in total from six to two.

3.2 These changes clearly reflect a reduction in the degree of administrative responsibility borne by the General Secretary at departmental level. Having been involved to some 15% to 20% of his time in wider departmental duties (his own estimate), the General Secretary was thenceforth freed to give that much greater attention to the Education remit itself. The Commission found evidence that this period 1998-2000 was a notably busy time for the Committee on Education (see paragraph 3.5 below).

3.3 In reviewing the current workload of the Committee the Commission noted the four main policy aims as set out in the Committee's Forward Plan 1999-2001:

(1) To represent the Church on all matters relating to Scottish education;

(2) To support people at local level e.g. Church representatives on local education authorities and school chaplains;

(3) To promote the place of Religious and Moral Education in Scottish schools;

(4) To maintain relations with other churches and other faith groups.

3.4 In relation to these aims the following areas of responsibility and operation may be noted:

(a) *Statutory*

Legislative regulations provide for the nomination by the Church of Scotland of a representative to the Education Committee of each of the thirty two Scottish Local Authorities and to the General Teaching Council of Scotland. The Executive of the Scottish Parliament recognises the Church's Committee on Education as one of the bodies to be regularly consulted on matters relating to education. In the name of the Church, the Committee has the responsibility of responding to such consultations promptly and with authority and seeks to maintain good relations with the Scottish ministers and parliamentary committees responsible for education and with HM Inspectors of Schools.

(b) *Operational*

Having pressed for long for a more assured place to be given to religious education in the day school curriculum the General Assembly has welcomed the introduction of the Religious and Moral Education Guidelines 5-14 and the Higher Still Certificate programme on Religious, Moral and Philosophical Studies, recognising that these developments place expectations on the Committee on Education in the name of the Church to produce appropriate teaching resources on a range of religious, social and moral topics. Recent examples of such resources are the video "Work and Worship in the Church of Scotland", a schools pack on "Perceptions of Jesus" and a Church of Scotland input to "What the Churches say on Moral and Social Issues" *(Religious Education Movement, Scotland)*.

The role and function of school chaplains is presently governed by guidelines under "Religious Observance" within the multi-cultural and multi-faith setting of the day school. This has required more attention to be given to the provision of support resources and training facilities. A regular Bulletin for school chaplains is published and circulated and conferences are held.

Support structures for exchange and information are provided also for the Church of Scotland representatives on the thirty-two local education committees.

(c) *Ecumenical*

The promotion of religious and moral education within a constantly changing setting involves co-operation with a variety of educational and ecumenical bodies e.g. the Catholic Education Commission and the Religious Education Movement (Scotland). Wider educational ideals are shared and developed through groups like the Forum on Scottish Education. A recent reflective report on "A Christian Vision for Scottish Education" has been produced by the education group of ACTS with considerable input from John Stevenson.

3.5 It might be thought that the reduced administrative workload of the Department of Education following from the demerger of 1998 would have left the General Secretary with greater leisure to address the educational remit as set out above. What could scarcely have been foreseen at the time but has become increasingly evident since is that education was set to rise strikingly to the top of the political and social agenda. The establishment of the Scottish Parliament in 1999 has produced a double ministerial brief in education with corresponding departments and parliamentary committees (Education and Enterprise and Life-long Learning), indicating an increased policy priority on education. Contentious matters like the abolition of Section 28(2a) regarding alternative lifestyles - on which the government sought and received a Church of Scotland statement - and the breakdown in the SQA, not to mention student fees, have kept educational concerns in the forefront of topical attention. Meantime, a flow of consultation documents on a wide range of educational issues has proceeded from the Scottish Executive inviting written response or oral evidence or both. As one of the bodies regularly consulted, the Committee on Education on behalf of the Church made response to no less than fourteen such documents in 1999-2000.

3.6 It will be clear that in these circumstances the Church would have been in an extremely disadvantageous position had it not been served by an alert Committee serviced by a Secretary who had the expertise, stature and flexibility to cope with this quickened pace of operation. It is the view of the Special Commission that such qualities will increasingly be required on the Church's part when dealing with the professional and personal issues inherent in the new Scottish educational enterprise.

3.7 A question arises, however, regarding the most suitable structure by which the Church's educational interest can best be served in the present circumstances. There seems no doubt about the distinctive need for such a body; as the Assembly Council expressed it in their review of the Committee on Education in 1992: *there is a continuing need to have a specialist committee able to deal promptly and knowledgeably with the complex and often technical issues that lie within its remit.*

In view of the changes which have overtaken the Department of Education since 1998 it is the view of the Special Commission that **the responsibility for representing the Church's interest in Education should now be vested in a Committee serviced by a Secretary rather than in a Department serviced by a General Secretary.**

3.8 It was made clear to the Commission that the person of the Secretary was valued, not only within the Church of Scotland but by other denominational bodies also, as a strong and constant voice in the cause of religious and moral education, the post constituting a spearhead for presenting the Church's interest in an ever-changing sphere. In this regard, and taking account of the workload of the Committee outlined above, the Commission would not envisage the post of Secretary as being anything other than full time and permanent.

4. The Committee on Education within the structures of the Church

4.1 The Commission has given attention, as required, to the location of such a Committee on Education "within the current organisational structures of the Church".

4.2 The possibility was considered of linking up Education with the Board of Parish Education. Although this was seen by some of our witnesses as "putting the clock back" pre-1992, there was a willingness to consider the proposition on the part of the Board representatives themselves. Recent collaboration in certain specialist topics (eg. special needs, sex education) showed commendable, if limited, co-operation. The matter of client group, however, seemed to constitute a separation between the two bodies, Education interfacing with the state, while Parish Education was perceived to be church-orientated as expressed in its prospectus: "to oversee the development of an education and leadership training service for the Church of Scotland". It seemed to the Commission that in view of the sensitivities which surround religious education in schools the specialist role of the Committee on Education will be better secured through a body independent of Parish Education.

4.3 The other structure with which the Committee on Education might be considered to have an affinity was the Church and Nation Committee. There was a ready recognition of a common aspect between the two bodies insofar as they both have dealings with government agencies and institutions. Some unofficial explorations had been done at various times about coming into closer administrative relationship with one another but negotiations had failed to develop due in part to the perceived distinctiveness of their spheres of labour. Evidence from the Church and Nation side made it clear that their recently appointed Secretary was already fully occupied with their own far-reaching responsibilities and that the Committee, as it stood, did not have the resources to encompass the work of Education. It seemed to the Commission that any move to merge the Committees would bring no saving and could involve a loss of concentration on education.

4.4 The Commission took note of the distinctive remit of the Committee on Education. Facing outward to the educational world, relating to the new parliamentary institutions and adjusting to an ever more direct style of consultation the Committee's work would not obviously be benefited, far less expedited, by a requirement to channel its operation through a Board or other agency. The need for flexibility and rapid response argue for **a Committee that is free-standing, utilising its expertise and experience aptly on the Church's behalf and accountable directly to the General Assembly.** The Commission recommend accordingly.

4.5 Such a free-standing Committee would not be without counterpart in the Church's structures. The Church and Nation Committee and the Committee on Ecumenical Relations operate on a similar basis. Although the terms of reference of the Commission preclude any proposal beyond existing structures, it may be not improper to envisage some future association of such free-standing committees and other agencies whose common concern is external affairs. Meantime, given a willingness to work co-operatively, such free-standing Committees may be encouraged to find their own opportunities for mutual support and beneficial collaboration at day-to-day levels.

5. The Secretariat: Terms and Conditions

5.1 The Commission consulted with the Personnel Manager concerning workload and terms of service, including the appropriate level of remuneration, relative to the appointment of a Secretary.

5.2 The procedure of the Personnel Manager in the matter of appointments is as follows. Having received assurances from the Board or Committee concerned that funds are available to support the post, he consults with them regarding the job description, fixes the salary scale, advertises the post and arranges for interviews.

5.3 Examination of the job specification as prepared for the advertisement in May 2000 revealed a proper concentration on the key responsibilities of the post viz. the servicing of the Committee as it acts for the General Assembly on all matters concerning education in schools, colleges and universities, the development of RME resources for schools, the support of personnel working in the field of RME teaching and school chaplaincy and the development of links with government departments and educational personnel. Some concern was felt regarding the multiplicity of representative duties in which the Secretary could be involved and it was suggested that a sharing of some of these duties could be achieved by a careful attention to the division of responsibilities as set out in the next section of this report.

5.4 The methodology employed in determining salary is based on a comparison of posts within the Church Offices taking into account factors of workload and responsibility with a possible additional factor in cases which might require professional qualifications, e.g. legal or financial. In the case of an education post, professionalism could be deemed to be a relevant factor as it is considered desirable to recruit someone who would be in a position to interface readily with senior educational executives in government or local authorities.

5.5. While acknowledging that the salary level is a matter for the Personnel Manager to fix and that in doing so he is dealing with a range of relativities it is the recommendation of the Commission that the salary scale should be comparable with that of salaries paid to the Secretaries of similar free-standing Committees within the Church offices.

5.6 The Commission envisages that the office support would continue as at present at the level of one Principal Assistant.

6. Division of Responsibility

6.1 Because the Secretaryship of Education benefits in its operation from good personal and professional relationships built up through steady contact, effective networking and the capacity to earn confidence and respect in a professional world, there will be a number of areas where the Secretary is the person of first choice to represent the Church in educational circles. Care, however, requires to be exercised that a proper attention is given to the division between the roles of Secretary and Convener.

6.2 A recent memo from the Principal Clerk set out the distinction as follows: *Generally speaking, the Board under its Convener is responsible for matters of policy. The Secretary is responsible for the administration of the department and the execution of policy. The relationship between Convener and Secretary is a key one and in the best of worlds they will co-operate in the work of the Church. At the same time, each should have regard to their separate spheres and respect for each other's responsibilities and expertise.*

6.3 The Convener and Secretary will therefore have a duty of vigilance in the sharing of representational roles appropriately between themselves and amongst the membership of the Committee itself.

7. Reflection

7.1 In the course of the foregoing review the Commission has found cause to criticise the Department of Education on a number of points, in particular:

(1)   their handling of the review procedure;

(2)   their failure to bring a promised report to the Assembly, and

(3)   their hastiness in advertising the vacancy in advance of the Assembly.

7.2 These criticisms stand but the Commission has also been aware of a number of circumstances which combined to exacerbate the situation in which the Department found itself. It is with no purpose of extenuation but to present some matters of concern with implications for the Church that the following observations are made:

7.2.1 It is, in the view of the Commission, a serious gap in the processes of the Church that there presently exists no standing body with the authority to adjudicate in regard to vacant appointments or adjustment of agencies. In this situation vacancies arising in departments are subject to no process of review other than an internal one. Thus, the Department of Education was left to conduct its own review.

As regards the adjustment of agencies or the querying of vacant posts the General Assembly, in the absence of a statutory review body, has no resort but to appoint a Special Commission which assesses the case and reports a year later, surely a heavy-handed way of dealing with matters which should be dealt with under standing procedures.

It seems to the Commission, therefore, that the General Assembly should move urgently to establish such a central reference body. Since issues are involved which bear upon administrative procedures it would seem that the agent to carry forward such an initiative should be the Board of Practice and Procedure.

7.2.2 Another circumstance affecting the Department of Education was the inconclusive arrangement made for their financial support beyond the year 2000. The temporary funding package of £30,000 p.a. for the years 1998-2000 was intended to fill the financial gap caused by the removal of the Committee on Education for the Ministry but as the year 2000 approached the issue of future funding was bearing down on the Committee of Education at the same time as they were immersed in their internal review and facing the impending retirement of their Secretary.

7.2.3 Any one of these issues would have been challenging enough but to have all three falling in at once tested the Committee to its limit. Each issue having a bearing on the others, a situation arose in which nothing was satisfactorily resolved.

7.2.4 These adverse circumstances cannot be said to have been due to deliberation on anyone's part but the effect was that the Department of Education felt itself to be in a very vulnerable position. This may in part explain the reluctance of the departmental review body to address some key internal issues and their precipitate action of going to press with the advertisement ahead of the General Assembly.

7.2.5 **To assist the process of recovery it is the Commission's view that an early meeting should be arranged between the Committee and the Board of Stewardship and Finance to discuss issues of funding.**

8. Recommendations

8.1 The Commission submits the following recommendations for the consideration of the General Assembly:

8.2. (1) Recognising education as a central concern of government and a continuing concern of the Church, the Assembly should now reaffirm the responsibility of the Committee on Education to represent the Church in all matters concerning education in schools, colleges and universities.

8.3. (2) Taking account of changes which have affected the Department of Education in recent years, the General Assembly should now resolve to abolish it and in its place constitute the Committee on Education as a free-standing committee reporting directly to the General Assembly, without prejudice to any future inclusion within a new administrative arrangement.

8.4. (3) Recognising the need for continuity within the Secretariat of the Committee, the Assembly should now authorise the Personnel Department to proceed with the appointment of a successor to the Rev John Stevenson, such an appointee to be designated Secretary to the Committee on Education.

9. Conclusion

9.1 The crucial question for the Commission has been: how can the Church most effectively promote the education and personal formation of the people of Scotland?

9.2 Today's Church must hold to the belief in education as an igniting factor in the power of a revived Christianity to serve the nation through enhanced values, purpose and sense of meaning. With the move in educational practice away from instruction and the delivery of packages of information to a system that invites young people to informed ownership of faith and philosophy it is essential that the Church continues in an ecumenical and inter-faith context to contribute the best of its mind and aspiration in that quest. To this end we are persuaded that, now as much as ever before, the Church needs a strong and effective Education Committee served by a Secretary of imagination, ability and dedication.

9.3 It need only be added that the findings of the Special Commission are unanimous.

In the name of the Commission

John H McIndoe, *Convener*

Appendix: Membership and Method

The members appointed to serve on the Special Commission anent the Department of Education were:-

Mr Kenneth Anderson
Rev. Charles Barrington
Rev. Marjory Macaskill
Rev. Gillian P Maclean
Miss Moyra McCallum
Very Rev. John H McIndoe, *Convener*
Professor Michael Meston

Miss Mary Macleod, Depute Solicitor of the Church, was in attendance and acted as Secretary to the Commission.

The Commission met on six occasions.

A visit was paid to the office of the Department of Education.

The following persons were interviewed:

Mr David Alexander (Member, Committee on Education)
Rev. Ronald S Blakey (formerly Secretary of the Assembly Council)
Very Rev. John B Cairns (Minister, Dumbarton: Riverside)
Mr George B B Eadie (Personnel Manager)
Rev. Jack J Laidlaw (Convener, Committee on Education)
Rev. Dr. Finlay A J Macdonald (Principal Clerk)
Rev. Alan D McDonald (Convener, Church and Nation)
Mr Leon M Marshall (Convener, Stewardship and Finance)
Mrs Agnes Mullen (Principal Assistant, Education)
Rev. Douglas Scrimgeour (Senior Lecturer, Religious Education)
Rev. Dr David Sinclair (Secretary, Church and Nation)
Rev. G Stewart Smith (Convener, Board of Parish Education)
Rev. John Stevenson (General Secretary, Department of Education)
Rev Professor William F Storrar (Christian Ethics, Edinburgh University)
Mr Iain W Whyte (Director, Board of Parish Education)

Written testimony was submitted by:

Rev. Dr Graham K Blount
Rev. Jack J Laidlaw
Rev. John Stevenson
Mr Henry Philip
Rev. John Taylor

INDEX

NOTES

NOTES

NOTES

NOTES

NOTES